Annals of the BODLEIAN LIBRARY

STATUE OF SIR THOMAS BODLEY
photograph © 2013 Tiger of the Stripe

Annals of the BODLEIAN LIBRARY

With a Notice of the Earlier Library of the University

WILLIAM DUNN MACRAY

REVISED SECOND EDITION

TIGER OF THE STRIPE
2013

First published 1868
Second edition published 1890

This edition first published 2013 by
Tiger of the Stripe
50 Albert Road
Richmond
Surrey TW10 6DP

ISBN 978-1-904799-64-1

Cover design by
Peter Danckwerts
based on a Victorian
chromolithograph
showing the interior of the
Bodleian Library

PREFACE.

WHEN this book was first published twenty-two years ago, it was found to appeal to the interest of so limited a class of readers, although one which in the course of years has gradually made it to become somewhat scarce, that the idea of publishing a second edition was never entertained by me. The accumulation of additional notes, indeed, continually went on, but it was with the idea of giving an enlarged copy some day to the Library in the belief that after my death it would be found useful. But it is owing to the present Librarian that this second edition now appears under my own eye and care. For the book had become a manual of such continual use in the Library that the Librarian was desirous that the additional matter should be rendered available while a last inheritor of some traditional information and a last associate in some details and labours under the management that existed fifty years ago still survives on the staff. And it is with much pleasure that I acknowledge the interest he has shown throughout, and the useful suggestions he has from time to time made. To Mr. Falconer Madan also, whose interest in the progress of the work has been equally sustained, I am indebted for frequent and cordial assistance. And to the Delegates of the University Press I desire to tender my thanks for liberally undertaking the publication.

The present volume exceeds its predecessor by considerably more than one-third, the text in the latter volume running to 344 pages and in this to 493. The history has been briefly continued from 1868 to 1880, its continuance to a later date being rendered unnecessary by the publication of Mr. Nicholson's Report of the work of the years during which he has held office. The fac-simile of the Shakespeare autograph which was given in the previous edition has been omitted, full and accurate photographs having been published in Germany (as mentioned at p. 380); but portraits of the Founder and of our great benefactor Rawlinson, together with a view of the old Reading-Room, are now for the first time supplied. The Bodley medallion portrait is photographed from the picture in the Library, but it was found impossible to reproduce satisfactorily more than the upper part of it, and the half-length portrait is consequently taken from Lodge's engraving, which slightly varies from the original. The portrait of Rawlinson is from a very scarce engraving, to which the Rawlinson arms, but no name, are attached, and which is affixed by Rawlinson to his own account of himself in his MS. continuation of Wood's *Athenæ Oxonienses*. The view of the Library is from a very successful water-colour painting, affording a view of a portion which has never before been so completely shown in illustrations, for the use of which I am grateful to the lady whose work it is.

Had I in the earlier years of my library-life contemplated the future compilation of these *Annals*, many an anecdote and much information which now cannot be recovered might have been noted down by myself and gathered from others. Especially from Dr. Bliss, amongst the former librarians and assistants then surviving, much might have been learned respecting the early years of this century, and the traditions of the end of the last, periods respecting which very little record remains. And in giving information for such an object one feels assured that Dr. Bliss would have felt lively interest and pleasure, as for an object of more than mere anecdotical reminiscence. For to all that traces and elucidates the progress of the Bodleian Library there attaches a real interest of its own. As a comprehensive history of the University Church of St. Mary will be a history of religious thought and movement in Oxford, so a history of the University Library can afford in some sort an outline of the progress of learning and of the development of studies. Upon the activity of the seventeenth century and the beginning of the eighteenth follows a period of general dulness and torpor; the little life that appears in the Library seems to be chiefly devoted to English antiquities, a worthy subject indeed, but hardly co-extensive with the work of a University or the objects of the Library. Then in the ever-extending range of acquisitions which marks the nineteenth century, we see a revival of the old activities within their wider sphere, and the place that was hallowed with the memories of the dead becomes consecrated anew by the use of the living.

And still, while around there cluster the necessary accretions of accruing years, the Great Room which Duke Humphrey helped to build and which Bodley enlarged, remains like the unmoved centre of a grand planetary system. As I remarked in the Preface to the former edition, the, in the main, still unaltered arrangement of this room 'often imparts an interest of its own to well-nigh each successive shelf of books; for each tier has its own record of successive benefactions and successive purchases to display, and leads us on step by step from one year to another.' The room is not, indeed, one fashioned and furnished after the newest plans, with abundance of iron and much glass, with easy chairs and all that appertains to modern ideas of convenience and fitness and to modern literary lounges; but it is in its old-world form the scholars' precious possession, uniquely grand, gloriously rich, marvellously suggestive. And not least suggestive in its very mode of entrance, albeit sometimes deemed unworthy, sometimes complained of as wearisome and tedious. From the quadrangle which tells by the storeyed buildings which enclose it that there is much wealth within, you enter, almost stooping, by a plain low door, and then begin to ascend a long, long, winding flight of stairs. You may rest as you go, here and there, on window-seats and benches, but still before you lies that winding ascent. At length you reach a simple green baize door; you open it—and the panorama of the world of learning is before you. Surely it is a very type of the way by which true knowledge is gained. By no railway-travelling in easy carriages, speeding swiftly and smoothly on, that requires little exertion and knows no delay, but by the real 'royal road' of humility that refuses no lowly beginnings, by the patience that is not disheartened by labour, by the perseverance that overcomes weariness, at last the door of knowledge is reached and opened;—and then all the toil is rewarded. It is the way which the true '*Mater Scientiarum*' teaches.

March 1890. W. D. M.

CONTENTS

ANNALS

OF THE

BODLEIAN LIBRARY

ANNALS

OF THE

BODLEIAN LIBRARY.

IN the north-east corner of St. Mary's Church, a church full of nooks little known to ordinary visitors, is a vaulted chamber (once dark because its windows had been built up), whose doors, when opened, only used to reveal the abiding-place of the University fire-engines[1]. Here of old sat the Chancellor of the University, surrounded by the Doctors and Masters of the Great Congregation, in a fashion which was formerly depicted in the great west window of St. Mary's Church, and is still represented on the University seal, which seal, in the early part of the last century, was adopted by Dr. Richard Rawlinson as his book-plate, being engraved from the impression attached to his own diploma in Civil Law[2]. Above this chamber there is another, lighted by four

[1] In 1871 it was fitted up as a Chapel for the Unattached Students; but its use for this purpose has been discontinued.

[2] The earliest known existing impression of this seal is attached to a deed preserved in the University Archives, which professes to be a bond from the Chancellor and Masters to the Prior and Convent of St. Frideswide in £200 that they will not molest any one within the convent precincts, dated on the f. of St. James, 1201. This is printed as the oldest existing University document in Brian Twyne's *Antiq. Acad. Oxon. Apologia*, 1608, pp. 234, 235. I saw this document for the first time in the year 1886, and a moment's glance showed the manifest forgery, the document having certainly been written in the fourteenth century, to which century also the seal in its whole character belongs. The seal is engraved in Ingram's *Memorials of Oxford*, iii. 17, where the old error is continued in describing the bond as being '*c.* A.D. 1200,' although its authenticity had been long questioned. See Mr. H. C. Maxwell Lyte's *Hist. of the Univ. of Oxford to* 1530, 1886, p. 248.

windows, forty-five feet in length and twenty in breadth, and now nominally assigned as the lecture-room of the Professor of Law. Here was begun about 1367, and finally established and furnished in 1409, the first actual University Library, called after Bishop Thomas Cobham, of Worcester, who about 1320 (seven years before his death) had commenced preparations for the building of the room and the making provision for its contents[1]. Wood tells us that before this time there were indeed some books kept in chests in St. Mary's Church, which were to be lent out under pledges, as well as some chained to desks, which were only to be read *in situ*; but *this* University chest soon gave way to the formal Library, as, at a later period, another University Chest was lost in funded investments and a banker's balance[2]. Another precursor of the general Library was found in the collection which came to Durham College (on the site of which now stands Trinity College) in 1345 from its first designer, the earnest lover and preserver of books, Richard of Bury; he of that charming book, that 'tractatus vere pulcherrimus,' the *Philobiblon*. He,—who apostrophizes books as the masters who teach without flogging or fleecing, without punishment or payment; as ears of corn, full of grain, to be rubbed only by apostolic hands; as golden pots of manna; as Noah's ark and Jacob's ladder, and Joshua's stones of testimony and Gideon's lamps and David's scrip; and who says that in the noblest monasteries of England he found precious volumes defiled and injured by mice and worms, and abandoned to moths,—gave strict injunctions for the care of the large collection, gathered from all quarters[3], with

[1] When Duke Humphrey's Library was completed, and the books were removed thither, this upper room took the place of that beneath it as the Convocation House, 'In which upper room,' says Hearne, 'was brave painted glass containing the arms of the benefactors, which painted glass continued till the times of the late rebellion.' (Bliss, *Reliquiæ Hearnianæ*, ii. 693.)

[2] The original treasure-chest, from which all academic money-grants are still formally said to be made, is preserved in the Bursary of Corpus Christi College, in which college it was kept in accordance with the statutes of the University, tit. xx. § 1.

[3] An indignant account of the way in which an abbot of St. Alban's with the assent of the convent, gave him four books, and sold to him thirty-two for £50, out of which the abbot

which his College was enriched[1]. It was to be free for purposes of study to all scholars, who might have the loan of any work of which there was a duplicate, provided they left a pledge exceeding it in value, but for purposes of transcription no volume was to go beyond the walls of the house. A register was to be kept, and a yearly visitation was to be held[2]. Some of these books, on the dissolution of the College by Henry VIII, are said to have been transferred to Duke Humphrey's Library, and some to Balliol College.

The Librarian of Cobham's Library was also entitled Chaplain to the University, and as such was ordered, in 1412, to offer masses yearly for those who were benefactors of the University and Library, and was endowed with half a mark yearly, as well as with £5 issuing from the assize of bread and ale, which had been granted to the University by King Henry IV, who was also a principal contributor to the completion of the Library, and who is therefore to this day duly remembered in the Bidding-Prayer at all the academic 'Commemorationes Solenniores.' But no trace remains of the devotional and sacred duties once attaching to the office, and laymen have been eligible to it from the time of Bodley's re-foundation. The old regal stipend, however, amounting at last to £6 13*s*. 4*d*., continued

took half, and assigned the other half to the refectory and the kitchen (thus devoting spiritual food, says the chronicler, the highest refreshment of cloistered men, to carnal uses), is given in Th. Walsingham's *Gesta Abbatum S. Alb.* (1867, ii. 200). He says, however, that Bury afterward, when bishop, 'ductus conscientia,' restored most of the books.

[1] The Bishop's *bibliomania* is thus noticed by a contemporary, W. de Chambre, in his *Continuatio Hist. Dunelm.* (*Hist. Dunelm. Scriptt. tres*; Surtees Society, 1839, p. 130):—'Iste summe delectabatur in multitudine librorum. Plures enim libros habuit, sicut passim dicebatur, quam omnes Pontifices Angliæ. Et præter eos quos habuit in diversis maneriis suis, repositos separatim, ubicunque cum sua familia residebat, tot libri jacebant sparsim in camera qua dormivit, quod ingredientes vix stare poterant vel incedere nisi librum aliquem pedibus conculcarent.' The bedroom of the late centenarian President of Magdalen College, Dr. Routh, was in this respect, *testibus meis oculis*, just like Bishop Bury's; and as the latter sent his library from Durham to be in some sort a nucleus for an University Library at Oxford, so the former bequeathed his to Durham that it might assist the development of the University Library there.

[2] *Philobiblon*, cap. xix, pp. 141–5 in Mr. E. Thomas's admirable edition.

to be paid to the Librarian, until in 1856, by the then revised code of statutes, various small payments were consolidated; it is found entered in the annual printed accounts up to that year.

But not a score of years had passed after Cobham's Library had been actually completed and opened before the building of a room more worthy of the University was commenced. In 1426 the University began to erect the present noble Divinity School for the exercises in that faculty; but as their own means for its completion soon failed, they betook themselves to all likely quarters to procure help. And Duke Humphrey of Gloucester, the patron of all learning[1], and the fosterer of the New School of theological thought, the protector of Pecock, responded so liberally to the petition of the University for aid to the fabric of their Material School, that he is styled (says Wood) in the Bedells' Book its Founder, while the roof to this day perpetuates his memory among the shields of arms of benefactors with which its graceful pendants terminate. His gifts of money for the School were quickly followed by still larger gifts of books for the Library. Between the years 1439 and 1446 he appears to have forwarded about 600 MSS., which were for the time deposited, some in chests, in Cobham's Library. The first donation, consisting of 129 volumes, was forwarded in November, 1439. The letter of thanks from Convocation is dated the 25th of that month, and on the same day a letter was sent to the House of Commons, to the 'ryght worshypfull syres, the Speker, knyghtes, and burges (*sic*) of the

[1] His love of literature was evinced by the motto which, according to Leland, was frequently written by him in his books: 'Moun bien mondain.' (Hearne's *MS. Diary*, xxxvi. 199.) Hearne, in his esteem for the memory of this 'religious, good, and learned Prince,' quaintly says that he used, whenever he saw his handwriting in the Bodleian Library (where it occurs several times), 'to show a sort of particular respect' to it. (*Preface to Langtoft*, p. xx.) Was this 'sort of respect' a reverential kiss, such as that with which (as Warton in his *Companion to the Guide* tells us) he saluted the pavement of sheep's trotters, supposed by him to be a Roman tesselated floor? Prefixed to the preface to the *Catalogus Manuscriptorum* of 1697 is an engraving from a painted window in the old church of Greenwich (which fell down in 1710) representing the Duke kneeling in prayer, with his shield of arms beside him.

worshepfull parlament,' informing them that the Duke had magnified the University 'with a thousand pounds worth and more of preciose bokes,' and therefore beseeching their 'sage discrecions to considere the gloriose gifts of the graciose prince . . . . . for the comyn profyte and worshyp of the Reme, to thanke hym hertyly, and also prey Godde to thanke hym in tyme comyng wher goode dedys ben rewarded.' Statutes for the regulation of the gift were made on the same day, prayers appointed, and provision made for the observance of the Duke's obit[1]. A catalogue of 264 of the MSS. is printed, from two lists preserved in the University Register, pp. 758–772, vol. ii. of Rev. H. Anstey's *Documents illustrative of Social and Academic Life at Oxford*, published in the series of Chronicles issued by the Master of the Rolls. The extent of these gifts rendered the room at St. Mary's quite insufficient for the purpose to which it was assigned, and the University therefore, in a letter to the Duke, dated July 14, 1444, informed him of their intention to erect a more suitable building, of which (as a delicate way, probably, of bespeaking his aid towards the cost, as well as of testifying their gratitude for past benefactions) they formally offered him the title of Founder. In the subjoined note is given an extract from this letter (copied from the Register of Convocation), which is interesting from its description of the inconveniences of the old room, and the advantages of the new site[2]. And this new building, first contemplated in A.D. 1444

[1] Register of Convoc. F. ff. 53ᵇ, 54ᵇ. The subsequent gifts are entered in the same Register as follows:—

1. Last day of Feb., 1440. A letter to thank the Duke for 126 volumes brought by John Kyrkeby. (f. 57ᵇ.)
2. Nov. 10, 1441. Letter acknowledging ten books (treatises of Augustine, Rabanus, &c.) received through Will. Say, proctor, and John Kyrkeby. (ff. 59ᵇ–60.)
3. Jan. 25, 1443. Letter of thanks for 139 volumes. (f. 63.)
4. Oct. 1443. Letter for another gift, number of volumes not specified. (f. 66.)
5. Feb. 25, 1443 (–4). Catalogue of 135 volumes. (ff. 67–68ᵇ.)
6. Feb. 1446. Letter of thanks for another gift, not specified. (f. 75ᵇ.)

[2] 'Nemo illos [libros] sine admiratione conspicit, cunctis una voce testantibus se nunquam libros tanta

and finished about 1480, forms now the central portion of the great Reading-Room, still retaining its old advantages of convenience and of seclusion 'a strepitu sæculari.'

The Duke's MSS. were, as became the object of his gift, very varied in character. With works in Divinity are mingled in the catalogue a large number in Medicine and Science, together with some in lighter literature, amongst which latter are found no less than seven MSS. of Petrarch and three of Boccaccio. Some additional MSS., being 'all the Latyn bokes that he had,' together with £100 towards the completion of the 'Divyne Scoles,' which the Duke had intended to bequeath, but the formal bequest of which was prevented by his dying intestate in 1447, were subsequently procured, although with considerable difficulty[1]. But only three out of the whole number of his MSS. are now known to exist in the present Library. One of these is a fine copy of books iv.–ix. of Valerius Maximus, with the commentary by D. de Burgo, and with an index by John de Whethamstede, abbot of St. Alban's (now marked, *Auctarium, F. infra*, i. 1[2]);

claritate conspicuos, tanta gravitate refertos, vidisse. . . . . Et ut per hoc, si quid maximo addi possit, tantæ munificentiæ gloria fiat illustrior, optamus sacram et celebrem scientiarum sedem reparari, ubi honorificentius et ad utilitatem studentium multo commodius libri vestri, ab aliis segregati, collocentur. Jam enim si quis, ut fit, uni libro inhæreat, aliis studere volentibus ad tres vel quatuor pro vicinitate colligationis præcludit accessum. Itaque locus huic rei nobis maxime videtur idoneus ubi venerabilis vir, modo Cancellarius noster, semper reverendus pater amantissimus, magister Thomas Chace, spectabilem novarum Scolarum fabricam ad cætera suæ virtutis testimonia insigni mensura ab humo erexit, quam nos cito, quoad exigua suppetebat facultas, promovimus. Hic locus, propterea quod a strepitu sæculari removetur, Bibliotecæ admodum videtur conveniens, cujus fundationis titulum, si Magnanimitati vestræ acceptabilis fuerit, cum omni devotione offerimus.' Register F. ff. 71b, 72. We find from an entry on the latter page that on January 13, 1444 (–5), 'liber Platonis in Phedro' (*sic*) was lent by Convocation to the Duke.

[1] They were not received by August, 1450, on the 28th of which month a letter was written from Convocation to Thomas Bokelonde, Esq., and John Summerset, M.D., on the subject. (Register F. ff. 88b–9.) An earlier letter bespeaking the aid of Will. of Wayneflete, then Provost of Eton, for obtaining the books, is printed from the same Register in Chandler's *Life of Wayneflete*, p. 321.

[2] It contains inscriptions recording its gift by Whethamstede 'ad usum

the second is a translation by L. Aretine of the Politics of Aristotle (marked, *Auct. F.* v. 27); and the third, the Epistles of Pliny (*Auct. F.* ii. 23). The first bears the Duke's arms; the second has an original dedication to him by the translator[1]; the last (which was restored to the University by Dr. Robert Master, Oct. 30, 1620) contains his own autograph. Six MSS. now in the British Museum, which formerly belonged to the Duke, are described in Sir H. Ellis' *Letters of Eminent Literary Men*, (printed by the Camden Society,) pp. 357–8. Two of these appear in the list of Humphrey's benefaction to Oxford; for Harl. 1705, which is a translation of Plato's Politics by Peter Candidus, or White, who gave it to the Duke, is doubtless the book entered at the end of the list as 'Item, novam traductionem totius Politeiæ Platonicæ;' while Cotton, Nero. D. v., the Acts of the Council of Constance, appears at fol. 67. Another of these six MSS., Harl. 988, is an anonymous commentary on the Canticles[2], which formerly belonged to Sir Robert Cotton, and which contains an inscription by him intended to commemorate his returning it to the University Library in 1602. It came into Harley's possession amongst Bishop Stillingfleet's MSS., all of which were bought by him. A letter from Wanley to Hearne, in which the book is mentioned, is preserved in the Bodleian in a Rawlinson MS. (*Letters* xvii.) under date of Oct. 13, 1714, Hearne's reply to which is printed by Sir H. Ellis, *ubi supra;* while Wanley's rejoinder is also found in the above MS., dated Oct. 27, in which he says, 'As for my Lord's MS. of the Canticles, designed for the Bodleyan Library by Sir Robert Cotton, I know not how you find it to have once belonged to Humphrey, duke of

scolarium studencium Oxoniæ,' with anathemas upon those who should alienate it, or steal were it but its title: 'Si quis rapiat, raptim titulumve retractet, vel Judæ laqueum vel furcas sensiat.'

[1] This dedication is printed by Prof. H. W. Chandler, pp. 41–4, of his *Catalogue of Editions of Aristotle's Nicom. Ethics in the 14th cent.*, 4°. Oxf., 1868. Of this privately issued work only 25 copies were printed.

[2] Two treatises on the Canticles, by Gilbert Porret and Musca, were contained in the Duke's first gift to Oxford. (Anstey, vol. ii. p. 759.)

Gloucester. My Lord has indeed two of his books, which we know to have been his, for certain; because one of them (which was given to his Lordship) hath a note therein of his hand-writing, and the other hath his armes and stile on the outside, as also his library-mark. This last (which was bought by Sir Simonds D'Ewes), together with the Cotton MS. of the Canticles, I besought his Lordship to give to the University for your Library, and I hope his Lordship will do so in a little time.' A copy of Wycliffe's Bible, in two volumes, which bears Humphrey's arms, is amongst the Egerton MSS. (617–8), Brit. Mus. And a Latin translation of treatises by St. Athanasius, made by Antonio Beccara, one of the Duke's secretaries, is now Royal MS., Brit. Mus., 5 F. ii. It has the Duke's autograph. Another of the Duke's books, being Capgrave's Commentary on Genesis, which occurs in the second list of those given to the University, is now in the library of Oriel College. One volume, containing, among other philosophical treatises, Plato's *Phædo*, *Timæus*, &c., with the Duke's autograph, 'Cest livre a moy Homfrey duc de Gloucestre' (given to him by the Abbot of St. Alban's) is in Corpus Christi College, 243. In the National Library at Paris are the following MSS. once the Duke's:—a magnificent Livy; *Panegyrici Veteres*; Cicero's *Epistolæ*; Bible-Histories [*qu.* Comestor ?], given to Humphrey by John Stanley in 1427, and bought at London by Philip de Loan in 1461; *Decameron*, given him by the Earl of Warwick; Reynard the Fox[1]. A metrical translation of Palladius *De re rustica* is in the library of Earl Fitzwilliam at Wentworth Woodhouse, Yorkshire, which contains a prologue descriptive of the varied contents of Humphrey's library 'at Oxenford,' and says that he

> 'In deskis xii hym selue as half a strete
> Hath boked thair librair universall.'

The MS. appears to have been a presentation copy to the Duke. In 1767 it was in the possession of James West[2]. Leland mentions

[1] Delisle's *Cabinet des MSS. de la Bibl. Imp.*, 4°. Par., 1868, vol. i. p. 52.

[2] For a very interesting notice of this MS. (deserving, however, con-

his having seen in the University Library a French translation of Barthol. Glanville's book *De proprietatibus rerum*, executed for the king of France, 'per Joannem Corbiconem,' which had been given by the Duke[1]. One of the MSS. of the old Library is now MS. 172 in the library of St. John's College; it contains the following inscription: 'Istum librum legavit magister Johannes Alwart, quondam rector ecclesie parochialis de Stoke Bruer, Universitati Oxon., ut oraret pro anima ejus, et animabus parentum et parochianorum ejus.' It appears from Bridges' *Hist. of Northamptonshire* that Alwart was rector of Stoke Bruerne from 1420 to 1457.

The large increase of treasures which these benefactions brought to the University probably caused the first institution of a formal Visitation. On Nov. 29, 1449, we find that Visitors were appointed by Congregation for the purpose of receiving from the Chaplain an account of the books contained in the Library[2].

Duke Humphrey was followed in the good work of the Divinity School and Library by another whose name still retains its place in the solemn list of benefactors, Bishop Thomas Kempe, of London, who, besides contributing very largely in money towards the completion of the former, sent some books to the latter in 1487[3], apparently one year before the new room was finally completed and opened for use[4]. And John Tiptoft, Earl of Worcester, who was beheaded in 1470, was also a donor in intention if not in fact[5].

siderable amplification) from which the above is derived, see an article by Mr. H. J. Moule in the *Athenæum* for 17 Nov. 1888, p. 664.

[1] Tanner, *Bibl. Brit.*, s. n. *Glanville*. A list of other MSS. seen by Leland is in his *Collectanea*, vol. iii. pp. 58–9, and is reprinted in my Appendix.

[2] Wood MS. F. 27. (Bodl. Libr.)

[3] J. Hales in his funeral oration on Bodley (*Bodleiomnema*, 1613, sign. N. 2) says that Kempe gave 500 (50?) volumes 'et intus argumenti scripturæque precio nobilissimis, et extra argento auroque operose fulgidis.'

[4] Maxwell Lyte's *Hist. Univ. Oxf.*, p. 322. Seven years after, according to Wood, *Hist.*, II. ii. 778, 918.

[5] In MS. 423 in Corp. Chr. Coll., Cambr., p. 69, there is a copy of a letter from the Univ. to Archbishop Neville of York, in which request is made that 'libros illos quibus a Wigorniæ comite nuperius defuncto Academia erat donata, ad valorem quingentarum ferme marcarum, eis obtinere summa sua prudentia dignaretur' (Nasmyth's *Cat. MSS. C.C.C.*, p. 395). In this same MS. there is a curious note by Archbishop Parker at

But Antony Wood (in whose pages records of other benefactors may be found) tells us that very few years passed before the Library began to lose some of its newly-acquired treasures; for Scholars borrowed books upon petty and insufficient pledges, and so chose to forfeit the latter rather than return the former[1], while tradition reported that Polydore Vergil, the historian, being at length refused any further opportunities of abstraction, obtained a special licence from Henry VIII for the taking out any MS. for his use[2]! From this traditionary report Sir H. Ellis, in his introduction to a translation of Vergil's history, printed for the Camden Society in 1844, endeavours to vindicate his author's reputation, but more by conjecture than evidence. In 1513 a Chaplain and Librarian was elected, named Adam Kirkebote[3]. The new Librarian, soon after, supplicated Congregation that on Festival Days he should not be bound to open the Library before twelve o'clock; a practice which, commencing at that day, does still unto this (the Library on those Holy Days during Term on which University sermons are preached being now not opened until the conclusion of the sermon, at eleven o'clock[4]) witness to the religious spirit which pervaded all the old institutions of Oxford. In 1527, when one Flecher was Chaplain, it is recorded[5] that 'Magister' Claymond (doubtless the President of Corpus Christi College, of that name) was permitted

p. 79, that 'the MSS. formerly kept in the Divinity Schools at Oxford were sold to Christ Church.' (*Ibid.*)

[1] A sale of a collection of (apparently) these forfeited pledges, or else of books deposited as securities for loans of money, took place in the year 1546. On Jan. 18, 1545-6, the following decree passed Convocation: 'Decretum est authoritate Convocationis Magnæ ut cistæ in domo inferiori sub domo Congregationis, et omnes libri pro pignoribus jacentes, aut etiam alii in eadem domo inventi, venderentur, secundum arbitrium quinque in eadem Convocatione eligendorum. Electi itaque sunt et a Vice-Cancellario admissi ibidem, Doctor Standishe, Mr. Parret, procurator, Mr. Slythers, Mr. Symonds, et Mr. Wattsone.' Reg. I. 107[b].

[2] See *infra, sub anno* 1634.

[3] Wood MS. F. 27.

[4] These Holy Days have now, in the wave of change which is gradually obliterating old religious landmarks in Oxford, become very few, sermons on Saints' Days having been abolished by a statute passed in Lent Term, 1872, except on those four special days on which they are preached in the Chapels of Merton, New, and Magdalen Colleges.

[5] Wood MS. F. 27.

by vote of Congregation to take Pliny's Natural History out of the Library. In 1543 Humphrey Burnford was elected Chaplain on Oct. 31, in the room of — Whytt, deceased[1]. It was probably during his tenure of office that the Library was destroyed. For in 1550 the Commissioners deputed by Edward VI for reformation of the University visited the Libraries in the spirit of John Knox, destroying, without examination, all MSS. ornamented by illuminations or rubricated initials as being eminently Popish, and leaving the rest exposed to any chance of injury and robbery. The traditions which Wood has recorded as having been learned at the mouths of aged men who had in their turn received them from those who were contemporaneous with the Visitation, are abundantly confirmed by the well-known descriptions of Leland and Bale of what went on in other places, and therefore, although no direct documentary evidence of the proceedings of the spoilers is known to exist, we may believe that Wood's account of pillage and waste, of MSS. burned, and sold to tailors for their measures, to bookbinders for covers, and the like, until not one remained *in situ*, is not a whit exaggerated[2]. One solitary entry there is, however, in the University Register (I. fol. 157[a]), which, while it records the completion of the catastrophe, sufficiently thereby corroborates the story of all that preceded, viz. the entry which tells that in Convocation on Jan. 25, 1555–6, 'electi sunt hii venerabiles viri Vice-Cancellarius et Procuratores, Magister Morwent, Præses Corporis Christi, et Magister Wright, ad vendenda subsellia librorum in publica Academiæ bibliotheca, ipsius Universitatis nomine.' The books of the 'public' library had all disappeared; what need then to retain the shelves and stalls, when no one thought of replacing their contents, and when the University could turn an honest penny by their sale? and so the *venerabiles viri* made a timber-yard of Duke Humphrey's treasure-house.

---

[1] Wood MS. F. 27, fol. 94[a].

[2] Of the ruin of the library John Pits says:—'Hæretici . . . . . libros illos omnes (ô irreparabile rei litterariæ dispendium) vel flammis tradiderunt, vel, ut alias perirent, dissipaverunt.' (*De illust. Angliæ scriptt.*, 1619, p. 38.) See *infra, sub anno* 1605.

But four years after the final despoiling of the Library there was an undergraduate entered at Magdalen College, who, by the good Providence which always out of evil brings somewhat to counterpoise and correct, was to be moved by the sight of the ruin and desolation to restore what his seniors had destroyed, and to reconstruct the old Plantagenet's Library on such a basis, and with such means for carrying on its re-edification, that the glory of the latter house should soon eclipse that of the former. All around him he doubtless found traces of the recent destruction; his stationer may have sold him books bound in fragments of those MSS. for which the University but a century before had consecrated the memory of the donors in her solemn prayers; the tailor who measured him for his sad-coloured doublet, may have done it with a strip of parchment brilliant with gold, that had consequently been condemned as Popish, or covered with strange symbols of an old heathen Greek's devising, that probably passed for magical and unlawful incantations. And the soul of the young student must have burned with shame and indignation at the apathy which had not merely tolerated this destruction by strangers, but had contentedly assisted in carrying it out to its thorough completion. Himself a successful student, he became eager to help others to whom thus the advantages of a library were denied; and, for a while without fee or reward, undertook a public Greek lecture in the Hall of Merton College, to which college he had been elected in 1563[1]. And when, after years thus spent in academic pursuits, Thomas Bodley betook himself to diplomatic service abroad, he still, amidst

[1] Bodley appears to have been altogether an accomplished linguist. James, in the preface to the first Catalogue of 1605, after speaking of his proficiency in the classical languages, adds, 'Linguas vero exoticas, veluti Italicam, Gallicam, Hispanicam, Hebræam præcipue, cæterarum omnium parentem, tam perfecte callet, ut illo neminem fere scientiorem invenies.' And in one of four letters addressed to him on the interpretation of passages in the Old Testament, which are printed among the Epistles of J. Drusius, *De Quæsitis* (1595, p. 40), Drusius says, 'Vere dicam, Bodlæe, et intelligis optime litteras Hebræas, et amas unice earum peritos.' The same volume contains also one letter to his brothers, Laurence, Miles, and Josias, on the *Pastor* of Hermas.

all the distractions of foreign and domestic politics, preserved his affection for the scenes and the studies of his early familiarity. So, when the days came wherein statecraft began to weary him and Courts ceased to charm, his thoughts reverted to the place where, free from these, he might still, although in a more private capacity, labour for the good of the commonwealth; he remembered the room once precious to students, 'scientiarum sedes,' as the University had called it of old, but now destitute alike both of sciences and of seats. And thus, says he himself, 'I concluded at the last to set up my staffe at the Librarie-dore in Oxon; being throwghly perswaded that, in my solitude and surcease from the commonwealth-affayers, I coulde not busie myselfe to better purpose then by redusing that place (which then in every part laye ruined and wast) to the publique use of studients[1].' So therefore, on Feb. 23, 1597–8, he wrote a letter to the Vice-Chancellor, offering that whereas 'there hath bin heretofore a publike library in Oxford, which, you know, is apparant by the roome itself remayning, and by your statute records, I will take the charge and cost upon me, to reduce it again to his former use,' first by fitting it up with shelves and seats, next by procuring benefactions of books, and lastly by endowing it with an annual rent[2]. This offer being accepted with great gratitude, other letters followed from him in March, in which he desired that delegates should be chosen to consider the best mode of fitting up the room, and mentioned an offer on the part of his own College, Merton, to provide timber for the purpose. At once, in 1598, upon the beginning of the work, a public expression of gratitude, 'in the name of the whole, which oweth you much more then my weakenesse is able to expresse,' was made by Rich. Haydocke of New College in a

[1] Bodl. MS. Addit. A. 186, f. 7 b; a contemporaneous copy.

[2] This letter (with subsequent correspondence and lists of the first donors) is printed by Hearne, at the end of the Chron. of John of Glastonbury, vol. ii. p. 612, from Reg. Convoc. M[a]. f. 31[a]. A box of original deeds exists in the Library, and copies of leases from Bodley respecting the farm at Cookham, Berks, and the tenements in Distaff Lane, London, which he conveyed to the Library, are entered in the earliest book of accounts.

dedication prefixed to his translation of Lomazzo's treatise on the Art of Painting. And in the engraved title of the book Haydocke inserts what seems to be a good portrait of Bodley[1]. And on March 6 in the same year Sir Dudley Carleton writes thus to John Chamberlain: 'Your friend Mr. Bodley has sent down to the University to signify his intentions to furnish their library, and his liberality has received very good acceptance and thanks by public letters. He is daily expected at Oxford to make good his word; the matter is generally approved here in the shire, and every man bethinks himself how by some good book or other he may be written in the scroll of the benefactors. My cousin Dormer would have been reckoned among the first, but his wife dissuaded him, and told him it would be ascribed to some planet which possessed all men with a sudden humour; for the chief benefactor, she does not greatly marvel at his purpose, in that he is taught by use to furnish a great desolate room' [*qu.*, what is the allusion?]. 'The books and shelves which were there before, she hears say, were all burnt; for those which he now puts in she wishes longer endurance[2].'

Two years were spent in the fitting up of the room and in the preliminary arrangements. These proved more costly than had been anticipated; for Carleton writes thus to his friend Chamberlain on 3 April, 1599: 'Bodley is looked for daily at Oxford; his library costs him much more than he expected, because the timber-works of the house were rotten, and had to be new made[3].' Amongst these preparations was the putting up the beautiful roof which to this day is such an object of deserved admiration. It is divided into square compartments, on each of which are painted the arms of the University, being the open Bible,

[1] So Hearne, in a note in one of his volumes of MS. papers (Raw. D. 316, f. 114) where a reference is given to the Selden copy of the book for this portrait; since the date of that note this title-page has been stolen, but the Library fortunately possesses now a perfect copy in the Douce collection. Wood says (*Ath. Oxon.*) the portrait is of Haydocke himself.

[2] *Cal. Dom. S. P.*, 1598–1601, p. 35.

[3] *Ibid.*, p. 174.

BODLEIAN LIBRARY.

HALF-LENGTH PORTRAIT OF THOMAS BODLEY

INTERIOR OF THE BODLEIAN

From a painting by E. Vaughan-Jenkins, 1888

Portrait of Dr R. Rawlinson

with seven seals[1], between three ducal crowns, on the open pages of which are the words (so truly fitting for a Christian School) 'DOMINUS Illuminatio mea[2];' while on bosses that intervene

[1] Most probably intended to refer to the Apocalyptic book (Rev. v. 1), and to signify the unsealing of Divine Revelation, the fountain of all wisdom, by our Blessed Lord. Sir J. Wake prefers to take the seven seals as representing the seven liberal arts; and dean Boyes endeavours to explain away more entirely all religious significance in this passage in his *Works*, (fol. Lond. 1638, p. 430):—

'My dear nurse the University of Cambridge hath for her armes *the book clapsed between foure Lions*; and her worthy sister of Oxenford, *the booke open betweene three Crownes*. Hereby signifying (as I conjecture) that Englishmen may study the Liberall Arts closely, and quietly, as also professe them openly and publikly, being guarded with the Lion and the Crown; that is, encouraged thereunto by royall charters and princely priviledges.'

But the Oxford antiquary Brian Twyne speaks more sensibly, and with more insight into the meaning of old symbols, in his *Antiq. Oxon. Apologia* (4°. Oxon., 1608, p. 201, lib. ii. § 216), in these words:—'Honoraria vero ipsius Universitatis Oxon. insignia sunt sacra in scuto cæruleo Biblia, septem sigillis ornata, non tamen clausa, sed ad Evangelium Sancti Johannis aperta, cum hac inscriptione Evangelica, *In principio erat verbum, et verbum erat apud Deum*; tres vero coronæ aureæ vel S. Trinitatis majestatem vel triplicem S. Scripturæ sensum representantes, quemadmodum in antiquissimis armorum delineationibus memini, adjunguntur; quæ insignia admodum antiqua esse vel illud convincit quod in turri in fano S. Sampsonis Greekladæ antiquissimo opere saxo insculpta reperiantur, a tempore translationis Græcladensium Schol. Oxoniæ usurpata.'

[2] The motto has varied at various times. 'Veritas liberabit, Bonitas regnabit,' is given with the University arms in the books printed by John Scolar at Oxford in 1517–8. In 1575 three mottos were recognised as alike used by the University. Laurence Humfrey, President of Magdalen College and Vice-Chancellor, speaks thus in his oration before Q. Elizabeth at Woodstock, on presenting her with a copy of the Bible: 'Hic liber nostræ Universitatis insignia continet, septem sigillis communitus . . . Sententiæ quæ describuntur symbola sunt Academiæ; una, *In principio erat Verbum, et Verbum erat apud Deum*; altera, *Dominus illuminatio mea et salus mea, quem timebo?* tertia, *Bonitas regnabit, Veritas liberabit*, sicuti in libris Oxoniæ, in vico Sancti Johannis quondam impressis vidimus.' (Nichols' *Progresses of Q. Eliz.*, 2nd edit., vol. i. p. 598.) A fourth motto, 'Sapientiæ et Fælicitatis,' is found in books printed at Oxford between 1587 and 1623, and also as 'Sapientia et Felicitate.' This latter form is found (with the arms) in 1671 on the title-page of Pococke's *Abi Jaafar*, printed at the University Press, and as late as 1684 on the title-page of the fourth edition of John Gregorie's *Works*, printed in London by Royston. It is incorrectly printed as 'Sapientia Felicitatis' on the title of [Fulman's] *Acad. Oxon. Notitia* in 1665. In an heraldic MS. of the seventeenth cen-

between each compartment are painted the arms of Bodley himself, being five martlets with a crescent for difference, quartered with the arms of Hone (his mother's family), two bars wavy between three billets; on a chief the three ducal crowns of the University shield, 'quarum merito gloriam ab Academia derivavit.' (Wake, *Rex Platon.* p. 12.) The striking motto 'Quarta perennis erit' was assigned to Bodley at the same time with this academic augmentation[1]. When, in 1610, the eastern wing of the Library was erected, a similar roof was added, as was also done to the Picture Gallery (built between 1613–1619); in the latter room the roof, having become decayed and out of repair, was unhappily altogether removed in the year 1831, and a plaster ceiling, divided into compartments, substituted. A few of the panels of this roof have been preserved, one bearing the figures of two cats, which used to be an object of interest to juvenile visitors, and a series bearing the letters which compose Sir Thomas Bodley's name, together with a portrait of him upon a centre panel. A high-backed arm-chair, the Librarian's seat of office in the Library, was formed out of oak from the roof, and an engraving hangs in the Gallery which represents the room before its change for the worse[2].

tury (Rawlinson, B. 60, fol. 81) it is singularly given as 'xx. Exod. Decem Dei omnipotentis mandata. Verbum Dei manet in eternum. Amen.' The motto from St. John i. 1, was in a window in St. Mary's Church (W. H. Turner's *Visitations of the County of Oxford*, 1871, p. 76). The great east window of the Library contains the arms with the three mottos: *Dominus*, etc., on a scroll above, *Sapientia et Fœlicitate* on the Book, and *Bonitas*, etc., on a scroll below. This is engraved in Ingram's *Memorials*, iii. 1; and the same design is stamped on the binding of the Library copy of Chandler's *Marmora Oxoniensia*, printed at the Clarendon Press in 1763.

[1] Wake notices it as a singular coincidence that the Library was first opened on the day of the 'Quatuor Coronati Martyres,' whom, however, by mistake, or in order to make the coincidence better, he calls 'Tres.'

[2] Mr. Davies Gilbert printed at his private press a memorandum that the box which contained his diploma for the degree of D.C.L. was made in June, 1832, from oak from this roof. (Gough Addits., Sussex, 8°. 41, Bodl. Libr.) With reference to this removal of the old roof, the following passage occurs in *The Popery of Oxford*, by Peter Maurice, D.D. (a valued friend for many years of the author).

'The book and its three crowns ought to be firmly impressed upon your minds. Those who built our noble library took care to make it sufficiently ob-

On June 25, 1600, Bodley wrote to the Vice-Chancellor, mentioning that, as the mechanical work was now brought to a good pass, he had begun to busy himself in the gathering of books, and had provided a Register for the enrolment of the names of all benefactors, with particulars of their gifts. This Register (formerly, like all the books in folio, chained to its desk), consisting of two large folio volumes, on vellum, now lies on a table in the great room, and is an object of notice by most visitors. The volumes are ornamented exteriorly with silver-gilt bosses on their massy covers, on which are engraved the arms of Bodley and those of the University, and interiorly in many places with the donors' coats of arms painted in their proper colours, and with various devices. Vol. i. extends from 1600 to 1688, containing 428 pages in double columns; and commences with a printed record of the gifts for the first four years, on pp. 1–90. The following printed title is prefixed: 'Munificentissimis atque optimis cujusvis ordinis, dignitatis, sexus, qui Bibliothecam hanc libris, aut pecuniis numeratis ad libros coemendos aliove quovis genere ampliarunt, Thomas Bodleius, eques auratus, honorarium hoc volumen, in quod hujuscemodi donationes, simulque nomina donantium singillatim referuntur, pietatis, memoriæ, virtutisque causa, dedit, dedicavit.' A paragraph follows, which mentions Bodley's own work of refitting and endowing, and notes that his own large gifts are not entered because he hopes throughout his life to make continually large additions. The whole of this title is printed in the preface to James' first Catalogue, issued in 1605, who was probably part-writer of it [1]. Wake (*Rex Platonicus*, p. 120) speaks of the Register, 'aureis umbilicis fibulisque fulgidum,' as always lying 'eminentissimo loco,' a pro-

vious to all that entered; they that among our learned ones enter within those walls cannot be mistaken when they lift up their eyes heavenward—the panelled roof declares with the tongue of the learned to all that can understand it, that light cometh from above. It has been reserved to this day of strange innovations to strip one of these rooms of their painted banners. Oh, may we never see it erased from the panels of our hearts!' (8°. Lond. 1837, pp. 83–4.) Dr. Maurice died 30 March, 1878, at his vicarage at Yarnton, near Oxford, aged 75.

[1] See *Reliquiæ Bodleianæ*, p. 158.

minent object of notice to all who entered the Library. Vol. ii. extends from 1692 to 1795, ending in the middle of the volume, on p. 216; but there are many omissions in the later portion of its period. Each volume has an index of names. The gifts of the principal donors, as recorded in this Register up to its close, are printed in Gutch's edition of *Wood's History*, vol. ii. part ii. pp. 920–950. It will not be necessary, therefore, to mention here the names of many, but of such only as are 'e principibus principes;' but in the Appendix will be found a list of all the other names which are recorded up to the year 1700. From the year 1796 inclusive, when the gifts of donors began to be entered in the annual printed catalogues of purchases and statements of accounts, this MS. Register ceased to be used.

Among the first and largest benefactors in the year 1600 occur Lord Buckhurst (afterwards Earl of Dorset), the Earl of Essex (see under 1603), Lords Hunsdon[1], Montacute, (editions of the Fathers), Lisle (afterwards Leicester, £100), and Lumley (High Steward of the University)[2], and William Gent, who gave a large collection of books, chiefly medical. Many volumes were given about this time by Bodley which had been collected in Italy by

[1] The books of Lord Hunsdon (who also gave £95 in 1603) bear his crest on the cover, a swan, with a crescent on its breast for cadency (he being the second son), and the garter round it. One of the volumes (4°. P. 106 Art) containing two books, came from Scottish hands. On the title-page of one, Major's *Hist. Brit.*, 1521, is the signature of 'Joannis Barton, decani Dunkelden,' and of another of the same family, 'Thomas Barton;' and on the title of the other, G. Lily's *Chronicon*, 1565, is written, 'Liber Nicholai Roscarrock.' A copy of Rob. Holcot's works (1497) among Selden's books (R. I. 23. Th. Seld.) was also the property of a Thomas Barton, 'in sacra pagina bacaularii ac monachi Westmonasterii, teste Kennio Hibernate.' The binding of this book is stamped with the Tudor rose and a dragon [Hen. VII ?].

[2] Three of the books given by Lord Lumley have the autograph of Cranmer, 'Thomas Cantuarien.,' on the title-page. One is *Sichardi Antidotum contra diversas omnium fere sæculorum hæreses*, fol. Bas. 1528; another, *Euclides*, &c., fol. Par. 1516; a third, *Ptolemæus*, &c., fol. Ven. 1493. His autograph is found also on the title-pages of two tracts in the vol. marked 4°. M. 9 Th., which did not form part of Lord Lumley's gift; one of these is *Eckii Apologia pro principibus Imperii*, 1542, the other an undated edition of the *Interim*.

Bill, the London bookseller, who was employed by Sir Thomas to travel on the Continent as his agent for this purpose.

The famous copy of the French *Romance of Alexander* (now numbered Bodl. 264) must have been one of the MSS. given by Bodley himself at the commencement of his work, as it is found entered in the printed Catalogue of 1605, but does not occur in the Benefactors' Register. It is decorated with a large number of beautiful paintings on a chequered background of gold and colour; but its special interest lies in the illustrations at the foot of about half the pages, which exhibit the most quaint and grotesque representations of customs, trades, amusements, dress, &c., of the time. Some of these were engraved by Strutt; and four specimens, together with one of the larger miniatures illustrating the text, are given by Dibdin in his *Bibl. Decam.* vol. i., where, at pp. 198–201, he discourses, in his own peculiar fashion, on the merits of the volume. A notice of the book may also be found in Warton's *Hist. of Engl. Poetry*, edit. 1840, vol. i. p. 142. At f. 208 is the following colophon, which is of much interest, as affording evidence that the work of the painter occupied upwards of five years:—

> 'Che define li romans du boin roi Alixandre,
> Et les veus du pavon, les accomplissemens,
> Le Restor du pavon et le pris, qui fu perescript
> Le xviii[e] ior de Decembre, lan M.ccc.xxxviii.
> Explicit iste liber, scriptor sit crimine liber,
> Xpristus scriptorem custodiat ac det honorem.

(*In gold letters.*) 'Che liure fu perfais de le enluminure au xviii[e] jour dauryl. Per Jehan de grise, Lan de grace, M.ccc.xliiij.'

A scribe's name is given in the following lines on f. 208, but in a hand apparently not that of any part of the book:—

> 'Laus tibi sit Christe, quoniam liber explicit iste.
> Nomen scriptoris est Thomas Plenus Amoris[1].'

[1] *Plenus-Amoris*, or *Fullalove*, seems to have been the name of a family of scribes. But the expression seems often also to have been used for the mere sake of rhyme. In the colophon of a translation of Alan Chartier in Rawl. A. 338, are these lines:—'Nomen scriptoris, Dei gracia, Plenus Amoris: Careat meroris Deus det sibi omnibus horis.'

Peter Plenus-Amoris was the scribe of Fairfax 6; Thomas, of Univ. Coll. MS. 142; William, of All Souls' 51; Geoffrey, of Sloane 513 (Brit. Mus.). John Plenus-Amoris writes arts. 1 and 2 in Digby MS. 77. 'Nomen

This is followed by a continuation (of later date) of the romance, in Northern-English verse, on seven leaves[1]; and lastly, by 'Livre du grant kaan de la graunt cite de Tambaluc,' which affords one of the earliest French texts of the travels of Marco Polo. Its first miniature gives a view of Venice, with the embarkation of the voyagers, of which a small engraving is at p. 134 of Mrs. Oliphant's *Makers of Venice* (1887), and the part representing the piazzetta is in vol. i. of Col. Hen. Yule's translation of Polo (second edit., 1875). At p. 520 of Col. Yule's second volume there is also a list of the thirty-eight miniatures which illustrate the MS.

The earliest owner's name occurring in the volume is that of 'Richart de Widevelle, seigneur de Rivières,' recorded in an inscription on the cover at the end, which proceeds to say that 'le dist Seigneur acetast le dist liure lan de grace mille cccclxvi. le premier jour de lan a Londres.' Rivers' own autograph follows ('Ryverys'), with some words in French, written in a perfectly frantic scrawl. Subsequent owners were 'Gyles Strangwayes' and 'Jaspere Fylolle' (whose signatures are engraved by Dibdin, *ubi supra*), and 'Thomas Smythe' (f. 215^{b})[2].

A.D. 1601.

It is from this date that our notes on the history of the Library can begin to assume an annalistic form. A gift of £20 from Herbert

scriptoris, Johannes Plenus-Amoris,' occurs in a MS. Sarum Missal, which was sold (for £160) at the sale of Mr. James Comerford's library, 24 Nov. 1881. One Richard Pleynamour, who died before 1317, held land at Gorleston, Suffolk (Muniments of Magd. Coll., *Spitlings*, Nos. 27, 106). In the following instances the name appears to be used only rhythmically:—'Nomen scriptoris est Jhon Wilde plenus amoris.'—(Rawlinson B. 214.) 'Nomen scriptoris Jon. semper plenus amoris, Esteby cognomen, cui semper det Deus homen' (*sic*).—(Bodl. 643.) 'Nomen scriptoris Charke plenus amoris, Totum nomen habes Johannem si superaddes, in etate 24.'—(Bodl. Addit. MS. A. 106.)

[1] Printed by Rev. J. Stevenson at the end of the *Romance of Alexander*, edited by him for the Roxburghe Club in 1849, from Ashmole MS. 44.

[2] Probably this book is the 'large liure en fraunceis tresbien esluminez de le Rymance de Alexandre,' once in the library of Tho. of Woodstock, Duke of Glouc. See Mr. Coxe's pref. to Gower's *Vox Clam.* (Roxb. Club, 1850,) p. 50.

Westphaling, Bishop of Hereford, was expended in the purchase of books with great success; no fewer than thirty were obtained, and amongst them were, 'Evangelia quatuor Saxonica, lingua et charactere vetustiss.,' being the MS. from which John Foxe had taken the text of the Saxon Gospels in the edition published at the expense of Archbishop Parker in 1571, and which was subsequently re-edited by Junius. It is now numbered, Bodl. MS. 441. 'Evangelia lingua Moscovitica' appear (but are not now to be identified) among some books given by Sir Henry Savile[1], whose brother-historian and antiquary, William Camden, is also registered as the donor of a few MSS. and printed books. Sir John Fortescue gave five Greek MSS. with other books. Thomas Allen, M.A., of Gloucester Hall, the astrologer, gave twenty MSS.[2]; the rest of his collection came subsequently to the Library, included in that of Sir Kenelm Digby, to whom Allen had bequeathed it[3]. One of the twenty now given is an extremely curious volume, chiefly written in the ninth century (marked Auctarium F. iv. 32), including in its contents an original drawing (engraved in Hickes' *Thesaurus*, p. 144) by St. Dunstan of himself as prostrate at the feet of the throned Christ[4],

[1] Savile's benefactions were continued in the years 1609, 1610, and 1615, (in which year he sent his own edition of Chrysostom), and in 1620 he sent a large number of Greek and Latin MSS.

[2] In the year 1604 he appears again as the donor of some printed books. A notice of one of his MSS. (now Bodl. 198), which once belonged to Bishop Grosteste, was by him given to the Friars Minor at Oxford, and by them, about 1433, to Gascoigne, who presented it to Durham College, is to be found in Warton's *Life of Sir T. Pope*, 1772, pp. 392-3. The volume contains MS. notes by both Grosteste and Gascoigne.

[3] A table showing the numbers of those Digby MSS. which previously were Allen's, being about 145 of the whole, is in Langbaine MS. xix. p. 583. When in Allen's possession, they were separate tracts, not bound together in volumes as they are now.

[4] Another relic of Dunstan is preserved among the Hatton MSS. No. 30 of that collection, 'Expositio Augustini in Apocalypsin,' written in Anglo-Saxon characters, has the following inscription in large letters on the last leaf: 'Dunstan abbas hunc libellum scribere jussit.' And Hatton 42, a ninth century MS. of Ecclesiastical Canons, is inscribed on the back in a 14th century hand, 'Liber S. Dunstani.' These Dunstan MSS. are described in Bp. Stubbs' Preface to his *Memorials of Dunstan*, 1874, pp. cx-cxii.

a grammatical tract by Eutychius (or Eutex, as the scribe calls him, while professing doubt as to the right form), with Welsh glosses (noticed by Lhuyd in his *Archæol. Brit.* p. 226); the first book of Ovid *De Arte amandi*, with similar glosses [1]; and lections in Greek and Latin from the Prophets and Pentateuch, amongst which is one from Hosea containing, in the Latin version, a line or two unlike any known early version (although faithful to the Hebrew), but found also in a quotation in Gildas [2]. Another of Allen's gifts was a MS. (now numbered Auct. E. iv. 9) which had formerly belonged to New College, and was previously (as appears from the royal arms painted on the first leaf) in the possession of Henry VIII. It is an anonymous Greek treatise in defence of the use of images, which has been cited by Steph. Durantus (in his book *De ritibus Eccl. Cathol.*) under the name of Nicetas [3]. It is entered as No. 98 in the Catalogue of the MSS. at New College in T. James' *Ecloga Oxon.-Cantab.* printed in 1600, where James adds that it had been stolen in the preceding year, 1599, during the *Comitia*, 'in concursu hominum qui undequaque confluebant ex omni parte ad videndum collegia et visendum bibliothecas . . . Deus novit plagium, ulciscatur hominem.' It is strange that a book stolen from New

[1] These glosses, with an 'Alphabetum Nemnivi' in Runic characters, (of which a facsimile is given in Hickes' *Thesaurus*, p. 168, and also in the App. to Hearne's pref. to Will. of Newburgh's *Chronica*), and some Welsh and Latin notes on weights and measures, are printed, with copious notes, by Zeuss in his *Grammatica Celtica*, 8vo. Leipz. 1853, vol. ii. pp. 1076–96. The glosses are also printed by Mr. Robinson Ellis, with a criticism on the MS. by the late Mr. H. Bradshaw, pp. 424–32, vol. xv., 1880, of the Berlin journal *Hermes*. The MS. is described in Wanley's Catalogue, p. 63, and an account of it, together with a facsimile from the Eutychius, is in Villemarqué's *Notice des principaux MSS. des anciens Bretons*, 8vo. Par. 1856. The Alphabet of Nemnivus, together with another, and somewhat later, Runic Alphabet (of 'winged' form), found in Bodl. MS. 572 (a very interesting MS., of Cornish origin and of cent. xi., which belonged to one 'Bledian,' and was given to the Library in 1607 by Ralph Barlow, B.D.), is printed at pp. 10–12 of the *Ancient Welsh Grammar of Edeyrn*, edited for the Welsh MSS. Soc. in 1856 by Rev. John Williams, ab Ithel.

[2] Pointed out to me by the late Rev. A. W. Haddan, B.D.

[3] Jo. Reynolds, *De Romanæ eccl. idololatria*, 1596, p. 607; Archbp. Ussher's *Adversaria*, Rawlinson MS. C. 850, fol. 47.

College in 1599, and noticed on account of the theft in 1600, should have come to the University Library, as a gift from a collector of MSS., in 1601 unquestioned. It is very possible that the donor was himself the thief; a third MS. of his gift (Bodl. 874) belonged to Brasenose College, and several, once in his possession, of the Digby MSS. belonged to his own College, Merton. Capt. Josias Bodley[1] gave an armillary sphere and other astronomical instruments in brass. One of these is a quadrant, about thirteen inches square, of most beautiful and delicate workmanship, with an ornamental border containing figures engaged in taking altitudes, and bearing this inscription, 'Christophorus Schissler geometricus ac astronomicus artifex Augustæ Vindelicorum faciebat anno Domini 1579.' Its original oak box is preserved. But the great benefactor of the year was the newly-appointed Librarian, Thomas James, who gave various MSS., chiefly patristic (which, however, Wood says, 'he had taken out of several College libraries'), and sixty printed volumes. From the first preparation of the new foundation Bodley had fixed upon James, then a Fellow of New College, as his Library-Keeper, who had no doubt become known to him as the man for the place by his editing R. de Bury's *Philobiblon*, and by his searches among the MSS. in the college libraries both of Oxford and Cambridge. The second edition of the *Philobiblon* (printed at Oxford by Joseph Barnes in 1599) has a long dedication to Bodley, in which, without any reference to the possible appointment of the writer to the charge of the new library, much is said in praise of the liberality of Bodley and of those who were assisting him in his foundation. The volume of letters published by Hearne (from Bodl. MS. 699) in 1703, under the title of *Reliquiæ Bodleianæ*, consists chiefly of those which the Founder addressed to James while his collection of books was in process of

[1] Afterwards Sir Josias, a younger brother of Sir Thomas, and Governor of Duncannon in Ireland, author of a humorous Latin tour in Lecale (a barony in the county of Down), which is not unfrequently met with in MS., and has been printed in the *Ulster Journal of Archæology*. His armillary sphere was temporarily lent to the Professor of Astronomy at the new Observatory, on 4 Dec. 1878.

formation, but unfortunately they have no dates of years, and Hearne printed them simply as they came into his hands, without any attempt to determine their order of sequence. We learn from these that James' salary at the outset was £5 13*s*. 4*d*. quarterly; but almost at once he threatened to 'strike' unless it were raised to an annual stipend of £30 or £40, while at the same time he demanded permission to marry. This latter requisition appeared particularly grievous to Bodley, who had made celibacy a stringent condition in his Statutes[1], and he forthwith expostulated strongly with his Librarian on these his 'unseasonable and unreasonable motions' (p. 52). The upshot, however, was that Bodley, very unwillingly, consented to become the 'first breaker' of his own institution, (which 'hereafter,' he says, 'I purpose to become inviolable,') and, for the love he bore to James, allowed him to marry[2]. But it was not until the year 1813 that the Statute was altered and the Librarian released from his obligation of perpetual celibacy, and even then, by a singular and unmeaning compromise, it was ordered that he, as well as the Under-Librarians, should be unmarried *at the time of election*. The whole restriction was, however, finally removed on the revision of the Statutes in 1856. But its infringement appears to have been again tolerated, in one instance, at least, during the last century, viz. in the case of Dr. Hudson. Hearne[3] enters the following 'memorandum' of uncharitable hearsay gossip respecting his quondam chief and friend: 'Dr. Hudson was married when he was elected Librarian. His first wife was one Biesley. That he hath now is his second. It is said that he was married to this Biesley when he was Taberder of Queen's. The Dr. hath been of a loose, profligate, and irreligious life, as I have often heard. The family of the Harrisons he is married into now is good for just nothing, being as stingy (if it can be) as himself.'

[1] These Statutes were probably drawn up by Bodley about 1600, and his English draft is printed by Hearne in the *Reliquiæ*. They were translated into Latin by Dr. John Budden. See under the year 1719, for the gift of a MS. copy.

[2] *Reliquiæ Bodl.*, p. 162. See also p. 183.

[3] *Diary*, vol. lviii. p. 157.

The poet, Samuel Daniel, in this year made the Library begin to be already celebrated in verse. To a 'newly augmented' edition of his *Works* now printed he prefixed many lines addressed 'To his booke, in the dedicating thereof to the Librarie in Oxford, erected by Sir Thomas Bodley, Knight.' They commence thus:

> 'Heere in this goodly Magazine of witte,
> This Storehouse of the choisest furniture
> The world doth yeelde, heere in this exquisite
> And most rare monument, that dooth immure
> The glorious reliques of the best of men;
> Thou, part imperfect work, voutsafed art
> A little roome, by him whose care hath beene
> To gather all what ever might impart
> Delight or Profite to Posteritie.'

And in this same year Charles Fitzgeoffrey, M.A., of Broadgate Hall, in his little volume of *Epigrammata*, printed at Oxford by Joseph Barnes, addresses the 'novæ bibliothecæ Oxon instauratorem' in eighteen Latin lines.

A.D. 1602.

The largest pecuniary donor of this year was Blount, Lord Mountjoy (afterwards Earl of Devon), who forwarded £100 to Bodley from Waterford[1]; which were expended upon books in most classes of literature, including music. Among various gifts of MSS. were some Russian volumes from Lancelot Browne, M.D., and (together with Persian, Finnish, &c.) from Sir Rich. Lee, ambassador in Muscovy. Lord Cobham gave £50 in money, with the promise of 'divers MSS. out of St. Augustin's library in Canterbury[2].' 'Biblia Latina pulcherrima,' 2 vols. fol. was given by George Rives, Warden of New College. This is probably a huge and magnificent specimen of twelfth-century work, now numbered Auctarium, E. infra, 1, 2[3]. But the year was specially marked by the donation of 47 MSS. (including, with some early English volumes, two probably ninth-century MSS., one, Bodl. 819, described in

[1] His letter is printed in Hearne's *Joh. Glaston.* ii. 626.

[2] *Reliquiæ Bodl.*, p. 92.

[3] See *ibid.*, pp. 137 and 219.

James' Catalogue only as 'Anon. in Parabolas Salomonis,' being Bede's Commentary on the Proverbs, and the other, Bodl. 426, 'Philippus Presbyter in Job'), from Walter (afterwards Sir Walter) Cope; and above all, by the gift, from the Dean and Chapter of Exeter to their fellow-countryman Bodley, of 81 Latin MSS. from their Chapter Library. By what right they thus alienated their corporate property no one probably cared to enquire; but, from the tokens of neglect still visible upon the books, we may conclude that only by this alienation were they in all likelihood saved from ultimate destruction: for they nearly all bear more or less sign of having been exposed to great damp, which in several instances has well-nigh destroyed the initial and final leaves[1]. Most of them are beautiful specimens of early penmanship, ranging chiefly from the eleventh century to the thirteenth; and amongst them is that precious relic of English Church offices [Bodl. 579], the Service-book given to Exeter Cathedral by Bishop Leofric in the reign of Edward Conf., described in the 'Registrum Benefactorum' simply as 'Missale antiquissimum'[2]. This is happily perfect; in size a small and thick quarto volume, written on very stout vellum, and containing 377 leaves. Four other volumes (possibly more) were also gifts of Leofric to his Church; they are now numbered Auct. D. II. 16 (the four Gospels), Auct. F. I. 15 (Boethius and Persius), Auct. F. III. 6 (Prudentius), and Bodley MS. 708 (Gregory's *Pastorale*). They each contain an inscription in Latin and Anglo-Saxon, varying in expression, but all to the following effect (as in the last-mentioned volume): 'Hunc librum dat Leofricus episcopus ecclesiæ sancti petri apostoli in exonia ad sedem suam episcopalem, pro remedio animæ suæ, ad utilitatem successorum suorum. Siquis autem illum inde abstulerit, perpetuæ maledictioni subjaceat.

[1] As Bodley's brother, Laurence, was a Canon of Exeter, it was no doubt by his means that these MSS. were transferred from their rightful place of deposit. Laurence himself gave books in 1605, and in 1611 £20. In 1566 the then Dean and Chapter had given to Archbp. Parker that well-known MS. of the Anglo-Saxon Gospels, also Leofric's gift to his Church, which was transferred by the Archbishop in 1574 to the University of Cambridge.

[2] Printed at the University Press in 1883, under the editorship of Rev. F. E. Warren, B.D.

Fiat. Ðaꞅ boc ʒeꝼ leoꝼꞃıc ƀ. ınꞇo scē peꞇꞃeꞅ mınꞅꞇꞃe on exanceꞅꞇꞃe þæꞃ hıꞅ bıꞅcopꞅꞇol ıꞅ· hıꞅ æꝼꞇeꞃꝼılıʒenꝺū ꞇo nıꞇꞇƿeoꞃðnıꞅꞅe· ⁊ ʒıꝼ hıʒ hƿa uꞇ æꞇbꞃeꝺe· hæbbe he ece ʒenıðeꞃunʒe mıꝺ eallū ꝺeoꝼlum. Ām̄.' To the MS. of the Gospels are prefixed very curious lists in Anglo-Saxon of the lands, vestments, books, &c., given by Leofric to his Church, and of relics given by King Athelstan (of which another copy is preserved in the Missal); these lists are printed in the Monasticon, and the titles of the books are given in Wanley's Catalogue (p. 80).

The Library being now supplied with upwards of 2000 volumes, it was solemnly opened on Nov. 8 (the day appointed for the annual visitation) by the Vice-Chancellor, with a procession of doctors and delegates. Meeting them at the door of the room, the Librarian hastily extemporized a short speech in honour of the occasion, 'in qua,' as the University Register records, 'tribus ferme versibus amplexus est omnia.'

A.D. 1603.

Sir Walter Raleigh appears in this year as a donor of £50. He is sometimes said to have procured for Oxford the library of Hieron. Osorius, which was carried off from Faro in Portugal (of which place Osorius had been bishop), when that town was captured by the English fleet under the Earl of Essex in 1596. Raleigh was a captain in the squadron, and probably influenced the disposal of the books; but no direct mention has been found of his name in relation to them, and they appear to be included in the gift made by the Earl of Essex in 1600, for in the account of his donation given in the *Regist. Benef.* many books published in Spain and Portugal are mentioned. Sir William Monson, in the account of the expedition given in his *Naval Tracts*, only says that the library 'was brought into England by us, and many of the books bestowed upon the new erected library of Oxford.' The Earl of Northumberland gave £100. Eleven MSS. were given by Sir Rob. Cotton, of which the list in the Register is printed in Sir H. Ellis' *Letters of Eminent Literary Men*, issued by the Camden

Society in 1843 (p. 103). One of these (Auct. D. II. 14) is the MS. of the Gospels, traditionally believed to be one of those two copies of the Vulgate sent by St. Gregory to St. Augustine in Britain, which were preserved in St. Augustine's abbey, Canterbury[1]; of which the other now exists among Archbp. Parker's MSS. in Corp. Chr. Coll. Cambr., No. 286[2]. They are both written in quarto, in uncial letters and double columns. Their date may possibly be somewhat later than that which is traditionally assigned; but at any rate they are certainly among what the historian Elmham calls 'primitiæ librorum totius ecclesiæ Anglicanæ.' On the last fly-leaf of the Bodley MS. is the following list of books in the hands, probably, of members of some abbey. 'Þas bocas haueð Salomon prst. Þis ƿecodspel tƿaht. ⁊ ƿemaƿtyƿluia. ⁊ ƿe (*erased*) ⁊ ƿe æȝlisce salteƿe ⁊ ƿe cƿanc ⁊ ðe tropere. ⁊ ƿulfmeƿ cild ƿeatteleuaui ('Ad Te levavi.') ⁊ pistelari. ⁊ ƿe (*erased*) ⁊ ðe imnere. ⁊ ðe capitelari. (*word erased*) ⁊ ƿe spel boc. ⁊ Siȝaƿ prst. ƿelece boc. ⁊ Blakehad boc. ⁊ Æilmer ðe ȝrete sateƿ. ⁊ ðe litle tƿopere ƿoƿbeande. ⁊ ðe donatum. xv bocas. Ealfric. Æilƿine. Godric. ⁊ Bealdeƿuine abb.[3] ⁊ Freoden ⁊ hu—(*torn*) ⁊ ðureȝisel.' Several leaves are wanting at the beginning and one at the end; the book commences at St. Matt. iv. 14, and ends in St. John xxi. 16. It now numbers 172 leaves, besides the fly-leaf, and contains 29 lines in a column; the Cambridge MS. has 25 lines.

Two Russian MSS. (a Bible, and 'Canones Patrum Moscov.') were given in this year by John Mericke, English Consul in Russia, and a collection of Italian books by Sir Michael Dormer.

When Ussher and Challoner were in London, in 1603, buying books for Trinity College, Dublin, they met Sir T. Bodley engaged upon the same work for his Library at Oxford; which began a correspondence between them, with a mutual interchange of good offices with regard to the procuring the best books[4].

[1] Wanley, p. 172. Elmham's *Hist. Mon. S. Aug.* 1858, pp. 97, 8.

[2] One of Archbp. Parker's MSS., bearing his signature, 'Matthæus Cantuar.' is now No. 3 of the MSS. called *Bodl. Orient.*

[3] *Qu.*, Baldwin, abbot of Bury, who died in 1098?

[4] Parr's *Life of Usher*, p. 10.

A.D. 1604.

On 18 Apr. Bodley became Sir Thomas, being knighted by the King[1]. And on June 20, letters patent were granted by James I, styling the Library by the founder's name, and licensing the University to hold lands, &c. in mortmain for its maintenance, to an amount not exceeding 200 marks *per annum*[2].

In the list of donors occur Sir Christopher Heydon, Sir Jerome Horsey (whose gift includes a printed copy of the (liturgical) Gospels in Russian, and rolls containing forms of letters, &c. mistakenly described as being in the autograph of the Czar Ivan Basilides), Sir Ralph Winwood (17 Greek MSS.), Robert Barker the printer, and Sir Henry Wotton (a MS. of the Koran).

A.D. 1605.

The bust of Bodley, which is seen in the large room, was sent by Sackville, Earl of Dorset, the Chancellor of the University. It attracted the notice of King James upon his entering the Library on Aug. 28, the fourth day of his visit to Oxford in this year, who, upon reading its inscription, indulged in the very mild pun that the Founder should rather be called Sir Thomas Godly than Bodly[3]. And, looking on the well-filled cases, he said he had often had proof from the University of the fruits of talent and ability, but had never before seen the garden where those fruits grew and whence they were gathered. He examined various MSS. of the Holy Scriptures, and especially of the old English version, as well as of the Ethiopic, on the authority of which, 'more suo, summo cum judicio disceptavit.' Then, taking up Gaguinus' treatise *De Puritate Conceptionis Virg. Mar.*, printed at Paris in 1498, he remarked that the author had so written about purity as if he wished that it should only be found on the title of his book; and said it had often been his desire that such objectionable writings (espe-

[1] Dugdale MS. R., fol. 201.

[2] Wood MS. F. 27.

[3] This would-be witticism is made the subject of a quatrain in the *Justa Funebria Bodlei*, p. 108.

cially on religious subjects) could be altogether suppressed rather than be tolerated to the corruption of minds and manners. He admitted, however, that probably there was no disadvantage from their being stored up in collections of this kind. Moved to a wonderful temper of liberality, the King then offered to present from all the libraries of the royal palaces whatsoever precious and rare books Sir T. Bodley, on examination, might choose to carry away; and promised that the grant should be made under seal, lest any hindrance should arise. It appears[1] that this (somewhat hasty) grant was actually passed under the Privy Seal about the beginning of November in the same year, and that Bodley expected to carry off a great many MSS. from Whitehall. Probably the full execution of his intentions was hindered, as he himself appears to have suspected might happen; at any rate, there is very little in the Library that tells of having come from the royal collections, except a few folio editions of the Fathers which once were in the possession of Hen. VIII, as his arms stamped upon the covers testify[2],

[1] *Reliquiæ Bodl.*, pp. 205, 339.

[2] His arms also occur in a Greek MS. now numbered Auct. E. 1. 15, and on the cover of Bodl. MS. 354 (which contains a Latin quatrain by Leland). And there is one volume among Selden's books (8°. A. 24, Art. Seld.) which appears to possess considerable interest as having come from the library of the many-wived king. It is a fine copy of Æsop, with the *Batrachomyomachia*, &c., printed by Froben in 1518, which may be conjectured, from initials on the binding, to have been a gift from Henry to Anne Boleyn. The cover is of embossed calf; on one side is the Tudor rose supported by angels, with the sun, moon, and four stars above, encircled by the lines:—

'Hec rosa virtutis de celo missa sereno,
Eternum florens regia sceptra feret.'

(These lines accompany the Royal arms on a leaf at the end of W. Burley's books, printed at Oxford in 1517 (Dec.) and 1518 by John Scolar. And arms and lines, with the initials R. L., are found also on the cover of a copy of the Injunctions of Edward VI, and of the Homilies printed in 1547, among Selden's books, 4°. I. 6, Th., and without initials on a copy of an Antwerp edition, without date, of the *Expos. Hymn. Sar.*, 4°. C. 4. 6. Linc. A book printed in 1509, preserved in the parish library at King's Norton, Warwickshire, has the same device on its cover, together with the pomegranate, the badge of Queen Katharine of Arragon: *Library Chronicle*, 1888, vol. v., p. 65). Below are the initials A.H., conjoined with a knot. On the other side is a representation of the Annunciation, with the same initials repeated. Two other books which belonged to Henry VIII are, a volume of Latin theological tracts (A. 7. 23 Linc.), which bears

and three or four MSS. which bear like evidence of having belonged to James I. Upon leaving the room, after spending considerable time in its examination, the King exclaimed that were he not King James he would be an University man; and that, were it his fate at any time to be a captive, he would wish to be shut up, could he but have the choice, in this place as his prison, to be bound with its chains, and to consume his days amongst its books as his fellows in captivity[1]. In the Librarian's congratulatory speech made to the King on this occasion (of which copies are preserved in Wood MS. D. 9, and, transcribed from thence, in Rawl. C. 866), he mentions that there were then in the Library books in at least thirty languages, and that it was frequented by Italians, Frenchmen, Germans, Danes, Poles, and Swedes.

An account of the King's visit to Oxford was written by one Anthony Nixon, under the title of *Oxford's Triumph*, and from a possibly unique copy in the British Museum the following extracts (for which I am indebted to Mr. Falconer Madan) are taken:—

1605. Aug. 30. Friday. [King James I towards the end of his visit to Oxford] 'mounted himself with diuers of his Nobles to see the Vniversities Librarie, which is in length all ouer the Diuinity Schoole. The scituation whereof is so pleasant, that the grounde whereon it is seated is Diapred with Floraes riches, yet is it farre more glorious, hauing placed within her circumference so famous a Monument of such worke, and workemanshippe.

'Round about, in forme of an Amphitheater, are placed Colledges, and in the forefront thereof, in the place of Oakes, Elmes, and Pine-trees, all which are comfortable trees to defende her from the furious wrathe of wind and weather, are planted the Schools of the seauen liberall Sciences, to adorn and beautifie her with the inward plenty of their wisedome and treasure.

'As for the Lybrarie itself, it hath a verie long, large, and spacious walk, ouer the schoole of Diuinitie, interseamed on both sides, from

his arms on both sides, impaling on one side Castile and Arragon, and a copy of an edition of Ptolemy in 1535 (Auct. K. iii. 13), which has on one side 'Redemptoris Mundi arma,' (cruelly half-effaced by the Library stamp), and on the other, arms, rose, and motto-lines, with initials 'H. R.' See also p. 24 *supra*, and under the year 1736.

[1] The account of the visit is given in Wake's *Rex Platonicus*, pp. 116-123.

the one ende vnto the other, very thicke with severall Partitions, with certaine seates and Deskes before them to sitte downe vpon and reade. These partitions are in euerie place filled full of shelues, and vnto the shelues are there many Bookes fastened with chaines of Iron: euerie volume bearing his name and title, written on paper or parchment, in faire Roman letters, and euerie partition hath an Inscription of the Faculties, As whether her bookes bee either of *Theologie*, *Philosophie*, *Astronomie*, *Geometry*, or any other Art, &c.

'The Bookes that are conteined within this Lybrarie, are verie rare, straunge and scarce, seldome or not at all to be heard of or seene in any place but there. All of them verie richlie guilded, and manye of them bossed either with Siluer or Golde.

'All these are so fairelie kept and maintained, as if the Goddesse of *Wisdome* hadde selected and reserued it a Paradice to entertaine the Muses: Therefore I conclude of it thus, that

Dignitatem eius, difficile est vt homo explicet sermone.

'This object being presented vnto the sight of his Maiestie, did so sensiblie discouer his delight therewith, that he reported it a most admirable ornament to the Vniuersitie: and gratiouslie promised himselfe, a royal friend and Patron for euer.'

In this year appeared the first Catalogue of the Library, compiled by Thomas James. It is a quarto volume, published by Joseph Barnes at Oxford, consisting of 425 pages, with an Appendix of 230 more; the Preface is dated June 27. The book is dedicated to Henry, Prince of Wales[1]. It includes both printed books and MSS. arranged under the four classes of Theology, Medicine, Law, and Arts, in a roughly alphabetical order according as they stood on the shelves, with lists of expositors of Holy Scripture, commentators on Aristotle, Hippocrates, and Galen, and in Civil and Canon Law. The legal and medical lists were added at Bodley's special desire[2]. A general alphabetical index of authors is added at the end. A continuation of this classified index, embracing writers on Arts and Sciences, Geography and History, is to be found in Rawlinson MS. D. 984. It was drawn up by James,

[1] At the suggestion of Bodley, who thought that more reward was to be gained from the Prince than from the King. (*Reliquiæ Bodl.*, p. 206.)

[2] *Reliquiæ Bodl.*, pp. 195, 256. The only copy of this catalogue now in the library is one, in very fine condition, which was given by Francis Wise while sub-librarian (1719–1747).

after his quitting the Library, for the use of young students in the faculty of Arts, in order to show his continued interest in them and in the place of his old occupation. In the preface he thus describes the arrangement of his book: 'Exhibeo, primo, libros distributos secundum facultates suas; secundo dissectos in minutissimas portiones vel sectiones, idque alphabetice; tertio, habetis cognitos et exploratos auctores singulos qui de singulis subjectis vel generatim vel speciatim scripserunt libros, tractatus, epistolas: postremo, ne quid desit, habetis editiones certas, et maxime ex parte ex pluribus selectas et meliores, cito parabiles, digitos ad pluteos et pluteorum sectiones intendendo.' This volume came into Rawlinson's possession from Hearne, who notes in it: 'This MS. came out of the study of Dr. Anthony Hall, of Queen's College, Oxford, who married the widow of Dr. John Hudson, to whom this book once belong'd.'

To foreign visitors copies of the catalogue were at first, as it seems, given, for in the book of visitors' names, after the entry of five Germans on 7 Feb. 1624, the following note is added:—'Hi duo postremi non habuerunt catalogum, erant enim aliorum famuli.'

Bacon, on the publication in this year of his *Advancement of Learning*, sent a copy to Bodley, with a letter, in which he said, 'You, having built an ark to save learning from deluge, deserve propriety in any new instrument or engine whereby learning should be improved or advanced.' In the Catalogue printed in 1620 the book is entered, but in that of 1674 it disappears, and there is only a copy which came with Selden's library, and which is still the only copy of the first edition. It is to be feared therefore that the author's donation copy was at some time parted with as a duplicate!

In this year the gossiping Sir John Harington thus notes in his *Nugæ Antiquæ* (1804, II. 110) a visit he paid to the Library:—'Before his Majesties comming to Oxford I was in Oxford librarie, and some of good qualitie of both the Universities; and one of their chief doctors said merrilie to a Cambridge man, that "Oxford had formerlie had a good librarie, till such time as a Cambridge man became our Chancellour, and so cancell'd our Catalogue and scatter'd our bookes, (he meant Bishop Cox in King Edward's time[1]), as from that time to this we could never recover them."' There seems little reason to doubt the truth of the tradition which represents this Chancellor of the University as having been foremost in zeal in destroying many of its treasures.

Henry Ball, gentleman, Bodley's stepson, was admitted to the Library on June 22[2].

A.D. 1606.

Chinese literature began to make its appearance even at this early date. Among the books bought with £20 given by Lady Kath. Sandys were, 'Octo volumina lingua Chinensi,' while two others, '*Excusa* in regno et lingua Chinensi,' were bought, together with the donor's own *Historie of Great Britaine*, with a gift of £5 from John Clapham, one of the Six Clerks in Chancery.

A.D. 1607.

Dr. Richard Mocket, in his bidding-prayer before a Latin sermon preached in this year, mentioned Bodley among the few University benefactors who were then commemorated, and spoke of him as 'de musis Oxoniensibus, si quem alium, optime merentem[3].'

A.D. 1608.

Sir Henry Lillo, who had been consul at Constantinople for the English merchants, gave two MSS. of some of Chrysostom's Homilies (with other books), which Bodley described as 'very fair and ancient.' Will. Burdet, of Sonning, Berks, gave thirty-four MSS.

[1] Cox, afterwards Bishop of Ely, was then Dean of Christ Church, and Chancellor of Oxford in 1547–1552.

[2] Wood MS. E. 5.

[3] Rawlinson MS. E. 154, fol. 58b.

A.D. 1609.

The permanent endowment of the Library was commenced by the Founder in this year, by the purchase, from Lord Norreys, of the manor of Hindons by Maidenhead, worth annually £91 10*s*., in which he reserved his life interest; to which at the same time he added 'certain tenements in London,' producing an annual rent of £40. From the former, now called Hindhay farm, in the parishes of Bray and Cookham, Berks, the Library received until 1882 an annual rent of about £220, but in that year it was advantageously sold (in pursuance of a decree of Convocation on 30 May) for £11,000; the latter, which consisted of houses in Distaff Lane, were sold in 1853, and the produce invested in £3455 10*s*. 3 per cent. Consols. Bodley's letter announcing his gift (of which a copy is entered in the Convocation Register K. fol. 36) is dated May 31, 1609.

Sir Thomas Smith, knt., bequeathed twenty marks and 'insigne quoddam instrumentum mathematicum deauratum.'

A.D. 1610.

The books having some time since begun to crowd the room provided for them, so that James, in his Preface to the Catalogue of 1605, said there already seemed to be more need of a Library for the books than books for the Library, the Founder commenced in this year an extension of his building. On July 16 the first stone was laid of the eastern wing, and of the Proscholium, or vestibule of the Divinity School, beneath; which were completed by 1612, as in that year several donations were placed in the new room[1].

[1] It is probably to aid given for the erection of this structure that the following passage refers: 'To the building Bodley's Library at Oxford a considerable sum was contributed by the Bishop of London, being his share of the moneys paid into court for commutation of penance.' Archd. Hale's Notes to the *Register of Worcester* (Camden Soc. 1855), p. cxxviii. Aid was also given by the Crown, for on May 3, 1611, an order was issued by the Lord Treasurer to the officers of the woods at Stow, Shotover, &c., near Oxford, to deliver to Sir T. Bodley, for enlarging the Library, the timber which was to have been employed for making the Thames navigable to Oxford, a work which did not proceed. (*Calendar of State Papers*, Dom. Series, 1611-18, p. 28.) Lord Norreys of Rycott gave twenty oaks, Ralph Sheldon £50, and Walter Bennet, D.D. £5. Convoc. Reg. K. *f*. 52.

An inscription in gold letters, in the front of this building, commemorates Bodley's work; having become barely legible, it was restored to its pristine lustre by the care of the late Librarian, Mr. Coxe. It runs thus: 'Qvod feliciter vortat. Academici Oxoniens. hanc bibliothecam vobis reipvblicæqve literatorvm T B P.' The noble east window contains some very curious and interesting relics in stained glass which were presented to the Library (with numerous other fragments, which adorn some of the other windows in the Library and partly fill two of those in the Picture Gallery[1]), in 1797, by Alderman William Fletcher of Oxford, a zealous local antiquary and Churchman of the good old school. The three principal fragments represent: 1. Henry II, stripped naked, and suffering flagellation with birch rods, at the hands of two monks, before the shrine of Thomas à Becket[2]. 2. The marriage (as supposed) of Henry VI with Margaret of Anjou, representing, says Dr. Rock[3], that portion of the ceremony which took place at the Church door; formerly in a window of Rollright Church, Oxfordshire. There is no evidence, however, to connect this representation with Henry VI, and it has been conjectured to describe his marriage chiefly from its corresponding in some very small degree to a representation of that event, formerly at Strawberry Hill, and described and engraved in Walpole's *Anecdotes of*

[1] See also under 1818.

[2] Representations of this scene are said to have been not uncommon in church windows. Probably our glass came from a window in Woodstock Chapel, which (as narrated in Froude's *Hist. of Engl.*, chap. xiv) contained such a representation, that chapel having undergone alteration a few years before the date of Alderman Fletcher's gift (Edw. Marshall's *Hist. of Woodstock*, 1873, pp. 334–6). A like window existed in the Hospital of St. Thomas of Acre in Cheapside (where Mercers' Hall and Chapel now stand), which was founded in Becket's honour by his sister Agnes and her husband Thomas Fitz Theobald, on land which had belonged to his father Gilbert, and the designation of which as of 'Acre' seems to favour the legend of his mother's eastern nativity. A letter from a 'reformed' friar, Robert Ward, to Cromwell, among the Cromwell correspondence of 1535 in the Record Office, describes this window in an exactly corresponding way; but the writer adds that he has seen this manner in divers places. See Mr. Gairdner's *Calendar of Letters and Papers of Hen. VIII*, vol. viii. 1885, p. 236.

[3] *Church of our Fathers*, i. 421.

Painting, i. 36. It is probably of an earlier date. 3. The doing homage by William, King of Scotland, with his abbots and barons, to Henry II in York Minster in 1171. Of the first of these, two coloured engravings, and of the second, one, are found in a copy of Gutch's Wood which came to the Library from the same donor, Alderman Fletcher, in 1818, illustrated with very numerous and curious engravings and drawings, as well as enriched with some MS. notes, and bound in seven large quarto volumes [1].

The large coats of arms appear to have been inserted in 1716, as in the accounts for that year we find, 'For paynted armes in the Library window, £5.' But one coat of arms was put up in the year 1771 (*q. v.*).

On 12 June the proposed statutes, which had been carefully considered by a delegacy, were submitted to Convocation and approved. It was also decreed that, in accordance with what had been the custom in former times, the Librarian should have livery given him of the best cloth worn by gentlemen ('liberatam de optima secta generosorum') from all those who customarily upon promotions or accumulations ('promoti vel cumulati') provided livery for University officials; subsequently commuted for a money payment. In the case of Grand Compounders the Librarian used to precede them in procession to the Convocation House. Dr. Bandinel was the last Librarian who took part in this ceremonial, which ceased with the abolition of the *status* of Grand Compounders (*i. e.* persons possessing landed property who paid extra fees for their degrees) in 1855.

At the same Convocation it was ordered that every one admitted to the Library should pay an admission fee of 12*d.*; eightpence to the Librarian and fourpence to the Under-Librarian.

[1] Mr. Fletcher died in 1826, at the age of eighty-seven, and was buried (in a stone coffin traditionally said to be that of Fair Rosamond) in the church of the village where he was born, Yarnton, near Oxford. His tomb is remarkable as exhibiting, before Architectural and Ecclesiological societies had been thought of, an anticipation of better days in monumental design than had yet appeared; a brass, upon a high altar-tomb, represents him clad in his aldermanic gown, with his hands clasped in prayer. A bust of him is in the Picture Gallery.

It was in this year that the Library began to be enlarged with the gift of copies of all works published by the members of the Stationers' Company, in pursuance of an agreement made with them by Bodley, which became the precursor of the obligations of the Copyright Acts. On Dec. 12 the Company made (by indenture sealed in Congregation Feb. 27, 1611) a grant of one perfect copy of every book printed by them, on condition that they should have liberty to borrow the books thus given, if needed for reprinting, and also to examine, collate, and copy the books which were given by others. An order of the Star-Chamber was made July 11, 1637, in confirmation of this grant[1]. The proposal of such an agreement emanated from the Librarian James; but in the effecting it Bodley says that he met with 'many rubs and delays[2].' Ayliffe says[3] that the agreement was very well observed until about 1640. He should rather have said 'about 1630,' for in that year, in a paper of notes made by the Librarian for the use of Archbishop Laud, as Chancellor of the University (in which the mention of a gift of books by Fetherston, a London bookseller, fixes the date), complaint is made that the Company were very negligent in sending their books, and it is suggested that a message from the Chancellor might quickly remedy that neglect[4]. In 1642, Verneuil, the Sub-Librarian[5], complained in the Preface to his *Nomenclator* of the neglect which had then begun; mentioning the names of several benefactors (*see under* 1640), he adds: 'These have beene more courteous than the Stationers of London, who by indenture are bound to give the Library a copy of every booke they print.' Not infrequent mention of disputes with the London booksellers is made in speeches delivered by Dr. Ralph Bathurst as Vice-Chancellor, sixty years afterwards, some of which were printed by T. Warton in 1761 at the end of his *Life*. In 1670 he uses almost the same words as we find him using in the following passage in July 1676 (taken from a copy made by Dr. Rich. Rawlinson, Rawl.

[1] Rushworth, iii. 315.

[2] *Reliquiæ Bodl.*, p. 350.

[3] *Univ. of Oxford*, i. 460.

[4] *Calendar of State Papers*, 1635–6, p. 65.

[5] See *sub anno* 1647.

MS. D. 275, fol. 6): 'Quanquam iniquissimos experimur bibliopolas Londinenses, quibus (mirum dictu!) vix aliud genus hominum academiis aut literatis infensius est; quanquam ingrati et versipelles, tum pactis cum ipso Bodlæo conventis, tum regni senatusconsulto, pertinaciter obluctantur, complures tamen libros Bibliothecæ Publicæ diu debitos, diu negatos, tanquam clavam e manibus Herculis extorsimus, aliosque continuo huc mittendos in posterum curavimus.' And in October of the same year (*Remains*, with *Life*, p. 77), after mentioning Justell's valuable gift of MSS., he again refers to his having procured some books 'a bibliopolis istis ingratis et versipellibus.' In the Visitation Order-book, under the year 1695, is the following 'memorandum' by Hyde, then Head Librarian: 'That in November, 1695, a copy of the indenture between Sir Thomas Bodley and the Company of Stationers, as also a copy of their By-Law to enforce their particular members to complyance, was sent up to the Master of the Company to be communicated and publicly read to the Company once every year, as is in the indenture expressed. The originall was also some years agon carryed up and shewed to the Master and Wardens, because some of them used to raile at the unjustness of the Act of Parliament in forcing them to give a copy of each book to the Bodleian Library; and therefore we shewed them that we had also another antecedent right to a copy of each book printed by any member in their Company. The Indenture mentions only the giving of books new printed, but the By-law mentions books both new-printed and also reprinted with additions [1]. We have been told that Sir Thomas Bodley gave to the Company 50 pounds worth of plate when they entered into this Indenture. But its not mentioned in our counter-part. Every book is to be delivered to the junior Warden within 10 dayes after its off from the press, and we are to appoint somebody to demand them of him. The obligation is upon every printer to give books; it were to be wished it had been upon every proprietor; for the proprietor must give them to us.'

[1] See *sub anno* 1612.

Owen Wood, dean of Armagh, bequeathed £66 13*s.* 4*d.* (100 marks), and Abbot, the archbishop of Canterbury, gave £50.

A.D. 1611.

The first book which came from the Stationers' Company, in pursuance of the Indenture made in Dec. 1610, was an anonymous catechetical work printed in this year by Felix Kingston for Thomas Man, entitled, *Christian Religion substantially, methodicallie, plainlie, and profitablie treatised.* It is now numbered 4°. R. 34 Th., and a note in Bodley's own handwriting records its presentation.

Twenty Arabic, Persian, and other MSS. were presented by Paul Pindar, Consul at Aleppo of the Company of English Merchants, whom Bodley three years previously had requested to procure such books[1]. They are entered in the *Reg. Benef.* under the next year.

Among other minor matters which called forth the care of Bodley, was the providing a bell for the purpose of giving notice when the Library was about to be closed. After it had been placed in the Library some accident appears to have happened to it, since we read in one of his letters to James[2], 'As touching the bell, I would have it cast again, and if my friends think it good, made somewhat better.' In 1616, and frequently in following years, a bell-rope was bought at the price of 1*s.* 6*d.*, and in 1655 for 1*s.* 4*d.* In 1637 £3 were paid for hanging it. Of late years, however, the Founder's bell had altogether disappeared, and the fact of its very existence was unknown, while a small hand-bell, suggestive of the old-fashioned muffin-man, and, more recently, a hand-bell taken from a Chinese temple outside Pekin, and presented by Major-Gen. Gibbes Rigaud [*dec.* Jan. 1, 1885], supplied

[1] Hearne's *Joh. Glaston.*, ii. 637, where Bodley's letter announcing this gift, and also Sir John Bennet's willingness to help in the enlargement of the Library and rebuilding of the Schools, is printed from Convoc. Reg. K. Copies of Bennet's own letters, dated 1 Apr. and 21 Jan. 1612, &c. are in Reg. K. at ff. 78[b], 80[b], 90[b]. Bennet promises to defray the tenth part of the cost.

[2] *Reliquiæ Bodl.*, p. 314.

its place. But in July, 1866, in the course of moving some boxes and rubbish buried under some stairs, a mouldy bell of considerable size was dragged to light, which proved to be the missing bell of the Founder. It was immediately put by the Librarian into the hands of Messrs. White, of Bessilsleigh, Berks, who fitted it with a frame and wheel; and now, restored to a conspicuous place in the great room, it daily thunders forth an unmistakeable signal alike for entrance and departure [1]. Around it, in gold letters, runs the inscription:—'Sir Thomas Bodeley gave this bell, 1611.' The bell-founder's initials, W. Y. (*i.e.* Will Yare), are accompanied by the device of a crown between three bells, on a shield [2].

Another relic of Bodley's furniture is a massy iron chest, fastened with three locks, two of which are enormous padlocks, for the preservation of the moneys of the Library, of which the keys used to be in the custody of the Vice-Chancellor and Proctors. This is now exhibited in the Picture Gallery, on account of the extreme beauty of the ironwork of the locks, which covers in its intricate ramifications the whole of the inside of the lid. On the outside are painted the arms of the University (with the motto 'Sapientiæ et Fælicitatis') and of Bodley. On 20 May, 1613, it was ordered that this chest should be kept in Corpus Christi College, in the same place with the University Chest [3]. It was brought back to the Library at the visitation in 1622, when 2*s.* were paid to two porters for carrying it, and 1*s.* 'to the buttler for beere and attendance at the farewell of the chest from C.C.C.'

A.D. 1612.

Two large donations of MSS. were received during this year; the one from the Dean and Chapter of Windsor (in imitation of

[1] From an allusion in a letter of Wanley's in 1699, it appears that the bell was then rung at the opening of the Library: Ellis' *Letters of Eminent Literary Men*, Camd. Soc., 1843, p. 292. In accounts for 1747–8 there is a payment for taking it down from some place *over* the Library.

[2] This device was used by Yare on bells at Reading in 1610–11, and on one of the bells of the Cathedral at Oxford, made by him in 1611; and was one in common use among bell-founders. It is engraved in the *Sussex Archæol. Collections*, vol. xvi, p. 172.

[3] Reg. Convoc. K. f. 123.

their brethren at Exeter), of 159 volumes, chiefly theological; and the other of a large collection of scientific treatises, chiefly astronomical and medical, about 120 in number, from Thomas Twine, M.D., of Lewes. Twelve MSS. were also given by Will. Harwood, prebendary of Winchester.

The agreement that was entered into by the Stationers' Company in 1610 having probably been found in some degree inoperative from the absence of any penalty upon non-fulfilment, the Company at the commencement of this year passed the following ordinance, which made it obligatory on every one of their members to forward their books to the Library. It is here printed from the original, preserved in the University Archives, marked A. 27 [1].

'*Vicesimo octavo Januarii* 1611 *nono regni regis Jacobi, at Stacõners Hall, in Ave Mary Lane in London. Present, the Masters, Wardens, and Assistants of the Company of Stacõners.*

'Forasmuch as this Companye out of their zeale to thê advancement of learninge, and at the request of the right worshipfull Sir Thomas Bodley, Knight, founder of the presente publique library of the University of Oxford, beinge readye to manifeste their willinge desires to a worck of so great pietye and benefitt to the generall state of the Realme, did by their Indenture under their common seale dated the twelveth daye of December in the eight yeare of his Maj.ts raigne of England, Fraunce and Ireland, and the foure and fortith yere of his raigne of Scotland, for them and their successors, graunte and confirme vnto the Chauncellor, Maisters, and Schollers of the Universitie of Oxford, and to their successors for ever, That of all bookes after that from tyme to tyme to be printed in the said Company of Stacõners, beinge newe books and coppies never printed before, or thoughe formerly printed yet newly augmented or enlarged, there should be freelie given one perfect Booke of every such booke (in quyers) of the first ympression thereof, towardes the furnishinge and increase of the said Library; Nowe therefore, to the ntent the said graunte maie take due effect in the orderlie performance and execucõn thereof, and that so good and godlie a worck and purpose maie not bee disappointed or defeated by any meanes, It is ordayned by this Company, that all and every printer and printers that from tyme to tyme hereafter shall

[1] For the use of this document the author was indebted to the late Keeper of the Archives, Rev. J. Griffiths, D.D.

either for hym- or themselves, or for any other, printe or cause to be printed any newe booke or coppie never printed before, or although formerly printed yet newly augmented or enlarged, shall within ten daies next after the finishinge of the first ympression thereof and the puttinge of the same to sale, bringe and deliver to the yonger warden of the said Company of Stacõners for the tyme beinge one perfect booke thereof to be delivered over by the same Warden to the recited use to the handes of such person or persons as shalbe appoincted by the said Chauncellour, Maisters and Schollers for the tyme beinge to receive the same; And it is alsoe ordayned that every printer that at any tyme or tymes hereafter shall make default in performance hereof, shall for every such default forfeite and paie to the use of this Company treble the value of every booke that he shall leave undelivered contrarie to this ordenance; Out of the which forfeiture, upon the levyinge and payment thereof, there shalbe provided for the use of the said Librarye that booke for the not delivery whereof the said forfeiture shalbe had and paid. And to the intent all printers and others of this Company whome it shall concerne maie take notice of this ordenance, and that any of them shall not pretend ignorance thereof, It is ordeyned that once in every yere at some generall assemblie and meetinge of the said Company upon some of their usuall quarter daies, or some other tyme in the yere at their discretion, this presente ordinance shalbe publiquely read in their Hall, as other their ordenances are accustomed to be read there.

'John Haryson	'William Leake
'John Norton, Mr. [Master]	'Robert Barker
'Richard Field } Wardens	'Thomas Mane
'Humphrey Lownes } Wardens	'Thomas Dawson
'Edward White	'John Standishe
'Humfry Hooper	'Thomas Adames
'Simon Waterson	'John Haryson[1]

'Ri. Collins, Clerk of the Companie.

'Havinge lately byn entreated, as well by the said Sir Thomas Bodley, Knight, as by the Maister, Wardens, and Assistants of the foresaid Company of Stacõners, to take some spetiall notice of this their publique acte and graunte, and (in regard of our beinge of his Maiestyes highe Commission in ecclesiasticall causes) to testifie under our handes with what allowance and good likinge we have thought it meete to be received, Wee doe not onlie as of merrit comend it to posteritie for a singuler token of the fervent zeale of that Company to the furtherance of good learninge and for an exemplarie guift and graunt

[1] Probably the son of the John Haryson who signs above.

to the Schollers and Studients of the Universitye of Oxford, But withall we doe promise by subscribinge unto it, that if at any tyme hereafter occasion shall require that we should help to maynteyne the due and perpetuall execucõn of the same, Wee will be readie to performe it, as farre as either of our selves thoroughe our present authoritie or by any whatsoeuer our further endeavours it maie be fitlye procured.

'G. Cant.	'Richard Moket	'Jo. Roffens
'Jo. London	'R. Cov. & Lich.	'George Montaigne (*sic*)
'Jo. Benet	'Jhon Boys	'Robt. Abbott
'Tho. Ridley	'Char. Fotherbye	'Henr. Hickman
'Tho. Edwardes	'Martin Fotherby	'John Dix
'G. Newname	'John Layfeilds	'Willm. Ferrand.'
'John Spenser		

A.D. 1613.

The death of the Founder occurred on Jan. 28[1], after long suffering from stone, dropsy, and scurvy, for which he is said to have been mis-treated by a Dr. Hen. Atkins[2]. Two volumes of elegiac verses were thereupon issued by the University, of which one (*Bodleiomnema*) was written entirely by members of Merton College[3]; the other (*Justa Funebria Ptolemæi Oxoniensis*) by members of the University in general. In the latter collection are Latin verses by Laud, then President of St. John's, and Greek verses by Isaac Casaubon. Illustrations of the fabric and arrangement of the Library are found in some of the verses in these volumes. Bodley was buried (according to his desire in his will) in the chapel of his old College, Merton, on March 29, with all the state of a public funeral; and one 'Oratio funebris' was delivered by Sir J. Wake, the Public Orator, in the Divinity School, and another in Merton College, by John Hales. He bequeathed the greater part of his property for the building of the west wing of the Library and the third story of the quadrangle, appointing Sir John Bennet and Mr. William Hakewill his executors. The former, however, proved in some measure an

[1] Wrongly given as 'quarto Cal. Feb.,' *i. e.* Jan. 29, in the very book published by his College on his death!

[2] *Calendar of State Papers*, 1611-18, p. 137.

[3] Of this no copy appears to have been in the Library until it came among R. Burton's books.

unfaithful steward. When prosecuted in Parliament in 1621, for gross bribery in his office as Judge of the Prerogative Court, some of Bodley's money (amounting to £751 1*s.* 0¼*d.*) was still remaining in his hands, and was mentioned in the charges brought against him. £150 were paid on 1 Aug. 1624. For the due payment of the remainder, by annual instalments of £150, the University, on June 28, 1624, accepted four bonds from him, witnessed by Thomas Coventreye, Matthew Bennet, and Henry Wigmore; only one of these was paid off, leaving an unpaid deficit of £450[1]. The entry of this debt is carried on, together with the loan made to King Charles I in 1642, in the Library accounts, from year to year up to 1782, when by order of the Curators the entries were discontinued. In the notice of the Library contributed (as it is said) by Dr. Hudson to Ayliffe's *Ancient and Present State of Oxford* (vol. i. p. 460), it is stated that the Library estate falls miserably short by reason of 'the fraud of his [Bodley's] executor, the loan of a great sum of money to Charles I in his distress, and by the fire of London,' that event, doubtless, necessitating the rebuilding of the houses in Distaff Lane. It appears from the accounts that an attempt was made in 1661–4 to recover what remained due on the bonds, but in vain.

Bodley was charged by some of his contemporaries, and

[1] A full account of Bennet's defalcations is given by B. Twyne, from the University Registers, in vol. vi. (pp. 120–4) of his *Collectanea*, now in the Univ. Archives. See also *Parl. Hist.* vol. v. p. 462. It appears from the first book of accounts (which extends from the foundation to 1676, and was discovered in 1878 in a box in the Coin Room) that two payments of £250 each were received from Hakewill on his separate account, 'being part of a greater summe remaining in his hands as executour to Sir Thomas Bodley,' in the year 1630, upon which a general acquittance was given to him. A statement of all the payments made by the executors out of Bodley's estate, and sums received up to March 28, 1618, is in Convoc. Reg. N. 23, ff. 57^b, 59^b, and subsequent entries are also to be found there, with copies of several letters from Bennet in 1624. In Bodl. Addit. MS. C. 206, f. 4, is a copy of a petition to the King praying for the assignment to the University of Bennet's 'possessionis Dawliensis' until his debt was paid, and promising that in that case no one should be able to enter the Library 'nisi inspecta prius hac Magni Jacobi praefatione.' Hence, probably, the figure of King James in the Tower of the quadrangle.

apparently with some justice, with sacrificing in his will the claims of relatives and friends too much to the interests of the Library. One Mr. John Chamberlain, a friend of Bodley, whose gossiping letters to Sir Dudley Carleton, Alice Carleton, and others, are preserved in the State Paper Office, does not spare his accusations on this head. In a letter dated Feb. 4, 1613, he says that Bodley has left legacies to great people, £7000 to the Library, and £200 to Merton College, but little to his brothers, his old servants, his friends, or the children of his wife, by whom he had all his wealth[1]. In another, dated June 23, 1613, he remarks that the executors cannot excuse Bodley of unthankfulness to many of his relatives and friends, he being 'so drunk with the applause and vanitie of his librarie that he made no conscience to rob Peter to pay Paul[2].' Some inferential corroboration of this is afforded by the following curious paper preserved among Hearne's gatherings (in a vol. now numbered Rawl. MS. D. 396), being no other than a petition for relief addressed by the grand-nephew and grand-niece of Bodley

[1] *Cal. of State Papers*, 1611–18, p. 169.

[2] *Ibid.*, p. 187. In a letter to Sir Ralph Winwood (who was by his marriage to Elizabeth Ball, daughter of Bodley's wife, Ann Carew [*ob.* 1611] by her first husband, connected with our founder) dated 29 Jan. 1612, Chamberlain is still more severe. 'Mr. Gent came to me this morning as it were to bemoan himself of the little regard hath been had of him and others; and indeed for ought I hear there is scant anybody pleased; but for the rest it were no great matter, if he had had more consideration or commiseration where there was most need; but he was so carried away (if a man may so say) with vanity and vain glory of his Library, that he forgat all other respects and duties almost of conscience, friendship or good nature; and all he had was too little for that work. To say the truth, I never did rely much upon his conscience; but I thought he had been more real and ingenuous. I cannot learn that he hath given anything, no not a good word, nor so much as named any old friend he hath but Mr. Gent and Tom Allen; who, like a couple of almsmen, must have his best and second gown and his best and second cloak; but to cast a colour or shadow of something upon Mr. Gent, he says, he forgives him all he owed him, which Mr. Gent protests to be never a penny. Neither can I deny but I have a little indignation for myself; that having been acquainted with him almost forty years, and observed and respected him so much, I should not be remembered with the value of a spoon or a mourning garment:' &c. Winwood's *Memorials of State*, 1725, vol. iii. p. 429.

in the year 1712 (as appears from the Library accounts) to the Heads of Houses and Curators of the Library, who appear both officially and individually to have been very parsimonious in their response :—

'To the Worshipful Mr. Vice-Chancellor and to all heads and governors of Colleges and Halls within the famous University of Oxon.

'The humble petition of William Snoshill of East Lockinge in the county of Berks, labourer, and of Jane the wife of Thomas Hatton of Childrey in the county aforesaid, labourer, sister of the said William Snoshill,

'Humbly sheweth,

'That your Petitioners being the grand-children of the sister of Sir Thomas Bodley, the munificent founder of the Bodleian Library in your University, being now reduc'd to a poor and low estate, do with all humility make bold to represent their distrest condition to your consideration, hoping that out of your tender pity and commiseration, and that regard you have for the pious memory of so great a benefactor to your University, to whom your poor Petitioners are so nearly allied, you will be pleas'd to consider them as real objects of your charity and compassion, and thereby you will lay an eternal obligation on them of praying for your present and future happiness.

'William Snoshill
'Jane Hatton.

'We, whose names are subscribed to this Petition, are well satisfied of the truth thereof.

'Thomas Paris, rector of Childrey
'John Holmes
'John Bell, vic. of Sparsholt
'John Aldworth, rector of East Lockinge
'Ralph Kedden, M.A., vicar of Denchworth, Berks.

'(*Mem.*) The Curators gave the Petitioners the sum of four pounds out of Sir Thomas Bodley's chest. Dr. Altham, Hebrew professor, and Dr. Hudson, Library-keeper, gave, each of them, ten shillings.'

The poverty of this branch of the family was caused by their ancestress, Bodley's sister, having offended her relations by a clandestine marriage with a clergyman of Exeter named John Burnett, who in consequence had to leave Devonshire, and died at Standlake in Oxfordshire in Sept. 1615, in a little chapelry near which village, named Shifford, he had officiated as curate. Letters to Hearne, which give full particulars, are found in vol. xxix of his MS. Diary, and these, together with extracts from the parish registers of Standlake and Ducklington, were communicated to *Notes and Queries* by me, where they may be found in vol. ii, sixth series, 1880, pp. 423–4.

An alphabetical catalogue was prepared in this year by James, but was not printed. The MS., in two small hand-books, remains in the Library.

It was ordered by the Curators, at the Visitation on Nov. 13, that 6*s*. 8*d*. be paid quarterly to the Bedel of the Stationers' Company as a gratuity for his trouble [1].

A Librarian's miscellaneous register-book, in small quarto, belonging to this year, contains many interesting matters :—

i. Lists of books sent to the binders.

ii. Lists of books bought second-hand, the large majority costing under 1*s*.

iii. Notes of promises of gifts.

iv. Orders of the Curators.

v. List of persons (Bachelors of Arts) suspended from the Library for three months, for coming up without their academical habits. (See under the year 1715.)

The Curators' orders were confirmed in Convocation on 13 Nov., and are entered in Reg. K. fol. 134, and other orders of 27 July, 1615, at fol. 168[b].

A.D. 1614.

Nine MSS. and other books were received from Edw. James, D.D., who had been a contributor already in the year 1601.

Various orders were made by the Curators at the Visitation on Nov. 10, which are prefixed to the small MS. 'hand-catalogues' made at that time for the use of those authorities. They resolve that the catalogues of newly-published works issued at Frankfort

[1] See also under 1624. When Bowles was Librarian (1719–1726) only twenty shillings *per an.* were paid to Joseph Collyer at Stationers' Hall for sending the books entered there. (Bodl. MS. Addit. C. vii. 8, ff. 10-14.)

in each spring and summer shall be examined by them within one week after their arrival. And they make an attempt to obtain possession of a gift presented through the Founder, which had never yet reached the place of its intended deposit. On Oct. 27, 1609, it had been reported to Convocation that there was about to be sent to the Library by Sir T. Bodley 'toga ex lana agni Tartarici ζωοφύτου, magni quidam valoris, ei data (ut in publica Bibliotheca conservetur) ab Richardo Lee, milite, qui eandem dono recepit ab augustissimo Imperatore Muscoviæ[1].' But the precious cloak had never yet arrived; the Curators therefore resolve 'quod literæ scribantur ad exequutores domini Fundatoris pro illo pretioso pallio ex zoophyto confecto, et legato ad nos per Ric. Leigh, militem, olim legatum apud Imperatorem Russiæ, et quod in cista ex ligno bene olenti, ad eam finem comparanda, reponatur in archivis, munita sera affabre facta; clavis permaneat semper apud Vice-Cancellarium vel ejus deputatum, nec cuiquam illud inspiciendi vel contrectandi potestas esto nisi in præsentia eorundem.' At this Visitation Joseph Barnes, the Oxford printer, appeared and promised to give a copy of every book which he might print. Complaint was made that the London Stationers had already begun to fail in the fulfilment of their agreement.

On Aug. 29 the King visited the Library on his way to Woodstock, and, asking for Fulke's *Annotations on the Rhemish New Test.*, pointed out the remarks at Rom. x. 15, on the calling of

[1] Reg. Conv. K. f. 43. Bodley mentions in a letter to James his expectation of exhibiting the 'lamb's-wool-gown' to the King. *Reliqq. Bodl.* 173. An account of this marvellous garment will be found in the Appendix. It was received on 2 Dec. 1615, when, as entered in the first book of accounts, xii*d.* were paid 'for bringing ye Moscovia gowne,' and vi*s.* for 'a litle chest' to keep it. In 1634 5*s.* were paid to a glover for mending it, and in 1643 10*s.* to a 'painter for drawing to life the picture of the Tartar lambe out of Duretts booke,' *i.e.* Cl. Duret's *Hist. admirable des plantes . . . miraculeuses en nature*, 1605. It proved a perpetual source of expense. In 1644 these entries are found in the accounts: 'For sewing, mending and ayring the Tartar lambes coate, and clensing and ayring the Turkey carpett, 3*s.* 6*d.* Item, for mending and putting on a paire of new hinges on the Russian boxe wherein the Tartar lambe coate is kept, 1*s.*'

ministers; 'deprehendit calumnias et imposturas quorundam pontificiorum de ordine et vocatione ministrorum [1].' In 1620 the editions of 1601 and 1617 of these *Annotations* were both in the Library, as appears from the Catalogue of that year, but in Hyde's Catalogue, published in 1674, only the edition of 1633 is found. This is one out of various instances which prove that, by a great miscalculation of literary value, later editions of a writer's works were thought to supersede so entirely the earlier, that the latter could be advantageously parted with. The Library has, however, since become re-possessed of the earlier editions, that of 1601 having been presented in 1824, and that of 1617 having been bought more recently. But the most remarkable example of this mistaken alienation of books occurs with reference to the first folio edition of Shakespeare. In the Supplemental Catalogue of 1635 the folio of 1623 duly appears; but in the Catalogue of 1674 we find only the third edition, that of 1664, which doubtless had been thought to be sufficient as well as best; upon its arrival, therefore, from Stationers' Hall, the precious volume of 1623 was probably regarded as little more than waste-paper. Nor was it until the year 1821, when Malone's collection was received, that a copy was again possessed by the Library [2].

A.D. 1615.

Richard Connock, auditor and solicitor to Prince Henry of Wales, gave a MS. book of *Horæ* [3], which had formerly belonged

[1] Wood's *Hist.* vol. ii. p. 319.

[2] The extraordinary *fancy* prices sometimes given for books, and their variations, are particularly exemplified in the case of the first folio Shakespeare. In 1778 Stevens said it was 'usually valued at seven or eight' guineas. (*Shakespeare*, second edit. vol. i. p. 239.) At the Roxburghe sale (a sufficiently bibliomaniacal one) in 1812 a copy was sold for £100; in 1864 the Baroness Burdett Coutts gave for Mr. G. Daniel's specially fine copy, £716 2*s.*; while in July, 1867, a copy was sold for £410; and one in Feb. 1878 for £480. In Dec. 1867 another copy was on sale at Mr. Beet's, a London bookseller, to which the owner very discreetly attached in his catalogue no specific sum. A fine and perfect copy was priced by Mr. Quaritch in 1887 at £785.

[3] The gift is omitted in the Benefaction-Register, apparently because it

to Mary I, and afterwards to Prince Henry. The donor, in a note prefixed, records that he gives the volume, 'not for the religion it contains, but for the pictures and former royall owners' sake.' It is a volume of the early part of the fifteenth century, in small quarto, containing 224 leaves, and ornamented with very beautiful illuminated borders and exquisite drawings in *camaieu gris*. Among these is one of the martyrdom of Becket, which, doubtless in consequence of the book being in the possession of the Princess Mary, has entirely escaped the defacement and obliteration ordered by her father to be made in all Service-books where the office for S. Thomas of Canterbury occurred. The following inscription (nearly effaced at its close by over-much handling in former years[1]), addressed by Mary to one of her ladies, whose name does not appear, to whom probably she presented the book, occurs in the blank portion of one of the leaves :—

'Geate you such riches as when the shype is broken, may swyme away wythe the Master. For dyverse chances take away the goods of fortune ; but the goods of the soule whyche bee only the trewe goods, nother fyer nor water can take away. Yf you take labour and payne to doo a vertuous thyng, the labour goeth away, and the vertue remaynethe. Yf through pleasure you do any vicious thyng, the pleasure goeth away and the vice remaynethe. Good Madame, for my sake remembre thys.

'Your lovyng mystres,

'Marye Princesse.'

This inscription (which does so much credit to its writer) was first printed by Hearne at the end of *Titi Livii Forojulien. Vita Hen. V.* (p. 228) and last, in Bliss' *Reliquiæ Hearn.* i. 105. The late Librarian, Mr. Coxe, noted (from *Alstedii Systema Mnemo-*

was a rule not to record donations of single volumes [*Reliquiæ Bodl.* pp. 91, 283]; consequently several books of the greatest value are omitted.

[1] The frequency with which it was handled is shown as early as 1629 by an entry in the accounts of 2*s.* 6*d.* being paid for 'mendinge the claspes of Queene Marie's booke'; and again in 1637 1*s.* 6*d.* were paid to 'Mr. Berry the goldsmith' for mending a clasp. The book is mentioned in Rous's speech on the reception of the works of James I, as being exhibited on the left hand at the entrance of the library. See p. 61.

nicum, 1610, i. 785) that the latter part is taken directly and literally from Musonius, while indirectly it comes from an oration by Cato[1]. Probably the first part may be traced to some similar source.

Another autograph inscription by Mary while Princess is found in a small book (Laud MS. Miscell. i.) of private prayers in Latin and English, which belonged to Jane Wriothesley, wife of Thomas Earl of Southampton, and which she seems to have employed as a kind of album. At f. 45[a] are these lines, which appear to form a triplet, although not written in metrical form by the Princess :—

'Good Madame, I do desyer you most hartly to pray,
That in prosperyte and adversyte I may
Have grace to keep the trewe way.
'Your lovyng frend,
to my . . . [power?]'

Unfortunately the conclusion, with the signature, has been cut off. A couplet, signed by Queen Katherine Parr, has an equal, and most regal, disregard of the restraints of metrical rhythm (f. 8[b]) :—

'Madam, althowe I have differred writtyng in your booke,
I am no lesse your frend than you do looke.
'Kateryn the Quene KP.'

Other inscriptions are inserted by Margaret Queen of Scotland, Mary Countess of Lennox and mother of Lord Darnley, and by the Countess of Southampton's daughters, Elizabeth, Mary, and Anne.

James Button, Esq., of the county of Worcester, gave, on March 28, a curious relic of the ancient language of Cornwall, being three Miracle-Plays of the Creation, the Passion, and the Resurrection, in Cornish, contained in a MS. on vellum, small folio, eighty-three leaves, written in the fifteenth century; now numbered Bodl. 791. A copy on paper of the Play of the Creation, written

[1] George Herbert expresses the same idea at the end of his *Church Porch* :—
'If thou do ill, the joy fades, not the pains;
If well, the pain doth fade, the joy remains.'
A collection of various parallel passages has been several times printed by Dr. Greenhill, of Hastings, on small leaflets entitled 'The Contrast.'

by John Jordan in 1611, is also in the Library, numbered Bodl. 219, which appears to have come from the library of King James I, having the royal crown stamped on the parchment cover, with the initials I.K. A second modern copy was presented in 1849 by Edwin Ley, Esq., of Bosahan, Cornwall, which is accompanied by a translation by John Keigwyn, made in 1695. The dramas were printed in two volumes at the University Press, with a translation, notes, and glossary, by Mr. Edwin Norris, in 1859.

In the Convocation Register, N. 23, under date of 25 Nov., are given particulars of the cost of building the third story of the Schools' quadrangle, now called the Picture Gallery, the total being £2497 10*s*.

A.D. 1616.

Some MSS. were given in this year by the three sons of Rich. Colf, D.D., and in 1618 twenty Greek volumes by Cecil Earl of Exeter.

A.D. 1617.

On Feb. 12 a delegacy was appointed to examine an inventory which the Vice-Chancellor had received of Bodley's goods, and to consider respecting the fulfilment of his will.

A.D. 1620.

At the beginning of May, James resigned the office of Librarian, but not, as Wood says, on account of his promotion to the subdeanery of Wells, since that took place in the year 1614. His appointment to the rectory of Mongeham, Kent, also mentioned by Wood, was in 1617. He continued, however, to reside in Oxford, and dying there in August, 1629, was buried in New College Chapel[1].

[1] In a deposition made by him in the Archdeacon's court in a suit relating to St. Aldate's parish in Oxford, in the year 1616, he says that he was then 42 years old, and had formerly been rector of St. Aldate's for twelve years, the then rector having been in possession for about two years (Arch-

On the 9th of the same month of May, John Rous, or Rouse, M.A., Fellow of Oriel, was unanimously elected James' successor. No account of him is given by Wood, possibly from dislike of his Puritanical principles, and of his continuing to hold office during the Usurpation. He appears to have discharged his trust in the Library with faithfulness, and, at least, to have deserved some mention at the historiographer's hands for the Appendix to the Catalogue which he issued in the year 1635 (*q.v.*)[1] He is best known as the friend of Milton, who, on Rous's application to him for a copy of his *Poems both English and Latin*, published in 1645, in the place of one previously given by Milton which had been lost, sent the volume, together with a long autograph Latin Ode, dated Jan. 23, 1646 (–7), and bearing the following title: 'Ad Joannem Rousium, Oxoniensis Academiæ Bibliothecarium, de libro poematum amisso quem ille sibi denuo mitti postulabat, ut cum aliis nostris in Bibliotheca publica reponeret, Ode Joannis Miltonj[2].' The volume is now numbered 8°. M. 168 Art. A facsimile of a considerable portion of the Ode (which Cowper translated into English, and which is said to have been the last of Milton's Latin poetical effusions) is given in plate xvii. of Sam. Leigh Sotheby's sumptuous volume, entitled *Ramblings in the Elucidation of the Autograph of Milton*, 4°. Lond. 1861; and at p. 120 there is a facsimile in full of Milton's inscription in another volume (4°. F. 56 Th.) which contains a collection of the political and polemical treatises published by him in the years

deacon's MSS. Records now in the Libr.). His presentation to the living in 1602 is noticed by Dr. Bliss in his edition of Wood's *Athenæ*.

[1] One fact to his credit is indeed mentioned by Wood in the *Fasti*, under the year 1648, viz. that he prevented the then Vice-Chancellor, Dr. Reynolds, and the Proctors from breaking open Bodley's chest in search of money, by assuring them that there was nothing in it. Hearne (*MS. Diary*, vol. xii. p. 13) says that Rous inserted a portrait of Sir Thos. Bodley, done at his own charge, in the window of the room which he occupied on the west side of Oriel College.

[2] Cowley followed Milton's example by inserting an Ode, in this case in English, in a folio copy of his *Poems* (numbered C. 2. 21. Art.), which he gave June 26, 1656. It is printed exactly from the original in *Reliquiæ Hearn.* ii. 921–3.

1641–5. This latter inscription, which gives a list of the contents of the volume, is addressed as follows: 'Doctissimo viro proboque librorum æstimatori Joanni Rousio, Oxoniensis academiæ Bibliothecario, gratum hoc sibi fore testanti, Joannes Miltonius opuscula hæc sua in Bibliothecam antiquissimam atque celeberrimam adsciscenda libens tradit, tanquam in memoriæ perpetuæ Fanum, emeritamque, uti sperat, invidiæ calumniæque vacationem; si Veritati, Bonoque simul Eventui satis litatum sit.' Warton tells the almost incredible story, in his edition of Milton's *Poems*, that about the year 1720 these two volumes were thrown out into a heap of duplicates, from which Nathaniel Crynes, who afterwards bequeathed his own collection to the Library[1], was permitted to pick out what he pleased for himself; fortunately, however, he was too good a royalist and churchman to choose anything that bore the name of Milton, and so the books, despised and rejected on both sides, by mere chance remained in the place of their original deposit! Such an incident, if true, goes far to justify the charges of ignorance and neglect of the Library which Hearne in his Diary constantly brings against Hudson, the Librarian at that time, and those whom he employed.

The second edition of the Catalogue was issued by James, shortly after his resignation of his office, with a Dedication to Prince Charles, and a Preface dated June 30. It consists of 539 quarto pages, with an appendix of 36 (containing the additions given or bought during the progress of the Catalogue), in double columns. It abandons the classified arrangement of the former Catalogue, and adopts that (followed ever since) of one alphabet of names. James, in his Preface, gives as his reason for this course, the frequent difficulty (already experienced even in so small a collection) of deciding to what class a book should be assigned,

[1] See *sub anno* 1745. One specimen of the duplicates which he selected may be seen in the book now numbered Crynes 169, which was formerly marked 8°. G. 114, Art., Priezac's *Vindiciæ Gallicæ*, 1638. Among old library lists and papers there is a list of books sold to Crynes in Feb. 1727 at prices fixed by Clements the bookseller, but neither the Milton volumes nor this book of Priezac appear in it.

and the inconvenience resulting from division of the works of the same author. He points out the value of the Library to foreigners, who can there consult 16,000 volumes for six hours a day, excepting Sundays and holidays[1]. As instances of the copiousness of its stores, he mentions that there are to be found above 100 folio and quarto volumes on Military Art, in Greek, Latin, and other languages; and that there are 3000 or 4000 books in French, Italian, and Spanish. He notes that heretical and schismatical books are not to be read without leave of the Vice-Chancellor and Regius Professor of Divinity; and makes some remarks on the method of keeping a Common-place-book. He gives as the reason for his quitting his post, his severe sufferings from stone and paralysis[2].

In anticipation of a visit from the King £1 4*s*. were given for a copy of his Works, as appears from the earliest book of accounts. It seems, however, that the King did not then visit the Library, but sent the folio edition of the book (edited by bishop Montague), on June 4. There appear to be two copies in the Library thus presented. The first (marked Arch. D. 35) is bound in red velvet, with the royal arms in gold stamped on the side, and the inscription given below, written in a formal hand, but headed by the King with his own autograph signature, and subscribed by Secretary Calvert. The other is bound in green morocco, also with the royal arms on the cover, and contains, besides the engraved title-page, the printed title and a leaf following with an engraving of the royal arms, both which are wanting in the first copy; and on its fly-leaf is an inscription written and signed by Sir Rob.

[1] At this time there were only two public libraries on the continent of Europe, both later in date than the Bodleian, viz. that of Angelo Rocca at Rome, opened in 1604, and the Ambrosian at Milan, opened in 1609. The next public library was that of Card. Mazarin at Paris, opened in 1643. Evidence of the consequent appreciation by foreigners of the advantages of the Bodleian Library is given under the year 1641.

[2] A second edition of the Appendix to the Catalogue was printed in 1635, *q.v.* The printing of the Catalogue cost £112 10*s*. (Convoc. Reg. N. 23, f. 93).

Naunton. The inscription in the first copy, the one normally presented in Convocation, is as follows :—

'Jacobus R. D.D.

Jacobus D. G. Magnæ Britanniæ, Franciæ, et Hiberniæ Rex, Fidei Defensor, qui maiorum titulis literarum decus addidit, et Musas pullâ lugentes in veste solio imposuit purpuratas; qui Catholicam fidem non ferro et igne (quod iis relinquit qui nihil sibi reliquerunt in veritate præsidii) sed stilo et voce asseruit; qui mitræ ambitione scriptis pessundatâ diadema sui fecit juris; Has Religionis et Sceptri vindicias, hoc regii otii negotium, sibi ideo voluit superesse, ut posteris suis impensi temporis ratio constaret, extaretque quod imitarentur, quandocunque res posceret exemplum. Itaque suæ Oxoniensi Academiæ, sanctissimo Mnemosynes fano, fido literariæ Reipubl. tabulario, hoc depositum credidit, monumentum bonæ mentis, æternumque amoris sui pignus, quo sic literas prosequitur, ut inter earum cultores in Bibliotheca publica locum ambiat, qui quotus qualisque futurus sit, Almæ Matris arbitrio permittit.

Georgius Calvert, Secretarius.'

The second copy (now marked B. 14. 17 Theol.) has the following inscription : —

'Jacobus Dei gratia Magnæ Britanniæ, Franciæ et Hiberniæ Rex, Fidei Defensor, etc., postquam decrevisset publici juris facere quæ sibi erat commentatus, ne videretur vel palam pudere literarum quas privatim amaverat, vel eorum seu opinioni seu invidiæ cedere qui Regis Majestatem literis dictitabant imminui, vel Christiani Orbis et in eo Principum judicia expavescere, quorum maxime intererat vera esse omnia quæ scripsit; circumspicere etiam cœpit certum aliquod libro suo domicilium, locum, si fieri possit, semotum a fato, æternitati et paci sacrum. Ecce commodùm sua se obtulit Academia, illa pæne orbi notior quam Cantabrigiæ, ubi exulibus Musis jam olim melius est quam in patria, ubi a codicibus famæ nuncupatis tineæ absterrentur legentium manibus, sycophantæ scribentium ingeniis.

In hoc immortali literarum sacrario, inter monumenta clarorum virorum, quos quantum dilexit studiorum participatione satis indicavit, in bibliotheca publica, lucubrationes has suas Deo Opt. Max., Cui ab initio devotæ erant, æternum consecrat, in venerando Almæ Matris sinu, unde contra seculorum rubiginem fidam illi custodiam promittit, et contra veritatis hostes stabile patrocinium.'

The book, which was carried to Oxford by a special deputation, consisting of Patrick Young, the Librarian at St. James's (to whom £20 was given by the University for his pains), and others, was received by the University with great ceremony. A Convocation was held in St. Mary's Church, on May 29, at which an oration was delivered by Rich. Gardiner, the Deputy-Orator (of which there is a copy in Bodl. MS. Add. C. 206, f. 115[1]), and at which a letter of thanks was approved (which is printed in Wood's *Annals*, ii. 336); from thence the Vice-Chancellor, attended by 24 doctors in their scarlet robes, and a mixed multitude of others, carried it in solemn procession to the Library, where the keeper, Rous, 'made a verie prettie speech,' says Patrick Young, 'and placed it *in archivis* . . . with a great deale of respect[2].'

Rous's 'prettie speech' was in the true style of the period, and now only sounds like satire. Thus, in polished Latin phrases, did it run: 'From the time of his election to his office there had come no gift that was worthy to be compared with this. If Bodley had ever dreamed before his death of such an honour to his library as that the King, laying aside his majesty for a while, would send, by the hands of a chosen delegacy, his own works, works perfected to a miracle, that godlike man would have prayed to be spared to enjoy that honour, from which those who were living derived now such incredible pleasure. This was but the one thing that had

[1] One line is enough as a specimen: 'Bibliotheca non literarum erit ædificium, sed miraculum, quia hunc orbis totius thesaurum continebit.'

[2] Nichols' *Progresses of James I*, vol. iii. p. 1105. The first presentation-inscription, and Rous's speech (with the University letter) are printed in Hearne's *Titus Liv. Forojul.* pp. 197–9. Young's short speech on delivery is in Smith MS. lxxvi. p. 153. See also Bliss's *Reliquiæ Hearnianæ*, *sub dat.* 9 Dec. 1705.

been wanting to complete Bodley's happiness; but probably even in the other world he shared in the glory of this day. But where should such treasures be deposited? Henry VIII wrote certain sheets against Luther, which were so valued at Rome, that to this day they hold no mean place in the caskets of the Vatican. But what are they, compared to the writings of James? Like tradesmen's tokens in comparison with good coins of the realm. ['*Distant æra lupinis.*'] Rous himself seven years before had seen in the Palatine Library [at Heidelberg] the history of K. Arthur translated from French into German by some Count or other, which was so valued that the great Gruter actually did not hesitate to show it to visitors as being one of the treasures of the place. If then such a man as he so admired the merest trifles which came from Kings and Princes, what place can be found good enough for so incomparable a treasure as this of K. James? Rous opens a door: lo! here the *sacrarium* of the Bodleian; nothing vulgar here, nothing common to the mass. On the right hand, the Breviary of Henry VII; on the left, the Breviary of Q. Mary; between these he deposits this gift, with that utmost reverence which befits something better and more noble. Behold this his act! and then, go, tell it to our King!'

No wonder that the King was greatly pleased with the formality and flattery with which his works were received, and the more so 'because Cambridge received them without extraordinary respect[1].'

[1] Letter from J. Chamberlain to Sir D. Carleton, June 28, 1620: *Calendar of State Papers*, 1619–23, p. 157. But if Cambridge received them without any 'extraordinary' outward formality or respect, at any rate the Public Orator, no less a person than George Herbert, returned thanks with extraordinary adulation and flattery in his Latin letter of acknowledgment, even outdoing Oxford completely. 'Now,' he says, 'that we are sprinkled with the royal ink, there is no subject too sublime for us; we can cut our way through all controversies, we can overcome all disputants. Would that some Jesuit might now be given us, in order that by mere friction against your Majesty's book, we might pulverize the man forthwith!' And then, with a jealous regard to Oxford and the stately room in which the King's Book would there be placed, he winds up with the following couplet, addressed 'Peregrinis academiam nostram invisentibus:'—

'Quid Vaticanam Bodleiumque objicis, Hospes?
Unicus est nobis Bibliotheca Liber'!

One whole leaf is devoted in the *Reg. Benef.* to the record of the gift.

Another gift in this year, presented by Thomas Neville, K.B., eldest son of Sir Henry Neville, Knt., is thus described in the Register: 'Elegantissimum libellum diversa scripturæ genera continentem, manu Esteris Anglicæ, characteribus exquisitis conscriptum.' This is the MS. of the Book of Proverbs, dated 1599, in which every chapter, as well as a dedication to the Earl of Essex, is written in a different style of caligraphy. It is now exhibited in a glass case containing curiosities of writing, and is an extremely beautiful specimen of the handiwork of Mrs. Esther Inglis, of whose skill the Library possesses another and smaller specimen (Bodl. 987), consisting of some French verses by Guy de Faur, Sieur de Pybrac, written for Dr. Joseph Hall (afterwards the Bishop of Norwich), in 1617. These are described in the account of Mrs. Inglis in Ballard's *Memoirs of British Ladies.* A third specimen of her work is in the Library of Ch. Ch.: it is a Psalter in French, presented to Queen Elizabeth in 1599, bound in embroidered crimson velvet, set with pearls [1].

The Douay Bible of 1609 was presented by Sir Rich. Anderson, of Penley, Herts, and a Persian MS. of the Liturgy of the Greek Church by Sir Thos. Roe. The first architectural model also was given in this year; but unfortunately it is not now extant. Its description is as follows: 'Clemens Edmonds, eques auratus, consilio Regis ab epistolis, donavit egregium παράδειγμα quinque columnarum, nunc primum inventum, secundum formam rusticam, ex alabastrite singulari artificio confectum.' In the book of accounts it is called a 'mathematical pillar,' and the liberal sum of £2 was 'given to Th. Fort the workman' who brought it.

For Minsheu's *Dictionary* £2 4*s.* were paid.

[1] An account of Mrs. Esther Inglis, and of all her known existing MSS., by David Laing, Esq., LL.D., of Edinburgh, is in vol. vi. of *Proceedings of Soc. of Antiquaries of Scotland*, pp. 284–309.

A.D. 1621.

A gift of £5 is noticeable as coming from the Girdlers' Company, 'Societas Zonariorum'; in the book of accounts it is entered as £4 'from Mr. Auberry, master of the company of the Girdlers.' Francis Bacon, visc. St. Alban's, occurs as a donor of his own books.

On Aug. 1 Convocation approved some orders made by the Curators, one of which provided that during the long summer vacation strangers might be admitted to study on the authority of such Curators as might be in Oxford, with the Vice-Chancellor and Proctors, and another that all and singular admitted to the Library should be bound to buy a copy of the Catalogue at the price of 2*s.*, to defray the expense of printing.

A.D. 1622.

One hundred pounds were received as a legacy from Charles Crooke, a gentleman of Cornwall, for books to be bought 'at the appointment of Dr. Prideaux,' and £27 from Rous for catalogues which had been sold[1]. For a new gate at the entrance under the Library £19 15*s.* 3*d.* were paid, and for setting up an inscription over the new gate, according to Sir T. Bodley's appointment, 30*s.*

A.D. 1623.

For eight Russia leather chairs for Sir T. Bodley's closet £5 16*s.* were paid, and for a Turkey carpet £3 10*s.*

Delegates were appointed by Convocation to consider 'de modulo frontispicii Bibliothecæ publicæ in parte occidentali versus collegium Exon[2].'

Already duplicates began to be sold, and the sum of £5 15*s.* 6*d.* was received in this year as the proceeds.

[1] In 1624 the sale of Catalogues produced £12 1*s.* 10*d.*; in 1625, £10: and in 1629, £4 11*s.* 6*d.*

[2] Reg. Conv. N. ff. 167, 169.

A.D. 1624.

'Williams, Bishop of Lincoln, and then Lord Chancellor of England, would have borrowed Paulus Benius Eugubinus *De dirimend. Controvers. de Grat. et Lib. Arb.*, but was deny'd[1].'

The first theft of a book from the Library occurred in this year. An account of it, and of several others, will be found in a note to the year 1654. See also 1647 and 1648.

The works of Socinus were bought either in this year or in 1625 for £4, and 'an old chronicle of St. Alban's' of 'Badger's wife' for 5*s*. Badger was the bedel of the Stationers' Company, who had an allowance of £1 6*s*. 8*d*. yearly for collecting books.

A.D. 1627.

Andrew James, of Newport, Isle of Wight, is recorded to have given 'duas capsulas in quibus asservantur scripta vetustissima, exotici et ignoti characteris, alia stylo, calamo alia, in corticibus exarata, ex orientalis Indiæ partibus allata[2].' An East India merchant, John Jourdain, gave four Arabic MSS., and Becon's *Works* [1564] were presented by Peter Ince, a bookseller at Chester. It appears from the Register and Accounts that Joseph Barnes, the Oxford printer and publisher, died in this year, or in 1626, as a legacy of £5 is entered as being received from his widow.

The copy of Bacon's *Essays* (1625) which was presented by the

[1] Barlow's Argument against lending books out of the Library; see *post, sub anno* 1659.

[2] At the end of the Barocci collection (numbered 245, 246, in the Catalogue of 1697) were two Javanese MSS., written on palm-leaves in two of the alphabets used in West Java: the one written with a reed, preserved in a box; the other written with a style, and having the leaves tied together as usual between two boards. When Lord Pembroke sent the Barocci MSS., he forwarded also (as we learn from Laud's letter) one book of his own 'like a bundle of thin laths,' of which Laud says 'none of us here can tell what to make of it'; but it would seem from the description of James's gifts that these were the MSS. placed with the Barocci collection, while Lord Pembroke's gift found a place elsewhere.

author to the Duke of Buckingham, was given to the Library by Lewis Roberts, a merchant of London. It is now exhibited in a glass case devoted to fine specimens of antique bindings, being clad in green velvet, embroidered with gold and silver thread, with the head of the duke worked in silk. One shilling was paid for a green baize cover for it in 1631. The same donor also presented the copy of Bishop Williams' Funeral Sermon on James I, which had been given to the same duke by the author. Several other embroidered bindings are preserved in the Library, which are all, it is believed, comprehended in the following list[1]:—

1. A part of L. Tomson's version of the New Test., printed by Barker, in 16°. (in 1578?), now marked MS. *e Musæo*, 242. This belonged to Queen Elizabeth, and is bound in a covering worked by herself, with various mottos, *e.g.* 'Celum patria,' 'Scopus vitæ Xpũs,' &c. And on a fly-leaf occurs this note in her handwriting: 'August[ine?]. I walke manie times into the pleasant fieldes of the Holye Scriptures, where I plucke up the goodlie greene herbes of sentences by pruning, eate them by reading, chawe them by musing, and laie them up at length in the hie seate of memorie by gathering them together; that so hauing tasted thy sweetenes I may the lesse perceave the bitternes of this miserable life[2].'

[1] A lady, graced with the appellation of 'heroina,' is recorded to have given to the University the Life of our Blessed Lord depicted in needlework, 'byssina et aurata textura ad vivum expressa,' which was duly presented in Convocation on July 9, 1636. [Reg. Conv. R. 24, f. 129[b].] It is not now preserved in the Library. The name of the 'heroina,' which is not found in the Reg., is given in the old book of accounts, where we find this entry:—'To Wynchester carrier for bringing certaine needle-worke peeces, being my Ladie [Elizabeth] Powlett's gift, 12*s*.' Due care was taken to preserve the pieces, for another item of payment follows, 'for 2 greene sey curtaines for the two needleworke peeces, 5*s*. 8*d*.' 'A curious piece of needlework' was formerly No. 346 in the list of the curiosities kept in the Anatomy School. Bodl. MS. 22 is a volume of verses (with one exception by members of New College) addressed to Lady Eliz. Powlet, in praise of her gift.

[2] This note is printed and the book described in Hearne's Appendix to *Titi Livii Forojul. Vit. Hen. V*, and, from thence, in Ballard's *Lives*; but not very correctly in either case. Also in Bliss's *Reliqq. Hearn.* i. 104. In a 16[mo]. book, printed on vellum in

2. Another of Elizabeth's bibliopegic achievements is the cover of her own translation from the French of *The Miroir or Glasse of the synnefull Soule*, executed when only eleven years old. She says that she translated it 'out of frenche ryme into englishe prose, joyning the sentences together as well as the capacitie of my symple witte and small lerning coulde extende themselves;' and prefixes a dedication, dated 'from Assherige, the laste daye of the yeare of our Lord God, 1544,' in which, 'to our moste noble and vertuous quene Katherin, Elizabeth her humble daughter wisheth perpetuall felicitie and everlasting ioye.' The volume consists of 63 small quarto leaves, and has the queen's initials K. P. embroidered within an ornamental border of gold and silver thread, on a ground of blue corded silk. It is numbered Cherry MS. 36.

3. *Dialogue de la Vie et de la Mort*, trans. from the Italian by J. Louveau, and printed in imitation of MS., second edit., 12°. Lyon, 1558. Red velvet, embroidered with gold and silver thread. A French inscription on a fly-leaf is in a handwriting resembling that of Queen Elizabeth. Bodl. MS. 660. Exhibited as above.

4. A very fine copy of the folio Bible printed by Barker in 1583, in which the initial letters of chapters are illuminated, and the woodcuts very delicately coloured. This is bound in an embroidered cover of very elegant floriated design, with gold and silver thread; and appears to have been a gift to Q. Elizabeth. It is in the Douce collection, and is exhibited as above.

5. A Testament in 16°, printed by Norton and Bill in 1625. Very thick and clumsy embroidery: on one side, David, in a flowing wig, playing on the harp, with a dog, dragon-fly, &c.; on the other, Abraham, in a similar wig and with a falling collar,

1562, *The Letany, wyth certayne other devoute and godlye meditations, very necessary to be dayly sayd of the faithfull Christians* there is a fly-leaf which has succeeded another, or more, torn out by some sacrilegious hand, which contains these concluding sentences in the hand of Q. Eliz.:—' . . vnto me and I will heare the, I will alwayes be with the in all thy tribulacōn. Behold I call vpon the oftner with myne hart then with my lippes. Lo how neare Tribulation cometh vnto me, and no bodie to deliuer me frō it, but thou o swete IESV. In this sure hoope and cōfidence I rest, deale with me fauorably o Christ accordinge to thy will.'

stopped in the sacrifice of his son. It was bought by Douce from Thorpe the bookseller, in whose catalogue for 1832 it appears as No. 11260, priced at £5 5*s*. It is there described as 'said to be bound in a piece' of a waistcoat of Charles I; but it is not known on what evidence this 'saying' rests, nor does the material seem likely to have been so employed. Exhibited in the glass case.

6. Bible, 8°. Lond. 1639. Landscape, &c., worked in silk, with embroidery in gold and silver thread. Arch. Bodl. D. subt. 75. Exhibited as above.

7. Prayer-book, New Test., and Metrical Psalms, 1630–1, bound by the nuns of Little Gidding. Exhibited as above. Bought in 1866 for £10 [1].

8. New Testament, printed at Cambridge in 1628, in 16mo. This was the first edition printed there of any portion of the Authorized Version, and only the second of any English translation [2]. The binding of the Library copy (which was bought, in 1859, for five guineas) is covered with silver filagree work.

9. Prayer-book, 8°. Lond. 1616. Purple velvet, embroidered in silver.

10. Bible, 8°. Lond. 1617, with Prayer-book, 1615. Needlework, with coats of arms in filagree; on one side, a cross az. between four eagles displayed, or; on the other, gules, a bend or between three crescents.

11. Bible, 12°. Lond. 1626. Needlework, very much worn.

Among Dr. Rawlinson's multifarious collections is a volume of curious early specimens of worked samplers, humorously lettered on the back, 'Works of Learned Ladies.'

[1] In the life of Rich. Ferrar, junior, in Wordsworth's *Eccl. Biogr.* (third edit. vol. iv. p. 232) a note is quoted from a MS. stating that a copy of Ferrar's *Whole Law of God*, bound by the nuns of Gidding in green velvet, was given to the University Library by Archbp. Laud. This is a mistake; the book in question was given by the Archbishop to the library of his own college, St. John's, where it still remains.

[2] The first was the Genevan Version, printed in 1591.

A.D. 1629.

The extremely valuable series of Greek MSS., called from its collector the Barocci Collection, comprising 242 volumes, was presented by Will. Herbert, Earl of Pembroke, and Chancellor of the University. The manner of its acquisition is recorded in Archbp. Ussher's correspondence. In a letter from Dublin of Jan. 22, 1628–9, Ussher says: 'That famous library of Giacomo Barocci, a gentleman of Venice, consisting of 242 manuscript volumes, is now brought into England by Mr. Featherstone the stationer[1].' He recommended that the King should buy it, and add to it the collection of Arabic MSS. which the Duke of Buckingham had bought of the heirs of Erpenius[2]. On April 13, 1629, Sir H. Bourgchier writing to Ussher, tells him that the Earl of Pembroke has bought the collection, for the University of Oxford, at the price of £700, and that it consists of 250 volumes[3]. It was forwarded to the University with the following letter, which is here copied from the Convocation Register, R. 24 (f. 9^b):—

'Good Mr. Vice-Chancelor,

'Understanding of an excellent collection of Greke manuscripts brought from Venice, and thincking that they would bee of more use to the Church in being kept united in some publick Librarye then scattered in particular hands; remembring the obligation I had to my mother the Universitie, first for breeding mee, after for the honor they did mee in making mee their Chancelor, I was glad of this occasion to repay some part of that great debt I owe her. And therefore I sent you downe the collection entire, which I pray present with my beste love to the Convocation house. And I shall unfaynedly remaine,

'Your most assured friend,

'PEMBROKE.

'Greenewich, the 25th of May, 1629.'

[1] In the following year (1630) Mr. Henry Featherstone, bookseller in London, gave to the Library a number of Hebrew books; and a pair of gloves, value 3*s.* 6*d.*, was given to Mr. Johnson 'for transcribing the register of the Rabbins of Mr. Fetherston's guift.'

[2] Parr's *Life of Ussher*, Letters, p. 400.

[3] *Ibid.* Quoted in Sir H. Ellis' *Letters of Eminent Literary Men*, Camden Soc., 1843, p. 130.

The MSS. were actually despatched from London by Laud two days later, with the following letter to the Vice-Chancellor:—

'To the Right Wor[ll]. my very worthie frend Doctor Fruyn, President of Magdalene Colledge and Vichauncellor of the University of Oxon, be these dd.

'Worthye Sir,

'I haue bye thiss carryer sent you downe those manuscripts which you haue longe expected; and hear inclosed you shall find a leter of my Lord Steward's, written with his owne hand to accompanye his gift; of whom I shall saye noe more but that he hath shewed himself your most Honourable Chaunclor.

'These books ar made up in three chests and one lesser trunke. They ar marked all with W. L. upon them, and directed to you. The catalogue of them (verye carefullye and exactlye taken bye the great paines of Dr. Lindsell and Mr. Patrick Younge) is with your Librarye Keeper allreadye, which I am verye glad of, because mye beinge at Court when they left London made it allmost forgotten.

'The waight of these is as you shall find in a paper mentioned. And the carridge for all is payed for. Thear is noe locke to anye of the chests but one; the other two ar nailed up. The keyes of that chest and of both the trunkes you shall receaue togeather with these leters in a litle boxe. In the chest which hath lockes on it you shall finde a boxe, and thearin a newe wheele, verye faire in velome, with his Majestyes hand to it, which mye Lord Steward desyers maye be kept carefully, and that the other with the Kings hand sent at first in paper maye be saflye sent backe to me.

I keepe the paper, but the sume totall is 53*s*. 6*d*.

'Amonge these manuscripts thear ar some that want bindinge, and I haue taken order that all or most of them ar putt togeather into the little trunke. Mye Lord was once purposed to haue them bound heare, but it was hard to find whome to trust with them, or whome wee should put to that paines to be a continuall ouerseer. If they should be mesplaced in the bindinge, it wear as much as manye of them wear worth, it would be soe hard to rectifye them againe. I thinke thearfore the safest waye will be to page them before they be taken asunder for newe bindinge. Mye Lord would haue them bound plaine, and as like their old felowes as maye be. I haue monye in mye hands to pay for that to; for mye Lord will possess the Universitye with thiss noble gift without puttinge them to anye chardge.

'I maye not omit to informe you to, that some of these bookes ar much worne with aige, and the leters in some places growne dimme, and if in some reasonable tyme they be not transcribed they will be lost to anye use. When they ar transcribed, the olde copye and the newe maye be sett togeather. But thiss I leaue to tyme and care.

'I had almost forgott to tell you that amonge mye Lord Stewards bookes you shall finde one of his owne, which his Lordship added to them he bought, thinkinge it a fitt monument for that Librarye. It is like a bundle of thinne laths. But what it containes he must tell that can; for none of us heare can tell what to make of it.

'In the other larger trunke ar some other manuscripts geven to the Universitye verye noblye & freelye bye Sir Tho. Rowe, whoe hath longe bine imployed in his Maiestyes seruice in Turkeye. These bookes ar in number twentye eight. One of these (the Arabicke booke in folio) must needs be newe bound; and one in 8[uo]. which is but in quiers. In the Arabicke booke you shall find some papers of direction bye the pains of Dr. Lindsell, which you maye keepe. With these bookes of Sir Tho. Rowe's you shall finde in the trunke a verye perfect catalogue of them made likewise & sent bye Dr. Lindsell. One booke of these ('tis as I remember a peece of St. Chrysostome vpon the Psalmes not yett printed for the most) you will find wantinge, but it was lent bye Sir Thomas himselfe to Dr. Lindsell, & thear is a paper with his hand to acknowledge it. He hath carryed it with him into the North to transcribe, and will bringe it safe.

'Vpon euerye of these bookes of Sir Tho. Rowe is written the donor's name as himeselfe directed. Vpon mye Lord Steward's nothinge is yett written, but I knowe you will thinke it fitt to doe bye his Lordship as the Vniuersitye worthelye doth to like Benefactours. And hauinge thuss dischardged all mye trust to that deare and honourable mother of myne, the Vniuersitye, I leaue you to the grace of God, and shall euer rest,

'Your verye louinge frend,

'GUIL. LONDON.

'London House, Maii 27, 1629.'

'But hauinge dischardged thiss trust, I am bold to become an humble suter for one Vniuersitye to another. The Vniuersitye of Cambridge ar att thiss tyme fitted with a verye learned, painfull, & able printer. They ar resolued to fall presentlye in hand with some manuscripts which Dr. Lindsell hath bye hime & makes readye. It will be a great honour to thiss church and kingdome, and was the grownd whye mye Lord Steward would haue his manuscripts for thiss vse vpon iust securitye to be borrowed out of your librarye. That which they desyer is the matrices of the Greeke leters giuen bye Sir Hen. Sauill. I thinke they purpose to haue some other made bye them. The desyer of that learned and worthye Vniuersitye will best appeare bye itselfe, & thearfore I make bold to send you heare inclosed a copye of the leters which the Heads sent to me. And I hartelye desyer you nowe at the Conuocation for the receit of the manuscripts to desyer them in mye name that the matrices maye be lent vnto them, and that if thear be anye ordinance to the contrarye they would be pleased to dispence with it. Mye Lord Steward vpon sight of these desyred me to ioyne his strength that thiss iust request maye not be denyed. The less I haue bine able to deserue of the Vniversitye, will bind me the more to theme for thiss their noblenes. If they be pleased to graunt & send the matrices to me, I will take order both for their saftye & returne. Thuss with mye hastye & affectionat remembraunce to all, and euerye one of that famous Bodye, especiallye to mye Bretheren the Heads of Houses, I againe take mye leaue, & rest

'Your assured frend,

'GUIL. LONDON.'[1]

The Earl was willing (as stated in Laud's letter) that the MSS. should, if necessary, be allowed to be borrowed. A further portion of the collection (consisting of 22 Greek MSS. and 2 Russian), which had been retained by the Earl, was subsequently purchased by Oliver Cromwell, and given by him to the Library in 1654. They still bear the Protector's name; but strange to say, no entry of the gift appears in the great Benefaction Book. A list of them, however, occupies pp. 41–67 of a small quarto register mentioned below under the year 1679. The list has this heading: 'My Lord Protector Cromwell's MSS. Vid. Dr. Langbaine's account of them in his MS. in 4°, whose note is D.'[2] These are all fully described in the first volume of the general Catalogue of MSS., published by Rev. H. O. Coxe in 1853. A Catalogue of the Barocci and Roe MSS., by Dr. Peter Turner, of Merton College, beautifully written, filling 38

[1] The original is preserved among some papers of Dr. Frewen, in the Muniment Room of Magd. Coll. Lord Pembroke's letter is not there; but the copy of the Cambridge letter is, and also a letter of thanks for the loan of the matrices.

[2] Richard Cromwell proposed at one time to perpetuate his own name in the Library, together with his father's, by sending a collection of the addresses which had been made to him, in order to show the temper of the nation, and the readiness of the greatest persons 'to compliment people on purpose for secular interest.' *Reliquiæ Hearn.* i. 263.

folio leaves, is bound up among Selden's printed books, marked AA. 1. Med. Seld.[1], and an Italian list of the Barocci collection, dated at Venice, 1618, is amongst Selden's MSS., numbered *supra* 80.

The MSS. given by Sir Thomas Roe (previously ambassador in Turkey, and afterwards, at the commencement of the Long Parliament, Burgess for the University, in company with Selden) were in number 29, all except three in Greek. One of the three exceptions is an original copy of the Synodal Epistles of the Council of Basle, with the leaden seal attached, which was added in 1630 to his original gift, and announced in Convocation on 6 Aug.; and another, a valuable Arabic MS. of the Apostolic Canons, &c., which is noticed at length by Selden in the second book of his treatise, *De Synedriis Hebræorum*[2]. The MSS. were forwarded by Laud from London together with the Barocci MSS., as told in his letter above. Roe proposed that his books should be permitted to be lent out to any one in England for purposes of printing, on proper security being given; a proposition which was accepted by Convocation on 16 Feb.[3] And licence to borrow Lord Pembroke's (the Barocci) and Roe's MSS. was granted by the donors themselves to Dr. Lindsell (afterwards Bishop of Peterborough and Hereford) and to Patrick Young, the Keeper of the King's Library at St. James's. The latter is found, from a memorandum at the end of the Register of Readers in 1648–9, to have used his privilege as late as Feb. and March, 164$\frac{7}{8}$, various volumes of Pembroke's MSS. being then lent to him, together with some marked 'Archbp.,' which were doubtless Laud's[4]. But one MS. in consequence suffered considerable injury[5]. After Roe's death in 1644 many coins were given by his widow by his desire.

[1] The Earl of Pembroke wrote to the University on 13 Feb. 16$\frac{29}{30}$, asking that leave should be given to Turner to take the Barocci MSS. to his rooms, upon giving security for them, for the purpose of making this Catalogue. Reg. Convoc. R. 24, f. 17[b].

[2] £1 5*s*. were paid for binding the 'Arabicke MS. of the Councells' in 1629.

[3] Reg. Conv. R. 24. 1628. f. 6.

[4] See *sub anno* 1635.

[5] See *sub anno* 1654.

Lucas Holstenius in his *Epistolæ* (edited by J. F. Boissonade, Par. 1817, pp. 115, 6) mentions the acquisition by England of the Roe and Barocci MSS. and the Arundel Marbles as being bitterly regretted by Card. F. Barberini. He enlarges the number of Roe's volumes to 200. Writing (from Aix) to Peiresc, he says:—

'Jesuita quidam, qui recens Constantinopoli venit, pro certo hic nunciavit, Oratorem regis Angliæ, sciente ac consentiente Cyrillo Patriarcha schismatico et μισολατίνῳ, ducenta volumina selecta ex Atho Monte secum in Britanniam detulisse . . . eodem tempore Marmora Arundeliana . . . quibus hactenus nihil simile in lucem prodiit, si Fastos Capitolinos excipias. Ita gemino stimulo illustrissimi Principis animus vehementius fuit commotus, quod hæreticos ex ultimo orbe Græciæ thesauros, ob Italorum incuriam neglectos, asportare videret, qui, ante aliquot menses, et Baroccianam bibliothecam Venetiis M.D. aureis, tum Mantuani Musei κειμήλια, aliquot scutalorum millibus, compararunt.'

Holstein himself had worked in the Bodleian (p. 124), and in other libraries at Oxford (p. 10),

'Veteres codices Græcos Latinosque sedulo excutiens, quibus nemo istic locorum negotium facessit'![1]

On Aug. 27, the Library was visited for the first time by King Charles and his Queen, little anticipating under what circumstances that visit would finally be repeated. He was received with an oration by the Public Orator, Strode, a copy of which is preserved in Smith MS. xxvi. 26, and which, in the exaggerated style of the Court-adulation of the time, began with words that sound blasphemously in our ears, '*Excellentissime Vice-Deus.*' From the Library the King ascended to the leads of the Schools; and there discussed the proposed removal of some mean houses in Cat Street, which then intervened between the Schools and St. Mary's Church. A plan of the ground and buildings was made at his desire, which was sent up to him at London.

In 1629–30 £5 15*s.* 4*d.* were received from the sale of books, and

[1] For these references to Holstein I am indebted to Mr. Ingram Bywater, M.A., of Exeter College.

£6 in fees from three undergraduates who were admitted to the Library.

A.D. 1630.

In this year Gerard John Vossius visited England, and came to the Library, but strange to say, his signature is not found among those of the 'Extranei,' in the *Liber Admissorum.* Pococke, who dedicates to him his Syriac version of the Catholic Epistles, published in this year, says that Rous told Vossius of Pococke's design, when he visited the Library, and that he approved of it.

A.D. 1631.

Charles Robson, B.D., of Queen's College, who had been Chaplain to the Merchants at Aleppo, gave a fine Syriac MS. of the Four Gospels, which he had brought from the East; it is now numbered Bodl. Orient. 361. Another MS. of his gift has been by some mistake placed amongst the Thurston MSS., No. 13.

£10 were paid to Hugh Davis, 'for making the modell to the new starecase and carrying it to London,' and 17*s*. to 'Wise, the painter, for limming my L. Steward's armes in the register,' &c.

In a MS. volume of travels by Jean Fontaine and Louis Schönbub, written in French, which is preserved in the Royal Library at Copenhagen (New Royal MS., 4°, 369), the travellers, who visited Oxford in 1630 or 1631, make the following notes on very common-place objects of curiosity which they saw in the Schools and Library, writing these notes (as well as a description of the 'Vita studiosorum') in Latin, out of regard, it may be presumed, to the character of the place. 'In Scholis publicis est, 1. bibliotheca, instructior reliquis omnibus; 2. superior ambulatio totius domus rotunda; studendi gratia facta est, ubi depicti Philosophi, Jurisconsulti, Theologi, &c., in parvulo cubiculo hujus ambulationis custodiuntur; 3. metalla, calendarium aureum, sigillum aureum ducis Moscovitarum, gladius Indicus, toga pellibus agninis, quæ crescunt in terra Tartariæ, facta, magnitudinis sunt pellis cuniculi; pictura Henrici Savilii, equitis aurati. 4. Schola medica eadem in domo, ubi 1. serpens Indicus 10 pedes longus; 2. pellis hominis totius; 3. collium (*sic*) album ex Mare Rubro[1].'

A.D. 1632.

William Burton, the historian of Leicestershire, gave the original MSS. of Leland's *Itinerary* (together with a transcript of some parts) and of his *Collectanea;* the former filling seven volumes in quarto[2], and the latter (including the book *De Scriptoribus Britannicis*) four in folio. He appears to have promised the gift originally about the year 1613[3]. The *Collectanea*, after the death of Leland, had been in the possession of Sir John Cheke, to whom Edward VI entrusted the custody of Leland's papers; on his going into exile in the reign of Queen Mary, he gave them to Humphrey Purefoy, Esq., whose son, Thomas Purefoy, presented them to Burton in the year 1612. The *Itinerary* was first published by Hearne in 1710–12, in 9 vols.; the *Collectanea* in 1715, in 6 vols.; the *De Scriptoribus*, by Ant. Hall, in 1709. The MS. of the *Itinerary* is much stained and injured by damp; but it is no longer in the perishable condition described by Hearne. There are, besides, five transcripts of it in the Library. The first (and best) of all, but imperfect, by John Stowe, in Tanner MS. 464; this also contains part of the *Collectanea*. Another (Bodl. 470), of part of the book, is a copy (mentioned above) which was made for Burton, and sent by him to Rous (and for which the Library paid Burton's clerk £2), with a letter dated 'Lindley, Leic. 17 July, 1632,' in which he describes it as being 'written, though not with so fine a letter, yet with a judicious hand.' He says that another part is 'now (as I heere) in the hands of Doctor Burton, Archdeacon of Gloucester, which he received by loane from a freind of mine, but never yet

[1] To this summary of a day's sight-seeing is added this note: 'N.B. Les querelles des Allemans dans l'hostellerie'!

[2] An eighth volume of the *Itinerary* was given by Charles King, M.A. of Ch. Ch. some time subsequently, having been lent by Burton and not recovered at the time of his own gift. In 1635 a copy of the Catalogue of the Library was sent to Burton, bound in vellum 'filleted with silke riband strings.' A 13th cent. MS. of 'Exempla,' which belonged to Burton in 1630, is among the Mareschal MSS.

[3] Register book of that year.

restored; the which, I thinke, upon request he will impart unto you;' and adds, 'Some more partes there were of this *Itinerary*, but through the negligence of him to whom they were first lent, are embesiled and gone.' He undertakes to send the three parts of the *Collectanea* and the book *De Scriptt. Angliæ*, according to promise, as soon as he has done using them. In 1642–3 £1 was given to 'Mr. Burton's sonne when he brought the 2 last parts of Leland's *Itinerarie*.' Another copy, made by Burton himself in 1628, was given to Dr. W. Stukeley by Thomas Allen, Esq., lord of Finchley, in June, 1758, and finally came to the Library with Gough's collection. It is now numbered Gough, *General Topog.* 2. It is injured by damp at the beginning, but has been repaired by Stukeley. The fourth copy is a later transcript, also in Gough's collection, and numbered *General Topog.* 1. And the fifth copy was bought in 1882 (now numbered *Top. Gen.* c. 5) which had been made by Browne Willis, when gentleman commoner of Ch. Ch. in 1704, in nine days, of which feat he gives an interesting account.

In the accounts for 1631–2 is this entry: 'Item, for a pastboard for a table for the Jesuits Pyramis given by Dr. Hakewyle, 6*d.*'; but what this Pyramid was does not appear.

Ten shillings were given to a Bachelor of Arts for transcribing a Catalogue of the Greek MSS.; and twenty shillings for a pair of gloves for Mr. Philip King 'by way of gratuitye for his great and continuall care and paynes to gather and pay in the rents of the Library.'

A fee of 40*s*. each was paid by four undergraduates for admission as readers in 1631–2 and by others in following years.

A.D. 1633.

A singular motto stamped upon the binding of three books, and it may be of more, within a border of cornucopiæ, &c., attracts the attention of the reader[1]. The books are, vols. i. ii. of Du Chesne's *Historiæ Francorum Scriptores*, 1636 (A. 2. 9. 10. Jur.), Halloix's *Ecclesiæ Orientalis Scriptores*, 1633 (G. 2. 3. Th.), and Jansen's *Augustinus*, 1641; the motto is, 'Coronasti annum bonitatis Tuæ,

[1] £1 3*s*. were paid for this stamp to an engraver in London in 1636.

Ps. 65. Annuo reditu quinque librarum Margaretæ Brooke.' An explanation is found in an entry in the Benefaction-Register under the year 1632 or 1633, where we read as follows: 'D. Margareta Brooke, vidua, quondam uxor Ducis Brooke [1], de Temple-Combe in comitatu Somerset, armigeri defuncti, donavit centum libras, quibus perquisitus est annuus reditus quinque librarum ad coemendos libros in usum bibliothecæ in perpetuum.' Probably the books thus stamped were the first that were bought after the final settlement of the gift, for which a pair of gloves, costing £2, was presented by the Library to Mrs. Brooke. In 1636 '5 great volumes of Mrs. Brookes' annuall gift' were bound by John Barnes for 16*s*., and in 1638 there is a similar payment of 12*s*. 6*d*. Other binders employed by the Library in 1636–7 were William Webbe, — Seale, — Bolt, and John Westall.

The Brooke rent arises from land at Wick-Risington, in Gloucestershire, and the sum duly appears to this day in the annual accounts of the Library. In 1655, the then Librarian, Barlow, makes a memorandum in his accounts that the University had not paid over this rent for several years; in consequence of his calling attention to this neglect, the arrears were paid up in 1658. At the same time the rents of the houses in Distaff Lane were heavily in arrear.

A (second) gift from Sir Henry Wotton consisted of the copy of Tycho Brahe's *Astronomiæ instaurandæ mechanica*, 1598, which the author gave to Grimani, Doge of Venice, containing several additional pages in MS., with two autograph epigrams; and also of a MS. of the *Acta Concilii Constantiensis*, which had formerly belonged to Card. Bembi, now numbered *e Musæo*, 25. For these thanks were returned by Convocation on 1 Sept.

£15 5*s*. were paid to Robert Martin for books bought out of Italy, and £7 16*s*. in the following year.

[1] Duke Brooke, esq., died in London 27 May, and was buried at Cobham, Kent, 10 June, 1606. As being lord of the manor of Romford, Essex, entries of his death and burial are, rather singularly, found in the register of that parish, as I have been informed by Rev. Edw. Fox, formerly vicar of Romford, and lately rector of Heyford Warren, Oxon.

A.D. 1634.

In this year Sir Kenelm Digby gave a collection of 238 MSS. (including five rolls) all on vellum, uniformly bound, and stamped with his arms, which still form a distinct series[1]. They are, for the most part, of the highest interest and importance, especially with reference to the early history of science in England. Amongst them are works by Roger Bacon, Grosteste, Will. Reade, John Eschyndon or Ashton, Roger of Hereford, Richard Wallingford, Simon Bredon, Thomas of New-Market, and many others. The oldest volume is one of astronomical tracts relating to the Paschal computation, written in Anglo-Saxon minuscules about the middle of the ninth century. The collection also comprises much relating to the general history of England, together with some early English and French poetical pieces, and is almost entirely written by English scribes. Many of the volumes had previously belonged to Thomas Allen, of Gloucester Hall, who himself was a liberal donor to the Library[2]. [*See* p. 23.] Two additional MSS., which formerly

[1] It was at Laud's instance, and through him as Chancellor of the University, that the gift was made. A letter from the Archbishop which accompanied it is printed in Wharton's collection of his *Remains*, vol. ii. p. 73.

[2] Allen bequeathed his literary collections to Digby, as mentioned by Rich. James in his dedication to the latter of Sir T. More's *Epist. ad Acad. Oxon.*, 4to. Lond. 1630. At the end of the Catalogue of the Digby MSS. I have printed from one of Wood's MSS. a list of such volumes as were once in Allen's possession, but are not now found in the Digby collection. Amongst these was one which had belonged to Duke Humphrey's Library, viz. two parts of Abbot John Whethamstede's *Granarium*, which the author had presented to his great ducal patron. Among Brian Twyne's vast MS. *Collectanea* (Ant. à Wood's great storehouse), preserved in the University Archives, in vol. xviii. pp. 117–141, is a history of the original Library, drawn from the University records, and of the foundation of Bodley's Library, written about 1620. Here, at p. 123, Twyne thus mentions Whethamstede's book: 'Duas partes priores eidem jam olim bibliothecæ [*sc.* Humphredi] ereptas, et vænum bibliopolis expositas, in privata magistri Thomæ Allani viri undique literatissimi, et alumni Aulæ Gloc. Oxoniæ meritissimi, bibliotheca ante paucos annos vidimus, et nos vicissim earum saltem titulos aliis videndos hoc in loco exhibebimus.' He then proceeds to describe the contents of the MS. At p. 124 in this account of the Library, Twyne gives an interesting confirmation from oral tradition of the story of Polydore Vergil's pillaging MSS. After mentioning the report, he adds, 'Et post, alii idem

belonged to Digby, and which each contain his inscription, 'Hic est liber publicæ Bibliothecæ academiæ Oxoniensis, K.D.,' were purchased in 1825. One of these, *R. Baconis opuscula*, was bought for £51; the other, a Latin translation, by W. de Morbeck, of Proclus' Commentary on Plato, for £31 10*s*. They are uniformly bound with the rest of the series, and are numbered 235 and 236 respectively. The MSS. all contain in Digby's hand the motto 'Vindica te tibi,' except one (No. 9) which has the inscription 'Vacate et videte.'[1] A Catalogue of the collection, by the author of these *Annals*, was printed in 1883.

The donor stipulated that his MSS. should not be strictly confined to use within the walls of the Library. Archbishop Laud says, in the letter (dated 19 Dec.) in which, as Chancellor, he announced the gift to the University, 'hee will not subiect these manuscripts to the strictnes of Sir Thomas Bodley's statutes[2], but will haue libertie given for any man of woorth, that wilbee at the paines and charge to print any of these bookes, to haue them oute of the Librarye vpon good caution giuen; but to that purpose and noe other[3].' But Digby afterwards left the University at liberty to deal as it pleased with his MSS. in this particular, as well as in all other questions that might arise concerning his books. In a letter to Dr. Langbaine, dated Nov. 7, 1654, he says: 'The absolute disposition of them in all occurrences dependeth wholly and singly of the University; for she knoweth best what will be most for her service and advantage, and she is absolute mistress to dispose of them as she pleaseth[4].' He mentions in the same letter two trunks of Arabic [and Hebrew] MSS. which he gave to Archbp. Laud to send to the University or to St. John's College, but he never heard whether they reached their destination or no[5].

fecerunt. Hoc solebat referre venerabilis senex Alexander Nowellus, a quo Tho. James illud accepit, et abs illo nos. Istius igitur Bibliothecæ occasus author primus fuit Polydorus.'

[1] The carrier's charge for bringing the MSS. from London was £1 9*s*. 11½*d*.

[2] See under 1654–9.

[3] Reg. Conv. R. 24, f. 102.

[4] [Walker's] *Letters by Eminent Persons, from the Bodl. and Ashm.*, 1813, vol. i. pp. 2, 3.

[5] They were received in 1639, but are entered in the Register with Laud's gift in 1640.

He promises also to send over some more MSS. from France when he has returned thither; as, when the troubles of the Rebellion drove him into exile, he carried his library with him[1]. Upon the Restoration, however, and his own return to England, he unfortunately left his books behind; and after his death they were confiscated by the French King as belonging to an alien, and subsequently sold for 10,000 crowns[2]. Doubtless the two MSS. acquired in 1825 were among those to which his letter refers. In Ballard MS. xi., from which Digby's letter was printed by Walker (as in the note on the preceding page), a rough draft follows in Langbaine's hand of a letter written by Langbaine to Digby, dated Aug. 26, 1656, in which he thus replies to the enquiry respecting the Oriental MSS. 'Those Arabick books which you consigned for our public Library about the beginning of the late warres, I finde upon search, did not wholly misse their way, though they do not confesse fully whence they came. For the arms and motto speake them yours, but the inscription and letters that came along with them from my Lord of Cant. put no difference but as if the whole tribe had bene his, and they are placed with the rest of his donation[3]. If you desire to have them retrieved, I shall pursue your directions to effect.' Langbaine refers also in this letter to enquiries

[1] Louis Jacob, in his *Traicté des plus belles bibliothèques* (published at Paris in 1649, which contains one of the earliest foreign notices of the Bodleian), says that Digby was living at the Court of the King of France in 1644, the year in which the author was writing his book, and that 'dans la guerre civile qui est aujourd'huy dans l'Angleterre, les Parlementaires ont entierement bruslez la bibliothèque des livres imprimez de ce Seigneur' (p. 267). 'Ce Seigneur' is called by Jacob 'le comte d'Igby.'

[2] Two are now amongst the 'MSS. Anglais' in the National Library at Paris, Nos. 55, 56. (Gaston Raynaud's *Cat. des MSS. Angl.* 1884, p. 20.) They are, 1. Verses in praise of col. John Digby, dedicated to his brother Kenelm; and 2. 'Peregrination of Sidnam Poynes,' being episodes of the Thirty Years' War, in 1624-36. Both these MSS. were formerly in the Gaignières collection.

[3] These amount to thirty-six, and Digby's motto, strange to say, is crossed out in them, and they are described as being of the Archbishop's gift. The present Librarian has now separated them from the Laudian MSS., and placed them under the name of the true donor. Two volumes containing the Arabic Dictionary of Algiauhari, which were given to the Library by Philip Williams, a merchant at Constantinople, in 1639, were also wrongly included in the Laud collection.

made by Digby about chemical books, and says, 'this place is very barren in books in that kinde . . . Amongst my acquaintance I know none who hath bene more inquisitive that way then Capt. Ashmole. Some old English pieces he hath published, and some more he reserves by him. Some I meet with in Sion Coll. library, but of what (treasure or coale) I am not so much a sonne of the art as to determine. Some there have bene in New Coll. library here, but embezeld of late yeres, and amongst them a piece of fryer Bacon in French. And having thus falne upon the mention of that author, give me leave to re-informe, that I retaine still a moneth's mind of publishing a good part of that man's works, to which I was first encouraged by a great admirer of his, Mr. Selden of honored memory. I transcribed out of Sir Tho. Cotton's copy his Epistle to Pope Clement the 4th, and so much as there was left of his *Compendium studii theologiæ* (for it was imperfect); and am now within kenne of the conclusion of his *Opus Majus* out of the Dublin copy, upon which I have sett Mr. Casaubon at work this yeere and upwards.'

This draft of Langbaine's letter is written, as it seems, on the blank leaf of a sheet containing twelve proposed rules for regulating the lending of Digby's books from the Library, which had been sent to Digby and returned by him, and to which he refers in his letter of 7 Nov. 1654. Langbaine proposed that books should be lent by the Curators for transcription in order to print, for collation, or for special perusal; on a bond for £100, or otherwise for double or treble value of the book, in which bond some member of the University should be bound with the borrower; a fixed time to be allowed; if the transcript be not printed, then to be deposited in the Library (— to this Digby objects, as too strict a requirement —); nothing to be transcribed except for the sake of printing; and two registers of the lent books to be kept, one with the Vice-Chancellor, the other in the Library.

The first stone of the western end of the Library, with the Convocation House beneath, was laid on May 13, 1634; it was fitted up with shelves and ready for use by 1640. Selden's books were placed here in 1659. The great west window was until recently a conspicuous example of the bad taste of the time; but about twelve years ago it was much improved by the introduction of some tracery, and the contrast with its opposite neighbour, the noble east window erected by Bodley himself, has become less marked. The dimensions of the Library, after this wing was added, are given as follows in a paper now to be found in Addit. MS. C. 78 (ff. 31, 32), and these are found to be very nearly correct as the present measurements:—

'From the South window at the entrance to the North, 89 feet.
From the East window to the West, 139 feet.
Height from the floor, 23 feet and a half.
[In the centre the height is now 22½ feet, the floor having there been raised.]
Breadth of the East side, over the Proscholium, 20 feet and a half.
Breadth of the middle, over the Divinity School, 31 feet 9 inches.
Breadth of Selden's library, 28 feet.
Length of Selden's library, 89 feet [or 88].'

The measurement of the three sides of the Picture Gallery was taken on Sept. 17, 1720, as follows:—

'North side, 138 feet.
West [*read*, East] side, 159 feet. [From this a small room has been cut off at the end.]
South side, 140 feet.
Breadth, 25 feet.'

Two undergraduates, Mr. Thinne and Mr. Knightley, paid admission fees of 40*s*. each.

A. D. 1635.

In this year Rous issued an Appendix to the Catalogue published in 1620, consisting of 208 pages in quarto, in double columns, and containing, as he says, about 3000 authors. It is called 'Editio secunda' on the title, with reference, no doubt, to the small Appendix attached to the Catalogue of 1620. At the end of the later one is added [by John Verneuil, then Sub-Librarian], an anonymous enlarged edition (which was also sold separately) of James' *Catalogus interpretum S. Script. in Bibl. Bodl.*, with an Appendix of authors who had written on the *Sentences* and the

Summa, on the Sunday-Gospels, on Cases of Conscience, on the Lord's Prayer, the Apostles' Creed, and the Decalogue. A book giving an account of all the copies of the Catalogue sold between 1620–47, with the names of the purchasers, still exists, the latter part being in the handwriting of Verneuil; but some leaves have been torn out at the year 1635. It appears from this book that the price of James' Catalogue was 2*s*. 8*d*., that of the Catalogue of Interpreters 6*d*., of the Appendix 2*s*., and of the whole series complete 5*s*. They appear to have been afterwards used as waste-paper; being cut up by the Library book-binders for fly-leaves, of which a specimen may be seen in the volume numbered 8°. C. 162 Th.

A legacy of £10 was received from Mr. Abraham Archdale.

A.D. 1635–1640.

The Register for these years presents a connected series of benefactions on the part of Archbishop Laud.

On May 22, 1635, he sent to the Library the first instalment of his magnificent gifts of MSS., which consisted of 462 volumes and five rolls. Among these were 46 Latin MSS., 'e Collegio Herbipolensi [Würtzburg] in Germania sumpti A.D. 1631, cum Suecorum Regis exercitus per universam fere Germaniam grassarentur' (*Reg. Benef.*). Laud directs, in his letter of gift, that none of the books shall on any account be taken out of the Library, 'nisi solum ut typis mandentur, et sic publici et juris et utilitatis fiant,' upon sufficient security, to be approved by the Vice-Chancellor and Proctors; the MS., in such cases, being immediately after printing restored to its place in the Library[1].

[1] Reg. Conv. R. 24, f. 109[b]. This permission, as soon as the donor was dead, and new authorities were taking the place of the old, was acted upon in one instance with considerable latitude, Laud's MS. of the Saxon Chronicle being lent to Sir S. D'Ewes without its being for the purpose of printing. The following formal acknowledgment is preserved in a folio leaf of paper, which was formerly among the Univ. Archives. 'Received by mee Sir Simonds D'Ewes, of Stowhall in the county of Suffolk, Knight and Baronet, out of the publique University Library at Oxford, one old manuscripte chronicle in the auntient English Saxon tounge, commonly called Chronica

In 1636, 181 MSS. formed the Archbishop's second gift, which were accompanied by five cabinets of coins in gold, silver, and brass, with a list arranged chronologically; an Arabic astrolabe, of brass[1]; two small idols, one Egyptian, the other from India; and the fine bust of King Charles I, 'singulari artificio ex purissimo ære conflatam,' which is now placed under the arch opening into the central portion of the Library. This beautiful work of art was believed by the late learned historical writer, Mr. John Bruce, who was engaged in researches into the life and productions of Hubert Le Sœur, the artist of the statue at Charing Cross, to be, (as well as the bust given by Laud to St. John's College,) a specimen of the skill of that famous craftsman. The existing arrangements of the Library being found insufficient for these large accessions, the lower end was fitted up in 1638–9 for the reception of Laud's books, for the cost of which £300 was voted by Convocation[2]. In 1639, 575[3] more MSS. were received, (with a letter of gift dated 28 June,) together with a magical wand or staff, and some additional coins. The wand is of dark polished wood, 2 feet 9 inches long, with a grotesquely-carved figure at the head, apparently of

Burgi Sancti Petri, my borrowing of it being for a publique use. And I doe faithfully promise to restore [it] againe whensoever it shalbee demanded. In witnes whereof to this presente writing I have hereunto put my hand and seale. Dated this 19th day of October, 1647. Simonds D'Ewes.' The seal has been cut out and stolen. Several volumes were also lent in 164⅞ to Patrick Young, the librarian at St. James's, as appears from an entry at the end of the Register of Readers in 1638–9.

[1] This was given to Laud by Selden, 'vir omni eruditionis genere instructissimus,' as Laud styles him in his letter of gift on June 16. Reg. Conv. R. 24. f. 128. £1 was paid to 'Hawkins the painter,' for limning the Archbishop's coat of arms in the Benefaction Register, and for an inscription over a closet where the MSS. were placed. £2 5*s*. 2*d*. were paid to Edgerley the carrier for bringing books and coins and the King's 'Statua' in 1636. Hawkins had 4*s*. for painting Sir K. Digby's arms in 1636, and the same sum was paid for a copy of the arms to a 'lymmer in London.' In 1668 Elias Ashmole gave a MS. Catalogue of Laud's coins.

[2] Reg. Conv. R. 24. 156^b. 169^b. The agreements with one Thomas Richardson for the work are found there.

[3] So stated in Laud's own letter, but entered as 555 in *Reg. Benef.*

Mexican workmanship. The last gift from the munificent Chancellor of the University came in the next year, 1640, and consisted of no more than 81 MSS.[1]; for troubles were beginning to gather now around the head of the Archbishop, and the Library at Oxford felt the blows which were levelled at Lambeth. This was accompanied with the following touching letter :—

'Viris mihi amicissimis Doctori Potter, Vice-Cancellario, reliquisque Doctoribus, Procuratoribus, necnon singulis in domo Convocationis intra almam Universitatem Oxon. congregatis.

'Non datur scribendi otium. Hoc tamen quale quale est arripio lubens, ut pauca ad vos transmittam, adhuc florentes Academici. Tempora adsunt plusquam difficillima, nec negotia quæ undique urgent faciliora sunt. Quin et quo loco res Ecclesiæ sint nemo non videt. Horum malorum fons non unus est; unus tamen, inter alios, furor est eorum qui sanam doctrinam non sustinentes (quod olim observavit S. Hilarius) corruptam desiderant. Inter eos qui hoc œstro perciti sunt quam difficile sit vivere mihi plus satis innotescit, cui (Deo gratias!) idem est vivere et officium facere.

'Sed mittenda hæc sunt, nec enim quo fata ducunt datur scire. Nec mitiora redduntur tempora aut tutiora querimoniis. Interim velim sciatis me omnia vobis fausta et felicia precari, quo tuti sitis felicesque, dum hic inter sphæras superiores stellæ cujuslibet magnitudinis vix motum suum tenent, aut præ nubium crassitie debile lumen emittunt.

'Dum sic fluctuant omnia, statui apud me in tuto (id est, apud vos spero) MS. quædam, temporum priorum monumenta, deponere. Pauca sunt, sed prioribus similia, si non æqualia, et talia quæ, non obstantibus temporum difficultatibus, in usum vestrum parare non destiti. Sunt vero inter hæc Hebraica sex, Græca undecim, Arabica triginta quatuor, Latina viginti et unum, Italica duo, Anglicana totidem, Persica quinque, quorum unum, folio digestum ampliori, historiam continet ab orbe condito ad finem imperii Saracenici, et est proculdubio magni valoris. Hæc per vos in Bibliothecam Bodleianam (nomen veneror, nec superstitiose) reponenda, et cæteris olim meis apponenda, cupio, et sub eisdem legibus quibus priora dedi. Non opus est multis [verbis] donum hoc nostrum nimis exile ornare, nec id in votis meis unquam fuit. Hoc obnixe et quotidie a DEO Opt. Max.

[1] An entry in the accounts shows that two more MSS. were brought down separately from London by the carrier Edgerley or Eggerley.

summis votis peto, ut Academia semper floreat, in ea Religio et Pietas et quicquid doctrinam decorare potest in altum crescat, ut tempestatibus quæ nunc omnia perflant sedatis, tuto possitis et vobis et studiis et, præ omnibus, DEO frui. Quæ vota semper erunt

'fidelissimi et amantissimi Cancellarii vestri,

'W. CANT.[1]

'Dat. ex ædibus meis
Lambethanis, 6to Nov. 1640.'

The collection, which contains in the whole nearly 1300 MSS., comprises works in very many languages: Hebrew, Chaldee, Syriac, Arabic, Persian, Turkish, Armenian, Ethiopic, Chinese, Russian, Greek, Latin, French, German, Italian, Irish, Anglo-Saxon, and English are all represented. It is impossible, in the limits of this survey, to point out many of the treasures with which the collection abounds; but that which is pre-eminently styled *Codex Laudianus* (numbered Laud Gr. 35) must not, of course, be omitted. It is a MS. of the Acts of the Apostles, in quarto, consisting of 227 leaves, and containing the text in both Greek and Latin, in parallel columns. Its date has been variously fixed by critics, from the sixth to the eighth century; Mr. Coxe placed it towards the end of the seventh century, with whom Dr. Tischendorf, who examined it in 1865, and for whom some photographs of portions were executed, was believed to coincide. Some leaves are wanting at the end, commencing at chap. xxvi. 29. It is the only MS. known to be extant which contains the peculiar readings (in number 74) cited by Bede in his Commentary as existing in the copy which he used; it has consequently been conjectured, with much reason, that this was the very MS. which he possessed. It was published by Thomas Hearne in 1715, printed in capitals corresponding line for line with the MS., but not with entire correctness; only 120 copies were printed, and it is therefore one of the rarest in the series of his works. A

[1] Reg. Conv. R. 24, 182^b. A translation of this letter and of the reply of the University on 19 Nov. was printed in 1641 in a small quarto pamphlet of 8 pp.

very fairly engraved facsimile of one verse (vii. 2) is to be found in T. H. Horne's *Introduction*, and a fac-simile of the whole, with a full introduction, was published by Tischendorf, at Leipzig, in 1870.

Another famous MS. (No. 636) is a copy of the Anglo-Saxon Chronicle, which ends at the year 1154, and appears to have been written in, and to have belonged to, the abbey of Peterborough, from its containing many additions relating thereto. And a third treasure calling for special mention is an Irish vellum MS. (No. 610), which contains the Psalter of Cashel, Cormac's Glossary, Poems attributed to SS. Columb-kill and Patrick, &c.[1] A fourth is a copy of Pope Gregory's *Pastorale*, probably of the ninth century, which has this colophon, 'Willibaldus diaconus scripsit. Amen:' too late to designate the saint of that name, as then the MS. would have been written about A. D. 730–740. The Greek MSS. of the collection are fully described in vol. i. of the *Catal. Codd. Bibl. Bodl.*, by Mr. H. O. Coxe, published in 1853; the Latin, Biblical, and Classical, with the Miscellaneous, in Part i. of the second volume, published by the same gentleman in 1858; the Oriental, in the various Catalogues of Uri, Nicoll, Pusey, Dillmann, and Payne Smith.

One of the Würtzburg books rescued from the Swedish soldiery is a magnificent Missal printed on vellum by Jeorius Ryser in 1481, with illuminated initials. On a fly-leaf is the following note: '1481, Johannes Kewsch, vicarius in ecclesia Herb[ipolensi] hunc librum comparavit propriis expensis, et pro omnibus, scil. pergameno, impressura, rubricatione, illinatura, et ligatione, xviii. flor.' Then follows a bequest, in his own hand, in 1486, of the book to the successive vicars of St. Bartholomew, which is repeated at the end of the 'Canon Missæ.' In the latter place four subsequent

[1] Four volumes of the miscellaneous collection on Irish affairs made by Sir G. Carew, afterwards Earl of Totness, are also to be found here. A list of their contents, as of those of the other volumes preserved at Lambeth and in University College, is printed in Sir T. Duffus Hardy's *Report to the Master of the Rolls on the Carte and Carew Papers*, 8º. Lond. 1864.

possessors, from 1565 to 1580, have written their names, the last of them adding, 'Omnis arbor qui non facit fructum bonum excidetur et in ignem mittetur.' The Library reference is now Auct. i. Q. i. 7. An account of this book is given in a letter from Wanley to Pepys, printed in the Camden Society's *Letters of Eminent Literary Men*, edited by Sir H. Ellis, 1843, pp. 280–2.

A.D. 1636.

£38 7*s.* 9*d.* were paid to Robert Martin for books bought in Rome and other parts of Italy.

On 31 Aug. King Charles visited the Library, and his visit is thus noted in the accounts: '— for certaine woemen and others imployed about the Librarie, and hearbs to strowe the windowes against his Majestie's coming, 5*s.* 8*d.*' Possibly these herbs were put as prophylactics against the danger of any infection, as the plague was then prevalent in London, and are not suggestive of any special mustiness in the Library.

In the course of an inaugural lecture delivered in this year by Henry Jacobs, of Merton College, upon his appointment to be public Reader in Philology in that College (published at Oxford by Henry Birkhead in 1652), reference is made to the large Oriental collection already existing in the Library; the Hebrew, Syriac, Coptic, Arabic, Armenian, Æthiopic, Persian, Chinese languages are all there represented, together with Taprobanic 'aliosque characteres suæ etiam Indiæ fere ignorabiles.' And the writer proceeds to sum up by adding: 'Heic denique qualescunque linguæ, vel figura insolentes, vel lectione inexpeditæ, vel captu tristes, vel solo longinquæ, vel raritate nobiles, vel antiquitate venerabiles, vel spatio diffusiores, vel usu commendabiles, omnes sedentariæ parantur helluationi aut parabuntur.' In an Appendix are added verses 'in bibliothecam Oxoniensem tertio amplificatam, 1636.'

A.D. 1637.

A Bachelor of Arts and Fellow of St. John's College, one Abraham Wright, published the results of his lighter reading in the Bodleian in a little volume printed by Leonard Lichfield, which he entitled, *Delitiæ Delitiarum, sive Epigrammatum ex optimis quibusque hujus et novissimi seculi Poetis in amplissima illa Bibliotheca Bodleiana, et pene omnino alibi extantibus*, ἀνθολογία.

In the accounts for this year are the following entries:—

'For a new Catalogue bound in vellum and sent to Sir H. Spelman by Mr. Jeremy .... (*blank*) advise and direction, when he sent us downe his Glossary	£0	5	0
'To 2 Bohemians that presented us with Vinselaus .... (*blank*) books for the Library . . .	0	5	0'

A.D. 1638.

A German law-student of Altdorf, whose MS. diary of his travels in 1633–40 was bought by the Library in 1882, visited Oxford in 1638. Of the Library he says that it is not 'in general so magnificent as it is reported,' but mentions some of the literary and miscellaneous curiosities which he saw. A translation of his description of Oxford was communicated to the *Athenæum* of 17 May, 1884, by Dr. A. Neubauer, sub-librarian; and the whole account of his English journey, translated into English by Herman Hager, is in vol. x. of Kölbing's *Englische Studien*, 8°. Heilbronn, 1886, pp. 445–453.

A.D. 1639.

A memorandum in the accounts records that £500 which had been borrowed from the Library Chest 'for the Anotomy (*sic*) purchase' was repaid on 26 July.

One shilling was paid 'to certeyne poore schollers for helping to tye books against the visitation of the Library.' This was continued in some subsequent years. In this year first appear payments for extra help in cleaning; fourpence a week are paid to a poor woman and her daughter for sweeping.

A.D. 1640.

On Jan. 25, 1639–40, died Robert Burton, of Ch. Ch., 'Democritus junior,' and bequeathed out of his large library whatever he possessed which was wanting in the Bodleian; in the words of his will, 'If I have any bookes the Universitye Library hath not, lett them take them.' A list of the Latin books thus acquired is given in the Benefaction Book, followed by this sentence: 'Porro [d. d.] comœdiarum, tragediarum, et schediasmatum ludicrorum (præsertim idiomate vernaculo) aliquot centurias, quas propter multitudinem non adjecimus.' These latter were just the classes of books the admission of which the Founder had almost prohibited, viz.,'almanacks, plays, and an infinite number that are daily printed.' Even if 'some little profit might be reaped (which God knows is very little) out of some of our play-books, the benefit thereof,' said he, 'will nothing near countervail the harm that the scandal will bring upon the Library, when it shall be given out that we stuffed it full of baggage books[1].' In consequence of this well-meant but mistaken resolution, the Library was bare of just those books which Burton's collection could afford, and which now form some of its rarest and most curious divisions. In his own address 'To the Reader' of his *Anatomy of Melancholy* he very fully describes the nature of his own gatherings. 'I hear new news every day; and those ordinary rumours of war, plagues, fires, inundations, thefts, murders, massacres, meteors, comets, spectrums, prodigies, apparitions, of towns taken, cities besieged in France, Germany, Turkey, Persia, Poland, &c. * * * * are daily brought to our ears; new books every day, pamphlets, currantoes, stories (&c.). Now come tidings of weddings, maskings, mummeries, entertainments, jubilees, embassies, tilts and tournaments, trophies, triumphs, revels, sports, plays; then again, as in a new shifted scene, treasons, cheating tricks, robberies, enormous villainies, in all kinds, funerals, burials, death of princes, new discoveries, expeditions; now comical, then

[1] *Reliquiæ Bodl.* p. 278.

tragical matters[1].' His books (of which a list exists in Selden MS. *supra* 80) are chiefly to be found in the classes marked 4°. Art. (particularly under letter L), Theol., and Art. BS. Amongst his smaller books is one of the only two known copies of the edition of *Venus and Adonis* in 1602. He is specially mentioned also in the preface to Verneuil's *Nomenclator*, 1642, as being (together with Mr. Kilby of Linc. Coll., Mr. Prestwich of All Souls', and Mr. Francis Wright, of Merton) a donor of Commentaries and Sermons. Besides his books, he bequeathed £100 'to purchase five pounds lands *per ann.* to be paid out yearely on books, as Mrs. Brookes formerly gave an hundred pounds to buy land to the same purpose' (*Will*); but the legacy, instead of being thus invested, was lent out at five per cent. interest. And eventually the money

[1] In his will (entered at Somerset House, in the register marked 'Coventry,' fol. 56) which is dated 15 Aug. 1639, 'beinge at this present I thanke God in perfecte healthe of bodye and mynd,' he directs his executors to dispose of all such books as are not included in bequests, 'with all such bookes as are written with my owne handes, and half my *Melancholy* copie, for Crips hath the other halfe.' He leaves 20*s*. to Rous the Librarian, with money-legacies to the Dean, Canons, servants, and M.A. Students, with 'a booke in folio, or twoe, apiece' to the latter. To Mrs. Fell, the Dean's wife, his English books of husbandry, one excepted (as below); to John Fell, the Dean's son, Student, 'my mathematicall instruments, except my twoe cross-staves, which I give to my Lord of Donnel (?), if he be then of the howse;' to Katherine, the Dean's daughter, six pieces of silver plate and six silver spoons; to Mrs. Iles, Gerard's *Herbal*; to Mrs. Morris, 'my *Country Farme*, translated out of French;' to Mr. Whistler, the Recorder of Oxford, 'all my English physick bookes;' to Mr. Jones, Chaplain and Chante., 'my surveighing bookes and instruments.' A statement connected with this will shows that Burton's death did not take place on Jan. 25, 16$\frac{39}{40}$, as stated by Wood, and also seems virtually to refute the story of his having committed suicide; for the will is attested by Dr. John Morris as having been shown to him by the testator as his last will, on Feb. 3, 1639-[40], some few days before his death. It was proved 11 May, 1640. Marshall MS. 132 (a little early 14th cent. volume of *Statuta Angliæ*) contains on its fly-leaf a very interesting series of notes of the Burton family from the time of Hen. VI. to 1642. The first name is that of Will. Burton, esq., standard-bearer to Hen. VI., who records his ownership of the book both in French and Latin, and who was killed at the battle of Towton in 1461. Our Robert Burton was in the fifth descent from this William, and was born 8 Feb. 1576. The names and dates of nine brothers and sisters are given.

was expended in the ordinary course of library charges. For in Barlow's Accounts for 1655, after mentioning the receipt of £40 paid by one Mr. Thomas Smith, occurs this '*Memorandum*:—that the £40 above mentioned amongst the *Recepta* is a part of an £100 given to the Library by Mr. Rob. Burton of Ch. Ch. It was first lent to Mr. Thomas Smith, and he (by bond) was to pay to the Library £5 per annum[1]. He breaking, or very much decay'd in his estate, and deade, this £40 was payd in by his executors, £50 more is to be payd us by University Coll. (it was owinge to Mr. Smith, and his executors assigned it over to us), and Dr. Langbaine hath in his keepinge a bond of one Spencer for £10 more.' The latter was paid in 1658, as appears from an entry, 'Recept. a Dno. Spicer (*sic*) et Hopkins, ex syngrapha;' and the former was paid Nov. 27, 1673, by Obadiah Walker, then Fellow of Univ. Coll., when it is noted that 'the bond could not be found.'

On a winter's day in this year a certain German Baron, weary, it may be, of quiet reading, seems to have warmed himself by a vigorous passage at arms with a (probably equally pugnacious) Welshman. Consequently, on the very next day, the fourth of Dec., came out the following order from the Vice-Chancellor for the Baron's expulsion from the Library.

'Bibliothecario Bodleiano Utrique, S.

'Quandoquidem D. Baro de Eulenbirg, die Jovis, 3 Dec. proxime elapso, publice, in Bibliotheca Bodleiana, coram pluribus testibus, quendam Th. Williams, scipione vel pugno usque ad sanguinis effusionem percussit, cum gravissima pacis perturbatione, ac statutorum tum Regni hujus tum Academiæ contemptu: Eapropter in tantæ contumeliæ pacisque violatæ pœnam, censeo atque edico eundem D. Baronem ab ingressu Bibliothecæ Bodleianæ posthac omnino arcendum atque amovendum, quoad D. Vicecancellario cæterisque Bibliothecæ Curatoribus aliter visum fuerit. Edico etiam, ne quis studiosus Anglus vel Advena, cujuscunque Nationis, Bibliothecam publicam cum baculis, vel scipionibus, vel ullo denique telo intrare ausit, sub pœna præ arbitrio infligenda.

'CHRISTOPHER. POTTER,

'Dat. e Coll. Reg., Dec. 4, 1640. Vicecan. Oxon.'

[1] The £5 were paid for the year 1644, when very little else came in.

The Register of Admissions to the Library shows that 'Tho. Williams, e societate Medii Templi,' was admitted on 17 March, 1636 (-7), and 'Botho Henricus, L. Baro ab Eulenburg' on 16 Jan. 1638 (-9). The latter must have been soon re-admitted after his expulsion, as he signs the Memorial to the Curators from foreign students noticed under the next year.

Payments of £8 8*s*. 4*d*. in this year, and £35 10*s*. 6*d*. in the following, were made to Rob. Mertin (*al.* Martin), 'stationer' (as in earlier years), for books out of Italy, and one of £1 16*s*. for books bought out of Mr. Lionell Daye's study. 5*s*. 6*d*. were paid 'to a poore scholar and labourers to help to remove my Lo. of Cant. my Lord Steward's, Sir Kenelme Digby's, and Sir Tho. Roe's MSS. into the new built end of the Library' from the Schools' Tower.

The booksellers ('stationers') from whom in most years about this time purchases were made were George Thomason and Octavian Pullen, with, occasionally, Samuel Browne, — Whittaker, Francis Bowman, Michael Sparkes, Edward Forrest, and Thomas Robinson. Thomason's name is well known as the collector of the series of Civil War tracts now in the British Museum, and in vain offered for purchase to our Library after the Restoration.

A.D. 1641.

The famous 'Guy Fawkes' Lantern,' which was until very recently such an object of interest in the Picture Gallery to most sight-seers, was presented to the University by Robert Heywood, M.A., Brasenose College, who had been Proctor in 1639. It came into his possession from his being the son of a Justice of the Peace who assisted in searching the cellars of the Parliament House, and arrested Fawkes with the lantern in his hand. In 1640 this Justice Heywood was wounded by a Roman Catholic when, while still holding office as a Justice for Westminster, he was engaged in proposing the oaths to the recusants of that city[1]. The following inscription is attached to it, engraved upon a brass plate: 'Lāterna

[1] Neal's *Hist. of the Puritans*, i. 688. Clarendon, *Hist. Reb.* iii. 180, where he is called *Hayward*.

illa ipsa, qua usus est et cum qua deprehensus Guido Faux in crypta subterranea, ubi domo Parlamenti difflandæ operam dabat. Ex dono Rob. Heywood, nuper Academiæ Procuratoris, Apr. 4, 1641.' From being for many years exposed to the handling of every visitor, it became much broken; but it has now for a long time been secured from further injury by being enclosed in a glass case [1]. In 1887, however, the lantern was transferred to the Ashmolean Museum as being a more appropriate place for it; where, however, amidst many other relics it can hardly be such a centre of popular attraction as when it occupied alone a whole window-seat in our gallery.

In May an order was made by the Curators that no strangers should have the use of any MSS. without finding sureties for the safety of the same [2], in consequence of a suspicion that whole pages had been in some cases abstracted. Hereupon a very earnest, and, in sooth, indignant, remonstrance was presented to the 'Curatores vigilantissimi' by the strangers then residing in Oxford 'studiorum causa.' The original document is preserved in Wood MS. F. 27, and is signed by eleven persons from Prussia and other parts of Germany, six Danes, and one Englishman (John Wyberd), a medical student. Some of these visitors are found, by reference to the Register of Readers, to have been students for a considerable time; one Ven, a Dane, for instance, having been admitted in 1633. The memorialists say that there is not even the very slightest ground for attributing such an offence to any of them, and that the Librarian himself candidly confesses that it has never been proved to him that strangers have ever done anything of the kind; they urge the difficulty of their finding sponsors for their honesty when they themselves are strangers and foreigners; they appeal to Bodley's own statutes as providing sufficiently for the

[1] A description and small engraving may be found in the *Illustrated London Almanac* for 1852.

[2] The original statutes of 1610 provided that some graduate should in such cases become responsible for the reader, and this order was consequently only a carrying out of this provision. It was re-enacted when the Library statutes were revised in 1856.

contingency by ordering the Librarian to number the pages of a MS. before giving it out, and to examine it when returned; they fortify their arguments by abundant references to the civil law; they upbraid those who,—'internecino exterorum atque advenarum odio æstuantes (O celebratam Britanniæ hospitalitatem!),'—have originated the calumny; and, finally, warn the Curators against giving occasion for suspicion to the learned men of the whole world that 'doctos Angliæ viros, priscæ hospitalitatis immemores, majori exterorum quam Athenienses Megarensium odio flagrare.' The memorial is endorsed: 'De hac re amplius deliberandum censebant Præfecti ult. Maii, 1641;' and no doubt the obnoxious order was soon repealed[1]. Half a century later, on Nov. 8, 1693, the order was in a certain degree renewed: it was then enjoined 'that no one be permitted to *transcribe* any manuscript, but such as have a right to study in the Library.' The revival, however, was not due to any revived fear of foreigners; the following reason is given in a letter of information on Library matters from Dr. Hyde to Hudson, his successor, written on the latter's appointment in 1701:—'Some in the University have been very troublesome in pressing that their Servitors may transcribe manuscripts for them, though not sworn to the Library, nor yet capable of being sworn; wherefore the Curators made an order (as you will find in the Book of Orders in the Archives) "that none were capable of transcribing, except those who had the right of studying in the Library," viz. Batchelors[2].' But no doubt this order also soon became dormant, even if it were not definitely repealed.

A.D. 1642.

'The Kinge, Jul. 11, 1642, had £500 out of Sir Th. Bodlyes Chest, as appeares by Dr. Chaworthes acquittance in the same box.'

[1] In 1663 one Esaias Fleischer, who had used the Library, as he records, for three and a half years, gratefully presented Huitfeldt's Danish Chronicle, in two folio volumes, as 'debitorum suorum partem.' But his debt of gratitude may have arisen, for all we know, from his working at printed books, not at MSS.

[2] [Walker's] *Letters of Eminent Men*, 1813, vol. i. p. 175.

(Barlow's Library Accounts for 1657. *MS.*) This loan was, of course, never repaid. It is regularly carried on in the Annual Accounts up to the year 1782. (*See* p. 47.)

On Sept. 15, the Parliament troops having entered Oxford under the command of Lord Sale and Sele, many Colleges were plundered of their plate, and entrance being refused at Magdalen College the painted windows of the Chapel there were beaten down until 'upon this assault the gates were opened.' 'Some of the most ignorant troopers went to the Schooles taking it for a colledge, and there lay searching and tumbling too and fro of the Library bookes.'[1]

Nov. 30. 'At night the Library doore was allmost broken open. Suspitio de incendio, &c.' (Brian Twyne's *Musterings of the Univ.*, in Hearne's *Chron. Dunst.* p. 757.)

It must have been about the close of this year or beginning of the next, while the King was in winter quarters at Oxford, that the visit was paid to the Library (if paid at all), which is the subject of the following well-known anecdote. It is here quoted from the earliest authority in which it is found, viz. Welwood's *Memoirs*, Lond. 1700, pp. 105–107:—

'The King being at Oxford during the Civil Wars, went one day to see the Publick Library, where he was show'd among other Books, a Virgil nobly printed and exquisitely bound. The Lord Falkland, to divert the King, would have his Majesty make a trial of his fortune by the *Sortes Virgilianæ*, which everybody knows was an usual kind of augury some ages past. Whereupon the King opening the book, the period which happen'd to come up was that part of Dido's imprecation against Æneas, which Mr. Dryden translates thus:—

"Yet let a race untam'd, and haughty foes,
His peaceful entrance with dire arts oppose,
Oppress'd with numbers in th' unequal field,
His men discourag'd, and himself expell'd,
Let him for succour sue from place to place,
Torn from his subjects, and his son's embrace.
First let him see his friends in battel slain,
And their untimely fate lament in vain:

[1] *The Cavaliers advice to his Majesty . . . with the relation of Oxford Schollers,* &c. 4°. Lond. 1642, pp. 6, 7.

And when at length the cruel war shall cease,
On hard conditions may he buy his peace.
Nor let him then enjoy supreme command,
But fall untimely by some hostile hand,
And lye unburi'd in the common sand."
(Æneid, iv. 881.)

It is said K. Charles seem'd concerned at this accident, and that the Lord Falkland observing it, would likewise try his own fortune in the same manner; hoping he might fall upon some passage that could have no relation to his case, and thereby divert the King's thoughts from any impression the other might have upon him. But the place that Falkland stumbled upon was yet more suited to his destiny than the other had been to the King's, being the following expressions of Evander upon the untimely death of his son Pallas, as they are translated by the same hand:—

"O Pallas, thou hast fail'd thy plighted word,
To fight with reason, not to tempt the sword.
I warned thee, but in vain, for well I knew
What perils youthful ardor would pursue;
That boiling blood would carry thee too far,
Young as thou wert in dangers, raw to war.
Oh! curst essay of arms, disastrous doom,
Prelude of bloody fields and fights to come."
(Æneid, xi. 230.)'

There is no copy of Virgil now in the Library amongst those which it possessed previously to 1642, which is 'exquisitely bound' as well as 'nobly printed;' it is not therefore possible to fix on the particular volume which the King consulted. But Archbishop Sancroft, in one of his numerous MS. note-books in the Bodleian Library (51, p. 29), assigns Windsor as the *locale* of the story. He says, 'There goes a story that Ch. I. a little before the Rebellion, being at Windsor, the company agreed to take their lots out of Virgil, and the King's was this:—

"At bello audacis populi vexatus et armis," &c.'

and a third report vouched for by Aubrey, the gossip-monger, assigns not the King but the Prince of Wales as the person concerned, and Paris as the place [1].

[1] See Lady Theresa Lewis' *Lives of the Friends of Clarendon*, 1852, vol. i, pp. 142-4 and 215-7.

A. D. 1643.

'Item, to buy a French standish to present Mr. Langbane for his paines about my Lord Steward's [the Earl of Pembroke's] Gr. MSS. . £1 0 0

'Item, to Mr. Chilmad for transcribing faire an alphabeticall catalogue of all the Greeke MSS. in the Librarie, and part of an other Catalogue . . . . 1 0 0'

A. D. 1644.

In the book containing copies of the annual accounts which is preserved among the University archives, there is a paper belonging to this year which is not entered in the corresponding book in the Library. It is a letter from the Chancellor of the University, the Marquis of Hertford, to the Curators, dated 7 Feb. 1643, in which he complains that many books are not yet chained or placed in order, that the MSS. are not properly arranged, and that there is no authentic register kept of the books bought (with their prices) or given. The reply of the Curators follows, to the effect that they have ordered all to be done that he recommends, but that the MSS. are already supplied with reference marks, and that the Librarian has kept for himself a register of accessions. But a proper 'leiger book' is ordered; and so we find in the accounts this entry:—'For 2 quier of paper to make a new leiger book for the use of the Librarie, 1*s*.'

The accounts for this year exhibit several marks of war and siege time, both in the non-payment of rents, and by such entries as the first two of these following:—

'To the widdowe Roche, late wife of Tho. Roche, porter of ye Librarie, towards ye hiring a man in his place one day in ye weeke to worke at ye bullworks, 31 weeks, 12^{d} per day, ut patet per billam £1 11 0

Item, to Francis Yong, ye present Porter, for a man to worke in his turne, the Underkeeper being weake, and then not able to goe up ye staires, 14 weekes 0 14 0

'Item, to one Sir Berriman, a Bachelor of Arts of Oriell Colledge, for supplying the Porter's place in his sicknesse, and ye Underkeeper's absence when his howse was infected, a fortnight at two shillings ye weeke . . . 0 4 0'

A. D. 1645.

No rents were received in this year or the following, and consequently no quit-rents were paid.

A small slip of paper, carefully preserved among the Clarendon Papers, is the memorial of an interesting incident connected with the last days in Oxford of the Martyr-King whose history is so indissolubly united with that of the place. Amidst all the darkening anxieties which filled the three or four months preceding the surrender of himself to the Scots, King Charles appears to have snatched some leisure moments for refreshment in quiet reading. His own library was no longer his; but there was one close at hand which could more than supply it. So, to the Librarian Rous, there came, on Dec. 30, an order, 'To the Keeper of the University Library, or to his deputy,' couched in the following terms: 'Deliver unto the bearer hereof, for the present use of his Majesty, a book intituled, *Histoire universelle du Sieur D'Aubigné*, and this shall be your warrant;' and the order was one which the Vice-Chancellor had subscribed with his special authorization, 'His Majestyes use is in commaund to us. S. Fell, Vice Can.' But the Librarian had sworn to observe the Statutes which, with no respect of persons, forbad such a removal of a book; and so, on the reception of Fell's order, Rous 'goes to the King; and shews him the Statutes, which being read, the King would not have the booke, nor permit it to be taken out of the Library, saying it was fit that the will and statutes of the pious founder should be religiously observed[1].' The story reflects, on the one hand, the highest credit both on Rous's honesty and courage, and shows him to have been fit for the place he held, while, on the

[1] Bp. Barlow's Argument against Lending Books. *MS.*

other hand, the King's acquiescence in the refusal does equal credit to his good-sense and good-temper. We shall see that this occurrence formed a precedent for a like refusal to the Protector in 1654 by Rous's successor, when Cromwell showed equal good feeling and equal respect for law. Rous is usually supposed from his friendship with Milton, as well as from his retaining his office by compliance with the Parliamentary visitors, to have been lacking in the loyalty which so nobly distinguished Oxford; but nevertheless, in a volume of undated papers among the Clarendon MSS., in a 'Skeme,' or list of persons who lent money to Charles I, and for whom letters patent, dated 4 July an. 19 (1643), were made for security, we find that at Oxford 'Rouse, Library-keeper,' contributed the very liberal sum of fifty pounds. To his character for truthfulness and conscientiousness we find the following testimony given by a distinguished foreigner twenty years later: 'inclytæ bibliothecæ Bodleyanæ Oxoniensis custos, cujus symbolum, "mentiri nescio; librum si malus est nequeo laudare[1]."'

'To Horne, executor of the last will and testament of William Fletcher ye Painter, for my Lord Primate's picture, allow'd & agreed upon by Mr. Vice-Chanc. & all ye Curators at ye last Librarye accompts . . . . . . £2 0 0'

This refers to a portrait not of the late primate of England, Laud, but of the primate of Ireland, Ussher, as appears by the following paper written by Rous, which is among old separate papers of Library accounts. 'March 27, 1645. There is due unto Simon Horne, executor unto the last will and testament of William Fletcher, late of Oxford, painter, for my lo. primate of Armagh his picture the summe of 45*s*. This was approved of and allowed at the last library accompt by the right worshipfull Dr. Pink, Vice-Chancelour, and all the Curators. The picture is in the closet, and yf I be not deceived is as good a piece for resem-

[1] Lambecius, *Commentt. de Bibl. Vindob.* 1665, vol. iii, p. 381; quoted in C. P. Cooper's *Appendix to Report on the Fœdera*, vol. A, p. 219.

blance as hath ben made by any man. And that was the opinion of the 2 reverend Judges of Irland. Ita testor, Jo. Rous, Biblioth.'

On June 20 in this year Rous buys Milton's *Liberty of Printing* and *Doctrine of Divorce*, various books by Prynne, Goodwin, and Burton, and even *Canterbury's Selfe Conviction*. He evidently was not afraid of royalist objections.

A. D. 1646.

'When Oxford was surrendered (24° Junii, 1646) the first thing Generall Fairfax did was to set a good guard of soldiers to preserve the Bodleian Library. 'Tis said there was more hurt donne by the Cavaliers (during their garrison) by way of embezzilling and cutting off chaines of bookes then there was since. He was a lover of learning, and had he not taken this special care, that noble library had been utterly destroyed, for there were ignorant senators enough who would have been contented to have had it so. This I doe assure you from an ocular witnesse, E. W. esq.'[1]

By the articles of the surrender of Oxford (dated June 20) it was stipulated that the Great Seal and the seals of courts, together with the sword of state, should be deposited in a chest 'in the Publick Library.' They were taken from thence to the Parliament on July 3, and the seals were broken in pieces[2]. It is said by John Walters (note on p. 40 of his *Poems* published in 1780; *v. sub anno*) that the Library walls still retained in 1780 marks of cannon balls discharged during the siege; but it is not now known to what marks he referred.

An account of the treatment of the Library on the surrender which is so strangely destitute of the slightest basis in fact as to be a pure invention of the imagination, is given in a small and (as may be supposed) interesting French volume on English History, entitled *Anecdotes Angloises*, which was published anonymously by one F. J. De La Croix in 1769. The writer, after

[1] Aubrey's *Lives*; in *Letters by Eminent Persons*, ii. 346.

[2] Rushworth, part iv, vol. i, 1701, pp. 281, 285.

describing under the year 1644 in a similarly imaginative way the ravages committed by Cromwell and his forces at Cambridge, brings the former direct from thence to Oxford, and there makes him destroy the whole Library in one vast conflagration! Thus (p. 529) writes the veracious story-teller: 'Après avoir ainsi maltraité la ville de Cambridge, Cromwel alla à Oxford, où il commit encore de plus grandes violences. Il fit allumer un grand feu, et y fit jetter toute la bibliothèque de l'université, composée de plus de quarante mille volumes, parmi lesquels il y avoit un grand nombre de livres rares et curieux, et beaucoup de manuscrits très-précieux, dont l'archevêque de Cantorbéry l'avoit enrichie.' Can this story have taken its rise from some confusion with that of the burning of Digby's printed books, noted under the year 1634?

'Item, for 8 bundles of pamphlets bought out of Mr. Branthwayt's study, conteyninge ye occurances of the times	£1	12	0
'Item, to ye painter that drew Sir Thomas Bodley's picture, and to Mr. Warren that made his medale, to each of them 2s, in toto . .	0	4	0
'Item, for a large Bible wherein is written downe all the Alterations of the last translacõn . .	0	13	4
'Item, to Dr. Langbane of Queenes Colledge for his assistance in helpinge me to catalogue and order the Greeke manuscripts, a paire of gloues	0	6	8
'Item, for the silver meddale of John Husse . .	0	5	0
'Item, for coppyinge out the life of St. Cutbert .	0	10	0
'Item, for transcribeinge and perfectinge a Catalogue with all addicõns of bookes brought into the Library since the printinge of the Appendix, together with a particular collection of all the French, Italian, Spanish, and other vulgar tongues for the use of all such as desire a transcript from time to time, a worke much desired by most gentlemen & strangers that come to the Library	1	10	0'

A banquet was given to the Chancellor of the University at the west end of the Library, for washing and preparing which end there is an entry in the accounts of a payment of five shillings. This banquet is not mentioned by Wood.

A.D. 1647.

John Verneuil, M.A., Sub-librarian (to which office he was appointed about 1618[1]), died about the end of September. He was a native of Bordeaux, and came into England as a Protestant refugee shortly before 1608. In that year he entered at Magdalen College, was admitted to read in the Bodleian 31 Jan. 160$\frac{8}{9}$ (Wood MS. E. 5), and was incorporated M.A. from his own University of Montauban in 1625. Besides his share in the Appendix to the Catalogue noticed under the year 1635, the following small book of a similar kind in English was issued by him: *A Nomenclator of such Tracts and Sermons as have beene printed, or translated into English upon any place or booke of Holy Scripture; now to be had in the most famous and publique Library of Sir Thomas Bodley in Oxford.* This is the title of the second and enlarged edition, which appeared in 1642 in a small duodecimo volume, printed at Oxford, by Henry Hall. The first edition (which was not entirely confined to books in the Library) was printed under the author's initials by William Turner in 1637. Some books communicated by friends are here cited (omitted in the second edition), which would, says Verneuil, have been accessible in the Bodleian, 'had the Company of Stationers beene as mindfull of their covenant as my selfe have beene zealous for the good of this our Library[2].' In an interesting undated letter from Sir

[1] See list of officers at the end of this book.

[2] Verneuil frequently went to London on the business of the Library, and the cost of his journey both ways was sometimes 10*s.*, sometimes 12*s.* Amongst the various old register books of accounts, &c., is a small quarto book in parchment cover, kept by Verneuil for 'the *sealing* of the catalogues,' by which the worthy Frenchman meant 'the *selling*.' It contains entries of all the copies sold, and of the money received for them from 21 Aug. 1620 to 9 Aug. 1647. And then follows this note, which shows that during his last illness he was careful to settle his account:—'Septemb. 4,

Richard Napier, Knt. (while apparently an undergraduate of Wadham College, before 1630) to his uncle the Rev. Richard Napier, which is preserved in Ashmole MS. 1730, fol. 168, is the following curious passage relating to the facilities for studying in the Library which were afforded to him by Verneuil :—

'I have made a faire way to goe into the Library privately when I please, and there to sitt from 6 of the clocke in the morneing to 5 at night. I have a private place in the Library to lay those bookes and to write out what I list, without being seene by any, or any comeing to me. I have made the second Keeper of the Library [*i. e.* Verneuil] my friend and servant, who promised me his key at all tymes to goe in privately, when as otherwise it is not opened above 4 houres a day, and some days not att all, as on Hollidays, and their eves in the afternoone, yett then by his meanes I shall [have] free accesse and recesse at all tymes. He hath pleasured me so farr as to lett me write in his counting house, or his little private study in the great publick library, where I may very privately write, and locke up all safely when I depart thence; he will write for me when I have not the leisure, or will transcribe any thinge I shall desire him, and if it be French translate it, for that is his mother tonge.'

Probably the practice here mentioned of admitting readers by favour into the Library at unstatutable times grew in the course of years to a considerable height, or was found (as might naturally be expected) productive of mischievous consequences, for on Nov. 8, 1722, it was 'ordered by the Curators that no person under any pretence whatsoever be permitted to study in the said Library at any other time than what is prescribed and limited by the Bodleian Statutes.'

One of Verneuil's last entries in any volume in the Library is to be found in a list of books of University Statutes borrowed for the Parliamentary visitation of the University, which had its actual commencement in October of this year. On a fly-leaf of a small copy of a Tamil translation of Bellarmine's Catechism

1647, Received this sum of two pound eleven shillings by the hands of Peter Vernueill, sonne to Mr. John Vernueill, under-keeper of the Publick Library. By me, Jo. Rous, Biblioth.'

(now numbered *Dravid. f.* 6), is the following memorandum in Verneuil's hand, hastily jotted down, as we may suppose, in the book he happened to have in hand at the moment of the borrowing, and intended to be transferred to a more formal register afterwards. 'The Parlament borrowed, Robert Hare, 108; Statuta Nova, 114; Statuta Antiqua, 115; Salamon, 116, *stollen*; 117 Epistolæ Oxon.; 174 Registrum.' The *stolen* book was one, apparently, taken by mistake, being very unsuitable for the work the Visitors came about, viz. 'Les Aprises de Salomon le sage'; it has never been restored, and its title is only found in the oldest catalogues.

Verneuil was succeeded in his office in the Library by Francis Yonge, M.A., of Oriel College, who had been Janitor. See p. 98.

Milton's gift of his *Poems*. See under 1620.

In 1647 and 1648 the distractions of the times hindered all keeping of accounts. Four pages are left blank in the book for entries never made.

A. D. 1648.

At the end of the Readers' Register for 1647–8, 1648–9, is a list of nine volumes 'olim surrepti,' of which five had been replaced by other copies. Entries are made in the same place of some coins which were given in 1648–50. At this period the Library appears to have been well attended by readers; about twelve or fifteen quarto and octavo volumes being daily entered, those of folio size being accessible (as, in regard to a portion of the Library, is still the case) by the readers themselves, and not registered because at that time chained to their shelves. The register for the next years (as well as those which followed, up to the year 1708) appears to be lost, so that it cannot be ascertained whether this daily average continued during the Usurpation; but thus far it seems that Dr. John Allibond's description of the state of the Library as consequent on the Puritan visitation of the University in 1648, is not borne out by facts. For that loyal humourist, in his *Rustica Academiæ Oxoniensis nuper reformatæ Descriptio*, which is supposed to commemorate the condition of Oxford in Oct. 1648, writes thus of our Library:—

'Conscendo orbis illud decus
  Bodleio fundatore:
Sed intus erat nullum pecus,
  Excepto janitore.

Neglectos vidi libros multos,
  Quod minime mirandum:
Nam inter bardos tot et stultos
  There's few could understand 'em.'

A few books were bequeathed by Lord Herbert of Cherbury. They are not entered in the *Reg. Benef.*, nothing being inserted there from 1641 to 1649. But they are noticed in a letter which was sold at the sale of the library of James West, Pres. R. S. in April 1773, and which is thus described in the auction catalogue, No. 3893, p. 198: 'An original letter from Dr. Ger. Langbaine to Mr. Selden respecting two boxes of books received by the University of Oxford, from Sir Hen. Herbert, as the legacy of Lord Cherbury, to their great disappointment; his Lordship having often expressed his intention of leaving them his whole library, &c. Qu. Coll. 12 Sept. 1648.' Some of his MSS. are in Jesus College.

John Bainbridge, M.D., the first Savilian Professor, who died in this year, bequeathed his own portrait and that of Sir Henry Savile. Both these are now in the Picture Gallery. They were to be delivered 'presently after the decease of my wife, with convenient curtaines of silke.'

A.D. 1649.

'The Jews proffer £600,000 for Paul's, and Oxford Library, and may have them for £200,000 more [1].' They wished to obtain the first for a synagogue, and to do a little commercial business with the second. It is said in Monteith's *History of the Troubles* (translated by Ogilvie, 1735, p. 473) that the sum they offered was

[1] London News-letter of April 2; printed in Carte's *Collection of Letters*, vol. i. p. 275.

£500,000, but that the Council of War refused to take less than £800,000: probably they afterwards increased this their original bid to £600,000[1].

Philip, Earl of Pembroke, the Puritan Chancellor of the University, gave a splendidly bound copy of the Paris Polyglott, printed in 1645 in 10 vols.

In a MS. table of the volumes in the Library under their several classes, apparently drawn up about this date (a small quarto, which came from the Ashmolean Museum, and is now kept among general Library records) the whole number is only reckoned as amounting to 15975; viz. in folio 5889, in quarto 2067, in octavo 4918, and MSS. 3101.

A.D. 1650.

8 May. A gift of £20 was received from 'Colonell [Jerome] Sanchy [*or* Sankey *or* Zanchy] fellow of All Soules Colledge,' who was Proctor that year, and who had served as a Colonel in the Parliamentary army. Dr. John Wilkins, the Warden of Wadham College, bought mathematical and philosophical books of Sam. Tomson, a London bookseller, to the amount of £8 2*s.*; and a 'great fraught' of books, to the value of £69 10*s.* (for which £1 was paid for carriage), was bought of George Thomason, the well-known London bookseller. Books were bought from Mrs. Degory Wheare 'out of her husband's study,' and, together with 'small pamphlets,' out of Dr. Clayton's study. In Feb. Sir Simonds D'Ewes borrowed 56 coins, giving to Rous a bond in £500 for their return on or before 31 Oct. The particulars, including a list of the coins, are to be found in Harl. MS. (Brit. Mus.) 298, f. 173.

A.D. 1652.

John Rous, the Librarian, died in the beginning of April, probably on April 3, as, the Statutes requiring the election of

[1] The *Jewish Chronicle* of 2 Nov. 1883, refers to this story as being discussed in the *History of St. Paul's* by W. S. Simpson, D.D., and quotes his conclusion that there is not 'a particle of real evidence' for it.

Librarian to take place within three days of a vacancy, it was on the 6th of that month that Thomas Barlow, M.A., Fellow of Queen's College, was unanimously elected to be Rous's successor. At the same time certain orders were read in Convocation which the Curators had made, for the formation by the Librarian of a Catalogue of the coins and other rarities, providing also that they should be regularly visited and verified by the Curators every November [1].

A legacy of £20 from Rous to the Library is entered in the Benefaction Register, under the year 1661, probably because it may not have been actually received until that year.

Peter Turner, M.D., of Merton College, dying in Jan. 165½, bequeathed many Greek MSS., of which a list (copied from one by Barlow) exists in Smith MS. 9. His books appear from the Library accounts to have been brought down from London in Sept. 1653.

The following entries occur in the accounts for this year:—

	£	s.	d.
'For a 3 hours glasse	£0	2	8
'For a piece of plate presented to Mr. Gellibrand for his pains in procureing the rents and arrears of Distaffe Lane	6	0	0
'To Mr. Ch. Halloway for counsell in that busines .	0	10	0
'To Mr. Walley, Clerk of the Company of Stationers, London, for transcribing a coppy [2] of all books printed for ten yeares last past .	2	0	0'

A. D. 1653.

Fifteen MSS., by Spanish authors, were given on Oct. 1 by Peter Pett, LL.B., Fellow of All Souls' College; and a sacred Turkish vestment of linen (Bodl. Or. 162) on which the whole of the Koran is written in Arabic, by Richard Davydge, an East India merchant. John Evelyn visited the Library on 11 July in the following year, 1654, and in his *Diary* he mentions this copy of the Koran as the 'rarest' curiosity, 'written on one large sheet of calico,

[1] Reg. T. 158-9.

[2] *i.e.* a list.

which is made up in a priest's vesture or cope, after the Turkish and Arabic character, so exquisitely written as no printed letter comes neere it.' (Edit. 1819, vol. i. p. 277.) Other rarities specially noticed by him are: Mrs. Inglis' Book of Proverbs, in a hand 'the most exquisite imaginable;' Roe's MS. of the Council of Basle, erroneously (the error probably that of the transcriber) said to be 900 years old; and a Mexican 'hieroglyphical table or carte, folded up like a map; I suppose it painted on asses' hide; extremely rare.'

Dr. Hammond's newly-published commentary on the New Testament was bought for £1 7*s.*; and £2 were paid to a B.A. of Queen's College, named Nanson, for transcribing the catalogue of Laud's MSS.

Dr. Wallis gave a volume (now *e Musæo*, 203) containing specimens of his decipherments of ciphered royal and royalist letters intercepted during the Civil War, and which he had unravelled for the Parliament. The particulars are so fully given from his own preface to this book in the common accounts of Wallis's life that they need not be repeated here. In Rawlinson's MS. continuation of the *Athenæ Oxon.* (at no. 634), there is the following entry which is said to be a true copy of a memorandum under Wood's own hand: 'March, 1660. The latter end of this month Dr. Wallis got by flattering good words, etc. his book of deciphering the King's letters, etc. from ye Publ. Libr. from Dr. Barlow, where he altered what he pleased.' The alterations, however, appear to be of the most trivial character, and the gift-inscription in the book testifies that he gave it 'reservata sibi in posterum potestate addendi vel emendandi.'

A.D. 1654.

'April last, 1654, my Lord Protector sent his letter to Mr. Vice-Chancellor to borrow a MS. (Joh. de Muris) for the Portugal Ambassador. A copy of the Statute was sent (but not the book), which when his Highness had read, he was satisfy'd, and commended the prudence of the Founder, who had made the place so sacred[1].'

Cromwell's gift of MSS. See under 1629. For this gift, and for ordering £100 per annum to a Divinity Reader, the University in September thanked the Protector (Whitelocke's *Memorials*, p. 588).

Twelve MSS. were bought of John Parry for £6, but no further particulars are given in the accounts.

A.D. 1654–1659.

The death of John Selden occurred on Nov. 30, 1654[2]. By

[1] Barlow's Argument against Lending Books out.

[2] As Aubrey (*Lives*, with *Letters by Eminent Persons*, ii. 532) has preserved a story that Selden on his death-bed refused, through Hobbes' persuasion, to see a clergyman (Mr. Johnson) who was coming 'to assoile him,' it is worth while to print the following notice of his death from Rawlinson MS. B. clviii. fol. 75, a volume containing a collection of biographical anecdotes, &c., written in a rather clumsy copyist's hand, about the beginning of the last century: 'Mr. Selden upon his deathbed disclaimed all Hobbisme and the like wicked and Atheisticall opinions, commanded that neither Mr. Hobbs nor Capt. Rossingham should be admitted to him, confessed his sins, and desired absolution, which was given him by Archbp. Usher; but amongst other things he much deplored the loss of his time in studying of things more curious than usefull, and wished that he [had] rather executed the office of a justice of peace than spent his time in that which the world calls learning.' And the following interesting account of his last hours is taken from a small quarto paper, preserved in a scrap-book of miscellaneous items relating to the Library. The paper has been torn, and the writing is in places much faded, and here and there altogether lost. In the deciphering I have been assisted by the acute help of Mr. Madan, sub-librarian. 'I have not many particulars of Mr. Selden's sickness, onely when he seemed near his end and believed it then he began to think [speak?] of religion and another world, and gave a strickt charge that neyther Rosingham nor Hobbs (his constant guests formerly) should be admitted unto him. A little before he dyed he assayed him to kneel in his bed to receaue the Communion . . . my Lord Primate, he that preacht his funerall sermon . . . he did it (?) with admirable devotion; and he sayd also that he was a great honor to Xtian religion; that whereas most men take it by course and custome and . . . [that he looked?] upon it by choyce as indubitably the . . beste . . , compendiating (?) all others. The Primate sayd though about 45 yeares ago he had . . . elements of the Eastern tongues from him, yet in most of them he came to be soe much before him as he was before the other when he came first to be instructed by him. The 4

his will the Library became possessed at once of his collection of Oriental and Greek MSS., together with a few Latin MSS. specially designated, as well as of such of his Talmudical and Rabbinical books as were not already to be found there. It has generally been supposed that no part of his library was received before the year 1659, and that none at all was actually bequeathed by Selden. The account usually given (taken from Burnet's *Life of Sir M. Hale*, p. 156[1]) is that Selden was so offended with the University for refusing the loan of a MS., except upon a bond for £1000, that he revoked that part of his will which left his library to the Bodleian, and put it entirely at the free disposal of his executors, and that they, when five years had passed, during which the Society of the Inner Temple (to whom it was first offered) had

executors, Justice Hales, Jewkes, Haywood, and Vaughan, may get they say £10,000 a peice if they please, since he gave not many legacyes, and to his sister's children not above £100 a peice, but they, proving as true friends as he took them for, endeavour to do much more than was injoynd them. They say 3 or 4 by-blowes appear, which beeing not mentioned in the Will they will yet duely (?) provide for. And for his invaluable library, though it bee in their power to divide most of it among themselves, yet they have offerd the Inner Temple that if they will build a library they will give them the bookes, which when refusd, 3 of them offerd to build the library and give the bookes too, and he is sayd onely to dissent that was thought to be neerest to him of all the 4, his old chamberfellow, who in former wills before his estate grew so unwieldy was ever made his sole executor. He was buryd privately in the Inner Temple (as he desird) but not so privately but that he had many mourners, which had eyther cloth or money to buy it given by the bounty of the executors. The famous monuments he had in Arabick and the Eastern languages he hath given to Oxford library, and his Arabick physick bookes to the College of Physitians in London. I doe not heare that he hath given ought to the Primate, but some report that the executors gave him £20, others £40, and some report they gave him £100. Some tell me that in a written book Mr. Selden gave directions to his executors to goe to every key and every trunck or chest wher his money or jewells or plate lay, which proved a right direction to all but one place wher they were directed for some thousands in gold, and ther they found just nothing, which made them suspect that some of his servants had been ther before them. If I heare any thing more you shall have it. The last I hear is that all his imperfect and unprinted papers and notes he caused to be brought out before him while he lay upon his deathbed, and saw them burned before his eyes.'

[1] See also Aubrey's *Lives*, *ut supra*, ii. 536.

taken no steps to provide a building for its reception, conceiving themselves to be executors not of Selden's passion but of his will, sent it in 1659 to its original destination[1]. But it is clear from Selden's will (as printed by Wilkins in his *Works*, vol. i. p. lv) that the books mentioned above were really bequeathed by him to Oxford; a line or two appears to be somehow omitted, by which the sense of the passage is lost, and in consequence of which the name of the Library does not appear, but there is a general reference to it both in the specification of such Hebrew books as are 'not already in the Library,' and in the mention of the '*said* Chancellor, Masters, and Scholars' of the University (although no previous mention of them occurs); while all other books not thus conveyed are left to the disposal of his executors. And a letter from Langbaine to Pococke, written from London only two days after Selden's death, furnishes proof positive; for there the former writes, having seen the will, that all the Oriental MSS., with such Rabbinical and Talmudical printed books as were not already in the Library, and the Greek MSS. not otherwise disposed of, are left to Oxford[2]. And in the annual accounts, under the year 1655, we find the following entries:—

'Pro vectura codicum MSS. a Londino Oxoniam .	£0	9	0
'D. Langbaine pro expensis cum Londinum petiit, libros a Seldeno legatos repetiturus . . .	5	0	0
'D. Ed. Pococke eodem tempore in rem eandem Londinum misso	7	0	0'

And in 1656 £6 were paid 'to Mr. Barlow for his journey to London about Mr. Selden's library.'

It is clear, therefore, that a portion of Selden's collection came to the Library by his bequest immediately after his death. And the reason why the whole was not bequeathed is

[1] Nichols (*Lit. Anecd.* i. 333) gives another and very different story, for which he produces no authority. He says that Selden had actually sent his library to Oxford during his lifetime, and hearing that they had lent a book *without sufficient caution*, he sent for it back again.

[2] Twells' Life of Pococke, in Pococke's *Theol. Works*, 1740, vol. i. p. 43. See also the note on the preceding page.

certainly not correctly stated by Burnet, nor even by Wood, who says that he had been informed that it was because 'the borrowing of certain MSS.' had been refused. For the Convocation Register shows that a grace was *passed* in Convocation, on Aug. 29, 1654, which sanctioned the giving leave to Selden to have MSS. from the collections of Barocci, Roe, and Digby (these donors having either expressed an opinion, or distinctly stipulated, that the rigour of the Library Statutes should sometimes be relaxed), provided he did not have more than three at a time, and that he gave bond in £100 (not £1000) for the return of each of them within a year[1]. Had these conditions been really the cause of Selden's taking offence, his executors would hardly have stipulated, as they actually did, in their own conditions of gift [see p. 121], that no book from his collection should hereafter be lent to any person upon any condition whatsoever. But there is certainly some little obscurity hanging over the matter. The writer of the sketch of the history of the Bodleian prefixed to Bernard's *Cat. MSS.*, after quoting Wood's account, only says, when barely more than forty years had elapsed, that he will not venture to speak rashly about the case of the lending of books; as if it were already forgotten how the facts stood. On the proposal to lend being first mooted, Barlow, the Librarian, drew up a paper on the general question, in which he opposed it both on the grounds of Statute and expediency; the original MS. of which still exists in the Library. Selden was at first mentioned in this paper by name, with distinct reference to his application; but the name was subsequently crossed out wherever it thus occurred, and the subject treated without any personal reference[2]. In this paper the Librarian objects to the

[1] Reg. Conv. T. p. 251. It is added, as an additional reason for the concession, 'porro spes sit virum, in rem nostram academicam optime affectum, hanc ei extra ordinem gratiam factam abunde olim compensaturum.'

[2] A copy also exists of this paper made by Hearne with a view to publication, and, as appears from a short preface by him, from a double motive; firstly, to prevent persons taking offence in his own day at refusals;

proposal, firstly, on the ground of precedent, since, though the University had power, with the joint consent of the Chancellor, Heads of Houses, and Convocation, to lend books, yet it had

secondly, to afford warning to persons with 'fanatical consciences,' who seem to have thought there was no harm done in carrying books away secretly, provided they returned them again. Unfortunately 'consciences' such as these still exist, and there is reason for quoting, with a present application, the words with which the warm-hearted Hearne concludes: 'Let these men consider seriously how they will answer this before God, and withall assure themselves that if they be found out, they will, besides the punishment like to come upon them hereafter (without an earnest, hearty repentance) be expos'd to all that infamy and disgrace which the Statute enjoyns to be inflicted upon such notorious offenders.' (Misc. MS. papers relating to the Library.)

The first actual theft of a book occurred in 1624. At the Visitation on Nov. 9, the Curators drew up a formal document, publishing and denouncing the deed, and exhorting the unknown doer to a timely repentance. A copy of it is preserved in volume xxiii of Brian Twyne's Collections, in the University Archives (p. 683), and runs as follows:—

'Cum in hac visitatione nostra anniversaria Bibliothecæ Bodleianæ, post diligentem et religiosam status ejus pro officii nostri ratione examinationem factam, compertum sit volumen unum (Jod. Nahumus, Conc. in Evangelia Dominicalia. Han. 1604. N. 1. 3[1]) in classe Theologica, catenâ abscissum et sacrilegâ nebulonis alicujus manu surreptum esse; Cumque ex fideli Bibliothecarii relatione (pensatis loci atque temporis circumstantiis) constet, non nisi a jurato aliquo facinus hoc detestabile perpetratum esse;—

'Nos Curatores, quorum fidei et inspectioni Bibliothecæ cura speciali nomine a Nobilissimo Fundatore concredita est, insolentis facti indignitate moti et perculsi, quamvis liber parabilis, exigui et pretii et usus sit, ne tamen lenti plus quam par est et frigidi in causa tanti momenti videamur, post maturam deliberationem, programmate affixo, facinus publicandum duximus;—

'Impense rogantes omnes et singulos cujuscunque ordinis et loci genuinos Academiæ alumnos, ut sicubi librum offendant, sive in privatis musæis, sive in bibliopolarum officinis, restituendum curent, unàque operam nobiscum conferant, ut, si fieri possit, hoc propudium hominis, Bibliothecarum pestis et tenebrio sacrilegus, e latibulis suis in lucem extrahatur; denique, odium et indignationem suam contribuant, saltem ut publicæ infamiæ tuba miser experrectus, misericordiam divinam tempestive imploret, conspecta vel Bibliothecæ porta posthæc attonitus resiliat, nec tanti putet libri contemptibilis acquisitionem ut animam pro qua mortuus est Christus ineptissime periclitari sinat.

Jo. Prideaux, Vice-Canc. et S. Theol. Professor Regius.

Tho. Clayton, Medic. Professor Regius.

Daniel Eastcot, Procurator Sen.

Ricardus Hill, Procurator Jun.

Edoardus Meetkerkius, Ling. Hebr. Professor Regius.

Johannes South, Græcæ Linguæ Prælector Regius.'

[1] This was never recovered, but a later edition, in 1609, was procured instead.

never thought fit to do so, except with regard to Lord Pembroke's MSS.; secondly, on the ground that if the rule were once broken, it would be impossible to refuse any person, without incurring great

To the entry in the Catalogue of 1747 of *Sermons* by James Johnson, 4° Camb. 1670, Dr. Bandinel has added in an interleaved copy the note, 'Stolen ages ago.' A volume containing four small books of the seventeenth century, which was numbered 8vo A. 19 Art. B. S., has been missing for over 150 years. And see also p. 156.

More serious abstractions, however, than such as these, have within the last forty or fifty years been committed. Two extremely rare tracts by Thomas Churchyard, viz. his *Epitaph of Sir P. Sidney*, and *Feast full of sad Cheere*, have been cut out of a volume of tracts in which they were bound up. May it be hoped that book-lovers, as well as lovers of honesty, will remember this, should unknown copies suddenly come to light? A book mentioned by Warton as being in Tanner's collection, *The Children of the Chapel Stript and Whipt*, is also not forthcoming; but no evidence that this tract was at any time actually within the walls of the Library has been found. As every separate volume and tract in the whole Library is now conspicuously stamped with the name of its *locale*, it is hoped that depredations of this character will henceforward be entirely checked.

A 12mo fifteenth-century Psalter amongst Rawlinson's MSS., which was given (as an autograph inscription testifies) by William, Viscount Beaumont, to his wife Elizabeth, March 5, 1498, has this note in the handwriting of Dr. Bliss: 'Stolen from the Library, and restored by Dr. Laurence, June 20, 1812, who purchased it at an auction in London.' It is not, however, entered in the list of donations for that year.

Two instances in which consciences (or more probably a single conscience) have been sufficiently awakened to make restitution of stolen goods, have occurred within the last forty years. In 185– (exact year forgotten), on a day on which a Convocation had been held on some exciting subject, which had consequently brought up country voters from all parts, the present writer happened to notice that a small book had been laid in a shelf of folios near the Library door. Taking it up, I found it to be a rare volume of tracts by J. Preston and T. Goodwin, printed at Amsterdam, and bearing a Library reference (Mareschal 397). On proceeding to restore it to its place, that place was found to be occupied by another book; this, of course, led to further examination, and it was then discovered that the former volume had been missing for so many years, that at last, all hope of its recovery being abandoned, its place had been filled up. The old register-books of readers were then ransacked, and at length an entry was found of the delivery of this book to a reader, who was still living at the time of this Convocation, on Feb. 14, 1807. A quarto volume was also found about the same time thrust in amongst other quartos in a shelf near the door, but the particulars of this case have been forgotten.

A third case of recovery, but of a different kind, occurred in 1851. In the year 1789 the Library was visited by Hen. E. G. Paulus, of Jena, afterwards the too-well-known author of the *Leben Jesu*, who copied from Pococke MS. 32 (a small octavo volume)

odium, while the gratifying all applicants would disperse into private hands the books intended for the public. He then proceeds as follows:—

'3. Suppose 3 bookes at a time be sent to any private man, 'tis true he is furnish'd, but 'tis manifestly to the prejudice of the Publick, the University wanting those books while he has them; so that if any forreigner coming hither from abroad desire to see them, or any at home desire to use them, both are disappointed, to the diminution of the honour of the University, in the one, and the benefit it might have by those books, in the other. And therefore it seems more agreeable to reason and the public good (and the declared will and precept of our prudent and pious Founder[1]) not to lend any books out

an Arabic translation of Isaiah made, in Hebrew characters, by R. Saadiah, which he published in the following year, transposed into Arabic characters. Thenceforward the MS. was lost from the Library, although no direct evidence of the manner of its disappearance appears to have been obtained. But after the death of Paulus in the year 1850, a bookseller at Breslau, to whom the volume had in some way been offered, entered into communication with the Librarian, Dr. Bandinel, and the result was that the missing MS. was at length restored, clothed in an entirely different German binding, and with all trace of its original ownership removed, to its right place. The theft of this MS. 'by an Oriental professor,' and its recovery, are mentioned, without further particulars, by Dr. Pusey, in his Evidence printed in the *University Report upon the Recommendations of the University Commissioners*, 1853, p. 171.

A German, named Meurer, was expelled about the beginning of the last century for stealing books: the initial of his Christian name is given by Hearne as 'A.', but the only reader with his surname found in the admission-register is 'Joannes Ulricus Meurerus, Wirtemburgensis,' who was admitted 14 Feb. 1699. Hearne in his *Diary* in 1706 speaks of A. Meurer as having been 'formerly a student in the Publick Library, but expelled for knavery' (vol. i., edited by C. E. Doble, M.A., 1885, p. 309), and in a letter to Dr. T. Smith in 1709 says, he 'is certainly a rascal, as he has plainly discovered not only by the violation of his oath to our Publick Library, from which he stole several books (which, however, were all happily recovered), but by other notorious and abominable crimes' (*ib.*, vol. ii., p. 205). Again, in vol. cxlv. of the MS. of his *Diary* (p. 48) Hearne says that H. Dodwell used to speak very well of Meurer so long as he 'had the character of a man of honesty; but being guilty of some fraudulent tricks at Oxford, he was slighted, and went off I know not whither.' Rawlinson MSS. D. 192, 193, are two volumes of A. Meurer's *Adversaria*.

[1] Bodley frequently in his letters expresses his positive determination not to allow books to be at all removed from the Library. He mentions the having connived at first at Sir H. Savile's having a book for a very short space of time, because he was like to

of the Library; for by not lending, private persons only want the use of those books which are another's, whereas by lending, the University wants the use of those books which are her own. Sure no prudent man can think it fit to gratify particular persons with the publick detriment.

'4. The Library is a magazine which the pious Founder hath fix'd in a publick place for a publick use; and though his charity to private persons is such that he will hinder none (who is justly qualify'd and worthy) to come to it, yet his charity to the publick is such that he would not have it ambulatory, to goe to any private person. And sure 'tis more rational that Mahomet should go to the mountaine, than that the mountaine should come to Mahomet.

'5. Lending of books makes them lyable to many casualties, as, I. absolute losse, either 1. *in via*, by the carrier's negligence, or violence offer'd him, or, 2. *in termino*, they may be lost by the person that borrows them; for (presuming the person noble, and carefull for their preservation, yet) his house may be burn'd, or (by robbers) broken open (as Mr. Selden's unhappily was not long since): or, (in case they scape these casualties) they may be spoyl'd in the carriage, as by sad experience we find, for above 60 or 100 leaves of a Greek MS.[1] lent out of *Archiva Pembrochiana* to Mr. Pat. Younge were irrecoverably defaced. Now what has happen'd heretofore may happen hereafter; and therefore to keep them sacredly (and without any lending) in the Library (according to our good Founder's will and statute) will be the best way for their preservation.'

become a very great benefactor; but declares that after the making the Statutes neither he nor any one else shall be allowed the same liberty upon any occasion whatsoever. (*Reliquiæ Bodl.* pp. 176, 264.) And in another letter he says, in reference to a particular application, 'The sending of any book out of the Library may be assented to by no means, neither is it a matter that the University or Vice-Chancellor are to deal in. It cannot stand with my publick resolution with the University, and my denial made to the Bishop of Glocester and the rest of the Interpreters [*i.e.* the Translators of the Authorized Version of the Bible] in their assembly in Christ Church, who requested the like at my hands for one or two books.' (*Ibid.* p. 207.) In 1636 the University refused leave to Archbishop Laud to borrow Rob. Hare's MS. *Liber Privilegiorum Universitatis* (compiled in 1592), when the Archbishop was prosecuting his claim to visit the two Universities as Metropolitan. But the refusal was doubtless rather from jealousy respecting their immunities (as Wood says) than from regard to the rules of the Library (Huber's *English Universities*, by F. Newman, vol. ii. p. 45). However, the book was at last produced before the Council. (Wood's *Hist. and Antiq.*, by Gutch, vol. ii. p. 403.)

[1] 'Μυριόβιβλος, num. 131' [Barocci].

Barlow adds finally, in the sixth and seventh places, that if all lending were declared unlawful, it would greatly encourage others to give more to the Library when they saw how religiously their gifts would be preserved, and that if no exceptions were made (save, as allowed by Archbp. Laud, for the purpose of printing), no applications would be made, and no one would take it ill if he were denied [1].

Another reason for Selden's withholding his library in its entirety has, however, been assigned, besides those mentioned above, and this, too, by closely contemporary writers. In July, 1649, the new intruded officers and fellows of Magdalen College found in the Muniment-room in the first cloister-tower of the College, a large sum of money in the old coinage called *Spur-royals* [2], or *Ryals*, amounting to £1400, the equivalent of which had been left by the

[1] This paper has been printed in full by Professor Chandler in his pamphlet *On lending Bodleian books and MSS.*, 1886. It had previously been printed in a folio sheet (which had, however, escaped all knowledge, but of which a copy has lately been found in the Library) about the year 1759, in opposition probably to an application then made, as is learned from another fly-sheet, for the loan of MSS. to Dr. Kennicott in connection with his Hebrew collations of the Old Testament. In the latter paper it is stated that the Librarian had declared that no injury whatever had been done to some MSS. which had previously been lent out. But this was only a happy accident.

A striking example of the danger of lending books from great libraries is afforded by the history of an unique MS. of Castilian poetry now in the National Library at Paris, which was sold in London at R. Heber's sale, but really belonged to the Escurial. It was lost by being lent for editing to the librarian of the Royal Library at Madrid, José Ant. Conde, and its story is shortly told in a memoir of him in C. Knight's *English Cyclopædia of Biography*.

A Greek MS. of the Gospels in Lincoln College Library was lent to the late Dr. S. T. Bloomfield, on one of his visits to Oxford, for collation. As it had not been returned when he left Oxford, the Librarian (Rev. O. Ogle, from whose mouth I have heard the story) visited his lodgings, and there found it tossed into a kind of coal or dust-bin, as being discarded rubbish left behind by the lodger! After the death of Rev. C. Marriott, B.D., of Oriel, a MS. belonging to the College Library was carried away with his library, and only by the accident of a literary enquiry being made for it, was it traced and recovered.

[2] These were gold coins, of the value of fifteen shillings, which derived their name from bearing a star on the reverse which resembled the rowel of a spur.

Founder as a reserve fund for law expenses, for re-erecting or repairing buildings destroyed by fire, &c., or for other extraordinary charges. This gold had been laid up and counted in Q. Elizabeth's time and had remained untouched since then; consequently, although some of the old members of the College were aware of its existence, to the new-comers it seemed a welcome and unexpected discovery, especially as the College was at the time heavily in debt. They immediately proceeded to divide it among all the members on the Foundation proportionately, not excluding the choristers, (who were at that time undergraduates,) the Puritan President, Wilkinson, being alone opposed to such an illegal proceeding, and being with difficulty prevailed upon to accept £100 as his share, which, however, upon his death-bed he charged his executors to repay. The spur-royals were exchanged at the rate of 18*s.* 6*d.* to 20*s.* each, and each fellow had 33 of them. But when the fact of this embezzlement of corporate funds became known, the College was called to account by Parliament, and, although they attempted to defend themselves, they individually deemed it wise to refund the greater, or a considerable, part of what had been abstracted[1]. Fuller, whose *Church History* was published in the year following Selden's death, after telling this scandalous story, proceeds thus (book ix. p. 234):—'Sure I am, a great antiquarie lately deceased (rich as well in his state as learning) at the hearing hereof quitted all his intention of benefaction to Oxford or any place else, on suspition it would be diverted to other uses, on the same token that he merrily said, I think the best way for a man to perpetuate his memory is to procure the Pope to canonize him for a saint, for then he shall be sure to be remembered in their Calender;

[1] Three-hundred-and-fifty of these coins were disposed of by the College in 1787 (Chandler's *Life of Waynflete*, p. 410), but a few are still preserved in an ancient chest in the same room where they were of old deposited. Here is also carefully preserved a very large and valuable collection of early charters, numbering over 13,000, including all which belonged to the Hospital of St. John Bapt. upon the site of which the College was built, and to several suppressed priories which were annexed to the College, reaching back to the twelfth century. Of all these I have made a MS. catalogue, for the use of the College.

whereas otherwise I see all Protestant charity subject to the covetousness of posterity to devour it, and bury the donor thereof in oblivion.' And the name of this 'great antiquarie' was supplied in 1659 by the Puritan writer Henry Hickman, who, as a Demy of Magdalen College, had shared in the spoils. He, in the Appendix to his *Justification of the Fathers and Schoolmen*, gives (in answer to a passage in Heylin's *Examen Historicum*) a full account of the dividing of the gold, adding, 'which, as is said, did hinder Mr. John Selden from bestowing his library on the University.' And Wood (*Hist. and Antiq.* by Gutch, ii. 942) says that he had been told that this misappropriation was one reason of Selden's distaste at Oxford. From all this it is clear that Burnet's narrative gives a very inaccurate account of the matter[1].

It was in the year 1659 that the great mass of Selden's collection was forwarded by his executors. In the accounts for 1660 appear payments to Barlow of £20 'for his paines in procuring Mr. Selden's books,' and of £52 for his expenses thereon. The bringing the books from London cost about £34, and the pro-

[1] In 1695 George Harbin, writing to Dr. Charlett, asserts that Sir Matthew Hale, one of the executors, was the real donor. 'The favour that I would obtain is this, that since Mr. Selden's books were properly the present of my Lord Cheif Justice Hales to your Publick Library, you would be pleased either in the preface to your Catalogue, or in the body of it, immediately before Mr. Selden's books, gratefully to acknowledge his Lordship's bounty, to which alone you owe them, which would be a lasting and endearing obligation on all his posterity. I am the more encouraged to ask this of you because upon enquiry I cannot understand that the University hath taken any care hitherto to accquaint the world that you owe so valuable a present to my Lord Cheif Justice Hales. You have neither his picture nor his coat of arms in your library, and the books, at home as well as abroad, are generally thought to be Mr. Selden's own gift.' (Letter to Dr. Charlett, 10 Jan. 169$\frac{4}{5}$, in Tanner MS. 25, and copied in Rawl. MS. C. 739, fol. 77^b.)

In the general Catalogue of MSS. published in the year 1697, Selden's MSS. are nevertheless distinctly described as being Selden's own gift. But probably Harbin only refers to the printed books; and the explanation of all the contradictory accounts may be found in this, that the MSS. really came by will, and the rest of the library by the assignment of the executors; as well as the marbles, which are said in an inscription on a tablet set over them, to have been given by the executors to the University.

viding chains for them £25 10*s*.[1] Unfortunately, during the interval, many books had been lost which had been borrowed in London, and were never returned. (Life, in *Works*, I. lii.) And a part, which somehow was not sent to Oxford, afterwards altogether perished, 'for the fire of the Temple destroyed in one of their chambers eight chests full of the registers of abbeys, and other manuscripts relating to the history of England; tho' most of his law-books are still safe in Lincoln's Inn[2].' Some medical books were bequeathed to the College of Physicians. Some of the original deeds relating to the gift were bought for the Library in 1837 for £1 1*s*.

About 8000 volumes were, in all, added to the Library by this gift, most of which bear Selden's well-known motto: 'περὶ παντὸς τὴν ἐλευθερίαν.' Amongst them are some which belonged to Ben Jonson, Dr. Donne, and Sir Robert Cotton. The number of miscellaneous foreign works, in several European languages, is noticeable, many of which had been published but a short time before Selden's death. In various volumes of Constantine Huygens'

[1] The conditions imposed by the executors (which are printed in Gutch's *Wood*, ii. 943, from the original MS., said by Gutch to be in the possession of J. Price, the Librarian, but really then of course, as now, in the possession of the Library itself, although Price has written his own name on the back of it, probably upon lending it to Gutch; and also printed elsewhere) expressly stipulated that the books should be chained. As late as the year 1751 notices occur in the Librarian's account-books of the procuring additional chains for the Library. But the removal of them appears to have commenced as shortly afterwards as 1757, and in 1761 there was a payment for unchaining 1448 books at one halfpenny each. In 1769 some long chains were sold at twopence each, and short ones at three-halfpence; and then *en masse* 19 cwt. of 'old iron' at fourteen shillings per cwt. Several of the chains are still preserved loose, as relics.

[2] Ayliffe's *Ancient and Present State of the Univ. of Oxford*, 1714, vol. i. p. 462. Pointer, in his *Oxoniensis Academia*, 1749, p. 136, quotes the account of the Bodleian given by Ayliffe as having been written by Dr. Hudson, under whose name it is also found in Macky's *Journey through England*, vol. ii. The fire here mentioned (if not the Great Fire of London) was probably that which occurred on 26 Jan. 16$\frac{79}{80}$, in which the chambers called the Paper-Buildings appear to have been destroyed, where Selden's original rooms were situated. At Lincoln's Inn some MSS. are now amongst Sir M. Hale's.

works, which he presented to Selden (apparently at the request of the latter) in 1651, the following laudatory verses are inserted:—

'Seldene, fulcrum sæculi labascentis,
Britanniarum grande phosphorum sidus;
Quò te Batavum credis anserem ignotum
Britannum olorem adire nemini ignotum?
Quò de throno sapientiæ, throno illustri,
Ubi literarum transmarine dictator
In Cismarinas sceptra prorogas musas,
Ad has cicadas usque ad hasce descendas
Picas rogare? nempe quò sciant nati,
Sciant nepotes olim, amiculos inter
Seldenianos Zulichemium patrem
Censum fuisse, sero, sed tamen censum.

Joanni Seldeno
viro supra laudem
amicit. auspic.
adscr. Aut.
CIƆ. IƆ. LI.'

In curious contrast to the character of the greater part of his collection (rich in classics and science, theology and history, law and Hebrew literature) there occurs one volume (marked 4° C. 39. Art. Seld.) which is priceless in the eyes of the lovers of old English black-letter tracts. It contains twenty-six tracts (most bearing the name of a previous possessor, one Thomas Newton) which are among the rarest of early popular tales and romances. As mere specimens of the collection may be mentioned, *Richard Cuer de Lyon*, *Syr Bevis of Hampton* (unique edit.?), *Syr Degore*, *Syr Tryamoure* (only two copies known), *Syr Eglamoure* (unique?), *Dan Hew of Leicestre* (unique?), *Battayle of Egyngecourt* (unique?), *Mylner of Abyngton* (unique?), *Wyl Bucke*, &c. In another volume numbered 4° Z. 3 Art. Seld. is one of three known extant copies of *Howleglas*, printed by W. Copland without date. This copy formerly belonged to Edmund Spenser, for on the back of the last leaf is the following note in the handwriting of Gabriel Harvey:—

'This Howleglasse, with Skoggin, Skelton and Lazarillo, giuen me at London, of Mr. Spensar, XX Decembris * * * [15]78, on condition [that I] shoold bestowe ye reading of them ouer before ye first of

January, imediatly ensuing; otherwise to forfeit unto him my Lucian in fower volumes. Whereupon I was ye rather induced to trifle away so many howers as were idely ouerpassed in running thorowgh the f[oresai]d foolish bookes: wherein methowght not all fower togither seemed comparable for suttle and crafty feates with Jon Miller, whose witty shiftes & practises are reported amongst Skeltons Tales [1].'

Among the MSS. is one of Harding's *Chronicle* (Arch. Seld. B. 10) which appears to have belonged to Henry Percy, Earl of Northumberland, from his arms being painted at the end, and which some have supposed was also a presentation copy to Edward IV. A curious map accompanies the description of Scotland (here given in prose, not, as in the printed editions, in verse), in which, next to Sutherland and Caithness, the author, who would have won Dr. Johnson's respect as being 'a good hater,' places 'Styx, the infernal flode,' and 'The palais of Pluto, King of hel, *neighbore to Scottz*.' This map was engraved for the first time in Gough's *British Topography*, vol. ii. pl. viii.; the description of it occupies pp. 579–583 in that volume. Another interesting volume is a copy of the Latin *Articles* of 1562, printed by Reginald Wolfe in 1563, with the autograph signatures of the members of the Lower House of Convocation (Arch. Seld. A. 76). One of the printed books is found away from the rest, numbered 4° W. 9. Th. BS; possibly this was acquired subsequently, or may have been overlooked when the collection was arranged. Fifty-four Greek MSS. are described in Mr. Coxe's Catalogue, vol. i. cols. 583–648. For the expenses connected with the transfer of the Selden books £143 13*s*. were collected in the University.

In October of 1654 Bulstrode Whitelocke, who had returned from his mission to Sweden in July, and had since been elected M.P. for Oxford, gave two Swedish honorary medals of gold and silver, which had been presented to him. Barlow's letter of acknowledgment, dated 22 Oct., is given by Whitelocke in his *Memorials*.

[1] This curious note was first observed by Mr. J. Payne Collier, who has printed it in vol. i. of his *Bibliographical Account*, &c. (1865), p. 381. Three words are mis-read in his copy, which are corrected above. The note is, in some words, almost obliterated.

A.D. 1655.

The stipends of the Librarian and Assistants at this time amounted jointly to £51 6*s*. 8*d*. Of this it appears from the account for 1657 that the Librarian received £33 6*s*. 8*d*., the Second Keeper, then H. Stubbe, £10, and [the janitor] — Skingleye[1] (?), £8. A volume of curious tracts, published during the early part of the reign of Charles I, now marked 4° *F.* 2 *Art. B. S.*, furnishes the name of a preceding janitor, by bearing the inscription, 'Liber Thomæ Roch, defuncti, quondam janitoris bibliothecæ.' He died in, as it seems, 1644; see under that year, *supra*. The janitor originally appointed by Bodley appears to be mentioned in the following passage in a letter from him to James: 'There is one Thomas Scott, under-butler of Magdalen College, that hath made means unto me for the Porter's place, whom I propose to elect[2].' Thos. Cooke was Janitor in 1624–1633, as appears by the accounts.

John Evelyn appears in this year, as well as subsequently, as a donor of books[3]. Nineteen MSS. were given by Peter Whalley, of Northamptonshire.

Three MS. volumes were transferred by vote of Convocation on 20 July, 1655, from the custody of the Keeper of the Archives to the Library. They consist of collections of the Charters and Statutes of the University, and include Rob. Hare's volume, and one from the collection of 'Dr. Darrell,' which is said in the Register of Convocation to have been placed in the Archives not long before.

A.D. 1656.

Cowley's *Poems*. See 1620.

[1] A Geo. Skingley took degrees at Merton Coll. between 1660–70.

[2] *Reliquiæ Bodl.* p. 263.

[3] A letter from Barlow, the Librarian, to Evelyn thanking him for a gift, and dated 17 March, 1654 [-5], is printed (singularly enough) in Rob. Bell's *Memorials of the Civil War* (from the Fairfax correspondence), 1849, vol. ii. p. 320.

A.D. 1657.

In this year the gifts to the Library, which since 1640 had been but few, begin once more to increase in number. Five hundred gold and silver coins were given by Ralph Freke, of Hannington, Wilts, and a cabinet for their reception, 'auro gemmisque coruscum,' by his brother William. Amongst various other donations occur a copy of Caxton's Description of Britain, 1480 (with other books), from Ralph Bathurst, M.D., [President of] Trinity College [1], and four Oriental MSS. from William Juxon, 'Londinensis olim Episc.' One entry in the Benefaction Register has been at one time carefully pasted over, and at another brought again to light; it is the record of a gift from *Hugh Peters*. 'Hugo Peters, serenissimo Britanniarum Protectori Olivero a sacris, pro sua in academiam et rempubl. literariam benevolentia, codices insequentes Bibl. Bodleianæ dono dedit Maii iiii°, Anno CIↃ. IↃC. LVII;' viz. the great Dutch Bible with annotations, 'edit. ult. [*scil.* Hague, 1637] auro sericoque compacta,' and the Æthiopic Psalter of 1513. A leaf which followed this entry has been removed from the Register, probably because it contained some further particulars of Peters' gift, or possibly the record of the MSS. presented by the Protector himself in 1654 [2]. The binding of silk and gold has now altogether disappeared, and the Bible is clad in a plain calf coat, with no note of its former condition or of its donor.

Francis Yonge, M.A. of Oriel College, the Sub-librarian, died in this year. In his place succeeded, through the influence of Dr. Owen, Dean of Ch. Ch., Henry Stubbe, M.A., the well-known violent and varying political writer, then a Student of that House. From the posts, however, of both Librarian and Student Stubbe was ejected in March, 1659, on account of the publication of his book entitled, *A Light Shining out of Darkness*, which was supposed

[1] The following note is added by Hearne's hand in the *Reg. Benef.*, 'Et supremo testamento legavit duas amicorum suorum picturas.' The portraits were those of Drs. Allestree and South (Warton's *Life*, p. 195). He again, some time after 1670, gave some books.

[2] See p. 110.

to attack the Universities and clergy[1]. It appears from a humorous passage in a 'Terræ Filius' speech delivered by South in this year, and printed in his *Opera Posthuma* (Lond. 1717, p. 40), in which Fuller the historian is ridiculed, that Fuller applied for the post on Yonge's death. The passage is as follows: 'Unum hoc superest notatu dignum, quod nuper vacante Inferioris Bibliothecarii loco, Academiæ nostræ supplicavit [Fullerus] per literas, ut sibi illum conferret: sed negavit Academia, nec illum admisit Bibliothecarium, ob hanc rationem, ne Bibliothecæ scripta sua ingereret.'

A.D. 1658.

Gerard Langbaine, D.D., the learned Provost of Queen's College, died on Feb. 10 in this year. Twenty-one vols. of his *Adversaria*, consisting chiefly of extracts from Bodleian MSS. and of notes concerning the arrangement of the books in the Library, were bought for £11[2]. Nine other volumes were bequeathed by Ant. à Wood in 1695. They are all fully described by Mr. Coxe in vol. i [cols. 877–888] of the General Catalogue of the MSS. of the Library, which appeared in 1853, as well as more briefly in Bernard's Catalogue. Besides obtaining his own autograph collections by purchase, the Library became possessed by bequest from him of the very valuable MS. (*e Mus.* 86) on the history of Wickliffe and his followers, entitled *Fasciculi Zizaniorum*, written by Thomas Walden. This was edited by the late Dr. Shirley in 1858, as part of the Master of the Rolls' Series of Chronicles. Dr. Shirley traced the volume to the hands of Bale and Ussher, but was not aware of the way in which it came to the Library.

The effect which civil war and confusion had had upon literature

[1] An account of Stubbe may be found in the last edit. of Welch's *List of Westminster Scholars*, 1852, p. 133. 'Mr. Stubbes, when Library Keeper, sate up at study till one a clocke, and rose at five, wondering any man would require more rest.' Rawlinson MS. D. 191, f. 10.

[2] Langbaine by his will (dated 19 Aug. 1647) had left five pounds' worth of books to the Library, with the right of pre-emption of any others.

may be commercially estimated by the fact that a gift of £5 from Joseph Maynard, B.D., of Exeter College, proved sufficient for the purchase of 28 printed volumes and 11 MSS., many of which were curious.

A crocodile, from Jamaica, was given by John Desborough, the republican Major-General, and brother-in-law to the Protector.

A.D. 1659.

Thomas Hyde, M.A., of Queen's College, was appointed Under-keeper on the expulsion of Henry Stubbe, as told above on p. 125.

Scroope album of engravings. See *Donations* in Appendix.

A.D. 1660.

Thomas Barlow, D.D. (who had been elected Provost of Queen's College in 1658), resigned the Librarianship on Sept. 26, in consequence of his appointment to the Margaret Professorship of Divinity. Thomas Lockey, B.D., Student of Ch. Ch., was elected in his place, on Sept. 28, by 102 votes to 80, over Mr. [John] Good, M.A., Balliol College[1].

In July William Wycherley was admitted as a reader in the Library, as a Student of Philosophy. He was persuaded to abandon the Roman Catholic religion by Barlow the Librarian[2]; but what religion he adopted in exchange, or what were the results of his conversion, cannot easily be discerned from his writings. The 'gain' in this case was certainly anything but 'godliness.'

A curious story is preserved by Wanley and Dr. Wallis, in memoranda, dated 1698–1701, on the fly-leaves of a copy of the rare *Index Librorum prohibitorum* printed at Madrid in 1612–14 (4° U. 46. Th.), respecting the visit of a Roman Catholic priest to the Library during the period of Barlow's headship. In the course of conversation with Barlow, the priest denied that such a book as this Index had ever been printed at Madrid (there being various discrepancies between it and the Roman Index), whereupon this

[1] Reg. Convoc. Tª. 27, p. 57. Lockey was created D.D. on Nov. 29 following upon a royal letter dated Nov. 6; *ib.* pp. 71, 72.

[2] Wood's *Fasti*, ed. Bliss, ii. 246.

copy was produced, bearing the names of several inquisitors who had from time to time possessed it. The visitor was extremely surprised, and, being very desirous of purchasing it, offered any sum for it that might be demanded, with the intent (as the somewhat suspicious tellers of the tale suggest) to destroy it; but the Doctor was above corruption. The vigilance of the Librarians being aroused, the book was removed from an exposed place where it had formerly been kept, to a less accessible situation in the gallery, and securely chained. Wallis adds that one fly-leaf, containing some of the previous owners' names, had since then been torn out[1].

A.D. 1661.

Bishop Brian Walton presented his *Biblia Polyglotta.* A gift by him of a second copy occurs in *Reg. Benef.* under 1662.

In the accounts for this year is the following interesting entry:

> 'For *polishing the rust* from the King's picture
> and setting it up againe in the Librarie . . £1 12 6'

It is also noted that on Sept. 11 it was decreed by the Curators 'that in consideration of having Mr. Selden's library kept clean and free from dust, henceforward forty shillings *per annum* be allowed for sweeping the library.'

Vinc. Viviani sent in April from Italy (with his own book *De max. et min.*) a portrait of Galileo.

Five Arabic MSS. and eight Chinese books were given by Will. Thurston, a London merchant, carriage of which from London cost 1*s.* 2*d.* By a mistaken arrangement of other small gifts, Thurston now passes as donor of forty Arabic, Persian, and Syriac MSS., instead of five. Several of these, at present all numbered as Thurston MSS., were given in 1684 by Jos. Taylor, LL.D., of St. John's College, one by Crewe, Bishop of Durham, in 1680, one by Benj. Polsted, a London African merchant, in 1678, one by Charles Robson, B.D., Queen's College, about 1630, and one is an Armenian

[1] The memoranda are printed in Mendham's *Lit. Policy of the Church of Rome*, second edit., pp. 152–4, and in Bliss's *Reliquiæ Hearnianæ*, i. 12–14.

poem of thanks for benefits received from the University, presented by the author, Jac. de Gregoriis, an Armenian priest, in 1674. One other volume (a mathematical MS. bought at Constantinople, by Const. Ravius, in 1641) was at one time, as it appears, abstracted from the Library, and was restored by means of Dr. Marshall, who, after the words 'Liber Bibliothecæ Bodleianæ Cxon.,' has added the following note: 'quem ex Ratelbandi cujusdam bibliopolæ officina libraria, prope novum templum Amstelodami, redimendum pretio persoluto curavit Tho. Mareschallus, e Collegio Lincolniensi apud Oxonienses.'

A.D. 1662.

A legacy of £50 was paid which had been bequeathed some time previously by Alex. Ross (who died in 1654), nowadays best known as the Ross of Hudibrastic memory. It is singular that a copy of the old printed quarto catalogue of the Library was amongst the books purchased with this gift; which shows that, within forty years after publication, it had become scarce even in the Library itself.

The first statutory obligation upon the Stationers' Company to deliver a copy of each book printed by them to this Library, together with that of Cambridge and the Royal Library, was imposed by the Act of 13 & 14 Chas. II. c. 33, for two years, which was renewed from time to time until the passing of the Copyright Act of 8 Q. Anne.

'For carriage of two pictures of the muscles[1] .	£0	4	0
For mending Joseph's coat[2]	0	2	0
For portage of Mr. Ogilvy's picture . . .	0	2	0'

To two assistants for 'making' [i.e. copying?] three catalogues of Selden's books £2 10*s*. were paid. In reference to this, in a letter dated 25 July, in apparently 1664, from Lockey to Archbp. Sheldon, in reply to inquiries from the latter respecting

[1] Two (entered as *three* in *Reg. Benef.*) anatomical pictures of the human muscles given by Thos. Highlow of London.

[2] This, no doubt, was a new fancy-name for the 'Muscovite Cloak' which had so often before needed repair. See also p. 131.

the Library (preserved in Tanner MS. 338, fol. 180) the Librarian says with respect to Selden's Library ('an accession of about 30,000 authors'), that 'I have *by mine owne paynes* disposed of [it] in a Catalogue to be inserted afterward in the General.' The work of a new Catalogue of Bodley's Library is, he says, 'distributed into the hands of fifty Masters of Arts . . . I presume in all probability that it will be ready for the presse by Michaelmas, and afterward wee suppose that it cannot possibly come forth thence to publike view under the compasse of a yeer.' It was not published till about 12 years afterwards.

£1 1*s.* 6*d.* (of which 8*s.* were in brass money) were paid for the exchange of £14 6*s.* of Parliament coin taken out of Bodley's Chest.

A.D. 1663.

The University was visited in September by Charles II and his Queen. And 'on Munday, September 28, about four in the afternoon, the University, being in their Formalities placed from Christ Church east-gate to the south gate of the publique Schooles, the King and Queen, the Duke and Dutches of Yorke, with the nobility and gentry attending, went to the Schooles, where the Chanceller, Vice-Chanceller and Heads of Houses received them, and invited them up to the Library; and Mr. Crew, the Senior Proctor, placed neer the globes, addrest himselfe to their Majesties in an oration upon his knees; which being ended, the King and Queen, with the Royal Family and nobility, were by our Chanceller, Vice-Chanceller, and the Heads of Houses, conducted to Selden's Library, and there entertained with a very sumptuous banquett[1].'

One pound was given 'to the Lady Newcastle's servant that presented her bookes.'

A description of the arrangement of the shelves and cases in the Library is given in the *Voyages* of a French traveller, M. Monconys, who was entertained at Oxford by Wallis, and lodged in Ch. Ch. with Pococke. The description of the Library is at pp. 51–2 of

[1] Reg. Convoc. T^a^. 27, p. 173.

part ii, 4°. Lyon, 1666. Amongst other things which he saw, he says, 'Dans un cabinet on nous montra une robe de peau de diverses couleurs, qui les oblige à dire que c'est celle de Joseph;' our old friend of the 'Tartar lambskin' under its new name.

In this year, also, Samuel Sorbière, a French physician, made a visit to England, of which he published a short account. At Oxford he had only a 'transient view' of the Library (as the translation published in 1709 words it), and simply mentions therefore the arrangement of the books on the tiers of shelves, for which he was ridiculed by Bishop Sprat, who criticised his observations upon England. He mentions also the (now removed) 'wooden stairs' to the galleries, 'very artfully contrived for to give light, in the middle and at the four corners' (p. 43; see *infra* under 1712). Sorbière, like Monconys, was lodged in Ch. Ch., and, like him again, says much about Wallis, and in his praise, but compares his manners, and those of the University in general (which he says need to become polite by being 'purified by the air of the Court at London') disadvantageously with those of 'Mr. Lockey, the Oxford Librarian, who had learnt at Court and in France to put on an obliging air and courteous behaviour,' and who conducted Sorbière over Oxford.

A.D. 1665.

Thomas Lockey, D.D., resigned the Librarianship on Nov. 29, 1665, in consequence of his appointment to a canonry of Ch. Ch. In the following year he gave some coins and the sum of £6 16*s*. In his place was unanimously elected, on Dec. 2, Thomas Hyde, M.A., of Queen's College, then Under-keeper. Upon Lockey's death, in 1680, books to the value of £16 15*s*. were bought out of his study[1].

Dr. Cornelius Burges, the well-known popular preacher on the side of the Parliament during the Rebellion, about three weeks before his death at Watford, where he lived after the Restoration in

[1] A biographical notice of Lockey is given in the last edit. of Welch's *List of Westminster Scholars*, 1852, p. 87. His formal resignation of the Librarianship, under his seal, is among official papers in the Library.

great poverty and suffering from disease, forwarded a gift of great value to the Library, with a touching inscription which evidences the sincerity of his attachment to the University. The inscription (which was first printed by Dr. Bliss in Wood's *Athenæ*) is on a fly-leaf of King Edward's First Book of Common Prayer, printed by Edw. Whitchurche in June, 1549, and is as follows:—

'I, Cornelius Burges, beeing a°. 1627 by my deere and much honoured mother the renowned University of Oxford, made Doctor in Divinity, am much greived that I am able to do nothing worthy of her, yet I humbly offer that I have, viz. this first Book of R. Edw. 6, as also the second Book of Cōmon Prayer in 5-6 Edw. 6, wherein this hath several alterations upon the censures of Bucer extant in his book *Scripta Anglicana*. I also adde a third Book of Com. Prayer renewed & established in 1 Elizab., which book is very hard to bee had that was then printed; I could never see any other of that edition. I also adde a 4th Book of Cōm. Prayer in 12°, wherein I have noted all the differences between that book established by this present Parliament, a°. 1663 and the former book established before.

All these I most humbly and thankfully give to my said Honourable Mother of Oxford, I beeing ready to dy, beseeching her to account of these 4 small mites as our Lord and blessed Saviour did of the poore widowes two mites, that, casting in that, cast in all that she had.

CORNELIUS BURGES[1].

Watford in Hertfordshire,
May 16, 1665.'

Sept. 8. The Earl of Manchester, Chanc. of Cambridge, visited the Library, 'and there Dr. Lockey the Custos of it spoke a speech before him, and when he was gone into the Gallery, the Earl of Clarendon, Canc. of Oxon., came to him, and discoursed with him concerning the University[2].'

A.D. 1666.

Twenty MSS. (including a copy of Wycliffe's Bible) were given by Sir Thos. Herbert, Bart., of York, and 14*s*. 6*d*. were paid for their carriage thence.

[1] Rawlinson MS. C. 797 contains an unpublished treatise by Burges on the Fruits of the Spirit, a commentary on Galat. v. 22, 23.

[2] Wood MS. D. 19, part iii. f. 20.

An East India merchant of London, one John Ken, gave (with other MSS.) the first 'Gentoo' or Sanscrit book ('lingua Gentuana,' Sansk. d. 23) which the Library possessed. It is noticeable what a real, although somewhat indiscriminating, interest the London merchants appear to have taken in the Library. Continual mention occurs not merely of books but of curiosities of all kinds, natural and artificial, which persons engaged in commerce, chiefly with the East Indies, sent as for a general repository. Most of these curiosities are now to be found, it is believed, in the Ashmolean Museum.

At some period between 1660 and 1667, *i.e.* during Clarendon's Chancellorship of the University, two volumes of MS. notes and observations upon Josephus, by Sam. Petit, the Professor of Greek at Nismes (who died in 1643), are said by Moreri to have been purchased by Clarendon, for 150 louis d'or, and given to the University. But in Bernard's Catalogue the volumes are said to have been bought by the University 'ære suo,' and had the Chancellor given them, we may be sure the gift would not have been omitted in the *Regist. Benef.* Dr. T. Smith remarks, in his life of Bernard, that when the latter was preparing to edit Josephus, he used 'Sam. Petiti largis commentariis, longe antea in bibliothecæ Bodleianæ gazophylacium ex Gallia transvectis,' but found that they were filled only with notes from Rabbinical writers. They are now numbered Auct. F. infra, I. 1, 2. One other MS. was certainly given by Clarendon, during his Chancellorship. It is a Greek *Evangelistarium* of the fourteenth century, formerly the property of a monastery described as 'τῆς παναγίας τῆς ἀχειροποιήτου,' which was given by Parthenius, Patriarch of Constantinople, to Heneage Finch, Earl of Winchelsea, when in Turkey, in 1661, as ambassador from England, and subsequently given by Clarendon to the University. On the cover is a silver crucifix, of Byzantine work. It is now numbered Auct. D. infra II. 12.

In this year an assistant began to be regularly employed in addition to the statutable officers. His salary was £8 *per an.*

A.D. 1668.

Lady Eleanor Roe gave a gold medal which had been struck by order of Charles I to commemorate the embassy of her husband, Sir T. Roe, to Sweden and Poland, and Thomas Philpott, D.D., the three-pound gold coin struck by Charles I at Oxford.

John Davies, of Camberwell, the storekeeper at Deptford dockyard, caused a chair to be made out of the remains of the ship, 'The Golden Hind,' in which Sir F. Drake accomplished his voyage round the world, which had been kept at Deptford until the timber decayed, and presented it to the Library. It stands now in the Picture Gallery, beside a chair which is said (but on what authority is not known) to have belonged to Henry VIII [1], and bears a plate on which are inscribed some verses, in Latin and English, by Abraham Cowley. An ode by Cowley on his 'sitting and drinking' in this chair is also printed in his Works. A good engraving of it is to be found in Lascelles' and Storer's *Oxford*, published in 1821 [2], and in the *Life of Drake*, published in 1828. In the folio Register of Benefactions the gift is thus entered:—'Anno MDCLXVIII. Dominus Johannes Davies de Cammerwell in agro Southreiensi, armiger, Regiæ Supellectilis navalis Depthfordiæ custos vigilantissimus, ex celeberrimæ illius navis Dracanæ reliquiis fabrefieri curavit Sellam seu Cathedram, quam, in tanti viri memoriam et nobilissimi facinoris monumentum, in Bibliotheca Bodleiana reponendam dono dedit.'

In the accounts for this year are the following entries:—

	£	s.	d.
'To Abendana for Hebr. MS. [*sic*; qu. MSS.?]	£37	0	0
Hebr. books of Rabbi Gaba	7	0	0
Descriptio Templi Stæ Mariæ Majoris . .	1	15	0
Hevelius his works [3], excepting his Selenographia	2	9	0

[1] The style of moulding on the back seems to point to a somewhat later date.

[2] A description, including a copy of the verses, and illustrated by a woodcut, is also to be found in vol. xxix. (1837) of the *Mirror*, p. 8, copied from the *Nautical Magazine*.

[3] But these are entered in the Register of Benefactions as being given by Hevelius himself.

Memorandum. Reditus domuum Badkin et Westley [*scil.* the houses in Distaff Lane] post Londini conflagrationem nos [*sic: read* non] receptos, et desperatos jam, in computum non perduci.'

In 1669 the houses are let to Mr. John Brace at a rent of £15 to commence a year after the building. The first year's rent was paid at Lady Day, 1671.

A. D. 1669.

The following purchases are worth noting:—

'Tycho's Observations, in folio	£1	9	0
Slusii Mesolabium, 4°	0	3	0
Arabick MS., bought by Mr. Bernard	10	15	0'

Nine MS. volumes, written by James Lambe, D.D., of St. Mary Hall, Canon of Westminster, who died in 1664, consisting of collections for an Arabic Lexicon and Grammar, together with the book of Daniel in Syriac, were given by Henry Beeston, LL.D., Head Master of Winchester School, and are kept in a small separate collection under Lambe's name.

A. D. 1670.

Thirteen Oriental MSS. (chiefly in their possessor's own writing) were bought from the heirs of Samuel Clarke, M.A., of Merton College, printer to the University and Esquire Bedel of Law, who died Dec. 17, 1669. He was greatly distinguished as an Orientalist, and assisted in the production of Walton's Polyglott. A list of his MSS. is given in Bernard's Catalogue, and another, by Prof. Nicoll, *Ath. Oxon.* iii. 885. He himself gave four printed Arabic books in 1663.

In this year James Alban Gibbes, or Ghibbes according to his own spelling, sent from Rome a gold chain and medal which had been given to him on his appointment as poet laureate to the Emperor Leopold, deeming them, in his overweening self-conceit, a gift honourable to the University as well as to himself. The Chancellor, Ormonde, thereupon recommended his creation as an honorary M.D. or D.C.L. in a letter dated 17 Jan. $167\frac{0}{1}$ [1], and he was in consequence created M.D. on 28 Feb., but the diploma was

[1] Reg. Convoc. Tª. 27, p. 314.

not actually passed until 10 Aug. 1673, a delay which greatly troubled the expectant doctor. The story is told by Wood in his *Fasti* under the year 1673[1]. The chain (of which the *Reg. Benef.* says, 'opus superat materiam') is preserved at present in the Coin Room.

A.D. 1671.

Upon the death of Meric Casaubon, on July 14, the Library became possessed, by his bequest, of sixty-one volumes of the *Adversaria* (chiefly consisting of notes on Greek criticism) of his father, Isaac Casaubon, who died in 1614. From these Jo. Christ. Wolf made some extracts when visiting the Library in 1709, which he published in the following year at Hamburgh, under the title of *Casauboniana*, with a preface giving some account of all previous collections of *Ana*, and with copious notes. The MSS. are catalogued in Mr. Coxe's first volume, cols. 825–850. The books apparently were not received until 1673, for in the accounts for that year is this entry:

'For bringing Dr. Casaubon's cabinett to the Schooles 0 0 6'

In 1674 portraits of the Casaubons and of Scaliger were given by Will. Jacob, M.D., of Canterbury.

About this year Edward Corbet, D.D. of Shrewsbury, gave the original MS. of Archbishop Abbot's commentary on the Epistle to the Romans, in four folio volumes.

'To Mr. Walker for ye Telescope	£1	10	6
For Sanson's Mapps	9	10	0
To Mr. Hide in part for transcribing the Catalogue	5	0	0
For a case for the great Crocodile . . .	0	12	0
To Mr. Nurse for a frame for Scotus his picture, and the carriage of it from London to the Library[2]	3	8	0
For carrying Chancellor Edgerton's picture[2] .	0	1	6

[1] A second letter from Ghibbes to H. Compton, besides the one mentioned by Wood, is preserved in Rawlinson MS., D. 397, fol. 429; it is dated from the palace of the Prince Giustiniani at Rome, 29 July, 1673.

[2] The donors of these pictures are not recorded. Hearne says (*MS. Diary*,

To Mr. Scott for severall bookes and MSS. brought into the Library . . . . 156 0 0'

A.D. 1672.

'To Mr. Hyde for finishing the transcript of the Catalogue £7 3 0

To Mr. Hyde, for ye transcript of Mr. Seldon's Catalogue for the Lord Chiefe Baron Hales . 1 10 0

For another copy for the Lord Chiefe Justice Vaughan by Mr. Vice-Chancellor . . . 1 10 0

To Mr. Hyde for bookes for ye Library . . 2 14 2

To Mr. Scott for severall bookes for ye Library . 29 7 6

For Joan. Antiochenus's MSS. 50 0 0

To Mr. Dugdale for his bookes 8 0 0

For the carriage . . . . 0 3 0'

About this year Will. Whorwood, esq., of West Bromwich, Staffordshire, gave £5, which were well laid out in the purchase of some thirteen MSS., which are found between Nos. 3525–3596 in the old general catalogue of MSS. They include Rob. Burhill's Latin treatise in defence of Monarchy and Episcopacy (Bodl. 58) and 'Historia Lichfeldensis' (Bodl. 204).

A.D. 1673.

Thomas, Lord Fairfax, to whose care the Library had been indebted for preservation in 1646, bequeathed to it on his decease, in November, 1671, twenty-eight very valuable MSS., including several early English books (Chaucer, Gower, Wycliffe's Bible, &c.) and works relating to the history of England, Scotland (Bp. Elphinstone[1]), and Ireland (Keating). But besides these, he gave that invaluable collection of genealogical MSS. known to all pedigree-hunters by the name of their indefatigable compiler, Roger Dodsworth, to whom he had allowed an annuity of £40 during his life, in order to enable him the better to prosecute his researches.

xx. 125) that Duns was 'drawn' by one Ashfield, 'from his own invention.' It has been attributed to Spagnoletto.

[1] A transcript of this Chronicle (usually called by Elphinstone's name, but probably written by one Maurice Buchanan,) is among the Jones MSS. It was publ. under the title of *Liber Pluscardensis*, in two vols. (text and translation) by Mr. F. Skene, in 1877–80.

This collection numbers 161 volumes (bound in 86) in folio and quarto[1], and consists of extracts bearing chiefly on the family and ecclesiastical history of Yorkshire and the North of England, with an innumerable mass of pedigrees, from all the authentic records within Dodsworth's reach, including many which were destroyed when the tower of St. Mary at York was blown up during the siege of that city in June, 1644. He appears to have commenced this wonderful series of notes about the year 1618, and not to have ceased before 1652, dying, in the seventieth year of his age, in August, 1654. Besides the very full catalogue of his MSS. which is given by Bernard (pp. 187–233), an extremely useful and original synopsis of their contents, prefaced with an account of Dodsworth's life and labours, and drawn up by Mr. Joseph Hunter, is to be found in the Report of the Record Commission for 1837; which was reprinted by Mr. Hunter, in an octavo volume, in 1838, together with a list of the contents of the Red Book of the Exchequer, and a Catalogue of the MSS. in Lincoln's Inn. After the MSS. were brought to the Library, they became in some way exposed to damp, 'and were in danger of being spoiled by a wet season.' Fortunately the danger was perceived by Ant. à Wood, who obtained leave of the Vice-Chancellor to dry them, which he accomplished by spreading them out in the sun upon the leads of the Schools' quadrangle. This cost him a month's labour, which, he says, he underwent with pleasure out of respect to the memory of Dodsworth, and care to preserve whatever might advantage the commonwealth of learning. The MSS. to this day give abundant proof, by their stains and tender condition, that, had it not been for Wood's unselfish labour, they would probably soon have perished. Some part of the collection appears to have been sent to the Library as late as 1684, for in the accounts of that year there is an entry of 4*s.* 10*d.* as having been paid for the 'carriage of Dods-

[1] No. 20 is a volume of Camden's collections, formerly in the Cotton Library, Julius B. x., from whence Dodsworth must have borrowed it, and whither, with an obliviousness too common in book-borrowers, he must have forgotten to return it. And No. 161 was given to the Library by Mr. Fras. Drake, the historian of York, in 1736.

worth's MSS.[1]' A list of both the Fairfax and Dodsworth MSS. is in the small quarto register noticed below under the year 1679. Fifty copies of a rough index of the names of persons and places occurring in the first seven volumes, compiled by Mr. W. H. Turner, were printed privately for the Library, in a quarto volume, in 1879. This index has been continued in MS. for a further portion of the collection by Mr. W. F. Thurland.

An interesting volume, written by the donor of these MSS., Fairfax, and entitled by him 'The Employment of my Solitude,' being metrical versions of the Psalms, with other poems, was bought, in 1858, for £36 10*s*., at the sale of the library of Dr. Bliss, who had purchased it at the Duke of Sussex's sale. It is described in Archdeacon Cotton's List of Bibles.

In the accounts are the following entries:

'To Dr. Marshall for the Armenian Bible and Testament	£20 0 0
To Mr. Hyde, for King Charles his Works . .	1 18 0'

A.D. 1674.

In this year appeared the third *Catalogus impressorum Librorum Bibliothecæ Bodleianæ*, in one folio volume, divided into two parts of 478 and 272 pages respectively. It is dedicated to Archbishop Sheldon, by Hyde the Librarian, not without reason, as being printed in that Theatre which the Archbishop had so lately built. The Keeper, in this dedication, speaks very feelingly of the daily weariness of mind and body which the compilation of the Catalogue had cost him, and tells how his very hours for refreshment had been spent among books alone, and how (*mirabile dictu!*) he actually had not shrunk even from the inclemency of winter[2]. In his

[1] 'A very extraordinary fiction connected with the name and family of Dodsworth appeared in the newspapers in July, 1826. It was pretended that in a snow-drift in Switzerland the body of a man was found frozen; that he was thawed, and being re-animated he announced himself [to be] . . . . Dodsworth, son of Roger the Antiquary, who had been lost in the snow on his return from Italy in 1660.' Dr. A. Gatty's edit. of Jos. Hunter's *Hallamshire*, fol. Lond. 1869, p. 43.

[2] Of the 'hyemis inclementia' before the present system of warming the Library was introduced, several of the staff of officers, who were living in 1868, when the first edition of these

preface he says that, on his entrance into office, he reckoned that the work of a new catalogue would occupy him for two, or at most three, years; six, however, had been spent in compilation and transcription, one in revision and enlargement, and, lastly, two in the actual printing. Yet, says he, he never withdrew his neck from the yoke, and postponed all considerations of bodily health. People little know, he proceeds, what it is to accomplish a work of this kind. What is easier, say they, than to look at the beginning of a book and to copy out its title? They judge only from one or two weeks' work in some little library of their own. But, what with careful examining of volumes of pamphlets (which of itself was labour perfectly exhausting), what with distinguishing synonymous authors and works, and identifying metonymous ones, unravelling anagrammatical names and those derived from places, and the like, the poor man declares he endured the greatest torment of mind ('maximo animi cruciatu') as well as waste of precious time. It is clear, from these pathetic lamentations, that Hyde had no great love for Bibliography for its own sake. But, after all his complaints, it is actually asserted by Hearne that he 'did not do much in the work besides writing the dedication and preface'![1] Hearne attributes the real compilation of the Catalogue to Emmanuel Prichard, or Pritchard, of Hart Hall, the janitor, who examined every book in the whole library, and wrote out the Catalogue, in two volumes, with his own hand. Hearne repeats this assertion frequently; it is found, *e.g.*, in his preface to the *Chronicon Dunstap.* p. xii, and in his *Autobiography* (1772, p. 11), where he adds that he was well informed of this by Dr. Mill and others. If this be true, the inditing such a preface, while totally suppressing Prichard's name, does little credit to Hyde. But see the statement mentioned under the year 1662 that 50 Masters of Arts were employed upon it[2]!

Annals was published, could speak as feelingly as Hyde. I remember, in particular, a time in one winter when, in consequence of the roof being under repair, the thermometer fell some eleven degrees below freezing point! And readers, naturally, were few and hasty and far between.

[1] *MS. Diary*, 1714, vol. ii. p. 193.

[2] Until the year 1760 a copy of this Catalogue, interleaved for additions, was the only one in use in the Maza-

Frequent mention of this Emmanuel Prichard is found between 1675 and 1699 as being employed upon the MSS., and as engaged in taking an account of duplicates, arranging Bishop Barlow's books, and writing a catalogue of Selden's books. In 1687, £20 were paid him for 'writing a Catalogue of MSS.' Probably this was the list upon which Hearne asserts that the index to the Bodleian MSS., in Bernard's Catalogue, was founded[1].' In 1686 he gave to the Library a copy of Latimer's *Sermons*, 4º. Lond. 1635. Hearne describes him[2] as being 'a very industrious, usefull man.' Although a member of Hart Hall, he never took any degree; but wore the gown of the now disused *status* of Student of Civil Law. He died in the Hall about 1704 or 1705, aged upwards of 70, and was buried in St. Peter's-in-the-East. He left £200 to the Vice-Principal of Hart Hall, which was partly spent in building a library-room[3].

Walter Charleton, M.D., gave portraits of Grotius and of Sir Martin Frobisher; the former had been painted by Grotius' order, when he was on an embassy in England in 1613, for Sir Theodore Mayerne, M.D.

In the accounts:—

'To Mr. Pullen for the portage of Dr. Plott's pictures to the Library	£0	4	9
To Mr. Walker of University College for books for the Library	5	2	6
To Mr. Scott for bookes for the library approved by Dr. Allestree	22	0	0
To Mr. Hyde for bookes for the Library . .	2	8	0'

A. D. 1675.

In the Register of Benefactions, on a page faintly headed in pencil with this date, is entered a gift from Christopher, Lord Hatton, 'Homiliarum Saxonicarum 4 volumina antiqua.' The donor was consequently the second baron, and first viscount,

rine Library at Paris, together with a small shelf-list. The copy is still preserved in that Library in two volumes, numbered 6750-1. (Alf. Franklin's *Hist. de la bibl. Mazarine*, 8º. Par. 1860, p. 132 *n.*)

[1] *Reliquiæ Hearn.* ii. 591. But see p. 164, *infra.*

[2] *MS. Diary*, li. 193.

[3] *Ibid.*, ciii. 38.

Hatton, who succeeded his father Christopher (a firm royalist, and close friend of Clarendon, as well as antiquarian, and friend of Dodsworth) in 1670, and died in 1706. Possibly this gift may have been made through the influence of his uncle, Capt. Charles Hatton, who appears to have been much interested in Anglo-Saxon studies, who himself gave three MSS. to the Library, which are still kept separate, and several of whose letters to Dr. Charlett in 1694–1707 are preserved in vol. xxxiii. of Ballard's MSS. These volumes of Homilies (written shortly after the Norman Conquest) were placed until recently among the Junian MSS., Nos. 22, 23, 24, 99, and their appearance in that collection is accounted for by Wanley (*Cat.* p. 43, where they are fully described at pp. 26–43) by a story which, he says, was often told him by Hyde, viz. that, immediately upon the arrival of the MSS. at the Library, they were lent to Dr. Marshall, who most probably in turn lent them to Junius; that, Marshall dying soon after, Junius kept them until his own death, when they returned to the Library with his own books, by his bequest. Junius himself frequently refers to them under the description of *Codices Hattoniani*.

The Library also contains a collection of 112 miscellaneous and valuable MSS., 'ex Codicibus Hattonianis,' of the presentation of which no record has been found[1], but which doubtless came about the same time from the same donor. A list, however, of 'my Lord Hatton's bookes' is found in the small quarto register mentioned below under the year 1679. Some precious Anglo-Saxon volumes form the special feature of this collection. Amongst them are, King Alfred's translation of Gregory's *Pastoral Care*, of which the King designed to send a copy to each cathedral church in the kingdom, this being, it may be, the copy sent to Worcester (No. 20); the translation by Werfrith, Bishop of Worcester, of Gregory's *Dialogues*, with King Alfred's preface (No. 76); and a version of the Four Gospels, written about the time of Henry II (No. 65). There is also a beautiful MS. of the *Regula S. Benedicti*, written

[1] The Register was evidently kept very irregularly and imperfectly during the time that Barlow and Hyde held the headship.

in uncials, most probably about the end of the seventh century (No. 48). And a collection of Canons (No. 42), of the recension called *Hibernensis*, which the late H. Bradshaw believed to have been written in Brittany in the ninth century, and to have belonged to Glastonbury Abbey. A letter from him on the subject is printed in the second edition of H. Wasserschleben's *Irische Kanonensammlung*, 8vo. 1885.

Henry Justell, afterwards Librarian at St. James's, sent to the University from France, through Dr. Hickes, three very precious MSS. of the seventh century, written in uncial characters, containing the Acts of the Council of Ephesus, the Canons of Carthage, Nicæa, Chalcedon, &c., which had been used by his father Christopher Justell in his *Bibliotheca Juris Canonici veteris*, 1661. They are now numbered, *e Mus.* 100–102. Several other MSS. given at the same time are preserved in the same series. In return for this valuable gift Justell was created D.C.L. by diploma.

On 7 Oct. a copy of the Catalogue was sent by decree of Convocation to Cosmo de' Medici, Grand Duke of Tuscany, together with Wood's *Hist. Univ.*, and Loggan's *Oxonia illustrata.* The Latin letter which accompanied the gift is entered in the Convoc. Reg. Tb. 28, p. 114.

Books were again bought on the recommendation of Obad. Walker, and by consent of Dr. Allestree.

'To Mr. Whitehall for portage of Sir Thomas Moore's picture to the Gallery[1]	£0	2	6
To John Hall for Father Walsh's booke in folio .	1	0	0
For bookes bought of Scholten the Dutch bookseller	6	2	0
For Peruta's Booke of Medalls and other bookes from Rome by Mr. Obad. Walker	7	16	4
To Dr. Yate for the case and portage of Archbp. Laud's picture	0	11	0
For two MSS. of Archbp. Usher's	30	0	0
To Mr. Walker for Ciacconius his *Columna Trajani*	3	15	0'

[1] This portrait by Mrs. Mary More, called Sir T. More's, is in reality a portrait of Cromwell, Earl of Essex!

John Lamphire, M.D., Principal of Hart Hall, gave a portrait of Bishop Andrewes, an Irish skull, about 100 coins, &c., about this year, but the date is not given in the Register.

A. D. 1676.

Some books were ordered by the Curators to be sold as duplicates in this year, among which was a copy of Rivola's *Dict. Armeno-Lat.* printed at Paris in 1633, which had been given in 1657 by — Needham, M.A., of Wadham College. This, however, still remains in the Library with a note signed by Thomas Hyde, that, 'I having added marginal observations, I do restore it again to the Library.' The notes chiefly consist of the addition of some Arabic, Persian, and Turkish synonyms. From this sale of duplicates the library at Ch. Ch. was furnished 'with a very good collection of Hebrew books,' as Prideaux tells us in his *Letters to J. Ellis* (1875, p. 54). This sale of duplicates is also referred to by Dr. R. Bathurst in his speech when resigning office as Vice-Chancellor, on 9 Oct. 1676 (printed by Warton with his *Life and Remains*, p. 77) in a passage commencing thus, 'Imo, non sine summo labore et tædio, tandem effectum est ut bibliotheca ipsa sibi benefica sit.' To Edmund (*sic*) Pritchard £2 17*s*. 6*d*. were paid 'by consent of the Curators' for his pains about these duplicates. Other payments in the accounts for the year are

'To Mr. Crossley, stationer, for Ravanell's *Bibliotheca*, 3 vol. fol.	£2	18	0
Bought of Dr. Allestree, *Memoires du Clergé de France*, 6 vol. fol.	5	16	6'

A. D. 1677.

The wonderful collection of early English poetry known as 'the Vernon MS.' was presented 'soon after the Civil Wars' by Col. Edward Vernon, of Trinity College, who had been an officer in the royal army. One who bore the same name, doubtless the same person, of North Aston, Oxon, was created D.C.L. Aug. 6, 1677; it was probably therefore about that time that the MS. was presented. The volume is described in Bernard's, Catalogue, 1697, p. 181, as being a 'vast massy manuscript;' and very correctly. Its measurements are these: length of page, 22½ inches; length of written text, 17½ inches; breadth of page, 15 inches; breadth of written text, 12½ inches. The greater part is in triple columns, on 412 leaves of stout vellum; and, having been clad of late years in a proportionate russia binding, is altogether a Goliath among books. In date it is of the latter part of the fourteenth century. Its first article bears the titles of 'Salus Animæ' and 'Sowle-Hele,' and its chief contents are Lives of the Saints, Hampole's *Prick of Conscience*, Grosseteste's *Castle of Love*, Hampole's *Perfect Living*, the treatise on *Contemplative Life*, the *Mirror of S. Edmund*, the *Abbey of the Holy Ghost*, the *Ancren Riwle*, and *Piers Plowman;* besides a multitude of smaller pieces, many of which have been printed by the Early Engl. Text Society[1]. Fifty copies of a brief list of the contents (numbering 161 articles) were printed by Mr. J. O. Halliwell in 1848. A MS., similar in size and contents, and apparently the work of the same scribe, was presented to the Brit. Mus. some years ago by Sir John Simeon. It is marked Addit. MS. 22, 283.

A.D. 1678.

Francis Junius, born at Heidelberg in 1589, who had passed a large part of his life in England as librarian to that Howard Earl of Arundel who collected the marbles which go under his name at Oxford, as well as the MSS. similarly entitled which are preserved in the British Museum and at Heralds' College, bequeathed to the Library, on his decease at Windsor in this year, all his Anglo-Saxon MSS. and his own life-long collections bearing on the philology of the Northern nations. Amongst these are some English relics of the greatest value and importance. The book of metrical Homilies on the Dominical Gospels, compiled by an

[1] This Society has also published Piers Plowman from this MS., edited by W. W. Skeat, M.A.

Augustinian monk named Orm, who thence called his book *Ormulum* ('þiss boc iss nemmnedd Orrmulum, Forrþi þatt Orrm itt þrohhte') is one of the chief of these. Its date is conjectured to be early 13th century. It is written on parchment, on folio leaves, very long and very narrow (averaging 20 inches by 8) in a very broad and rude, but very regular, hand, with many additions inserted on extra parchment scraps. Twenty-seven leaves appear to be wanting[1]. The whole work was first published in 2 vols., at the University Press in 1852, under the editorship of R. M. White, D.D., formerly Professor of Anglo-Saxon. Cædmon's metrical paraphrase of Genesis and other parts of Holy Scripture, illustrated with numerous curious drawings, is another of the gems of this collection. The MS. is of the end of the tenth century, and the work itself is maintained by the generality of recent German critics to be, in the main, not the production of the earliest English poet, the Cædmon noticed by Bede (iii. 24), who died towards the close of the seventh century, and who probably wrote only a small portion, but, as Hickes first conjectured, of some later writer or writers[2]. The MS. first came to light in the hands of Archbp. Ussher, by whom it was given to Junius. The latter published it at Amsterdam in 1655, and it was re-edited by Mr. Benj. Thorpe in 1832; several English and German translations have also appeared. Many of the drawings were engraved and published in 1754, as illustrations of the manners and buildings of the Anglo-Saxons; and the whole of them have been engraved in vol. xxiv. of the *Archæologia*, with some remarks by Sir H. Ellis. MS. 121 is an extremely valuable collection of the Canons of the Anglo-Saxon Church, written in the tenth century, which belonged to Worcester Cathedral; and there were included four valuable volumes of Homilies, which, however, were really part of Lord Hatton's gift to the Library. (See under 1675.)[3] Besides books, Junius left to the

[1] It belonged in 1659 to Janus Vlitius. On a fly-leaf is a Runic alphabet called 'Alphabetum Anglicum,' with the equivalent transliteration.

[2] See Ten Brink, *Gesch. der englischen Literatur*, 8°. Berl., 1877; trans. in 1883 in Bohn's Stand. Library series.

[3] Parts of MSS. 4 and 5, which had

University six founts of Gothic, Saxon, and other types, together with the moulds and matrices.

Fifty-five MSS. and printed books, chiefly Oriental, were purchased in this year from the library of Dr. Thomas Greaves, Deputy-professor of Arabic, who died May 22, 1676. It appears from the list in Bernard's Catalogue that sixty-five volumes were purchased, but that ten of these were never sent. With Greaves'

been stolen from the Library, were recovered, in 1720, in the manner recorded in the following entry in the Benefaction Book: 'Vir doctissimus Joannes Georgius Eckardus, bibliothecæ Brunsvicensis præfectus, pro singulari sua humanitate, folia quammulta MSS. Dictionarii Fr. Junii, continentia sc. litteras F. et S., a nequissimo quodam Dano jam olim surrepta, propriis sumptibus redemit et Bibl. Bodl. ultro restituit.' The following draft of a letter from Hyde, acknowledging the restitution of the fragments, has lately (1882) been found.

'Sir,—The very worthy Master of University College, having kindly imparted to me the letter which you receiv'd from Mr. Eccard, that learned gentleman must accept of my thanks for his care in endeavouring to restore to our Library that part of Junius's MSS. which had so luckily fallen into his hands. If all other persons, whether foreigners or Englishmen, who have, or pretend only to, any knowledge in books, would act upon the same honourable principles, there would certainly be good reason for the keepers of Publick Librarys to treat them with more freedom and humanity. The good opinion which I must have of Mr. Eccard and yourself (tho' not personally known) will make me ready to do you all the service I can. And, sir, you must be so kind as to assure your correspondent from me that when the MS. of Junius sent over by Mr. Bernstorfius shall be safely restored into my custody, I shall use my best endeavours to procure him transcripts from the rest as he has directed. Whatever you shall be pleas'd to communicate, so much I can confide in the Master's goodness, it will come safe to me thro' his hands; or, if you shall be unwilling to give him more trouble than is necessary, your directions will be observ'd by, Sir, ——.' It does not appear to whom this letter was addressed.

Some further portions of Junius' papers (including some which had formerly been in the Library) are recorded to have been given in 1753 by the Provost and Fellows of Queen's College. To these papers the following extract refers.

'What we have lately discovered at our College is an index drawn up by Junius to his edition of Cædmon, which in the Bodleian Catalogue is said to have been stolen; but we suppose that, as Junius's MSS. were formerly kept in a closet in the School-gallery, Mr. Thwaites might borrow it from thence; and, it being afterwards found in his study, was, with his other papers, inadvertently reposited in our archives.' Letter from E. R. Mores to Ducarel, dated at Queen's College 13 Jan. 1753: Nichols' *Literary Anecdotes*, vol. v. 403.

own books were obtained also the MSS. of Richard James, of Corpus Christi College, nephew of Thomas James, the first Librarian, which had come into the possession of his friend Greaves upon his death in Dec. 1638. These amount to forty-three volumes, entirely written by James himself, in a large bold hand; they consist chiefly of *Collectanea* bearing on the history of England from various MS. Chronicles, Registers,' and early writers, particularly with reference to the corruption of the Church and clergy before the Reformation, and in opposition to Becket. A full list of their contents, drawn up by Tanner, is given at pp. 258–263 of Bernard's Catalogue. The price paid for the books bought out of Greaves' library was £55.

Fifteen shillings were paid, as appears from the accounts, for the carriage of a whale from Lechlade, which, strange to say, had been caught in the Severn, and was presented by Will. Jordan, apothecary at Gloucester[1]. Ten shillings were also paid for a 'sea elephant.'

A.D. 1679.

In a quarto register of donations of MSS. to the Library, which appears to have been commenced by Barlow on his appointment in 1652, and continued for some forty years thereafter, four MSS. are noted as having been 'Restored to Salisbury by order of the Curators, 1679.' They were all of them collections of Lives of Saints, and very probably may have been stolen from the Chapter Library during the Civil War. They do not, however, appear in the list of the Salisbury MSS. in the *Cat. MSS. Angl.*, 1697, and are not there now. But see under 1696.

In May, Robert Ward, of Northampton, a surgeon, who had returned from the East Indies, gave a large gold coin of Japan, 'eorum lingua dictum *Coopangue*.'

A. D. 1680. [See A.D. 1665.]

Sir W. Dugdale gave copies of his own works. About two hundred coins were given by Dr. George Hickes.

[1] In the Benefaction Book this gift is assigned to the year 1672.

A. D. 1681.

In this year John Rushworth, of Lincoln's Inn, the historian of the Long Parliament, was a member of the Parliament held at Oxford. Probably it may have been at this time that he presented to the Library one of its most precious κειμήλια, called, from its donor, 'Codex Rushworthianus.' (Auct. D. 2. 19.) In 1665, Junius mentions it in the Preface to his *Glossarium Gothicum*, as being then in Rushworth's own hands[1]. It is a MS. of the Latin Gospels, written by an Irish scribe, Mac-Regol (who records his name on the last leaf, 'Macregol dipincxit hoc evangelium,' &c.), and glossed with an interlinear Anglo-Saxon version by Owun and by Færmen, a priest at Harewood. The volume is traditionally reported to have been in Bede's possession, but since the Irish annals record the death of Mac Riagoil, a scribe and abbot of Birr in 820, the volume must be about a century too late. It has been published in full, together with the Lindisfarne Gospels, by the Surtees Society in 4 vols., under the editorship of Rev. J. Stevenson and George Waring, Esq., M.A., and the interlinear version, chiefly edited by Prof. Skeat, at Cambridge, also in 4 vols., 1858–78. A description is given in Prof. Westwood's *Palæographia Sacra Pictoria;* and a fac-simile of the first page of St. John's Gospel in Mr. J. T. Gilbert's *Fac-similes of National MSS. of Ireland.*

Nine shillings were paid for the carriage of a mummy from London, probably one of those which are now in the Ashmolean Museum[2]. It was given by Aaron Goodyear, a Turkey merchant, who gave also a model of the Church of the Holy Sepulchre at Jerusalem, and various little images and other curiosities, and in 1684 more than forty coins.

Thomas Smith, D.D., of Magdalen College, gave, on his return from Constantinople, a MS. of the Psalms in Russian, with 'Religio Brachmanorum, Malabarice,' and a Turkish MS.

[1] It is strange that no entry of the gift of this priceless volume is found in the Register of Benefactions, any more than of that of the Vernon MS.

[2] The following note is added in the Register: 'Dictum mummiatum cadaver ad Repositorium novum translatum est.'

When the Parliament met at Oxford in this year, the House of Lords sat in the Picture Gallery, and the House of Commons in the Convocation House.

A. D. 1682.

Richard Davis, M.A., of Sandford, Oxon, gave the portrait of Margaret, Countess of Richmond, a book of Russian laws, and the Runic Calendar, or Clog Almanack, which is now exhibited in the glass case in the first part of the Library. The Calendar is thus described in the Register: 'Calendarium ligneum, tam materia quam usu perpetuum, unius ligni quadrati angulis incisum, more antiquo.'

Dr. John Morris, Regius Professor of Hebrew, who died in 1648, bequeathed five pounds annually to the University, to be paid to some Master of Arts of Ch. Ch., chosen by the Dean, for a speech 'in Schola Linguarum,' in honour of Sir Thomas Bodley, 'and as a panegyric and encouragement of the Hebrew studies,' on Nov. 8, in the presence of the Visitors of the Library after the conclusion of the annual Visitation. The bequest was to take effect after the death of his wife, which happened on Nov. 11, 1681; and on Oct. 6, 1682, Convocation fixed 3 p.m. as the hour for delivery of the Speech on the Visitation-day.

The Speeches are continued annually, and are delivered in the Library, after the Visitation, before the Curators and officers. Until within about the last fifteen years they were delivered semi-publicly in a lecture-room in the Old Clarendon Building, although for want of any public notice, very few persons ever knew of their delivery, and they were consequently very scantily attended. It is to be wished that formal notice of speech and speaker were given in the *University Gazette*, and the old public lecture-room again used. If provision had been made for the regular deposit of the Speeches in the Library after delivery, they might possibly have formed an interesting and accurate record of its growth, and of many passing events which, for want of such a record, are soon forgotten, and might have greatly assisted the compilation of these

Annals. Only one of the older speeches appears to be preserved in the Library: it is that delivered on Nov. 8, 1701, by Edmund Smith, M.A., and is very beautifully written in imitation of typography. But in this case nothing is recorded of the history of the preceding year, the speech being simply a panegyric of the Founder. It has been printed among Smith's *Works*, a pamphlet of 103 pages dignified with that name, of which the third edition appeared at London in 1719[1]. Since 1879, however, the MSS. have been kept in the Library, and the wish expressed in the former edition of this book is now happily annually fulfilled. Dr. Rawlinson endeavoured to compile a list of the Speakers; for Bishop Tanner, in a letter to him dated Oct. 11, 1735, from Ch. Ch., says he will enquire them out, if he can, but that they are not entered upon the Chapter books, since they are not appointed by the Chapter, but privately by the Dean or Hebrew Professor, and paid by the Vice-Chancellor, in whose accounts alone their names are probably entered[2]. And, as the subjoined list shows, Rawlinson was able to procure the names, with the omission of the single year 1691.

The names of the Speakers up to the year 1690 are given in Wood's *Athenæ* (ii. 127) as follows. They were all M.A., and Students of Ch. Ch.:—

1682 Thomas Sparke
1683 Zach. Isham
1684 Chas. Hickman
1685 Thos. Newey
1686 Thos. Burton
1687 Will. Bedford
1688 Rich. Blakeway
1689 Roger Altham, jun.
1690 Edward Wake

The following list from 1692 to 1739 is copied from a list supplied to Rawlinson by Dr. Conybeare, Dean of Ch. Ch., on 24 Jan. $17\frac{38}{40}$. From 1706 to 1734 the names are also found in Hearne's *MS. Diary*:—

1692 Francis Gastrell
1693 Francis Hickman
1694 George Smalridge
1695 John Pelling

[1] A long account of Smith is given in Johnson's *Lives of the Poets*.

[2] *Letters of Eminent Persons*, &c., ii. 111.

1696 Mich. Thompson
1697 Rob. Cock
1698 George Bull
1699 Edward Wells
1700 William Percivale
1701 Edmund Smith
1702 Anthony Alsop
1703 William Adams
1704 John Robinson
1705 Peter Foulkes
1706 Rich. Newton
1707 Thos. Terry
1708 Will. Periam
1709 Rich. Sadlington
1710 Richard Frewin
1711 Charles Aldrich
1712 Gilb. Lake
1713 Hen. Cremer
1714 Chas. Brent
1715 John White
1716 Edw. Ivie
1717 Hen. Gregory
1718 Thos. Fenton
1719 George Wigan
1720 Thos. Foulkes
1721 Will. Le Hunte
1722 Hen. Sherman
1723 Matthew Lee
1724 Christopher Haslam
1725 Will. Davis
1726 Edw. Blakeway
1727 David Gregory
1728 Rob. Manaton
1729 Hen. Jones
1730 John Fanshaw
1731 Oliver Battely
1732 Dan. Burton, B.D.
1733 Fifield Allen
1734 Pierce Manaton, M.D.
1735 Bernard Dowdeswell
1736 John Whitfeld
1737 Walter W. Ward
1738 Thomas Burton
1739 Anthony Parsons.

From my own early diaries I can supply the following :—

1843 Rob. Hussey, B.D.
1847 P. Butler.
1851 T. P. Rogers.

The speeches for these years following are now preserved among the Bodley Additional MSS. :—

1879 W. H. Payne Smith
1880 W. Warner
1881 J. H. Onions
1882 F. Paget
1883 H. B. Hodgson
1884 F. York Powell
1885 R. E. Baynes
1886 A. Hassall
1887 W. Hobhouse
1888 W. O. Burrows.

Wood has preserved in one of his MSS.[1] an amusing story of a

[1] It is quoted as being from Wood's MS. E. 32, by Huddesford, in some MSS. notes by the latter in a copy of his edit. of the *Life of Wood*, but the reference which he gives is wrong, and I have not been able to correct it.

singular gift to the Library, which was then regarded as a general receptacle of miscellaneous odds and ends.

'At Ducklington, neare Witney in Oxfordshire, hath been a custom for forty or fifty years not to give the parson gloves at weddings. But if the persons married shall at the year's end after marriage say that they repent not of marriage, then shall they give, and the parson claime, a pair of gloves. In 1682 a pair was given to the parson by a couple that had been married a year. Wherefore Walter Bayly, the parson, sometime fellow of Magd. Coll., did shew them to his friends for a rarity, and being persuaded to give them to the archives in Bodley's Library at Oxon, did so, and these verses following (made by Ant. Hodges, rector of Wytham neare Oxon, 1682) were pin'd upon them :—

Chirothecas connubentes
Anno post non pœnitentes
Has dederunt nuptiales:
Quis ostendat mihi tales?

Wedded a year, we ne're repented,
But to the Preist these gloves presented.
Let Oxford archives never dare
To shew me such another paire.'

The 'Parson of Ducklington' (as the writer of this volume can personally testify) nowadays receives no gloves at all, either at the wedding itself or at its 'year's-mind.' It is to be hoped that the postponement of the gift for the eventful year has not led to a vain repetition of the cry, 'Quis ostendat mihi tales?' ever since!

Two pounds were paid in this year to one Robert Hawkins for painting in gold and blue the archive-cupboards now called Arch. E and F, and 6*s*. 8*d*. and 5*s*. for painting the arms of lord Fairfax and H. Justell, respectively, in the Register of Benefactors.

A.D. 1683.

Five MSS., containing three copies of the Samaritan Pentateuch, the Syriac Pentateuch, and the Syriac Old Testament, were purchased at the cost of the University.

A. D. 1684.

Nine Oriental and Russian MSS. were given by Joseph Taylor, LL.D., of St. John's College. Dr. John Radcliffe, the physician, gave two gold coins, of Edw. Conf. and Hen. I; and Geo. White, an East Indian merchant, gave a Chinese map of the heavens, and also a map of China. And Sir Rob. Viner, Bart., the loyal alderman of London, favoured the Library with a human skeleton, a tanned human skin, and the dried body of a negro boy! 'A Blackmoore mummied' was formerly no. 190 of the Curiosities in the Anatomy School, to which Viner's gifts were, no doubt, transferred, which was then the room now called the *Auctarium*.

A. D. 1685.

Thomas Marshall, or Mareschall, D.D., Rector of Linc. Coll., and Dean of Gloucester, who died Apr. 18, bequeathed his MSS., and such of his printed books as were not already in the Library. The MSS. amount to 159, chiefly Oriental, including some valuable Coptic copies of the Gospels, &c., procured for him by Huntington, with a few in Dutch, and others miscellaneous in language and subject. They are in Bernard's Catalogue, pp. 272–3 and 373–4. Both printed books and MSS. are still kept under his name.

A. D. 1686.

Dr. John Fell, the learned and pious Bishop of Oxford, who died July 10, bequeathed a few MSS. They consist of a collection of *Vitæ Sanctorum* in four folio volumes, of a transcript (in nine fol. vols.) of a *Glossarium Septentrionale* by Fr. Junius, Dionysius Syrus in Latin by Dudley Loftus, and two Greek MSS., Damascius and Euthymius Zigabenus, described at col. 907 of Mr. Coxe's Catal. of the Greek MSS. One other MS. has somehow been incorporated with these (numbered 21–23) which does not belong to them. It is a *Clavis Linguæ Sanctæ*, or explanation of all the Hebrew, and some Chaldee, roots found in the Old Testament, by Sir Nicholas Trott, in three fol. volumes, written with great care and neatness. This, of which Part I. had been printed at Oxford in 1719[1], was sent to the Library in 1746, as appears from the following letter, preserved (without address) in a parcel of papers relating to the Library:—

'MY LORD,

'My wife's grandfather Judge Trott, cheif justice of South Carolina, desired on his death bed that his forty years' labour relating to the Hebrew root might be sent as a present to the Publick Library at Oxford. I proposed to have carried it, but my time has allways been taken up at a disagreeable series of Court Martials, and now I am again going to the West Indies. That I must beg your Lordship will order or give it a conveyance to the University, and I am, with great respect, my Lord,

'Your Lordship's most humble servant,

'23 *Nov.*, 1746.' 'THOS. FRANKLAND.'

It appears, however, from accounts, &c., that the MS. was not delivered until 1748 or 1749, when it was received through Dr. Hunt.

Fell's volumes of *Vitæ Sanctorum* are without doubt those which were ordered to be returned to Salisbury in 1679. How they came into his hands instead, remains to be discovered. Vols. i–iii are in a hand of the early part of the twelfth century; vol. iv in another hand a little later in the same century. From the first vol. the Rev. James Raine took the text of Eddi's Life of St. Wilfrid in vol. i of his *Historians of the Ch. of York* (Rolls Series), 1879[2]. Vol. ii has a very full life of St. Remigius, at ff. 184^{a}–235^{b}; and to vol. iv is prefixed, in a hand of the thirteenth century, a life of St. Edm. Riche, occupying twenty-two leaves.

A few of Fell's MSS. came subsequently to the Library among those of his nephew, the Rev. Hen. Jones[3], to whom they were be-

[1] Aid had been sought subsequently from the General Assembly of the Church of Scotland towards completing the printing of the book. In the Index of the unprinted *Acts of the Assembly* for the year 1725, there is notice of its being referred to the Commission to consider 'what encouragement may be proper to be given' towards its publication, and this reference was renewed in 1730.

[2] I see that Mr. Raine in his preface anticipates my supposition that the MSS. belonged to Salisbury, from finding that this text of Wilfrid's Life has been quoted by Mabillon and Gale as from a Sarum MS.

[3] Hearne's pref. to John Ross, p. 1. See under the year 1700.

queathed by Fell, and who was a successor to the Bishop's father (his own grandfather), Dr. Sam. Fell, in the rectory of Sunningwell, Berks.

At the Visitation on Nov. 8, it was ordered that notice be given that 'Nullus in posterum quemlibet librum aut volumen extra Bibliothecam asportet,' and that monition be sent to every College and Hall for the return of any books taken out within three days. Several books appear to have been reported in previous years as missing; hence, doubtless, the issue of this order.

A.D. 1687.

On the occasion of the visit of King James II to Oxford, chiefly, but unsuccessfully, made for the purpose of overawing the fellows of Magdalen College, who had refused to elect as president his nominee, Anth. Farmer, he was invited by the University to partake of a breakfast or collation in the Library. For this purpose he came hither on the morning of Sept. 5, between nine and ten, where, at the south part of the Selden end, a banquet was prepared which cost the University £160, consisting of 111 dishes of meat, sweetmeats, and fruit. The King sat here for about three quarters of an hour, and held some conversation with Hyde about a Chinese, 'a little blinking fellow,' who had recently visited the place, and about the religion of China; but asked no one to join him at the table. Upon rising to depart, a scene of strange indecorum, as it would now appear, ensued; the 'rabble' (as they are described) of courtiers and academics rushed upon the mass of untouched dainties, and began a disorderly scramble, in which they 'flung the wet sweetmeats on the ladies' linnen and petticoats, and stained them.' The King watched the scramble for two or three minutes, and then departed, commending to the Vice-Chancellor and doctors his chaplain, W. Hall, who had preached before him the day previous, and delivering a most fatherly homily on the sin of pride, the virtue of charity, and the duty of doing as they would be done to. Good, gossiping, Ant. à Wood gives in his *Autobiography* a full account of all that passed, from which are taken the above quotations[1].

After recording the fact of the 'sumptuous banquet' the Univ. Reg. (B. 29, f. 173) only adds, 'After that entertainment was over his Majestie departed hence, and went immediatly towards Cyrencester.'

A.D. 1688.

Dr. Hyde went to London in this year to demand personally of the Company of Stationers the books due to the Library by Act of Parl. (1 James II, cap. 17, for seven years, continuing previous acts), but which they had neglected to send. His expenses were £6 5*s*.

A.D. 1690.

Thirty pounds were paid in this year to Ant. à Wood for twenty-five MSS. out of his library[2]. These are volumes of great value, including Chartularies of the Abbeys of Glastonbury and Malmesbury, and of the Preceptory of Sandford, Oxon, copies of Papal bulls relating to England, and a register of lands in Leicestershire *temp.* Hen. VI. The rest of Wood's MSS., and his printed books, came to the Library, from the Ashmolean Museum, in 1860.

It is said that Wood in this year estimated the number of MSS. in the Library at 10,141; the number probably of books, not volumes, as the latter appear from Bernard's Catalogue to be in 1697 about 6700.

A.D. 1691.

On Oct. 8, died Dr. Thomas Barlow, Bishop of Lincoln, who, retaining his attachment for the place over which he had presided from 1652 to 1660, bequeathed to it a considerable number of MSS. (which are now bound in fifty-four volumes), and all the printed books in his collection which the Library did not possess, the remainder going to Queen's College. They appear

[1] See also Miss Seward's *Anecdotes*, Supplement, 1797, p. 72.

[2] In Bernard's Catalogue the purchase is said to have been made in 1692, but this is an error, as it is entered in the accounts of 1690.

to have been received in the years 1693–4, as large payments for the carriage are found in the accounts then. His MSS. are described in the old Catalogue of 1697[1]. The quarto and octavo printed books, which are particularly rich in tracts of the time of Charles I and the Usurpation, are still kept distinct, being called *Linc.*[2]; ending, in the 8o. series, at about the middle of the shelves marked with the letter C in that division[3]. They were placed in a gallery on the left hand of the great central room, which was removed in 1877, when the books were transported to one of the lower rooms. The corresponding gallery on the right, which contained law-books, was removed at the same time. These galleries are seen in the old views of the interior of the Library. Barlow's folios, which were not numerous, are dispersed amongst other folio volumes. Amongst them is a Roman Missal, printed at Paris in 1684, which belonged to James II, or was used in his private chapel. Pasted in it, at the end, is a printed form of prayer, in Latin, appointed by John [Leyburn], bishop of Adramyttum, the Vicar Apostolic, to be used during the pregnancy of James's Queen in 1688, with a MS. collect for the Pope as well as the Royal Family, which may possibly be in Leyburn's own hand. One of Bp. Barlow's chaplains, named Offley, was said by Wanley to have narrated that it was taken out of the King's chapel at the Revolution. Two copies of the prayers, one by H. Gandy, the Non-juring bishop, described as being taken from 'K. James's Masse-book, now in the University Library at Oxford, amongst Bp. Barlow's books,' are in Rawl. MS. D. 680, ff. 164b, 165. Barlow's legacy included a copy of the famous *Exposicio Sancti Jeronimi in Simbolo Apostolorum*, which was printed at Oxford in 1468 [1478?], and completed, as the colophon states, on Dec. 17. This volume was given to Barlow, as he notes at the beginning, by Bishop Juxon, July 31, 1657. It is exhibited

[1] No. 49 formerly belonged to Sir R. Cotton, and several volumes consist of papers of Archbp. Ussher.

[2] Apparently it was at first intended to designate Barlow's books (like his MSS.) as *Barl.* instead of *Linc.* Sandford's *Coronation of James II.* (now G. 2, 8 Jur.) was at first marked 'A. 1, 1 Barl.'

[3] In most of them is inscribed the motto, αἰὲν ἀριστεύειν.

in a glass case. The Library possesses also seven other productions of the early Oxford press. They are as follow:—

1. *Ægidius Romanus de Peccato Originali*, dated March 14, 1479. This was one of Rob. Burton's books. Only two other copies are known to exist.

2. *Textus Ethicorum Aristotelis, per Leonardum Arretinum translatus*, 1479. One of Selden's books.

3. *Expositio Alexandri* [*de Hales*] *super tertium librum* [*Arist.*] *De Anima.* 'Impressum per me Theodericum rood de Colonia in alma universitate Oxon.' Oct. 11, 1481.

4. *Joh. Latteburii Exposicio Trenorum Jheremie*, July 31, 1482. No place, but printed with the same type as the last.

5. *Liber Festivalis*, [by John Mirke or Myrcus] in English, printed by Rood and Hunt, 1486. Two copies, both very imperfect. The more imperfect one of the two formerly belonged to W. Herbert, and was bought for £6 6*s*. in 1832; two additional leaves have been inserted by Mr. Coxe, which were found among Hearne's scraps, having been given to him as fragments of a Caxton by Bagford. The other copy was bought in 1852, at Utterson's sale, for £6 10*s*.

6. *Opus Wilhelmi Lyndewoode super Constitutiones Provinciales.* No place or date, [*c.* 1483] but identified by the type.

7. *Vulgaria quedam abs Terentio in Anglicam linguam traducta.* Without place or date, [*c.* 1483] but also identified by the type. The following note, which corroborates the identification, is written in red ink on a fly-leaf in the volume (which includes several other tracts): '1483. Frater Johannes Grene emit hunc librum Oxon. de elemosinis amicorum suorum[1].'

[1] This last book is described by Dr. Cotton in the second series of his *Typographical Gazetteer*, published in 1866, from a copy in the University Library at Cambridge. It forms part of a *Compendium totius Grammaticæ* (conjectured to have been written by John Anwykyll, Waynflete's first Grammar Master at Magdalen College), of which several other fragments have been discovered. Mr. H. Bradshaw, the late lamented Librarian of the University of Cambridge, whose knowledge of early typography was so wide and so accurate, found and identified, at Cambridge, two leaves in the University Library in 1859, two more in Corpus Christi in 1861, and two in St. John's in 1866. Four other leaves were discovered by myself in 1867, bound up as fly-leaves in a volume in the library of Viscount Dillon, at Ditchley, Oxfordshire. Mr. Bradshaw supposed the book to have been printed about 1483. In the library of Bramshill House, Hants, Sir William Cope, the owner, found about twenty years ago in the fly-leaves of a volume containing tracts printed between 1498 and

A list of sixty-six books, which Hunt, the Oxford printer and bookseller, had in his hands for sale in 1483, is preserved in his own writing on a fly-leaf in a copy of a French translation of Livy, Paris, 1486, which was bought for the Library from Mr. C. J. Stewart, in Dec. 1860, for £12. The list is headed thus: 'Inventorium librorum quos ego Thomas Hunt, stacionarius universitatis Oxoniensis, recepi de Magistro Petro Actore et Johannis (*sic*) de Aquisgrano ad vendendum, cum precio cujuslibet libri, et promito (*sic*) fideliter restituere libros aut pecunias secundum precium inferius scriptum, prout patebit in sequentibus, Anno Domini M°. CCCC°. octuagesimo tercio [1].'

A. D. 1692.

Thirty-eight Persian and Arabic MSS., with one printed book, were bought from Hyde, the Librarian. They are entered in Bernard's Catalogue, pp. 286–7. Being bought out of the funds of the University, no mention of the price paid for them is found in the Library accounts.

In Smith MS. 11 (p. 35) we meet with the following suggestions made by Dr. Bernard:—

'*Oct.* 8, 1692.

Proposals to the Curators of the Bodleian Library:—

1. That cases be made in the Gallery or in the great Library for some new books.

2. That the Cromwell, Hatton, Fairfax, Junius, Casaubon, Greaves,

1503, two sheets, in the Oxford type, of Cicero's oration *Pro Milone*, marked b iij and e iij, in small quarto, with wide margins. He gave these to the Library in 1872. There is also one leaf of a volume of treatises on logic.

An exhaustive account of the work of the Oxford Press in the fifteenth century will form part of a bibliographical catalogue of all Oxford-printed books and tracts, on which Mr. Falconer Madan, M.A., Sub-librarian, has been for some time engaged. To him, for editing the curious account-book of John Dorne, a Dutch bookseller in Oxford in 1520, the members of the Oxford Historical Society are much indebted.

[1] This list has been printed by Mr. Falconer Madan, at the end of Dorne's Day-book, pp. 141–3, vol. i. of the Oxf. Hist. Soc. *Collectanea*, 8vo. Oxf. 1885.

and other MSS., with those of Pocock and Huntington, be figured, entered in the Curators' books, and yearly examined.

3. That the Catalogue of the MSS. be printed by the Librarians, they being paid for it per sheet by the Delegates for printing.

4. That no person be in future obliged to take a copy of the Cat. of printed books on his admission to the Library, there being but few copies left, which may be wanted for presents or otherwise.

EDWARD BERNARD.'

A. D. 1693.

The Oriental MSS., in number 420, of the famous Edward Pococke, Regius Professor of Hebrew (who had deceased Sept. 10, 1691), were purchased by the University for £600. They are chiefly in Armenian, Hebrew, and Arabic, with three volumes in Æthiopic, a Samaritan Pentateuch, and a Persian Evangeliary. A list is given at pp. 274–278 of Bernard's Catalogue. In 1822 the Library became possessed of a portion of Pococke's collection of printed miscellaneous books, by the bequest of Rev. C. Francis, M.A., of Brasenose College. They are chiefly small volumes in Latin, on historical subjects; and are, for the most part, placed in the shelves marked 8°. Z. Jur. [Arabic version of Isaiah, *see* p. 115 *n.*]

Another large Oriental collection was added in this year by the purchase, from Dr. Robert Huntington, for the sum of £700, of about 600 MSS. These he had procured while holding the post of chaplain to the English merchants at Aleppo [1]. The collection is one of very great value and rarity. No. 1 is a fine and ponderous Syriac volume, containing the works of Gregory Abulpharage. No. 2 is a very fine folio Arabic MS., written in the year of the Hegira 777 (=A.D. 1375), and dedicated to the Sultan Almalek Alashraf Shalian ben Hosain; in it, as Uri says in his Catalogue, 'variæ Ægypti regiones recensentur, agrorum cujusque regionis

[1] He had previously given thirty-five MSS. in the years 1678, 1680, and 1683. He died on Sept. 2, 1701, only twelve days after his consecration as Bishop of Raphoe.

mensura definitur, et annui redditus exponuntur.' Dibdin[1] describes it in his own exaggerated style, as follows:—'One of the grandest books— . . . a sort of Domesday compilation—which can possibly be seen. . . . The scription is in double columns, with the margins emblazoned only in stars. The title, on the reverse of the first leaf, is highly illuminated, in a fine style; not crowded with ornaments, but grand from its simplicity. At the end, we observe that it is (rightly) called *Munus Pretiosum*, and that the author was Sherfiddin Iahia ben Almocar ben Algiaian. The inspection of such a volume, on the coldest possible morning, even when the thermometer stands at *zero*, is sufficient to warm the most torpid system.' No. 80 is a copy of Maimonides' *Yad Hachazaka*, revised by the author, with his autograph signature at the bottom of fol. 165, and a MS. note by him on fol. 1. Of these an engraved facsimile is given in *Treasures of Oxford, containing Poetical Compositions by the ancient Jewish Authors in Spain, and compiled from MSS. in the Bodl. Libr. by H. Edelman and Leop. Dukes; edited and rendered into English by M. H. Bresslau:* part i. 8°. Lond. 1851. A second part of this work was to have contained prose selections from MSS. in the Huntington, Pococke, Michael, and Oppenheim collections, but it was never published. Among Huntington's books there are also three, of no great antiquity, in the Mendean character, of which Dr. T. Smith narrates in his life of Bernard (1704, p. 21) that [the originals of] two were said to have been given by God to Adam, and the third to the angels, 330,000[2] years before Adam. And one volume (No. 598) is in the Ouigour language, a Tartar dialect, of which very few specimens are known to exist. M. Arm. Vambéry, the traveller in Tartary, who was engaged in forming a Chrestomathy of this dialect, came in 1866 to England for the purpose of examining this volume, as one of the few on which his work could be based. Three MSS. exist at Paris; but that in the Bodleian is said to be the most beautiful of all as a specimen of writing, as well as the most

[1] *Bibliogr. Decam.* iii. 472.

[2] Or, with more moderation, 33,000; *Life of Pococke*, edit. 1816, p. 326.

ancient. It is a version of the *Bakhtiar Nameh*. A description of it, with an engraved facsimile, is given in Davids' *Turkish Grammar*, 4°. Lond. 1832, pref. p. xxxi.

An exchange of some duplicates was made with the Library of Queen's College, and in 1695 the duplicates of Bishop Barlow's collection were transferred, in accordance with his will, to the same Library.

Among the verses recited at the Encænia on 7 July was a poem, 'carmine heroico,' by Henry Ewer, of Ch. Ch., entitled 'Bibliothecæ Bodleianæ auctarium.'

A. D. 1694.

A Mr. Clarke was employed in this year in making a catalogue of Pococke's and Huntington's MSS., for which he altogether received between £13 and £14.

A. D. 1695.

Books were bought from Jacob Bobart, the Professor of Botany, and at the auction of the library of Sir Charles Scarborough, M.D.

Mr. Anderson, the Keeper of the University Library at Edinburgh, gave a copy of the protest of the Bohemian nobles against the burning of John Huss, of which the original is preserved in that Library. The copy is numbered Bodl. 598.

Stationers' Company. See 1610.

MSS. from Wood. See 1658.

A. D. 1696.

From this year until 1700, Humphrey Wanley was an assistant in the Library, at an annual salary of £12. He had also £10 at the end of this year 'extraordinary, for his paines already past,' and £15, at the beginning of 1700, 'for his pains about Dr. Bernard's books.' Possibly this grant may have been in consequence of the interposition of Bishop Lloyd of Worcester, who, in a letter to Wanley of Jan. 6, in that year, promises to speak to the Bishop of Oxford to see whether he can get his place in the Library made better for him[1]. Wanley was no favourite with Hearne. The following passage from the MS. *Diary* of the latter[2] is a specimen of the censure which he (with considerable injustice) on several occasions passes on him: 'Humphrey Wanley appears from several passages to be a very illiterate silly fellow. He committed strange and almost incredible blunders when he was employed by Dr. Charlett and some others in printing the catalogue of the MSS. of England and Ireland, which work was committed first to the care of Dr. Bernard; but he being then very weak and otherwise employed, he could not take so much pains about it as he would, had he not been thus hindered.' The very accurate, although too brief index, however, to this Catalogue was Wanley's work, as he tells us in a MS. account of the Catalogue and of the index, which remains in the Library. Another, much fuller, index was made to the whole catalogue from the proof-sheets by Bernard,

[1] [Walker's] *Letters by Eminent Persons*, i. 102. It is pleasant to find that Wanley in more prosperous days evinced his gratitude for the help he had received in the Library, by giving, in the year 1721, £7 7*s*., together with a MS. Latin Bible, as testified by the Benefaction Register. The way in which he made the gift is shown in the following paper, which is now preserved in Bodl. Addit. MS. C. vii. 8. fol. 15:—

'20 Oct. 1721.

'Whereas about twenty years ago, being then in London, at the instance of Dr. Charlet, and with the consent of Dr. Hans Sloane, I compared many thousands of his books with Dr. Hyde's Catalogue, and after long labor during several weeks found out a great number of books which were duplicates in Dr. Sloane's library, and yet wanting in the Bodleyan, of which books I also took a list, and was assisting at their putting up, when Dr. Sloane gave them to the University; which services I then valued at seven pounds and ten shillings, which money remaineth still due to me, notwithstanding a demand I made of it to Dr. Mander when he was Vice-Chancellor: If the now reverend and learned the Vice-Chancellor, the King's Professors and the Procurators, being the Curators of the Bodleyan Library, after so many years elapsed, shall judge it meet to gratifie me for my labor and my good will also, at the rate that then I valued my time at, it is my desire that the said seven pounds and ten shillings be employed in the procuring of some one or more good and useful book or books to be put into the said Library, wherein I have served to my great benefit (both of information and maintenance) without the trouble of any entrance into the Benefaction-book.

Witness my hand,

HUMFREY WANLEY.'

[2] 1714, vol. li. p. 193.

and written with his own hand, 'uti ab illo accepi,' says Dr. T. Smith in his Life (1704, p. 48), which includes, besides, the contents of eight of the great foreign libraries, but not the Royal Library at Paris, the catalogue of which he was unable to obtain. This index, which is in the Library, is in one thick folio volume [1].

A.D. 1697.

On the death of Edward Bernard, D.D., the Savilian Professor of Astronomy (which occurred on Jan. 12), the University became the purchaser from his widow of the greater part of his library. A selection from his printed books, made on behalf of the Library by H. Wanley, comprising many rare Aldines and specimens of the 15th century, was bought for £140, and his MSS., many of which were valuable copies of classical authors, together with collated printed texts and his own *Adversaria*, for £200. Of 218 of the latter, Bernard has given a very brief list in his own invaluable *Catalogus Manuscriptorum Angliæ* (vol. ii. pp. 226–8), which appeared posthumously, in the year of his death, and in which all the MSS. then in the Library are catalogued. The original draft of the *Epistola* prefixed to this Catalogue is in the Library (in a hand not yet identified) from which it appears that it was addressed to Dr. Arthur Charlett. The Life of Bodley, also prefixed to the Catalogue, is by Edmund Gibson. The bulk of Bernard's books are dispersed in various parts of the Library; and amongst these there are about thirty volumes of his *Adversaria.* A very full account, by H. Wanley, of the purchase of the collection exists in MS. in a folio volume among the Library registers, with a list of the books and their prices; and the text of this account is printed by Dr. Bliss in his notes to the *Ath. Oxon.* (iv. 709), who adds that this addition 'contained many of the most valuable books, both printed and MSS., now in the Library.'

[1] In the previous edition it was supposed that Bernard's index was the one actually printed, but this has been found to be a mistake. Wanley, in his MS. account, states that he was strictly ordered to make his own index as brief as possible, and describes the difficulties which he as a young beginner found in the work.

In the discharge of his duty of selection, Wanley came into sharp collision with his chief, Dr. Hyde, as is shown by a curious paper, in Wanley's handwriting, which was transcribed by Dr. Rawlinson from the original in Dr. Charlett's possession[1]. The paper gives a list of books for not securing which, together with others, out of Bernard's collection, blame had been thrown upon Wanley, and which Hyde had said must by all means be bought at the auction which was to be held in October, 1697. To the title of each book so specified Wanley appends some caustic remarks, exposing Dr. Hyde's little acquaintance with the Library or with the books themselves; and sums up thus at the close:—

'This is what I have to say to these 13 books, one whereof I look upon as imperfect, two more I was charged not to meddle with, and the other ten are in the Library already. I shall wave all unmannerly reflections, as whether this be not in you *insignis insufficientia*, for which you are liable to be turned out of your place; or [whether,] if you had been employed to bring in a list of Dr. Bernard's books wanting in the Library, and took the same method as now, the University would not have bought a fair parcel of duplicates, and such like; but I pass them by. Tho' it must be owned that the University being willing to lay out but 140 pounds, some different editions of the Bible, Fathers, Classicks, &c. were preferr'd to some books not at all in the Library, but they were at the same time judged to be of less moment, and likely to be given to it by future benefactors[2].'

The quarrel, however, soon ceased; for, in the following year, Hyde was anxious to see Wanley appointed as his successor. The

[1] Rawlinson's copy is now in MS. Rawl. D 742. For knowledge of it I was indebted to Mr. W. H. Bliss.

[2] Others beside Wanley had a very low opinion both of Hyde's character and of his abilities. Humphrey Prideaux, dean of Norwich, is very bitter against him in his *Letters to J. Ellis* (edited by the Camden Society in 1875 by E. Maunde Thompson). Under date of Oct. 1675, he tells a scandalous story about the 'poor fool' and his wife, a low and violent woman. In 1682 he speaks (pp. 132, 133) of Hyde as 'soe egregious a donce . . . who doth not understand common sense in his own language, and therefore I cannot conceive how he can make sense of anything that is writ in another;' and that 'he hath the least skill' in the Arabic language 'of any that pretend to it in the University.' He however admits that Hyde 'can do something in Persian.' (Hyde was a candidate for the Professorship of Arabic in 1682, and was appointed to the office in 1691). On the other hand, Greg. Sharpe in his *Prolegomena*

latter, in a letter to Dr. Charlett, dated Oct. 10, 1698[1], repeats a conversation held with Hyde on the previous evening, in which the Librarian said 'that he is heartily weary of the place of Library-keeper; that he must use more exercise in riding out, &c., if he intends to preserve his health; which will of necessity hinder his attendance there. He had rather I succeeded him than anybody else, which I cannot do untill I am a graduate; that, if I have any friends amongst the heads of houses, they cann't do better for me than in procuring for me the degree of Batchellor of Law, that I may be in a condition to stand for his place with others, which he will resign as soon as I have obtain'd the said degree, and (for my sake) will communicate his intentions to nobody else in the mean time. He presses me to get this degree as soon as possible, urging that he does not care how soon he is rid of his place.' Wanley asks for Charlett's advice; what that was does not appear, but, at any rate, he did not obtain the degree which he desired, and consequently did not become eligible as Hyde's successor.

Sixteen MS. treatises on Mathematics, Astronomy, and Ancient History, by Thomas Lydiat, were given by Will. Coward, M.D. They are amongst the Bodl. MSS., chiefly between Nos. 658–671.

A. D. 1698.

Alexander Brown, an East Indian merchant, living in Fifeshire, gave a Chinese printed map of China, with eight other Chinese and East Indian papers and books, of which a list is given by Hearne in one of his volumes of *miscellanea*, Rawl. D. 261. p. 362, as

to his collected edition of Hyde's *Dissertationes* (printed at Oxford in two quarto vols. in 1767) praises Hyde in the highest terms. He there prints (pp. x, xi) two letters from Hyde to James Watson, a young Scottish student, who had collected some Coptic and other MSS. in the East, but died at an early age in 1677, together with a letter to his father at Dundee proposing to purchase the MSS. for the Library. They were not, however, obtained; and Sharpe says that some had come to his hands, and that he believes others were used by Dr. Marshall.

[1] Ballard MSS. xiii. 45.

well as in the Benefaction Register. The latter book records also the gift of various Oriental books, together with a portrait of Aurungzeb, by Rev. John Lewis, chaplain at Fort George.

The surveillance exercised at this time over strangers in the Library is shown by a passage in a letter from Edw. Thwaites in Sept. of this year, in which he says that 'Palthenius has a great desire to read [Tatian], and he cannot have the use of that in the Library unless a Master of Arts or Dr. sit by him[1].'

A.D. 1699.

Mr. Timothy Nourse, M.A., Univ. Coll., of Newent, Gloucestershire, who died 21 July in this year, bequeathed upwards of 500 coins, 'in thankful remembrance of the obligations I have' to the University[2].

A.D. 1700.

Considerable fears were entertained for the safety of the Divinity School and that portion of the Library which is built over it. About thirty-two years before, some failure had been observed in the roof of the former, which was rectified under the superintendence of Sir Christopher Wren. When Bishop Barlow's books were brought to the Library, in 1692 or 1693, the galleries on either side of the middle room were erected; and, as the beams of the roof of the School were then observed to give from the wall, they were anchored on both sides, under the direction of Dr. Aldrich. But the tight bracing had now caused the south wall, that which adjoins Exeter College garden, to bulge outwards, so that the book-stalls were found to have started from the wall by three and a-half inches at the top and two and a-half at the bottom; the wall itself was seven and a-half inches out of the perpendicular, and the four great

[1] MS. Eng. Hist. c. 6. f. 112.

[2] On a small slip of paper containing the extract of his gift from his will, made by Abr. Morse, rector of Huntley, is added this enumeration of the coins: 'gould peeces, 2, white, 121; copper, 409; in all, 532. A brass buckle.' See T. Hearne's *Diary* (or *Remarks and Collections*) as printed by Oxf. Hist. Soc., vol. i., pp. 3, 198.

arches of the vault of the School were all cracked. Hereupon Dr. Gregory, the Savilian Professor, was despatched to London to consult Sir C. Wren again, and, by his advice, additional buttresscs of great depth and strength were erected on the south side, the weight of the bookstalls was removed from the roof of the School by their being trussed up to the walls with iron cramps; and the cracks in the vault were filled with lead or oyster-shells, and in some places with the insertion of new stones, and were then 'wedged up with well-seasoned oaken wedges.' This work went on through the summers of 1701 and 1702; and in 1703 some similar repairs were executed in some of the other Schools. The letters and papers of Wren on the subject, with the draughts, and reports of the workmen employed, are preserved in Bodley MS. 907. They are printed in [Walker's] *Oxoniana*, iii. 16–27.

Between 1700 and 1738 Sir Hans Sloane is recorded to have given considerably more than 1400 volumes, together with his picture in 1731; but the majority of them do not appear to have been considered of much value, and only 415 are specified by name in the Benefaction Register[1]. Dr. Hyde, in a letter to Hudson, which accompanied a list of the books for which the latter had asked with a view to registration, says he scarce thinks the entry to be 'for the credit of the business, *nos inter nos*[2].' But Hudson appears to have thought that the omission proceeded rather from carelessness, for, in a letter to Wanley, he says that he thinks Hyde assigned '*non causa pro causa*[3].'

Five Oriental MSS. were given by Moses Amyrault.

A. D. 1701.

The long-entertained idea of resigning the Librarianship was at length carried out by Dr. Hyde in this year, for the reasons given in the following letter, which was addressed by him to the Pro-Vice-Chancellor, probably Dr. Charlett. It is here printed from a

[1] See also under the year 1710.

[2] [Walker's] *Letters by Eminent Persons*, i. 173.

[3] Ellis's *Letters of Eminent Literary Men*, Camd. Soc. pp. 302–3.

copy sent by Hyde to Wake, then Rector of St. James, Westminster, and preserved amongst the Wake Correspondence in the library of Ch. Ch.[1]:—

'*March* 10, $\frac{1700}{01}$,
'CHRIST CHURCH, OXON.

'SIR,—I being a little indisposed by the gout, acquaint you thus by letter, that what I long agoe designed (as you partly knew) I am now about to put in execution. That is to say, I shall shortly lay down my office of Library-keeper, about a month hence, which resolution I do now declare, and I do hereby give you timely and statuteable notice of the same as Pro-Vice-Chancellor, entreating that, as the Statute requires, you will in two days order Mr. Cowper to draw a Programma to be set up at the Schools to the sence of the enclosed paper, he best knowing forms and lawyers' Latin.

'Among the Bodleian Statutes in the Appendix, in the Statute *de causis amovendi aut libere recedendi*, you will find that upon the Library-keeper's notice thus given, you are in two days' time to fix up the programma preparatory to make it known that about a month hence (which is about the end of this term) that office will be actually resigned and void.

'My reasons for leaving the place are two, viz. one is because (my feet being left weak by the gout) I am weary of the toil and drudgery of daily attendance all times and weathers; and secondly, that I may have my time free to myself to digest and finish my papers and collections upon hard places of Scripture, and to fit them for the press[2]; seing that Lectures (though we must attend upon them) will do but little good, hearers being scarce and practicers more scarce.

'I should have left the Library more compleat and better furnish'd but that the building of the Elaboratory[3] did so exhaust the University mony, that no books were bought in severall years after it. And at other times when books were sometimes bought, it was (as you well know) never left to me to buy them, the Vice-Chancellor not allowing me to lay out any University mony. And therefore some have blamed me without cause for not getting all sorts of books.

'Before the Visitations I did usually spend a month's time in prepar-

[1] Resolutions of the Curators follow, dated 11 March, 1700/01, that marriage after election should vacate the post, and that the offices of Keeper and Curator were incompatible. A letter from Hyde to Archbishop Tenison on the subject, in the same month, is in Lambeth MS. 953, f. 67.

[2] These were left in MS. at Hyde's death, and have never been published.

[3] *i.e.* the Ashmolean Museum.

ing a list of good books to offer to the Curators; but I could seldom get them bought, being commongly (*sic*) answered in short, that they had no mony. Nay, I have been chid and reproved by the Vice-Chancellor for offering to put them to so much charge in buying books. These things at last discouraged me from medling in it. But, however, I leave the Library three times bigger than I found it [1], and furnished with a Catalogue of which I found it destitute. I wish the University a man who may take as much pains and drudgery as I have done whilst I was able to do it.

'I entreat you with all speed to cause the Register to put up the programma signed with your name, that so things may be regularly and statutably dispatched in order, until the time of actuall resignation shall come.

'In the mean time I remain,

'Your humble servant,

'THOMAS HYDE.'

John Hudson, M.A., of Queen's, afterwards D.D. and Princ. of St. Mary Hall, was elected in Hyde's room; he was opposed by J. Wallis, M.A., of Magd., the Laudian Professor of Arabic, but was chosen by 194 votes to 173 [2]. A letter to him from Hyde on his election, with advice about the entering of Sir H. Sloane's books in the Register, the augmentation of Mr. Crabbe's salary, the Catalogues and the Statutes, is printed in [Walker's] *Letters by Eminent Persons*, i. 173. He had previously, in 1696–98, given seventy books to the Library, and in 1705–10 he added nearly 600. Hyde did not long survive his resignation, dying before two years had elapsed, on Feb. 18, 170$\frac{2}{3}$. He was buried at Handborough, near Oxford.

In this year Thomas Hearne, the famous antiquary, was appointed Janitor, or Assistant, in the Library. He tells us in his *Autobiography* (p. 10) that, from the time of his taking the degree of B.A. in Act term, 1699, 'he constantly went to the Bodleian Library every day, and studied there as long as the time allowed by the Statutes would admit,' and that the fact of this his 'diligence

[1] Hyde was greatly mistaken here, as a calculation made by Hearne in 1714 (*q. v.*) showed that the Library had then little more than doubled since 1620.

[2] *Reliqq. Hearn.* ii. 616.

being taken notice of by all persons that came thither, and his skill in books being likewise well known to those with whom he had at any time conversed,' occasioned Hudson's appointing him to be an Assistant immediately upon his own election as Librarian. It appears from the Visitors' Book that a payment of £10 was made to him in this year, and that in the next year £30 were voted to him for his assistance in making an Appendix to the Catalogue of printed books [1], and for enlarging and correcting the Catalogues of MSS. and Coins. Extra payments of 50*s*. were also made to him in 1704 and 1706, and of 20*s*. in 1709.

The Bodley Speech. See 1682.

A. D. 1702.

On Dec. 3, 1702, Tho. Hyde writes to Dr. Hudson telling him that he has examined two Chinese MSS., *Miscellanea Sinica* and *Dictionarium Germanico-Sinicum*, and thinks them well worth £6 or £7 as between man and man, but would advise him to give £10 rather than lose them, 'because they are really a rarity, and there is not yet any thing of that kinde in the Public Library, to which they will be an additional ornament [2].'

A considerable number of printed books were given by Steph. Penton, B.D. Fifteen shillings were paid 'for a Hyrogliffick Board to the Museum.'

A. D. 1704.

The name of John Locke appears in the Register, as the donor of his own works (which he gave at Hudson's request), together with some others, including, with an honourable fairness, those of Bishop Stillingfleet written in controversy with himself. As Locke's expulsion from Ch. Ch., in 1684, by royal mandate, for political reasons, is sometimes, with an injustice which he himself would doubtless have warmly repudiated, represented as if it had

[1] For an account of Hearne's Appendix, see 1738.

[2] Bodl. MSS. Addit. c. 78, fol. 6. An entry in the Accounts for the year sets down £7 1*s*. as allowed to Hudson, possibly for this purchase; but I have not traced the books themselves, and they very likely were not bought.

been the act of Oxford itself, it is worth while to quote the language in which this gift from him, twenty years afterwards, is recorded, and recorded, too, by the pen of the earnest and conscientious Jacobite, Thomas Hearne: 'Joannes Lock, generosus, et hujus Academiæ olim alumnus, præter Opera ab ipso edita, ob ingenii elegantiam, doctrinæ varietatem, et philosophicam subtilitatem, omnibus suspicienda (*here follow the titles of his own works*), insuper ex suo in optimas artes amore, animoque ad supellectilem literariam augendam propenso, Bibliothecæ huic dono dedit libros sequentes;' *scil.* Churchill's *Voyages and Travels*, 4 vols., 1704, Stillingfleet's *Vindication of the Doctrine of the Trinity*, Stillingfleet's *Answer to Locke*, and Rob. Boyle's *History of the Air*. Locke desired, in a codicil to his will, that in compliance with a second request from Hudson, all his anonymous works should also be sent to the Library [1].

William Raye, formerly consul at Smyrna, presented about 600 coins, chiefly Greek, which E. Lhwyd (who reported their number to be about 2000) said he had been told had been collected at Smyrna by his cook [2]. But the Benefaction Register records that they were obtained by Raye from the widow of one 'domini Dan. Patridge,' who had himself intended to present them to the University. They were put in order, and a Catalogue made of them, some years afterwards, by Hearne, who intended to have given the Catalogue to the Library, 'had not,' he says, 'the ill usage he afterwards met with there obliged him to alter his mind [3].' But, happily, this Catalogue, as well as two copies, is in the Coin-room of the Library (having doubtless been included in Rawlinson's bequest), in a folio volume, very neatly written, which contains also catalogues of the Laud, Freke, Nourse, and other collections. Raye also gave a Turkish almanac.

'Our Public Library, which for some years had stood still, is now in a thriving condition by the active diligence and curiosity of Dr.

[1] Lord King's *Life of Locke*, edit. 1830, vol. ii. p. 51.

[2] [Walker's] *Letters by Eminent Persons*, i. 137.

[3] *Life*, p. 13, in *Lives of Leland, Hearne, and Wood*, 1772.

Hudson, who spares no author, no bookseller, but solicits all to augment that vast treasure. Our anniversary Visitation is the 8th of November, the day of opening, when the Curators inspect the whole number. I visited in behalf of Dr. Jane, who is indisposed. The Vice-Chancellor and Curators very much applauded the successful pains of the Librarian.' (Letter from Dr. Charlett to Dr. Lister, 22 Nov. 1704, in Lister MS., Bodl. Libr., 37, No. 34.)

A. D. 1705.

Rev. Abednego Seller bequeathed a MS. of the end of cent. xv containing William of Malmesbury *De Gestis Pontificum* (a copy as yet uncollated by editors), and the *Chronicon Lichfeldense*. It is now numbered Bodl. 956. Hearne says that a gentleman had 'offered to give at least 150 guineas for it[1].'

Rev. Lewis Atterbury, LL.D., having published in this year some letters relating to Sarpi's *Hist. of the Council of Trent* from Father Fulgentio, Archbp. Abbot, etc., to Sir Nath. Brent, the original publisher of the History, which he had obtained from Basil Brent, the son of Sir Nathaniel, presented the originals to the Library. They are now numbered Bodl. MS. 659. A MS. of Tacitus was given by Charles Bernard, a distinguished surgeon; and various printed books by Dr. George Hickes.

A. D. 1706.

The supposed original MS. of *The Causes of the Decay of Christian Piety*, by the author of *The Whole Duty of Man*, was given by Mr. Keble, the London bookseller. It is now numbered Bodl. MS. 21. Dr. Aldrich was of opinion that it is not in the author's own hand, but copied in a disguised hand by Bishop Fell. Hearne thought it to be in a disguised hand of Sancroft's; but the resemblance is very slight indeed[2].

[1] Rawl. MS. C. 867, f. 36b.

[2] See *Letters by Eminent Persons*, vol. ii. pp. 133–4. The claim of Dr. Rich. Allestree to the authorship has been strongly urged by Mr. C. E. Doble, M.A., in letters to the journal entitled the *Academy* in the year 1882, pp. 348, 364, 382.

A. D. 1707.

Seven volumes of Archbishop Ussher's *Collectanea*, with another MS. which had belonged to him, were given to the Library by James Tyrrell, the historian, who was the archbishop's grandson, together with his own *History of England.* He had placed them previously in the hands of Dr. Mill, for use by him in his edition of the Greek Test., and it was about a week before Mill's death, June 21, 1707, that they were transferred (together with a gift from Mill of various printed books) to the Library[1]. They are placed among the Bodl. Additional MSS., and one volume containing various readings in the Greek Test. is numbered Auct. T. v. 30. Other volumes of Ussher's MS. collections are Barlow, 10 and 13; *e Musæo*, 46 and 47; Rawl. Letters, 89; Rawlinson C. 849, 850, and several in Rawlinson D, all of which came to Rawlinson by Tyrrell's having given them to Hearne. Hearne has printed some extracts at the end of *Gul. Neubrig.* iii. 804. Six Samaritan and other MSS. which belonged to Ussher are now in the class called *Bodl. Orient.*

By the bequest of Dr. Humphrey Hody (who died 21 Jan.) the Library acquired some 400 or 500 volumes, being all those in his own collection which were wanting here, together with his MS. *Collectanea*. These last, amounting to twenty-three volumes, are now numbered Bodl. Addit. A. 65–85, C. 44–6, and Gr. Misc. 330.

Thomas Wardapiet (which is the very doubtful name by which he is entered in the Convocation Register, Bd. 32, f. 33b), Archbishop of Gocthan, in Armenia, visited England on an errand which seems to have justly excited great sympathy and attention. Sensible of the low condition of his fellow-countrymen, through their want of means of instruction, and being earnestly anxious to do something towards their elevation, he had spent some forty years in travels through Europe and Asia for the purpose of procuring books, establishing printing-presses, educating young men, and obtaining help for the furtherance of his Christian and patriotic

[1] Hearne's *MS. Diary*, xv. 24.

projects. His first printing establishment, at Marseilles, was ruined by the mismanagement and fraud of those to whom it was entrusted. He then, for ten years, carried on a press at Amsterdam, where he printed, in Armenian, the New Testament, the Prayers and Hymns of the Church, a translation of Thomas à Kempis, and several other theological works, together with some in geography, history, and science. But troubles and trials again overtook him; disputes and law-suits involved him in debt; one hundred books, which he shipped for Armenia in 1698, were taken at sea, and so never reached their destination. And so, poor and sorrowful, in extreme old age, the Archbishop came to England to seek for help, recommended by Dr. John Cockburn, the English minister at Amsterdam. He was well received by the Archbishops, and Sharp, of York, procured him an interview with the Queen, who gave him some assistance. Then, recommended by Bishop Compton[1], of London, he came to Oxford. What he received in the way of the help which he most of all needed, deponent sayeth not; let us hope it was not small. What he received in the way of honour, and what he did to cause the introduction of his name in these *Annals*, Hearne tells, in his own interesting way, in his *Diary*[2]:—

'May 24. Last night came to Oxon one of the Armenian Patriarchs. He is Patriarch of the Holy Cross in Gogthan (near Mount Ararat) in Greater Armenia. He subscribes himself in his speech to the Queen in the last month, by translation, Thomas. The next day he was attended to the publick Library by Dr. Charlett, Pro-Vice-Chancellor. At the entrance, Dr. Hudson, the Keeper, made him a handsome complement in Latin; but the Patriarch, being about 90 years of age, and understanding no Latin, nor Greek, nor any European language but Italian, took but little notice of any thing. He afterwards was carried to Dr. Charlett's lodgings, where he was treated.

'May 29. This day was a Convocation in the Theatre, when the Archbishop of the Holy Cross in Gocthan was created Doctor of

[1] And by the good Robert Nelson (*Letters by Eminent Persons*, i. 167, 9), who had also obtained ten guineas for him from the Christian Knowledge Society (Secretan's *Life of Nelson*, pp. 113-4).

[2] Vol. xiv. pp. 64, 68.

Divinity, and his nephew, Luke Nurigian, and Mr. [Patrick] Cockburn, son of Dr. Cockburn, were created Masters of Arts. The day before, the Archbishop presented to the publick Library several books in Armenian which he has caused to be printed. Mr. Wyatt, the orator, spoke a speech in his commendation, and presented him, the Queen having been pleased to let us be without a Professor. During the Convocation, several papers printed at the Theatre were given to the Doctors, Noblemen, and some others, entitled, *Reverendissimi in Christo Patris Thomæ, Archiepiscopi Sanctæ Crucis in Gocthan Perso-Armeniæ, peregrinationis suæ in Europam, pietatis et literarum promovendarum caussa susceptæ, brevis narratio; una cum dicti Archiepiscopi ad serenissimam Magnæ Britanniæ Reginam oratiuncula ejusque responso. Accedunt de eodem Archiepiscopo testimonia ampla et præclara.* Printed upon two sheets, folio [1].'

In another volume of memoranda [2], Hearne adds the following notice of one of the books given by the Archbishop: 'Amongst other books which he gave to the Bodleian Library is a History, at the beginning of which the Archbishop's nephew put the following memorandums: "*Historia Nationis Armeniæ, a Moise Chorenensi grammatico doctore Armeno.* Amst. 1695. Maii 28, 1707, Bibliothecæ Bodleianæ dono dedit reverendiss. Thomas Archiep. S. Crucis in Majori Armenia. Per manum ejusd. reverendiss. nepotis, Lucæ Nurigianidis." Underneath which is written, at the motion of Dr. Charlett, and by the direction of the said Archbishop's nephew: "Auctorem istius libri floruisse traditur seculo quarto post Christum."' The book is now numbered, 8º N. 134 Th.

A.D. 1708.

In this year died Henry Jones, M.A., Vicar of Sunningwell, Berks [3]. He bequeathed to the Library sixty volumes in MS., very miscellaneous in character, and chiefly of the 16th and 17th

[1] A copy of this tract is in V. 1. 1 Jur.

[2] Rawlinson MS. C. 876, p. 44.

[3] His will is dated 25 Oct. 1707, and was proved 20 Apr. 1708 (Somerset House; *Barrett*, 95). In Steele's *MSS. Collections for Berks*, Gough MS. 27, he is erroneously said to have died in 1700. Perhaps he resigned his living in that year. He is included in the list of Non-jurors printed at the end of Kettlewell's *Life*.

centuries. Some of them had belonged to Bishop Fell. It was from a modern transcript among these that Hearne edited the *Historia Regum Angliæ* of John Ross or Rouse; and seventy-one documents from No. 23, which is an Hereford Chartulary, were printed by Rawlinson at the end of his *History of Hereford*, 8o. Lond. 1717. One volume has for many years been missing from the collection, viz., a funeral oration, by John Sonibanck, on the death of Queen Elizabeth of York, in 1503. A list of the MSS. is printed from the Benefaction Register, in Uffenbach's *Commercium Epistolicum*, pp. 200–208.

A.D. 1709.

In this year the first Copyright Act was passed, which required the depositing of copies of all works entered at Stationers' Hall at nine libraries in England and Scotland. This number was increased upon the Union with Ireland to eleven, but finally reduced to five (British Museum; Oxford; Cambridge; Advocates' Library, Edinburgh; and Trinity College, Dublin) by 6 & 7 Will. IV. c. 110. The Act now regulating the claim is 5 & 6 Vict. c. 45.

A.D. 1710.

Dr. Richard Middleton Massey, formerly of Brasenose College, gave (with a few other books) a very curious and valuable series of Registers of the Parliamentary Committee for augmentation of poor vicarages, from 1645 to 1653, in eight folio volumes. To local antiquaries these proceedings are full of interest, while their historical and biographical value is equally great. They are now numbered Bodl. MSS. 322–329. Of the donor the following account is given in Hearne's *Diary*, vol. xxix., pp. 178–9, under date of 9 June, 1711:—

'Last night I was with one Mr. Middleton Massey, formerly of Brase-nose College, and one of the Keepers of the Museum Ashmoleanum. He took no degree, being a Non-juror. He now practises Physick with good reputation at Wisbich, in the Isle of Ely. He is a man of good curiosity and well skilled in drawing. He collects divers coyns, MSS., and other things of that nature. He is communicative, and corresponds with some men of learning. He has given us something to the Bodleian Library, and designs other benefactions. He gave divers things also formerly to the Museum Ashmoli, but he complains that he cannot now find them, and indeed several other things are there missing.'

Dr. Massey gave in 1726 a large number of printed books, and in 1730 a portrait of Nicolas Harpsfield. Of the printed books, most of those in octavo were placed at the end of Bishop Barlow's books, in the shelves marked *D. Linc.*

Three thousand pounds were offered by the University, through Dr. Rich. Bentley, for the library of Isaac Vossius, but refused. But the books were shortly afterwards sold to the University of Leyden for the same sum[1].

Among some books given by Sir Hans Sloane in this year were two MS. volumes of collections of Bp. Bale relating to the history of the Carmelite order. These were brought to the Library by T. Tanner, then Chanc. of Norwich, and are mentioned by Hearne in 1715 as being there then. But in 1726 an entry in an old hand-list of the 'Bodl.' MSS. records that one of the two vols. was missing at the Visitation in that year, and unhappily it has never been found since. The two vols. are entered in the *Cat. MSS. Angl.*, 1697, as being then in the possession of Dr. Francis Bernard.

A. D. 1711.

A watch which had belonged to Dudley, Earl of Leicester, is said to have been presented by Mr. Ralph Howland, of Maidenhead. It is not now in the Library, or in the Ashmolean Museum, and must therefore have been lost.

Grabe's *Adversaria.* See 1724.

'1711 Nov. 12. Mond.

'Dr. Hudson having lately, by leave (as he says) of the Vice-Chancellor, erected a study over the staircase by the Jurisprudentia School, (the charges of which came to about twenty pounds) on Tuesday last

[1] *Reliquiæ Hearn.* i. 205, 6.

Nov. 6 the Delegates of accounts order'd the same to be pull'd down again, and voted it a nusance. Accordingly Will. Sherwin one of the yeomen-beadles was sent to Dr. Hudson to acquaint him with the resolution, and to tell him that the study must be pull'd down on Monday Nov. 12 immediately following. The Dr. took this very much amiss, but thought that upon better consideration they might give a counter-order. But instead of this on Saturday last, Nov. 10, Sherwin comes again to the Library, and tells the Dr. that the study must down on Monday, and therefore desir'd him to remove his things. The Dr. immediately upon this remov'd all his things, and this day the study was pull'd down. That which, I believe, chiefly mov'd the Delegates and Curators was this, that the study was built without their consent, that it very much defac'd and darken'd the stair-case, that the Dr. turn'd a good part of the study into a ware-house for holding his own books that he printed, and that there was no manner of occasion for a new study, there being two studys already for the Librarian, one in the Library, and the other (a large one) in the Gallery, the latter of which Dr. Hudson had for several years turn'd into a ware-house, and not put to its proper use [1].'

A.D. 1712.

'July 19, Died Mr. Joseph Crabb, Under-keeper of the Bodleian Library, having kept in ever since this day sennight. He died of a rheumatism, occasion'd by a careless sort of life. He was, however, an honest harmless man. He was buried on Monday night following (between 7 and 8 o'cl.) in Haly-well Church-yard, very privately. Upon his coffin was put, *I. C. ag.* 38. 1712; but I heard him say some time since he was 39 years old [2].' He is described in the following caustic terms by Zach. Conr. Uffenbach, in a letter written in 1713, and printed in his *Commercium Epistolicum* [3]:—

'Alteri [præfecto Bibliothecæ], nomine Crab, caput vacuum cerebro est, lepidum alias, dignusque homo quem ridiculo illo encomio, quo

[1] Hearne's *MS. Diary*, xxxii. 21–24.

[2] *Ibid*, xxxvii. 180.

[3] 1753, p. 182. For the reference to this passage the author is indebted to Dibdin's *Bibliogr. Decam.* iii. 281. The same volume of Uffenbach's contains some criticisms on Bernard's Cat. of the MSS., chiefly with relation to the Barocci collection, and extracts from additional entries in the *Reg. Benef.*

tamen multi serio egregios viros onerarunt, ornetur, vociteturque Helluo, non librorum tamen sed præmiorum, quæ ab exteris Bibliothecam hanc invisentibus avide excipit, statimque cauponibus reddit pro liquore, ad guttur colluendum purgandumque a pulvisculo, qui librorum tractationem velut umbra aut nebula comitari solet: quamvis non ejus, sed tertii infimique Bibliothecarii, hoc sit muneris, ut libros in loculos reponat, quævis in ordinem redigat atque emundet.'

In vol. iii. of the same author's *Reisen*, printed in 1754, there is a very long and minute account of his stay in Oxford during three months in the year, 1710, and of his frequent visits to the Bodleian[1]. He there describes Crabb in still more severe terms as being a very ignorant and 'gold-hungering' man, who knew little or nothing of the Library, was unable to read MSS., and (as said also in the passage quoted above) only cared for the exorbitant fees which he extracted from visitors to spend in drink. His account of Hudson corresponds with that which is quoted from his letters under the year 1718, *infra*. The whole story of Uffenbach's life at Oxford is curious, amusing, and life-like. An abstract of it is given in an elaborate appendix to an as yet unfinished and therefore unpublished edition of the *Life of Ambrose Bonwicke*, prepared by Rev. J. E. B. Mayor, of St. John's Coll., Cambridge, pp. 374–9, 386, 391. The same volume contains an abstract of Fr. Burman's Travels in England in 1702, in which visits to the Bodleian are mentioned.

The date of Crabb's appointment has not been ascertained, but it was previous to 1692, as he is mentioned as holding the appointment in that year in the quotation from Sam. Wesley, which will be found on page 183. On Nov. 8, 1699, an order appears in the Visitors' Book for an extra payment to him of

[1] At p. 91 Uffenbach gives an engraving of the light, elegant, and convenient stair-cases which formerly gave access on either side of the library to the central galleries of *Jur.* and *Linc.* which were very unfortunately removed with the galleries in 1877, although actually still needed for access to other galleries. It is the only distinct representation of these stair-cases in existence. The stair-cases to the galleries in the Sheldonian Theatre were probably copied from these in their design, or *vice versa*.

£10[1]; other additional payments of £5 and 50*s*. are made to him annually until 1710. Two vols. of an index to texts of printed sermons, ending about the year 1708, (now Bodl. MSS. 47 and 657,) which were, doubtless, intended to form a continuation of Verneuil's little book, are said in an old entry in the Catalogue to be by 'Mr. Crabb.' The following brief account of him is given in Rawlinson's MSS. collections for a continuation of Wood's *Athenæ*:—

'Joseph Crabb, son of Will. Crabb, clerk, born at Child-Ockford in Dorsetshire on —— 1674; educated in grammar learning at ——; matriculated as a member of Exeter College, 18 July 1691: took the degree of B.A. 17 Oct. 1695; became Sub-librarian at the public library; removed to Gloucester Hall, where he became M.A. 4 July 1705, and died ——.'

Rawlinson goes on to attribute to him (as his solitary claim to a place in the *Athenæ*) a *Poem on the late Storm*, Lond. 1704, fol., but this was written (as well as a Latin poem *In Georgium reducem*, Lond. 1719, fol.) by his brother John Crabb, Fellow of Exeter College (B.A., Oct. 15, 1685; M.A., June 19, 1688), who was also a Sub-librarian at an earlier period, but the date of whose entrance into office as well as of quittance is not known[2]. It was before or about 1677, as he is mentioned as 'Mr. Krabbe, vice-bibliothecarius, vir humanissimus,' in a volume of Travels in England in 1677–8, by Oliger Jacobæus, a Dane, preserved in MS. in the Royal Library, Copenhagen, new Royal MS. 4°. 375 (*see* Append. ii. to 46th Report of the Dep. Keeper of Public Records, p. 72). Samuel Wesley, of Epworth (the father of John and Charles) refers to him as being sub-librarian at the time of his own entrance into the University, which must have been

[1] This was granted at Hyde's urgent request, 'in regard of his great pains in entering books in the Catalogue, and of the smallness of his place.' Letter from Hyde to Hudson, in Walker's *Letters*, i. 174.

[2] He is mentioned in a volume of miscellaneous collections by Hannibal Baskerville (Rawlinson, MS. D. 810), in a note on Exeter College, as being a scholar of that college and 'one of the University Library-keepers' in 1686.

about 1684, as Wesley took his degree in 1688. It is in an autobiographical letter [to Dr. Peter Barwick?] which accompanied the original MS. of Wesley's *Account of dissenting Academies*, and which is dated Aug. 22, 1692, that this notice of John Crabb occurs. After mentioning the drunken habits which generally prevailed at Oxford, Wesley proceeds thus:—

'However, even then I found 'twas possible to live soberly there, as I know severall did when I came thither, addressing myself to Mr. Crabb, a Dorsetshire man and my countryman, who was then second librarian, as his brother is now (or was lately); with whom I had severall discourses on the subjects in controversy between the Dissenters and Church of England, and was pretty well satisfied in many things, tho' not so well as to come quite over at that time..... [Returning to Oxford, I] arrived there Sept. 22, 1684, addressing myself to Mr. Crabb, who received me with great humanity and kindness, and I having spent about 20*s*. of my small estate' (only £3 altogether) 'in my journey, and the purchase of a servitor's cap and gown, he supplied me with 20*s*. more, which made up my caution money.'

When ready to take his degree, Wesley 'was employed to transcribe some manuscripts in the Bodley, by which I gott money enough to take my degree, and had besides ten guineas in bank.' A copy of this letter, as yet unpublished, is in Rawlinson MS. C. 406.

John Crabb became incumbent of the donative of Breamore, Hants in 1709, where he died in 1748 at the age of eighty-five. He is remarkable for having married four wives, all of whom lie buried with him in his church. The third of these, Grace Shuckbridge, became his wife when he was aged seventy-six and she was forty-nine; the last (who survived until March 13, 1777) was thirty-six when she took him, at the age of eighty-one, for better or worse. There is a handsome marble tablet to his memory on the north wall of the chancel of Breamore Church, bearing the following inscription, and surmounted by his arms (*scil.*, on a field gules a chevron, in chief two fleur-de-lis, in base a crab displayed or; crest. a demi-lion rampant or) in their proper tinctures:—

'H. S. E. Reverend. Johan. Crabb, A.M. è Coll. Exon quondam Socius Oxon., Bibliothecæ Bodleianæ Sub-Librarius, et a sacris olim Episc.

Fowler, hujus Parochiæ Minister residens amplius XXXVIII ann. Vir doctus, pius, generosus, in Ecclesiâ orthodoxus, in Republicâ fidelis, et omnibus liberalis. Author Georgianæ et aliorum Carminum celebrium Latine et Anglice. Obiit tandem XIII Id. Martii, Anno ætat. suæ LXXXV., Æræ Christianæ MDCCXLVIII [1].'

On July 22, Thomas Hearne was appointed Second-keeper by Dr. Hudson, in the room of Joseph Crabb, while still retaining his post as Janitor, 'with liberty allow'd him of being keeper of the Anatomy schoole, or Bodleian repository, on purpose to advance the perquisites of the place, which are very inconsiderable [2],' but with the proviso that the salary of the janitor's place should go to an assistant officer. By this arrangement Hearne retained the keys, so that he could go in and out when he pleased [3].

'Sept. 16, Dr. Hudson told me to-day that some have complain'd that books in the Public Library are not so easily come at as usual. I am glad there is such a complaint. I am afraid the complainers are such as us'd to steal books from the Library, and, upon that account, are concern'd that they are more strictly look'd after than formerly [4].'

A.D. 1713.

The learned and munificent Narcissus Marsh, Archbishop successively of Cashel, Dublin, and Armagh, on his death, Nov. 2, in this year, bequeathed to the Library a very large and valuable gathering of Oriental MSS., which had been chiefly procured for him in the East by Huntington, and at the sale of Golius' library, at Leyden, in October, 1696, by Bernard. They were received at

[1] For the above particulars of John Crabb's history subsequent to his leaving Oxford the author was indebted to the late Rev. Dr. J. H. Blunt, once Curate in charge of the parish of Breamore, who mentioned with reference to Crabb's connubial experiences, the parallel case of Bishop John Thomas, Bishop of Lincoln and afterwards of Salisbury, 1743-61. At his fourth wedding that prelate had the good taste and feeling to present his friends with memorial rings inscribed with the couplet:—

'If I survive
I'll make them five.'

But the lady did not afford him the wished-for opportunity. See Nichols' *Lit. Anecd.* iv. 732.

[2] Hearne's *MS. Diary*, xxxvii. 191.

[3] *Life*, 1772, p. 14.

[4] *MS. Diary*, xxxix. 120.

Oxford in August, 1714[1]. The collection numbers at present 714 volumes, but probably some of these may have been books added for convenience sake from other sources. Many of them bear the motto of some former owner (*qu.* Golius?), somewhat like Selden's in form, but better in spirit, 'πανταχῆ τὴν ἀλήθειαν[2].' It is strange that no notice of this liberal gift is found in any of the Library Registers, and it is only from a passing mention in Hearne's preface to Camden's *Elizabeth* (p. lxvi) that we find it was a death-bed legacy, and consequently learn the date of its acquisition[3]. Hearne there says that the books were placed in the Library 'in tenebris in angulo quodam Bibliothecæ;' and this expression was made one of the subjects of complaint against him when prosecuted in 1718 in the Vice-Chancellor's court on account of that preface. He then replied that the expression was correct, for that they were placed in a dark corner to which access was only had through a trap-door, but that he himself had put them there for want of a better place. He had wished to deposit them in one of the rooms in the Picture Gallery, but Dr. Hudson kept that for his own purposes[4].

At this period every stranger admitted to read in the Library had to pay nine shillings in fees, of which 1*s.* went to the Head Librarian, 3*s.* 6*d.* to the Second Librarian, 1*s.* 6*d.* to the Janitor, 2*s.* to the Registrar (for an order for admission, but in the Long Vacation this fee went to the Second Librarian), and 1*s.* to the Proctor's man[5]. In 1720 the fee to be received from every visitor not qualified to read was fixed at one penny, to be paid to a

[1] Convoc. Reg. B[d]. 31, f. 113.

[2] Gilbert Wakefield's book-motto was a combination of the two; below an engraved representation of the hart panting after the water-brooks were the words, 'Αλήθειαν καὶ 'Ελευθερίαν.

[3] The Archbishop held frequent correspondence with Dr. Thomas Smith, and his letters are to be found in vol. lii. of Smith's MSS. while copies by the latter of his own letters are to be found in vol. lxiv (formerly lviii). One long letter from the Archbishop contained in the former volume, relative to the Irish version of the Old Testament, was printed with notes, by Dr. J. Henthorn Todd, in the Dublin *Christian Examiner* for 1833, new series, vol. ii. pp. 761–772.

[4] Hearne's *MS. Diary*, vol. lxxi. May 20.

[5] *Ibid.*, vol. xlvii. p. 89.

porter who was then first appointed to the charge of the Picture Gallery. It subsequently rose by a silent custom to the exorbitant sum of a shilling; but some twenty-five years ago the Curators fixed the charge to visitors at threepence each, unless accompanied, and in consequence *franked*, by some member of the University in his academic dress. Since this moderate sum has been fixed, the number of ordinary sight-seeing visitors has, naturally, much increased[1].

The suppression, by an order of the Heads of Houses, dated March 23, 171$\frac{2}{3}$, of Hearne's edition of Dodwell's tract *De Parma Equestri Woodwardiana*, was attributed by Hearne himself to (as the remote occasion) an incident connected with his office in the Library which is related very fully by himself in vol. xliv. of his *MS. Diary*. On Feb. 20, Mr. Keil, the Savilian Professor of Geometry, brought to the Library an Irish gentleman named Mollineux, recommended by Sir Andrew Fountaine, to whom he requested Hearne to show the curiosities of the place. As Keil was 'a very honest gentlemen,' Hearne little suspected that his friend was possessed with the 'republican ill principles' and 'malignant temper' of Whiggism, and consequently was not very guarded in his talk. After showing him various MSS. and coins, he took the visitor into the Anatomy School[2], where all kinds of odds and ends were preserved; amongst which was (as Hearne gravely notes in another place) a calf which, being born in the year of the Union, 1707, had (it is to be presumed in consequence thereof) two bodies and one

[1] In an account of a visit to Oxford by an American tourist, which appeared in 1867 in the *New York Times*, and was copied into English journals, written with the warm-hearted tone of one who could rightly appreciate the interest of the place, although (like many Transatlantic visitors) he spent but twenty-four hours in it, the following comment is made upon the smallness of this Bodleian fee:—'The gentleman [i. e. the late Janitor, Mr. John Norris] who showed me through this noble collection, and gave me the most interesting explanations, politely informed me that the charge was 3*d*. It went against my conscience to give a gentleman of his civility and erudition the price of a pot of beer, and I added a small testimonial, for which he seemed more than sufficiently grateful.'

[2] This was the room which is now attached to the Library under the name of the *Auctarium*.

head. What followed during the exhibition of this museum is worth relating in the diarist's own words:—

'I mentioned a picture engraved and hanging there with horns and wings, and underneath, *uxor ejus ad vivum pinxit.* This picture many had said was Benjamin Hoadley, the seditious divine of London: but, for my part, I gave no other description of it than this, that 'twas the picture of one of the greatest Presbyterian, republican, anti-monarchical, Whiggish, fanatical preachers living in England. And this description was enough to exasperate him. And yet, for all that, he did not discover any passion, nor give the least hint that he was a Whig himself. Neither did he give any hint of it afterwards till I came to mention a tobacco stopper tipped with silver, and given to me by a reverend divine, who had informed me that it was made out of an oak that lately grew in St. James's Park, but was destroyed by the D. of M. for the great house he was building near St. James's, and that the said oak came from an acorn that was planted there by King Charles II, being one of those acorns that he had gathered in the Royal Oak, where he was forced to shelter himself from the fury of the rebells after the fight at Worcester. Mr. Mollineux was at the other end of the room when this was shew'd, and the said story told; but hearing it he comes immediately to the tables, and expresses himself in words of this kind, viz. *that 'twas a bawble, and that an hundred such things were not worth the seeing.* Mr. Keil however thought otherwise, and said that he thought my collection was better than that in the Laboratory. Some mirth passing after this, I went on with my description, and had not yet formed an opinion that Mr. Mollineux was a Whig; but finding that he was still inquisitive after other curiosities, and that he pretended to much skill in good ingraving and drawing, I produced the picture of a beautifull young man, over the head of which was ΕἸΚῺΝ ΒΑΣΙΛΙΚΗ', and underneath, *Quid quæritis ultra?* I did not tell them whose picture it was, but said that I shew'd it them as a thing excellently well done, which they all allow'd and view'd it over and over, and seemed to be mightily taken with it, and Mr. Mollineux in particular was pleased to say that 'twas admirably well done, and deserved a place amongst the most exquisite performances of this kind, at the same time asking how long I had had it, and whose picture I took it to be. To the former of which questions I reply'd, about a quarter of a year, to the latter that I did not pretend to tell who it was designed for. Yet Mr. Keil was pleased to laugh, and to tell Mr. Mollineux, *They are all rebells, Mr. Mollineux, they are all rebells in this place*, speaking these words in a merry joking way, and not with any intent to do me an injury. Mr. Mollineux took the words upon the picture down, which I did not deny him, not thinking that 'twas with a design to inform against me, as it afterwards proved. Yet from this time I began a little to suspect his integrity, and that he was not one of those good men I exspected from Mr. Keil, whom I had always found to be a man of honesty.'

Hinc illæ lachrymæ! Poor Hearne was reported to Dr. Charlett the same afternoon for showing the 'Pretender's' Picture; a meeting of the Curators of the Library was threatened; but eventually the matter seemed to pass over by his being desired by the Vice-Chancellor to give up the key of the Anatomy School, in order that the determining Bachelors might meet there, by which change Hearne was mulcted of the fees which he obtained for showing the room, and was sometimes detained one hour, or two, later than usual in order to see to the locking up of the staircase on which it is situated. On March 23, however, he was summoned before the Heads of Houses for remarks made in his preface to Dodwell's abovementioned tract, and, after a sharp discussion, in which reference was made to his exhibition of the portraits, he was ordered to suppress his preface, and re-issue the book without it; to which he consented. He was pressed to make a formal retractation of the passages to which objection was made, but this he stiffly refused to do. He says in a letter to Sir Philip Sydenham that the only form of retractation or expression of sorrow he could have been prevailed on to sign (strongly resembling in spirit the famous apology of a middy to an insulted naval surgeon) would have been some such form as this:—'I, Thomas Hearne, A.M., of the University of Oxford, having ever since my matriculation followed my studies with as much application as I have been capable of, and having published several books for the honour and credit of learning, and particularly for the reputation of the foresaid University, am very sorry that by my declining to say anything but what I knew to be true in any of my writings, and especially in the last book I published, intituled, *Henrici Dodwelli de Parma Equestri Woodwardiana Dissertatio*, *&c.*, I should incurr the displeasure of any of the

Heads of Houses, and as a token of my sorrow for their being offended at truth, I subscribe my name to this paper, and permitt them to make what use of it they please[1].'

In this year John Christian Pepusch was created Mus. Doc. by recommendation from the Chancellor (the Duke of Ormonde), who in his letter dated 28 May, says that Pepusch, 'a foreigner and Protestant, who hath long resided in England, who is a person of good learning and singular skill as well in theory as the practice of musick, humbly prays, in consideration of his design shortly to publish a treaty[se] of musick from severall tracts now in the Bodleian Library, and other collections of his own already made, he may have the degree of Doctor of Musick conferred on him[2].' This proposed treatise does not seem, however, to have been ever published.

A.D. 1714.

An evidence of the increased intercourse which sprang up between Denmark and England, in consequence of the marriage of Queen Anne, is probably to be found in the number of Danish readers who frequented the Library in the interval between her marriage and her death. Between the years 1683 and 1714, forty-nine Danes are entered in the *Liber Admissorum*, besides many from Sweden, Norway, and the North of Germany[3]. The total number

[1] Hearne's *MS. Diary*, xlviii. 22. The retractation and apology which Hearne afterwards actually submitted to the Vice-Chancellor in Court in 1718, when in trouble again for his preface to Camden's Elizabeth, was very similar in style to this. But he was not allowed to read it. *Ibid.* lxxi. 3 May.

[2] Reg. Convoc. Bd. 31, f. 98. At the same time W. Croft was recommended for his degree, 'in consideration of composing, and, at his great charge, performing, the entertainment of musick for the Encænia.'

[3] Several volumes of travels by Danes who visited Oxford during this period are noted in my Report on MSS. in the Royal Library at Copenhagen, printed in the 46th Report of the Deputy-Keeper of the Public Records. To the notice there given (p. 73) of a visit in 1714, I may add that the writer (who lodged in Oxford at the house of a bookseller named Kibbelwhite, opposite St. Mary's Church) gives the rules of the Library, a copy of the Vice-Chancellor's notice expelling the Baron von Eulenberg (see p. 92) and presentation inscriptions in several books given by Danes.

of foreigners admitted within the same period was no less than 244.

'In the year 1714 were in the Bodleian Library:—

30169 pr. vols.
05916 MSS. vols.

In all 36085.'

(Hearne's *MS. Diary*, vol. xci. p. 256.)

It is strange that, notwithstanding Selden's and Laud's large additions, the Library had therefore very little more than doubled since 1620.

It is recorded in vol. li. of the same *Diary* (p. 187) that the old series of portraits which were painted on the wall of the Picture Gallery was renewed in November of this year. These portraits, amounting in number to about 222, ran round the gallery, immediately under the roof; many of them were fancy-heads of ancient philosophers and writers, but besides these there were some real portraits of English writers and divines, up to the time of James I. A list of the whole series, as well as of the oil paintings in the Gallery, was printed by Hearne together with his *Letter containing an Account of some Antiquities between Windsor and Oxford.* Of the renovation of the wall-paintings he thus speaks in his preface to *Rossi Historia Regum Angliæ* (1716): 'Non possim quin bibliothecæ Bodleianæ Curatores laudem, qui pictori Academico [*scil.*—Wild-goose] in mandatis dederunt, ut veteres effigies renovet nitorique pristino restituat: quippe quas eo pluris æstimandas esse censeo, quod eas in galeria depingendas jusserit ipse Bodleius, Loci Genius.' When the Gallery was re-roofed in 1831, all these paintings were, however, removed [*see* p. 18].

About the end of this year the Arundel Marbles (together with some given by Selden and by Sir George Wheeler), which, strange to say, had been exposed to the open air within the enclosure of the Schools, in niches in the walls that then shut in the Theatre, ever since they were given to the University, were removed into the Picture Gallery, and in 1749 into one of the rooms on the ground-floor, from which they were removed in 1888 to the University Galleries, a much more suitable place. It was said that they had suffered more 'since they were exposed to our air, than they did in many hundred years before they came into it[1].' But the influence of the air was not all they had to contend against, for Hearne tells us that the defacing of the Marble Chronicle (of which there are portions that were read by Selden which can now no longer be read at all) and some others, was owing not merely to exposure to the weather, but 'to the abuses of children who are continually playing in the area, and of other ignorant persons[2].'

Of their subsequent removal from the Gallery to the ground-floor H. Owen writes thus to Dr. Rawlinson, in a letter (bought in 1876) dated 27 Oct. 1749[3]:—

'I have been extremely busy this last summer in attending the workmen who were to remove the Arundel marbles out of the Schooles Gallery. As the removing of them was necessary in order to make room for the wainscotting the Gallery in a regular manner, which our honoured and worthy benefactor and friend, the Duke of Beaufort, undertook to do at his own expence, I was, as Librarian, charged with the care of seeing them properly placed in one of the ground-Schooles, which I prevailed upon the V. Chanc. and Delegates to allot for that purpose, being the only one well lighted, and that had an immediate communication with the Library by the staircase at the N. west angle of the quadrangle within the Schooles. I have placed them there, I hope to the satisfaction of every one that has seen them, in such a manner as to leave two sides of the room open to receive future benefactions.'

Wood tells us in his *Life* (*Ath. Oxon.* ed. Bliss, I. xli.) that the Selden marbles were distinguished by the letter S. and the Arundel by H. (for *Howard*).

A.D. 1715.

We learn from Hearne's *MS. Diary* [vol. liii.] that differences between him and Dr. Hudson (of which he makes frequent mention) increased during this year. He was reported to the Vice-Chancellor in April for absence from the Library through his duties as

[1] *Letters by Eminent Persons,* 1813, vol. i. p. 297.

[2] *Ibid.*, vol. i. p. 204.

[3] Rawl. MS. D. 912.

Bedel, by reason of which readers had difficulty in obtaining books lodged above stairs. To this complaint his reply was that he was not bound, as Second Librarian, exclusively to do such 'drudgery,' but that Dr. Hudson was himself obliged by statute to deliver out such books as were under lock-and-key, and books in quarto and octavo, either personally or by his own special deputy. At the same time a complaint was made against him by three Bachelors of Arts of Queen's College, for refusing books to them which were outside the faculty of Arts prescribed to them by the Statutes of the Library. Hearne's only reply to the Vice-Chancellor in this case was the asking whether they had, also in accordance with the Statutes, come to the Library in their hoods, if under two years' standing; at which 'he smiled.' It appears, therefore, that this requirement had already become obsolete[1]. Dr. Hudson, however, regarded the matter more seriously, and threatened that Hearne should be turned out of both his places.

April 15. (Good Friday!) 'This morning Dr. Hudson went out of town, and that pert jackanapes Bowles (who is Dr. Hudson's servitor) came to tell me that he is gone, and that the sweeper of the Library being dead, I must not admitt any one to sweep the Library as formerly. I returned answer I had nothing to do in that case. In the afternoon I was at study in the Library, and Bowles brings up a woman and girl, and set them to sweeping, and left them there, tho' this should not have been, they being not sworn nor admitted as sweepers. Indeed all things are now done very irregularly in the Library by the permission of Dr. Hudson, and by the impudence of this pert, silly servitour, and I am afraid much mischief is done withall. The whole Library and galleries and studies and the Anatomy School used to be swept this day; they began about eight, and had not done till four or five in the afternoon. But now the Library only below stairs was swept over,

[1] The wearing full academical costume had been at first rigidly enforced. A leaf in the first register-book of work done by the binder for the Library contains memoranda of six instances during the years 1613–1616, in which Bachelors of Arts appeared in the Library 'sine pileo et habitu,' for which offence they were in three of the cases excluded from the Library for a period of three months. One of the offenders (—Bray, of University College) was afterwards censured again for reading books which did not bear on his prescribed branches of study, whereupon 'in præsentia doctoris Buddeni verba brigosa dedit, et admodum insolenter se gessit.'

and that very slightly, and all things were left in a bad condition, to my very great concern[1].'

At the Visitation on Nov. 8, the Curators passed a resolution that the places of Under-librarian and Bedel were inconsistent, and that on St. Thomas' day Hudson should be at liberty to appoint some other person to Hearne's office. Hereupon Hearne immediately, without a moment's delay, resigned both the offices of Architypographus and Superior Bedel of Civil Law, and claimed to remain in the Library; but Hudson had fresh locks put on the doors, of which Bowles kept the keys, so that Hearne was unable to go in and out as before. However, he continued to execute his office whenever the Library was open until Jan. 23, 1716, when the Act which imposed a fine of £500, with other penalties, upon any one who held any public office without having taken the Oaths, came into operation. Then at once, all worldly interests, all affection for the old place of his studies and his care, gave way to the honest and unwavering dictates of his conscience; the Non-juror withdrew, and, with singularly hard measure, in spite of his representations, his place was ordered by the Curators to be filled up at Lady-Day, not on the ground of his own retirement, but on that of *neglect of duty!* His successor was Rev. John Fletcher, M.A., Chaplain, and afterwards Fellow, of Queen's College. Hearne states that his salary was, with great unfairness, withheld from him for the whole half-year preceding Lady-Day, together with some fees which were due[2]. But to the end of his life he maintained that he was still, *de jure*, Sub-librarian, and, with a quaint pertinacity, regularly at the end of each term and half-year, up to March 30, 1735[3], continued to set down, in one of the volumes of his Diary, that no fees had been paid him, and that his half-year's salary was due.

On Hearne's announcing John Ross's *Historia Angliæ* for publication in this year, W. Whiston forwarded to him a MS. of a

[1] Hearne's *MS. Diary*, liii. 124, 5.

[2] *Life*, 1772, pp. 18-20.

[3] He died on June 10 in that year.

Latin historical poem entitled *Britannica,* written in 1606 by an author of the same names as the forth-coming historian, with the following note inserted :—

'This book was written, as I think, by my great uncle, Mr. John Rosse, rector of Norton-juxta-Twycross in Leicestershire, where I was myself born. If it may be of any use to Mr. Hern at Oxford in his intended edition of this or some other work of the same author now advertis'd, or may be thought worthy of a place in the publick library of that University, it is hereby freely given thereto by

'WILLIAM WHISTON.

'London, December 12, 1715.'

Hearne adds that (of course) the author was altogether different from the Ross of his editing, and that the poem had been printed at Frankfort in 1607, as he learned from a MS. Catalogue of Mr. Richard Smith's books lent him by Bp. Fleetwood of Ely[1]. Whiston's MS. is now numbered Bodley 573.

A learned tailor of Norwich was in this year recommended by Dr. Tanner, then Chancellor of Norwich Cathedral, for the Janitor's place in the Library should it be vacant. Although but a journeyman tailor of about thirty years of age, who had been taught nothing but English in his childhood, Henry Wild had contrived within seven years to master seven languages, Latin, Greek, Hebrew, Chaldee, Syriac, Arabic and Persian, to which Tanner adds, in another letter to Dr. Rawlinson, Samaritan and Ethiopic. The application appears to have been unsuccessful so far as the holding office in the Library was concerned; but Wild found some employment in the Library for a time in the translating and copying Oriental MSS.[2] He removed to London about 1720, and died in the following year, as we learn from an entry in Hearne's *MS. Diary,* (xcii. 128–9,) under date of Oct. 29, 1721, where we read:—

'About a fortnight since died in London Mr. Henry Wild, commonly called, *the Arabick Taylour.* I have more than once mentioned him

[1] This catalogue was sold at the auction in 1855 of the MSS. of Dr. Routh, who had bought it at Heber's sale.

[2] *Letters by Eminent Persons,* i. 271, 300. [On p. 270 for *Turner,* read *Tanner.*]

formerly. He was by profession a taylour of Norwich, and was a married man. But having a strange inclination to languages, by a prodigious industry he obtain'd a very considerable knowledge in many, without any help or assistance from others. He understood Arabick perfectly well, and transcrib'd, very fairly, much from Bodley, being patroniz'd by that most eminent physician, Dr. Rich. Mead. He died of a feaver, aged about 39. He was about a considerable work, viz. a history of the old Arabian physicians, from an Arabick MS. in Bodley. The MS. was wholly transcrib'd by him a year agoe, but what progress he had made for the press I know not [1].'

Five MSS., including the Leiger Book of Malmesbury Abbey, together with a large number of printed books, were given on May 7, by William Brewster, M.D. of Hereford, a well-known antiquary [2].

A thick quarto volume (1052 pages) containing a Latin treatise by Adam Zernichaus on the controversy between the Eastern and Western Churches, concerning the Procession of the Holy Ghost, was forwarded to the Library through Sir Robert Sutton, ambassador at Constantinople, by Chrysanthus, Patriarch of Jerusalem, nephew and successor of Dositheus, an autograph Greek epistle from whom, occupying seven pages, is prefixed. At the end is a list of eleven German scribes who were employed upon the transcription of the volume, with the payments they severally received. It appears from the Benefaction Register that the volume was not actually received at the Library until 1722; and in 1731, an entry in the catalogue records that the MS. 'was restored to Sir Robert Sutton, by order of the Vice-Chancellor;' but no reason or explanation is given. For more than a century the Patriarch's gift was consequently lost from the place of its destination; but in Dec. 1864, having turned up for sale among the well-known stores of the late Mr. C. J. Stewart [*ob.* 1883], it was secured by the late Librarian at the cost of £5 15*s.* 6*d.*, and is once more to be found in its legitimate quarters, numbered MS. Bodl.

[1] Descriptions by him of some Arabic MSS. are given in the sale catalogue of Tho. Rawlinson's MSS. in 1734, pp. 78-81.

[2] Hearne's *Diary*, liii. 148.

1032. Chrysanthus also gave, in 1725, a copy of Dositheus' History of the Patriarchate of Jerusalem, which was printed, in Greek, in 1715.

A.D. 1716.

On Aug. 23, a legacy of £100 from Dr. South (who died July 8), for the purchase of modern books, was paid to the Vice-Chancellor [1].

At a Convocation held Dec. 13, a Chancellor's letter was read dispensing with one term's residence for the B.A. degree in the case of Joseph Bowles, commoner of St. Mary Hall, 'an assistant in the Publick Library,' in consideration of his having performed all exercises for the degrees of both bachelor of laws and bachelor of arts, 'and on account of his great pains and service in the Publick Library [2].' In 1719 he became Librarian.

Arms in the window. See 1610.

A.D. 1718.

One Mr. Hutton appears to have been employed in the Library during this year. It seems, from a passage in a letter of C. Wheatly's, printed in *Letters by Eminent Persons*, ii. 116, that the learned commentator Samuel Parker, son of the Bishop of Oxford, was also at some time employed in the Library; for Wheatly expresses a wish that S. Parker's son, then (1739) an apprentice to Mr. Clements the bookseller, might, if the accounts of his extraordinary proficiency be true, be placed 'in his father's seat, the Bodleian Library.' As Parker was a non-juror, his employment must doubtless have been at some earlier period than this, but his name is not met with in any of the old Account-books or Registers. One Thomas Parker occurs in the Library accounts in 1766 and in 1772.

The degree of B.D. was conferred (in pursuance of a Chancellor's letter in June) on Rev. John Reynolds, M.A., of King's College,

[1] Hearne's *Diary*, lix. 141; *Reliqq. Hearn.* i. 366.
[2] Reg. Convoc. Bd. 31, f. 137.

Cambridge, in return for his having 'lately presented to the Bodleian Library a very valuable collection of antient coyns[1].'

A. D. 1719.

Dr. Hudson died, on Nov. 27, of dropsy. And at one o'clock on the afternoon of the very next day, Joseph Bowles, M.A., of Oriel College, was elected in his room.

The bitter terms in which Hearne frequently, in the course of his *Diary*, condemns Hudson's management, or rather mismanagement, of the Library, may be supposed to be owing in a considerable degree to personal pique and quarrel[2]. But they meet with very singular and abundant confirmation in the letter of Z. C. Uffenbach, quoted above (p. 180), where the writer expresses, in the following strong language, his opinion of Hudson's neglect and incapacity, and of the general condition of the Library under his management:—

'Perpende, quæso, mecum, vir eruditissime, quantus thesaurus ex solius Bodleianæ Bibliothecæ codicibus elici possit, nisi Proto-Bibliothecarii Hudson negligentia ac pertinacia obstaret. Is enim muneri abunde satisfecisse, imo eximie ornasse Spartam, videri vult, dum tot annis unico scriptori, Thucydidem ejus puto, omni Bibliothecæ cura plane abjecta, insudavit, cum hoc, quod supra dixi, potius agendum fuisset. Nefandam hujus insignis Bibliothecæ sortem (ignosce justæ indignationi) satis deplorare nequeo. Inculta plane jacet, nemo ferme tanto thesauro uti, frui, gestit. Singulis sane diebus per trium mensium spatium illam frequentavi, sed, ita me dii ament, nunquam tot

[1] Reg. Convoc. Bd. 31, f. 152.

[2] In one passage, Hearne says that such was Hudson's self-esteem that he reckoned himself equal to Erasmus or Sir Thomas More, while all that was curious in his books was gained from Hearne himself or others. (*MS. Diary*, vol. lviii. p. 158.) But Hudson appears to have had, as every one in his office ought to have, a real *amor loci*, although a love as ill-regulated as his care: for in a copy of the English version, entitled *Celestial Worlds discovered*, of Huygens' book Κοσμοθέωρος, which belonged to him and subsequently to Sub-librarian Bilstone, and is now to be found in the Library, he subjoins the following line to the inscription of his name, 'satis beatus unicâ Bodleii bibliothecâ.' How ignorant in the midst of his books if he knew of no better and more enduring beatitude!

una vice homines in illa vidi quot numero sunt Musæ, vel saltem artes liberales. De librorum studiosis loquor; nam puerorum, mulierculelarum, rusticorum, hinc inde cursitantium, voluminumque multitudinem per transennas spectantium mirantiumque, cœtum excipio.... De Proto-bibliothecarii incuria jam dixi, ejusque stupendam in historia literaria librariaque, inprimis extra Insulam ultraque maria, ignorantiam taceo.'

Of Hearne, however, Uffenbach writes in the following different strain:—

'Hîc scholaris, ut hîc loqui amant, esse solet, atque etiamnum est, nomine Hearne, qui, præ reliquis, diligentiam suam non modo scriptis, sed in novo etiam Bibliothecæ catalogo confitiendo, typis proxime exscribendo, probavit; ast, quod dolendum, ad exemplum prioris, qui satis jejunus, inconcinnus, erroribusque innumeris scatens est.'

Hudson's successor, Bowles, had previously been his Assistant for some years, and as, while Hearne was Under-keeper, he had come into sharp collision with that irascible antiquary (see under 1715), his election now was a matter of sore annoyance to the latter. Hearne dwells upon it in his *Diary* with great bitterness and at great length: 'Competitors were Mr. Hall, of Queen's, and that pert conceited coxcomb Mr. Bowles (who is not yet Regent Master) of Oriel College. Bowles carried it by a great majority, having about 160 votes, and Mr. Hall about 77[1]. I think it the most scandalous election that I have yet heard of in Oxford.' Of Bowles' supporters he speaks thus:—'Charlett and such rogues, who contrived to bring in that most compleat coxcomb Bowles to be Head-Librarian, to the immortal scandal of all that were concern'd in it[2].' And even, when ten years later he records Bowles' death, he indulges, in forgetfulness of charity to the departed, in the following strain: 'Of this gentleman (a most vile, wicked wretch) frequent mention hath been made in these Memoirs. He took the degree of M.A. Oct. 12, 1719. 'Tis incredible what damage he did to the Bodl. Library, by putting it into

[1] The Register of Convocation gives the votes as being these numbers exactly.

[2] Vol. lxxxiv. pp. 59, 60.

disorder and confusion, which before, by the great pains I had taken in it (&c.), was the best regulated library in the world[1].' Bowles' name never occurs in the *Diary* without some opprobrious epithet being attached to it, which may be accounted for partly from his having taken the oaths of allegiance after declaring he would never do it (a defection which Hearne never forgave in any one), and partly also from his having personally excluded Hearne from the Library, when the latter refused to resign his keys in 1715, by procuring new locks and keys, which he kept in his own custody. But there appear also to have been graver reasons (see under 1729).

Three or four days after Bowles' election, Mr. Fletcher, the Sub-librarian (disliking, no doubt, the appointment of his junior over his head), resigned his office, to which Bowles appointed the well-known antiquary, Francis Wise[2]. Upon this appointment Hearne comments thus: 'Bowles put in Mr. Wise, A.M., of Trin. Coll. (a pretender to antiquities), tho' he had promised it to one of Oriel Coll., that came in fellow of Oriel when he did, and was very serviceable to him in getting the Head Librarian's place; for which Bowles is strangely scouted and despis'd at Oriel, as a breaker of his word, and a whiffling, silly, unfaithfull, coxcomb.' It must be allowed that the portrait of Bowles in the Library bears out in some degree Hearne's last epithet, by giving

[1] Vol. cxxii. p. 158.

[2] The following is the account of Wise, furnished by himself to Dr. Rawlinson for the collections made by the latter for a continuation of Wood's *Athenae.* It is strange that he makes no mention of his appointment as Sub-librarian. 'Francis Wise, son of Francis Wise, mercer in Oxford, born in All Saints parish in Oxford, on Julie 3, 1695, educated in grammar learning at New College School, admitted Commoner of Trin. Coll. Jan. 3, 1710, matriculated Jan. 15, 1710, Scholar May 31, 1711, Prob. Fellow 12 June, 1718, Actual next year, as usual. Was ordained Deacon by the Bp. of Oxford at Cuddesden the third of Sept. 1721; Priest at the publick ordination at Oxford 24th of the same month. Presented by Francis Lord Guildford to the curacy of Wroxton in Oxfordshire, 1723, and afterwards by the said Lord to the Vicarage of Harlow in Essex in 1726, which he soon resigned, choosing to live in Oxford, where he had been chosen *Custos Archivorum* of the University 26 April the same year upon the death of Dr. Gardiner.'

him the appearance rather of a fine clerical gentleman than of a student. But Des Maizeaux says in a letter dated London, Aug. 29, 1720, that he has 'heard much good said of Mr. Bowles,' and that no one is better able than he is to satisfy the expectation of the public for an accurate Catalogue of the Library. (Bodl. MS. Addit. C. 78. f. 9.)

Baskett, the printer, presented to the Library, through the Delegates of the Univ. Press, 27 May, 1719 (Hearne's *Diary*, vol. lxxxiii. p. 27), a magnificent copy on vellum of the 'Vinegar' Bible, printed by him in 1717. Only three copies were so struck off; the second was placed in the King's Library, and the third was sold to the Duke of Chandos, for five hundred guineas, at whose sale, in 1747, Lord Foley purchased it for £72 9*s*.

Thomas Girdler, D.D., of Wadham College, gave a roll containing '*ἀρχέτυπον*, ut videtur,' of the Library Statutes.

Henry Massey, M.A., Queen's Coll., gave three coins: a gold one of Edw. III, found at Cirencester Abbey; a brass of the Emperor Tacitus, found at Devizes, 'tertium, argenteum (majoris formæ) ab Olivari Cromwelli (nunquam satis execrandi) braccis vulgo nominatum.'

A.D. 1720.

About this time, one John Hawkins, a highwayman (who was executed in May, 1722), is said by an accomplice, Ralph Wilson, who published an account of his robberies, to have defaced some pictures in the Library. The University is said to have offered £100 for discovery, and a poor Whig tailor was taken up on suspicion, and narrowly escaped a whipping. No particulars, however, of Hawkins' act are given in the pamphlet, and no further notice of it has been found elsewhere.

Joseph Swallow, B.A., who died in this year, is found from the Accounts to have been employed, for some short time, in the Library.

In this year the titles of all books which were bought out of the Library funds begin to be recorded, together with their prices; they are entered in a Register marked with the letter C.

Visitors' Fees. See 1713.

A.D. 1721.

The inscription on the Schools' Tower, beneath the statue of James I, was renewed in this year[1]. It was again renewed, and all the sculpture repaired, in the year 1884.

Sir Godfrey Kneller presented his own portrait to the Gallery.

A.D. 1722.

Mrs. Mary Prince is recorded to have presented heads of our Blessed Lord and of King Charles I, painted by herself. They appear to be two paintings upon paper, mounted on copper. Beneath that of our Lord is the following inscription: 'This present figure is the symylytude of our Lorde Jesus our Saviour, imprinted in amyrald by the Predecessors of thė Great Turke, & sent to Pope Innocent ye Eight at the cost of the Great Turke for a token, for this caus, to redeme his brother that was taken prisner.' The inscription is, of course, if the painting be Mrs. Prince's work, reproduced *literatim* from some older copy.

The attachment to the old Stuart family, which was so warmly cherished in Oxford, appears to have lingered in the Bodleian notwithstanding Hearne's departure, who himself would scarcely have thought that a vestige of it had been left behind. For in the Benefaction Register for this year, the gift of a portrait of Sheffield, Duke of Buckingham, from his widow Catherine, a natural daughter of James II, is entered as coming from 'filia Regis Jacobi II, τοῦ μακαρίτου.'

Chrysanthus, Patriarch of Jerusalem. See 1715.

[1] Hearne's *Diary*, xci. 196.

A.D. 1723.

The noble brass statue of William Herbert, Earl of Pembroke, (who was Chancellor of the University from 1617 to his death in 1630, and was the donor of the Barocci MSS.,) which forms such a conspicuous feature in the Picture Gallery, was presented this year by the earl's great nephew, Thomas, the seventh Earl of Pembroke. It was cast by the famous artist Hubert le Soeur, from a picture by Rubens, and is said to weigh about 1600 lbs.[1]. The letter of thanks from the University was read in Convocation on April 17; it is criticized by Hearne in his *Diary*[2] in the following terms: 'I am told that this letter is very silly and poor, and that, among other things, his Lordship is told in it that the statue is placed *in æde immortalitatis.* Now what this *ædes immortalitatis*, church, temple or chappel of immortality is, I cannot conceive, but am sure that the statue is at present fix'd in the Picture Gallery, adjoyning to the Bodl. Library.' The exact words of the letter (Convoc. Reg. Bd. 31, f. 196) are, 'in æde ipsa immortalitatis, nimirum Bodleiana.'

Mrs. Sarah Bilstone, of Cirencester, gave a Roman gold ring with some coins.

A.D. 1724.

The MSS. *Adversaria* of Dr. J. E. Grabe came to the Library in this year after the death of Bishop Smalridge (Sept. 27, 1719), in accordance with the will of their writer, who at his death (Nov. 12, 1712) bequeathed them first to Hickes and next to Smalridge, with the final reversion to the Bodleian. They form forty-three volumes. Some account of them is given in Hickes' *Discourse* prefix'd to Grabe's *Defects and Omissions in Whiston's*

[1] The head is said to be removable, and a story is told in John Walters' *Poems* (p. 48;—see *infra*, under the year 1780—) that it was brought by two members of the University from Wilton, at once upon the first intimation of the Earl's intention to give it, separately from the body, in order to prevent any possible change of purpose.

[2] Vol. xcvi. p 101.

Collection of Testimonies, &c. (8º. Lond. 1712), and they are fully catalogued by Mr. Coxe in vol. i. of the general Catalogue of MSS., cols. 851–876. In a written list of them, preserved in the Library, Dr. Bandinel has noted that several volumes of the series were purloined before they came to Oxford, while remaining in the possession of a friend after Grabe's death. It appears that this friend was a Dr. David Humphreys; for a draft of a peremptory letter from Bowles to him, requiring the return of some books of Grabe's, which he had borrowed from Hickes under a bond to return them to Hickes or Smalridge or the Vice-Chancellor for the Bodleian Library, dated 9 Nov. 1726, is preserved in Bodl. MS. Addit. C. 78, a volume of letters relating to the Library, fol. 24.

A Zend MS. very well and clearly written (dated in the year 1005 of the era of Yezdegird, *i.e.* A.D. 1635), of the *Leges Sacræ Ritus, &c. Zoroastris*, was received from G. Bowcher, a merchant in the East Indies. It was given in 1718, but not forwarded until 1723, when it was brought from India by Rev. Rich. Cobbe, M.A. It is now numbered Bodl. Or. 321. And a Coptic Lexicon, compiled and prepared for the press by Rev. Thos. Edward, M.A., a former Chaplain of Ch. Ch., was bought for the sum of ten guineas, which was specially granted from the University Chest. It is now numbered Bodl. Or. 344. The author was originally of St. John's College, Cambridge, and tells us in his preface that Bishop Fell, who was also Dean of Ch. Ch., meeting him there in the house of Dr. Edmund Castell, with whom he was living, brought him to Oxford by appointing him a Chaplain of the Cathedral, with the view of carrying on the study of the Coptic language, which had fallen to the ground upon the death of Dr. Marshal of Lincoln College. But just when Edward was prepared to begin printing the results of his labours, his patron, the Bishop, died; and, as he found no one else cared for the subject, he took the College living of Badby in Northamptonshire, and quitted Oxford. He finally became Rector of Aldwinckle in the same county, and died there in the year 1721. His book is dated 1711. It is cited by Archdeacon Tattam in his *Lexicon Ægyptiaco-Latinum.* Another MS. Coptic Lexicon, in two volumes, was purchased in 1857.

John Frederick, a commoner of University College, gave an ostrich egg, 'manu quadam Americana affabre cœlatum.'

A.D. 1725.

On 7th May a copy of the surreptitious edition of John Flamsteed's *Historia Cœlestis,* printed in 1712, was received from Sir Robert Walpole, which is described as one 'quod in Thesauraria Regia adservabatur, et, cum paucis aliis, vitaverat iram et ignem Flamsteedianum.' The 'wrathful burning' here mentioned does not appear to be elsewhere noticed, and must have been a destruction of the greater part of the impression as being one unauthorized by Flamsteed. In this copy a letter from his widow, Mrs. Margaret Flamsteed, dated at Greenwich, March 22, 1726, to the Vice-Chancellor (Dr. Mather, of Corp. Chr. Coll.), is inserted, in which, after referring to the acceptance by the University of the three volumes of the edition of the *Historia* printed in 1725, and transmitted by the late Bishop of Chester (Gastrell), she says:—

> 'I have since been told that there remains in your Public Library one volume printed in the year 1712, which passes as the genuine work of Mr. Flamsteed's. I most humbly entreat you will please to order that single volume to be removed out of your Public Library, the greatest part of which is nothing more than an erronus abrigment (*sic*) of Mr. Flamsteed's works, he not being concerned in the printing any more of that book than 97 sheets, the rest being done without his knowledg or consent. . . . I am under an obligation not only to doe justice to the memory of Mr. Flamsteed, but alsoe to prevent the world's being imposed upon by a false impression.'

In this year Alex. Pope gave his *Iliad* and *Odyssey*, but without any special inscription in the copies.

A.D. 1726.

A large collection (in twenty-five volumes) of the tracts on the Roman Catholic controversy which appeared between 1680–1690, was given by Will. Smith, M.A., of Univ. Coll., and Rector of Melsonby, Yorkshire. £7 1*s*. were paid to Mr. Wise by order of the Curators, but for what services is not specified.

An advertisement was inserted in the *London Gazette* of 15 Oct., No. 6520, notifying that Messrs. Will. and John Innys, of London, booksellers, had been appointed by the University and Keeper of the Library to collect the copies of books due under the copyright Act of 1710 which had not been as yet delivered, and to receive books in future from Stationers' Hall; with a warning that proceedings would be taken against defaulters. In a subsequent advertisement in the *Gazette* of 12 Nov., No. 6528, the name of John Brooks, of the University of Oxford, gent., was substituted as that of the collector.

A.D. 1727.

Thomas Perrott, D.C.L., of St. John's College, gave nine volumes of MSS., the most important of which is a copy-book of the letters written by Sir John Perrott, Lord Deputy of Ireland, in 1584–6. Another is a book of orders from the Privy Council to the officers of the Customs of London, 1604–18: a third, notes of a sermon preached by Ussher at the Temple, July 2, 1620. A few political and miscellaneous tracts, *tempp. Eliz.—Jac. I*, and two heraldic MSS., complete the number. The MSS. are noticed in the return printed in the Record Commission Report for 1800, p. 348.

Some Greek MSS. were bought which had been brought from Mount Athos; three of them were placed amongst the Cromwell MSS., Nos. 15, 16, and 27, and three others are numbered Miscell. Gr. 137–9.

Sale of Duplicates. See 1745.

A.D. 1728.

The degree of D.C.L. was conferred by diploma on 9 Feb. upon the Count Conrad à Dehn, ambassador from the Duke of Brunswick-Wolfenbüttel, in return for the gift of some gold and silver medals; and on 28 June that of B.C.L. on Christ. Fred. Weichmann, for the gift of some German poetical volumes, and his own portrait[1].

Gen. Charles Ross, of Balnagowan, in Ross-shire, gave a MS. copy of the Solemn League and Covenant, with the signatures of eighteen peers (including the Great Montrose), in 1639. It is now numbered MS. *e Mus.* 247[2].

Sir James Thornhill gave some pictures, which, from the largeness of a blank space left in the *Reg. Benef.* for their enumeration, but never filled up, would appear to have been many in number. But only two portraits are now recorded as having come by his gift, one of Erasmus, and a full-length of the first Duke of Ormonde.

A.D. 1729.

Mr. Bowles, the Librarian, died at Shaftesbury, the place of his birth, and was buried there on Nov. 25[3]. On Dec. 2, Mr. Robert Fysher, B.M., Fellow of Oriel College, was elected his successor

[1] Reg. Convoc. B^{d}. 31. ff. 253^{b}–4, 259.

[2] A copy of the Covenant as printed by Evan Tyler at Edinburgh in 1643, is among the Clarendon MSS. It has many signatures, and is now exhibited in one of the glass cases.

[3] In the churchyard of Trinity parish, in the grave of his grandfather and grandmother. He was only thirty-four years old. Hearne, who in vol. cxxx. (p. 32) of his *Diary* notes this under date of June 1, 1731, adds,

'His father is still living, being a taylor at Shaftesbury, very poor and indigent. His name is likewise Joseph. His said wretched son, who was pupil to Mr. Davys when he (Bowles) was of Hart Hall, might have been a support to his father, had he acted the part of a sober, virtuous man. But his being cry'd up at first, and strangely caress'd and admired, and being withall naturally giddy, heady and conceited, drew him into the utmost folly and the height of wickedness, which shortened his life.'

To what course of conduct Hearne refers, there is no evidence to show.

by 100 votes to 85 over Francis Wise, B.D., the Under-librarian. Mr. John Bilstone, M.A., Chaplain of All Souls' and Janitor of the Library, was also a candidate, but retired before the election, in the hope of securing Wise's return. As Wise held Hearne's old place, and was regarded by him as an usurper, and as Bilstone held in his possession the new keys which Bowles originally procured to render Hearne's old ones useless, the latter consequently regarded them both with great disfavour, and rejoiced greatly at the result of the election. His account of it is printed in the *Reliqq. Hearn.* vol. ii. p. 712.

Forty-seven MS. volumes came to the Library by the gift (upon her death) of the widow of the early patron and constant friend of Hearne, Mr. Francis Cherry, of Shottesbrooke, Berks, together with a portrait of the latter [1]. Cherry himself died Sept. 23, 1713, and Hearne says that he had intended to give his MSS. to himself, his old *protégé*. As this was not done, Hearne had offered to buy them of the widow. They are not, for the most part, of very great value, but among them are various volumes by Dodwell; and a book written and bound by Q. Eliz. is described above, under the year 1628. Hearne was greatly annoyed at a paper of his own, containing reasons for taking the oath of allegiance, which he had written in 1700, coming into the Library amongst these books; he endeavoured in vain (although now in these days his legal right to stop a transfer would be at once recognized) to recover it, and it was published, to his still greater annoyance, by the Whigs, under the editorship of Mr. Bilstone, the janitor. An account of Hearne's endeavours to regain it, together with a notice of Mrs. Elizabeth Cherry's gift and of the MSS., is to be found in Dr. Bliss's Appendix to his *Reliqq. Hearn.* ii. 899–906 [2]. No mention of the MSS. is made in Mrs. Cherry's will, which is dated 25 Dec. 1725, and was proved 3 Sept. 1729.

[1] In the Benefaction Register they are entered as coming by the bequest of Mr. Cherry himself, probably because he may have so provided (although not by will) for their ultimate disposition.

[2] See also Hearne's *Life*, 1772, pp. 29–30.

In the Register of Readers admitted by favour occurs, under date of April 19, the name of 'C. Wesley, Ædis Xti alumn.,' written in a neat and clear hand. The name of his great brother is not found in any register extending over the period of his stay in Oxford. At this time the Library appears to have been almost entirely forsaken. Between 1730–1740 it rarely happens that above one or two books are registered to readers in a day, while often for whole days together not a single entry occurs; and since in the register for this period, the books are noted down by three hands, it can hardly be possible that the blanks are due to the negligence of a librarian (as might have been supposed were the same handwriting found throughout) rather than to the lack of students.

A.D. 1730.

A portrait of Dr. Will. Jane, Dean of Gloucester (1685–1707), was given by Peter Foulkes, D.D.

A.D. 1732.

Portraits of George Buchanan, Ben Jonson, and Dryden, were given by George Clarke, D.C.L., of All Souls' College. He had previously given, in 1724, a portrait of Mich. Montaigne, and in 1727 one of Hugo Grotius.

A.D. 1735.

On June 10, 1735, Thomas Hearne died. Fifteen of the MSS. of Thomas Smith, D.D., of Magdalen College, the well-known and learned non-juror, came hereupon to the Library, Smith having bequeathed them to Hearne on this condition. With them came also copies of Camden's *Britannia* and *Annales Eliz.*, with MSS. notes by their author. The rest of Smith's MSS. appear to have come to the Library together with the mass of Hearne's collections, as included in Rawlinson's bequest in 1755. They amount altogether to 140 thin volumes, containing notes, extracts and letters on all kinds of subjects. Among them are two volumes of notes on Ignatius in

Bp. Pearson's hand. There is a very full *written* catalogue of their contents, in two volumes.

Another volume in quarto, containing Smith's own original diary of the proceedings against Magdalen College in 1687–8 (hitherto only known from a copy among the Hargreave MSS. in the British Museum), was bought in 1888.

Three Greek MSS. were given by Smith himself on his return from his travels in the East about 1681; and in 1708 he gave a very interesting little volume which, he says, he had bought at an auction in London twelve years before, containing a treatise (in Greek and Latin, with the author's autograph signature in three places) of Cyril Lucar's, ('reverendissimi viri ac fortissimi martyris') 'De articulis orthodoxæ fidei,' with a portrait of the Patriarch very carefully depicted (Bodl. MS. 12).

A.D. 1736.

The Library was now enriched with the collections of the well-known antiquary, Thomas Tanner, Bishop of St. Asaph, who died on Dec. 14, in the preceding year. By his will, dated Nov. 22, 1733, he bequeathed his MSS. to the Library together with such printed books, not already there, as the Curators and Library-keeper should think fit to accept. But he directed his executor to burn all his sermon-notes, 'and other little pieces and attempts in divinity,' as well as all his own private papers and letters. The largest portion of his MSS. (nearly 300 volumes out of 467) consists of the papers which he himself says he 'bought of Archbishop Sancroft's executors,' but which it is said in the *Gent. Mag.* for 1782 (cited by Gough in his *British Topography*, i. 126) he bought for eighty guineas of the bookseller Bateman, to whom Sancroft's executors had sold them[1]. Together with these, and perhaps not

[1] There is in addition to the above-noted volumes, a long series (numbering 140 volumes) of small pocket common-place books filled with notes and extracts by Sancroft. Of these I made a MS. hand-catalogue some years ago. Eighteen other volumes of Sancroft's MSS. are to be found in the Harleian collection, Brit. Mus., and a few among Wharton's books at Lambeth.

now to be distinguished, are some of the collections of Dr. Nalson between 1640 and 1660. To the latter a claim was made through Archdeacon Knight, in 1737, by Dr. Williams of St. John's College, as grandson of Nalson; but the Bishop's brother replied (as we learn from a copy of his answer and of another letter written by him in 1753) that the Bishop had bought them at Ely, where they had lain neglected for many years, and he thought possibly from some one living in the house which Nalson inhabited when Prebendary of Ely. The matter ended by Dr. Williams waiving any claim which he had, in consideration of the place of deposit being the Bodleian[1]. Sancroft's and Nalson's papers together comprise a large series of letters of the time of the Civil War, of the highest interest and value, from most of the leading personages on both sides, including Charles I, Rupert, the Protector Oliver, and Hampden. There are also collections relating to various dioceses, with very much that illustrates both the ecclesiastical and literary history of the seventeenth century[2]. A selection from the Civil War letters was published, in 2 vols. in 1842, by Rev. Henry Cary, M.A. (a son of the translator of Dante, and at that time an assistant in the Library), under the title of *Memorials of the Civil War;* but the transcripts were very carelessly made, and scarcely a single letter can be trusted as faithfully and *verbatim* representing the original. Another volume of selections from Sancroft's papers was published, with much better care, by Will. Nelson Clarke, D.C.L., 8º. Edinb. 1848, entitled, *A Collection of Letters addressed by Prelates and Individuals of high rank in Scotland, and by two bishops of Sodor and Man, to Archbishop Sancroft, in the reigns of Charles II and James VII*[3]. A catalogue of the MSS., compiled by the Rev.

[1] Thirty-one other volumes of Nalson's papers were offered for sale through Thos. Carte to Dr. Rawlinson in 1751 (Letter to H. Owen, Rawl. MS. C. 989. fol. 169). Four volumes which belonged to Bp. Moore's library were restored to Cambridge out of Tanner's collection in 1741; two of them were registers of the Abbeys of St. Edmund's-bury and Langley.

[2] Some collections for Wiltshire made by Tanner did not come to Oxford with his library, but were forwarded by his son in 1751.

[3] Dr. Clarke appears not to have been aware of the existence of an interesting volume of letters from Scottish Bishops to Bishop Compton of

Alfred Hackman, M.A. (afterwards Sub-librarian) was published in 1860, in a thick quarto volume, forming vol. iv. of the general Catalogue of MSS. The several volumes are described in brief in the body of the work; but a very full Index is subjoined, in which the contents of all the letters and papers are entered in detail. The printed books (upwards of 900) contain many, by the Reformers and their opponents, which are of the utmost rarity in early English black-letter divinity. One of these is an unique copy (as it is believed) of an edition, printed without place or date, of the *Pore Helpe*, of which there is also an unique copy of another edition, equally without place or date, among the Douce books. It has not hitherto been remarked that two copies, or two editions, exist of this metrical satire. Another volume, which contains several tracts printed by W. de Worde and Gerard Leeu, has also two by Caxton, hitherto unnoticed as exhibiting his type, and described in the printed Catalogue simply as being books without place or date. The merit of their discovery as Caxtons was due to the research of Mr. Bradshaw, the late Librarian of the Cambridge Library. The one is a clean and perfect copy of the *Governayle of Helthe*, with the verses called *Medicina Stomachi*, of which the only copy known to Mr. Blades is in the library of the Earl of Dysart at Ham House; the other a wholly unknown quarto, *Ars Moriendi*, in the same type.

Unfortunately, when Tanner was removing his books from Norwich to Oxford, in Dec. 1731, by some accident in their transit (which was made by river) they fell into the water, and were submerged for twenty hours[1]. The effects of this soaking are only too evident upon very many of them[2]. The whole of the printed

London, among Rawlinson's MSS. (C. 985), which was rescued by Rawlinson, with the rest of Compton's papers, from being destroyed as waste paper. Other letters, including a large number from Archbishop Burnett of Glasgow, addressed to Archbishop Sheldon, are in a volume of the Sheldon papers.

[1] *Gent. Magaz.* 1732, p. 583.

[2] None of them, however, are now in the state described in a note in *Letters by Eminent Persons*, ii. 89, where it is said that many 'have received so much injury as to be altogether useless, crumbling into pieces on the slightest touch.' Perhaps the unique

books were uniformly bound in dark green calf, apparently about seventy years ago; the binder's work was well done, but, most unhappily, all the fly-leaves, many of which would doubtless have afforded much of great interest, with regard to the books themselves and their former possessors, were removed[1]. Many of Tanner's own letters are to be found amongst the Ballard and Hearne MSS., as well as scattered here and there in other collections; and one volume of them was purchased in 1859. Some coins were given by him in 1733. We learn from the Accounts that Thomas Toynbee, an undergraduate of Balliol College (B.A. 1743, M.A. 1745), received £12 12*s*., in 1741, for making a list of Tanner's MSS., and that E. Rowe Mores, the subsequently well-known antiquary, arranged some of his deeds in 1753-4.

A. D. 1738.

The fourth Catalogue of the printed books appeared this year in two volumes, folio, of 611 and 714 pp. respectively. It is still a Catalogue of great use and value, from its remarkable

copy of *The Children of the Chapel Stript and Whipt* which Warton says was amongst Tanner's books, but which has never appeared in any Bodleian Catalogue, may have perished from this cause. For a notice of the disappearance of two of Churchyard's tracts, see under the year 1659.

[1] A few other volumes from Tanner's library are to be met with dispersed in various parts of the Library, which possibly may, for the most part, have been gifts from him during his lifetime. A copy of *Sallust*, printed at Lyons by John Marion, in 1519, which had belonged to him, and was given to the Library by Mr. [William] Williams of Brasenose College (marked DD 68. Art.) was once, as shown by the arms on the binding, in the library of Henry VIII. On one side of the cover are the arms of England impaling Castile, Leon, Arragon, Sicily, and Granada, with two angels as supporters; below, a garden. On the other side, the arms of England alone; supporters, a gryphon and a greyhound, regardant; above them, the Tudor rose between two angels, and below, two portcullises. Some English and Latin words are interlined in the earlier part of the text in two or three contemporary hands, and some of these interlineations may possibly bear resemblance to the handwriting of Henry VIII. The book may have been one of the school-books of Princess Mary.

A volume of collections for Suffolk by Tanner was sold (No. 649) at Mr. Craven Ord's sale in 1829.

accuracy, and from the abundance and minuteness of its cross-references. The secret history of this Catalogue, however, as of the preceding one, is related by Hearne. By him, as he himself frequently tells us[1], the greater portion of it was virtually prepared soon after his appointment as Janitor, in 1702 (although no mention of his name is made in Fysher's preface), and to him, therefore, its accuracy is most probably in a great measure due[2]. He compared every book in the Library with Hyde's Catalogue, and corrected many mistakes, adding notes here and there about anonymous and synonymous authors, and, as the Vice-Chancellor (Dr. Mander, of Balliol) was anxious to have an Appendix issued, he transcribed for this purpose all his corrections and additions into two folio volumes, 'which' (to take up now Hearne's own account in his *Diary*, vol. lxii. p. 58, under date 1717) 'now lye and are to be seen in the Library. . . . But at last Dr. Hudson thought it more convenient with respect to himself that both Dr. Hyde's Catalogue and my Appendix should come out together as one intire work, so that he might have the honour of all. Upon which he employed one Moses Williams, his servitour[3] (the Dr. being then Fellow of University College), to transcribe it, the said Williams being in the Dr.'s debt. When Williams had done, he demanded the remaining part of his money, which was about ten or twelve pounds, the rest having been

[1] Pref. to *Chron. de Dunstaple*, p. xii. *Autobiogr.* p. 11, &c.

[2] It is fair to say that Fysher remarks in his preface that experience proved how entirely vain and foolish were the reports which had been spread abroad of the little or the nothing which, after the labours of their predecessors, would remain for the then editors to do.

[3] Moses Williams took his degree as B.A. in 1708. One John Williams (probably the one of that name who is entered in the Register of Graduates as having taken the degree of B.A. at Oriel in 1704) may possibly have been a colleague of Hearne's in some employment in the Library, about 1704. For in a letter written by Williams to Hearne, March 20, 170$\frac{5}{6}$, one year and a-half after he had quitted Oxford, in which he mentions his having been appointed to the Head-mastership of Ruthin School in November, 1705, he refers to 'our dear friends that are in irons at the Bodleian Library, there being several, I suppose, that have been manacled in that pleasing prison since my being there.' (*Rawlinson Letters*, vol. xii. f. 1.)

stopped by the Dr. for the debt just now mentioned. The whole was fifty lbs. which he bargained for with the Dr. But when Williams desired the said ten or twelve pounds, of which he had immediate occasion to discharge the fees and charges for the degree of Bachelor of Arts, the Dr. was in a very great passion, and refused to pay it. Upon which Williams moved the matter so far that the Catalogue was laid before the Delegates of the Press, and the Dr. was called before them to his very great mortification, and they told him that 'twas highly unreasonable to stop the poor lad's money. Upon which the Dr. in a great rage and fury paid him; otherwise Williams had most certainly put him into the Court. This Catalogue was last summer ordered to be printed, and the Dr. was refunded his money; but 'tis not yet put to the press, the Dr. being unwilling it should be printed till such time as he hath done Josephus.' But Hudson died before his Josephus was finished, and the proposed new Catalogue was consequently begun, and only begun, by his successor, Bowles. The latter printed as far as p. 244 of vol. i. and p. 292 of vol. ii.[1] His successor, Fysher, upon his appointment, engaged the assistance of his friend, Emmanuel Langford, M.A., Vice-Principal of Hart Hall, who completed the second volume, while Fysher himself finished the first. At the end of the second volume appeared an announcement of a supplemental Catalogue, as being ready for the press, containing the books existing in College Libraries but wanting in the Bodleian. This, however, never appeared, and nothing is known of the MS. from which it was to have been printed: [see under 1794]. Fysher's Catalogue appears, from the University Accounts, to have occupied from 1735 in preparation, for which, and for transcribing it for the press, £194 5*s.* were paid to him[2].

[1] In a letter to John Lewis of Margate, dated 16 June, 1727, Bowles says, 'Thus have I endeavour'd to answer your queries as soon as my constant business in the Bodleian Library, and my attendance on the press during my publishing a catalogue of all the Bodleian printed books, would permit me.' (Rawl. MS. D. 376, f. 202^{b}.)

[2] In Gough MS. Oxfordshire 83 (a note-book apparently of Archbishop Secker's) there is a memorandum (at

Alexander Pope gave in this year a curious volume, containing a series of 178 portraits of East Indian Rajahs and Great Moguls, down to Aurung-Zebe. It is now numbered MS. Sansk. d. 14.

This MS. is described in detail in the following letter (apparently a copy of the original) which has been recently inserted in the MS. It is endorsed by Owen the Librarian, as having been addressed 'To Mr. Everard, F. Br. N. Coll., and deliver'd to the Librarian by Mr. Mayo, Fell. of Brazen-nose College.'

'London, 8 July, 1760.

'With great pleasure it is, Sir, that I comply with your intimation to me of a desire to know some particulars of that collection of the miniature-portraits of the sovereigns of Indostan, presented by Mr. Pope to the Bodleian Library at Oxford, inscribed with his name and mine.

'While I was in India, sometime before the year seventeen hundred and forty, one of the Mogul's generals was with an army incamped before the town of Surat, of which Tegbeg-Khawn was then governor for the Mogul. On those occasions the general never enters the town himself, but deputes certain officers to the governor, under pretext of taking cognizance of his conduct, but, in fact, to receive a bribe, in form of present, not to make too strict a scrutiny. Tegbeg-Khawn, who was far from being on good terms with the Court, being obliged to proportion his present to the need he stood in of absolution for the past and protection for the future, sent the general some lacks of rupees, not less than to the amount of some three or four hundred thousand pounds. But that such a transaction may not appear too barefacedly, what it always is, a corrupt bargain, the general usually makes the governor some present which is to pass for a return. On this occasion, then, the Mogul general sent Tegbeg-Khawn a sabre set with rubies, emeralds and diamonds, worth perhaps at most three or four thousand pounds, together with this book, containing a set of miniature-portraits of the successive sovereigns of Indostan for several ages back. They are in colors, on vellum leaves, and are copies from a series of originals, in the Mogul's palace.

'That they are not fancy-pictures there is great reason to believe, independent of the presumption in their favor from the circumstance

p. 525) that of this fourth catalogue 'few of them [were] sold; only 8 sold in Holland and France, of 100 sent abroad.'

of their being a present on so capital an occasion from one great officer of state to another; it being well-known that such a set of pictures actually exists in the royal palace, it hardly seems improbable that a copy was taken from them. And here it is observable that the Mogul-Moors have nothing of that aversion to images or pictures which is even a point of religion to the Mahometans in general. But these Moguls retain so much of their Tartarian origin as to tolerate all religions, and even to incorporate theirs of the *Thien*, such as the Court of China also professes, with the predominant religion of whatever country they conquer, for the greater ease of preserving their conquests by this political conformity.

'The portrait of Tamerlan (Timur-lang) in this collection, and perhaps the only one extant in Europe on which any dependence for genuineness may be reasonably had, seems to favor the belief of its authenticity, in that you may very clearly remark in it the distinctive Tartar lineaments, a broad flattish face, with small eyes. These in his son and successor are somewhat less conspicuous, and, as the line of descent proceeds, they melt by degrees wholly into the softness of the Indian features.

'It may also be observed that the Moors or Mahometan sovereigns of Indoostan are in this collection distinguished from the Gentoo ones, by the fashion of the skirts of their robes, which, in the Gentoos, hang on each side, cut at bottom into an angular form, as all the Rajahs wear them to this day for an insign of royalty.

'However, this book, such as it is, was by the governor Tegbeg-Khawn made a present of to Mr. Frazer, the same who, at my instance and request, translated from a Persian manuscript the account of Shah Nadir's (the famous Thamas Kooly-Khawn) expedition into India, and who brought home a curious collection of oriental manuscripts, most of which once belonged to the royal library of Ispahan, and had escaped the rage and barbarism of the Aphgoons or Aghuan invaders under Emir Veiss and his successors.

'Mr. Frazer having parted with this set of portraits to me, I sent it to Mr. Pope, with whom I was then in correspondence, and who wrote me that, judging it too great a curiosity for his private study, he had done it the honor of presenting it to the Bodleian Library.

'I need not, I presume, insist on how agreeable such a disposal must be to one so penetrated as I have ever been with sentiments of veneration for an University which, in quality both of a spring-head of learning and of a noble conservatory of literature, is so justly considered as a national ornament and honor. But I now receive from that circumstance a fresh pleasure in its furnishing me an occasion of the assuring yourself of the truth with which I most respectfully am, Sir,

'Your most obedient humble servant,

'JOHN CLELAND[1].'

The following is Pope's autograph inscription on a fly-leaf:—

'This book containing one hundred and seventy-eight portraits of the Indian Rajahs (continued to Tamerlane and the great Mogols his successors, as far as to Aurengzebe), was procured at Surat by Mr. John Cleland, and given to the Bodley Library, as a token of respect, by

'ALEX. POPE, 1737.'

On following fly-leaves is a somewhat different account of the MS. in another hand, of which the following extract forms the greater part:—

'The accompanying collection of portraits was procured by a Banyan merchant, broker to the Dutch at Surat. Upon his going up to Dehly, the present residence of the Great Mogull, by making great interest he got permission to have copys taken from the collection of originall paintings, as they are preserved at that Court. By the death of the broker this collection fell by great chance into an English gentleman's hands, at a time that Mirza Golam Mahomet, brother to the Governor of Surat and the sole manager of all affairs in that city, was enquiring it out as a present to the Ghonim generall, who was encamped near the city with his forces. All the merchants to whom it has been shown, esteem it a great rarity, and the like not procurable in all Surat.

'It will easily occurr that the first series or century of kings must, both in their history and effigies, be wholly considered as fable and fiction; and the visible sameness of the face and lineaments shews that the painter was at no pains to vary the invention. But it is an undeniable truth that the face and peculiar habits of the late monarchs of Indostan have been religiously preserved. . . . The temper and qualitys of the severall Kings, whether Gentoo Rajahs, or Moors, or Mogulls,

[1] This letter, together with a copy of Pope's inscription, is printed pp. xxv–xxviii, of the Introduction to Major Davy's translation of the *Institutes of Timour*, edited by Prof. Joseph White (where also the portrait of Timur is engraved from the MS.), 4°. Oxf. 1783.

are attempted to be respectively exprest and denoted by certain symbols; a warrior is figured by his sword or target, a lover of justice or prayer by a book or beads, a hunter by a hawk, a luxurious, effeminate Prince by a rose, flower, or betel-box, a drunkard by a cup, and the like. . . . The sketches of the line of Mogulls from Tamerlane inclusive, No. 157, down to Aurengzebe, the last in this collection, are in all probability just and true, as they have been compared severally with other loose detached copys of the same originalls. . . .'

At the end of a folio book of Library accounts from 1676 to 1813 is entered a notice of an application from the Earl of Oxford in this year for the loan of the portrait of Sir Tho. Bodley for the purpose of having it copied in London. The Vice-Chancellor replied

'that Mr. Twells had lately made the like request; but it being judged that the practice of lending pictures out of the gallery might probably be attended with ill consequences, withdrew his petition, and was contented with a copy of Dr. Pocock, taken by an Oxford hand.'

It was added that if still the Earl should persist in his request, nothing could be denied him; but that if, upon this representation, he 'would send any one to take a copy, the person so sent should be properly accommodated; and in so doing his lordship would effectually put a stop to all future requests of this nature.' A copy of the following reply is then subjoined:—

'Dover Street, Dec. 7, 1738.

'Reverend Sir,

'I received the favour of your letter in answer to my request sent by Mr. Wise to you, to have Sir Thomas Bodley's picture to London, to have a copy of it; designing at the same time to have it clean'd and new framed. Had I known the resolution you mention, I should have been far from offering my request. Give me leave, Sir, to tell you that I not only entirely acquiesce, but that I most heartily rejoyce that you are come to this resolution; for I think it is the true way to preserve what you have, and to gain future benefactions. The preservation of the noble Bodleian Library is owing to the not lending books out, and the annual Visitations. The high honour and regard I have always entertain'd, and always shall, for the University of Oxford, will make me extreamly carefull not to do any thing that might in the least be construed to her prejudice; and heartily wish it was in my power to do her any service.

'I am with true respect,

'Reverend Sir,

'Your most obedient humble servant,

'OXFORD.'

James Heany, a poor Irish bookbinder, (one employed, in his own words, in 'clothing naked authors') having come to Oxford, after being, as he says, '*almost* shipwrecked between the *inevitable* rocks of Ruin and Distress,' and having travelled 'so far that I could scarce put a shilling between my head and the firmament,' published a 'poem' on 'Oxford the seat of the Muses,' which, happily we may hope for the author's pocket as well as for the readers' amusement, reached a second edition. To the Library the following lines are devoted:—

'A Publick Library, that all must own
The like at present in the world's not known;
In goodly piles and great variety
Records and books promiscuous [!] here do lye.'

The names of various persons (most, probably, undergraduates) employed in the Library about this time are learned from the Accounts:—1738, Mr. Hall; 1740–1, Mr. Allen[1]; 1740, Mr. Toynbee (Ball. Coll., B.A., 1743); 1743, Mr. Jessett (All Souls', B.A., 1745); 1747, John Foot, M.A., Balliol[2]; 1747, Mr. Thomas Winbolt (All Souls', B.A. 1748); 1748, — Roberts[3]. Other names, found in the Register of Readers, are Robert Davy and John Sydenham [B.A. All Souls', 1747].

[1] John Allen, afterwards M.A. and Vice-Principal of Magd. Hall. He died in 1784. In an obituary notice in the *Gentleman's Magazine* for Jan. 1785, it is stated that 'he was for many years Under-librarian of the Bodleian Library;' but in the MS. notes of Ald. Fletcher in his copy of Gutch's *Wood* in the Bodleian Library, this statement is described as incorrect. However, it appears from the above entry that he was at one period an officer of the Library. He took the degree of B.A., as a member of All Souls' College, 6 Feb. 1740, and that of M.A., as of Alban Hall, 11 Feb. 1746.

[2] Note in the Register of Readers.

[3] 'Roberts succeeded Winbolt, Nov. 16, 1748:' note, *ibid.*

A.D. 1739.

Notification was given to the Vice-Chancellor, on June 9, (and on July 5 Convocation accepted the bequest,) that thirteen pictures (of no great value) were bequeathed to the Gallery by Dr. King, Master of the Charter House, by his will dated July 28, 1736, together with £200 for the cleansing, and repairing the frames, of the pictures already in the Gallery, 'which are very visibly in decay.' A list of these thirteen pictures is given in Gutch's transl. of Wood's *Annals*, vol. ii. pp. 969, 970. They are now in the Randolph Gallery. Dr. King also left a legacy of £400 to the University to prepare a complete and handsome edition of Zoroaster's Works, in Persian, with a Latin translation and notes; but this portion of his bequest was not accepted.

A.D. 1740.

A copy of the Byzantine historian Pachymeres was restored in this year, by order of the Curators, to Emmanuel College, Cambridge, from which it had by some means been removed; but the College paid £4 4*s*. for its restoration.

A.D. 1745.

In this year died Nathaniel Crynes, M.A., Fellow of St. John's College and Superior Bedel of Arts, to which latter office he had been elected Jan. 26, $17\frac{15}{16}$[1]. He bequeathed to the Library all such books out of his own valuable collection as it did not already possess, the rest going to his own College. His books in octavo and smaller sizes, with a few quartos, are still kept distinct, under his own name, and number 968 volumes, many of which are of great rarity. Seven MSS. were presented by him in 1736, and six more came with his legacy. In 1727 he purchased

[1] He left a benefaction to his successor in that (now suppressed) office, which produces £13 6*s*. 8*d*. yearly.

some duplicates from the Library, for £3 16*s*. 8*d*., and a story, told by Warton in connection with this purchase, of his fortunately rejecting books which bore the name of Milton, will be found under the year 1620. There is a biographical notice of him in J. Haslewood's Introduction to Juliana Barnes' *Boke of St. Alban's*, Lond. 1810, pp. 86–7. In the Accounts for 1746 occur special payments to Fr. Wise, and to one Mr. Gerard Bodley, for cataloguing and arranging Crynes's books.

A. D. 1746.

Trott's *Clavis Linguæ Sanctæ*. See under 1686.

A. D. 1747.

Dr. Fysher, the Librarian, died on Nov. 4, at Mr. Warneford's, of Sevenhampton, Wilts, and was buried, on Nov. 7, in Adam de Brome's chapel in St. Mary's Church, Oxford. And on Nov. 10, Rev. Humphrey Owen, B.D., Fellow of Jesus College (afterwards D.D., and chosen Principal of his College in 1763), was unanimously elected his successor[1]. Rawlinson mentions, in a letter to Owen of April 15, 1751, that he had heard a complaint that in Fysher's time 'there was a great neglect in the entry of books

[1] Memorandum by Owen himself, in reply to a question from Rawlinson, Rawl. MS. C. 989, f. 205. This volume contains a collection of letters to Owen, chiefly from Browne Willis and Rawlinson, between the years 1748-1756. It affords proof that Owen was what his correspondents would call an 'honest' man, *i. e.* a Jacobite. In one letter (f. 1), Willis sends him a Latin inscription in praise of Flora Macdonald, which he says is 'on a fair lady's picture, in an honest gentl. seat in the province of St. David's;' in another (f. 170), Rawlinson sends him, as a contribution to the Oxford collection of verses on the death of Frederick, Prince of Wales, this Jacobite epitaph:—

'Here lies Fred., Down among the dead;
Had it been his Father, Most had much rather;
Had it been his Brother, Better than any other;
Had it been a Sister, More [*lege*, None?] would have mist her;
Wer't the whole generation, Happy for the nation;
But since it is only Fred., There is no more to be said.'

into the Benefactors' Catalogue, and into the interleaved one of the Library; as to these objections, my answers were as ready as true, at least I hope so, that Dr. Fysher's indisposition disabled him much from the duty of his office, and that I did not think every small benefaction ought to load the velom register[1].' And in a previous letter (of 27 Oct. 1749) from Owen to Rawlinson (in which the writer explains the circumstances of many books of Rawlinson's gift having been left uncatalogued by the fact of Fysher's having been fully occupied with the publication of the new Catalogue, and by the coming of Bp. Tanner's and N. Crynes's books, as also by his having been hindered by bad health) Owen remarks that 'no man could have the faithfull discharge of his office more at heart than he had, as I can assert from my knowledge of the man's personal character, and from the minutes I find in the Library as his successor.'

A. D. 1748.

A volume of exquisitely delineated maps of Flanders, by the Sieur Naudin, a French engineer, was received from the ex-Chancellor, the attainted and expatriated Duke of Ormonde, who had died three years before, but who had thus testified, as it would seem, by a last gift, to his continued regard for the University. The entry in the Benefaction-Register describes the donor as being 'Honorabilissimus nuper Dux Ormondiæ;' but there is nothing to explain the apparent delay in the receipt of the bequest, if bequest it were.

A. D. 1749.

A Runic Primstaff, or Clog Almanack, was given by Mr. Guy Dickins, a gentleman-commoner of Ch. Ch., for several years previously ambassador in Sweden, where doubtless he obtained it. It is now exhibited, together with another given in 1682 (*see* p. 150), in a glass case in the Library. Pointer, in his *Oxoniensis Academia* (p. 143), mentions that an explanation of the Primstaff was given

[1] Rawl. MS. C. 989, f. 166 b.

by himself, in a manner that implies that he was the actual donor of the clog; and the Accounts show that the gift of the explanation was also in this year; it is numbered Rawl. D. 707.

A number of coins were added to the Numismatic museum which had been collected by the late Librarian, Fysher.

A.D. 1750.

A copy *on vellum*, with illuminated initials, &c., of vol. i. (reaching to the Psalms) of the Vulgate Bible, printed by Fust and Schoeffer in 1462, was bought for £2 10*s.*! The volume was imperfect at the end, ceasing at Job xxxii. 5, and seven leaves followed in contemporary and beautiful MS., which also ended imperfectly at Ps. xxxvi. 9, with one leaf wanting at the end of Job. But when the Canonici collection of MSS. was received from Venice in 1818, among some fragments which were found in one of the boxes were fourteen leaves of a Bible, which were at once recognised as being part of those wanted to complete this book, and which left only four still deficient! The volume itself originally belonged to the collection of Nic. Jos. Foucault, 'Comes Consistorianus,' many of whose MSS. and printed books came to the Library by Rawlinson's bequest; but through how many hands the missing leaves had passed in the seventy subsequent years ere they were thus marvellously restored to their place, it is impossible to tell[1].

Edward Edwards was [under] Janitor in this year, as deputy for the Rev. John Bilstone. They both sign receipts for fees and salary in October as being then in office.

A.D. 1751.

A benefaction from Lord Crewe, Bishop of Durham, of £60 to the Librarian and of £10 for the purchase of books, appears for

[1] The story of this recovery is related by Archd. Cotton in his *Typographical Gazetteer*, p. 339, where by mistake he refers the original purchase to the year 1752.

the first time in the Accounts for this year. These sums (which are still annually paid into the General Fund) proceed from a bequest of £200 *per ann.* from Crewe (who died Sept. 24, 1721) to the University. A proposal to give these same sums to the Library, with other assignments for the remainder, was brought forward in Convocation on June 5, 1723, but the scheme was then rejected[1]. And thus nearly thirty years seem to have elapsed from the time of the bequest before the share for the Library was definitely fixed and paid.

Charles Gray, M.P. for Colchester, presented a MS. Roll, containing a Survey of the estates of the Abbey of Glastonbury at the Dissolution, which is printed by Hearne in his Appendix to Langtoft's *Chronicle*, vol. ii. pp. 343–388, from a copy made from this original; and an inscription, in the Phœnician language, upon a white marble stone, which was brought, with many others, from Citium, in the island of Cyprus, by Dr. Porter, a physician of Thaxted in Essex. The stone measures 12 inches in length, by three in breadth, and three in depth. It has been frequently engraved: first by Pococke (*Travels in the East*, vol. ii. pl. xxxiii. 2); next by Swinton (*Inscriptiones Citieæ*, 1750, and *Philos. Trans.* 1764); afterwards by Chandler, Barthélemy, &c.; by Gesenius (for whom former copies were collated with the original, and corrected, by Mr. Stephen Reay) in his *Scripturæ Linguæque Phœniciæ Monumenta*, published in 1837, where the inscription is described at pp. 126–133, part i., and engraved at pl. xi. part iii.; and in Renan's *Corpus Inscriptt. Semit.*, 4°. Par. 1881, vol. i. pp. 67–8. It appears to be an epitaph by a husband for himself and his wife.

Thomas Shaw, the well-known Eastern traveller, bequeathed his collection of natural curiosities, which was sent to the Ashmolean Museum, and the MS. of his own travels, with corrections, and other papers. Copies of Caxton's *Game of the Chesse* and *Recuyell of Troye* were given by Mr James Bowen, of Shrewsbury, painter[2].

[1] Hearne's *Diary*, xcvii. 12.

[2] A MS. vol. of collections by him relating to the history of Shropshire, dated 1768, is among Gough's books, Salop MS. 20.

Dr. Philip Hayes, Professor of Music, gave a very large 'prospect' of London and Westminster [by John Rocque, engraved by John Pine in 1746], which still hangs where it was originally placed, on the wall outside the Library door.

A.D. 1753.

In May of this year died Henry Hyde, Lord Cornbury, son of Henry Hyde, Earl of Rochester, and great-grandson of the great Earl of Clarendon. He had made a will bequeathing all the Chancellor's MSS.[1] to Secker, Bishop of Oxford, and others, in temporary trust for the University of Oxford, to print at their press whatever might be thought fit, and the profits to be devoted to a school for riding and other athletic exercises in the University (in pursuance of an idea suggested by his great-grandfather in his dialogue *On Education*), should such an institution be accepted, or else to other approved uses. Dying before his father, through the effects of an accident, his bequest was void, as he was never actually in possession of the papers to which it referred; but after the death of his father in Dec. following, his sisters, who were the co-heiresses, carried out his will[2], by sending all the Clarendon MSS. in their possession to the University on the same conditions[3].

[1] These comprised everything except the *Hist. of the Rebellion*, of which the original autograph copy appears to have come to the Library at some earlier date from the hands of Dean Aldrich. It was not in the Library in 1711 (Hearne's *Diary* under date of 28 June in that year), but was then supposed to be about to be deposited there; but in 1743 Rawlinson speaks of it as being in the possession of the University (Ballard MS. ii. 68).

[2] In a letter (without date) to Owen, the Librarian, Rawlinson writes, 'It is said here that Lord Hyde has left all the Clarendonian MSS. to Bodley, £10,000 for building a repository for the printed books, and fine pictures.' (Rawl. MS. C. 989, f. 139.)

[3] On Feb. 4, 1868, a scheme for the appropriation of the accumulated fund (then amounting to about £12,000), which had been approved by the Clarendon Trustees, was accepted by Convocation. The money has been applied to the erection of laboratories, &c., at the University Museum, for the Professor of Experimental Philosophy. The original proposal for a riding-school, &c.,

From these was published in 1759 (in which year the papers were deposited in the Library) the *Life* of the first Earl, reprinted in several editions up to the year 1827. This was followed, in 1767–73, by the publication, under the editorship of Dr. Rich. Scrope, of Magd. Coll., of vols. i., ii. of a selection from the *State Papers*; of which vol. iii. appeared under the editorship of Mr. Thos. Monkhouse, of Queen's Coll., in 1786. During the progress of this publication, however, the original collection of MSS. papers was very largely increased by the acquisition of various portions which had long before been detached. Some were obtained, before the publication of vol. i., from the executors of Rich. Powney, LL.D.; and many were presented to the University, before the publication of vol. ii., by the Radcliffe Trustees, who had bought them for £170 when sold by auction in 1764 by the executors of Joseph Radcliffe, Esq., one of the executors to Edward, third Earl of Clarendon, who died in 1723. Dr. Douglas (afterwards Bishop of Salisbury), who was employed in the latter purchase, himself bought and gave some MSS. which had belonged to Mr. Guthrie, and was instrumental also in procuring some letters from Viscountess Middleton, &c. Again, before the publication of vol. iii. many further papers were purchased by the Radcliffe Trustees from a Mr. Richards, near Salisbury (from whose father Mr. Powney had obtained his portion), and from Mr. W. M. Godschall, of Albury, Surrey. And lastly, about thirty years ago, several boxes (including Clarendon's own iron-bound *escritoire*), containing miscellaneous papers, were forwarded by the Clarendon Trustees in final discharge of their trust [1].

was one which had been warmly pressed at various times, and a full account of all the schemes will be found in the preface by Mr. T. W. Jackson, M.A. to a letter from Dr. Wallis against Mr. Lewis Maidwell, one of the projectors, printed in 1885 in the first vol. of the Oxf. Hist. Society's *Collectanea*.

[1] Three letters from the Duke of York to Henry, Earl of Clarendon, in 1680, four from his Duchess to the Queen of Charles II in 1679–80, and two from Laurence Hyde, while ambassador at the Hague in 1678, to the Earl of Danby and Secretary Williamson, were added to the collection by the gift of Mr. Charles H.

A MS. of the *History of the Rebellion,* being a copy made for the printer, in seven volumes, together with one of the *Contemplations on the Psalms,* in three volumes, was forwarded in 1785 or 1786 by the Duke of Queensbury. The former MS. appears to be that from which the first edition was printed by the Earl of Rochester[1].

Three volumes of a Calendar of the *Clarendon State Papers* were issued in 1869–76, which extended to the end of the year 1657. Unfortunately the sale of these volumes was so limited that the continuation of the Calendar was suspended, notwithstanding the great importance and interest of the work. Of the papers of 1658 and of 1659 to the month of July, and of portions of 1660–1 the Calendar however exists in MS. As far as the work has advanced, it has proved, on the whole, the good judgment and the extreme correctness with which the old printed selection was made; but as that selection ended with the Restoration, while

Radcliffe, of Salisbury, in Dec. 1888. They had formed part of a parcel of papers which appear to have remained in possession of the family of the Joseph Radcliffe mentioned above, and which with the accidental exception of these nine letters were all burned (nothing being known of their contents) after the death of Geo. Radcliffe, D.D., Prebendary of Salisbury, in 1849, in unhappy accordance with his most unfortunate directions. The nine letters which had been saved were printed by Mr. Fr. R. Y. Radcliffe, M.A., of All Souls' College, in the *National Review* for Aug. 1888, pp. 748–61, and in consequence of a communication which I addressed to him thereon, that gentleman liberally procured their restoration to the collection to which they had no doubt originally belonged. The letters of the Duke and Duchess all bear endorsements in the handwriting of Henry, the second Earl of Clarendon.

[1] In the Benefaction Book this gift is entered under 1793, but it is mentioned in the Preface to vol. iii. of the *State Papers*, dated May 29, 1786, as having been '*lately*' given. But the promise of papers from the Duke is mentioned, together with the Radcliffe and Powney gifts, as early as April, 1764, in a letter from Rev. C. Godwyn. (Nichols' *Lit. Anecd.* vol. viii. p. 242.) Another copy of books i.–vii. of the *History*, chiefly written by William Edgeman, who was Hyde's secretary at Scilly and during his first exile, and no part by Hyde himself, came to the Library among Rawlinson's MSS., by whom it was bought at the sale of the Chandos Library in 1747 for £1 10*s*.! Dan. Perkins, who drew up the Chandos Catalogue (see under 1755), wrote to Rawlinson, 'I am very positive that it is an original and not a copy, and that it is wrote by the Earl's own hand.'

the papers of the great Earl reach on to 1667, the year of his exile, and those of his family some years later, the subsequent portion, which has scarcely ever been touched, will be found to contain much of fresh interest[1].

It was in this year also that the first portion of the MSS. of Thomas Carte, the 'Englishman' and historian, came to the Library. It has been hitherto universally supposed that his voluminous and invaluable collections came *en masse* subsequently to his death, but the Library Register shows that Oxford was indebted to him for a considerable and important portion during his life. In this year we find that he sent the papers which relate to the life of the great Duke of Ormonde, with a large number of others bearing on the history of Ireland from the time of Queen Elizabeth, comprised in thirty volumes folio and quarto. In the following year, shortly before his death (which occurred on April 2, 1754) he forwarded twenty-six more of his Irish volumes, in folio, marked A, B, C, D, &c. And in 1757 nine more of the same series were forwarded by his widow from Caldecot, near Abingdon, according to an entry in the old Catalogue, which appears to correspond to one in the annual Register to the effect that four more boxes were forwarded by the executors, 'by order of Rev. Mr. Hill.' The remainder of his collections were left in the hands of his widow, who, re-marrying to Mr. Nicholas Jernegan, or Jerningham (of the family seated at Cossey, Norfolk), bequeathed them, upon her death, to him, with the reversion to the University of Oxford. While they were in Mr. Jernegan's possession they were largely used by Macpherson for his publication of *State Papers*, for which use of them £300 were paid; and the agreement entered into by the publisher Cadell, when borrowing some of them for this purpose, is preserved in the MS. Catalogue of the collection. On April 30, 1771, a delegacy, consisting of nine persons, was appointed by the University in

[1] From these later papers I printed in 1880 the hitherto unknown poem by George Wither, entitled *Vox Vulgi*.

Convocation 'qui de libris manuscriptis egregii viri Thomæ Carte in usum Academiæ conservandis deliberent et determinent, cum relatione ad hanc venerabilem [domum], et approbatione ejusdem'; but no report from them appears to be on record[1]. In 1778, however, Mr. Jernegan disposed of his life-interest to the University, for (as Nichols[2] was informed by Price, the Librarian) the sum of £50, and the remainder were consequently at once transferred to the Library. The collection numbers altogether 180 volumes in folio, fifty-four in quarto, and seven in octavo, besides several bundles of Carte's own papers; and is accompanied by a very full list of contents, compiled by Carte himself, in one folio volume. The mass of papers relating to Ireland which these volumes contain is enormous, drawn chiefly from the stores accumulated by Ormonde at Kilkenny Castle; to which are added miscellaneous historical collections derived from Lords Huntingdon, Sandwich, and Wharton. There are, also, several volumes of extracts and papers, collected with immediate reference to Carte's *History of England.* And a third, and especially interesting, portion consists of the papers of Mr. David Nairne, under-secretary to James II during his exile, which reach from 1692 to 1718, and fill two volumes in folio and eight or nine in quarto. It was from these that Macpherson chiefly compiled the Stuart portion of his *Original Papers*, published in 1775, in 2 vols., 4°.[3] A Report upon the contents of the collection, with special reference to Ireland (omitting the Nairne papers) was made to the Master of the Rolls by [Sir] T. Duffus Hardy and Rev. J. S. Brewer in 1863, and was printed in the following year (8vo., pp. 101), together with an extremely useful summary of the contents of the various volumes, and a reference-table of the letters &c., printed

[1] Reg. Conv. Bl. 36, p. 181.

[2] *Lit. Anecd.* ii. 514.

[3] In addition to the papers there printed in full, the appendix contains lists of contents of several of Carte's volumes. Many of the Irish papers (as well as various others amongst the Clarendon MSS.) have been printed recently by Mr. John T. Gilbert in his two works dealing with the period of 1640–52, entitled *Contemporary Hist. of Affairs in Ireland*, and *History of the Irish Confederation*.

by Carte in his Ormonde volumes. In consequence of this Report, two Commissioners, the Rev. Dr. Russell, President of Maynooth (deceased 26 Feb. 1880), and J. P. Prendergast, Esq., were appointed to examine the whole series, and select for transcription all official papers of interest relating to Ireland, with a view to the preservation of copies in the Record Office at Dublin, whose further Report, which includes copious extracts, was printed in 1871 (8vo., pp. 236). Several transcribers were therefore continuously employed for some years in transcribing for this purpose (under the direction of the late Mr. H. S. Harper), the papers selected by the Commissioners. Some notice of the MSS. is to be found in the Record Commission Report for 1800, p. 354. A calendar was made for the Library in the years 1877–83, by Mr. Edward Edwards (the author of the *Memoirs of Libraries*, who died in 1886); but unfortunately this remains, and must remain, unprinted, having been found on subsequent examination to require such an amount of revision, enlargement, correction, and re-arrangement, as was quite unexpected and disappointing.

In this year ornamental stucco-work was put up in the Picture Gallery under the Tower at a cost of £116.

A.D. 1754.

In this year the MS. collections of Rev. John Walker, D.D.[1], of Exeter (son of Endymion Walker, of Exeter; born 1674, dec. 1747[2]), from which he compiled his valuable and laborious work, *The Sufferings of the Clergy*, were forwarded to the Library by his son, William Walker, a druggist in Exeter, as appears from a letter from the latter preserved among papers relating to the Library in the Librarian's study. The annual accounts, however,

[1] He was M.A., and at one time a fellow, of Exeter College, and was created D.D. by diploma on 7 Dec. 1714, in pursuance of a letter from the Chancellor, in acknowledgment of his book on the *Sufferings of the Clergy*. (Reg. Convoc. Bd. 31, f. 116.)

[2] His successor in his Exeter prebend was appointed in that year.

mention the gift under the year 1756. Dr. Walker had expressed in his book (*pref.* p. xliii) his intention to deposit his papers in some public repository, and his purpose was fortunately thus carried out. The papers have recently been bound, and now form twelve volumes in folio and eleven in quarto.[1] A large number of letters from many among the sufferers and their representatives are here preserved; but, unfortunately, Walker's own handwriting is often very hard to decipher. Many pamphlets which belonged to him (identified by the peculiar handwriting in MS. notes) are amongst a vast series recently bound and placed in continuation of the Godwyn Tracts; and several volumes of pamphlets written by Dissenters were given by himself in the years 1719–21.

The name of Hogarth occurs in the list of donors, as presenting his two engravings of the *Analysis of Beauty*, which he had published in the preceding year.

A.D. 1755.

This year is remarkable for the number and variety of the collections with which, during its course, the Library was enriched, comprehending those of Rawlinson, Furney, St. Amand, and Ballard.

On April 6 died Richard Rawlinson, D.C.L., a Bishop among the Non-jurors, notwithstanding that he passed in the world as a layman. From the time of Bodley, Laud, and Selden, he was the greatest benefactor the Library had known; and his only rivals since his own day have been Gough and Douce. In point of numbers, his donation of MSS. far exceeded all. From the short autobiographical notice of himself, given in his own collections for a continuation of the *Athenæ Oxon.* (where he has inserted a small portrait of himself, engraved, without his name, by Van der Gucht), we learn the following particulars. He was born Jan. 3, 16$\frac{89}{90}$, in

[1] In answer to an enquiry in *Notes and Queries* in 1862 (3rd series, i. 218), I said that these papers were amongst the *Rawlinson* MSS. This mistake arose from the fact that the least important portion had then been recently found in a mass of papers belonging to that collection, but they did not at any time themselves form part of it.

the Old Bailey, his father being Sir Thos. Rawlinson, who was Lord Mayor of London in 1706. On March 9, 170$\frac{7}{8}$ (having been previously at St. Paul's School and Eton), he was matriculated as a commoner of St. John's College; but in consequence of the death of his father in the same year, he became a gentleman-commoner in 1709; B.A., Oct. 10, 1711[1]; M.A., July 5, 1713; Governor of Bridewell and Bethlehem Hospitals, 1713; F.R.S., 1714; ordained (among the Non-jurors) Deacon, Sept. 21, and Priest, Sept. 23, 1716[2]. He then travelled through the whole of England, except some of the northern parts, and in 1719 went into Normandy, where, while staying at Rouen, he received from Oxford the degree of D.C.L. by diploma of June 30. Thence he went to the Low Countries, where, in Sept., he was admitted into the Universities of both Utrecht and Leyden, and returned into England in Nov. On June 12 in the following year, he started on a longer journey, which he extended through Holland, France, Germany, the whole of Italy, and Sicily, to Malta; and returned on the death of his elder brother Thomas, also a well-known book-collector, in 1726. During his six years' travels, he had seen, he remarks, four Popes[3]. Admitted F.S.A. May 10, 1727. On March 25, 1728, he was consecrated Bishop, by Bishops Gandy, Doughty, and Blackbourne, in Gandy's chapel[4]. Appointed a Governor of St. Bartholomew's Hospital in March,

[1] This date is from the *Register of Graduates*; Rawlinson himself only says, Mich. Term, 1710.

[2] By Bishop Jeremy Collier, in Mr. Laurence's chapel on College Hill, London. (See a communication from me in *Notes and Queries*, 3rd series, iii. 244.) He appears to have endeavoured to conceal from the world his clerical character. In a letter to T. Rawlins, of Pophills, Warw. in 1736, he requests him not to address him as *Rev.* (Ballard's MSS. ii. 6.) Some volumes of Sermons in his handwriting are among his MSS. His writing is of a very broad, rude, and clumsy character; and it is singular that his brother Thomas wrote a hand very similar. Richard usually signs only with his initials, separated by a cross, 'R + R.'

[3] The small note-books kept on his journeys, containing epitaphs, inscriptions, accounts of places visited, &c., are preserved (but, unfortunately, in an imperfect series) among his MSS. in class D.

[4] See *Notes and Queries*, 3rd series, i. 225.

1733. He resided at London House, Aldersgate, so called from having been in early days a mansion of the Bishops of London. During his lifetime he was a constant benefactor to the Library; in the years 1733-4-5-7-8-9 and 1750, he is entered in the great Register for special gifts of coins, books, and pictures, and onward to 1754 in a small quarto register. Some hundreds of printed books, now in the series called '*Jur.*,' and elsewhere, were given by him at these times; while many of the Holbeins and other valuable portraits in the Picture Gallery came from him[1]. A few MSS. also came from him during his lifetime which are now placed in the general Bodley collection. But at his death all his collections came *en masse*[2]; collections formed abroad and at home, the choice of book-auctions, the pickings of chandlers' and grocers'

[1] Two beautiful oval miniature portraits of James Edward, son of James II, and his wife Clementina Sobieski, which could not, probably, at the time be safely exhibited, were exhumed by Mr. Coxe from the obscurity to which they had been consigned, and are now hung in the Picture Gallery. [Two miniatures of these royal personages, possibly of corresponding character, were sold at a sale of curiosities which had belonged to Hon. Francis Forbes, at London in March, 1874; that of the Princess for £79, but that of the Prince for only £10 10*s*.] In Feb. 17$\frac{49}{50}$, Rawlinson sent Kelly's 'Holy Table,' a marble slab, covered with astrological figures (engraved in Dr. Dee's *Actions with Spirits*), which, he says, had been subsequently in the possession of Lilly. It is now in the Ashmolean Museum.

[2] By the terms of his will, dated June 2, 1752, and printed in 1755, he bequeathed all his MSS. of every kind (excepting private papers and letters) to the Chancellor, Masters, and Scholars of the University, to be placed in the Bodleian Library, or in such other place as they should deem most proper, for the use and benefit of the University, and of all other persons, properly and with leave resorting thereto with a view to the public good; and to be kept separate and apart from every other collection. With these he gave also all his books printed on vellum or silk (of which latter kind there are two or three small specimens), all his deeds and charters, and all his printed books containing any MSS. notes, together with various antiquities and miscellaneous curiosities. His MS. and printed music he bequeathed to the Music School. Of the Musical library preserved in this room, a MS. Catalogue was made some years ago by Rev. Robert Hake, M.A., then Chaplain of New College, afterwards Precentor of Canterbury and Vicar of Aylsham, and now English Chaplain at Buda-Pesth. The library was placed under the custody of the Librarian of the Bodleian in 1885; see the Librarian's *Report* printed in 1888, p. 22.

waste-paper, everything, especially, in the shape of a MS., from early copies of Classics and Fathers to the well-nigh most recent log-books of sailors' voyages[1]. Not a sale of MSS. occurred, apparently, in London, during his time, at which he was not an omnigenous purchaser; so that students of every subject now bury themselves in his stores with great content and profit. But history in all its branches, heraldry and genealogy, biography and topography, are his specially strong points. The printed books bequeathed by him in selection from his whole library (of which those in quarto and smaller sizes are still called by his name) amounted to between 1800 and 1900[2], but the MSS. to upwards of

[1] *Apropos* of log-books, it may be mentioned that whereas it appears from the eighth Report of the Deputy-Keeper of the Records, p. 26, 1847, that the earliest log among the Admiralty Records is of the year 1673, there are several of about the same date and a little earlier to be found in Rawlinson's collection.

[2] Among the printed books are two copies of Archbp. Parker's rare *De Antiq. Eccl. Brit.*, 1572. One of these is the identical copy described by Strype in his *Life of Parker*, and which was then in the possession of Bp. Fleetwood of Ely; the other (which was given to the Library by Jos. Sanford, B.D., Balliol Coll., in 1753) was presented to Rich. Cosin by John Parker, the Archbishop's eldest son, Jan. 5, 1593. Owen, the Librarian, notes on the cover that Dr. Rawlinson tells him this copy was bought at the sale of the library of his brother, Thos. Rawlinson, by the Earl of Oxford, for £40. A collection of the original broadside-proclamations issued during the whole of the reign of Queen Elizabeth, in beautiful condition, forms a remarkable and splendid volume; the collection is complete, except that a few proclamations, of which printed copies are wanting, are supplied in MS. As far as the year 1577 they are printed by Richard Jugge, sometimes alone and sometimes in conjunction with John Cawood; thenceforward they are printed by the two Barkers, first by Christopher, and afterwards by Robert. They appear to have been collected in the reign of James I. A printed chronological table of contents is prefixed, together with a portrait of the Queen, engraved by Fr. Delaram, with six lines of verse by 'Jo. Davies, Heref.' At the year 1559 a leaf is inserted containing the arms of Q. Mary of Scotland quartering those of England (the assumption of which by Mary gave irreconcileable offence to Q. Eliz.), beautifully painted, with the note, 'Sent out of Fraunce, in July, 1559,' and these lines below:—

'The armes of Marie Queene Dolphines of ffraunce,
The nobillest Lady in earth for till aduaunce:
Off Scotland queene, and of Ingland also,
Off Ireland als, God haith providit so.'

This leaf is one of two copies executed for Cecil and Q. Eliz. Two,

4800, besides a large number of old charters and miscellaneous deeds[1].

The staff of the Library being very small at the time, as well as ill-paid[2], and such an accession being completely overwhelming, the officers appear to have contented themselves with duly entering the printed books, while leaving the MSS. entirely neglected. About the beginning of the present century some steps were

almost unique, 'red-letter' books are also among the rarities of Rawlinson's printed collection. The one is a Sermon on Ps. iv. 7, preached before Charles I at Oxford by Josias Howe, B.D., of Trinity College. It is printed entirely in red, and has no title. It was bought, included in a volume of miscellaneous sermons, out of Dr. Charlett's library, by Hearne, who says in a MS. note that only thirty copies were printed. A description of it is given by Dr. Bliss in his *Reliquiæ Hearn.* vol. ii. pp. 960–1, where Hearne's note is printed in full. The other is a volume entitled, *The Bloody Court; or, the Fatal Tribunal*, being an account of the trial and execution of Charles I. The lengthy title is printed by Dr. Bliss, *ubi supra*. This tract was reproduced in photo-lithography by Jul. Guggenheim, a photographer at Oxford, in 1882. A third tract printed entirely in red was published in 1652 by Samuel Chidley; it is entitled, *A cry against a crying sinne*, and is a protest against the infliction of capital punishment for theft. Some few of Rawlinson's printed books came to the Library among Gough's, in 1809.

[1] With reference to his collections Rawlinson says in a letter of 25 June, 1743, 'I go on digesting and binding up my papers, as I think you should Dr. Charlet's correspondence, least these kind[s] of things should be lost, as disregarded by those who come after us. As in all collections, making for thirty years together, there must necessarily be a quantity of rubbish, I shall begin to sift them and contract my quarters.' (Ballard MS. ii. 83.)

[2] The salaries being miserably insufficient, the recognised duties of the officers appear to have been simply the cataloguing the few books that were received in ordinary course, and attending upon the readers. Consequently for any other work, for arranging or cataloguing any new collections, &c., special payments were always made. A somewhat amusing instance of this occurs under the year 1722, when the Librarian craved payment for making with his own hand certain new hand-lists, &c., but was refused. However, he carried on his claim from year to year until it was admitted to the amount of £5 15*s*. 6*d*. in 1725. And as the funds were insufficient to defray in this way the extra cost of cataloguing such a collection as Rawlinson's, hence, doubtless, came the neglect which it experienced. Such work was so clearly understood to form no part of the Librarians' regular duties, that Rawlinson says, in a letter to Owen, Apr. 15, 1751 (MS. C. 989), 'I think large benefactors should pay the expense of entries into the Bodleian, as their books are useless till so entered.'

taken towards a Catalogue, and a portion were arranged and numbered; still later, considerably more was done. But it was only on the accession of Mr. Coxe to the Headship, that the full extent of Rawlinson's collections was ascertained. Every corner of the Library was then examined, and cupboard after cupboard was found filled with MSS. and papers huddled together in confusion, while, last not least, a dark hole under a staircase, explored by me on hands and knees, afforded a rich 'take,' including many writings of Rawlinson's Non-juring friends. The whole number of volumes thus brought to light amounted to about 1300.

The classes into which the whole collection of MSS. is now divided are the following:—

1. *Class A:* 500 volumes, chiefly of English history, with a few theological books. Amongst these are the *Thurloe State Papers*, in sixty-seven volumes, of which all of importance were published by Birch, in seven vols. folio, in 1742. These papers were found after the Revolution concealed in the ceiling of garrets in Lincoln's Inn, which belonged to the rooms formerly occupied by Thurloe; and they still bear too evident marks of the damp to which they were there exposed. They passed through Lord Somers' and Sir Jos. Jekyll's hands into those of a bookseller, Fletcher Gyles, from whom Rawlinson obtained them in 1751, and who, as Rawlinson says (Rawl. C. 989, f. 169^{b}), asked at first an 'immoderate price' for them. Another series is that of *Miscellaneous Papers of Sam. Pepys*, in twenty-five volumes, containing his correspondence, collections on Admiralty business, &c.[1] Of these,

[1] It was chiefly from these that the two volumes published in 1841 under the title of *Life, Journals, and Correspondence of S. Pepys* were compiled. Unfortunately the editor, or his copyist, appears to have been sometimes unable to read the MSS., and at other times very careless; his book therefore abounds with errors. The following is one of the worst, as it libels the memory of a statesman who deserved better treatment: Sir R. Southwell is represented as saying in a letter to Pepys (vol. i. p. 282) that he has lost his health 'by sitting many years at the *sack*-bottle,' whereas the poor man had lost it by sitting many years 'at the *inck*-bottle.' A line or two farther on, Southwell's occupation with 'some care and much sorrow,' is changed into 'love, care and much sorrow.' Certain '*Novelles*,'

together with many other volumes which belonged to Pepys, including many curious dockyard account-books of the times of Henry VIII and Queen Elizabeth, Rawlinson says, 'They were collected with a design for a Lord High Admiral, such as he [Pepys] should approve, but those times are not yet come, and so little care was taken of them that they were redeemed from *thus et odores vendentibus.*'[1] Of another acquisition Rawlinson writes thus:—

'There was lately an auction here of Mr. Bridgeman's books, curiosities, and MSS., who was formerly clerk of the Council to K. James II, and register to the Ecclesiastical Commission. Here I laid out some pence, and picked up some curiosities; the original minute-book of the High Commission, the proceedings every session with the names of those present[2], by which it appears that Bp. Sprat was not so innocent as he would persuade us in his letter to the Earl of Dorset to think, and that notwithstanding all his shiftings he sat to the penultim. Session of that Court;' [Letters canvassing the nobility, gentry, justices of the peace, &c., in favour of the repeal of the Penal Laws and the Test, which Rawlinson describes as 'a fine picture book (as one may properly call it) of all the great men, who were canvassed by the Court'] '3 letters from the D. of Monmouth, two to the King and one to the Queen, desiring an audience in which he would give them such satisfaction as would agreeably surprise them . . . very pathetic, and deserved at least some attention[3]; . . . several volumes of treaties, . . . instructions to ambassadors . . . Very remarkable are those to Lord Castlemain on his going to Rome, the King's two letters to the Pope, a third of

or newspapers, which Mr. Hill sends to Pepys are explained (vol. ii. p. 135) to have been the *Novellæ* of Justinian! Throughout the book proper names are frequently made to become anything but proper to their owners.

[1] Letter from Rawlinson to T. Rawlins, Jan. 25, 17$\frac{49}{50}$; Ballard MS. ii. 115.

[2] These notes have been printed by J. R. Bloxam, D.D. in his *Magdalen College and K. James II*, printed for the Oxf. Hist. Soc. in 1886, pp. 50, 53, 56, &c.

[3] The same volume (now A. 139[b]) also contains Monmouth's acknowledgment, written and signed by himself on the day of his execution, that Charles II had declared that he was never married to his mother; witnessed by Bishops Turner and Ken, together with Tenison and Hooper. This is now exhibited in the glass case at the entrance to the Library. The Monmouth letters were printed for the Camden Society by Sir G. Duckett in 1879, and the papers about the Penal Laws were privately printed by him in 1882–3.

revocation, all personal, a complement, but no embassy of obedience. Copy-books of letters, private and public, wrote by K. Charles and K. James II, from which might be collected such a fund of true tho' secret, history, that the prize is not to be valued[1], and will, I hope, be a standing monument of great events, and preserved in Bodley's repository, with the papers of Bp. Turner and other great men at and since the year 1688. But no more of what too much can't be said[2].'

There are also some papers in this class and in class C which belonged to Archbp. Wake. Probably it is about these that Rawlinson writes, on June 24, 1741[3]:—

'A gent. last week met with some papers of Archbp. Wake's at a chandler's shop; this is unpardonable in his executors, as all his MSS. were left to Christ Church. But quære whether these did not fall into some servant's hands who was ordered to burn them, and Mr. Martin Folkes ought to have seen that done. They fell into the curate's hands of St. George, Bloomsbury.'

2. *Class B* numbers 520 volumes numerically, but really, including double numbers, 534. They comprise heraldry and genealogy (including MSS. of Sir Richard and Sir Thos. St. George, W. Wyrley, Guillim, Ryley, Glover, Le Neve, and other heralds) English and Irish history, and topography, including several monastic chartularies. Among the genealogical MSS. is a remarkable collection of pedigrees, in twelve volumes, which I ascertained to have been compiled by Thomas Wilkinson, Vicar of Laurence Waltham, Berks, between about 1647 and 1681. They are arranged alphabetically, as far as the letter P in tolerable order and regularity, but thenceforward only in a rough and incomplete state. Unfortunately the handwriting is far from clear, and bad ink has often made it worse. Among the volumes relating to *Essex*, *Norfolk*, *Suffolk*, &c., are twelve or thirteen which belonged to William Holman, a voluminous collector for the first-mentioned county, who incorporated the gatherings of Rev. John Ousley

[1] In his delight at his new purchase, Rawlinson seems to have considerably exaggerated the interest of the volumes of copies of letters.

[2] Letter to T. Rawlins, Feb. 24, 174$\frac{2}{3}$; Ballard MS. ii. 78.

[3] To the same; *Ibid.* 59.

and Thos. Jekyll. Morant, the historian of Essex, obtained the larger portion of Holman's books; some are in the British Museum; and the remainder ('the refuse,' says Morant) were bought by Rawlinson in 1752 for £10[1]. Besides the above-mentioned volumes, there are a large number of Holman's MSS. which are kept distinct, and which have been bound in fourteen folio volumes, eleven quarto, and five octavo. Under *London* are some volumes of Diocesan papers which belonged to Bp. John Robinson. They formed (with one volume in class A and several in class C) a mass which are described by Rawlinson as follows[2]:—

'I lately rescued from the grocers, chandlers, &c. a parcel of papers once the property of Compton and Robinson, successively Bps. of London. Amongst those of the first were original subscription and visitation books, letters and conferences during the apprehensions of Popery amongst the clergy of this diocese, remarkable intelligences relating to Burnet and the Orange Court in Holland in those extraordinary times before 1688[3], minutes of the proceedings of the Commissioners for the Propagation of the Gospel, and a great variety of other papers. Amongst those of Bp. Robinson, numbers of originals relating to the transactions at the treaty of Utrecht, copies of his own letters to Lord Bolingbroke, and originals from Lord Bolingbroke, Lord Oxford, Electress and Elector of Hanover, Ormonde, Strafford, Prior, &c.; letters from the Scots deprived Bishops to Compton, and variety of State papers. They belonged to one Mr. [Anth.] Gibbon, lately dead, who was private secretary to both the afore-mentioned prelates.'

Of some other ecclesiastical papers (now in Class B) which were obtained in a similar way, Rawlinson writes thus:—

'Last week I met with a collection of ecclesiastical causes, several of notes (*sic*), which formerly belonged to Sir John Cooke, Advocate-General and Dean of the Arches. They were sold by his nephew's widow to support pyes, currants, sugar, &c., and I redeemed as many

[1] Gough, *Brit. Topogr.* i. 370, 345.

[2] Letter to Thos. Rawlins, of Pophills, Warw., June 24, 1741; Ballard MS. ii. 59.

[3] Including some letters from Ken while Chaplain to Princess Mary. These papers of Compton are in class C.

as came to 12*s.* at 3*d.* per pound, which I intend to digest and bind up. Amongst the rest are the causes of Bp. Watson, the Dutchess of Cleveland, with the whole process, sentence, original letters, &c.[1]'

Under *Bucks* are Rawlinson's own collections for a history of Eton College, and under *Middlesex* and *Oxon.* his parochial collections for those counties. The *Irish* MSS. include many of great antiquity and value which formerly belonged to Sir James Ware, *e.g.* Tigernach's Annals, Annals of Ulster, Lives of Saints, Dublin Chartularies, Arms of Irish families, Irish poems, &c., which came from the Chandos sale. Among them is the often noticed Life of St. Columba by Magnus O'Donnell, written in 1532, which was bought by Rawlinson for twenty-three shillings.

3. *Class C* comprehends 989 MSS. of very miscellaneous character, but chiefly consisting of law, history and theology, with a few medical works. Among the theological portion are papers of John Dury, the zealous labourer for union amongst Protestants in the time of Charles I, papers of Bedell and Ussher, some volumes of John Lewis of Margate[2], and some interesting Service-books of English use, including a Pontifical given to Salisbury Cathedral by Bp. Roger de Martivale between 1315–1329, and an early Oseney book. Several volumes consist of papers of Dr. Chamberlaine (author of *Notitia Angliæ*) and Mr. Henry Newman, secretaries of the Societies for the Propagation of the Gospel, and Promoting Christian Knowledge, which Rawlinson says in a letter dated April 28, 1744 (Ballard MS. ii.), he had then recently purchased. Some seventeen or eighteen volumes came from the library of Bp. Turner of Ely (together with others in the classes called D. and *Letters*), containing papers of Bp. Gunning, of Turner himself, and of his brother, Dr. Thomas Turner, Dean of Canterbury. These were obtained by Rawlinson in 1743, who in them became master, as he says, of a considerable treasure

[1] Letter to T. Rawlins, 13 July, 1739; Ballard MS. ii. f. 28[b].

[2] A volume of collections by him relating to the early versions of the Bible was bought in 1858 for five guineas. Other papers of his were transferred to the Library from the Clarendon Press in 1886.

for ten guineas[1]. Early English poets are represented by Lydgate, Rolle of Hampole, William of Nassyngton, and others[2]; and one volume contains a few Welsh verses. The volumes relating to English history in classes A and C are noticed in the return printed in the Record Commission Report for 1800, pp. 348–353.

Of the three classes A, B, and C, a catalogue compiled by myself was printed in two volumes in quarto in 1862 and 1878, with a full index to the contents of the MSS., as well as to the catalogue itself[3].

4. The class formerly entitled *Miscellaneous*, but now D, numbers about 1400 volumes, and includes the greater part of those which were discovered in 1861. Of these a catalogue by myself is now in gradual progress, as the main part of my work. They are so entirely miscellaneous that it is impossible to give in a few lines a real idea of their nature. History, travels, biography, and religious controversy largely prevail. There are papers of Sir Thos. Browne, Dr. Dee, Maittaire, Peter Le Neve, Ashmole[4], John Dunton, and Bagford, with a very large mass of *Hearniana*[5]. Of the Nonjurors, there are papers of Grascome, Gandy, Spinckes, Hickes, Fitzwilliams, Howell, and Dean Granville. Some nine or ten volumes are occupied with the accounts of the Royal Surveyor of Works from 1532 to 1545. The Churchwardens' accounts of Sutterton, Lincolnshire, from 1493 to 1536, and of St. Peter's, Cornhill, from 1664 to 1689, are also found here[6]. There is a

[1] Ballard MS. ii. 87.

[2] One curious volume is described by Sir F. Madden in his preface to *Syr Gawayne*, printed by the Roxburghe Club in 1839.

[3] For the description of the contents of three of the Irish volumes (C. 475, 477, and 512) I was indebted to an experienced Irish scholar, Standish Hayes O'Grady, Esq.

[4] With relation to these Rawlinson says, in a letter dated Feb. 25, 1736–7, that he had bought, about two years since, some of Ashmole's papers from his heirs, including some of Dugdale's (Ballard MS. ii. 11).

[5] Among these last were discovered the hitherto unknown first and second parts of the series of Cambridge plays of the *Pilgrimage to* and *Return from Parnassus*. These I edited for the Clarendon Press in 1887.

[6] For Parish Registers, see under 1821.

large collection of MSS. in foreign languages, chiefly French, Spanish, and Italian; some of the latter of which bear on English history, as containing copies of reports made to Rome by Papal agents and to Venice by ambassadors, together with the proceedings at many conclaves. These, which number twenty volumes, and were obtained originally in Italy and elsewhere by Addison during his travels[1], were bought by Rawlinson at Sir Jos. Jekyll's sale of the Somers' MSS. in 1739, for £3 15*s*.[2] There is also a mass of papers of J. J. Zamboni, Resident in England for the Duke of Modena and Elector of Hesse Darmstadt, and a friend of Maittaire[3]. A considerable number of autograph signatures, barbarously cut out from various books by Thomas Rawlinson, were found in loose papers; these have now been mounted and bound in two volumes. There are not, however, many of interest among them, except several of Ben Jonson.

5. Of *Letters* there are upwards of 100 volumes, comprising all the multifarious correspondence of Hearne with Anstis, Bagford, Baker, Barnes, Dodwell, Smith, &c., the correspondence of Rawlinson, Dr. Thomas Turner, and Bishop Francis Turner, Philip Lord Wharton, and Sir Edm. Warcupp. One volume contains a few

[1] See a note in Rawl. MS. D. 610.

[2] Two MS. volumes of copies of the Relations of Venetian Residents in various countries in the latter half of the sixteenth century were given to the Library by Will. Gent, in 1600, and Sir Rich. Spencer, in 1603 (Bodl. MSS. 880, 911).

[3] Zamboni died on Apr. 8, 1753, very much (and deservedly) in debt and difficulty, and his papers were bought by Rawlinson (as the latter states in a memorandum attached) of one Mr. Charles Marsh, by whom they had been seized. They remained tied up in the bundles in which Zamboni himself had placed and labelled them, unopened, until 1878, when the writer of these Annals took them in hand for arrangement for binding. They now make twenty-one volumes in folio (of which four consist of letters from and to the sovereigns of Modena and Darmstadt), and one in quarto. They are chiefly in Italian, French, and English, with a few in Spanish and German, but are of no great interest; a large proportion are merely mercantile, or relative to speculations in books, pictures, and jewellery, and some relate to Zamboni's debts and gross immoralities. He is said in the notice of his death in the *Gentleman's Magazine* to have been 'a friend to many gentlemen under misfortune,' and numerous begging letters addressed to him seem to attest the correctness of this statement.

letters by Dryden, Pope, Edw. Young, &c. There is also a series of letters in three vols. relating to Dr. John Polyander, of Kerckhoven, Professor of Divinity at Leyden, and twelve volumes of G. J. Vossius' correspondence, being the originals from which the folio volume published at London in 1691 was printed[1].

Of a volume now numbered 73 Rawlinson thus writes:—

'I don't remember whether I mentioned a copybook of letters wrote by Jesuits to one another from Naples to Rome and St. Germains-en-lay, and *vice versa*, in which are very curious notitia relating to our English Travellers' (*i.e.* the exiled Royal Family), 'and others abroad, but they are not so perfect as one could wish.' He then adds: 'There are also originals of the Duke of Perth's, Berwick's, F. Saunders, Sabran, Polton, &c., a sketch of a life of K. James II, an original renuntiation of Popery by one John Gordoun a Jesuit, and other uncommon papers, which I rescued from the chandlers, &c.[2]'

These last papers are mostly to be found in D. 21.

6. The class of *Poetry* contains 246 volumes, including Chaucer, Hoccleve, Lydgate, Capgrave (Life of St. Catherine), and Rolle of Hampole, with Piers Plowman and the Romance of Parthenope of Blois (both imperfect). The majority are miscellaneous poems and plays of the seventeenth century. One volume, containing the words of anthems with the composers' names, is supposed to be the Chapel-book used by Charles I.

Of the three last-mentioned classes, a brief MS. list was drawn up with great neatness and accuracy by Dr. Bliss, in 1812 (reaching in the case of the *Miscell.*, or *D*, only as far as No. 407). In continuation of this a short index has been made to the later additions.

7. Of *Sermons* there are about 220 volumes; many of which are by Non-jurors (*e.g.* Bishops Hickes and Hawes), including three by Rawlinson himself. Ten volumes are by Dan. Price, Dean of St. Asaph, 1696–1706; and three volumes contain sermons by

[1] In Bodl. Addit. MS. C. 78, f. 30 is a memorandum by Dr. Rich. Allestrei (*sic*) of the receipt by him from Eton on Apr. 28, 1679, of thirteen boxes of letters from 'Dr. [Isaac] Vossius.' These do not appear to have been presented to the Bodleian, and where they now are I do not know.

[2] Letter of June 25, 1743; Ballard, ii. 83.

Leighton, apparently from notes taken by some auditor at the time of delivery. These were published by Rev. W. West, formerly of Nairn, N.B., now rector of Rendlesham, Suffolk, in his edition of Leighton's whole works, in six vols., 1869–75. Others are by Bishops Walton, Sanderson, and Turner, by Tho. Lydiat, Horneck, and eleven volumes by Tho. Swadling, D.D. Of Nonconformists' sermons there are many volumes; *e.g.* of Edm. Calamy, 24 of Robert Fleming the Presbyterian, 11 of — Beaumont (an Independent at Rotherhithe), Sam. Ogden; at Crosby Square and Exeter.

8. A selection of Biblical and Classical MSS., with a few others, amounting to 199, are marked with the reference 'Rawl. BN.' Amongst these are a few Greek volumes, with critical *Adversaria* of Maittaire, Josh. Lasher, and J. G. Grævius. Early copies of Statius, Ovid, Virgil, &c. form part of the classics; while among the Biblical MSS. is a grand eighth-century copy (written in half-uncials, in the same style as the Rushworth book) of the Gospels of St. Luke and St. John, and a beautiful eleventh-century Psalter with the commentary of St. Bruno. One other fine book is a Psalter written for Ch. Ch. Cathedral, Dublin, by the care of Stephen Derby, Prior, about A.D. 1360–80, with remarkable miniatures illustrating Psalms xxxix, liii, lxix, lxxxi, and xcviii [1].

9. Of *Missals*, *Horæ*, and other Service-books, there are (besides some which are scattered in Classes C. and BN.) about 130. These (many of which are of French origin, bought out of the library of Nic. Jos. Foucault [2], of Flemish, or of Italian) were for a time incorporated with a large collection of Liturgical books, consisting chiefly of part of the Canonici collection purchased in 1818, under the general title of *Miscell. Liturg.*, but they have now been again separated.

[1] Three plates of fine fac-similes are given from this volume in the collection of *Fac-similes of National MSS. of Ireland*, edited for the Master of the Rolls in Ireland by Mr. John T. Gilbert in 1874–84. Specimens from many Bodleian MSS. are to be found in this work.

[2] From this library Rawlinson also obtained some French editions of the *Horæ*, printed on vellum.

10. A small collection of *Statutes*, comprising sixty-five volumes. They consist of the Statutes of various Colleges at Oxford and Cambridge, of the Cathedrals of Lichfield, Hereford, Worcester, Chester, Manchester, Canterbury, Exeter, and the Abbey of Westminster; of the Order of the Garter (various copies); of Hospitals at Croydon, Chipping-Barnet, and Chichester; of the Gresham Charities; together with the Charters of London and Bristol; Statutes made by the Chapter of Paris for the Church of the Holy Sepulchre there in 1421, and an eighteenth-century transcript of the Statutes of the College at Bayeux. But the volume of most interest in this class is the rare printed volume of the Statutes of Thame School, issued in 1575. Of this, only five other copies are known, one kept at the School itself, a second in the custody of the Warden of New College (the Visitor of the School), a third in the Royal Library, Brit. Mus., and the fourth and fifth, both on vellum, in the possession of the Earl of Abingdon and in the Grenville Library, Brit. Mus. Rawlinson's copy, which wants the title, has in it the book-plate of John, Duke of Newcastle.

11. Of the MSS. of Dr. Thomas Smith, the Non-juror, of Magd. Coll., Oxford, there are 138 volumes, which (with the exception of a few bequeathed by Smith himself) came into Rawlinson's hands together with the rest of Hearne's collections. They are noticed above, under the year 1735.

12. Besides the multitude of books, scattered throughout every class of Rawlinson's library, which belonged to Hearne or were written by him, there are about 150 small duodecimo volumes of Hearne's daily diary and note-books, commencing in July, 1705, and ending on June 4, 1735, the last actual entry being on June 1, and his decease occurring on June 10. The character of this diary is well known from the two volumes of Extracts published by Dr. Bliss in 1857, with the title *Reliquiæ Hearnianæ.* But these volumes are of course far from comprehending all that deserves publication; the diary throughout is full of like curious personal history and anecdote, antiquarian gleanings and amusing gossip, mixed, as a matter of course, with a good deal of occasional acri-

mony against those with whom Hearne came in collision, either from differences in academic or literary matters, or from their being friends of the 'Elector of Hanover.' There is scarcely a subject falling within its writer's scope of observation on which this diary may not be consulted; and as it is written in his usual plain and neat hand, with an index to each volume, it is fortunately easy for reference. The publication of the whole diary has now been commenced by the Oxford Historical Society, and three volumes, reaching to 1712, have been issued, under the careful editorship of C. E. Doble, M.A., who adds under each day abstracts of the letters of the same date written by or to Hearne. To the volumes copious notes are attached. Hearne bequeathed all his MSS., and books with MSS. notes, to Mr. William Bedford, son of the well-known bishop among the Non-jurors, Hilkiah Bedford; the legatee died on July 11, 1747, and Rawlinson bought them of his widow for £105. Hence it was that they came finally to the place where Hearne would himself have rejoiced to see them deposited. The autobiographical sketch of Hearne's own life, which Huddesford published in 1772, in conjunction with the lives of Leland and Wood, is preserved among the D. MSS. Of this Rawlinson says, in a letter dated June 19, 1740[1]: 'Tom's own life was so low and poor a performance that I recommended it to Bedford to burn.' On account, probably, of the numerous reflections which the diary contained on living persons, Rawlinson ordered in his bequest that it should not be open to inspection until after the lapse of seven years. He laid also the same restraint upon the use of his own papers noticed in the next paragraph.

13. Large collections were made by Rawlinson for a continuation of Wood's *Athenæ Oxon.* These contain much valuable biographical information, derived in very many cases from the actual information of the persons noticed, letters from many of whom are inserted. There are, in all, twenty-five volumes, folio and quarto; among the folios there are two series of notices

[1] Ballard MS. ii. 41.

arranged alphabetically, and one volume (also alphabetical) of notices of Cambridge men admitted *ad eundem;* the quartos contain 1331 notices, numbered but not arranged in any other order, with one general alphabetical index. These collections, together with Hearne's Diaries, and Rawlinson's Non-jurors' Papers, and notes of his own Travels, were included in a fourth and last codicil, dated Feb. 14, 1755, which directed that all these papers should be kept locked up during a period of seven years. By the same codicil also were conveyed numerous engravings by Vertue, portraits of Englishmen, some paintings, and a collection of Roman, Persian, Italian, and English medals[1]. Some of the Italian medals, particularly a fine set in copper of the members of the House of Medici, are now exhibited in a case in the Picture Gallery[2]. By a codicil of June 17, 1752, Rawlinson had previously bequeathed a series of medals of Popes, of which he remarks, 'as they are, I take them to be one of the most complete collections now in Europe;' together with twenty shillings *per annum* for enlarging and continuing the set[3].

14. Finally (as regards MSS.), Rawlinson left a mass of ancient charters (five hundred of which were catalogued by the late Mr. Coxe), and of vellum deeds and documents of all kinds, chiefly of the seventeenth and eighteenth centuries. These are for the most part, if not entirely, included in the *Calendar of Charters and Rolls*, edited by the late Mr. W. H. Turner in 1878. He left, also, copper-plates of engravings of some of his ancient documents and other curiosities, as well as a large number of impressions from these plates. Some of these impressions were given to Lord

[1] The clock still in use in the Library, made by Robinson in Gracechurch Street, was one of the items comprised in this codicil, where it is described as a 'table clock,' then in the custody of Mr. John King, a bookseller, in Moorfields.

[2] These were bought, 'very cheap,' at Mrs. Kennon's sale, Feb. 24, 1755, by a dealer named Angel Carmey, who sold them to Rawlinson for £10 10*s*. Carmey's letter conveying his offer of sale is preserved in Rawlinson's copy of the sale catalogue. Carmey gave portraits of Charles XII of Sweden and of Fred. Will. I of Prussia to the Library in 1762.

[3] It does not appear, however, that this sum was ever paid.

Mountstuart in 1773, in exchange for Buffon's Natural History and two botanical works[1]; and many were sold at the sale of Bodleian duplicates in 1862. The copper-plates were added to his bequest by a second codicil, dated July 25, 1754, in which he desired that impressions should be taken from them, to be sold in one volume for the use and benefit of the University.

15. A last item in Rawlinson's miscellaneous gifts (besides various bas-reliefs, figures, a Jewish vessel, Muscovite cup[2], &c.) was a large collection of matrices of ancient episcopal, conventual, and personal seals, chiefly foreign[3]; together with impressions of seals, ancient and modern, in metal and wax, 'most of which,' it is said

[1] MS. list, in 8vo, by J. Price of benefactions during a portion of his time, beginning at 1765 and ending at 1786.

[2] Both the vessel and the cup were engraved by Rawlinson in 1742. The vessel is a two-handed pot of bell-metal, with three legs, which was found by a fisherman in a brook in Suffolk about 1698; it was sold by the executors of Dr. John Covel, Master of Christ's College, Cambridge (who died in 1722), to the Earl of Oxford, and Rawlinson bought it at the sale of the earl's pictures and curiosities in March 1742, for £1 5*s*., as noted in his own copy of the sale catalogue. It appears to have been a sacred offering for some purposes of ablution, given by one Joseph ben Yehiel (as appears from a Hebrew inscription), who was a Jew of Colchester, probably about the middle of the 13th century. It is described in Tovey's *Anglia Judaica*, 1738, pp. 248-9, where it is engraved; in Dr. M. Margoliouth's *Vestiges of the Anglo-Hebrews in East Anglia*, pp. 47-54, and in a review of that book by Dr. A. Neubauer, which appeared in the *Academy* for April, 1870. It was exhibited in the Anglo-Jewish Exhibition in London in 1887, where it attracted much notice, and was frequently mentioned in articles at the time in the *Jewish Chronicle*. Other articles purchased by Rawlinson at the same sale of the Earl of Oxford's curiosities were the following: portrait of T. Baker, of St. John's College, Cambridge, three-quarters, £2 10*s*.; drawing by Faithorne of Sir Rob. Peake's head, 5*s*.; John Bagford, by Hugh Howard, three-quarters, £1 1*s*.; a Greek inscription on Parian marble in honour of certain women celebrating sacred mysteries, £1 19*s*., which Rawlinson calls 'a noble relique of antiquity from Smyrna,' (Ballard MS. ii. 69); some Roman medals, and 'the zodiac medals.' He says that the portraits of Baker and Bagford are 'the only original pictures' of those worthies (Ballard MS. *ib.*).

[3] Of these he says in a letter to Thos. Rawlins, Apr. 8, 1741: 'I believe I have of these kind[s] of seals, foreign and domestic, the largest collection in Europe, at least in England, though I never saw Lord Huntington's. Ballard MS. ii. 69.

in the Will (p. 4), 'were of the collection of Mr. Charles Christian, the celebrated seal engraver.' A selection from the wax impressions is now exhibited in the Picture Gallery.

16. Distinct from Rawlinson's other printed books is a curious series of Almanacs, in 175 volumes, extending from 1607 to 1747, which were sent to the library in 1752–5. Some volumes in continuation, from 1747 to 1768, were given by Sir Rob. H. Inglis, Bart., in 1846[1]. Another series, between 1571 and 1663, is in the Ashmole collection.

By his second codicil, of July 25, 1754, Rawlinson bequeathed a fee-farm rent of £4 *per annum* to the Under-librarian, in consideration of his taking charge of the MSS., but clogged with the strange conditions that he should not be a doctor in any faculty, married, or in Holy Orders[2]. The receipt of this sum is entered in the Accounts for 1756, but in no subsequent year.

The following is an alphabetical list of the principal libraries from which Rawlinson's MSS. were collected, with the dates (so far as ascertained) at which these libraries were dispersed :—

Acton (Oliver), of Bridewell Hosp.

Bacon (Thos. Sclater), 1737.

Bridgeman (Will. & Rich.), 1742. [see p. 237].

Britton (Thos.), 'the small-coal man,' 1714–15.

[1] A curious, and probably unique, little 'Almanacke for XII yere, after the latytude of Oxenforde,' printed in 48° (measuring two and a-half inches by one and three-quarters), by Wynkyn de Worde, 'in the fletestrete,' in 1508, was presented by David Laing, LL.D., the late eminent Librarian to the Writers to the Signet at Edinburgh, in 1842. The Library also possesses two copies of a sheet Almanack, by Simon Heuringius, for 1551, printed by John Turck, at London; and other almanacs for 1564, 1567, and 1569. A volume containing five almanacs for the year 1589 was bought in 1857.

[2] With the same perverse eccentricity he ordered that the recipients of his endowments for the Keepership of the Ashmolean Museum and the Professorship of Anglo-Saxon, should be unmarried (in the former case only M.A. or B.C.L.), not a native of Scotland, Ireland, or the Plantations, nor a son of such native, nor, in the case of the Museum, even educated in Scotland, and not a member of either the Royal Society or the Society of Antiquaries. These restrictions have all been of late removed in the general re-construction of University Statutes.

Chandos (Duke of), 1747 [1].
Clarendon (Henry, Earl of). Through *Chandos*.
Clavell (Walter), 1742.
Compton (Bishop). See p. 239.
Foucault (Nic. Jos.), 'Comes Consistorianus [2],' 1721.
Gale (Samuel), 1755.
Graves (Rich.), of Mickleton. Through *Hearne*.
Halifax (Montagu, Earl of), 1715.
Hearne (Thomas), 1747.
Holman (William). See p. 238.
Jekyll (Sir Joseph), 1739. See p. 236.
Le Neve (Peter), 1731.
Lewis (John, M.A.), 1749.
Maittaire (Mich.), 1748.
Mead (Richard, M.D.), 1754–5.
Murray (John), 1749.
Oxford (Harley, Earl of), 1743–5.
Pepys (Samuel). See p. 236.
Pole (Francis), March 1751 [3].
Powle (Henry), of Shottesbrooke, Berks, in 1689 Speaker of House of Commons. Through *Halifax* [4].
Rawlinson (Thomas), 1734 [5].
Robinson (Bishop). See p. 239.
St. George (Sir Thomas).

[1] The sale catalogue of the Chandos library was drawn up by one Daniel Perkins. Rawlinson wrote to him respecting the volume of Clarendon's *History*, which he purchased out of that library (*see under* 1753), and in two out of three letters in reply, dated from Whitchurch, Aug. 25 and Nov. 8, 1747 (which are preserved in that volume), Perkins says, 'I own that I had the chief management of the MS. Catalogue of the library. . . . But I absolutely disown it as it appear'd in print. It went out of my hands with all the accurateness and care that is usual, and much more than that, in a catalogue of books. But I was totally denied the liberty of conducting it through the press, and Cock and the two booksellers who assisted me in making the catalogue . . . . so alter'd and mangled it, and through their ignorance so entirely defaced between it's going out of my hands and it's coming into the world, that I entirely disclaim it.' He says that twenty-two days and a half were spent over the whole catalogue, of which only eight were given to the MSS., and that 'I labour'd every day from morning to night, without either eating or drinking;' that he had not been paid for his work, and was employing a lawyer to obtain payment.

[2] Autobiographical memoirs by Foucault, extending to 1719, were published under the editorship of F. Baudry, 4°. Paris, 1862, in the French Government series of *Documents inédits sur l'Histoire de France*. The editor remarks in the preface (p. xli), 'On ignore en quelles mains la bibliothèque de Foucault passa après sa mort [1721]. Le P. Le Long nous apprend seulement qu'elle fut vendue, et probablement dispersée.'

[3] He died Nov. 6, 1750.

[4] He died in Jan. 1692. Mr. John Bruce, in his preface (p. iii) to the *Correspondence of the Earl of Leicester*, printed by the Camden Society in 1844, says that his MSS. went to Lord Somers, and thence to Jekyll and to Yorke, Lord Hardwicke, and that some are in the Lansdowne collection. But those acquired by Rawlinson came from Lord Halifax's sale.

[5] The catalogue of T. Rawlinson's MSS. was drawn up by his brother, who says that but few copies were

Somers (Lord). Through *Jekyll.*
Spelman (Sir Henry).
Spinckes (Rev. Nathaniel), 1727.
Thoresby (Ralph)[1].
Turner (Bishop). See pp. 240, 242.
Ussher (Archbishop). Through *Hearne.*
Wake (Archbp.). See p. 238.
Ware (Sir James). Through *Clarendon* and *Chandos.*
Whiston (William).

On July 15, a bequest of printed books and MSS. was received from Rev. Richard Furney, M.A., Archdeacon of Surrey (who had

printed (Rawl. MS. D. 390, f. 99). Hearne notices the extraordinarily low prices (even for that time) at which T. Rawlinson's MSS. were sold in his *Diary*, vol. cxliii. p. 100. Of the unhappy private life of T. Rawlinson (the Tom Folio of Steele's *Tatler*, No. 158), some account is given in a letter from Dr. Rawlinson (signed A. B., in which he speaks of himself, for the sake of disguise, in the third person), dated Aug. 18, 1743, to his friend Thomas Rawlins, of Pophill, Warwickshire, which is preserved in Ballard MS. ii. 68. He ends this account by saying, 'Thus have I unburthened my friend's case, but hope you'll not let it be handed down to posterity by preserving it.'

[1] A copy of Hearne's *Vindication of . . . the oath of allegiance* now in the possession of Mr. Falconer Madan has some curious anonymous MS. notes, which have been found to be in the handwriting of Thomas Wilson, once a bookseller at Leeds, and afterwards (as it seems) a schoolmaster and F.S.A.; from which it appears that many of Thoresby's MSS. came to Rawlinson through him. The following are extracts. 'I suppose the Dr.'s [*i. e.* Rawlinson's] benefactions to Oxford are worth above 30,000 pounds. I gave the Dr. all the antient deeds collected by the Leedes antiquary Mr. Thoresby, which I purchased of his son, and my own collecting for 30 years past, in number about 1000; because I knew he wou'd dispose of them for a publick good; and I am glad he reposited them in the finest Library in the world. Also I sent him my collection of MSS., which will be some addition to the Bodleian Library.

'During the Doctor's stay at Oxford in 1754 he repaired Mr. Hearne's tomb, and built a curious vault for himself at St. Giles's there, where his body was buried, but he ordered his heart to be buried in St. John's College Chapel, his dear *Alma Mater*, often so called in his letters to me.

'The remainder of his fine library was catalogued by Mr. Baker, bookseller and auctioneer, consisting of above 10,000 books, most rare impressions in antiquities, history, &c., of all nations and in all languages, being the most curious collection ever sold in England by auction, begun 29 Mar. 1756, and continued the 50 following days.'

It is singular that if Wilson's gifts to Rawlinson were as large as he here represents, no record or mention of them should as yet have been elsewhere found.

been schoolmaster at Gloucester, 1719–1724, and who died in 1753), by the hands of the Rev. John Noel, of Oriel College. The printed books (nineteen in all) consisted almost entirely of early editions of classics. The MSS. (six folio volumes) are thus described in a list made by the Librarian, Humphrey Owen, at the time of their receipt:—

'1, 2, 3 and 4 contain collections relating to the history and antiquities of the city, church and county of Gloucester. 5, 6 a fair copy, seemingly prepared for the press, of the history and antiquities of the said city, church and county, by the Arch-deacon himself, or some friend of his from whom these papers came into his hands.'

The gift comprised also two ancient brass seals, and eighteen original deeds, amongst which is a confirmation charter (the genuineness of which is questioned by some, from its being probably an eleventh century copy) granted to Gloucester Abbey, by Burgred King of Mercia, in 862. This deed was printed for the first time in Haddan and Stubbs' *Councils*, vol. iii. p. 652, is accurately reproduced in part II. of Sanders' *Facsimiles of Anglo-Saxon MSS.*, and, lastly, is printed in Mr. De Gray Birch's *Cartularium Saxonicum*, ii. 109. It is written in seventeen lines, with five lines containing seventeen signatures, and measures sixteen inches in width and ten and one-third in length. There are also original grants to the abbey from Hen. II and Stephen, and three confirmations of Magna Charta, dated respectively 1 Hen. III, 21 Hen. III, and 29 Edw. I, which last has a magnificent and perfect impression of Edward's beautiful Great Seal attached. All these three were printed by Sir W. Blackstone, accompanied by engravings of their respective seals, in his edition of *The Great Charter and Charter of the Forest*, 4°. Oxf., 1759. The deeds are noticed in the Report on the Public Records for 1800, p. 354.

By the death on Sept. 5, 1754, of James St. Amand, Esq.[1]

[1] A record of his birth and baptism is entered in a family register kept by his father on the fly-leaves of a splendid copy of the folio Prayer-

(formerly of Lincoln College), a bequest of books, MSS., coins, &c. which had been made by a will dated Nov. 9, 1749, accrued to the Library, being received in the year 1755. The books consist chiefly of the then modern editions of the classics, and of the writings of modern Latin scholars; such of them as the Library did not need were to go to Lincoln College. The MSS., sixty-eight in number, comprise various papers relating to the history chiefly of the Low Countries[1], together with notes and indices by St. Amand himself to Theocritus and other Greek poets, Horace, &c. They are described by Mr. Coxe, in vol. i. of the Catalogue of MSS., cols. 889–908. The main part of the residue of his property was bequeathed to Christ's Hospital, together with a picture of his grandfather James St. Amand, done in miniature and set in gold, with the singular proviso that the picture should be exhibited, and the part of the will relating to these bequests be read, at the first annual court of the Hospital, and also that the picture be shown annually to the Vice-Chancellor of Oxford, if required. Should a refusal to show the picture be persistently made, or any of the conditions of the will be avoided, then all the residue was to be given to the University, first to increase the stipend of the chief Librarian to £120 and of the second Librarian to £70, but only so long as both of them were unmarried, and then to be devoted to the purchasing of books and MSS., specially of classic authors.

There is a book-plate in many of his books, which I have

Book of 1662. He was the second son; born in Covent Garden, Apr. 7, 1687; bapt. Apr. 21, by Dr. Patrick, the sponsors being Major-Gen. Werden, Sir Peter Apsley and the Countess of Bath. Prince George of Denmark was one of the sponsors to his elder brother, George. He had also a sister, Martha. An account of him is given in the preface to Thos. Warton's edition of Theocritus, publ. at Oxford in 1770; an edition which was chiefly based upon St. Amand's collections. A James St. Amand, no doubt our donor's father, was one of the witnesses for the birth of the Prince of Wales in 1688.

[1] Amongst these is a large collection of MS. news-letters written from various places abroad about the years 1637–1642; one of these, containing particulars of movements of the Swedish and Imperialist armies, is printed, as a specimen, in *Letters by Eminent Persons*, 1813, vol. i. pp. 15–17.

ascertained to be that of Dr. Arthur Charlett; being the initials A. C., interlaced with the same repeated in an inverse way, surrounded by piles of books, and with the motto, 'Animus si æquus, quod petis hîc est[1].' There were said to be amongst MSS. papers which he ordered his executors to destroy as not relating either to literature or to his estate, 'very curious collections relating to the finances of this kingdom[2].'

By the bequest of George Ballard (the author of the *Memoirs of Learned Ladies*), who died on June 24, the Library became enriched with forty-four volumes of Letters, chiefly addressed, by ecclesiastical and literary personages of all ranks, to Dr. Arthur Charlett, Master of University College, between the reigns of James II and George I. There is also one volume of letters from Dr. Rawlinson to Thomas Rawlins, of Pophills, and to Ballard himself, which abounds with interesting notices. For the biographical and bibliographical history of the time these volumes are full of information; it was from them that the *Letters by Eminent Persons*, published in 1813, by Rev. John Walker, M.A., Fellow of New College, were chiefly drawn. No printed catalogue of them has yet appeared, but the Library possesses a MS. index to the contents of each volume, and a general and fuller MS. index has been in recent years completed[3]. Besides the Letters, Ballard bequeathed some other MSS., in number twenty-three, among which is a volume of various voyages and expeditions, 1589–1634; Sir Edm. Warcupp's autograph account of the treaty in the Isle of Wight[4]; a dialogue between a tutor and

[1] I have been informed by Sir W. H. Cope that the same library-stamp was used by Anth. Cope, whose books are at Bramshill House.

[2] Letter from Rob. Vansittart to Owen the Librarian, Nov. 8, 1754, Bodl. MS. Add. A. 64, f. 293^b.

[3] References to many particulars relative to Thoresby, Bp. Gibson, White Kennett, Hickes, and a few others, are given in J. Nichols' notes to the *Letters of Archbp. Nicolson* (2 vols. 1809), an interesting and varied biographical miscellany, but guilty of the capital crime of omitting an index.

[4] This ought, apparently, to have reached the Library much sooner, through the hands of Dr. Charlett; since it has the following inscription on the fly-leaf: 'Given by the Honble.

his pupil, by Lord Herbert, of Cherbury; the second book of the *Supplication of Soules*, by Sir Thos. More, a little volume of 103 closely-written duodecimo pages; the *Universitie's Musterings*, by Bryan Twyne; collections by Ant. à Wood; a small volume of Gloucestershire notes, supposed by Guillim; and several volumes written by Mr. Elstob and his sister. An extract from Ballard's will, with a list of his MSS., is in the Register marked 'C,' and a transcript has lately been made from the original enrolment at Somerset House[1].

S^r^. Edmund Warcup (being all writ wth his own hand at ye Isle of Wight at ye Treaty) to the Public Library in Oxford, to be placed there when I thought fitting.

'AR. CHARLETT.

'Univ. Coll. Nov. 25, 97.'

[1] In the volume of Wills marked 'Paul, 232.' The will is dated in April, 1754, and was proved Sept. 3, 1755. He leaves to Francis Wise two heads drawn with crayons by Mrs. Elstob of herself and her brother, to be given at Wise's death to the Bodleian gallery, 'as being the most proper place for such curiosities.' (These are now in the Picture Gallery.) To John Loveday, of Caversham, formerly gentleman commoner of Magdalen College, a 'beautiful old Missal, finely printed upon vellum, and elegantly illuminated,' and the scarce printed Lives of Becket and Cantilupe. With regard to his collection of Letters, which he says 'I very carefully bound up with my own hands,' he directs 'that not any one of these MSS. may be shewn to, or consulted by, any person upon any occasion whatsoever, until six years after my decease, under the penalty of forfeiting all the MSS. to my executor.' To his friend Willis's coin-cabinet in the Bodleian, he gives five Anglo-Saxon coins, and 'a fair silver medal of Prince Henry' of Wales, 'given, or rather forced upon, me by one John Wyckham, then of Corpus Christi College, now fellow of Baliol College, who afterwards most ungratefully, barbarously, and villanously attempted to take away my reputation on this occasion by reporting in most infamous language that he did not give me this medal, but exchanged it with me for a coin in large brass of Tiberius; a most impudent lye this; whether he invented it to get the medal off me again or to get a Tiberius in large brass, a coin I never possessed, and if I had I should have been thought very unskilful by those who understand such curiosities to have made such an exchange, he knows best. I suppose in the heat of forging and hammering it out for his vile purpose he forgot that John Bridge, esquire, gentleman commoner of Corpus Christi College, a person of great probity and integrity, was both an eye and ear witness of everything that passed between us at the time when he gave me this medal, and he has publickly declared, particularly to the rev. Mr. Timothy Neve, fellow of Corpus Christi College, and will I am confident depose it upon oath if required, that this malicious accusation is intirely false. But I forgive him

Ballard was originally a stay-maker or mantua-maker at Campden, Gloucestershire; but, following the study of antiquities with great ardour, became well known and highly esteemed amongst all of like pursuits. At the age of forty-four he was appointed one of the eight clerks of Magdalen College, being matriculated Dec. 15, 1750, but he never took any degree. He bequeathed to the College Library some of his books which were there wanting. The fullest account of him will be found in vol. ii. of *A Register of St. Mary Magd. College*, by J. R. Bloxam, D.D., 1857, pp. 95–102. Some letters from him are printed in Nichols' *Lit. Hist.* iv. 206–226.

The very valuable MS. of the letters of Gilbert Foliot, Bishop of London (which are of great importance for the illustration of the history of Thomas à Becket), now numbered *e Musæo* 249, was given by Sir Thomas Cave, Bart. It is described in the Benefaction Book as 'liber rarissimus; per totam Angliam unum hoc tantum modo exstat exemplar.' The letters were first printed by Dr. J. A. Giles, together with the Lives of Becket, in his series of *Patres Ecclesiæ Anglicanæ*, in 1845.

A. D. 1756.

Dr. Samuel Johnson presented the account of Zachariah Williams' attempt to ascertain the longitude at sea, which he had published under Williams' name in the preceding year; and, as Warton noted[1], he entered it with his own hand in the Library Catalogue. The entry is still to be seen, with a memorandum of its being in Johnson's hand, in an interleaved, and now disused, copy of the Catalogue of 1738.

A. D. 1758.

Rev. John Douglas, afterwards Bishop of Salisbury, transmitted

(? *after all the preceding strong language!*) as I hope to be forgiven. The reason for my taking notice of it in this manner may be seen in the rev. Mr. Seed's Sermons, vol. i. p. 345.'

[1] Boswell's *Life of Johnson*, edit. 1835, vol. ii. p. 54.

to the Library from Sir Henry Bedingfeild a collection of original letters and documents upon which Douglas' exposure of Archibald Bower, the ex-Jesuit, was based in the pamphlet-war which had been carried on between them two or three years previously. These papers, which are very curious, are now bound in a volume numbered MS. Bodl. Addit. C. 49.

A.D. 1759.

Above forty Syriac, Greek and Arabic MSS. are recorded in the Registers to have been presented by Henry Dawkins, Esq., of Standlynch, Wilts, who had collected them while travelling in the East with Robert Wood, whose works on Baalbec and Palmyra he presented at the same time. There are now *sixty* MSS. in Syriac alone which pass under the name of Dawkins, some of which are of great age and value. They are described in Dr. R. Payne Smith's Catalogue of the Syriac MSS. Mr. Dawkins died in London, June 19, 1814, aged eighty-six.

Swedenborg's *Arcana Cœlestia*, published anonymously, in 8 vols. were sent 'by the author, unknown.' The same donor, still unknown, sent in 1766 *Selecti Dionys. Halicarn. tractatus.*

In this year and in 1761 published music began to be received from Stationers' Hall, and to be entered in the Register. It remained piled up in cupboards until about 1845, when it was all disinterred and carefully arranged by Rev. H. E. Havergal, M.A., then Chaplain of New Coll. and Ch. Ch., and an assistant in the Library (afterwards Vicar of Cople, Bedfordshire, who died in Jan. 1875), and bound in some 300 or 400 volumes. Since that time two further series of musical volumes have been arranged and bound; and all that comes is now duly catalogued and bound.

A meagre list of the pictures, &c., in the Picture Gallery and Library was printed by the Under-janitor, Nathaniel Bull, and 'sold by him at the Picture Gallery[1].' It fills twelve duodecimo

[1] Bull was Under-janitor, or door-keeper of the gallery, 1757–67. The post of Janitor was until a little later held by an assistant in the Library, and a porter had the care of the gallery (see pp. 185–6), with a salary of £2 and fees.

pages. A new edition, 'with additions and amendments,' including the pictures in the Ashmolean Museum, was issued by him in 1762, in sixteen octavo pages. This was, as it seems, the first list that had been issued since Hearne printed his original Catalogue in his *Letter containing an Account of some Antiquities between Windsor and Oxford.* A list, equally meagre with Bull's, was published by William Cowderoy, Janitor, in 1806[1]. He was succeeded in office about 1826 by Maurice Lenthall; on whom (who died in October, 1835, aged 69[2]) followed John Norris[3]. The present Janitor, Charles Coppock, was appointed in 1875, in which year at Lady Day Norris retired on a pension. By the latter (who died 21 March, 1877, aged 70) a new Catalogue, enlarged with biographical notices (written for him by, I believe, Dr. Bliss), was issued, filling sixty pages; which was re-issued, with a few alterations, in 1847, when such of the pictures as were not portraits had been removed to the new Randolph Gallery. As all the portraits were some years ago distinctly labelled, no new edition has consequently been called for by visitors, useful as a carefully-prepared list would be[4].

A.D. 1760.

The MSS. of the eminent antiquary, Browne Willis, who died

[1] He appears from receipts in a note-book of Price's to have been appointed in 1785. 'W. Cowderoy, June ye 18th, 1792,' is written on a pane of glass in the window of the last study on the right hand. He is remembered by Rev. R. Eden (*see under* 1825) as having been at one time employed at sea, and as wearing knee-breeches to the end of his life. His successor, Lenthall, had been butler to Dr. Isham, Warden of All Souls' College.

[2] He is entered (Oct. 15) in the burial register of St. Mary the Virgin as having lived in St. Mary Hall Lane, and it is worth mentioning in connection with Oxford street nomenclature that (as pointed out to me by the Vicar, Rev. E. S. Ffoulkes) the Lane ceases to bear this name in the register at the end of Mr. Newman's tenure of the incumbency, and from 1843 onwards is called Oriel Street.

[3] With Norris there was an Under-janitor named Saunders.

[4] A catalogue of all the portraits to be found in the University buildings and in College halls, is among the many valuable works proposed for publication by the Oxford Historical Society.

on Feb. 5, in this year, came to the Library by his bequest. They were received from his executor, Dr. Eyre, on April 24. There are altogether fifty-nine volumes in folio, forty-eight in quarto, and five in octavo, consisting chiefly of Willis's own collections for his various works, with much correspondence intermingled and a few older historical papers. There is much of value for general ecclesiastical topography and biography, besides his large collections for the county of Bucks, and special volumes relating to the four Welsh Cathedrals. He desired in his will that the books should be placed in the Picture Gallery, 'next to those of my friend Bishop Tanner;' but both collections were long since removed to the floor below. Many of his letters are to be found among Ballard's and Rawlinson's papers, and show throughout both the warm interest which he took in ecclesiastical renovation and religious work generally, but particularly in the state of the Church in Wales, and the continual efforts which he made to rouse slothful and negligent dignitaries to a sense of their duties and responsibilities. The restoration of the then ruined and desolate Cathedral at Llandaff was an object especially dear to him. By his will, which was dated Dec. 20, 1741, he bequeathed to the University, besides his MSS., all his numerous silver, brass, copper and pewter coins, and also his gold coins, if purchased at the rate of £4 per oz., as the best return he could make for the many favours he acknowledged to have been conferred on him and on his grandfather, Dr. Thomas Willis, Professor of Natural Philosophy. This latter provision of his will was at once carried into execution; in the following year the University purchased one hundred and sixty-seven gold coins for £150 at £4 4*s*. per oz., and two more in 1743 for £8 5*s*. His other coins were given by him in the years 1739, 1740, 1741, 1747 and 1750; and by a codicil to his will dated Feb. 5, 1742, he desired that the whole collection should be annually visited on the Feast of St. Frideswide (Oct. 19), which day he had himself been wont annually to celebrate in Oxford. His first gift to the Library was in the year 1720, when he gave ten valuable MSS., chiefly historical (now placed among the general *Bodley* series), together with his grandfather's portrait[1].

A bequest of £70 towards the purchase of an orrery, was received from Rev. Jos. Parsons, M.A., of Merton College.

A folio MS. containing the account of the moneys laid out in building the Sheldonian Theatre was given by Mr. Abraham Tucker.

A.D. 1761.

Kennicott's collations of Hebrew Biblical MSS., made during the years 1759–60, were received from him on Dec. 17, in this year, according to an entry in the Register. But all his MSS., collations, correspondence, and miscellaneous books (including one in Zend, upon cloth), were subsequently deposited in the Radcliffe Library, whence they were removed, in 1862, together with the other contents of that collection, to the place of their present deposit, the New Museum.

Q. Elizabeth's translation of Ochini: *see* list of special objects of interest, in the Appendix.

A.D. 1762.

The west, or Selden, end of the Library was re-floored at a cost of £66.

A.D. 1763.

In this year the late Janitor, Rev. John Bilstone, M.A., who had been deprived of his office by Owen, the Librarian, on account of his neglecting to perform his duties in person, brought an action for arrears of salary against Owen[2]. He appears to have been appointed before 1729. He died Feb. 13, 1767, at which time he held three livings, besides a Chaplaincy at All

[1] In 1716 Hearne says, in vol. lix. of his *Diary*, 'Mr Willis' collections are wonderful, and much surpass my expectation, tho' I knew before that they were extraordinary.' But in an earlier volume of his *Diary* he had said, when he knew the collections only by report, and when Hudson had been to see them, that it would be 'easy to stuff the Library with such rubbish as that'!

[2] 'See papers in *Files*; Archiv.' Note in Dr. Bliss's MS. *Collectanea.*

Souls' College[1]. John Price, Owen's successor, had been appointed Janitor in Bilstone's place before 1757. One John Jones succeeded Price in 1761, and still held the office in 1768.

A. D. 1764.

The *Editio princeps* of Homer, printed at Florence in 1488, was bought for £6 6*s*.

A. D. 1767.

It is noted at the beginning of the Register for 1768 that Dr. Owen had omitted in his last account of benefactions to enter some books bequeathed by Benj. Heath, Esq., of Exeter, and received from his son, Mr. Benj. Heath, of Eton, 10 Apr. 1767. These consisted of a folio vellum MS. of Chaucer (now Bodl. MS. 414), and three printed books, one of which contained the *Achilles* of Statius, collated with a MS. at Eton.

The Earl of Radnor gave a MS. Chronicle of France to the time of Philip of Valois. It is a volume very beautifully written and illuminated, bound in crimson velvet, with gold bosses and ornaments, and enclosed in a curiously knitted bag, now sadly torn. It was written for Charles, Count of Maine and Guise, who was appointed Governor of Languedoc (one of the titles by which he is here described) in 1443, and is entitled *Mirouer historial abregie de France*. It is now numbered Bodl. 968.

A. D. 1768.

H. Owen, the Librarian, and Principal of Jesus College, died in March of this year, and was buried in his College Chapel.

[1] Two, at least, out of his three livings were very poor. The Lord Chancellor Henley once promised him a bishopric, but eventually only gave him the rectory of St. Clement's, Oxford. (Letter from Rev. C. Godwyn to Rev. C. Hutchins, printed in the latter's *Hist. of Dorset*; second edit., vol. iv. p. xvii.) He was also minister of Chiselhampton and Stadhampton, in Oxfordshire, the stipend of which perpetual curacy was reduced in 1743 from £26 to £20, as he noted in the parish register. (*Transactions of Oxf. Architect. Soc.*, new series, vol. vi. p. 37.)

In his room was elected the Rev. John Price, B.D., of Jesus College, 'after a severe contest with Mr. Cleaver, of Brasenose, afterwards head of that College and Bishop of St. Asaph, who used to say that he was indebted to Mr. Price for his mitre, for had he obtained the Bodleian he should have there continued, instead of becoming tutor in a noble family, and so placed in the road to advancement. In this election the votes were equal, and Mr. Price, being senior, was nominated by the Vice-Chancellor[1].' By a strange omission no entry of the election is found in the Register of Convocation! Price had been employed in the Library as Janitor before, and in 1757, and onwards to 1761, when he was appointed Sub-Librarian[2]. He ceased to be Sub-Librarian in 1763, but appears as Acting-Librarian in 1765-7, receiving Owen's salary in his place, and keeping a note-book of donations, &c.

Benjamin Hall [M.A. Jesus Coll., afterwards D.D., dec. 1825] was Sub-Librarian in 1767-8, as appears from notes of accounts by Price.

On Nov. 23 a printed order about the hours of opening and shutting the Library was issued 'by order of Convocation, for the following year.' No copy of this order has been found in the Library, but I have seen one which is preserved in Moldenhawer's MS. account of his visit to Oxford in 1783, in the Library at Copenhagen (New Royal MSS., fol., 132). The order was passed in Convocation on 16 Nov., and is entered in the Register for that year at p. 74. It provides that 'in annum sequentem' the Library shall be open in the winter half-year (on ordinary days) from 9 to 3, and in the summer half-year from 8 to 2 and 3 to 5. Forty pounds are granted in augmentation of the salaries of the Librarian and his assistants for their increased attendance. These experimental alterations met with approval, and were embodied in a statute passed 15 Dec. 1769.

See under 1776 and 1799.

[1] Note by Dr. Bliss in the edition of Wood's *Life*, published in 1848 by the Eccl. Hist. Soc., p. 88.

[2] He acted as Owen's deputy at Kingston Bagpuze, Berks (where Owen was curate to one Mr. Richard King), in 1762-3, with a stipend of £20 *per an.*

A.D. 1769.

In this year H. Liden, Professor of History at Lund, visited the Library, and gives in his MS. *Dagbok* preserved in the library of the University of Upsala (vol. iii. p. 457) a notice of his visit. He speaks of Price as 'en flitig och arbetsam man' (a diligent and hard-working man), and says that he met with much civility from him. He had a letter of introduction to Uri from Dr. Archibald Maclaine, the translator of Mosheim, of the Hague, and notices his work upon the Oriental MSS.

Dr. Kennicott applied to Convocation for leave to borrow eight Hebrew MSS., four at a time, from the Library, on depositing £500 as security; but it was refused in Convocation on 14 Feb.[1]

A.D. 1770.

The Library was largely enriched with books which were then modern, in which it appears to have been very deficient, by the legacy of the library (as well as the coins) of Rev. Charles Godwyn, M.A., Fellow of Balliol College, whose will was dated 28 Feb.[2] The collection, which is still in the main kept undivided (although a few folio and quarto volumes are placed in the general class marked *Art.*), consists chiefly of works in English and general history, civil and ecclesiastical, published in the eighteenth century, and includes, besides, the later Benedictine editions of the Fathers. There is also a series of theological and literary pamphlets[3]; to which have been added of late years upwards of 2400 volumes, of all dates and on all subjects, which are now all alike numbered, for convenience sake, in connection with Godwyn's own. The

[1] Reg. Convoc. B[1] 36, p. 83.

[2] A copy of his will is entered in the Register of Convocation for this year, p. 134. He ordered all the MSS. and papers in his own handwriting to be burned except the catalogues of his books and coins, and his books of accounts.

[3] These pamphlets were not entered in the catalogue until about forty years afterwards! A note in the eleventh volume records that they were entered by A. H. M[atthews], who was appointed a Sub-librarian about 1807.

residue of his property, after payment of all claims and bequests, formed a further portion of his legacy; and the interest upon £1050 [£1005 19*s*. in 1783, when the business of the bequest was finally settled] which accrued from this source, still forms part of the annual income of the Library.

A.D. 1771.

A payment of £2 12*s*. 6*d*. was made in this year (or rather, at the close of 1770) to a glass-painter, named Brooks, for one of the coats of arms in the great east window. A portrait of Robert Nelson was given by Rev. J. Craven.

A.D. 1772.

The following inscription, dated Oct. 24, 1772, is found in the first volume of a copy of the edition of St. Augustine's *Opera* printed at Paris in 1586 (A. 4. 1. Th.): 'These books were presented to the Bodleian Library by the Rev. John Clayton, A.M., Fellow of the Collegiate Church of Manchester, who bought them out of Dr. Deacon's catalogue, who purchased them out of Dr. Rawlinson's library, who bought them from the sale of Archbp. Sancroft's books, to whom they had been given by Archbp. Juxon, who received them as a present from Archbp. Laud.' The volumes contain the autograph of 'William Laud,' and MS. notes by him; and also the autograph of the non-juring bishop, 'Tho. Deacon, 1740.' They are not mentioned in the MS. list of donations to the Library in 1772, or in any subsequent year! It is not easy to understand how Dr. Deacon could in 1740 have purchased them from Dr. Rawlinson's library, unless as a special purchase from a friend of a special book. There was a twenty-five days' sale in March, 1727, of books of Rawlinson's, but no catalogue of this sale exists in our Library, and in a MS. list of purchasers and prices (Rawl. MS. D. 661) the name of Deacon does not occur. Thomas Rawlinson's sales were in 1727–8 and 1734, but the book is not found in the catalogues of these sales.

A. D. 1774.

July 19. Pursuant to an Act of the last session of Parliament the Curators examined the money in Bodley's chest, and found twenty-seven guineas so deficient in weight that they were no longer current; they were exchanged by weight for £25 16*s*. 6*d*.

A. D. 1775.

Twenty-four Oriental MSS. and bundles of papers which had been found in the study of Rev. Dr. Thos. Hunt, Reg. Prof. of Hebrew, who died in the preceding year, were given by various persons.

A. D. 1776.

Lord North, the Chancellor of the University, presented to the Library the observations made by Dr. James Bradley, while Astronomer Royal, at Greenwich, 1750–62. These had been given to him by Mr. John Peach, son-in-law to Dr. Bradley, while a suit was pending between the Board of Longitude on behalf of the Crown and Mr. Peach respecting his right to their possession. The claim of the Crown had been first made in 1765, on the ground that they were the papers drawn up by Bradley in discharge of his public and official duties, but the executor, Mr. Sam. Peach, refused to resign them except for some valuable consideration. But after his death, his son, Mr. John Peach, who married Dr. Bradley's daughter, presented them to Lord North, with the understanding that the latter should give them to the University, on condition that they should be forthwith printed. They were, consequently, immediately put into the hands of Dr. Hornsby, the Savilian Professor of Astronomy, for publication; but the work progressed very slowly, in consequence of his ill-health, and a remonstrant correspondence ensued between the Board of Longitude, the Royal Society, and the University, which was printed by the Board, together with a statement of the whole case and of the steps taken by them for the recovery of the papers, in 1795. Several letters from Sir Joseph Banks, as President of the Royal Society, to Price the Librarian, in 1785, on the slow progress of the work, are preserved in a volume of MS. Letters to Librarians, Bodl. MS. Addit. A. 64. The first volume at length appeared in 1798, in folio, and the second, edited by Prof. A. Robertson, in 1805, with an appendix of observations made by Bradley's successor, Rev. Nath. Bliss, and his assistant, Mr. Charles Green, to March, 1765, which had been purchased by the Board of Longitude, and were presented by them to the University in March 1804. Some further remains of Dr. Bradley were, after Dr. Hornsby's death, found among the papers of the latter, and these (having been restored to the University by his family, on application, about 1829) were published in 1831, under the editorship of Prof. S. P. Rigaud, in one vol. quarto, entitled *Miscellaneous Works and Correspondence of Rev. J. Bradley.* In 1861, a fresh application for the return of the Observations was made to the University, by Mr. Airy, the Astronomer Royal, on the ground that they were the only volumes wanting in the series preserved at Greenwich, and that they were frequently needed there for reference. By a vote of Convocation, on May 2, this application was acceded to, and thirteen volumes of Observations were returned to what was certainly their legitimate place of deposit. Some miscellaneous papers, making about thirty parcels, still remain in the Library. In 1768 Miss Bradley gave a portrait of her father the Astronomer Royal.

George and John Reinhold Forster sent copies of their books of travels, &c., and at the same time sent to the Ashmolean Museum various weapons, dresses, &c., from the islands of the Pacific, collected during Capt. Cook's voyages. Their Latin letter of presentation, dated 1 Feb. 1776, is entered in the Convocation Register for that year at p. 371.

A.D. 1778.

Carte's MSS.: *see* 1753. Some Oriental and other MSS. were bought out of the collections of John Swinton, B.D.

A.D. 1780.

On Jan. 22, a Statute was passed which imposed an annual fee of four shillings[1] on all persons entitled to read in the Library and on all who had exceeded four years from matriculation, as well as assigned to the Library a share of the matriculation fees. The preamble of the Statute alleges that the funds of the Library were so insufficient for their purpose, that of works of importance daily published throughout the world 'vix unus et alter publicis sumptibus adscribi possit[2].' The Statute also provided for the holding of regular meetings by the Curators, and the issuing of an annual Catalogue of the books purchased during the year, with their prices, together with a statement of accounts. The commencement of the annual printed purchase-catalogues dates in consequence from this year.

In a letter from Thomas Burgess, afterwards Bishop of St. David's and Salisbury, to Mr. Tyrwhit t, the editor of Chaucer, dated Corp. Chr. Coll., Nov. 16, 1779, the plan for increasing the funds of the Library, established by this Statute, is mentioned as a scheme 'much talked of,' the defects of the Library being such as 'we are now astonished should have been of so long continuance[3].' A paper in behalf of the proposal was circulated among Members of Convocation, upon a copy of which, preserved by Dr. Bliss with his set of the annual catalogues, the latter has noted that it was written by Sir William Scott, afterwards Lord Stowell.

The exquisite portrait of Sir Kenelm Digby, supposed to be

[1] By the Statute passed in 1813, and by that on Fees passed in 1855, an annual payment of *eight* shillings was ordered to be made to the Library out of the total sum (now £1 6*s*.) paid by each graduate whose name is on the University Books. But these individual fees, varying with the numbers on the Books, were consolidated, in 1861, in one fixed annual sum, from the University Chest, of £2800.

[2] A letter from the Chancellor, Lord North, sanctioning the proposal of this Statute, dated 24 Nov., 1779, is in the Convocation Register, Bk 37, p. 88.

[3] Note by Dr. Bliss, in his MS. *Collectanea*, bequeathed by him to Rev. H. O. Coxe, and by the latter to the Library.

by Vandyke, was given by Edw. Stanley, Esq. It is now in the Picture Gallery; and, having within late years been cleaned and covered with plate-glass, appears in all the freshness of its original perfection[1].

The Sub-librarian at this time was John Walters, an undergraduate Scholar of Jesus College. He published in this year a small volume of *Poems* ('written before the age of nineteen'), the chief portion of which consists of a description of the Library, written with a warm admiration of his subject, and by no means destitute of poetic feeling. It numbers 1188 lines, and is illustrated with some well-selected notes. Walters alludes in his preface to the probable employment of his future leisure in arranging and preparing for the press 'a large portion of miscellaneous information, in print and MS., which tends further to elucidate the former and present state of the Library.' It were very much to be wished that these materials could now be found. In 1782, when B.A. and still Scholar of his College, he published *Specimens of Welsh Poetry in English verse, with some Original Pieces and Notes.* He took the degree of M.A. in 1784, and died in 1791[2]. We learn from a MS. note in a copy of his *Poems*, presented to the Library by the Rev. W. Dyke, B.D., of Jesus College, that he was the son of John Walters, Rector of Llandough (author of a Welsh Dictionary, 1794), by Hannah his wife, and that he was baptized there, July 9, 1760.

A. D. 1783.

The Library was visited by D. G. Moldenhawer, the librarian of the Royal Library at Copenhagen, whose notes on it are to be found in his account of his visit to England now amongst the MSS. in that Library, numbered New Royal, folio, 132. *See* p. 262.

[1] Another portrait of Sir Kenelm, which hangs in the Library, was given, in 1692, by Mr. William Pate, a woollen-draper of London. To this Mr. Pate, Thos. Brown dedicated, in 1710, as 'his honest friend,' his translation from the French of *Memoirs of the Present State of the Court and Councils of Spain.*

[2] Nichols' *Lit. Anecd.* viii. 122.

A. D. 1785.

George III and Queen Charlotte visited the Library, from Nuneham, on Oct. 13. Price, the Librarian, was in attendance, and kissed hands.

Several Assistants, whose names are not mentioned in the Library records, were perpetuated by inscriptions written by successive generations on the old oak staircases which ran from their studies to the galleries above. In June of this year, Thomas Whiting, of Jesus College (B.A. also in this year), did in this way transmit the memory of his service to posterity; unhappily, when these light and elegant staircases were removed with the galleries in 1877, no care was taken to preserve any portion. [See also *sub anno* 1807.]

A 'Mr. Price' occurs as an assistant in the Library in 1786, in an octavo book of notes of benefactions and payments kept by the Librarian, J. Price. He enters there a small loan to this assistant, which was repaid in the following year.

A. D. 1787.

On May 31, the Reader in Chemistry, Thomas Beddoes, M.D., of Pembroke College, issued a printed Memorial to the Curators 'concerning the state of the Bodleian Library, and the conduct of the Principal Librarian.' The utmost laxity appears from this statement to have prevailed with regard to attendance, and to the hours of opening the Library; the Librarian was always absent on Saturdays and Mondays, as on those days he was occupied in journeys to and from a curacy eleven miles distant[1], which he held

[1] Wilcote, a very small parish in Oxfordshire. He became curate here to one Dr. Nichol in 1775, as appears from the MS. Visitation Records now in the Library, and his name disappears from the lists after 1810. He is erroneously described in Nichols' *Literary History*, vol. viii, p. 471, as rector of the parish. He had previously been curate of the adjoining parish of North Leigh from 1766 to 1773, assisting a vicar named David Price. This parish was unfortunately a loser as regards its records by his ministrations, for in the sale catalogue of his library (sold in London by auction in June, 1814), no. 662, is this MS., 'Northleigh Book of Benefactions'!

together with a living more remote (the rectory of Wollastone, Gloucestershire); and the Library which should then in summer have been opened at eight was found unopened between nine and ten, and unopened also after University sermons[1]. The Librarian is charged besides with having discouraged readers by neglect and incivility, with being very careless in regard to the value and condition of books purchased by the Library[2], and with having but little knowledge of foreign publications. An anecdote is related (amongst others) of his lending *Cook's Voyages*, which had been presented by King Geo. III, to the Rector of Lincoln College, and telling him that the longer he kept it the better, 'for if it was known to be in the Library, he (Mr. Price) should be perpetually plagued with enquiries after it.' And it is said that until recently the only book of Dean Swift's to be found in the Library had been his *Polite Conversation*![3] In consequence of these complaints, the Curators, in 1788, resolved to hold terminal meetings for inspection of booksellers' catalogues and the ordering of books, &c., and also prepared a new form of Statute, while the Heads of Houses on their part prepared another. This separate action led to a paper war between the two bodies, in which the Regius Professors of Divinity, Law, Medicine, Hebrew and Greek, (Randolph, Vansittart, Vivian, Blayney and Jackson) appeared on the Curators' side of the question, and, as the Hebdomadal Board persisted in pressing their own scheme, they at length (with the exception of Blayney) adopted the strong step, on the day when the

[1] Edw. Morgan, the Sub-librarian, writing to Price (when absent) from the Library, on July 27 in this year, witnesses to the good effect of this complaint by saying, 'every thing goes on smoothly at the Library. Mr. Williams and myself attend so regularly that if the little Dr. (*i.e.* Beddoes) was in Oxford, disposed as he is to complain, he would have nothing to allege against us.' Bodl. MS. Addit. A. 64, f. 180. The name of this Mr. Williams has not been met with elsewhere as employed in the Library. Nearly all Mr. Price's assistants appear to have been Welshmen, and (naturally) from his own College.

[2] Among other instances the purchase (in 1784) of Sir John Hill's *Vegetable System*, at the cost of £140, is mentioned.

[3] It appears incidentally, from this pamphlet, that three o'clock was the dinner-hour at almost every College at that time.

rival plan was proposed in Convocation (June 23, 1788), of formally protesting before a notary public against this violation of their privileges. The consequence was that the Statute was withdrawn, and the proposal for a new code was in December abandoned by both parties. The chief points of difference were, that the Curators objected to the proposal being put forward as 'cum consensu Curatorum' instead of 'ex relatione Curatorum,' to the increase of the Librarian's stipend to £150 (a sum which they said 'might be a temptation to improper persons to become candidates for the place, and to endeavour to make a party for themselves in the University to compass their end'), to the appointment of two Sub-librarians instead of one, and to the leaving the appointment of these in the hands of the Librarian (in accordance with Bodley's own Statute) instead of assigning it to the Curators.

Eleven Arabic and Persian MSS. were given by Turner Camac, Esq., co. Down.

A first part of a Catalogue of the Oriental MSS., comprehending those in Hebrew, Chaldee, Syriac, Æthiopic, Arabic, Persian, Turkish and Coptic, was issued in this year, in folio. It was compiled by John Uri, a Hungarian, who had studied Oriental literature under Schultens, at Leyden, and who was recommended for this purpose to Archbp. Secker, by Sir Joseph Yorke, then Ambassador in the Netherlands. Many years were occupied in the preparation of this volume, as Uri appears to have commenced his work in 1766, his signature occurring in the 'Registrum admissorum' under Feb. 17, in that year[1]. Sixty closely-printed folio pages of corrections and additions are, however, supplied by Dr. Pusey, in the second part of the Catalogue, which he completed after Dr. Nicoll's death and published in 1835. In his preface to this part, Dr. Pusey remarks that Uri frequently copied with carelessness; and that the whole series of Arabic MSS. was found to

[1] He died suddenly at his lodgings in Oxford, Oct. 18, 1796, aged upwards of seventy: *Gent. Magaz.* vol. lxvi. p. 884, and *Oxford Journal* of 22 Oct.

need re-examination, from the discovery that all kinds of cheats and impositions had been played upon all the purchasers of Eastern MSS., Pococke alone excepted, by the cunning sellers with whom they dealt, particularly in the passing off of supposititious works for genuine. And upon carrying out this re-examination, the following was found to be the result:—

'Varias errorum formas deprehendi, titulis nunc charta coopertis, nunc atramento oblitis, nunc cultro pæne abrasis; auctorum porro nominibus paullulum immutatis quo notiora quædam referrent; numeris etiam, quibus singula volumina signata sunt, permutatis, quo quis opus imperfectum pro integro habeat, paginis denique pauculis operi alieno a fronte assutis.'

A.D. 1789.

The Anatomy School, on the Library staircase, was fitted up in this year as a room for receiving the Greek and Biblical MSS., and fifteenth-century editions of classics. In 1794 it was ordered that it should be distinguished by the name of the *Auctarium*, a name which it still retains. Mr. John Thomas, of Wadham College, (B.A. 1790, M.A. 1793) was employed in 1790 in arranging the room and making a list of its contents. The name of one E. Thomas with the date of 1790 was formerly to be found on one of the gallery staircases.

Many early editions of the classics were purchased at the sale of the library of Mapheo Pinelli, at Venice. To enable these purchases to be made, the Curators made a public application in a printed circular dated 1 Dec., for loans, to which a liberal response was returned, as noted under the following year.

The increased attention which began to be paid to the Library about this time is thus mentioned in a letter from Mr. Dan. Prince, the Oxford bookseller[1]:—

'Our Bodleian Library is putting into good order. It has been already one year in hand. Some one, two or three of the Curators work at it daily, and several assistants. The revenue from the

[1] A short extract from this letter is given in *Gent. Magaz.*, lix. ii. 664.

tax on the Members of the University is about £460 per annum, which has existed 12 years. This has increased the Library so much that it must be attended to, and a new Catalogue put in hand. They have lately bought all the expensive foreign publications. A young man of this place is about making a Catalogue of all the singular books in this place, in the College libraries as well as the Bodleian . . . . . We have a young man in this place, his name is Curtis, who was an apprentice to me, who has hitherto only dealt in books of curiosities, in which he is greatly skilled, superior in many respects to De Bure, Ames, or his continuator. He has been employed five or six years in the Bodleian Library, and since at Wadham, Queen's and Balliol. He purposes to publish a Catalogue of little or not known books in Oxford, particularly in Merton, Balliol and Oriel [1].'

Curtis is mentioned in Beddoes' pamphlet in 1787 as being the only one in the Library who could answer questions or find books; but he has been charged with gross dishonesty, in stealing various rare portraits from books in the Bodleian and other libraries. In 1797 James Caulfield, the well-known publisher of portraits and memoirs, projected the first publication of Aubrey's biographical anecdotes from the MSS. in the Ashmolean Museum, with illustrative portraits, under the title of *The Oxford Cabinet*, and engaged Curtis to make the necessary transcripts, for which leave was given by the Keeper of the Museum. Of this work, however, only the first part was published, the leave to make transcripts being withdrawn; and in the Bodleian copy of this part there is the following note, in the handwriting of Dr. Philip Bliss: 'This undertaking was prevented from proceeding through the interference of Mr. Malone, who probably knew the character of Caulfield and his friend Curtis to be such as not to entitle them to admission into any repository of prints or papers. Of Caulfield we know nothing; but of Curtis a great deal too much, since most, if not all, of the depredations that have been committed in the Bodleian were ascribed to the confidence placed in him by Mr. Price, and which he most unworthily abused.' Caulfield published a pamphlet about Malone's procuring the withdrawal of the per-

[1] Nichols, *Lit. Anecd.* iii. 699, 701.

mission which had been given him to make copies, in which he ascribed the interference to a jealous fear that his plan might clash with a similar project of Malone's. In the Bodleian copy of this tract, Dr. Bliss has inserted a further note about Curtis's dishonesty. To the mention, at p. 17, of 'the gentleman who kindly undertook the office of transcribing the papers,' he adds, 'Curtis, no doubt; a rogue who was employed to catalogue books in the Bodleian, St. John's, Worcester College, and other libraries, and who stole all the rare heads he could lay his hands on.'

A. D. 1790.

A very large number of *Editiones principes* and other early-printed books were purchased at the sale at Amsterdam of the library of P. A. Crevenna. The first entire Hebrew Bible, printed at Soncino in 1488, was purchased for £43 15*s*.; and Fust and Schoeffer's first *dated* Latin Bible (Mentz, 1462) for £127 15*s*. In June, 1873, a copy sold at the Perkins' sale for £780; the same copy had previously at Watson Taylor's sale brought £250. At the Sunderland sale in 1881 a copy sold for £1600. To enable the Library to make the purchases of this and the preceding year, benefactions were received to the amount of nearly £200, and upwards of £1550 were lent by various bodies and individuals. The repayment of the loans was completed in 1795. The names of all the contributors are given in Gutch's edition of Wood's *Annals*, II. ii. 949–50.

£120 were received for duplicates sold to Messrs. Chapman and King. Other small receipts from similar sales are found under the years 1793, 1794, and 1804[1].

Books received from Stationers' Hall were by an order of the Curators on 19 May appointed to be looked over by any two Curators 'for the purpose of separating such as are useless.'

[1] In 1721 Wanley wrote that Lord Oxford wished to buy duplicates. Bodl. Add. MS. A. 64, f. 16.

A.D. 1791.

From this year onwards until 1803, inclusive, the name of Mr. Edward Lewton, of Wadham College (B.A. 1792, M.A. 1794), is found as that of an Assistant employed upon the Catalogues. Further benefactions to the amount of £232, for the purpose of aiding the purchase of early-printed books, were received in this year.

A.D. 1792.

The collections of notes and various readings made by Joseph Torelli, of Verona, in preparation for his edition of Archimedes, were deposited in the Library, (F. *infra*, 2. *Auct.*). They were given to the University after his death (in 1781) by his executor, Albert Albertini, partly through the instrumentality of Mr. John Strange, Envoy to Venice, upon condition that the University undertook the publication. The work was consequently printed at the University Press, and issued in a handsome folio volume in this year.

A.D. 1793.

A magnificent copy of the [Gutenberg?] Bible, not dated, but supposed to have been printed about 1455, fresh and clean as if it had just come from the hands of the men of the New Craft, carefully set at their work, was bought for the very small sum of £100. It is exhibited in a glass case in the Library. This is the edition often called the *Mazarine Bible*, from the circumstance that the first copy which obtained notice was found in the Mazarine Library at Paris. A copy on paper sold at the sale of the library of Mr. Perkins, of Hanworth, in June, 1873, for £2690, and a vellum copy, wanting at least one leaf, for £3400; and at the Syston Park sale in Dec. 1884 a paper copy for £3900!

A.D. 1794.

The *Editio princeps* of the Bible in German, printed by Eggesteyn about 1466, was bought for £50.

A chronological Catalogue, in two folio volumes, of a very large and valuable collection of pamphlets (which had hitherto been kept in the Radcliffe Library), extending from 1603 to 1740, was made in 1793–4, by Mr. Abel Lendon, of Ch. Ch. (B.A. 1795, M.A. 1798). In a note, apparently by Archbp. Secker while bishop of Oxford, in Gough MS. Oxford 83 (p. 524) we read: 'Mr. [Humphrey ?] Bartholomew, of University College, hath given a collection of 50,000 pamphlets to be put into Radcliffe's Library.' The gift was in 1749, for in a letter from Dr. Rawlinson to Owen, the Librarian, dated 16 Nov. in that year, that unbending antiquary says: 'we had a report here of an offer to Dr. Radcliffe's Library of 50,000 pamphlets, but I suppose the Trustees will not accept of such trash'! (Rawl. MS. C. 989, f. 124.) The *trash* includes a collection of pamphlets of the Civil War period that may perhaps rank second to the Thomason collection in the British Museum.

Mr. Rich. S. Skillerne, of All Souls' (B.A. 1796, M.A. 1800), was employed in the Library.

With a view to the formation of a new Catalogue, the Curators at the end of the annual list made a first application for returns of such books existing in the several College libraries as were not in the Bodleian, in order thereby to accomplish what would be a most useful work, and is still a great *desideratum*, a General Catalogue of all the books in Oxford.

A.D. 1795.

A brief list (filling sixty small octavo pages) was printed at the Clarendon Press, of the *Editiones principes*, the fifteenth-century books, and the Aldines, then in the Library. The name of the compiler does not appear, but it was 'ascribed to the late bishop of London (Dr. Randolph) and the Rev. Dr. Will. Jackson.' (Horne's *Introd. to Bibliography*, 1814, p. 628.) It is entitled,

'Notitia editionum quoad libros Hebr., Gr. et Lat. quæ vel primariæ, vel sæc. xv. impressæ, vel Aldinæ, in Bibliotheca Bodleiana adservantur.'

Four cabinets of English coins were presented by Thomas Knight, Esq., of Godmersham, Kent. Among them was an ornament said to have been worn by John Hampden when he fell at Chalgrove Field[1]. It consists of a plain cornelian set in silver, with the following couplet engraved on the rim:—

'Against my King I do not fight,
But for my King & Kingdom's right.'

The Curators renewed the request, made ineffectually in the previous year, that the several Colleges would make out returns for the Library of all such books in their own collections as did not appear in the Bodl. Catalogue. In the year 1801 they acknowledged the receipt of such lists from Magdalen[2], Balliol, Exeter, and Jesus; Oriel sent a list subsequently (in 1808?); but these were all that were ever forwarded.

A. D. 1796.

A few *incunabula* and Aldines were purchased at Göttingen, at Baron Kulenkamp's sale. Amongst them, the Aldine Homer, 1504, with some leaves wormed and dirty, and with MSS. notes, was bought for 4*s*. 6*d*.

The annual list of donations was, for the first time, printed in

[1] Lord Nugent, in his *Memorials of Hampden*, mentions this as being preserved in the Ashmolean Museum. This statement is erroneous, for the jewel has never been transferred to that depository. He also repeats two mistaken readings first given in Miss Seward's *Anecdotes*, 1796, iv. 358 (a volume dedicated to Price, the Librarian, and which contains extracts from Bodl. MSS. and from Aubrey's collections), where a small woodcut of the ornament is given.

[2] A complete Catalogue of the Library of this College, compiled by the late Rev. E. M. Macfarlane, M.A., of Linc. Coll., was issued by the College, in three handsomely-printed quarto volumes, in 1860-62. The books of all writers belonging to the College are entered separately in an Appendix in vol. iii. Of other Colleges there are now printed catalogues for Balliol, Merton, and Hertford, with lists of special portions at Worcester and Oriel.

this year. It does not include, however, a large gift which was partly received now, the actual presentation having been made in the year preceding. It was the gift by Rev. Dr. Nath. Bridges of the MSS. collections made by Mr. John Bridges for his *History of Northamptonshire*. They number thirty-seven volumes in folio, eight in quarto, and one in octavo; and consist chiefly of extracts from Public Records and from the Episcopal Registers of Lincoln, the volumes in quarto containing church notes for the several parishes. Some account of them is given in Mr. Whalley's preface to vol. i. of Bridges' *History*, published in 1791.

A.D. 1797.

A MS. German Bible (Bodl. 969, 970), in two ponderous folio volumes, with large brass bosses, written at Nuremberg by one Heinrich Kun in 1441–52, was bought for £21 10*s*. In 1623 it belonged to George Stolzer, pastor at Steudenitz, who states in a long note that it had been treasured in the Stolzer family for upwards of 80 years. Subsequent possessors were, Paul Gryphius in 1658, Gottfr. Bose, archdeacon of Leipzig, and on his death his brother, Casp. Bose, a merchant there, who gave it in 1699 to Franc. Jul. Lütkaus. On outer cases, in which the brass-bossed bindings are enclosed, is stamped a coat of arms (quarterly, 1 and 4 three mullets, 2 and 3 a lion ramp. bearing a banner with cross of St. George; on an escutcheon of pretence a lion ramp.), with a marquess's coronet, and two eagles as supporters, and, below, an elephant (*qu.* the Danish Order?).

A.D. 1798.

Henry Ellis, an undergraduate Fellow of St. John's College (which he entered in 1796), afterwards well known as the historical antiquary, Sir Henry Ellis, D.C.L., was appointed in this year, by his friend the Librarian, to be one of the Assistant-librarians; commencing thus early the studies and pursuits which eventually led to the post, so long and honourably held by him, of Principal Librarian of the British Museum. In a letter which I received from him (*'jam senior, sed mente virens,'*) in 1868, Sir Henry (who died 15 Jan., 1869, aged 92) mentioned that the Rev. Henry Hervey Baber, of All Souls' College (B.A. 1799, M.A. 1805), who was afterwards one of his colleagues in the Museum, and lastly Vicar of Stretham, in the Isle of Ely, and who died (*ætat.* 93) 28 March, 1869, was his senior in the Bodleian, as Coadjutor-under-librarian, by a year or two. In consequence of the insufficiency of the statutable staff, the place of the one Under-librarian was at this time, and subsequently, shared by two occupants. In 1800 Mr. Ellis signed, in conjunction with Mr. Price, the return printed in the first Record Commission Report relative to the Historical MSS. possessed by the Library.

A.D. 1799.

Some MSS. papers of the eminent French divine, Pet. Franc. Le Courayer, were bequeathed by Rev. Bertrand Russel. Courayer's portrait, representing him in his alb, was given by Courayer himself in 1768 [1], who also at other times gave several books.

A.D. 1800.

The chief purchases in this year were of English and foreign maps, purchases which were continued in 1802 and 1804. For

[1] The gift is noticed in a note-book kept by Price, and in a letter from C. Godwyn in that year. Godwyn says that Courayer originally gave the picture to Bishop Atterbury. (Hutchins' Dorset, second edit. vol. iv. p. xxi.) Courayer's letter to the Vice-Chancellor accompanying his gift is copied in the Register of Convocation, B[i]. 36, p. 73; it is dated at London, 8 Nov. 1768. In it he says, 'As I do expect every day to receive from Holland the last volume of my French translation of the Memoirs of Sleidan about the origin of the Reformation, I propose to send a copy of the whole to the University Library; and if you do me the honour to accept of it, to join one for you, as a pledge of my regard for you and of my thanks for the trouble I give you. This is the last tribute I shall be able to pay to your respectable and learned society, because the decay of my sight and of my other faculties renders me now entirely unable to apply myself to any sort of reading, and reduces me by this misfortune for the remainder of my days to a state of idleness more conform to my present situation than to my inclinations.' (Courayer died 16 Oct. 1776, aged 95.) A letter of thanks from the University for his gift was passed in Convocation on 25 Nov., to which Courayer replied on 8 Dec.

Maraldi's and Cassini's *Atlas of France*, in 2 vols., no less than £104 was paid! The interest now taken in French politics was also shown by the purchase of a set of the *Moniteur* from 1789, which was bought for £66.

A. D. 1801.

A large and valuable collection of MS. and printed music was received, at the beginning of this year or the close of the preceding, by the bequest of Rev. Osborne Wight, M.A., formerly a Fellow of New College, who died Feb. 6, 1800[1]. The MSS. number about 190 volumes. They contain anthems, &c., by Arnold, Bishop, Blow, Boyce, Croft, Greene, Purcell, &c.; a large number of the works of Drs. Philip and William Hayes; with very many madrigals and motetts by early Italian and English composers, and some of Handel's compositions. The printed volumes consist chiefly of the original folio editions of Handel, Arnold's and Boyce's collections, and the works of Playford, Purcell, Croft, Greene, and other English composers. A MS. Catalogue of the whole was made by Rev. H. E. Havergal, M.A., about 1846, when the collection was put in order. The Library also possesses full band and voice parts of several of the odes and other compositions by both Philip and William Hayes. Besides his books Mr. Wight also bequeathed £100 in the 3 per cents. 'to defray expenses.' No large additions have been made in the class of old music since his gift. Some rare sets of madrigals have been purchased, specially, in 1856, those of Morley, Watson, Weelkes, Wilbye, and Yonge, for £24 14*s.* 6*d.*; Mr. Vincent Novello gave, in 1849, MSS. of Handel's *Te Deum in D*, and Greene's anthem, 'Ponder my words,' and in the following year a MS. of part of the ancient Gregorian Mass, 'De Angelis,' harmonized by Sam. Wesley, in 1812; the Professor of Music, Sir F. Ouseley, Bart.,

[1] A short memoir of this gentleman is given in *Gent. Magaz.* for 1800, p. 1212, where it is said that 'he was eminently skilled in the practice and composition of music, and was probably excelled by no one, whether *dilettante* or professor, as a sightsman in vocal execution.'

gave some French *Cantates* in 1856; and two or three volumes were added by the present writer.

A.D. 1803.

An Arabic MS., in seven volumes, written in 1764-5, and containing what is rarely met with, a complete collection of the Thousand and One Tales of the *Arabian Nights' Entertainments*, was bought from Capt. Jonathan Scott for £50. Mr. Scott published, in 1811, an edition of the Tales, in six volumes, in which this MS. is described. He obtained it from Dr. White, the Professor of Hebrew and Arabic at Oxford, who had bought it at the sale of the library of Edward Wortley Montague, by whom it had been brought from the East. It is noticed in Ouseley's *Oriental Collections*, vol. ii. p. 25.

A.D. 1804.

The payment of various fees was re-arranged in Convocation on 21 June, in pursuance of a letter from the Chancellor, and the fee payable by graduates on admission to the Library was raised to eleven shillings.

A.D. 1805.

In this year the last volume (numbered 142) of Dr. Holmes' Collations of MSS. of the Septuagint-Version, was deposited in the Library. This great and important work had been commenced in the year 1789; it was intended to embrace collations of all the known MSS. of the Greek text, as well as of Oriental versions; and for seventeen years, by the help of liberal subscriptions, in spite of the difficulties interposed by the continental wars, the collection of the various readings from MSS. in libraries throughout Europe was carried on. And each year's work was, on its completion, deposited in the Bodleian. During this period, annual accounts were published of the progress of the work, which possess both critical and bibliographical interest; and the results of the whole are seen in the fine edition printed at the Clarendon Press, in five vols., folio, 1798–1827.

The MSS. of the distinguished classical scholar, James Philip D'Orville, who died at Amsterdam, Sept. 14, 1751, were bought for £1025. After the purchase was completed, a question arose whether the University of Leyden were not, by the terms of his will, entitled to them after the death of his son, but it was ascertained that this provision was only made in case his son did not reach manhood. The collection numbers about 570 volumes, containing many valuable Greek and Latin Classics, together with numerous collations of texts, and annotated printed copies. A few volumes were received in 1821 by gift from J. C. Banks. Thirty-four volumes contain correspondence (autograph and in copy) of Is. Vossius, Heinsius, Cuper, Paolo Sarpi, Beverland, and the letters addressed to D'Orville by all the great scholars of his time. And thirty-eight volumes, in folio and quarto, contain *Adversaria* (chiefly legal) of Scipio and Alberic Gentilis. There are also six Turkish and Arabic MSS. The gem of the collection is a quarto MS. of Euclid, containing 387 leaves, which was written 'χειρὶ Στεφάνου κληρικοῦ,' A.M. 6397 = A.D. 889. It contains a memorandum by one Arethas of Patras, that he bought the book for four (or, more probably, fourteen,) *nummi*. A Catalogue of the MSS., compiled anonymously by Dr. (then Mr.) Gaisford, was printed in quarto, in 1806. D'Orville's signature occurs in the Admission-book as having been admitted to read on Aug. 18, 1718. He visited the Library again in 1725.

A form of new Statute was put out on March 28, which was promulgated in Congregation on 6 May, and proposed in Convocation on 9 May; but it was then rejected on a division, and no fresh Statutes were enacted until 1813. The staff was proposed to be increased to the number which was adopted in the latter year, but with smaller salaries; and the Library was to be open from nine to three, throughout the year. By decree of Convocation on 21 Feb., the old Anatomy and Law Schools were annexed to the Library, and the latter was fitted up in 1817 for the reception of MSS.

A.D. 1806.

Fifty pounds were paid for some 'Tibetan MSS.' of Capt. Samuel Turner, E.I.C.S., who had been sent by Warren Hastings on a mission to the Grand Llama in 1785. Of this mission he published an account, in a quarto volume, in 1800. His MSS. consist chiefly of nine bundles of papers and letters in the Persian and 'Tartar' languages, written in the last century, together with a few Chinese printed books. Capt. Turner died Jan. 2, 1802; but as one of his sisters was married to Prof. White, it was probably through him that the papers were now purchased.

A beautiful copy of the *Koran* (Bodl. Or. 793) which had been in the library of Tippoo Sahib was presented, together with another MS. from the same collection, by the East India Company. Dibdin speaks of it as a work 'upon which caligraphy seems to have exhausted all its powers of intricacy and splendour,' and adds the following description:—

'The preservation of it is perfect, and the beauty of the binding, especially of the interior ornaments, is quite surprising. The first few leaves of the text are highly ornamented, without figures, chiefly in red and blue. The latter leaves are more ornamental; they are even gorgeous, curious and minute. The generality of the leaves have two star-like ornaments in the margin, out of the border. Upon the whole this is an exquisite treasure, in its way[1].'

The *Catholicon* of J. de Janua, printed at Mentz, in 1460, was bought for £63.

The following singular memorandum, relating to this year, is preserved on a small paper:—

'Oxford, Aug. 29, 1806. Borrowed this day, of the Rev. the Bodleian Librarian, the picture given to the Library by Mr. Peters, which I promise to return upon demand.

'JOSEPH WHITE.

'*Mem.* Not returned, June 24, 1807.

'Nor as yet, Oct., 1808. J. P. (*i. e.* J. Price).

'And never to be ret^{d}.' (Added at some later period.)

[1] *Bibliogr. Decam.* iii. 472.

This picture must have been the portrait of Professor White himself, which was painted and presented by Rev. Will. Peters, R.A., in 1785[1]. It has never been restored. Price gave in this year a portrait of Q. Elizabeth, which had been given to him in 1801 by Mr. R. H. Beaumont, of Whitley Hall, Yorkshire[2].

On the morning of Saturday, April 19, probably but little after eight o'clock, the statutable time for the opening of the Library, (see p. 294, *n.*), some zealous student stood at the door, but could get no further. No one appeared to give him entrance; the Librarian himself never came on a Saturday, and his Assistants were not scrupulous in punctuality; at any rate, the expectant student stood and expected in vain. But ere he departed, he denounced a 'Woe' which perpetuates to this day the memory of his vain expectancy; he affixed to the door the following text, which doubtless seemed to him naturally suggested: 'Οὐαὶ ὑμῖν, ὅτι ἤρατε τὴν κλεῖδα τῆς γνώσεως· αὐτοὶ οὐκ εἰσήλθετε, καὶ τοὺς εἰσερχομένους ἐκωλύσατε.' The paper is now preserved over the door of one of the Sub-librarians' studies, with this note added: 'Affixed to the outer door of the Library by some *scavant inconnu*, April 19, 1806.'

A. D. 1807.

A list of the books printed during the year at the University Press is added to the annual account. This was not repeated.

A copy of the *Speculum Christiani*, printed by Will. de Machlinia, was given by Rev. A. H. Matthews, of Jesus College, Sub-librarian.

Amongst the names of Assistants, written by them, *more Anglico*, on the wood-work of their studies, occurs the name of 'Rob. Fr. Walker, New Coll., Dec. 1807.' Mr. Walker (Clerk of both Magd. and New Colleges, B.A. 1811, M.A. 1813) was subsequently Curate of Purleigh, Essex, where he was buried in 1854.

[1] Gutch's *Wood*, II. ii. 979.

[2] A parcel of interesting family letters was also given by Beaumont to Price, which I edited for the Roxburghe Club in 1884, and in the preface to the volume an account is given of the curious discovery of the papers in the Library in 1881.

He was known as translator of a *Life of Bengel*, and of other works, from the German. A memoir of him was published by Rev. T. Pyne, from which an account given by Dr. Bloxam in his *Register of Magd. Coll.* ii. 115–117, is chiefly taken. In 1810, John Woodcock (B.A. 1817, M.A. 1818, Chaplain of New College) appears, from the same evidence as Mr. Walker, to have been an Assistant, one Will. John Lennox in 1808, and John Jones, (Ch. Ch., B.A. 1801, M.A. 1815), in 1809.

A. D. 1808.

The Latin Bible printed by Ulric Zell, at Cologne, in two volumes, about 1470, was bought for £47 5*s*. The Bible printed at Rome, by Sweynheym and Pannartz, in 1471, had been bought, in 1804, for £35; and in 1826 a Strasburg edition, printed with Mentelin's types, without date, was obtained for £94 10*s*.

In this year Dr. Philip Bliss, the editor of Wood's *Athenæ*, entered the Library as an Assistant, as noted by himself in *MS. Topogr., Oxon.* e. 21, fol. 39, and in 1810 the entries in the register of books received from Stationers' Hall are partly made by him, in his very clear and neat hand.

A set of the Oxford Almanacks, from the commencement in 1674 to this year, was given by a frequent donor, Alderman Fletcher[1].

A. D. 1809.

The death of the eminent topographer and antiquary, Richard Gough, on Feb. 20, 1809[2], brought into operation the bequest made to the Library in his will, dated ten years previously. This

[1] A limited number of copies of the engravings of these Almanacks, from the original plates which remain in the University Press, were re-issued in 1867, under the superintendence of Rev. John Griffiths, M.A.

[2] A very full memoir of him is to be found in the *Lit. Anecd.* vol. vi. pp. 262–343, and 613–626. His miscellaneous library was sold by auction in 1810. Two drawings in sepia, by F. Lewis, of his house at Enfield, were bought in 1861.

consisted of all his topographical collections, together with all his books relating to Saxon and Northern literature, 'for the use of the Saxon Professor,' his maps and engravings, and all the copper-plates used in the illustration of the various works published by himself[1]. The transmission of this vast collection was accomplished by Mr. J. Nichols, the executor, in the course of the year; and some of his correspondence on the subject (as well as Gough's previous correspondence with Price) is printed in his *Illustrations of Literary History*, vol. v. pp. 555-561[2]. The collection (which numbers upwards of 3700 volumes) was placed in the room formerly the Civil Law School, that room having been assigned to the Library a few years previously, and fitted up (at a cost of about £675) for the reception of various historical collections. In the same room were until lately the Carte, Tanner, Junius, Walker, and a portion of the Rawlinson, manuscripts, with those of Dodsworth and Willis which still remain there; the name proposed to be given to it, and by which it was designated in Gough's will, was 'The Antiquaries' Closet,' but it is now occupied entirely by topographical collections. Gough's library consists, firstly, of a large series of maps[3] and topographical prints and drawings, in elephant-folio

[1] He had offered the whole to the British Museum in 1804, on condition of his retaining personal use of his copper-plates, but his offer was received somewhat ungraciously, and he in consequence altered his intention. See Nichols' *Illust. of Lit. Hist.* v. 571-7.

[2] Original letters from him to Price are in Bodl. MS. Addit. A. 64.

[3] One of these is a very curious manuscript map of England and Scotland, executed in the fourteenth century, which now hangs, framed and glazed, in the eastern wing of the Library. It was bought by Gough at the sale of the MSS. of Mr. Thomas Martin, of Palgrave, Suffolk, in 1774. A facsimile (engraved by Basire) and a description are given in the *British Topography*, 1780, vol. i. pp. 76-85; and it has been photozincographed in part III of the *Facsimiles of National MSS. of Scotland*, by Mr. W. B. Sanders, who has described the Map in the 32nd and 34th (p. 288) Reports of the Deputy Keeper of Public Records. Another object of interest among the maps is a piece of tapestry, in three fragments, containing portions of the counties of Hereford, Salop, Staffordshire, Worcestershire, Warwickshire, Gloucestershire, Middlesex, &c. They are said by Gough, in a MS. note in his collections for a third edition of his *Topography*, to be parts of the three great maps of the Midland Counties, formerly at Mr. Sheldon's house at Weston, Long Compton, Warwickshire, which are

volumes; of this a very brief outline-list is given in the printed catalogue, but a full list in detail exists in MS.[1] Secondly, of printed books and MSS., arranged under the heads of General Topography, Ecclesiastical Topography[2], Natural History, the several Counties (with London, Westminster, and Southwark) in order[3], Wales, Islands, Scotland, and Ireland. Thirdly, of 227 works connected with Anglo-Saxon literature and that of the Scandinavian races generally. Fourthly, of an extremely large and valuable series of printed Service-books of the English Church before the Reformation, together with a few MSS., chiefly *Horæ*. The value of this series may be gathered from the following statement of the Missals, Breviaries, Manuals, Processionals, and Hours,

the earliest specimens of tapestry weaving in England, the art having been introduced by William Sheldon, who died in 1570. They are described in vol. ii. of the *Topography*, pp. 309–10. They were brought by Lord Orford at a sale at Weston for £30, and presented by him to Earl Harcourt, whose successor, Archbishop Harcourt, gave them to the Museum of the Philosophical Society at York (where they now are) in 1827. In Murray's *Handbook for Yorkshire*, they are said to have been made in 1579. One guinea was given by Gough for his fragments.

[1] This list was drawn up about 1844–6 by Mr. Fred. Oct. Garlick, then an assistant in the Library (afterwards of Ch. Ch., B.A., deceased 1851).

[2] Mr. A. Chalmers gave, in 1813, the second volume of a copy of Wharton's *Anglia Sacra*, with MSS. notes by White Kennett, of which the first volume was in this division of Gough's library. But both volumes had been bought by Gough for £1 1*s*. at the sale of J. West's library in 1773, at which sale he procured, besides, several other books with Kennett's notes. There are also volumes with MSS. notes by Baker (the 'socius ejectus'), Cole, Rowe Mores, and other well-known antiquaries. Three MSS. containing the Form of Coronation used at the coronations of James II, Q. Anne, and Geo. II, came to the Library among the MSS. of F. Douce, and amongst the printed books of the latter (D. 133) is a volume of theological tracts which also belonged to Gough.

[3] The County Histories are in many instances enriched with various notes and papers in print and MS. The Berkshire MSS. were increased in 1868 by the addition of the collections of the late Will. Nelson Clarke, D.C.L., of Ch. Ch., author of the *History of the Hundred of Wanting* (4°. 1824), which were presented to the Library by Mr. Coxe, to whom they were given by the collector, his cousin, when the latter relinquished the idea of writing a history of Berks. They consist of a Parochial History of the county, transcripts of Heralds' Visitations and of early records, and miscellaneous note-books and papers.

which it comprises, besides which there are Graduals, Psalters, Hymns, Primers, &c.

Missals,	Salisbury use	30
,,	York ,,	4
,,	Rouen ,,	1
,,	Roman ,,	3
,,	'pro sacerdotibus in Anglia, &c. itinerantibus'	1
Breviaries and *Portiforia*,	Salisbury use	18
,, ,,	York ,,	2
,, ,,	Hereford ,,	1[1]
Manuals,	Salisbury use	10
,,	York (MS.) ,,	1
Processionals,	Salisbury use	10
,,	York ,,	1
Hours,	Salisbury use	24
,,	Roman ,, (besides several MSS.)	1

Of several of these books there are more than single copies.

A fifth division of Gough's library consists of sixteen large folio volumes of coloured drawings of monuments in churches of France, chiefly at Paris, in Normandy, Valois, Champagne, Burgundy and Brie, and at Beauvais, Chartres, Vendosme and Noyon. They form part of a large collection extending through the whole of France, which was made by M. Gagnières, tutor to the sons of the Grand Dauphin, and given by him to Louis XIV in 1711. Of this collection, now preserved in the National Library, twenty-five volumes were lost amid the troubles of the French Revolution, between 1785 and 1801; but in what way, out of the twenty-five, these sixteen came into Gough's hands has not been clearly ascertained.

[1] The splendid and, as it is believed, unique vellum copy of the *Hereford Missal* ('ad usum eccl. Helfordensis,' fol. Rouen, 1502) which the Library possesses, came to it from Rawlinson among the books of T. Hearne, to whom it had been given by Charles Eyston, Esq., of East Hendred, Berks. (Hearne's pref. to Camden's *Annales Eliz.* I. xxvii.) This Hereford volume is described, together with many of Gough's books, in a book by Ed. Frère, entitled *Des Livres des Églises d'Angleterre imprimés à Rouen dans les* xv. *et* xvi. *siècles*, 8°. Rouen, 1867.

The collection is of great value, as most of the monuments were defaced or destroyed by the revolutionary mobs. Gough's volumes contain about 2000 drawings, of the whole of which facsimiles were made in 1860 by M. Jules Frappaz, by direction of the French Minister of Public Instruction, (who made application for the purpose, through Mr. J. H. Parker, in 1859) for the purpose of so far supplying the deficiency in the series at Paris[1].

The copy of the *British Topography* which Gough had prepared for a third edition (of which a considerable part of vol. i. had been printed, but was burned in the disastrous fire at Mr. Nichols' printing-office in Feb., 1808,) was bought by the Curators of Mr. Nichols in 1812 for £150[2]. It has been bound in four very thick volumes. A fifth volume contains the proof-sheets of that portion of vol. i. which had been printed, extending to *Cheshire*, p. 446. The collections for the first edition make three volumes.

By Gough's bequest the Library became also possessed (as mentioned above) of the very valuable copper-plates which illustrated his *Sepulchral Monuments*, and other works. In 1811, one hundred guineas were paid to Basire, the engraver, for cleaning and arranging 380 of these plates. Amongst these was the actual brass effigy of one of the Wingfield family in the fifteenth century, from Letheringham Church, Suffolk, of which an impression is found in the *Monuments*.

The Catalogue of the collection was issued from the University Press, in a quarto volume, in 1814. It was chiefly compiled by Dr. Bandinel, to whom fifty guineas were paid for it, in 1813; but Dr. Bliss has noted[3] that the first 136 pages were prepared by himself. In the *Bibliographical Decameron* (vol. i. p. xcv) Dibdin has made honourable mention of the 'perseverance, energy, and exactness' with which he found Dr. (then Mr.) Bandinel working on a very hot day in the year 1812, in the arrangement

[1] See *Gent.Magaz.* for 1860, p. 406.

[2] So in the Library Register of accounts. Nichols (*Lit. Hist.* vol. v. p. 559) says £100.

[3] In his MS. *Collectanea*, bequeathed by him to Rev. H. O. Coxe, and by the latter to the Library.

of the collection, 'in an oaken-floored room, light, spacious, and dry.'

Some account and survey-books, belonging to University and Magdalen Colleges, which came to the Library among Gough's MSS., were restored by vote of Convocation on March 9, 1814.

The MSS. which the well-known traveller, Rev. Edw. Dan. Clarke, LL.D., had collected during his journeys through a large part of Europe and Asia, were purchased from him in this year for £1000. A first portion of a Catalogue, comprising descriptions of fifty volumes, of which fifteen are in Latin, two in French (Alain Chartier, one being the printed edit. of 1526), and the rest in Greek, was published in 1812, in quarto, by Dr. Gaisford, who printed in full some inedited Scholia on Plato and on the Poems of Gregory Nazianzen. A second part of the Catalogue, containing a description of forty-five volumes in Arabic, Persian, and Ethiopic, was issued by Dr. Nicoll, in 1814. The special feature in the collection is a MS. of Plato's Dialogues, from which the Scholia are printed in the Catalogue, written (on 418 vellum quarto leaves) by a scribe named John (who styles himself *Calligraphus*) in the year 896, for Arethas, a deacon of Patras, for the sum of thirteen Byzantine *nummi*[1]. The D'Orville MS. of Euclid was also written for this Arethas (*see* p. 282).

A.D. 1810.

In March, the Prince Regent forwarded to the University four rolls of papyrus, brought from Herculaneum, burned to a state resembling charcoal, together with engravings of rolls hitherto deciphered, and many facsimile copies, in pencil, of inedited rolls[2].

[1] On the inscriptions which are found in this MS. and in the D'Orville Euclid, and on the prices paid to the scribes, see *Mélanges* (*à la mém. de Ch.*) *Graux*, 8° Par. 1884, pp. 751–2.

[2] Copies of the Prince's letter to Lord Grenville, the Chancellor of the University, dated 9 March, and of a long letter from the latter of 11 March, on forwarding the gift to Oxford, are entered in the Register of Convocation.

A committee was appointed on 5 Feb., 1811, from the Curators of the Library and Delegates of the Press, to have the charge of this gift, and £500 were granted towards publication. Two volumes of lithographed facsimiles were in consequence published at the Clarendon Press, in 1824–5. Some further selections from these papers have been published by a German scholar, Dr. Th. Gompertz; and a descriptive catalogue, with facsimiles, &c., by Walter Scott, M.A., was issued by the Clarendon Press in 1885. And in the present year (1889) the Oxford Philological Society has issued photographic facsimiles of all that are yet unpublished.

On Nov. 15, it was resolved in Convocation to restore to the Chancery at Durham, on the application of the Bishop of Durham, the MS. Register of Richard Kellawe, Bishop of Durham, 1311–16, containing also a portion of the Register of Rich. Bury, 1338–42, which had come to the Library among Rawlinson's collections, and was the only volume wanting at Durham in an unbroken series of Episcopal Registers, of which this was the first. It was borrowed in $16\frac{39}{40}$, as it appeared, by an agent of the Marquis of Newcastle, for the purpose of production in some law-suit affecting his property; remained through the Civil War in his hands; fell subsequently into those of the Earl of Oxford, and was bought by Rawlinson from Osborne the bookseller, in whose sale-catalogue of the Harleian Library in 1743 it was numbered 20734. Kellawe's Register was printed in the Master of the Rolls' series of chronicles, under the editorship of Sir T. D. Hardy, in four volumes, in the years 1873–78[1].

Bulkeley Bandinel, M.A., entered the Library in this year. To him, for a list of a portion of the Rawlinson MSS., £26 5*s*. were paid in 1812; in which year also his colleague and life-long friend, Philip Bliss, drew up short lists of the Rawlinson *Poetry*,

[1] The return of this register was appealed to, as a precedent, but unsuccessfully, in an application made by the Dean and Chapter of Lichfield in 1884 for the return to them of Ashmole MS. 794, which contains the Chapter-Book for the years 1321–1356 (*Athenæum*, Dec. 27, 1883, p. 860).

Letters, and a small part of the *Miscellaneous* MSS., as well as of the St. Amand MSS., for which a payment was made to him of £21. Dr. Bliss afterwards quitted the Library for the British Museum, but returned in 1822, as Sub-librarian, for a short time.

A.D. 1811.

Only eighteen books were purchased in this year! The list, scantly filling one page, is consequently the *minimum* in the series of annual catalogues.

A.D. 1812.

Proposed alteration of statutes: *see foot-note to the following year.*

A.D. 1813.

The Rev. John Price, B.D., the Librarian, died on Aug. 11, aged seventy-nine, after forty-five years of office as head Librarian. A short biographical notice is given in the *Gentleman's Magazine* for Oct., 1813, p. 400, and a fuller account, together with many letters, and an engraved profile-portrait (the only one in existence, from a sketch taken in 1798 by Rev. H. H. Baber[1]), with facsimile signature, in vols. v. and vi. of Nichols' *Illustrations of the Lit. Hist. of the 18th Century*. The following character of him with regard to his discharge of his official duties is there given (vi. 471), which in some respects forms a strong contrast to the representation of Prof. Beddoes in the year 1787 (*see* pp. 269–70). 'In the faithful discharge of his public duties in the University, he acquitted himself with

[1] It represents him as wearing a very solid pair of spectacles, with rather curious circular endings to the arms of the frame. To a late dear friend, John Rigaud, B.D., Fellow of Magd. Coll., I owe the possession of a similarly solid pair of silver spectacles, which were worn to the end of his life by the old President of our College, Dr. Routh, whose quaint and venerable figure (never seen, even by his study fire, without wig, gown, bands, cassock, and silver buckles) is ever fresh in my remembrance. My last interview with him was on 9 Nov. 1854, only six weeks before his death, when I called because he wished to consult me respecting a catalogue of his library.

the highest credit, and deservedly conciliated the esteem of others by his readiness to communicate information from the rich literary stores over which he presided, and of which he was a most jealous and watchful guardian. He was, from long habit, so completely attached to the Library, that he considered every acquisition made to its contents as a personal favour conferred upon himself.' It was chiefly owing to his assiduous attention to Mr. Gough and his frequent correspondence with him, that the Library was enriched with the bequest of the latter's splendid topographical collections. But there is not much existing to tell of personal work in the Library during his long tenure of office, and the fact that nothing was done till near the close of that period towards arranging and cataloguing the Rawlinson MSS., seems to prove that there was no great activity in the Library under his management. This is corroborated also by the wonderful difference which is immediately seen in the annual catalogue of purchases; the Catalogue for 1813 grows at once from the two folio pages of the preceding year to seventeen, while the sum expended becomes £725 in the place of £261[1]. And the list of books forwarded from Stationers' Hall, and hitherto received only twice yearly, at Lady-day and Michaelmas, becomes in 1815 largely increased, while in the year 1822 the number of yearly parcels is increased to eight. At the present time books are received tri-monthly.

The Rev. Bulkeley Bandinel, M.A. (D.D. in 1823), of New College, was elected Librarian by Convocation on Aug. 25, without opposition. He had been appointed Sub-librarian in 1810, by Mr. Price, who was his godfather; and for a short time previously had been a Chaplain in the Royal Navy, having served with Adm. Sir James Saumarez on board the 'Victory,' in the Baltic, in 1808.

The appointment of a new Librarian was followed by the enacting of a new Statute, passed by Convocation on Dec. 2, which provided for the increase of the Librarian's stipend to £400, exclusive of his share of fees from degrees; for the appointment

[1] Among the purchases is a set of the *Gentleman's Magazine* to the year 1810 for £52 10*s*.

of two Sub-librarians, instead of one, and these not under the degree of M.A., with salaries of £150; of two assistants, Bachelors of Arts or undergraduates, with salaries of £50; and of the Janitor, with a salary of £20. An additional annual grant, calculated at £680, equal to that which resulted from the provision made by the Statute of 1780, and to be paid, like that, out of the yearly fees of graduates whose names are on the books, was sanctioned, with the triple object of providing for this enlarged staff, for the commencement of a new Catalogue, and for repairs hitherto defrayed out of the general University funds. The state of the roof and ceiling were said to be such as to justify an apprehension that they must at no distant period be entirely constructed anew; happily this reconstruction was only carried out with respect to the Picture Gallery, and the roof of the Library remains as a precious relic still.

The hours at which the Library should be open, were fixed to be from 9 to 4 in the summer half-year, and 10 to 3 in the winter; the changes since made have been the enacting, in 1867, that nine o'clock shall be the invariable hour of opening on all ordinary days[1], and in 1874, that the hour of closing should be three in the months of Nov.—Jan., four in Feb., March, Aug.—Oct., and five in April—July.

The junior assistants in the Library in this year were Mr. Francis

[1] The alteration of hours had been previously proposed in a Statute which was to have been submitted to Convocation on Dec. 11, 1812, but which appears to have been withdrawn ere the day came, probably because this larger measure of revision of the old Statutes was already in contemplation. A blank is left in the Convocation Book under that date, by the then Registrar, Mr. Gutch; and his successor, Dr. Bliss, has added a pencil-note to the effect that he supposes from the blank not being filled up, that the proposal was previously abandoned. The Statute of 1769 had required that the Library should be open in summer from 8 to 2 and from 3 to 5, but it was stated in some remarks which accompanied the proposed enactment that these injunctions had 'long been disregarded in practice,' and that the Library had been open throughout the year from nine to three o'clock. But it was added that 'experience' had 'shewn that there is no occasion for requiring the attendance of the Librarians before ten in the winter season;' and it is seldom that experience bears other testimony now.

L. Thurland, of New and Magd. Colleges (B.A. 1812, M.A. 1814, died 31 Jan. 1838), and Mr. Sam. Slack, of Ch. Ch. (B.A. 1813, M.A. 1816).

A.D. 1814.

The nomination of the Rev. Henry Cotton, M.A., then Student of Ch. Ch., afterwards Archdeacon of Cashel, as Sub-librarian, was approved in Convocation on March 9. Of the interest which he took in his work, of his qualifications for it, and of the advantages which the bibliographical world has derived from it, his *Typographical Gazetteer* and *List of Editions of the English Bible* afford abundant testimony[1]. He remained in the Library eight years, quitting it when his friend Dr. Laurence, on his appointment to the Archbishopric of Cashel, carried him with himself to Ireland, where his *Fasti Ecclesiæ Hibernicæ* testified, as one proof amongst many, to like interest in duty and regard for his work, and where he died on 3 Dec., 1879, aged 89.

During his continuance in the Library, a descriptive Catalogue of the *Editiones principes* and *Incunabula* was projected by him and Dr. Bandinel, but never carried out; of a specimen page, which was printed in octavo, a copy has been preserved by Dr. Bliss with his set of the annual catalogues. But in 1826 an alphabetical list of these books, similar to that issued in 1795 (*see* p. 276),

[1] In a clever and amusing little squib of four pages, which he printed anonymously in 1819, and which is preserved in the Library-collection of University papers, and was reprinted in Peter Hall's *Crypt* [vol. i. N.S., 1829, pp. 150–4], professing to be a 'Syllabus' of treatises on academic matters, to be printed at the University Press in not more than thirty vols., elephant quarto, Mr. Cotton thus satirized himself and his colleagues. (—In my former edition I added 'doubtless with the more readiness because with no reason,' but I have since had some grounds for thinking that the satire may have had some little basis of fact.—) '21. De Bibliothecario et ejus adjutoribus. *Captain.* What are you about, Dick? *Dick.* Nothing, sir. *Captain.* Tom, what are you doing? *Tom.* Helping Dick, sir.' Treatise 24 has for its title the few but emphatic words, '*De Dodd,*' and nothing more. Lest some future delver in Oxford antiquities should be lost in a maze of conjectures as to the personality and history of this worthy, so evidently then well known, let it here be told that Dodd was the *Clerk of the Schools.*

was completed by Dr. Bandinel and printed in small octavo, but never finally struck off. His MS. and proof copy (extending to 100 pages) are in the Library, and why he again never completed his task is not known. The list would have been useful. The date of its printing is ascertained from the fact of its including books bought in 1826, while those purchased in 1827 are added in MS.

Alex. Nicoll, M.A., of Balliol College (a native of Monymusk[1], in Aberdeenshire), was appointed Sub-librarian at the early age of twenty-one; the nomination was approved in Convocation on April 27. He at once devoted himself to the study of Oriental languages, and became a proficient in Hebrew, Arabic, Persian, Syriac, Ethiopic, and Sanscrit. His facility in acquiring languages must have been truly marvellous, for, in addition to these Eastern tongues, and although his death occurred at the early age of thirty-six, it is said that 'he spoke and wrote with ease and accuracy, French, Italian, German, Danish, Swedish, and Romaic.' In 1822 he was, much to his own surprise, appointed, at the age of twenty-nine, to the Regius Professorship of Hebrew, by Lord Liverpool, on the recommendation of Dr. Laurence, who vacated that post in consequence of his appointment to the see of Cashel[2]. Nicoll held the Professorship for only seven years, dying on Sept. 24, 1828. The records of his labours in the Bodleian are found in the Catalogue of Clarke's Oriental MSS. noticed under the year 1809, and in his second part of the General Catalogue of Oriental MSS., published

[1] His father was a humble maker of wooden dishes (*Scottice,* noggins) in that parish. From the parish school the future professor went to the University of Glasgow, where he obtained a bursary; and from thence came to Oxford as a Snell Exhibitioner at Balliol College, through the influence of Bishop John Skinner of Aberdeen, his family being staunch Episcopalians. This information was given to me by my late venerable friend Alexander Keith, D.D., the well-known writer on Prophecy, who knew Nicoll in his boyhood as well as in later life. A brother of Dr. Nicoll's became an advocate in Aberdeen.

[2] It was said that Nicoll kept the letter of the Prime Minister offering the appointment in his pocket for several days unanswered, believing it to be a hoax: but this story is contradicted in a memoir prefixed to a volume of Sermons printed at Oxford in 1830. Mr. Robert Eden (*see under* 1825) tells me that he had a remarkably weak and 'mouse-like' voice, hardly above a whisper.

in 1821, *q. v.* The examination and arrangement of the Canonici MSS. engaged him in 1818.

The total receipts and expenditure of the Library were for the first time fully stated in the annual accounts. Hitherto the practice had been to omit the Bodley endowment and the Crewe benefaction, &c., which were devoted to salaries, repairs and other ordinary expenses (including also the occasional purchase of MSS.), and only to report the amount received from University fees and expended on printed books and incidental charges.

Some MSS. collections of Sam. Pegge, LL.D., the antiquary, were given by his grandson, Sir Christopher Pegge, M.D., Regius Professor of Medicine.

A.D. 1815.

Cedunt arma togæ! The effect which the cessation of the war produced, in diverting to quiet academic channels the stream of youth which hitherto had flowed in the turbid currents of continental strife, is shown by the large increase of the Library receipts derived from matriculation fees. These, which previously fell below (and often far below) £250, rose in 1814, on the first sign of peace, to £424, and in this year, on its final establishment, to £633.

In January, Mr. John Calcott, of Lincoln College (B.A. 1814, M.A. 1816, B.D. 1825; Fellow of Linc.; deceased 1864) was appointed *Minister* in the room of Mr. Francis Thurland, of New College, resigned. Mr. Calcott, however, only held the office for one year, being succeeded, in Feb. 1816, by Mr. Sam. Fenton, of Jesus College (B.A. 1818, M.A., Ch. Ch. 1821).

A.D. 1816.

An interesting MS., with relation to Scottish history, was placed in the Library on Dec. 5, in this year. It is a transcript (from the originals,) by Col. Nathaniel Hooke, agent in Scotland for

James II[1], of all his political correspondence between the beginning of the year 1704 and the end of 1707. It forms two folio volumes, but is unfinished, as the second volume ends with the commencement of a letter from James Ogilvie, of Boyn, to M. de Torcy, Dec. 26, 1707. A brief narrative of Hooke's negotiations, which contains copies of a few of the letters here given, was published at the Hague, in the French language, and a translation was printed in a small volume at London in 1760, and reprinted both at Edinburgh and Dublin in the same year; but the whole of the correspondence was edited by me for the Roxburghe Club in 1870 in two thick volumes. The MS. came to the Library in pursuance of a bequest from the Rev. J. Tickell, Rector of Gawsworth, Cheshire, and East Mersea, Essex, who died at Wargrave, Berks, July 3, 1802. The bequest was to take effect upon the death of his wife, which occurred towards the close of 1816[2].

The Curators reported, at the end of the annual list, that considerable progress had been made towards the formation of a new general Catalogue. Further progress was reported in the following year; in which year also Dibdin announced[3] that the Catalogue would be finished, in four folio volumes, by Messrs. Bandinel and Cotton under the superintendence of Professor Gaisford[4]. He adds, 'The Prince Regent hath munificently given a considerable sum towards the completion of these glorious labours.' There is no record in the annual accounts of any such donation; but in 1823 and 1824 payments amounting to £420 were made to the Librarian, Sub-librarians, and Assistant, for their work on the new Catalogue[5], out of 'the Prince Regent's benefaction.' On the proposition of the Chancellor, Lord Grenville, in 1814,

[1] Hooke in 1685 was one of the chaplains attending Monmouth in his rebellion! *Lockhart Papers*, 1817, vol. I. p. 148.

[2] *Gent. Magaz.* vol. lxxv. ii. 569.

[3] *Bibliogr. Decam.* iii. 429.

[4] Portions of the letters A F and P which had been thus prepared were subsequently printed, but the whole work was then for some years suspended, and afterwards commenced *de novo*. And nearly thirty years elapsed before it was finally completed.

[5] Previous grants amounting to £260 had been made in 1820.

Mr. Vansittart, the Chancellor of the Exchequer, had expressed his willingness to apply to Parliament for a grant of £5000 for the purpose; probably this idea was abandoned for the more easily practicable one, and much more limited one, of a grant from the Privy Purse.

Four Greek MSS. were presented in this year by Rev. —— Hall, Chaplain at Leghorn[1]; a copy of Lucan's *Pharsalia*, with MSS. collations by Joseph Addison, by Dr. Peter Vaughan, Warden of Merton College; and a large collection of books in Oriental literature, printed in Bengal, by the East India Company.

A.D. 1817.

The large Canonici collection of MSS. was obtained from Venice in this year, for the sum of £5444, a purchase unprecedented in greatness in the history of the Library[2]. The collection was formed by Matheo Luigi Canonici, a Venetian Jesuit, who was born in 1727 and died in Sept. 1805 or 1806. Indefatigable in his passion for antiquities, he first formed a Museum of statues and of medals at Parma, but, in consequence of the Jesuits being expelled from the State, this was sold to the government. He then at Bologna set himself to collect religious objects of interest, and had succeeded to some extent, when the rector of his society observed to him that such a collection was little suitable to a poor monk, and he consequently disposed of it to a Roman prince. Finally, at Venice, he commenced the gathering of a library, in which it is said, as one evidence of its extent, there were more than four thousand Bibles in fifty-two languages[3].

The MSS. purchased by the Bodleian amount in number to

[1] Three of these are described in Mr. Coxe's Catalogue, cols. 812–14.

[2] The money was raised by loans of £2000 from the Radcliffe Trustees and £3644 from the University Bankers. They were both repaid by the year 1820.

[3] De Backer's *Bibliothèque des écrivains de la comp. de Jésus*; quatr. série, p. 93. 8vo. Liège, 1858.

about 2045. Dibdin, almost immediately, noticed the acquisition thus[1]:—

'They have recently acquired a very curious and valuable collection of MSS., which formerly belonged to an ex-Jesuit Abbé, who intended (had he lived to have seen the restoration of the order of the Jesuits) to have presented them to the Jesuits' College at Venice. Neither pains nor expense were spared among his brethren, in all parts of the world, to make the collection, on that account, as perfect as possible.'

In Greek there are 128 volumes, chiefly of the fifteenth and sixteenth centuries, with a few of earlier date, including two *Evangelistaria* assigned by Montfaucon to the ninth century. Of Latin classical authors and mediæval poets there are 311 volumes; some of those of the former class are of great age and value, notably a Virgil of the tenth century (No. 50). Ninety-three MSS. form the class of Latin Bibles; the finest of these are, one written in 1178 for the church of SS. Mary and Pancras in Ranshoven, and another, in five very large folio volumes, written and illuminated in France in the years 1507–1511. Of Latin ecclesiastical writers and Fathers there are 232 volumes; and of Latin miscellanies (chiefly in medicine, philosophy and science, theology, and *belles lettres*, with scarcely anything of an historical character), 576 volumes. Of all these classes a catalogue was published by Mr. Coxe in 1854, forming part iii. of the new general Catalogue of MSS.

Another division consists of Liturgical books. In this class there are about 250 volumes; about 130 were added by Mr. Coxe, chiefly from the Rawlinson collection, but these have been restored to their original places by his successor. They consist chiefly of *Horæ*, Breviaries, Missals, and Psalters, with a few other service-books; most of them being 'secundum usum Romanum.' No catalogue of this series has as yet been made.

A sixth division comprehends 295 Italian MSS., with five in Spanish, of which a very elaborate catalogue was compiled, as a labour of love, by the Count Alessandro Mortara, during the

[1] *Bibliogr. Decam.* iii. 429.

years of his stay in Oxford[1]. His MS. was bought after his death from his executor the Abate Giuseppe Manuzzi, of Florence, for £201, in the year 1858; it was afterwards put to press under the care of his intimate friend the late Dr. H. Wellesley, then Principal of New Inn Hall, and appeared, with an Italian preface by him giving some account of the whole collection, in one volume quarto (158 pages,) in 1864.

The last portion of the collection consists of 135 Oriental MSS., chiefly valuable Hebrew books on vellum. One of these (No. 78) is a copy of Maimonides' Commentary on the Law, in fourteen books, which is dated 1366. Seven of the Biblical volumes are noticed in De Rossi's *Variæ Lectiones Veteris Testamenti*. The few Arabic MSS. are described in Dr. Pusey's continuation of Nicoll's Catalogue; and the Hebrew in Mr. Neubauer's general Catalogue of the Hebrew MSS.

A curious story of the recovery, amidst these books, of some leaves belonging to a printed vellum Bible existing in the Library, has been already related under the year 1750. A few other MSS. from Canonici's library, with some from Saibante's, were sold by auction in London, in 1821. And many relating to Italian and Venetian history, which were at first retained by one of the heirs, passed afterwards into the hands of the Rev. Walter Sneyd, of Baginton, Warwickshire. A MS. volume of notices of the Canonici library, drawn up by Signor Lorenzi, of Venice, was bought by the Bodleian, in 1859, for ten guineas[2].

[1] See under the year 1852.

[2] Fifteen MSS. of Dante came in the Canonici collection; with the exception of one (a late fifteenth-century copy) which came with the D'Orville MSS. in 1805, they were the first which the Library possessed. This fact is worth mentioning, on account of an extraordinary story told by Girolamo Gigli, in his *Vocabolario Cateriniano*, p. cciii (a book the printing of which was commenced at Rome in 1717, but which was suppressed, by bull, before completion), that in the Bodleian Library at 'Osfolk,' there was a MS. of the *Divina Commedia*, which, from being employed in enveloping a consignment of cheese (and so imported into England by a mode of conveyance said to have been usually adopted by Florentine merchants, with a view of spreading at once a knowledge of their luxuries and their literature), had become so saturated with a caseous savour as to require the constant guardianship of two traps to

A MS. of Suidas, of the fifteenth century, was purchased for £220 10*s*. Another acquisition was a French translation, made in 1417, by Laurens de Preme, of the *Ethics*, *Politics*, &c. of Aristotle[1]. Some specimens of the Javanese language were given by Capt. L. H. Davy.

Among printed books, the most noticeable purchase (besides the *Edd. Pr.* of Livy, 1469, Lactantius, 1465, &c.) was that of a vellum copy of the first edition of the Hebrew Pentateuch, printed at Bologna in 1482, for £17 10*s*. Some sets of controversial and political tracts, with other books, which had belonged to Thomas Brande Hollis and Dr. John Disney, were bought at the sale of the library of the latter.

The old Law School was fitted up in this year as an additional room for MSS. A duplicate portrait of Lord Chancellor Ellesmere was given to Brasenose College in exchange for a portrait of Dean Nowell, of St. Paul's, which is now in the Picture Gallery.

A.D. 1818.

A return was made to the House of Commons of such books received since 1814, in pursuance of the Copyright Act, from Stationers' Hall as it had not been deemed necessary to place in the Library. The list is but a trifling one, consisting chiefly of school-books and anonymous novels, with music; but, nevertheless, it is sufficient to show the great need of caution in rejecting any books excepting such as are of the simplest elementary character, and the advantage of erring rather on the side of inclusiveness than exclusiveness. Miss Edgeworth's *Parents' Assistant*, Mrs. H. More's *Sacred Dramas*, Mrs. Opie's *Simple Tales*, and an edition of *Ossian*, were all consigned to the limbo of 'rubbish.' But the Cambridge return (which is

protect it from the voracity of mice. Hence, according to this marvellous traveller's story, the MS. went by the name of *The Book of the Mousetrap!* (See *Notes and Queries*, first series, i. 154.)

[1] Bodl. MS. 965.

much more detailed than that from Oxford[1]) shows a recklessness of rejection which speaks little for the judgment of the Librarians for the time being. Besides school-books and music, a large number of pamphlets figure in the list, including some by Chalmers and Cobbett; the *Theology* includes Owen's *History of the Bible Society;* the *History* includes *Memoirs of Oliver Cromwell and his Children;* the *Poetry*, Byron's *Siege of Corinth*, L. Hunt's *Story of Rimini*, and Wordsworth's *Thanksgiving Ode;* and the *Novels*, [Peacock's] *Headlong Hall*, one by Mrs. Opie, and—*The Antiquary!* The wiser plan is now carried out in the Bodleian[2] of rejecting nothing; even the elementary works and worthless trifles that certainly do not need entering in the Catalogue were for many years so kept that access could be had to the mass at all times and examination made, while now everything alike *is* entered; and the music is catalogued and bound. And this plan was commenced in the year of which we are writing; for, (in consequence, of course, of this return being called for by the House of Commons,) the Curators ordered, on May 27, that *all* publications sent from Stationers' Hall should in future be entered and preserved.

A very valuable and curious series of original editions of Latin and German tracts, issued by the German Reformers between 1518 and 1550, in eighty-four volumes, was bought for £95 15*s*. Additions have been made to this collection at various times subsequently, so that now it probably comprises as complete a gathering of these controversial publications, so easily lost or destroyed from their small extent and often ephemeral character, as can anywhere be found. A kindred collection (although not of like value or interest) was obtained through the gift by

[1] The minuteness of specification is such that '*Turner's Real Japan Blacking, a Label*,' is duly entered.

[2] With regard to this word *Bodleian* let it be noted that in this year a writer in the *Gent. Magaz.* who signed himself F.R.S. (part i. p. 519), charged the *Annual Biography* for 1817 with 'flippancy and vulgarity' for speaking of 'the Public Library at Oxford by the slang term, the Bodleian!' It is strange that this its familiar *apocopized* name should ever have been regarded as 'slang'; and it would seem by this censure to have been only coming into use about this time. Another instance complained of was the calling Sir Joshua Reynolds 'Sir Joshua.'

Mr. A. Müller, of Amsterdam, of a series of tracts, in sixty-two volumes, and chiefly in the Dutch language, on the controversy with the Remonstrants in 1618–19. Of these there is a MS. catalogue, by Mr. Müller, dated March 3. Besides the books, Mr. Müller gave a few coins, including one struck on leather during the siege of Leyden in 1574, and some natural curiosities, which latter are now preserved in the New Museum. A *black negro baby*, preserved in spirits (!), has, however, unaccountably disappeared; let us hope it was decently buried. Seventeen panes of painted glass, probably by disciples of Crabeth, who painted the windows in the church of Gouda, also formed part of this very miscellaneous donation; these, most probably, are included among the curious fragments which decorate some of the Library windows.

Six Persian MSS. were given by the Principal of Magd. Hall, and Lord Almoner's Reader in Arabic, Dr. Macbride. This gentleman, who died 24 Jan., 1868, aged 88, was admitted to read in the Library while an undergraduate of Exeter College, on May 10, 1797.

Alderman Fletcher's copy of Gutch's Wood. See under 1610.

Mr. John Walker, Queen's College (B.A. 1820; Chaplain of Magd. and New Colleges, M.A., 1823, died 20 March, 1834), succeeded Mr. Fenton as *Minister* in July.

A.D. 1819.

A copy of the extremely rare Polish version of the Bible, made by the Socinians at the expense of Prince Nich. Radzivil, printed in 1563, was bought for £45[1]; and the second edition of the Mentz folio Psalter, printed by Fust and Schoeffer in 1459, (finished Aug. 29), on vellum, for £70[2]. The second vellum printed book in the Library is a copy of Durandus' *Rationale*, printed by the same printers in the same year, but completed on Oct. 6. This was bought in 1790 for £80 10*s*. Large additions were made to the series of Aldines.

[1] The rarity of this edition was caused by its being bought up and destroyed by the sons of Prince Radzivil.

[2] A copy of this edition was sold in 1884 at Sir J. Thorold's sale for £4950, which in 1824 was sold for £136 10*s*.

The name of Lady Hester Stanhope occurs among the benefactors as presenting an Arabic MS. of the Romance of Antar, in thirty volumes.

A.D. 1820.

From Messrs. Payne and Foss was bought, for £150, the famous MS. of the Greek New Testament called, from its former possessor, the 'Codex Ebnerianus.' It is a small quarto, containing 425 leaves of fine vellum, in excellent condition and well written, and ornamented with eleven rich paintings, besides occasional arabesque borders, &c. It comprehends all the books of the New Testament except the Apocalypse, and is assigned in date to the twelfth or thirteenth century. The former owner, whose name it perpetuates, Jerome William Ebner von Eschenbach, of Nuremberg, obtained it, it is said, when first brought from the East 'ex singulari Numinis providentia.' While it was in his possession, a small descriptive volume, comprising forty-four pages and an engraved facsimile, was published by Conrad Schoenleben, under the title of *Notitia egregii codicis Græci Novi Testamenti manuscripti*, &c. 4°. Norib. 1738. This was incorporated by De Murr in his *Memorabilia Bibliothecarum publicarum Norimbergensium*, published in 1788, part ii. p. 100, who added thirteen well-engraved plates of the illuminations, binding and text. It was formerly bound in leather-covered boards, ornamented with gold, with five silver-gilt stars on the sides, and fastened with four silver clasps. This cover being much decayed, Ebner cased the volume in a most costly binding of pure silver, preserving the silver stars, and affixing on the outside a beautiful ivory figure (coæval with the MS.) of our Saviour, throned, and in the attitude of benediction. Above the figure, Ebner engraved an inscription in Greek characters, corresponding to the style of the MS., praying for a blessing upon himself and his family[1].

[1] This MS., with forty-six others of the illuminated MSS. (including many noticed in the Appendix to this volume), is described in Dr. Waagen's

A MS. of Terence, of the eleventh or twelfth century, which also belonged to Ebner, was bought from Payne and Foss, at the same time, for ten guineas. It is described in De Murr, *ubi supra*, pp. 135–7.

Fifty Greek manuscripts were bought for £500, which had formerly been in the possession of Giovanni Saibante, of Verona. The library of this collector is noticed in Scipio Maffei's *Verona Illustrata* (fol. 1731), part ii. col. 48[1]. The MSS. purchased by the Library are described in Mr. Coxe's Catalogue, cols. 774–808.

A collection of Arabic tracts and papers, which had formerly belonged to Dr. Kennicott, was given by Shute Barrington, Bishop of Durham.

A.D. 1821.

The great event of this year was the reception of the famous and extensive collection of English dramatic literature and early poetry, formed by Edmund Malone[2]. It was bequeathed by him on his decease (May 25, 1812) to his brother, Lord Sunderlin, with the expression of a wish that, if not retained as an heirloom in the family, it should be deposited in some public library. In fulfilment of this wish, Lord Sunderlin communicated to the University, in 1815, his intention to transfer the collection to the Bodleian so soon as Mr. James Boswell, to whom it was entrusted in order to assist him in the preparation of a new edition of Malone's *Shakespeare*, should have finished his use of it. That edition being at length issued in 1821, the library was sent

Treasures of Art in Great Britain, 1854, vol. iii. pp. 65–111. And a specimen-facsimile, taken from the commencement of St. Luke's Gospel, is given, with a notice of the MS., in Shaw's *Illuminated Ornaments*.

[1] Some MSS. which had belonged to Saibante, together with some of the Abate Canonici's collection, which had been brought to England by the Abate Celotti, were sold by auction, in London, in 1821. The sale of a further portion, which had passed into the hands of P. de' Gianfilippi (also of Verona), took place at Paris in January, 1843.

[2] Malone was the son of an Irish Judge. He was born in Dublin, Oct. 4, 1741, was educated at Trin. Coll., Dublin, where he took the degree of B.A. in 1762 and became a barrister, but soon retired from legal practice. He was created an honorary LL.D. at Dublin in 1801.

to Oxford in the same year. The character of the collection is too well known to need description; suffice it to say that it contains upwards of 800 volumes, of which by far the greater number are distinguished by their rarity[1]. There are first quartos of many of Shakespeare's plays, and second editions of others[2]; of his collected works there are both the first and second folios. Barnfield, Beaumont and Fletcher, Chapman, Decker, Greene, Heywood, Ben Jonson, Lodge, Massinger, John Taylor the water-poet, and Whetstone are amongst those who are most fully represented. There are also a few MSS.[3] A Catalogue of the collection, in folio (52 pp.), with a life of Malone by Boswell (previously printed in *Gent. Magaz.* and Nichols' *Lit. Hist.*), was published in 1836; and, in 1861, Mr. J. O. Halliwell printed fifty-one copies of a small *Hand-list* of the early English literature preserved in it. Various volumes of Malone's own MSS. collections have been subsequently added by purchase; viz. in 1836 some papers relating to the life and writings of Pope; in 1838, his collections for the last edition of his *Shakespeare* and for the illustration of ancient manners, together with a portion of his literary correspondence; in 1851 a volume of letters written to him by Bishop Percy, between 1783 and 1807; in 1858 three octavo volumes of collections made by him at Oxford; in 1864 a volume of letters to him from Dr. Johnson, Mrs. Siddons, and others; and in 1878 a collection of 300 letters to him, with papers in his own hand and books, from Mr. A. Russell Smith, of Soho Square, London, for £40. In consequence of this purchase being noticed in the *Athenæum*, Mr. L. Sharpe, Librarian of the Guildhall Library, London, presented to our

[1] No. 217 belonged to K. Charles I, and has a list of contents in his handwriting; it contains nine plays by Beaumont and Fletcher. Malone has inserted in it a blank commission, on parchment, signed by Charles II and dated at Bruxelles, 2 March, 1659, *an.* xi, appointing county commissioners for levying forces against those in rebellion.

[2] For notices of the purchase of several early quartos, wanting in this series, see 1834.

[3] At the end of one of these (a notebook of extracts by Malone, No. 34) is an annual summary of the amount spent by him on his library in books and binding from 1771 to 1808; the total is £2121 5*s*. From 1780 to 1808 on pictures and prints he spent £839 9*s*.

Library several letters from Malone to his grandfather. A large series of pamphlets, chiefly relating to Irish history and to literary matters, comprised in seventy-five volumes, was also purchased in 1838[1]. Almost all his books are uniformly bound in half-calf, with 'E. M.' in an interlaced monogram on the back; a very few have a book-plate consisting of his coat-of-arms within a square of books, with the inscription (in imitation of Grolier's) 'Edm. Malone et amicorum,' and a motto from the *Menagiana*.

A curious instance of the variableness and uncertainty of the prices of books is afforded by the purchase-list of this year, when contrasted with prices paid at the present time. A copy (wanting the preliminary leaves and a few others) of one of the Antwerp editions of Tyndale's New Test. in 1534 (which had belonged to Mr. Benj. Ibott, and is mentioned in Herbert's *Ames*, vol. iii. p. 1543), was bought for nineteen shillings; Mr. H. Stevens in 1855 priced another imperfect copy at fifteen guineas. But, on the other hand, £63 were given in this year for the rare *Ed. Pr.* of Virgil, printed by Sweynheim and Pannartz in 1469[2]. A somewhat similar instance occurred also in 1826, when Daye's edition of the Apocrypha, printed in 1549 (being vol. iv. of his edition of the Bible in that year), was obtained for fifteen shillings, while £73 10*s*. were paid for an edition of Virgil printed at Venice about 1473.

The very rare German Bible, printed at Strasburg about 1466, was bought for £42, and a perfect copy of the first edition of the Bishops' Bible, in 1568, for £7 7*s*.[3] A volume of interest in typographical history was presented by T. H. Scott, M.A., in the first book printed in Tasmania. It is entitled *Michael Howe, the last and worst of the Bush Rangers of Van Dieman's Land; narrative of the chief atrocities committed by this great murderer and his associates during a period of six years in Van Dieman's Land:* it extends to

[1] These are now incorporated with the large collection called *Godwyn Pamphlets*. A copy of Wood's *Ath. Oxon.* with MSS. notes by Malone, was given by Mr. B. H. Bright in 1835.

[2] Various other *editt. princ.* were bought in this year, with some Aldines. Also a collection of modern Greek works printed at Venice.

[3] Offor's copy sold for £41; Lea Wilson's for £61 10*s*.

thirty-six small octavo pages, and was printed at Hobart Town, by Andrew Bent, in Dec., 1818[1].

The Catalogue of the Oriental MSS., commenced in the year 1787 by Uri, was continued in this year by the publication by Mr. Nicoll of the first part of a second volume, containing notices of 234 additional Arabic MSS. His premature death occurred before the publication of the second part, which he had printed as far as p. 388; this was completed and edited (with nine lithographic plates of specimens of Arabic MSS.) by his successor in the Hebrew Professorship, Dr. Pusey, in 1835. It contains altogether descriptions of 296 Arabic volumes, together with copious additions by Dr. Pusey to Uri's first portion, which are noticed above, p. 271.

The Parish Registers of Newington, Kent, and of Bures, in Suffolk, which had come into the Library among Dr. Rawlinson's books, were rightly restored to their respective parishes by a decree submitted to Convocation on Nov. 9. In the Register of Convocation itself, by a singular omission, no mention of the former of these parish books is made (although included in the proposal), and the restoration of that of Bures is alone recorded. But by enquiry addressed to the Vicar of Newington, I ascertained that one of the Registers contains a memorandum of its having been returned by vote of Convocation on the day in question[2].

[1] I have in my possession an early newspaper printed in New Zealand, the *Auckland Times*, No. 41, for Apr. 6, 1843, not merely curious in relation to the history of the colony, but also as a typographical relic. Its crowning interest is to be found in its colophon (if such a classical word may be applied to the imprint of a newspaper), which states that it was '*Printed in a mangle.*'

[2] There remains among the Rawl. MSS. (D. 796) a most carefully written volume of 317 leaves (No. 14 of a series), containing a Register of christenings, churchings, publication of banns, weddings, burials, and 'whatsoever done in the parishe church of St. Buttolphe's without Aldgate, London,' from 11 June, 1596 to 5 Oct. 1597. The other things recorded are vestry-meetings, number of communicants at monthly communions, with list of names at Easter, excommunications, briefs, the proceedings for building a vestry-house 'before the upper pane of the window on the sowth syde of the church,' burial-fees, weekly sermons, &c. For the monthly communions the elements were provided at the cost of the parish; for the Easter communions, 'according to auntient

By a vote of Convocation on July 7, the rooms on the first floor of the Schools' quadrangle, which were formerly used as the Hebrew and Greek Schools, were assigned to the Library; the former (on the south side) now contains, in two rooms, the Bodley, Rawlinson, and other collections of MSS.; the latter (on the north side), also in two rooms, foreign and English periodicals[1].

On May 25, a plan for warming the Library was, for the first time, adopted. It consisted in introducing hot air simply at two small gratings at one end of the Library, from pipes communicating with a stove placed (with the consent of Exeter College) where the furnace of the present apparatus is situated, in the wall between the north-west corner of the Library and the Ashmolean Museum. As a means of warming the Library generally the system was wholly ineffectual, no benefit being experienced except by those who remained in the immediate vicinity of the gratings[2].

custome,' at the cost of Thomas Dow, the farmer of the rectory. At five Easter communions there were 713 communicants, for which thirteen gallons and three quarts of claret were provided, and two shillings' worth of bread. A long account is given of the baptism of a black maid-servant aged 20. The curate and lecturer when the book commences is Christopher Threlkeld; he was inhibited in Dec. 1596 for marrying without license or banns, but was restored as curate on 2 Feb. following: he, however, died on 10 July, 1597, aged 53, 'of inward griefe of mind, or of a thowght' (*sic*), and was buried the next day. Mr. William Hubbuck, preacher at the Tower, was chosen lecturer on Feb. 6; he preached twice on Sundays, whereas Threlkeld only preached once. The latter was succeeded in the curacy by Paul Bushie, appointed by Thomas Dow, the farmer of the rectory. (The living being a donative, no names of incumbents are given in Newcourt's *Repertorium Londinense.*) With considerable acquaintance with the contents of parish registers, I can say that I have never met with another volume so full of miscellaneous matters of interest as this. There is also a vol. of copies of vestry-books, 1583–1666.

[1] In Lascelles' Account of Oxford, published in this year, it is said that the printed books in the Library were computed at 160,000, and the MSS. at 30,000. The former estimate was tolerably correct; the latter greatly exaggerated. Prof. S. P. Rigaud, in a letter written in 1817 (communicated to me by his son, the late J. Rigaud, B.D., of Magd. Coll.), gave a much more correct account of the MSS. when he said that they were then about 10,000 or 12,000, and the printed books 150,000.

[2] I well remember how on cold winter days Professor Reay, the aged Sub-librarian, would stand for half-hours together over these gratings, in but half-successful endeavours to free himself from the chills incurred by sitting in his unwarmed study at the further end of the Library.

It remained, however, in use until 1845, when pipes were laid down through a considerable part of the Library for the purpose of warming it by steam. This plan, however, did not give satisfaction, either on the ground of safety or of effectiveness. In 1855 Mr. Braidwood, the then distinguished head of the London Fire Brigade, was brought down to survey the apparatus and to examine generally how the Library could best be secured against fire; and, by his advice and that of Mr. G. G. Scott, the pipes were enclosed in slate casings, so as effectually to hinder contact with any inflammable materials, and two fire-proof iron doors were inserted at the entrances to the great Reading-room, in order to cut it off from the rest of the building[1]. But in 1861 steam was discarded for the safer and more effectual system, now in use, of warming by hot water; new pipes (partially cased in slate) were laid down by Messrs. Haden and Son, and were carried through the then Examination Schools on the ground-floor of the quadrangle, as well as through the reading-room of the Library.

In Feb. Mr. John Phillips Roberts, New College (B.A. 1821, M.A. 1826, afterwards Minor Canon of Chichester, deceased 12 Dec. 1882, aged 84) was appointed *Minister*, *vice* Mr. P. Barrett, Wadham College (B.A. 1828); and Mr. Robert Eden, of St. John's College (Corp. Chr. Coll. B.A. 1825, M.A. 1827, now Vicar of Wymondham, Norfolk), was appointed *vice* Walker. From this time there appear to have been two Assistants, although it was not until 1837 that that number was formally allowed by Statute.

Bequest by Rev. Charles Francis, M.A., rector of Mildenhall, Wilts, of printed books and MS. papers of Edw. Pococke; *see under the year* 1693.

A.D. 1822.

In July, the Rev. Dr. Bliss returned to the Library as Sub-librarian, in the room of Mr. Nicoll, appointed Regius Professor of

[1] Mr. Braidwood's report was printed in 1856, together with one from Mr. Scott, on the extension of the Library, and the means of rendering it fire-proof.

Hebrew. And in October the Rev. Rich. French Laurence, M.A., of Pembroke College, succeeded Dr. Cotton, who quitted Oxford for Ireland.

'Tuesday, August 6, 1822, I was at the Library the whole day, and not a single member of the University came into the room, excepting Mr. Eden, the assistant. Oxford race-day[1].' This note occurs in vol. x. of Dr. Bliss's MS. antiquarian and miscellaneous memoranda. Considering that the time of the year was well-nigh the middle of the Long Vacation, it does not seem surprising that on one day there should have been no academic readers in the Library, even if there may have been academic riders at the race-course. The two occurrences have so little correspondence with each other that one would hope that the zealous Sub-librarian (who has deemed the same want of readers worth commemorating also in another note) assigned *non causa pro causa.*

A.D. 1823.

By the exertions of the brothers J. S. and P. B. Duncan, Esqs., Fellows of New College, distinguished for their efforts to promote the study of the Arts and Sciences in the University, a subscription-fund was raised for the purpose of adorning the Picture Gallery with plaster models of some of the finest buildings of Greek and Roman antiquity. The result was that in the present year the following series, by Fouquet, of Paris, was placed in the Gallery, at a total cost of about £400:—The Arch of Constantine, the Parthenon, the Temple of the Sibyl at Tivoli, the Maison Carrée at Nismes, the Erechtheum and Lantern of Demosthenes at Athens, the Theatre of Herculaneum, and the Temple of Fortuna Virilis at Rome.

A large number of works by foreign authors, chiefly theological, was bought (for £375) at the sale at Leyden of the library of Jonas Wilh. Te Water, professor of Eccl. Hist. in that University.

[1] On May 2, 1889, Mr. Eden tells me he has no recollection of this day as having been specially remarked. See note under 1825.

A separate catalogue, occupying twenty-three folio pages, was issued of these books.

Some odd volumes were sold 'for waste paper' for £15 6*s*.

Mr. Edw. P. New, of St. John's College (B.A. 1822, M.A. 1825, B.D. 1831), was appointed in December to assist in the compilation of the new Catalogue; he remained in the Library until his decease (from cholera), 28 July, 1832.

A.D. 1824.

A collection of valuable original papers relating to affairs in Church and State, which had belonged to Archbishop Sheldon, were sold by his great-nephew, Sir John English Dolben, of Finedon, Northamptonshire, to the Library for £40 5*s*. They are now bound in six volumes, of which three are lettered *Sheldon*, and three *Dolben*. Of the first three, two contain letters from English, Welsh, Scotch, and Irish Bishops, and the contents of the other are miscellaneous; of the second three, one contains miscellaneous letters and papers commencing at 1585, another has similar papers from 1626 to 1721, and the third contains miscellaneous ecclesiastical letters and documents. Some of the letters are addressed to the Archbishop's secretary, Miles Smyth, Esq. A short letter from Sir John Dolben to Dr. Bandinel, relating to his disposal of these papers, dated Oct. 12, 1824, is preserved in Bodl. MS. Addit. A. 64. f. 57. He had previously given, in 1822, a fine copy of a quarto Bible which had belonged to Sheldon, containing (1) the Prayer-Book and Metrical Psalms, printed at Cambridge in 1638, (2) the Old Test., printed by Field at London in 1648, and (3) the New Test., Cambr. 1637. At the end are some memoranda by the Archbishop of the births, baptisms, and deaths of members of the Sheldon and Okeover families, and of the legitimate children of Charles II and the Duke of York. The Library more than a century before had received benefactions from a member of the same family of Dolben; Gilbert Dolben, of Finedon, having given some printed books in 1697, together with a manuscript of Gower. And twenty vols. of Chamberlaine's *State of Great Britain* were given by Mr. J. E. Dolben in 1796. An additional volume of the Sheldon correspondence was given to the Library in 1840, by Dr. Routh, the President of Magdalen College. It is a copy-book of business-letters written by the Archbishop. In a note to Dr. Bandinel which accompanied the gift, and which is now fixed in vol. i. of Burnet's autograph copy of his *Own Times*, Dr. Routh says :—

'The President takes the opportunity of sending a volume containing the first draught of letters sent by Archbp. Sheldon to different persons, together with a few other contemporary papers. They were put into the President's hands by the late Sir John English Dolben, and as the University purchased of that gentleman what were commonly called the Sheldon Papers, he thinks they cannot be deposited anywhere more suitably than in the Bodleian Library.'

To the annual catalogue for this year was attached a special list, filling thirty-two folio pages, of the books (upwards of 1500 in number) which were bought at the Hague, at the sale of the library collected by the distinguished Dutch scholars and lawyers, Gerard and John Meerman. The sale-catalogue is a volume of more than 1200 pages. The books bought for the Library were chiefly such as supplied deficiencies in foreign history and law, together with some Greek[1] and Latin MSS., for the most part

[1] These, in number thirty-eight, are described in Mr. Coxe's Catalogue, cols. 724-773. A copy of Eusebius' *Chronicon*, which appears to be of the sixth century, and which is in that case the oldest MS. *book* in the Library, is among the Latin MSS. A few of the MSS. came from the Jesuit College at Clermont, Meerman having bought the collection belonging to that college in 1764 on the suppression of the Order. In a letter to me of 21 April, 1869, Mr. David Laing, the late eminent Librarian of the Signet Library at Edinburgh, furnished me with the following interesting reminiscence of this sale in connection with the then Regius Professor of Greek, afterwards Dean of Christ Church, who was until his death in 1855 the leading Curator of the Bodleian: 'He attended most assiduously during the sale at the Hague, and managed to get the London booksellers to withdraw their opposition to his acquiring many of [the Greek] MSS. unless at exorbitant prices. Having assisted at the end of the sale in packing his books, I will not readily forget the Greek Professor standing without his coat and his hands clasped, so anxious in overlooking the packing, without being able to render any actual assistance.'

patristic and classical. The sum expended was £925. Some rare Spanish historical books (in which class of literature, thanks to Dr. Bandinel's care in keeping it steadily in view, the Library is now very rich) were bought at the sale of Don J. Ant. Conde.

But the chief distinction of this year lies in the acquisition, by bequest of Mrs. Eliza Dennis Denyer (widow of Mr. John Denyer, of Chelsea, who died in 1806) of a most valuable collection of early editions of the English Bible, numbering altogether about twenty-five. To show the rarity and worth of this collection, it will be sufficient to mention but a few of the volumes which it contains. *Imprimis*, Coverdale's second edition, 1537; Cranmer's, in April, 1540 and in 1541, and by Grafton in 1553; Matthew's, by Becke, in 1551; Tyndale's New Testament, in 1536 [1], and another of his earliest editions; Hollybush's English and Latin Testament, 1538, and Erasmus' Testament, 1540, on yellow paper [2]. Besides the Biblical collection, Mrs. Denyer also bequeathed twenty-one English theological works, nearly all printed before 1600; including a beautiful copy of Fisher on the Penitential Psalms (by Wynkyn de Worde) and books by (amongst others) Bale, Bonner, Brightwell, Erasmus, Hooper, Joye, and Tonstall.

Mr. L. E. Judge, New College (B.A. 1827, M.A. 1830; Chaplain; deceased 1853), succeeded Mr. Roberts, in March, as Assistant; but in July of the next year retired, and was succeeded by Mr. W. Bailey, also of New College (B.A. 1829).

A.D. 1825.

The sale at Paris of the library of L. M. Langlès, the Keeper of the Oriental MSS. in the Bibl. Royale, afforded a considerable

[1] A letter from W. Herbert to Mr. Denyer in 1786 is inserted in this volume. Two or three of the Denyer books have Herbert's autograph of ownership in them.

[2] In several instances Mrs. Denyer has inserted very good facsimiles in pen and ink of title-pages and leaves wanting in the Bibles.

accession of books in that branch of literature which was his specialty. Amongst these was a 'Vocabulario de Japon,' printed in quarto, on silk paper, at the College of St. Thomas in Manilla in 1630, for which 599 francs were given. (Cotton's *Typogr. Gazetteer*, second edit. 1831, p. 161.) For another book printed at Manilla see the year 1833.

Mr. Sim. J. Etty, New College (B.A. 1829, M.A. 1832, afterwards Vicar of Wanborough, Wilts, deceased 4 July, 1879, aged 71), was appointed assistant in the room of Mr. Eden[1]. Mr. Etty remained in the Library until the year 1834. The Catalogue of *Dissertationes Academicæ*, which appeared in 1834, was in a great measure his work[2].

Two MSS., intended of old for the Library by Sir K. Digby, were bought in this year. To the account which is given of them at p. 79 *supra*, it should be added that the Library left in France by Digby on his death (from which, no doubt, these volumes came) was bought back by George, Earl of Bristol, and finally sold by auction at London, in April and May, 1680. Sixty-nine MSS. were included in this dispersion.

An offer made from Paris (through C. T. Longley, afterwards Archbishop of Canterbury) for the sale of some MSS. containing the history of the proceedings of the Inquisition in Rome and Italy was unfortunately declined by the Curators![3]

[1] During Mr. Eden's time of service in the Library (1820–25) there were very few readers to be found at any time in the Library. The most frequent attendants were, as I am informed by him, the eminent Greek scholar Peter Elmsley (described as being a big heavy man with a remarkably pleasant and musical voice), Augustus Hare, Dr. Will. Wilson (afterwards vicar of Holy Rood, Southampton), James Parsons (father-in-law of Alex. Nicoll), while engaged in completing Holmes' Septuagint, Vaughan Thomas of C.C.C., and Jeremiah Wiffen, the translator of Tasso. In the month of May, 1889, I have had the pleasure of hearing from Mr. Eden's lips, at the age of 85, his recollections of his early days, including not only reminiscences of Bodley, but of many such other things as the preaching of Robert Hall and Chalmers and John Foster.

[2] This he told me himself, on our casually meeting one day in Oxford, and it is also noticed in the Curators' minute-book.

[3] Bodl. MS. Add. A. 64. f. 167.

A.D. 1826.

There is not much to notice in the acquisitions of this year. A few Persian and other Oriental MSS. were purchased, and more in the two following years; and some Burmese MSS. were given by Sir C. Grey, Chief Justice of Calcutta. A curious volume of manuscript and printed papers relative to the siege of Oxford in the years 1643–46 was presented by Mr. W. Hamper, of Birmingham. In January, the Rev. Chas. Hen. Cox, M.A., Student of Ch. Ch. (afterwards rector of Oulton, Suffolk, deceased Oct. 1, 1850, aged 52) was appointed Sub-librarian in the room of Mr. Laurence.

A.D. 1827.

A very large collection of Academic Dissertations published in Germany (with many published at Leyden, and some in Sweden), amounting to about 43,400, was bought at Altona for £332 16*s.* Of these a folio catalogue was published in 1834, which, by a singular error, bears on its title the date 1832, as the year in which this accession came to the Library. In 1828, 160 volumes of the same character were added, and other large additions were made in 1836 and 1837, but particularly in 1846, when no fewer than 7000 were purchased[1].

[1] There is scarcely an imaginable subject in law, Roman and German, on which something may not be found in this vast collection, with much in theology and history. The *something* may often be meagre and superficial, but it is as often curious, and even in the former case it may be useful as pointing to sources of further information. In days of Ritual controversy, one party or another may be glad to know that in 1725, Geo. Heinr. Goetz, D.D., wrote on the interesting question whether a clergyman might officiate in his furred night-gown,—*Num Verbi ministro toga cubicularia* (Schlaffpeltze) *induto officio sacro defungi liceat?* Those who know what curses were invoked of old upon the heads of stealers of books, may be interested in hearing what one Pipping had to say on the subject in 1721, in his *Diss. de Imprecationibus libris ascriptis;* while

Mr. Henry Forster, New College (B.A. 1832, M.A. 1834; Esquire Bedel of Divinity; deceased 1857), succeeded Mr. Bailey, in March, as Assistant.

A.D. 1828.

A collection of 153 Northern MSS., chiefly in the Icelandic and Danish languages, formed by Finn Magnusen, was purchased from him for £350[1]. Amongst them are many curious volumes in poetry and history. A catalogue written by Magnusen himself (56 pp. quarto) was published in the year 1832. Other

the title of Sam. Schelging's discourse in 1729, *De Apparitionibus mortuorum vivis ex pacto factis*, will have attraction for not a few. Sometimes the dryest subjects were lightened up at the close with ponderous jokes, or unexpected turns were given to the matter in hand; *e.g.* those worthy Germans who had gone to sleep at Jena, in 1660, during the reading of a dissertation *De Jure et Potestate Parlamenti Britannici*, by one J. A. Gerhard, (who must have taken unusual interest in the history of the English Rebellion,) were wakened up at the end by the discussion of the following novel questions in law:—
'Casus ex jure privato.

'I. Titius ducit uxorem Caiam. Caia, elapso uno vel altero anno, transmutatur in virum. Q. an Caia hæc, soluto per hanc metamorphosin matrimonio, possit repetere dotem? Dist.

'II. Sempronia, defuncto marito Mævio, nubit Titio. Mævius divinâ potentiâ in vitam resuscitatur mortalem. Q. an Mævius hic, secundùm vivus, uxorem Semproniam et bona sua repetere possit? Aff.' Sir T. Browne in his *Religio Medici*, § xxi, says that he can read the history of Lazarus without raising such a question as this.

It was usual for the friends of the candidate who defended the thesis of the Dissertation (generally written for him by the *Præses*) to attach some complimentary letters or verses. In the case of those published at Upsala, the zeal of the encomiasts frequently breaks out into wild compositions in Hebrew, Greek, French, German and English, affording in the latter instance (and it may be in others) very curious specimens of the language. A laborious trifler, named P. Wettersten, compliments a friend, who had read at Upsala, in 1742, a dissertation by Prof. Peter Ekerman on the antiquities of the town of Norkoping, with a kind of acrostic in twenty-five lines on the verse, 'Nunc erit et seclis Norcopia clara futuris,' which, starting from the centre of the page, may be read upwards, downwards, and in every form of mazy irregularity; every way, in short, except the right. On the occasion of J. C. *Guttbier's* taking a medical degree at Erfurt in 1713, the Præses on the occasion, a physician named L. F. Jacobi, wrote for him very aptly 'Dissertatio exhibens *cerevisiæ bonitatem*.'

[1] Some notes by G. J. Thorkelin on Northern Antiquities were bought in 1846.

collections of MSS. were also sold by him to the British Museum and to the Advocates' Library at Edinburgh.

A large number of Aldines were obtained at the sale of the collection of M. Renouard, the Aldine bibliographer, which took place in London, June 26–30. And the rare first edition of John Knox's *Historie of the Church of Scotland* was purchased for sixteen guineas.

Some additional rooms on the second story of the Schools' quadrangle, on the north and east sides, which went by the names of the Schools of Geometry and Medicine, were permanently attached to the Library, by vote of Convocation, on June 5.

On June 26, the nomination of the Rev. Stephen Reay, M.A., of St. Alban Hall (afterwards B.D., and Laudian Professor of Arabic in 1840), as Sub-librarian in the room of Mr. C. H. Cox, was approved in Convocation. Mr. Reay was appointed to the charge of the Oriental department, his knowledge of Hebrew qualifying him for the care of the yearly increasing mass of Rabbinical lore. To this branch he added, and retained to the close of his life, the care of the 'Progress' Room, or room containing the publications, foreign and English, which appeared in parts. And on Dec. 20, the Rev. John Besly, M.A., Fellow of Balliol (afterwards D.C.L., and Vicar of Long Benton, Northumberland, deceased April 17, 1868, aged 68), was confirmed as Mr. Reay's colleague, in the place of Dr. Bliss.

A. D. 1829.

The great Hebrew collection, which at present forms so distinguished a feature in the contents of the Library, was virtually commenced in this year by the purchase at Hamburg, for £2080, of the famous Oppenheimer library, consisting of upwards of 5000 volumes, of which 780 are MSS.[1] Many Hebrew

[1] One MS. which had strayed from Oppenheimer's library previously to its transfer to the Bodleian, was purchased and restored to its place in 1847. A notice of this collection, and of the other Hebrew portions of

works had, it is true, come with Selden's library, in 1659; but little or nothing had been done since that period to advance upon that beginning. The additions made in this department from 1844 up to about the year 1857, are said, in Dr. Steinschneider's introduction to his catalogue (*col.* 50), to have numbered no fewer than about 2100 volumes; and the additions since then may be reckoned as about 1500.

David Oppenheimer, or Oppenheim, Chief Rabbi at Prague, devoted more than half a century to the formation of his library. On his death, Sept. 23, 1735, it came into the possession of his son, a Rabbi at Hildesheim, and thence into the hands of Isaac Seligmann at Hamburg. Several catalogues were issued during this period, the last being one in octavo, at Hamburg, in 1826, an index to which, compiled by Dr. J. Goldenthal, was printed at the expense of the Library in 1845. The collection would have been dispersed by auction had it not been bought *en masse* for Oxford. It possesses extreme interest and value in the eyes of Jewish students, so that for a series of years the Library was never without several foreign visitors engaged in its examination. A very elaborate catalogue of all the printed Hebrew books contained in it, and throughout the whole of the Library, was compiled by Dr. M. Steinschneider during the years 1850–1860, and printed at Berlin, where it was published in the latter year in a very thick quarto volume. The book is divided into two parts: the first containing a description of the Biblical, Talmudical, liturgical and anonymous volumes; the second containing the works of miscellaneous authors, in the alphabetical order of their names. Prefixed is a brief list of the Hebrew MSS. in the Library, with the numbers at present attached to them, and re-

the Library, is given in the preface to vol. viii. of Fürsts's *Bibliotheca Judaica*, 8°. Leipz. 1863, pp. 42–51. (The *Catalogus Interpretum S. Script.*, by Thomas James, in 1635, is here metamorphosed into one by Thomas *Jones*, in 1735.) In 1827 Dr. Nicoll visited Hamburg in order to negotiate for the purchase of the collection, but met at that time with insuperable legal impediments from interests involved in the property. (Memoir prefixed to his *Sermons*, p. xl.)

ferences to the old catalogues in which they were described. Of several rare books in the Oppenheimer library there are duplicate copies, varying in condition and ornamentation; of some there are copies on red, yellow, and blue paper. Distinguished amongst all is a copy of the Talmud, printed in 1713–28, in twenty-four folio volumes, entirely on vellum. 'Perhaps,' says Archdeacon Cotton, 'this work is the grandest and most extensive vellum publication extant [1].'

Mr. Robert Bowyer, miniature painter to Queen Charlotte, who had devoted a considerable part of his life to the collection of drawings and engravings illustrating the Holy Scriptures, put forward a proposal for their purchase by subscription with a view to their being deposited in the Bodleian. Their number amounted to nearly seven thousand (including 113 drawings by Loutherbourg), described as being in fine condition and of great value; and they were inserted as additional illustrations in a copy of Macklin's folio Bible, which was enlarged thereby from its original extent of seven volumes to forty-five. Hence the collection passed, and passes, under the name of Bowyer's Bible. Mr. Bowyer, who had spent upon it upwards of three thousand pounds, proposed to dispose of it for £2500, and a committee was formed in London, upon which appeared the names of many distinguished persons, to raise a subscription for the purpose. But upon Mr. Bowyer's despatching an agent to Oxford, the matter met with so little encouragement here, the Librarian, in particular, being (as Dr. Bliss has noted upon his copy of the original proposal) unfavourable to it, that the project fell to the ground. The reasons why Oxford made so little response do not appear; probably the value set upon the collection was deemed to be greatly exaggerated. After the death of Mr. Bowyer (June 4, 1834, aged seventy-six) the Bible came into the hands of one Mrs. Parkes, of Golden Square, by whom it was disposed of, in 1848, in a lottery (together with a few other prizes) for which four thousand tickets were issued at one guinea each. The successful speculator

[1] *Typographical Gazetteer*, p. 349.

was Mr. Saxon, a gentleman-farmer, near Shepton Mallet. In 1852 it was in the hands of Messrs. Puttick and Simpson, the well-known book-auctioneers, for sale. By them it was announced for an auction on Feb. 26, 1853, and was disposed of, about that time, to Messrs. Willis and Sotheran, the booksellers, for £405. In 1856 it was sold at an auction at Bolton to Mr. Robert Heywood for £550[1].

A. D. 1830.

A copy of the rare edition of Luther's translation of the Bible printed at Wittemberg in 1541 was bought, through Messrs. Payne and Foss, for fifty guineas, at the sale, in London, of the library of the Archdeacon de la Tour, of Hildesheim, which was said to have been formerly the property of the English Benedictine monastery of Landspring, and which was then, it appears, in the possession of Mr. — Solly. It contains some texts on the fly-leaves in the autograph, and with the signatures, of both Luther and Melanchthon, which seem to have been unnoticed at the time of the sale. A facsimile of a part of Luther's inscription is given in plate xxxi. in Mr. Leigh Sotheby's *Illustrations of the Handwriting of Melanchthon*[2].

A. D. 1831.

In December of this year, Viscount Kingsborough[3] presented a magnificent coloured copy (being one of four which were printed

[1] Allibone's *Dict. of Eng. Lit.* i. 718.

[2] A copy of this edition, with MS. notes by Luther, Melanchthon, Bugenhagen and Major, was sold to the British Museum, at Hibbert's sale in 1829, for £267 15*s.*!

[3] This learned and spirited nobleman died of typhus fever in 1837, in a debtor's prison in Dublin, where he was confined for liabilities incurred on behalf of his father, the Earl of Kingston. It is stated in the Sale Catalogue issued in 1886 of the first portion of the library of printed books of the late Sir Thomas Phillipps, Bart., that the work was undertaken by the encouragement and with the advice of Sir Thomas, in whose collection of MSS. many of the MSS. and drawings used in it are preserved, although not mentioned in the book; and that Lord Kingsborough spent upwards of £30,000 upon it. The account of the book there given and of its author, ever, it is said, to 'be lauded by the world,' is noteworthy.

on vellum) of the *Antiquities of Mexico,* being facsimiles, collected and edited by Guillelmo Dupaix and Aug. Aglio, and executed at Lord Kingsborough's expense, in seven folio volumes, of Mexican paintings and hieroglyphics preserved in the libraries of Paris, Berlin, Dresden, Vienna, Rome, Bologna, and Oxford (in Laud's and Selden's collections), together with preliminary dissertations. This sumptuous book is exhibited in a case made expressly for its reception.

On June 30, the nomination, as Sub-librarian, of Rev. Ernest Hawkins, M.A., of Balliol, afterwards Fellow of Exeter, (and subsequently well known for his labours in the cause of Missions, as Secretary to the Society for the Propagation of the Gospel, who died 5 Oct., 1868), was approved by Convocation. He succeeded Dr. Besly, who had taken the Balliol College living of Long Benton, in Northumberland.

The Picture Gallery was re-roofed and re-floored in this year (*see* p. 18), and a small part was cut off at the further end to form an additional room for the Library. The alterations were carried out under the direction of Sir R. Smirke, and the correspondence and accounts of expenditure, which had remained at Exeter College in consequence of the Vice-Chancellor at the time having been the Head of that College, were only transferred to the Library in 1888.

A. D. 1832.

A twelfth-century MS. of Scholia on the *Odyssey* was purchased for £105. The collection of Bibles, which had during some time past made some slow progress, was increased by copies of various early printed versions in European languages, and its further enlargement was steadily kept in view in succeeding years.

Six guineas were given for copies of Servetus' treatise *De Trinitatis erroribus* and his *Dialogi de Trinitate,* printed in 1531 and 1532, which are of very great rarity, in consequence of their having very generally shared the fate of their author.

A fine copy of Didot's beautiful edition of the *De Imitatione*

Christi, printed in 1788 (said to have been formerly in the Library of the King of France) was presented by Mr. Nathaniel Ogle, 'who,' as he has recorded in an inscription on the fly-leaf, 'with his partner, William Altoft Summers, brought on the 14th of August, 1832, the first steam carriage which ever enter'd the city of Oxford, from Southampton.' A list of friends and servants who accompanied these, 'the patentees and inventors,' is subjoined to the inscription.

A. D. 1833.

Some precious Shakespearian volumes, consisting of the *Venus and Adonis* of 1594 and 1617, the *Lucrece* of 1594 and 1616, with a subsequent edition of 1655, and the *Sonnets* of 1609, were presented by the well-known collector, Mr. Thomas Caldecott, who had been formerly a Fellow of New College. They are now incorporated with the Malone collection. Several MSS. of Sir William Jones were presented by the brothers Augustus and Julius C. Hare. An interesting and large collection of tracts on the Roman Catholic disabilities, affairs in Ireland, &c., in forty-five volumes, was purchased at the sale of the library of Charles Butler, of Lincoln's Inn.

An anonymous pamphlet, entitled, *A Few Words on the Bodleian Library*, appeared in this year; its author was Sir Edmund Head, M.A., Merton College. The object was to urge the desirableness of allowing books to be borrowed from the Library, after the example of Cambridge. One of the arguments by which the author supported the proposal, viz. that College tutors were unable to visit the Library in term time during the hours at which it is open, has since been entirely removed by the attachment of the Radcliffe Library as a Reading-room, which remains open until ten o'clock at night. The pamphlet was reprinted in the Report of the University Commission in 1852.

The large sum of £73 10*s*. was paid to Messrs. Payne and Foss for a fine copy of the edition of Ovid, printed at Parma in 1477, on account of its containing many MSS. notes by Ang. Politian, with his autograph signature in Greek, ''Αγγέλου κτῆμα Πωλιτιανοῦ καὶ τῶν φίλων.' At the foot of the first page of the text is this note: 'Liber conventus S. Marci de Florentia, Ord. Praed., habitus a syndicis die 19 Januarii 1497 pro compensatione librorum qui commodati ab eodem conventu fuerant D. Angelo Politiano, et in ejus morte amissi sunt.' Politian died at Florence 24 Sept. 1494.

A translation, by Ant. de Borja, into Tagala (the principal language of the Philippine islands) of the history of Barlaam and Josaphat by John of Damascus, printed at the Jesuit College at Manilla in 1712, was purchased for six guineas.

A. D. 1834.

Numerous purchases were made during the sale of Mr. Heber's library. Amongst these were some rare English tracts of the Reformers, Bale, Becon, Tyndal, Knox, &c.; a large and valuable collection of booksellers' catalogues and sale catalogues of books and coins between 1726 and 1814[1]; and a mass of some 1100 or 1200 plays, published in the seventeenth and eighteenth centuries[2]. Numerous early Shakespeare editions were also obtained; *inter alias*, the first edition (1594) of the first part of the *Contention betwixt the Houses of Yorke and Lancaster*, for £64; *Richard III*, 1598, £17; fourth edit. of *Henry IV*, 1608, £12 12*s*.[3], &c. The greater part of the collection of editions of Horace up to the year 1738, formed by Dr. Douglas, a collection which was used in the preparation of the edition published at London, by James Watson, in 1760, was bought for £20. It consists of twenty-seven vols. in folio, thirty-nine in quarto, and 248 in octavo and smaller sizes. Dibdin (*Introd. to the Classics*) says that the whole collection consisted

[1] Another collection of sale catalogues in forty-five vols. was purchased in 1836.

[2] Another collection, in twenty-eight vols., of plays chiefly dating from 1630 to 1707, was bought, in 1842, for £6 17*s*.

[3] In 1837 *Romeo and Juliet*, printed by Smethwicke, n. d., was bought for £9 10*s*.; in 1840, *Richard III*, 1605, for £21, and *Hamlet*, 1611, for £10 10*s*.; and in 1841 the first edit. 1595, of part iii. of *Henry VI*. was bought at Chalmers' sale for £131!

of 450 editions. A Prayer-Book of 1707, with MSS. collations by Rev. John Lewis, of Margate, of alterations in editions between 1549 and 1637, was bought for £8 8*s*. One of the chief gems formerly in the Picture Gallery was bequeathed by James Paine, Esq., being the portrait of his father, James Paine, the architect[1], while instructing his son in drawing, by Sir Joshua Reynolds. This beautiful picture long retained its freshness of colour more perfectly than most of Sir Joshua's paintings; and under the direction of the late librarian, Mr. Coxe, it was carefully cleaned, and protected with glass and a curtain, in hope that thus its brilliancy might incur no deterioration. It was removed to the Randolph Gallery some years ago. But this year is chiefly distinguished in the Annals of the Library by the bequest of the

Douce Collection.

Francis Douce, the donor of this magnificent library (who died on March 30, in this year, aged 77) is said to have been induced to make this disposition of his treasures through the courteous reception afforded him by Dr. Bandinel, upon the occasion of a visit, in company with Isaac D'Israeli, to Oxford, in 1830[2]. The gatherings of a lifetime with which the Bodleian was thus enriched, consist of 393 manuscripts, ninety-eight charters, about 17,000 printed volumes, a very large collection of early and valuable prints and drawings, and many coins[3]. For the most part, the books

[1] Mr. Paine died in France in 1789, aged 73 years. The picture was painted by Reynolds in June, 1764. Among the buildings erected by Paine were Brocket Hall, Herts; Wardour Castle, Wilts; and Richmond Bridge.

[2] *Gent. Magaz.* 1834, vol. ii. p. 216.

[3] To the British Museum Mr. Douce bequeathed his own correspondence, note-books, and miscellaneous papers, to remain sealed up until Jan. 1, 1900, in order probably that all of his own and the succeeding generation may have passed away before the personal histories which they undoubtedly contain are brought to light. He was for a short time (about 1804) Keeper of the MSS. in the Brit. Mus., and catalogued the Burghley papers in the Lansdowne collection, as contained in part i. of the fol. Lansdowne Catalogue printed in 1819. In Nov. 188[illegible] two annuities of £40 and £20 respectively were granted by the University to two collateral descendants of Douce, who had inherited very little of their

which thus came were of classes in which the Library was then deficient. Nearly all the finest specimens of Missal-painting which it now possesses are found among the Douce MSS., several of which are exhibited in a glass case in the Library. Among the chief of these are three volumes of *Horæ*, one executed, perhaps by Giulio Clovio, at the beginning of the sixteenth century for Leonora Gonzaga, Duchess of Urbino, a second possessed by Mary de' Medici, and the third completed in 1527 for B. Sforza, second wife of Sigismund I. of Poland. These are priceless gems, rivalled only by such as the Bedford Missal. A Psalter on purple vellum, probably of the ninth century, came from the old Royal Library of France, and has, from this circumstance and its age, been sometimes called Charlemagne's Psalter. The printed books are rich in history, biography, antiquities, manners and customs, and the fine arts[1]. In Bibles (English and French), Horæ, Primers, Books of Common Prayer and Psalters, the collection is very strong. Among the Psalters is a copy of Archbishop Parker's rare metrical version. Early French literature is also a conspicuous feature, in which the Library had previously been very deficient. Of fifteenth-century typography there are no fewer than 311 specimens. The finest of these is a magnificent copy of Christoforo Landino's Italian translation of Pliny's Natural History, printed on vellum by Nic. Janson, at Venice, in 1476. It is enriched with exquisite illuminated borders at the commencement of each book, a specimen of which, together with a description of the volume, is given in Shaw's

relative's wealth, in consequence of estrangement which existed (little, it is to be feared, to his credit) between him and members of his own family, as well as his wife.

[1] In the majority of instances the books bear MS. notes by Douce, which are often valuable for the references they afford to other works and sources of further information. A few specimens of some of the fuller notes of this kind were contributed by the present writer to the early volumes of the second series of *Notes and Queries*. One book, viz. John Weever's *Epigrammes*, 1599, containing notes by Douce, which had somehow escaped from his library before it came to Oxford, was purchased in 1838, for £24 10*s*. A letter written by Douce in 1804, dated from the British Museum, was bought in 1864, and a few other papers in 1866. Four or five of his less important MSS. were bought by him at Gough's sale in 1810.

Illuminated Ornaments, pl. xxxviii[1]. There are also a large number of fragments of works by early English printers, including two by Caxton which are unique. One of these is a portion (two quarters of an octavo or duodecimo sheet) of an edition of the *Horæ*, conjecturally assigned by Mr. Blades to 1478, and the other is of an edition of the *Booke of Curtesye*, probably printed in 1491, consisting of two quarto pages. There is also one of the two known copies of a curious placard, issued by Caxton, inviting those who were disposed to buy 'ony pyes of two and thre comemoracions of Salisburi vse' to come to him at Westminster, and they should have them 'good chepe[2].' The other copy is in the possession of Earl Spencer. Very different, but still very curious, items are large collections of chap-books and children's penny books of the last century and commencement of the present, and of playing cards; and two folio volumes are filled with black-letter ballads. A catalogue of the library was published in one volume, in folio, in 1840; the part containing the printed books was the work of Mr. H. Symonds, of Magdalen Hall (B.A. 1840, M.A. 1842, afterwards Precentor of Norwich, now Rector of Tivetshall, Norfolk), and Rev. Arthur Brown, M.A. Ch. Ch., and that which describes the Fragments, the Charters and the Manuscripts was drawn up by Mr. Coxe. From the year 1839 until the commencement of 1842, Mr. Thomas Dodd, formerly a well-known London dealer in prints, and author of the *Connoisseur's Repertory*, was employed in making a catalogue of the Douce prints and drawings[3]. This catalogue still remains in MS. Four grand studies of heads, drawn either by Raffaelle or Giulio Romano, were some time since removed to the University Galleries, whither the prints, &c. have also been transferred.

On June 25, Convocation sanctioned the transfer to the Library of the room immediately over the entrance in the gateway-tower

[1] In the same beautiful volume are facsimiles from three of Douce's MS. *Horæ*.

[2] A facsimile of this advertisement is given in the catalogue of the Douce library.

[3] A memoir of Mr. Dodd, with a portrait, is given in the *Gent. Mag.* for Nov., 1850.

of the quadrangle, (now called the *Mason Room*) which had been hitherto assigned as the 'Savile Study,' on condition that a small room in the adjoining south-east angle of the quadrangle should be prepared at the expense of the Bodleian for the reception of the MSS. and printed books, instruments, &c., which were given to the University by Sir Henry Savile for the use of his Professors. This is the room in which the Savile library (which includes also some books given by Dr. Wallis and Sir Christopher Wren) is still preserved, which was incorporated with the Bodleian Library in 1884.

On July 5, Convocation confirmed the nomination of Rev. William Cureton, M.A. of Ch. Ch. (afterwards so well known for his Syriac studies, which gained him the patronage of the Prince Consort and a Canonry at Westminster, and who died 17 June, 1864), to the Sub-librarianship vacated by Rev. E. Hawkins.

Mr. Edmund Grove, of Magdalen College (who never graduated), was appointed Assistant in April, *vice* Mr. Stephen Exuperius Wentworth, of Balliol (B.A. 1833, M.A. 1835; dec. 29 Apr. 1866). Mr. Wentworth appears to have succeeded Mr. Forster in 1832.

A.D. 1835.

The original MS. of Burnet's *History of my Own Times*, with a copy prepared for the press, a portion of his *History of the Reformation*, and some other papers by him, was purchased, from a family descended from the Bishop, for £210. An account of these MSS. may be found at p. 474 of the Appendix to Burnet's *History of James II*, being an extract from the *Own Times* which Dr. Routh edited, with additional notes, when ninety-six years old, in 1852. In a letter from Rawlinson, dated Aug. 18, 1743, it is said that Dr. T. Burnet had expressed his intention of depositing the MS. of his father's *Life and Times* in some public library, 'but *quando* is the case': and then Rawlinson adds, 'I purchased the MSS. of a gentleman[1] who corrected the press where that book

[1] Rev. John Blackbourne, a non-juring bishop.

was printed, and amongst his papers I have all the castrations, many of which I believe he communicated to Dr. Beach's son, whom T. Burnet had abused in a life of his father at the end of the second volume[1].' The omitted passages were printed in 1826 from other copies in Dr. Routh's edition of the *Life and Times*.

The MS. of Lewis' *Life of Wyclif*, with some additions by the author, was bought for £4 14*s*. 6*d*. Various other MSS. by Lewis were already in the Library among Dr. Rawlinson's collections, and five volumes were transferred from the Clarendon Press in 1887, which had been bought of Mr. Gutch, a bookseller at Bristol, in 1820. The purchases of printed books were chiefly of early editions of classics (Juvenal, Ovid, Virgil, &c.), Fathers (Augustine, Jerome), Schoolmen, and a very large series of fifteenth-century editions of the Decretals, Digest, Institutes, and other works in Canon and Civil Law. These were obtained at the sale of the famous library of Dr. Kloss, of Frankfort.

A curious collection of papers and pamphlets, printed and MS., relating to Spanish affairs, of much interest to students of Spanish history, contained in 32 volumes in folio and 80 in quarto, was purchased for £40. It was lot 4583 in Heber's sale, by whom it had been bought at the Yriarte sale for more than £100.

A.D. 1836.

Aubrey's collection of notes and drawings concerning Druidical and Roman antiquities in Britain, together with some miscellaneous historical notes, entitled by him *Monumenta Britannica*, in four parts (now bound in two folio volumes), was purchased, for £50, of Col. Charles Greville. Accounts of Abury and Stonehenge, which are important from their early date (the former being the earliest known), are to be found in these curious and interesting volumes[2]. The remainder of Aubrey's MSS. came to the Library

[1] Ballard MS. ii. 88.

[2] A short description of them will be found in Gough's *Brit. Topogr.* vol. ii. pp. 369–70, and a fuller account in Britton's *Memoir of Aubrey*, 1845, pp. 87–91. Mr. Britton, however, strange to say, was not aware that the volumes had been for nine years in safe custody

in 1860, upon the transfer of the books from the Ashmolean Museum. See *sub anno* 1858.

A collection of about 300 tracts, relating to American affairs and the War of Independence, in forty-one vols., formed by Rev. Jonathan Boucher[1], was bought for £8 18*s.* 6*d.* These are now included in the series of tracts called *Godwyn Pamphlets*, in continuation of those which came, in 1770, from the donor so named. Another large gathering of American tracts, collected by Mr. George Chalmers, when engaged in writing his *History of the Revolt*, was bought in 1841 for £24 13*s.*; at the same time, the first and only volume of his *History*, which itself was never actually published, was bought for £2 7*s.*

Sale Catalogues. See 1834.

When the new Copyright Act was introduced into Parliament in this year, it was proposed to allow £500 *per annum* to the Bodleian, in the manner adopted with regard to six other libraries, in lieu of the old privilege of receiving a copy of every book entered at Stationers' Hall. The Curators, however, on May 27, resolved that it would be highly desirable to retain the privilege, but that, should an alteration be made, it would be inexpedient to receive an annual grant by way of compensation; and in consequence of this opinion, the proposed abolition of the privilege was abandoned.

A.D. 1837.

The magnificent series of historical prints and drawings which is called, from the name of its collectors and its donor, the Sutherland collection, was presented to the University on May 4 in this year, although it was not actually deposited in the Library until

in the Bodleian, and consequently deplores their unfortunate disappearance! He describes their contents from an abstract in the Gough collection.

[1] An account of Mr. Boucher, who quitted America on account of his royalist principles, and afterwards was Head-Master of a well-known school at Cheam, will be found in *Notes and Queries* for 1866, vol. ix. pp. 75, 282.

March, 1839[1]. The six volumes of the folio editions of Clarendon's *History of the Rebellion* and *Life*, and of Burnet's *Own Times*, are inlaid and bound in sixty-one elephant folio volumes, and illustrated with the enormous number of 19,224 portraits of every person and views of every place in any way mentioned in the text, or connected with its subject-matter[2]. The gathering was commenced in 1795 by Alexander Hendras Sutherland, Esq., F.S.A.; on his death (May 21, 1820) it was taken up by his widow[3], who spared neither labour nor money to render it as complete as possible, and by whom its contents were, consequently, nearly doubled. At length, desiring, in accordance with her husband's will, that the results of her own and his labour should be always preserved intact, Mrs. Sutherland presented the whole collection to the Bodleian. Its extent may be in some degree appreciated when it is mentioned that there are (according to Mrs. Sutherland's statement in the preface to the Supplementary Catalogue) 184 portraits of James I, of which 135 are distinct plates; 743 of Charles I, of which 573 are distinct plates, besides sixteen drawings; 373 of Cromwell (253 plates); 552 of Charles II (428 plates); 276 of James II; 175 of Mary II (143 plates); and 431 of William III, of which 363 are separate plates[4]. There are also 309 views of London and 166 of Westminster. Amongst those of London is a drawing on many sheets, by a Dutch artist, Antonio van den Wyngaerde, executed between 1558–1563[5]. It affords a view which extends from the Palace at

[1] MS. note by Mrs. Sutherland in the Library copy of her catalogue.

[2] As early as 1819 the collection numbered 10,000 prints, bound in 57 volumes. Clarke's *Repert. Bibliogr.* pp. 574–577.

[3] Mrs. Sutherland died March 18, 1852.

[4] In Mrs. Sutherland's own copy of the catalogue (now added to the collection by the gift of E. L. Hussey, Esq.), some of these numbers are enlarged in MS. as follows: Charles II, 554, being 432 plates; Cromwell, 379, 255 plates; William III, 436, 367 plates. Amongst the portraits there are frequently numerous copies of the same plate, being impressions in all its different states. In a few instances (particularly with regard to Charles I) some of the prints entered in the catalogue have not been found in the volumes.

[5] This map was originally in the Plantin Museum at Antwerp, was sold about 1820 to one colonel Roettiers,

Westminster to that at Greenwich, both included; and comprehends also Lambeth Palace and part of Southwark, with the palace there of the Protector Somerset, in which the Mint was situated. The whole amount expended on the formation of the series is estimated at £20,000.

The collection is accompanied by a handsomely printed Catalogue, compiled by Mrs. Sutherland, and published in 1837 in three volumes quarto, two containing the portraits, and one the topography[1]. A Supplement to this was printed in the following year, in the preface to which Mrs. Sutherland records her transfer of the collection. She adds that 'the University of Oxford, by the manner in which it has received the collection, has afforded her the high gratification of witnessing the fulfilment, in their utmost extent, of the wishes of its founder; and in the liberal step which its future conservators have taken, to insure a direct and easy means of reference to the prints, she finds proof of their intention to comply with her own earnest desire, that the books should be as freely open to those really interested in them as may be consistent with their safe preservation. Under the superintendence of the compiler, but at the expense of the University, a copy of the Catalogue has been prepared, in which every print is marked with the page which it respectively fills in the volumes; by means of this, every difficulty of reference, and every doubt as to the print intended to be described, is obviated, and the manuscript indices will be preserved from the injury of constant use. In order to prevent the possibility of disappointment in

who subsequently disposed of it to Messrs. Colnaghi, the art-publishers, in London, from whom it was purchased by Mrs. Sutherland. It is noticed in Dallaway's *Discourses on Architecture*, 8°. 1833, p. 389. See *Notes and Queries*, second series, viii. 292, 331. A fac-simile was issued by the London Topographical Soc. in 1881-2, with a description by Mr. Hen. Wheatley.

[1] Ten copies were printed of a larger and finer edition, for presentation to various Libraries, but as only four of these (Bodleian, Cambridge University, British Museum, and Bibl. Royale, Paris) acknowledged the gift (the letters from which are preserved in one copy of the catalogue), no more than five copies were printed of the Supplement. Consequently those Libraries which did not return thanks for the gift have now an imperfect book.

referring from this marked catalogue, every print (with four exceptions only) of which the page has not been ascertained, has been struck out, although probably several of the portraits not at present found are still in the volumes.' The following letter of thanks was addressed by Convocation to the donor [1]:—

'To Mrs. Sutherland, of Merrow, in the County of Surrey.

'MADAM,—We, the Chancellor, Masters and Scholars of the University of Oxford, feel ourselves called upon to acknowledge, in a public and formal manner, the splendid donation recently made by you to our Bodleian Library.

'It is doubtless a source of much gratification to us that our University should have been selected by you as the fittest depository of so valuable a collection; but we are not, on that account, less disposed to appreciate and admire the feeling which has led you to make so considerable a sacrifice, and to relinquish the possession of what has been to you, for many years, an object of constant interest and occupation.

'We shall prize the matchless volumes about to be committed to our care, not merely as being embellished with the richest specimens of the graphic art, but as possessing a real historical character; as enhancing, in no slight degree, the value of works which we have long been accustomed to regard as most important contributions to the annals and literature of our Country.

'Given at our House of Convocation, under our Common Seal, this first day of June, in the year of our Lord one thousand eight hundred and thirty-seven [2].'

[1] It is here printed from the original (written in the beautifully neat hand of the late Registrar, Dr. Bliss,) which is now in the possession of a nephew of Mrs. Sutherland, Edw. Law Hussey, Esq., of Oxford, M.R.C.S. It is sealed with the old University seal, described on p. 1 of these *Annals*, enclosed in a gold box. The late Rev. R. Hussey, Regius Professor of Ecclesiastical History, was one of the brothers of Mrs. Sutherland.

[2] A very erroneous notice of the collection, written in a singularly depreciatory tone, was inserted in an article in the *Quarterly Review*, in 1852, vol. xci. p. 217. The writer appears to have confounded the facts connected with Gough's preference of the Bodleian to the British Museum (as told in Nichols' *Lit. Hist.*), or possibly Douce's, with the totally different circumstances of Mrs. Sutherland's gift, whose husband had left the collection entirely at her disposal, provided only that it were not dispersed.

A few other books were sent by Mrs. Sutherland at the same time, including Boydell's *Shakespeare*, Heath's *Chronicle*, Scott's edition of Dalrymple's *Preservation of Charles II*, Faber's *Kit-Cat Club*, Wilson's *Catalogue of an Amateur*, &c. And in 1843 she increased her former gift by the presentation of copies of a large number of illustrated, biographical, and historical works, many of which are in a like manner enriched with additional engravings. Chief amongst these is a copy of Park's edition of Walpole's *Royal and Noble Authors*, enlarged from five vols. 8°. to 20 vols. 4°. by the insertion of prints, portraits, and some of the original drawings. Similarly enlarged copies of Dr. Dibdin's works are also included; together with framed oil-portraits of Frederic, King of Bohemia, and of Mr. Sutherland.

A curious collection of rare Dutch tracts, in two vols., printed at Amsterdam between 1637 and 1664, and relating to English, Irish, and Scottish affairs, chiefly during the Civil Wars, was bought for £2 13*s.* And an enormous gathering of English pamphlets, on every kind of subject, in prose and verse, between about 1600 and 1820, said to number 19,380 articles, and which had accumulated in the stores of the well-known bookseller, Mr. Thomas Rodd, was bought of him for £101 14*s.* 6*d.* These exceeding, from their number, the powers of the then very slender staff of the Library for arrangement and cataloguing, remained piled up in cupboards for about twenty-five years. But a general clearance out of all neglected corners taking place on the appointment of the late Librarian Mr. Coxe to the headship, they were then sorted (to a certain extent), bound, numbered, and incorporated in the general Catalogue; when they proved to be a valuable addition to the pamphlet-literature, comparatively few of them being found to be duplicates.

In this year appeared at Heidelberg a volume of Greek Byzantine Law, the *Prochiron* of the Emperors Basil, Constantine and Leo, edited by Dr. Zacharias, a legal graduate of that University. The publication of such a volume would not seem likely to call for mention here; but, curiously enough, the editor, in consequence of his having visited the Library for the purpose of collating some MSS., and of having his interest in the place thereby greatly aroused, added to his book, not merely a notice, occupying some twelve pages, of the MSS. bearing on his subject, but also a preliminary historical 'Commentatio de Bibliotheca Bodleiana,' in fifteen pages. In the course of this, he objects to the rule forbidding extradition of books, which, he says, 'tam pietate erga fundatorem atque benefactores, quam propter odium Oxoniensibus adversus omnes innovationes commune, adhuc servatur.' He gives quotations from several English letters respecting the Library which were addressed to him by Dr. Bandinel, notes of the then existing Catalogues, and a somewhat minute list, compiled from Bernard's Catalogue, the Benefaction-Register, and the annual Catalogues, of the various donations and purchases of MSS. The Library is reported, he says, to contain 180,000 printed volumes.

Shakespeare; Romeo and Juliet. See 1834.

Sanscrit MSS. See 1842.

A grant was made by Convocation of £400 annually, for five years, towards the expense of the new Catalogue, the printing of which was commenced in the summer. A statute also was passed providing that there should be two 'Ministri,' or Assistants, instead of one, with salaries regulated by the Curators.

The Rev. Herbert Hill, M.A., Fellow of New College (now Master of Lord Leicester's Hospital, Warwick), was approved by Convocation, on Oct. 26, as Sub-librarian, in the room of Mr. Cureton, who removed in this year to the British Museum. Mr. Hill, however, only held the office for one year. And Mr. Richard Firth, New College (B.A. 1839, M.A. 1849, from 1850 to 1868 a Chaplain in the diocese of Madras, and now Vicar of Widdrington, Northumberland), became *Minister* in the room of Mr. F. J. Marshall, New College (B.A. 1834, M.A. 1837, Chaplain of New College, deceased 1843), who had probably entered the Library in 1834 in the place of Mr. Etty.

A.D. 1838.

The well-known portrait of Q. Mary of Scotland, which had been given by Alderman Fletcher in 1806, was cleaned by one S. Collins, on the recommendation of Sir D. Wilkie, and a former portrait, which had been painted over, was brought to light, and that which had always passed as the 'vera effigies' of the murdered Queen was (perhaps rather questionably) removed. Fortunately the latter had been engraved; but it remains an open question as to which of the two pictures really represented the Queen whose name it bears.

One of the 'curiosities of literature' was obtained by the purchase (for £10 10*s.*) of the *System of Divinity, in a Course of Sermons on the first Institutions of Religion*, by Rev. Will. Davy, A.B., Vicar of Lustleigh, Devon. It is a work in twenty-six volumes, of which only fourteen copies were printed, entirely by the hands of the indefatigable author himself, between the years 1795 and 1807. It is very roughly executed, the author having purchased only just so much old and worn-out type as sufficed for the printing of two pages at once; accomplishing in this way the work upon which he had set his heart, 'arte meâ, diurno nocturnoque labore' (as he says in a Latin preface), in consequence of having failed to procure in any other way the publication of his book. The copy in our Library is distinguished by having many additions inserted, printed (in many cases with later and better type) upon small slips[1].

[1] Mr. Davy has had a rival, with much more success, within late years in the Rev. Tho. R. Brown, M.A., Vicar of Southwick, Northamptonshire (dec. 1876). The Library possesses three works out of six or seven written by him and printed in his own house. The first is entitled, *A Grammar of the Hebrew Hieroglyphs applied to the S. Scriptures, containing the History of the Creation of the Universe and the Fall of Man*, 8°. 1840. This appears to have been partly *composed* in type, literally as well as technically, for the author says that 'a considerable part of the mental composition is coeval with' the manual labour, which last was entirely performed by himself. A second book appeared in 1841, *Elements of Sanscrit Grammar*. A third, *A Dictionary, containing English Words of difficult Etymology*, tracing

A set of the *Monthly Review*, from the commencement to 1828, in 200 volumes, in which the names or initials of the contributors are appended in MS. to their several articles, together with a volume of Correspondence with the editor, Ralph Griffiths, LL.D., between 1758 and 1802 (now numbered MS. Add. C. 89), was bought for £42.

Among the donations were: 1. A collection of twenty-one Oriental works, printed between 1808–1835 by the East India Company, presented by the Directors, and, 2. A valuable series, MS. and printed, of the Statutes of various Italian cities, presented by George Bowyer, Esq. (the late baronet, who succeeded to the title in 1860 and died in 1883), who also in the years 1839, 1842, and 1843, forwarded large additions to the printed series. These volumes are now kept distinct as a separate collection. Altogether there are seventy-eight printed volumes, besides four MSS.

On Nov. 15, a Statute was approved by Convocation which raised the stipend of the Sub-librarians from £150 to £250.

From the year 1825 an annual folio Catalogue had been printed, containing, in one list, all the accessions accruing in each year from purchases, gifts, and the supply of new publications from Stationers' Hall. The issue of these catalogues was discontinued after the appearance of that for the years 1837 and 1838 jointly; except that in 1843 one for that year was printed in octavo.

A form of declaration and promise for due use of the privilege

them chiefly to Sanscrit roots, appeared in two vols. 8°. 1843. Of this the author certifies that only nine copies were printed, and the one now in the Library was bought of Mr. Lilly (who had it from the author) for £5 5*s*. in 1855. The execution of all these volumes does the reverend printer great credit. The Rev. Dr. J. A. Giles (deceased 24 Sept. 1884, aged 75) had also a private press for some time in his house at Bampton, Oxon, while curate of that parish, which he taught some of the village children to work, and from which issued some of the publications of the Caxton Society, as well as his Histories of Bampton and Witney, but the results were far from being generally satisfactory, although probably quite as good as could be expected from such juvenile compositors. At Elgin in 1822 a lad 15 years of age collected and translated various passages relative to the natural history of bees, cut the type, and then printed and bound his little book.

of admission to the Library, to be made by all graduates upon taking their first degree, in lieu of the oath formerly required, was approved by Convocation on June 9[1]. In accordance with this form as altered in 1874, each person admitted to read now promises, 'me libros ceteramque supellectilem sic esse tractaturum ut superesse quam diutissime possint, animum ad studia et silentium accommodaturum, et, quantum in me est, curaturum nequid Bibliotheca detrimenti aut incommodi capiat.' The statutable penalty for any wilful mutilation or abstraction of any book, or portion of a book, is immediate expulsion from the Library and University, 'sine ulla spe regressûs.'

On the resignation of Rev. H. Hill, Sub-librarian, in this year, he was succeeded by Rev. H. O. Coxe, M.A., of Worcester College, who had previously worked for five years and a-half in the Department of MSS. in the British Museum[2]. Mr. Coxe's nomination was approved by Convocation on Nov. 16.

A. D. 1839.

An application was made by Magdalen College for the return of a copy of the Statutes of the College, found among the Rawlinson MSS., but it was refused by the Curators, on the ground that sufficient evidence was not produced of its having ever been the property of the College.

A. D. 1840.

Ninety specimens of the Aldine press, together with other volumes chiefly printed at Venice by A. de Asula, were purchased at the sale of the library of Dr. Samuel Butler, Bishop of Lichfield. From the same library was purchased, in the following year, a collection of portions of more than twenty of the very

[1] A previous proposal of this alteration had been rejected by Convocation on March 17, 1836.

[2] Mr. Coxe had a considerable share in the compilation of the folio catalogue of the Arundel MSS. preserved in the Museum.

earliest editions of Donatus' *De Octo Partibus Orationis*, many of which were unknown; these had previously come from the library of Dr. Kloss. A ninth-century MS. of St. Gregory's *Sacramentary* was purchased for £63; and early MSS. of Juvenal, Lucan, &c. A fine and perfect copy of Caxton's *Dictes or Sayengis of the Philosophres*, printed in 1477, was purchased for £50. It had previously been sold, at Dr. Vincent's sale in 1816, for £99 15*s.*; this sum, which is marked in pencil on a fly-leaf, having been altered by some feeble practical joker, by the insertion of a figure, to £199 15*s.*, Mr. Blades has in consequence recorded that as being the price at which the Library secured the volume[1].

The Rev. Rob. J. M'Ghee, Rector of Holywell, Hunts, deposited in the Bodleian (as also in the University Library at Cambridge, and in that of Trinity College, Dublin,) a collection of thirty-one volumes relating to the controversy with the Church of Rome, and to the moral theology taught at Maynooth. The volumes consist of editions of the Douay and Rheims versions, of some Irish diocesan statutes, of Bailly's *Theologia Moralis*, and Delahogue's dogmatic treatises, and of various Irish polemical pamphlets; and they are enclosed in a mahogany case, with glass door. In consequence of reference having been made to this collection by the donor, at a county meeting held at Huntingdon, Dec. 28, 1850, upon the occasion of the 'Papal Aggression,' some slight degree of public attention was called to it; and a controversial volume was in consequence published by Mr. M'Ghee, in 1852, entitled, *The Church of Rome; a Report on the Books and Documents on the Papacy, deposited in the University Library Cambridge*, &c.

[1] As Mr. Blades' valuable work on *The Life and Typography of Caxton*, 1863, gives most accurate descriptions of all the copies and fragments of our great printer's works which are preserved in the Library, it is only necessary to refer the reader to it for detailed information. A notice of two, however, which were unknown to be Caxton's at the time of Mr. Blades' investigations, will be found in the account of Bishop Tanner's books, p. 211, and two fragments, among Douce's books, are mentioned at p. 328.

Shakespeare; Richard III and *Hamlet.* See 1834.

The first non-academic *Minister* was appointed in Mr. H. S. Harper (*vice* Mr. Firth), who had acted for three years previously as an under-assistant, and of whose valuable services and acquaintance with details the Library for fifty years enjoyed the benefit. Just at the close of those fifty years (only previously exceeded by the Librarian Price, who ended his fifty-two years in 1813), he was, almost suddenly, removed on Sept. 23, 1887, at the age of 66; directly after sitting for his likeness, which the officers of the Library were about to present to him, and which consequently became only a gift to his family.

A. D. 1841.

The very large and valuable MS. collections of the Rev. John Brickdale Blakeway, relating to the history of Shropshire, were presented by his widow. Mr. Blakeway was minister of St. Mary's Church, Shrewsbury, for thirty-two years, and died March 10, 1826. He was long engaged in gathering materials for a county history, and published one or two volumes in connection with it, and his collections now form fifteen closely-written volumes in folio, nine in quarto, and two in octavo, arranged, and lettered on their backs, according to their several subjects, viz. pedigrees, county history, parochial history, &c. A list of them is given at the end of the Annual Catalogue. They were supplemented in 1850 by the purchase (for £42) of a copy of Mr. T. F. Dukes' *Antiquities of Shropshire* (4°. Shrewsbury, 1844), divided into two large volumes, and enriched by the author with many MS. additions and copies of ancient deeds, and with upwards of 700 portraits and original drawings of churches, fonts, &c. relating to almost every parish in the county. As Mr. Blakeway's collections are not accompanied with engravings or drawings, these volumes largely assist to make the materials for the history of this county complete.

A parcel of 136 early French and Anglo-Saxon coins was presented by Her Majesty the Queen, out of a mass of upwards of 6700 which were found in digging at the bank of the river Ribble, at Cuerdale, in Lancashire, and were adjudged to belong to Her Majesty in right of the Duchy of Lancaster. The largest part of the Saxon coins were of the reigns of S. Edmund of East Anglia (in number 1770) and of Alfred (793); of the Continental, of Charles le Chauve (712) and, apparently, of Charles le Simple (2942).

Some rare and interesting books issued by English printers about the middle of the sixteenth century were acquired in this year; among them, the *Boke of Common Prayer*, printed by Oswen, at Worcester, in 1552, bought for the very moderate sum of £3 16*s*. Two rare American Psalters were purchased, the one called *The Massachuset Psalter*, printed at Boston in 1709, for £2, and the other, the Psalms in blank verse with tunes, printed at Boston in 1718, for £1 19*s*. A copy of the very scarce fragmentary *History of Cornwall* by William Hals, printed at Exeter [in 1750], was bought for £15.

Shakespeare, Henry VI. See 1834.

American Tracts. See 1836.

Donatus. See 1840.

The hitherto somewhat narrow funds of the Library received in this year a welcome increase by the bequest of £36,000 in the Three per Cents. from Rev. Robert Mason, D.D., of Queen's College, deceased Jan. 5. He bequeathed also a further sum of £30,000 for a new library to his own College. In commemoration of this munificent legacy, one room, devoted to the reception of costly illustrated works, and works of some degree of value or rarity in various languages, has been styled the *Mason Room* (see p. 329). The elegant model of the Church of the Holy Sepulchre at Jerusalem now exhibited in the Gallery came by his bequest, together with a painting of the Zodiac of Tentyra, or Denderah, in Egypt.

A. D. 1842.

Seven Sanscrit MSS. had been given to the Library in 1837 by B. H. Hodgson, Esq., the British Resident in Nepaul, before which time there were but a very few works in that language scattered through some of the various Oriental collections, and most of them recently acquired[1]. But in this year the real foundation of the present very large and valuable collection was laid, by the purchase for £500 of the MSS. obtained by Professor H. H. Wilson (dec. May 8, 1860) during his residence in India, numbering 616 works and 540 volumes, of which 147 are MSS. of the Vedas. A brief list of them is attached to the Annual Catalogue for 1842, and the non-Vedic are fully described in the catalogue of the Sanscrit MSS., compiled by Theod. Aufrecht, M.A., now Professor of Comparative Philology in the Univ. of Bonn, the second and last part of which was published in 1864. The greater part of Mr. Wilson's collection consists of MSS. written in the last and present centuries.

Some small collections towards the history of Cheshire, made by Rev. F. Gower, were purchased in this year and in 1846.

In printed books the chief purchase was a copy (at the price of fifty guineas) of the original and hitherto unknown edition of the poems of Drummond, of Hawthornden. It is in quarto, with a portrait, having the letter-press only on one side of the page, and was printed at Edinburgh by Andro Hart in 1614. There are three or four small corrections in Drummond's own handwriting[2].

Bowyer. *Italian Municipal Statutes*. See 1838.

Laing. *Almanac by W. de Worde*. See 1755.

Old Plays. See 1834.

In March, Mr. J. B. Taunton, All Souls' College (B.A. 1843,

[1] The gift of the first Sanscrit book (described in the Benefaction-Register as being 'Gentuanâ linguâ') in 1666, is noticed at p. 133.

[2] A copy of Blackwood's *Martyre de la Royne d'Escosse* (Edinb. 1587), among Rawlinson's books, has an autograph of Drummond: 'Gũi. Drũmond, a Paris, 1607.'

M.A. 1848), was appointed Assistant *vice* Mr. F. E. Thurland, New College (B.A. 1841, M.A. 1846, now Rector of Thurstaston, Cheshire), who was made an *extra*, in the place of Mr. Symonds, resigned. Mr. Thurland had succeeded Mr. Grove in 1837.

The stipend of the Librarian was increased by £150, by a statute which passed on May 6. By the same statute an annual payment was ordered of £20 to the Janitor, in lieu of fees hitherto taken for showing the Library or Picture Gallery to members of the University. These, undergraduates as well as graduates, have now, if wearing their academical dress, the right of free entrance for themselves and friends; other visitors are admitted, by a regulation made about 1862, at the very moderate fee of threepence each person. (See p. 186.)

A. D. 1843.

The valuable collection of Oriental MSS. formed by the celebrated traveller, James Bruce, of Kinnaird, was purchased for £1000. It consists of ninety-six volumes, of which twenty-six are in Ethiopic, and seventy in Arabic; there is also one Coptic MS. on papyrus. Included in vol. iv. of an Ethiopic copy of the Old Testament is one of the three copies of the Book of Enoch which were brought by Bruce from Abyssinia, and which were then (if they be not even still) the only manuscripts of the book to be found in Europe. One of the three had been given by Bruce himself to the University, in 1788, through the hands of Dr. Douglas, Bishop of Salisbury; it is written on forty leaves of vellum, in triple columns. It was from this MS. that Dr. Laurence, afterwards Archbishop of Cashel, first made the translation which he published in 1821, and then subsequently, in 1838, published the original text. The second copy ('elegantissimum et celeberrimum') was given by Bruce to Louis XVI, and is now in the National Library at Paris. By the purchase of the third, the Bodleian became, therefore, the possessor of two out of the three.

Two unsuccessful attempts had previously been made to dispose of this collection by auction. It was first announced for sale by Mr. Christie, for May 17, 1827, to be disposed of in one lot; and a list was issued, abridged from the catalogue made by Dr. Alex. Murray, the editor of Bruce's *Travels*. The result of this proposed sale is recorded by Douce in the following MS. note (much in error in its estimate of the value of the MSS.) on his copy of the auction-catalogue: 'These MSS. were put in by the owner at £5500, and after an elaborate eulogium on them by Mr. Christie, no bidding or advance took place, and they were of course withdrawn. Had the owner offered them for £500, I should think the same result would have happened.' The second attempt was made in 1842, when the MSS. were offered for sale by Mr. George Robins, on May 30, but it appears that even all the eloquence of that most moving of auctioneers failed to elicit a bid corresponding to the expectation of the seller; and so the collection fortunately remained intact, to be disposed of to our Library in the year following.

A catalogue of the Ethiopic MSS. of the collection was issued in a small quarto volume (eighty-seven pages), in 1848, as part vii. of the General Catalogue of MSS. It was compiled by a German scholar, well acquainted with this branch of Oriental literature, Dr. A. Dillmann, and contains, besides Bruce's books, three of Pococke's MSS., one of Laud's, one of Clarke's, and three others; in all thirty-five.

Valuable materials for the history of Devon were secured by the purchase (for £90) of the collections made for that purpose by Jeremiah Milles, D.D., Dean of Exeter, and President of the Society of Antiquaries. The library of dean Milles (who died Feb. 13, 1784) was sold by auction by Mr. Leigh Sotheby, in April; and these collections, comprised in eighteen volumes in folio, one in quarto, and one in octavo, formed a principal feature in the sale.

In this year a new Catalogue of the general library of printed books, exclusive of the Gough and Douce libraries and the collections of Hebrew books and Dissertations, of which already special catalogues were in print, was completed and published in three folio volumes. It had been commenced in the year 1837, and was prepared by the Rev. Arthur Browne, M.A., Chaplain of Ch. Ch. (afterwards a chaplain in the Royal Navy, dec. 23 March, 1889, aged 79), whose share comprises the letters P—R, and the commencement of S; the Rev. Henry Cary, M.A. (son of the well-known translator of *Dante*, then incumbent of St. Paul's, Oxford, but afterwards, by returning to his previous profession of the Law, a barrister in Australia, who died 30 June, 1870, aged 66, professing himself at the last a Roman Catholic), who was responsible for the letters F—K, and part of L; and Rev. Alfred Hackman, M.A., Chaplain and Precentor of Ch. Ch., and afterwards Sub-librarian (*see under* 1874), who completed the greater part of it, viz. the letters A—E, L (from *London*)—O, S (from *Shakespeare*)—Z[1]. The whole charges of the printing of

[1] *Humanum est errare.* With a full personal sense of the truth of this aphorism, and trusting that I shall not hereby lay myself open to any severe application of the proverbs about 'an ill bird,' or dwellers in 'glass houses,' I may venture to amuse readers with a few choice blunders which I have gathered out of this catalogue. The pursuivant John Pine Bluemantle is supposed to bear an azure name instead of an azure robe. C. W. *Bach.*-[elor of Laws] is made to stand as if he were of some kin with the great German composers Bach. Two writers (one being Will. Shelley, *alias* de Conchis) who were supposed in their books to be hidden under the dark disguise of *Aneponymos* are on the contrary supposed in the catalogue to answer in good faith 'Nameless' to the question, 'What is thy name?' A Minorite who describes his book as being 'por F. Ant. Daza, indigno frayle Menor,' would hardly know himself in the Catalogue under the name of 'Porf. Ant. Daza Indigno,' or be likely to approve of his being thus treated as 'unworthy' of his own name, and reduced as it were from a Minorite to a Minim. Under *Naples*, a guide for foreigners, 'signori forastieri,' becomes Signor Foreigner's (Forastieri's) guide. Under *Kempis*, 'Fevrier' becomes a place where a book is printed; under *Peyrerius*, 'l'auteur mesme' loses his identity, and sings 'I'm not meself at all,' on becoming 'L'Auteur Mesme;' under *Defos*, a history of the 'Comté de Castres' and of the 'comtes d'icelvy' is made to give the counts another county, entered in the Catalogue under the distinct head of 'Icelvy.' Even in the Supplement 'Sermones Socci' [sive Succi], *i. e.* Marrow Sermons, sermons of the marrow of Holy Scripture, are entered as if they were 'Soccus's Sermons.'

the Catalogue amounted to £2990 12*s.*[1]; the previous cost of compilation was about £2000. The preface, although signed with Dr. Bandinel's name, was written by Dr. Gaisford, the Dean of Ch. Ch.

Bowyer. Italian Municipal Statutes. See 1838.

Sutherland. Illustrated Books. See 1839.

A. D. 1844.

Sir William Ouseley, the editor of the three volumes entitled *Oriental Collections* (brother to Sir Gore Ouseley, whom he accompanied when he went as ambassador to Persia in 1810), gathered, during some forty years spent in accumulation, about 750 Oriental MS. works or parts of works, chiefly in Persian, but including also a few in Arabic, Sanscrit, Zend, &c. Of these, in 1831, a catalogue (in 24 pp. quarto) was issued by the owner, who wished to dispose of them collectively, but no purchaser was then found, and they consequently remained in Sir William's possession. After his death, however (in Sept. 1842), they were again proposed for sale *en masse*, and the Library became a purchaser in this year for the sum of £2000. Many of the volumes are specimens of the best styles of Persian writing and illumination, while others are of great antiquity and rarity. The printed Oriental collection was also increased by various works printed in the East Indies in 1830–1839, which were presented by the Asiatic Society of Bengal, and by some Sanscrit and Mahratta books given by Rev. G. Pigott, Chaplain at Bombay.

A. D. 1845.

This year is rendered noticeable in the later annals of the Library by the fact that not a single MS. was purchased during its course. But a very valuable collection of Arabic, Persian and Sanscrit MSS. formed by Brigadier Gen. Alex. Walker, during his

[1] MS. note by Dr. Bliss.

service in India, was presented by his son, Sir Will. Walker, of Edinburgh[1]. These are kept as a distinct collection, like other donations or purchases of similar extent; the Sanscrit portion is described in the catalogue compiled by Prof. Aufrecht. The collection of printed Hebrew books was increased by the purchase (for £176 14*s.* 6*d.*) of 483 volumes from the library of the celebrated lexicographer, Gesenius, of Halle, who died Oct. 23, 1842, and whose library was sold by auction at Halle, in Jan. 1844. Two curious collections of tracts were also bought; the one in English, consisting of 300 volumes, ranging from 1688 to 1766, and chiefly treating of the case of the Non-jurors, the Bangorian controversy, and the affairs of the city of London (for £22 10*s.*); and the other in French, consisting only of four small volumes, but containing a very large number of '*Merveilles*,' strange histories of strange wonders, between 1557 and 1637, of great rarity and singularity. These were obtained at the sale of the library of Mr. Benj. Heywood Bright, No. 3796, for £13.

On Dec. 23, the author of these *Annals* (then an academical Clerk of Magdalen College) was appointed Assistant, *vice* Mr. Taunton, after upwards of five years' previous service as a supernumerary, having first entered the Library in July, 1840.

A. D. 1846.

The original MS., or first copy, of Wood's *History and Antiquities of Oxford*, in English, was purchased for the moderate sum of £8 8*s*. Already the Library possessed the corrected copy, in the author's autograph, in two large folio volumes, which had formed part of his collection in the Ashmolean Museum, but which had been transferred to the Bodleian as early as the year 1769. The volume now obtained had been in the possession of Edw. Roberts, Esq., of Ealing, a letter to whom from Mr. Joseph

[1] Gen. Walker, who in the beginning of the century was Governor of Baroda, in Guzerat, died at Edinburgh in 1832. His MSS., in the words of Prof. Aufrecht, 'integritate et antiquitate eminent.'

Parker, of Oxford, is inserted, dated July 4, 1827, in which he mentions the sale of the book to Mr. B. Roberts [Barré Charles Roberts, of Ch. Ch., Oxford?], and says that it was purchased at a sale at Burford, in 1797 or 1798.

A curious and valuable account-roll (56½ feet long) of Sir John Williams, Knt., Master of the Jewels to Henry VIII, which specifies all the treasures from dissolved religious houses which were in his custody at the accession of Edw. VI, was bought for £25[1]. It is numbered MS. Addit. E. 3.

The department of Italian topography, antiquities and art was largely enriched by the purchase from Rev. R. A. Scott (for £234 6*s*.) of a collection of 1426 volumes made by his brother George C. Scott, Esq., during ten years' residence in Italy.

Dissertations. See 1828.

Gower's Cheshire. See 1842.

Thorkelin. See 1828.

A.D. 1847.

A valuable MS. of Star-Chamber Reports, from June 17, 1635, to June 4, 1638, was purchased for £11. Several similar volumes of Reports are among the Rawlinson MSS. A series of State special Forms of Prayer, from 1665 to 1840, was bought for £10 10*s*.

Works relating to the history of America, in which the Library is now very rich, begin in this year to form a specially noticeable feature in the catalogue of purchases. Many rare

[1] Part of an original account, by the same Master of the Jewels, of the plate and jewels received for the King's use from a few dissolved monasteries in the year 1540–1542, is preserved in MS. *e Musæo*, 57; it is signed on several pages by the King. It was given to the Library about 1650. Strange to say, it was printed in 1713, in one of the little duodecimo books printed on London Bridge, entitled *Memoirs of the Antiquities of Great Britain relating to the Reformation*, &c. (pp. 46–75) 'printed by H. Tracy, at the Three Bibles;' a very curious little volume, with plates, including a view of Godstowe Nunnery.

tracts had been of old in the Library, but much of the completeness of the present collection is due to the energy of the late well-known American bibliophilist, Henry Stevens (dec. 28 Feb. 1886).

A.D. 1848.

A collection of Hebrew MSS., numbering 862 volumes and nearly 1300 separate works, was purchased at Hamburg for £1030. It had been amassed by Heimann Joseph Michael (born Apr. 12, 1792, deceased June 10, 1846), who had devoted thirty years to the formation of his library. One hundred and ten vellum MSS. are included in it, written for the most part between 1240 and 1450. Michael's printed books amounted to 5471; these were purchased by the British Museum. A short catalogue of the collection, drawn up from the owner's papers, was issued at Hamburg in 1848, with a preface by Dr. L. Zunz, and an index to the MSS. by Dr. M. Steinschneider. They have all been fully catalogued, together with all the other Hebrew MSS. in the Library, by Dr. Neubauer, who in 1868 commenced his important task, and in 1886 saw the completion of it (with the addition of such MSS. as are in College libraries) in the publication of a thick quarto volume, together with a portfolio of facsimiles.

A.D. 1849.

The valuable collection of Oriental MSS. formed by Rev. W. H. Mill, D.D., Regius Professor of Hebrew at Cambridge, during his residence in India as Principal of Bishop's College, Calcutta, was purchased from him for £350. A small remaining portion of his collection, comprising thirty-six volumes, was bought in 1858, after his death, for £35. In all there are 160 volumes, of which 145 are in Sanscrit. These latter are fully described in Prof. Aufrecht's Sanscrit Catalogue.

The chief purchases of printed books were made at the sale at Berlin, in May, of the library of Professor C. F. G. Jacobs, the editor of the *Anthologia Græca* (who died March 30, 1847), whence a large number of classical dissertations, many of them authors' presentation copies, were obtained[1], and at the sale of the library of Rev. Hen. Francis Lyte (deceased 1847) which took place in July. A collection of 360 sermons, published by Non-juring divines between 1688 and 1750, is an interesting item in the year's list; another is a copy of Pliny's *Historia Naturalis*, printed at Rome by Sweynheym and Pannartz in 1473, with a MS. collation of three very early codices made by Ang. Politian in 1490, which was bought for £21, at an extremely curious sale at Messrs. Leigh Sotheby's, in Feb., of books 'selected from the library of an eminent literary character' (M. Libri).

The two statutable Assistants at this time and for some short time previously were Mr. J. M. Price, All Souls' College (B.A. 1849, M.A. 1852, now Vicar of Cuddington, Bucks,) and Mr. W. W. Garrett, New College (B.A. 1849, M.A. 1874, for many years a Naval chaplain, and now Vicar of Cramlington, Northumberland). The former of these was succeeded about 1850, by Mr. J. C. Hyatt, Magd. Hall (B.A. 1852, now Vicar of Queensbury, Yorkshire). From that time, in consequence of the difficulty of reconciling attendance on College lectures, &c. with attention to the continually increasing work of the Library, the Assistants were, as a rule, for a considerable period, taken from the City instead of from the undergraduate members of the University, as had been generally the case hitherto; but the old practice is now, with great advantage, restored, so far as regards the statutable *Ministri.*

In pursuance of an address from the House of Commons, Sept. 4, 1848, on the motion of Mr. Ewart, various returns relative to public libraries were obtained, which were printed by Parliament in 1849, State Paper, No. 18. The following is the reply from Dr. Bandinel there printed:—

[1] A separate list of the books purchased at Jacobs' sale is appended to the annual Catalogue.

'BODLEIAN LIBRARY,
January 9, 1849.

'SIR,—In compliance with your letter, dated Oct. 27, 1848, desiring certain Returns respecting the Bodleian Library, I have to state—

'1. As to the number of books received under the various Copyright Acts, no distinct register of the books so received has been kept, but they have, at the end of each year, been incorporated into the general collection, so that I am unable to give the number of the books so received.

'2. The number of printed volumes in the Bodleian Library amounts to about 220,000; but this statement will very inadequately express the real extent of the collection, as so many works have been bound together in one volume.

'3. The number of manuscripts is about 21,000.

'4. All graduates of the University have the right of admission to the Library; other persons must apply for admission to the regular authorities.

'5. No register is kept of persons consulting the Library; accordingly, the number of students who have frequented it during the last ten years cannot be ascertained.

'I have, &c.

'BULKELEY BANDINEL,
'*Bodleian Librarian.*

'George Cornewall Lewis, Esq.,
'Under-Secretary of State, Whitehall.'

The estimate of printed volumes here given is believed to be as nearly accurate as it was possible to make it, since considerable pains were taken in forming the calculation. The number of separate printed books and tracts may be reckoned as at least treble the number of volumes. With regard to the reply to the fifth enquiry some explanation is requisite. A register is kept of all the octavo and most of the quarto volumes taken out for readers, of all the volumes from special and separate collections, and of all the MSS.; but no account used to be kept of the folios and other books on the ground-floor of the great room, which are accessible to readers themselves, and which are still frequently used by them without the help of the assistants. Consequently, any return of the number of readers entered on the register would not at that date represent the whole number of students who used the Library, although, of course, it would, with a margin for allowance, afford a very fair approximation. No record, however, of separate *visits* of readers is kept, as distinct from the books required; so that although a reader may be at work for many days or weeks together, yet, if he continue to use only the same books as at first, one entry alone will be made of his name.

A.D. 1850.

The Hebrew collection was still further increased in this year by the purchase of sixty-two MSS., of which fifty-seven had been brought from Italy; and in 1851, by the purchase of some printed books collected by Dr. Isaac L. Auerbach, of Berlin, who had recently deceased. Every year about this time saw additions to this branch of the Library[1], made chiefly through the agency of Mr. Asher, a then well-known Jewish bookseller at Berlin, and also through Hirsch Edelmann, a learned Rabbi, who was for some years a frequent reader in the Bodleian, from whence he commenced the publication of a series of extracts (see under the year 1693)[2]. A series of works illustrating the history, civil and ecclesiastical, the geography, &c., of Hungary, Transylvania, Croatia, and other neighbouring provinces of the Austrian Empire, amounting to 400 volumes, was purchased for £78; and a similar but much larger collection, relating to the history of Poland, numbering no fewer than 1200 volumes, was purchased for £366. Three hundred and twenty volumes of early printed works, some of which were fine specimens of *incunabula*, were obtained at the sale of the duplicates from the Royal Library at Munich. It

[1] In 1845, about 320 printed volumes were purchased from a catalogue issued at Berlin by A. Rebenstein, or Bernstein, and D. Cassel.

[2] Mr. Edelmann died some time after 1860 in Germany.

was announced at the end of the Annual Catalogue that a special list of these, together with a catalogue of the Hebrew MSS. noticed above, and of the Hungarian and Polish collections, would be printed and circulated in the following year; this, however, was not done.

A series of 600 English sermons, printed between 1600 and 1720, bound separately, was purchased for £59.

Various specimens of the first beginning of printing in one of the Friendly Islands, Vavau, consisting of the Bible in the Tonga language, and of several elementary books, were presented by Capt. Sir Jas. Everard Home, R.N., as also some elementary books printed at Apea by the natives, under the direction of the Missionaries, for the use of the natives of the Navigators' Islands.

Dukes' Shropshire Collections. See 1841.

A.D. 1851.

At the sale of the books of the poet Gray, by Messrs. Sotheby and Wilkinson, on Aug. 28, his copies of Clarendon and of Burnet's *Own Times* (vol. i.), with many MSS. notes written by him in the margins, were bought for £49 10*s.* and £2 18*s.* respectively[1]. Perfect specimens of facsimiles, which would defy detection, were obtained for the completion of Coverdale's Bible of 1535, which came to the Library among Selden's books; being pen and ink copies of the title, from Lord Leicester's copy, and of the map of Palestine, from Lord Jersey's copy, executed with admirable skill by the late well-known facsimilist, Mr. J. Harris[2].

A Supplemental Catalogue of the printed books, comprehending all the accessions which had been made during the years 1835–1847, was published in this year, in one folio volume, under the editorship of the Rev. Alfred Hackman, M.A., by whom the

[1] The Clarendon had been previously sold at an auction on Nov. 29, 1845, by Messrs. Evans, with other books which had belonged to Gray.

[2] A pen and ink facsimile title had been previously supplied by Mrs. Denyer from a copy in her possession.

greater part of the earlier Catalogue had been compiled, as mentioned at p. 346.

On March 27, Convocation voted an addition of £50 *per annum* to the stipends of the Sub-librarians.

Recovery of Pococke MS. 32. See pp. 115–6 *n.*

Malone's Correspondence. See p. 307.

A.D. 1852.

In the Report of the first University Commission, which was issued in this year, various suggestions were embodied which had been made by several witnesses. Sir Edmund Head renewed his plan of allowing books to be taken out of the Library by readers, and was supported by the opinions of Professors Wall and Jowett; but the proposal was met with the strong counter-testimony of Mr. H. E. Strickland[1], Prof. Vaughan, Dr. W. A. Greenhill (at that time a constant reader in the Library), Prof. Donkin, Mr. E. S. Ffoulkes, and others. And the Commissioners were not prepared to report in favour of a plan which would at once lessen what was described as being one of the great advantages of the place, namely, the certainty of finding within its walls every book which it possessed. At the same time, they were disposed to recommend a relaxation in some instances of the strictness of the rule, and concurred in a suggestion made by Dr. Macbride and Mr. Story-Maskelyne, that duplicates should be allowed to circulate. Most, however, of the suggestions for extension of facilities to readers, as well as of the reasons alleged

[1] Several important suggestions were made by this gentleman. One, that the Library Books should all be stamped with a distinguishing mark, has now been carried out. Another, respecting the great importance of collecting the most ephemeral local literature, especially for the county of Oxford, and of procuring books printed at provincial presses, relates to a subject which has received much more attention of late years than formerly. A third, on the desirability, acknowledged (as we have seen) in the last century, of having a general Catalogue compiled of the books found in College Libraries which are wanting in the Bodleian, has unfortunately as yet seen no accomplishment.

for alteration of system, have now been answered by the opening (through the liberality of the Radcliffe Trustees) of the Radcliffe Library as a noble reading-room for both day and evening. As the hours during which the Library may be used extend now, in consequence of this addition, from nine a.m. to ten p.m., it is at once apparent that the Bodleian presents greater advantages to students than can anywhere else be enjoyed; to which is to be added the readiness and quickness (specially testified to, in 1852, by Dr. Greenhill) with which, under all ordinary circumstances, readers are supplied with the books which they require. The Commissioners in their Report called attention to a suggestion of Sir Henry Bishop, then Professor of Music[1], for the establishment of a classified musical library, which should comprehend, not merely the music received by the Bodleian from Stationers' Hall, but all superior foreign music as well, of every school and every age. Such collections the Professor said were only to be found at Munich and Vienna.

The Report and Evidence upon the recommendations of the Commissioners, which were issued by the Hebdomadal Board in the following year, did not differ widely in testimony or suggestions from those of the Commission. Dr. Pusey ('*clarum et venerabile nomen*') and Mr. Charles Marriott (both of them habitual readers, for whom the Library was indeed a fitting treasure-house, and for whose use separate studies were specially reserved), agreed

[1] I recall with pleasure the acquaintance which I made with this popular composer during his very infrequent professorial visits to Oxford; and remember the taking part in singing with him several of his own beautiful glees, on one occasion, in my room at New College. It was reserved, however, for his successor, the (alas! late) distinguished professor, Rev. Sir Fred. A. Gore Ouseley, Bart. (dec. 6 Apr. 1889, aged 63), to revive the study of music as a science in the University, and by procuring statutory changes in the examinations to restore our musical degrees to their due credit as real evidences of knowledge and ability. In the performance of his exercise, the oratorio of 'St. Polycarp,' for the degree of Mus. Doc., on 9 Nov., 1854, I took part, with many others of his friends, among the chorus-singers; in Oct. 1888, I heard once more from him upon the Hereford Cathedral organ, at my request, his own rendering of that stately march which is one of its distinguishing features.

in deprecating the allowing removal of books, speaking (as did several of the witnesses before the Commission) from their own actual experience; and Dr. Bandinel mentioned, in a paper of observations which he contributed, the fact that he had been told by the Librarian of the Advocates' Library at Edinburgh that between 6000 and 7000 volumes appeared to have been lost there from the facilities afforded to borrowers. A comparative tabular statement respecting the arrangements and rules of the libraries at Berlin, Dresden, Florence, Munich, Paris and Vienna, drawn up by Mr. Coxe from the Parliamentary Report on Libraries, which showed very favourably in behalf of the Bodleian, was subjoined by Dr. Bandinel to his evidence.

The great feature of this year was the acquisition of the Italian library of the Count Alessandro Mortara, consisting of about 1400 volumes, choice in character and condition, for £1000. The Count, who was distinguished for his literary taste and knowledge of the literature of his own country, had, although holding the nominal office of Grand Chamberlain to the Duke of Lucca, taken up his abode in Oxford some ten years previously, on account of his desire to examine the Canonici MSS. and of his friendship with Dr. Wellesley, the late Principal of New Inn Hall. He became a daily reader in the Bodleian, where the interest which he took in the place, together with his polished, yet genuine, courtesy, made him a welcome and popular visitor. It was upon returning to Italy (where he died, June 14, 1855, at Florence), that he disposed of his valuable collection. A catalogue, compiled by himself, with occasional short notes, was issued with the purchase-catalogue for the year. He also drew up a catalogue of the Italian MSS. in the Canonici collection, which was published, in a quarto volume, in 1864. (See under 1817[1].)

[1] It is worth mentioning that in 1853 the Count, who had served as a colonel in the armies of the first Napoleon, presented to the second Emperor, when dining with him shortly after his marriage to the Empress Eugénie, a thin tractate of eight octavo pages (printed at Paris

Among miscellaneous purchases were a few volumes which were wanted to make the Library set of De Bry's *Voyages* complete, an imperfect copy of the Oxford *Liber Festivalis* (see 1691), and a large collection of Dr. Priestley's writings (believed to have been made by himself), in thirty-nine vols.

A. D. 1853.

A portion of the collection of Hebrew MSS. formed by Prof. Isaac Sam. Reggio, at Goritz, amounting to about seventy-two volumes, was purchased for £108. Many other MSS. in this class of literature occur yearly in the accounts at this time. But the great acquisition of 1853 was the *Breviarium secundum regulam beati Ysidori, dictum Mozarabes,* printed *on vellum* at Toledo, by command of Cardinal Ximenes, in 1502. £200 were given for this book, which is the only vellum copy known, and which is in most immaculate condition. It is of extreme rarity even on paper, as it is believed that only thirty-five copies were printed. A copy of this book (described as 'the rarest book in the whole world') was on sale at T. Osborne's, the well-known London bookseller's, in 1750–1 for £35. The Missal and Breviary together were sold at the sale of the library of Mr. Perkins, of Hanworth, in June 1873, for £295.

An imperfect copy of Caxton's *Chronicle*, 1480, was bought for £21; and a large gathering of Norfolk tracts was obtained at the sale of Mr. Dawson Turner's library.

On 26 Sept. in this year Dr. Constantine Simonides, the notorious forger of ancient MSS., visited the Library in the hope of disposing of some of the products of his Eastern ingenuity, but

'by E. Brière, rue Sainte-anne, 55') bearing the following inscription as its title: 'Napoleoni III Francorum Imperatori Pio Felici Augusto Europæ Tutamini Alex. Mortara, Napoleonis I. jam Miles, CH DDD': and containing Latin verses by 'Aloisius Chrysostomus Ferruccius,' Italian by 'prof. ab. Giuseppe Arcangeli' and by the Count himself, and English by my father, then Librarian of the Taylor Institution, Oxford. Of this little *brochure* probably not more than a dozen copies are in existence.

failed here, as also at the British Museum (whence warning notice of his movements had been received), although successful in most other quarters. It is much to be lamented that the talent, learning, and ability which he undoubtedly possessed in no small degree were devoted to such unworthy purpose as his history discloses. The story of his interview with Mr. Coxe, then Sub-librarian, was at the time, and is still, well known. It was reproduced in an article in the *Cornhill Magazine* for Oct. 1867 (p. 499); and as the version there given appears to be substantially correct, it will be sufficient to borrow it from its pages:—

'On visiting the [Bodleian Library, Mr. Simonides] showed some fragments of MSS. to Mr. Coxe, who assented to their belonging to the twelfth century. "And these, Mr. Coxe, belong to the tenth or eleventh century?" "Yes, probably." "And now, Mr. Coxe, let me show you a very ancient and valuable MS. I have for sale, and which ought to be in your Library. To what century do you consider this belongs?" "This, Mr. Simonides, I have no doubt," said Mr. Coxe, "belongs to the [latter half of the] nineteenth century." The Greek and his MS. disappeared.'

An account of this visit was given in the *Athenæum* for March 1, 1856, and another version in *Gent. Magaz.* for Nov. 1856, p. 593; and a full narrative, including a letter from Sir F. Madden respecting the dealings with Simonides on the part of the British Museum, is to be found in S. L. Sotheby's *Principia Typographica*, vol. ii. pp. 133–136 f[1].

A.D. 1854.

A very interesting series of eighteen autograph letters from Henry Hyde, the second Earl of Clarendon, was presented to

[1] A notice of his forgeries was communicated by my father to the *Gent. Magaz.* for Oct. 1856, pp. 440–2. His death, from the terrible disease of leprosy, was announced as occurring at Cairo in 1867. In 1883 an attempt to rival his forgeries was made by the Jewish expert Shapira in the production of his famous fragments of a Phœnician copy of Deuteronomy, which followed his 'discovery' of the pseudo-Moabite pottery now at Berlin. I saw the fragments while they were under careful temporary keeping at the British Museum.

the University by our late honoured Chancellor, the Earl of Derby[1]. They are best described in the following letter to the Vice-Chancellor, which accompanied the gift, and which is now bound in the same volume :—

'KNOWSLEY, *Oct.* 17, 1854.

'MY DEAR SIR,—In looking over some old papers here the other day, I found (how they came here I know not) some original and apparently autograph letters, which appeared to me to be curious. They are private letters, addressed by Lord Clarendon, to the Earl of Abingdon, as Lord Lieutenant of Oxfordshire, during, and on the suppression of, the Duke of Monmouth's Rebellion. I have no doubt of their genuineness ; and if from the connexion of the University with the writer[2], as well as the locality, you think they would be worth depositing in the Bodleian Library, I shall have great pleasure in offering them to the acceptance of the University for that purpose ; and in that case would send with them a miniature pencil drawing of the Duke of Monmouth, which is not too large to be let into the cover of the portfolio which should contain the letters, and for the authenticity of which I can so far vouch that it has been in this house since 1729, at least; since it appears in a catalogue of the pictures and engravings here which formed the collection at that time.

'I am, my dear sir,

'Yours sincerely,

'DERBY.'

The portrait in question, which is a beautifully executed drawing, in an oak frame, marked on the back, 'Duke of Monmouth, by Foster,' is now fixed, as desired, in the present morocco binding of the volume.

A collection of early editions of the Prayer-book (including Whitchurch's May and June editions of 1549 and that of 1552), of the Metrical Psalter, and of Visitation Articles (amongst others, Edward the Sixth's Articles of 1547. and Injunctions of the same year), with a few miscellaneous books, was bought of the Rev.

[1] A portrait of Lord Derby, in his Chancellor's robes, painted by Sir F. A. Grant, was given by him to the University about 1858, and now hangs in the Picture Gallery. He died Oct. 23, 1869.

[2] The Earl was High Steward of the University.

T. Lathbury, M.A., the well-known writer on English Church history (who died 11 Feb., 1865, aged 66), for £300. Various rare English books were purchased at Mr. Will. Pickering's sale, and foreign dissertations, &c. at that of the library of Professor Gottfried Hermann, the Greek editor and commentator (who died 31 Dec., 1848), at Leipsic, in April.

A.D. 1855.

Three Greek Biblical MSS. of great antiquity were obtained from the collection of Prof. Tischendorf, being Nos. 3–5 of the volumes described in a small quarto catalogue issued (anonymously) by him of *Codices Græci*, &c. One of these three (Auct. T. *infra*, II. 2) is of the ninth century, containing the Gospel of St. Luke, with portions of the other Gospels, which was bought for £125; another (Auct. T. *infra*, I. 1) of the eighth century, containing the whole of St. Luke and St. John, bought for £140; the third (Auct. T. *infra*, II. 1), also of the eighth century, containing the greatest part of Genesis, for £108.

Rev. T. R. Brown's Dictionary, &c., printed by himself. See under 1838.

A.D. 1856.

A volume containing two autograph letters of Luther was bought for £20, together with a large collection (formed by — Schneider, of Berlin) of printed books relating to him and the German Reformation, with various editions of his works, for £300. Another volume, with some small additional papers in the Reformer's hand, was subsequently obtained.

The ever-increasing Bible collection received the addition of the very rare *ed. princ.* of the Bohemian Bible, printed at Prague in 1488, which was obtained for £17 10*s.*, and a still more rare edition of the Pentateuch, with New Test., &c. printed at Wittemberg in 1529, obtained for eighteen guineas. A Roman Missal, printed 'ad longum, absque ulla requisitione,' (*i. e.* in a kind of 'Prayer-book-as-read' form,) Lyons 1550, was obtained for £20.

It was arranged by Nicholas Roiller, Chanter of the Church of S. Nicetius at Lyons, with the view of avoiding difficulties and delays, 'sacerdotesque expectantibus molestos reddentes, ipsosque erga dictos circumstantes scandalum generantes, qui existimant illos non solum ignaros sed nescientes quid agendum vel faciendum habeant;' and was issued with the papal *imprimatur* of Paul III. But as Pius V and Clem. VIII subsequently forbade any variation whatsoever from the authorized Roman form, this Missal, like the Breviary of Card. Quignones, was, with others, suppressed. And hence its rarity.

Fifty guineas were given for a very large collection of Chinese works numbering altogether about 1100, which had been gathered by Rev. F. Evans, for some time a missionary in China. Some of the Chinese books in the Library were subsequently examined and catalogued by Professor Summers, of King's College, London; and the work has been recently continued by Professor Legge.

A large and important collection of books and tracts relating to the history of the Jansenists, which had been gathered by the Jansenist Archbishop of Utrecht, van Nieuwen Huysen, was purchased in two portions, in this year and in 1858, for £151.

On May 22, a new body of Library Statutes was confirmed by Convocation, after a complete revision of the previous regulations. The principal changes, besides the omission of various obsolete requirements, were the adding five elected Curators, holding office for ten years, to the old *ex officio* body of eight; the providing for the removal of books to the extra-mural 'Camera,' or reading-room, about to be added; the fixing the stipend of the Librarian (including all the former fees and small separate payments) at £700, and that of the Sub-librarians at £300, and the assigning to the former a retiring pension after twenty years' service of £200, and after thirty years', of £300, and to the latter, after thirty years', of £190; and the making a few alterations with regard to the times at which the Library should be closed, these times being lessened by about one week in the course of the year.

A report from the eminent architect, Mr. (afterwards Sir) G. G.

Scott, on the means which might be adopted for the enlargement of the Library, and for rendering it fire-proof, dated in Dec. 1855, was printed in this year, together with one from Mr. Braidwood on the warming apparatus (see under 1821). Mr. Scott's report contained suggestions for the extension of the Library throughout the whole of the quadrangle and adjoining buildings, including the Ashmolean Museum, and proposed that the Divinity School should be assigned as a reading room, for which the great degree of light afforded by its large windows appeared peculiarly to fit it. The subsequent assignment, however, of the Radcliffe Library as a reading-room for the Library, removed the immediate necessity for any other extension. In 1858 a paper on the subject, illustrated with a plan of the Library, was printed by the late Dr. Wellesley, who, after considering the various modes then suggested for the enlargement of the Library, recommended the adoption (from the British Museum) of presses running up direct from the ground through all the floors, by which the dangers attendant upon the increase of weight of the wall-pressure would be obviated.

A.D. 1857.

A collection of manuscripts, more interesting as to their history than as to their actual contents [1], was presented by William and Hubert Hamilton, in memory, and in accordance with the wish, of their celebrated father, Sir William Hamilton. It comprises fifty-eight volumes (thirty-nine in folio, sixteen in quarto, and three in octavo) from the library of the Carthusian monastery of Erfurt, famous as the place of Luther's early abode. A short catalogue of them, by Joh. Broad, was printed at Berlin in 1841, with a prefatory notice, from which we learn that they were preserved at Erfurt until 1805, when the library was broken up and dispersed

[1] For the most part, they consist of mediæval sermons and theological treatises by writers of no great fame, together with some of the works of Aquinas.

on the occupation of the city by the French army, who stabled their horses in the place where the books were deposited, and burned many of them for fuel, while others were carried away and secreted with a view to their safety. Some of the latter were bought by the Count von Bülow, on whose death they were purchased from the subsequent possessors by Broad, and finally sold by him to Sir W. Hamilton. 'Nunc in eam terram demigrant,' says the bibliopolist, 'quæ, quodcunque alicujus pretii est aut materialium aut spiritualium rerum, in suo gremio accumulare a Providentia Divina destinata videtur.' Another collection of MSS. from the same library at Erfurt, was on sale by Mr. J. M. Stark, a well-known bookseller at Hull, and afterwards in London, in 1855, who issued a small catalogue of them in duodecimo.

A valuable collection of Italian and Spanish MSS., amounting to thirty-seven volumes, came to the Library by the bequest of Rev. Joseph Mendham, M.A., of Sutton Coldfield, who died Nov. 1, 1856. The most important part of these is a series of twenty-eight volumes relating to the Council of Trent, which were purchased at the sale of the Earl of Guildford's library in 1830 by Thorpe, the bookseller, for £35, and re-sold by him to Mr. Mendham in 1832 for fifty guineas. It was chiefly from the materials afforded by these that Mr. Mendham drew up his *Memoirs of the Council of Trent*, published in 1834. They are described in Thorpe's Catalogue of MSS. on sale in 1831, and in the preface to Mr. Mendham's book.

On June 18, the Rev. Robert Payne Smith, M.A., of Pembroke College (now D.D., and Dean of Canterbury), was appointed an Assistant Sub-librarian for the Oriental department, in consequence of the increasing infirmities of the aged senior Sub-librarian, Mr. Reay.

A.D. 1858.

On Oct. 30, an offer made by the Trustees of the Ashmolean Museum for the transfer of the printed books, coins, and MSS. there contained to the Bodleian, in order to facilitate the devotion of a part of the building to the purposes of an Examination School, was accepted by the Curators; but a similar offer with regard to the antiquities was declined. The latter consequently remain in their old repository, but the collections in Natural History were transferred to the New Museum. It was not, however, until 1860, that the books were actually received into the Library, where they now fill one small room. Altogether they amount to upwards of 3700 volumes, forming five different series. First are those of Elias Ashmole himself, numbering originally 2175, but reduced by losses before the transfer to 2136, of which about 850 are MSS.[1] This collection is extremely rich in heraldic and genealogical matter, together with an abundance of astrology. The printed books are chiefly scientific and historical; these, with the books in the following collections, are now incorporated with the rest of the Library in the new General Catalogue. A list of the MSS. is given in Bernard's catalogue, A.D. 1697; but a very elaborate and minute account, forming a thick quarto volume, was drawn up by Mr. W. H. Black, the well-known antiquary (dec. 1872), and published in 1845. As this, however, was destitute of an index, it remained comparatively useless until 1866, when a full Index, edited by me, with the help for the larger part of my valued friend Mr. Henry Gough, was published under the direction of the Delegates of the University Press.

The next collection is that of Anthony à Wood, containing about 130 MSS. and 970 printed volumes[2], which were bequeathed to the Museum by the owner on his death in Nov. 1695. The former are of extreme value for the history of Oxford and the neighbourhood; among the latter are most curious sets of the pamphlets of the time, with ballads, fly-sheets, chap-books, almanacks, &c. just such 'unconsidered trifles' as most men suffer to perish in the using, but a few, like Wood, lay up for the amuse-

[1] This number includes some fifteen or sixteen volumes given by subsequent donors, but incorporated with Ashmole's own books.

[2] About fifty volumes out of Wood's whole number were missing when the Library became possessed of them.

ment and information of future generations. There are also seven volumes of his own correspondence, including letters from Dugdale, Evelyn, &c. Of the MSS. a list is to be found in the old Catalogue of 1697; a fuller and better one, compiled by William Huddesford, M.A., the Keeper of the Museum, was printed in a thin octavo volume, in 1761, which was reprinted by Sir Thomas Phillips, at Middlehill, Worcestershire, in 1824. There were also bundles of charters and deeds, chiefly monastic, but nearly all more or less mutilated or injured by damp and dirt, so as to be partially illegible. These have been cleaned and repaired and bound, as far as possible, and are included in the Catalogue of Charters, by Mr. W. H. Turner, which was published in 1878.

The third collection is that of Dr. Martin Lister, physician to Queen Anne, who died Feb. 2, 171½. Besides his books, he was the donor of various other gifts to the Museum, in return for which he was created M.D. of Oxford, in 1683. The books are chiefly medical and scientific, and number in a written catalogue 1451 volumes (including thirty-two MSS., some of which consist of correspondence, given by Dr. John Fothergill in 1769), but thirty-five of these were missing when the transfer from the Museum was made. A few printed books came with the MSS. given by Fothergill.

The collections of Sir William Dugdale, which form a fourth series, number forty-eight volumes. A list of these is in the old Catalogue of 1697.

In the fifth place there are the MSS. of the well-known antiquary, John Aubrey. These are about twenty in number, of which fifteen are in his own hand, and are described in Britton's Life of him, printed for the Wilts Topographical Society, pp. 88–123. Collections for the history of Wiltshire, entitled *Hypomnemata Antiquaria*, form one of Aubrey's own works[1], but unfortunately the second volume (marked with the letter B) is missing. It was

[1] These were printed by the Wiltshire Archæological Society in 1862, in one volume quarto, under the editorship of Rev. John Edw. Jackson, M.A., rector of Leigh Delamere, Wilts.

borrowed from the Museum, in 1703, by William Aubrey, the author's brother, and was never returned. A paper on the subject was inserted by Rev. J. E. Jackson, in 1860, in vol. vii. of the Wiltshire Archæological Magazine, and a reward for information as to the present *locale* of the missing volume was subsequently publicly offered, but to no purpose, by the same gentleman; and yet the volume was sold as recently as 1836 in Rich. Heber's sale! It appears in part xi. of his catalogue, as No. 48, and was sold to Thorpe, the bookseller, for £9. It may therefore be regarded as tolerably certain that it will some day come to light again. A small MS. of *Horæ*, which had belonged to Sir Thomas Pope, the founder of Trinity College, is among Aubrey's books. A MS. of Matthew of Westminster (now *e Mus.* 149) had been given to the Library by Aubrey, June 1, 1675, through Ant. à Wood.

There are also five or six MSS. which were given to the Museum by William Kingsley before 1700. Some few others, which were given by E. Lhuyd and Dr. W. Borlase, together with Lhuyd's own correspondence, given by Dr. John Fothergill in 1769, and a volume of W. Huddesford's correspondence, are now incorporated with the Ashmole MSS., and are described in Mr. Black's catalogue; as well as the latest gift of this kind which was made to the Museum, *viz.* a little volume of *Private Thoughts*, by Bishop Wilson, of Sodor and Man, which was presented in 1824 by Lieut. Brett, R.N.

Thirty-nine choice Persian and Arabic MSS., which had formed part of Sir Gore Ouseley's collection, were bought from his son, the late Rev. Sir Fred. Gore Ouseley, Bart., for £500. The rest of the collection came by gift, as will be seen under the following year.

At the sale (in June—Aug.) of the library of Rev. Dr. Philip Bliss, (who died 18 Nov. 1857, aged 70), a large number of volumes (still kept separate) were purchased, including a volume of original letters of Charles I, Clarendon, &c., and poems by Lord Fairfax (see p. 139); together with many from the series of books of *Characters* collected by Dr. Bliss, and from two other series, the one of books printed in London shortly before the fire of 1666, and the other of books printed at Oxford. The Library obtained by his bequest his own interleaved copy of the *Athenæ*, with many MS. additions[1].

A copy of the octavo Bible printed by Barker in 1631 (not 1632, as generally said), in which the word 'not' was omitted in the seventh commandment, was bought for £40. For this error (which looks very much like a wicked jest) the printer was fined 1000 marks by the High Commission Court[2], and the edition was rigidly suppressed, all the copies which could be found being condemned to the flames.

Another purchase was a large collection of political tracts in seventy volumes, chiefly relating to foreign affairs, which had been formed by Mr. — Hamilton, of the Diplomatic Service.

A.D. 1859.

Numerous MSS., chiefly classical, patristic, or Italian, were purchased at the sale of M. Libri's collection in London, in March. Amongst them was a Sacramentary, of the commencement of the ninth century, which was obtained for £43; and a copy of S. Cyprian's Epistles, also of the ninth century, for £84. Four volumes of the correspondence of Scholars at home and abroad with E. H. Barker, of Thetford, were also added to the Library from the sale of Mr. Dawson Turner's library. They are now

[1] A very valuable Index of notes and references on all kinds of biographical, historical, and antiquarian matters, contained in forty small covers, which had been the growth of the many years of Dr. Bliss's literary researches, was bequeathed by him to Mr. Coxe, and by the latter in 1881 to the Library. Several references are made to this Index in the earlier part of this volume. The slips which compose it are now mounted and bound in three folio volumes.

[2] In Burn's *High Commission Court*, 1865, it is said (from the Reports of proceedings in the Court) that the fine inflicted on Barker was £200 and on Lucas £100. 'With some part of this fine Laud causeth a fair Greek character to be provided, for publishing such manuscripts as time and industry should make ready for the publick view; of which sort were the *Catena* and *Theophylact* set out by Lyndsell.' Heylin's *Cyprianus Anglicus*, p. 228.

numbered Bodl. MSS. 1003–1006. And the munificent gift of a very valuable collection of 422 volumes of Arabic and Persian MSS. was received from Mr. J. B. Elliott, of Patna. These chiefly consist of the MSS. which Sir Gore Ouseley (who died Nov. 18, 1844,) obtained during his diplomatic service in the East, commencing his collection when stationed at Lucknow, and completing it while ambassador in Persia; of which Mr. Elliott had been the purchaser. A small remaining part had previously been bought by the Library, as noted under 1858. In 1860, Mr. Elliott added to his former gift a series of Eastern coins, and various handsome specimens of Eastern weapons; the latter are now exhibited in a case in the Picture Gallery. Six Sanscrit MSS. (in 7 volumes) were also received from Mr. Fitz-Edward Hall, of Saugur (afterwards Librarian at the India Office), who, at the same time, expressed his munificent intention of presenting hereafter the whole of his large collection; an intention, unfortunately, not carried out. It was at this gentleman's suggestion that Mr. Elliott's MSS. were presented to the Library.

In this year, after considerable enquiry had been made respecting different modes of cataloguing, and Mr. Coxe had reported on the arrangements adopted in the great libraries at home and some of those abroad, it was resolved by the Curators, upon that gentleman's recommendation, that the plan in use in the British Museum should be immediately introduced, for the purpose of commencing a new General Catalogue of all the printed books (excepting the Hebrew, of which a separate Catalogue had been made) in the whole Library. By this plan, three or five copies, according as the case may be that of a single or double entry, are written simultaneously on prepared paper, as with a manifold-copier, the transcribers writing out the entries of titles which have been previously examined and corrected by the cataloguers. The separate titles are then mounted, arranged in alphabetical order, and bound in volumes. In this way two copies of the Catalogue are at once written with the labour of one, while surplus slips are also provided for the formation of a classified

Catalogue as well. The use of the Catalogue, however, is thus confined to the Library itself; and the literary world in general can only refer to the printed Catalogues of 1843 and 1851, and go no further. The new undertaking was commenced in this year; but it was not until 1862 that a full staff of assistants was employed, and the work completely organized. By the year 1868 the letters A—E, G—H were catalogued[1]; and the whole was completed in 1878. The number of volumes of which the Catalogue now consists is 741; for the relative proportions of letters, it may be mentioned that A, B, and C fill twenty-eight, sixty-four, and sixty-five volumes respectively. All the books were seen and examined separately; anonymous authors, in many instances, traced out; and many errors and omissions in previous Catalogues were corrected.

A.D. 1860.

The resignation of the Librarianship by Dr. Bandinel, after forty-seven years of office in the capacity of Head, and a total of fifty of work in the Library, forms a leading feature in the Bodley Annals of this year. At the age of seventy-nine the natural infirmities of age were felt by himself to incapacitate him for the duties which he had so long and so regularly discharged; while at the same time the continually increasing pressure of work and requirements of the Library made those duties much more onerous than they had been even a quarter of a century before. And so he resolved to withdraw at Michaelmas from the place to which he had been so heartily attached, and which under his headship had been doubled in contents. The parting was not without a great struggle; it was the abandoning what had been the occupation of his life, and with the ceasing of

[1] The preparation of the letters G and H, with half of I, fell to my share, as being then general superintendent of the new Catalogue; but early in 1871 I returned to my former work upon MSS., after ceasing, on accepting the rectory of Ducklington, twelve miles distant, to reside in Oxford. I thereupon became a 'half-timer' in the Library, and my attendance since 1870 has been on three days in the week.

that occupation he felt a certain foreboding (which he expressed to me) that the life would soon cease as well. A well-merited tribute was paid to him by Convocation in June, in both increasing the amount of his statutable pension, so that he retired on a full stipend, and in specially enrolling him among the Curators of the Library. But he was seldom seen in the old place after his resignation; on two or three occasions only did he again mount the long flight of stairs which had of late tried both his strength and breath severely; and then, when only seven months had elapsed, on Feb. 6, 1861, he passed away. And little more than a fortnight previously, on January 20, his old colleague, Professor Reay, departed this life, at the age of seventy-eight. He also had retired on his pension at Michaelmas, 1860, and had been succeeded as Oriental Sub-librarian by Rev. R. Payne Smith (Assistant-librarian in the same department since 1857), whose appointment was confirmed by Convocation on Nov. 22. Memoirs of Dr. Bandinel and Mr. Reay are given in the *Gentleman's Magazine* for 1861 (pp. 463–6), which do justice, in the case of the former, to his solicitude for the Library and his thorough acquaintance with it[1]; and in the case of the latter (evidently from intimate personal acquaintance), to his great kindliness of heart and simplicity and gentleness of character.

The Convocation for the election of Dr. Bandinel's successor was held on November 6, when, with unanimous consent, the Rev. H. O. Coxe, M.A., Sub-librarian since 1838, was appointed to the office.

A most seasonable and valuable enlargement of the Library was effected by an addition which henceforth marks an æra in our Annals. On June 12 Convocation thankfully accepted an offer from the Radcliffe Trustees (which had been first mooted

[1] In one element of a good librarian's character, it must, however, be admitted that Dr. Bandinel was sometimes wanting; viz. in the general courtesy which should be exhibited to all duly qualified readers alike. The Library too often seemed to be regarded as a rich preserve for favoured students, while the unfavoured were viewed somewhat jealously, not to say suspiciously. And all the staff trembled at Jupiter's nod.

by Dr., now Sir H. W., Acland in 1856), of the use, as a Bodleian reading-room, of the noble building hitherto under their control, the existing contents of which had (for the most part) been removed to the New Museum. Dr. Radcliffe's own original intention had been the building an additional wing to the Bodleian rather than the erecting a library of his own[1]; and subsequently the idea had been entertained of devoting his structure to the exclusive reception of manuscripts[2]. Its appropriation, therefore, to the Bodleian upon the removal of the library of medicine and natural

[1] Rawlinson says in a letter to T. Rawlins of Apr. 1, 1749, 'I am told it is designed for the most modern books in all faculties and languages not in the Bodleian Library,' and that Carte's *History* will be the first book placed in it. Ballard MS. II. 113.

[2] In prosecution of this idea several valuable collections of Oriental MSS. were obtained, which long formed part of the stores of the old Radcliffe Library. They consist of the Arabic, Persian, and Sanscrit MSS. collected by — Fraser and by Sale, the translator of the Koran, which were obtained (as we learn from Sharpe's *Prolegomena* to Hyde's *Dissertationes*, 1767, vol. i. p. xvii) through Professor Thomas Hunt, at the suggestion of Dr. Gregory Sharpe; and of the collations of the MSS. of the Hebrew Old Test. by Dr. Kennicott (Librarian 1767–1783), together with his correspondence and miscellaneous *codices*. The Sanscrit MSS. of Fraser and Sale are described in Prof. Aufrecht's Catalogue. All these MSS., amounting to between 400 and 500, were transferred to the Bodleian, May 10, 1872, upon condition that a Catalogue should be printed, and that if at any time they should be reclaimed, the cost of the Catalogue should be repaid. For notice of a collection of pamphlets, see 1794. Other collections still in the Radcliffe Library in the New Museum are the classical and historical (as well as medical) books of Dr. Frewin, a physician and Camden Professor of Anc. History; and the law books of Mr. Viner, founder of the Vinerian Professorship and Scholarships; together with the works of J. Gibbs, the justly famous architect of the building in which they were kept. Some coins bequeathed by Wise, the first Librarian, have been transferred to the Bodleian. Two volumes of Clarendon MSS. were bought for the Library in 1780, but were united some years since to the mass of those papers preserved in the Bodleian. It was not until the year 1811 that the Library was specially assigned to Medicine and Natural History. (See *Report on the transfer of the Radcliffe Library to the Univ. Museum*, by Dr. Acland, 1861.) The proposal to assign the Library as a depository for the MSS. of the Bodleian is mentioned with great approbation by Blackstone in his Introduction to his edition of the *Great Charter*, 1759, p. [illegible]; and a further proposal by Blackstone to bring all the MSS. of the various College Libraries together is advocated by Greg. Sharpe, *ubi supra*.

history, was, in some sort, a return to the Founder's first design. And the return came most seasonably, when the old walls of the Schools' quadrangle were well-nigh bursting from a plethora of books, and still the cry 'They come' daily caused fresh bewilderment as to whither those that came should go. It was resolved that the new reading-room thus opportunely gained should be appropriated to new books (arranged under a system of classification) and magazines; that it should be called the 'Camera Radcliviana;' and that it should be open from ten A.M. till ten P.M., thus affording the facilities for evening use of the Bodleian which had often been desired for those who were occupied in college work during the day. It was at the close of the year 1861 that the building began to be filled by its new occupants, and on Jan. 27, 1862, (the necessary alterations and preparations having been completed in the short space of the Christmas vacation) it was announced by the Vice-Chancellor to be open as a Reading Room in connection with the Bodleian. A grant of £200 *per annum* towards the expense of management was made by Convocation on Nov. 28, 1861, which was increased to £300 in 1865, the remainder of the charge, consisting of the incidental expenses, being defrayed from the general fund of the Library.

A large additional space for the reception of books was gained by the closing up the open ground-floor (through which was the former entrance to the reading-room), converting the spaces between the outer arches into windows, and lining the walls within with book-shelves, thus affording accommodation, according to the reckoning at that time, for about 50,000 volumes. The whole building may be reckoned as capable of containing altogether about 130,000 volumes[1].

The terms on which the Radcliffe Trustees made their offer,

[1] An account of this assignment and arrangement of the Radcliffe Library, as also of the transfer of the Ashmolean books to the Bodleian, appeared in the *Athenæum* for Jan. 1865, p. 20. At the beginning of 1885 the building contained 97,101 volumes. *Report* of the Librarian printed in 1888, p. 3.

and which were accepted by the University, were these :—1. That the Radcliffe Building should be a reading-room to the Bodleian, or be used for any other purpose of the Bodleian Library. 2. That it should remain the property of the Trustees, being esteemed a loan to the University. 3. That no alteration should be made in the building without consent of the Trustees or of a Representative approved by them. 4. That the expense of maintaining the building should be borne by the Trustees.

The transfer of this magnificent room afforded a rare opportunity for developing the usefulness of the Library to which it became attached, and all who frequented it acknowledged that that opportunity was well and worthily improved under the direction of the late Librarian.

On Oct. 25, leave was granted by Convocation for the lending two Laud Manuscripts, 561 and 563, being copies of the *Historia Hierosolymitana*, by Albert of Aix, to the French Government.

At the sale of the library of Dr. Wellesley, Principal of New Inn Hall, a copy of Boccaccio's *Corbaccio*, 1569, was purchased, on account of its possessing the autograph of Sir Thomas Bodley, to whom it had been given by the editor, J. Corbinelli. This is now exhibited in a glass case at the entrance of the reading-room.

A rare Salisbury *Primer*, or *Horæ B. M. V.*, printed at Rouen by Rob. Valentin in 1556, was purchased for £22. Its title (in common with many of the Rouen editions of the *Horæ*) affords an amusing specimen of a foreigner's mode of printing English; it runs thus—*This prymer of Salisbury vse is se tout along with houtonyser chyng, with many prayers & goodly pyctures.* It is intended hereby to be conveyed to the English reader that, without any searching, he will find his prayers and psalms set out in their proper order.

A.D. 1861.

One hundred and four volumes of Tamil MSS. were purchased; as well as four Samaritan MSS. of the Pentateuch, of the twelfth century, which had been brought to England by a native of Samaria.

The Syriac MSS. of the well-known Orientalist, Dr. Bernstein, were purchased by the Delegates of the Press, with a view to assisting in the great work of a Syriac Lexicon by Dr. R. Payne Smith, now Dean of Canterbury, upon which the Dean is still engaged.

The printing of the Annual Catalogues of purchases was discontinued, after the issue of the Catalogue for this year, and only a list of donations and donors, with the statement of accounts, continued to be annually printed for circulation in the University and amongst the donors. But since the year 1885 the list of donations has ceased to be printed, on account of the great increase of small gifts. It would be very useful, however, if from time to time a list of all the MSS. purchased or given were issued, after the custom of the British Museum. Written registers are now kept in the Library of all the books added, whether by purchase or gift, in the course of each year.

A.D. 1862.

A large collection of British Essayists and Periodicals was presented by the Rev. F. W. Hope, D.C.L., (who died 15 Apr. in this year, aged 65), a munificent benefactor to the University Museum, the founder of the Professorship of Zoology, and the donor also of a large collection of engraved portraits and other prints[1]. The collection was one which had been formed by John Thomas Hope, Esq., the donor's father. It contains some

[1] These engravings are now deposited in a room on the ground-floor of the Old Schools' quadrangle (formerly the Philosophy School) whither they were removed from the gallery of the Radcliffe reading-room in 1888. They are under the charge of a separate Keeper, the Rev. J. S. Treacher, M.A., and do not belong to the Bodleian. The collection contains upwards of 210,000 portraits, and is constantly being increased by purchases and gifts. There is also an art library containing some 4000 volumes.

760 specimens of its class of literature, belonging chiefly to the eighteenth century. Special thanks for the gift were returned by Convocation, on Feb. 20. A Catalogue, which had been drawn up for Mr. Hope by Mr. Jacob Henry Burn, containing notices in detail of the various publications, was printed at the University Press, in 1865, in an octavo volume.

A Hebrew MS. of the Pentateuch, probably of the thirteenth century, was bought for £32 10*s*. Some tracts relating to the period of the Great Rebellion were bought at the sale of Dr. Bandinel's extensive Caroline collection.

On March 4, the Curators accepted the gift of a bust of Rev. F. W. Robertson, late incumbent of Trinity Chapel, Brighton, which had been purchased by subscription. It is now placed in the Picture Gallery.

A large number of purchase-duplicates, which had accumulated during the course of many years, were removed from the Library and sold by auction, in London, by Messrs. Sotheby and Wilkinson, in May. Among them were some of great rarity. The sale, which lasted five days, produced £766 2*s*. 6*d*.; of which £110 5*s*. were given for a specimen of the St. Alban's press, the *Rhetorica Nova* of Gul. de Saona, printed in 1489. A second and smaller sale, containing many English works of the sixteenth and seventeenth centuries, took place on April 12, 1865, at which a copy of Chettle's *Kind-Harts Dreame* (1593), produced £101, and Decker's *Guls Horne-Booke*, 1609, £81. The proceeds of this second sale amounted to £750 18*s*. 6*d*.

The Rev. Alfred Hackman, M.A., Chaplain and Precentor of Ch. Ch., and P. C. of St. Paul's, Oxford, and an Assistant in the Library of twenty-five years' standing, was approved by Convocation, on April 12, as Mr. Coxe's successor in the Sub-librarianship; after a discussion which led to the abrogation by Convocation, in February, of a provision in the Statutes forbidding the holding cure of souls in connection with that office or that of Head-librarian without special licence from the Curators, a provision which was, however, re-enacted, without any qualification whatever, on June 14, 1873. The abrogation was strongly supported by Dr. Pusey.

A.D. 1863.

Among the purchases made in this year were the following: Card. Ximenes' rare treatise entitled *Crestia*, printed at Valentia in 1483 (£25); Court-Rolls of Tamworth, Solihull, and other neighbouring places, obtained from Mr. J. O. Halliwell-Phillipps[1]; and a collection, in three thick folio volumes, of placards, hand-bills, &c., relating to the town of Coventry, formed by Mr. W. Reader, a printer in that place.

Capt. Montagu Montagu, R.N., who died at Bath on July 3 in this year, bequeathed a collection of about 700 volumes, in various branches of literature, which was received at the Library about the beginning of 1864. There are about ninety editions and versions of the Psalter, with works on Psalmody, including a metrical version by Capt. Montagu himself; a large number of editions of Anacreon, Horace, Juvenal, Phædrus, Petrarch, Boileau, and La Fontaine's *Fables*; a few MSS. of Juvenal, Petrarch, &c., with a large series of autograph letters, chiefly obtained at Upcott's sale. There are, besides, a number of topographical and biographical works illustrated, *more Sutherlandico*, with additional engravings, together with many parcels of separate prints arranged for the same purpose. One item of particular interest which accompanied the collection is a small sketch of Napoleon I, in profile, admirably executed by the well-known Italian artist, Giuseppe Longhi. It now hangs, framed and glazed, in the Library, together with a letter from Longhi himself, in French, dated at Milan, June 4, 1828, in which he narrates the occasion on which it

[1] They were sold by that gentleman for the benefit of the fund then being raised for the purchase of Shakespeare's house at Stratford-on-Avon. By the death of Mr. Halliwell, on 3 Jan., 1889 (aged 68), I lost a friend who, in 1844, gave me his first Shakesperean publication (printed in 1841), the *Essay on the character of Sir J. Falstaff*, and with whom my acquaintance then begun continued during the forty-four years that followed.

was taken. He attended, in 1801, at Lyons, as a member of the 'Consulte Cisalpine,' for the settling the affairs of the Republic of Italy, under the presidency of the First Consul. It happened that during the delivery of a long harangue, full of tedious flattery, Napoleon sat *vis-à-vis* with the orator; and Longhi saw that an opportunity for exercising the cunning of his pencil had come. The light, which streamed in through the great window of the church (!) where they were assembled, brought out the profile very clearly; there was little fear of being cut short by the speaker's suddenly ceasing his declamation, or of being interrupted by movement on the part of the unconscious subject of the operation, for the latter sat immersed in thought upon matters far away, while regarding the speaker with a pensive air; and so, while Napoleon sat pondering, Longhi sat sketching. And everybody, both at Lyons and Paris, he declares with a pardonable pride, pronounced the likeness to be excellent. A small bust of Napoleon came to the Library at the same time. A catalogue of Captain Montagu's books, comprising forty octavo pages, was printed and circulated with the Annual Statement for 1864.

A. D. 1864.

The chief acquisitions in manuscript books were various Hebrew volumes (for £159), and a series of letters to Malone from Dr. Johnson, Mrs. Siddons, and others; and in printed books, a perfect copy of Cromwell's Great Bible, printed by Grafton in 1539, which was bought of Mr. Fry, the well-known collector, for £100.

A sixth part of the General Catalogue of MSS. was issued, containing the Syriac, Carshunic and Mendean MSS., in number 205, which had been drawn up by Rev. R. Payne Smith, M.A., and to which several facsimiles were appended. And the eighth part, (of which a first *fasciculus* was issued in 1859), containing the Sanscrit MSS., in number 854, appeared under the editorship of Theodore Aufrecht, M.A., now Professor of Sanscrit in the University of Bonn[1].

A. D. 1865.

At the beginning of January, a sale was held in London by Messrs. Sotheby and Wilkinson, of the stock of the late Mr. William Henry Elkins, a bookseller, of 41, Lombard Street. At this sale, the Library was the fortunate purchaser of what appears to be a genuine Shakespeare autograph. The book is Ovid's *Metamorphoses*, printed by Aldus, at Venice, in October, 1502, in octavo; and on the title is the signature 'W^{m}. Sh^{e}:', or perhaps 'Sh$^{e\tilde{r}}$:', in a hand bearing no resemblance whatever to that of the Ireland forgeries, but not unlike that of the signature attached to Shakespeare's will. Opposite to the title, on a leaf pasted down on the original binding of the book, is this note, most certainly a genuine memorandum of the date to which it professedly belongs:—'This little Booke of Ovid was giuen to me by W Hall who sayd it was once Will Shaksperes. T N 1682.' That the note itself is no forgery is admitted by all who have examined it; the volume, therefore, is certainly, by tradition, one which belonged to the poet. The only question is, whether the signature may not have been forged in consequence of the existence of this note. To this, which is the opinion of some, it may fairly be replied, that, seeing no contracted form of Shakespeare's signature is known to exist, a forger would hardly have invented one for the occasion, but would have given the name in full; while, on the other hand, if the signature be real, what more natural than that a subsequent owner should record the tradition that the indefinite 'Sh^{e}.' of this unimportant title-page was no other than the very definite 'Shakspere' himself? The name mentioned in the note is a name, as every one knows, connected with the poet's history. *Hall* was the marriage name of his daughter Susannah, to whom he left his house in Henley Street; and one William Hall, a

[1] The catalogue of a further portion of the Oriental MSS., viz. the Persian, has been completed in the present year, 1889, by Dr. H. Ethé.

glover, appears from the Stratford Records printed by Mr. Halliwell-Phillipps, to have had a house in that street in 1660, and also, from another entry discovered in 1869 by that gentleman, to have been still living there in 1684. He, doubtless, was the donor of the volume. Susannah Hall's daughter, Elizabeth, was married to a Thomas Nash, who died in 1647; but though he died without issue, the initials 'T. N.' may well stand for some member of the family who bore the same names. That, therefore, a Hall should possess the book, and subsequently give it to, very possibly, a Nash, goes far to establish its genuineness as a Shakespeare relic[1]. In a full account of the volume, supporting its pretensions, which appeared in the *Athenæum* for Jan. 28, 1865 (p. 126), it was pointed out that the two references to the story of Baucis and Philemon which are found in Shakespeare's Plays show that he was not unacquainted with the *Metamorphoses*. To this may be added a better proof of his knowledge of Ovid's writings in the fact that two lines from the *Amores* (I. xv. 35, 36) form the motto to the *Venus and Adonis*. As the volume is somewhat dirty, and has a well-worn air, it may possibly have been used by Shakespeare during those school-keeping experiences of which Aubrey tells us; possibly, however, the wear and tear may be due to an older owner, who has plentifully interspersed his MS. notes in, apparently, a foreign hand, on many of the pages. Owing to a generally-entertained suspicion throughout the auction-room on the occasion of the sale of the volume that the autograph must be a forgery, the Library became its possessor for the small sum of £9! An article by Dr. F. A. Leo maintaining the genuineness of the book as being 'Shakespeare's Ovid,' is printed pp. 367–375, vol. xvi. of the Berlin *Jahrbücher der Shakespeare-Gesellschaft*, 1880, accompanied by photographs of the fly-leaf, of the

[1] Mr. W. Salt Brassington has found in the Library of the Grammar School at Birmingham, which was founded by Thomas Hall, of King's Norton, Warwickshire, a copy of Camden's *Britannia*, 1590, stamped on the cover with the initials 'W. S.' A conjectural inference at once suggests itself as a bare possibility.

title-page, and of p. 47 of the book, which contains some small MS. notes [1].

A small volume, containing several papers in the handwriting of Luther, was bought for £45. The first edition of Coverdale's New Testament, printed at Antwerp, by Matthew Crom, in 1538, was added to the Biblical collection. Two interesting and important series of newspapers were obtained; the one, a set (not quite perfect) of the *London Gazette*, from 1669 to 1859, bought for £200 [2]; and the other, a collection of London newspapers, from 1672 to 1737, arranged in chronological order in ninety volumes, obtained also for £200. This very curious collection had been formed by Mr. John Nichols; its escape from destruction by the disastrous fire at his printing-office in 1808, is mentioned at p. 99 of the *Gentleman's Magazine* for that year. It is accompanied by a MS. index, drawn up by Mr. Nichols himself. Many unknown contributions by Defoe to the journals of his time, have been traced in this series by the biographer of Defoe, Mr. W. Lee.

Considerable assistance in completing the Library sets of the Public and Private Acts of Parliament was afforded in this year by the late Mr. W. Salt.

Specimens of the first books printed in the Dyak language, which were issued at Singapore in 1862, were given by the late Rev. J. Rigaud, B.D., of Magdalen College.

On the appointment of Dr. Jacobson to the see of Chester, Mr. R. Payne Smith became his successor in the office of Regius Professor of Divinity. Professor Max Müller, M.A., was thereupon nominated to take Mr. Smith's place as the Sub-librarian in special charge of the Oriental department, and the nomination was confirmed in Convocation on Nov. 7.

[1] The purchase of the book, as of a relic 'which there is little doubt is genuine,' was noticed in an article on Books and Book-collecting in the *Cornhill Magazine* for Oct. 1867, p. 496.

[2] The only portions of the *London Gazette* previously to be found in the Library were of the reign of Charles II; and these only came by the transfer of the Ashmolean Library.

A.D. 1866.

There is not much to notice under this year, save that the *Vulgaria quedam abs Terencio in Anglicam linguam traducta*, printed at Oxford before 1483, was obtained, in a volume containing also two tracts printed by J. de Westphalia, at the sale of the library of Mr. Thomas Thomson, of Edinburgh, for £36. Although complete in itself, it must have formed a part of a larger work, as the signatures run from *n* to *q*, in eights; and most probably that larger work was John Anwykyll's *Compendium totius Grammaticæ*.

A.D. 1867.

This year (the closing year of the first edition of these *Annals*) was distinguished by the acquisition of a volume described by Archdeacon Cotton, in his *Typographical Gazetteer*, as being 'of the very highest rarity.' It is a fine copy of the *Breviarium Illerdense*, printed at Lerida, in Spain, in 1479, by Henry Botel. Besides being remarkable from its rarity, there is special interest attaching to the volume from the fact that it was printed at the sole expense of the bell-ringer of the cathedral! The colophon states that 'Antonius Palares, campanarum ejusdem ecclesiæ pulsator, propriis expensis fieri fecit.' The volume was bought from Mr. Boone for £36.

A somewhat imperfect copy of the rare Bible printed at Edinburgh by Arbuthnot and Bassandyne in 1579, being the first edition printed in Scotland, was another purchase of the year; as were also two thick volumes of recent transcripts of the Stuart correspondence preserved in the Imperial Library at Paris, chiefly consisting of the letters of Q. Mary of Modena. These are now being printed for the Roxburghe Club under the editorship of Falconer Madan, M.A.

Within the last few years preceding 1867 considerable attention had been paid by the Librarian to the formation of a series of editions of the English Bible. The number collected by the end of 1870 was very large, and approached very nearly to a complete gathering of every edition before 1800 which has any claim to regard either from date, imprint, variety of size, correctness, or incorrectness. In 1869 £82 10*s.* were paid to Mr. Fry for a copy of Cranmer's Bible of 1541. Early Quaker tracts had been largely collected, together with editions of Cotton Mather's works and of John Bunyan, some of the early editions of whose works were also acquired in 1869.

A portrait of the Prince of Wales, in academic dress, painted by Sir J. Watson Gordon, was presented towards the close of the year to the University by the Prince, in memory of his undergraduate days, and now hangs conspicuously at the entrance of the Picture Gallery.

Prof. Max Müller having resigned his Sub-librarianship on account of health, the Rev. J. W. Nutt, M.A., Fellow of All Souls' College, was approved by Convocation, on June 25, as his successor in the charge of the Oriental department.

The number of printed *volumes* in the Library in 1867 was estimated at nearly 350,000. It was returned to Parliament in 1848 as being then about 220,000; and with a view to that return a calculation as nearly accurate as possible was then made. In 1867 an estimate was made of the additions received since 1848; and it appeared that some 79,500 additional volumes had been placed in the old Library and 45,000 in the *Camera Radcliviana*, making a total for the whole collection of about 345,000 volumes. Within the same period about 5000 additional manuscripts had been obtained, making a total of nearly 25,000. The number was returned in 1848 as being about 21,000, but this seems to have been somewhat in excess of the fact. The proportion was singularly over-estimated in 1819, for Clarke, in his *Repertorium Bibliographicum* published in that year (p. 68), states that the Library contained upwards of 160,000 volumes, of which 30,000 were manuscripts!

A.D. 1868.

Three folio volumes of treatises in Canon and Civil Law, printed between 1502 and 1511, were given by Rev. David Royce, M.A., Vicar of Nether Swell, Gloucestershire, to which a very curious history attaches, of a kind which would have seemed almost impossible to have become a history in the latter half of this century. On the death of the owner of a certain old estate, it was thought wise by heirs or executors to destroy *en masse* certain old writings, books, and papers, which they could not read or understand, and which they were unwilling should pass into other hands, as they themselves did not know what their contents might be. So these wise men of Gotham made a fire, and condemned the books to be burned. But the soul of the village cobbler was moved, for he saw that vellum might be more useful as material for cutting out patterns of shapely shoes and as padding than as fuel; and so he hurried to the place of execution, and prayed that he might have a cart-full from the heap; and his prayer was granted. Some time after, Mr. Royce heard of what had occurred, and by his means the cobbler was 'interviewed,' and all that was left of the precious load was obtained from him. And among vellum fragments were the three above-mentioned books on paper, perfect copies, books which the Bodleian did not possess. And by the gift of my old friend who was the means of their rescue, I have myself some fragments of a fine early 13th century MS. of one of St. Augustine's treatises, cut and marked for the measure of some rustic foot. That a remnant of an old monastic library perished on this occasion, there is only too much reason to fear.

A grant of £360 was made by Convocation in January for the purchase of some supposed Samaritan MSS., but the purchase was not completed, for it was found on examination by the late Mr. George Waring, M.A., of Magd. Hall, that the MSS. were really only Arabic texts written in Samaritan characters. They were subsequently purchased by Lord Crawford.

Another Samaritan MS., a copy of the Pentateuch, which went by the name of 'the fire-tried MS.,' was offered for the modest sum of £500, but the offer was declined. A legend which gave it its name reported that it had been once cast into the flames and had been miraculously preserved. It is now at St. Petersburg. A fine thirteenth-century MS. of a part of the Talmud, with a commentary, which had been brought from Poland, was bought for £25.

A rare Quaker book, written by one Caleb Pusey, in opposition to George Keith, entitled *Proteus Ecclesiasticus*, which was printed at Philadelphia, by Raynier Jansen [in 1703], was bought for £12 12*s*.

A.D. 1869.

A fragment of a Samaritan Targum, containing part of the books of Leviticus and Numbers, was bought, together with two Hebrew MSS. of prayers, for £200. It is believed to be the oldest (*i.e.* earlier than the thirteenth century) of the known copies. It was edited in 1874 (with an introduction on Samaritan history and literature) by Rev. J. W. Nutt, M.A., then Sub-librarian.

A.D. 1870.

A collection of 74 Arabic works, printed at the Egyptian government press at Boulak in Cairo, was given by the Khedive of Egypt, Ismail Pasha, through his son Prince Hassan, who was then an undergraduate at Oxford. A list of them is given in the printed List of Donations for this year.

A MS. of H. Purcell's Songs and Hymns was purchased at a sale at Puttick and Simpson's for £7 10*s*., and the original MS. of Dr. Crotch's grand Oratorio *Palestine* for the very small sum of £3 5*s*.

A.D. 1871.

Three volumes of Thomas Delafield's MSS. Collections for Oxfordshire were given by Mr. L. L. Hartley, of Southampton. The writer, an industrious local antiquary, was born of poor parents in the parish of Haseley in 1690, and became vicar of Great Milton in the same county, and afterwards master of Stokenchurch School. He is supposed to have died about 1760, but, strange to say, no record of death or burial has been found at either of the above-named places. His large collections for the parish of Haseley were already in the Library in the Gough Collection, having been bought by Gough at the sale of the library of a Mr. Cooper of Henley[1].

A.D. 1872.

A collection of original letters almost entirely of the time of Q. Eliz. and James I, in number about 500, was given by Hon. G. M. Fortescue, of Boconnoc, Cornwall, and Dropmore, Bucks. They include letters from James I, Q. Elizabeth of Bohemia, Bacon, Buckingham, Bishop Williams, and many others of the leading men of the period. A calendar of them is given at pp. 49–62 of the Second Report of the Historical MSS. Commission, printed in 1871.

A.D. 1873.

Important alterations were made in the Library Statutes by a revision which was finally accepted by Convocation on 14 June, which increased the stipend of the Head Librarian from £700 to £1000, and those of the Sub-librarians from £300 to £400, increasing also the scale of retiring pensions for them. But the holding any cure of souls was altogether forbidden in the case of these three officers should they be in Holy Orders (*see under* 1862). A special provision was, however, made on 26 June in favour of Mr. Coxe, by which he was allowed to retain his rectory of Wytham while receiving the augmentation of salary. It was also enacted that the Curators should have power to lend ('*mutuari*') books, printed and MSS., both to members of the University and to others. A wider license for borrowing was proposed by many,

[1] Brewer's *Beauties of Engl. and Wales*, vol. xii. Oxf. p. 366.

but happily was rejected on a division in Congregation on May 20 by 43 to 35. In 1886, however, attention was called to the dangers attending the practice of lending books, and to its questionable legality, in a series of criticisms upon this statute by the late Prof. H. W. Chandler, M.A., of Pembroke College, one of the Curators; and the final result was that all power of lending books of any kind, except in such few cases as might be sanctioned by a special vote of Convocation, was abolished (by vote, on 31 May, of 106 to 60) by a statute which finally passed Congregation on 25 Oct., and Convocation on 10 Nov., 1887. In saying that I heartily rejoiced at this termination of the controversy, I am only expressing the opinion on the subject of book-lending which I had formed many years previously. A subsequent proposal to authorize the lending books to certain professors in University institutions, which was strongly opposed by Mr. Falconer Madan in a pamphlet circulated among the members of Congregation, was rejected by the decisive majority of 126 to 37 on 8 May, 1888.

One other provision of the statute passed in 1873 was, that on occurrence of a vacancy the Librarian should always be elected in full Term.

At Michaelmas a well-known face, and a face welcomed wherever it was seen, was lost from the Library by the resignation of Rev. A. Hackman, who had been engaged in it altogether for thirty-six years, during eleven of which he had been a Sub-librarian. Paralysis had attacked his limbs, not by a sudden stroke but by gradual failure of power; and for some little time previous to his resignation he had been brought to the Library in a wheel-chair, and then assisted up the stairs to his old place. Together with his office here he resigned also the incumbency of St. Paul's parish and his chaplaincy at Ch. Ch., and retired to a brother's house in Middlesex, where he died on 18 Sept. 1874, aged only 63, having been born on 8 Apr. 1811. He was brought to the cemetery attached to his old parish in Oxford for burial[1]. In his place Adolf Neubauer,

[1] I add here in a note some reminiscences of Mr. Hackman which are not concerned with his Library work. His earnest, stirring, pulpit-addresses,

Ph.D. of Leipsic, who had long been engaged in the Oriental department of the Library, was nominated by Mr. Coxe, and the nomination was approved in Convocation on 30 Oct. He had been created M.A. by diploma, 18 Feb. in this year.

Sir Frederic Madden, Keeper of the MSS. in the British Museum, who died 8 March in this year, bequeathed to the Bodleian his journals, with other private papers, on condition that the box in which they were and are securely enclosed shall not be opened until 1 Jan. 1920. It may well be inferred from this that much of contemporary gossip, of literary controversy, and probably of personal matter relative to the Museum, lies hidden here until all who lived in Sir F. Madden's time shall have departed.

Various Aristotelian volumes from the library of George Grote, with MS. notes by him, were given in this year and in 1875 by his widow. And seventeen volumes of lithographed transcripts of the Irish Brehon Laws, which had been made by Dr. O'Donovan and Prof. O'Curry for the Brehon Law Commission, were presented by Dr. Graves, Bishop of Limerick, who had been Secretary to the Commission.

and the life and spirit which (aided by like-minded curates) he threw into the services at his church, have never been forgotten by those to whom they were known. While I was an undergraduate I frequently hurried away from the Sunday dinner in Hall to reach St. Paul's Church, and thereby supplement the beautiful and stately services of Magdalen Chapel with the hearty worship of a crowded parish congregation, all moved by the energy of one who to natural power in speech added oratorical movement and gesticulation, to which he had become habituated by early education in France. And like spirit and vivacity marked also all his intercourse with friends; a story from his lips became a marvel of laughter-moving mirth, while kindliness of heart and most self-forgetting charity characterized alike his words and deeds.

During all the time of his service in the Library he had used as a cushion in his plain wooden arm-chair a certain vellum-bound folio, which by its indented side, worn down by continual pressure, bore testimony to the use to which it had been put. No one had ever had the curiosity to examine what the book might be; but when after Hackman's departure from the Library it was removed from its resting-place of years, some amusement was caused by finding that the chief compiler of the last printed Catalogue had omitted from his Catalogue the volume on which he sat, of which too, although of no special value, there was no other copy in the Library!

A.D. 1874.

A collection of circular letters, written in the name of the University, to many great personages soliciting help in money towards the building of the Schools' quadrangle, was given by Mr. Jos. Mullings of Cirencester. The letters are of the years 1611–1613, and contain the request that any sums contributed may be paid over to Sir John Bennet. These are accompanied by a few letters subsequent to his fall and bankruptcy, up to the year 1626 (including the petition to the King noticed *supra* under the year 1613); and there are also a few earlier academic letters in 1575–6, which appear to be in the handwriting of Bodley himself, who was then acting as Public Orator. The whole collection is very curious and interesting. It is now included in the volume marked Bodl. MS. Add. C. 206. The same donor gave also in the year 1879, three letters written by Alb. Gentilis from Oxford in 1603.

Mr. Frederick Morrell, of Oxford, gave a valuable set of the Oxford Journal newspaper for 110 years, from 1762 to 1873.

A spotless copy of the 'Somme rurale' (a *Summa* of French law), printed at Bruges by Colard Mansion in 1479, was purchased of Mr. B. Quaritch for £210. It is in most perfect condition, fresh and clear as when it issued from the printer's press. Of Mansion's types the Library previously possessed only specimens in two small fragments.

A.D. 1875.

The Lancashire collections were increased by the gift of seventeen manuscript volumes compiled by the Rev. John Watson, M.A., of Brasenose College, who died in Jan. 1875. They were presented, in accordance with what was known to have been his wish, through his sister, Mrs. George Robinson.

Capt. (now Sir Charles) Warren presented to the Numismatic room upwards of 700 Eastern coins, to which in the following year he added others, collected during his surveying operations in the Holy Land[1].

A.D. 1876.

The books relative to the Anglo-Saxon language and literature which were in the library of the late Anglo-Saxon Professor, Rev. J. Bosworth, D.D. (who died 27 May, in this year, aged 87), were given by his executors. Professor Edwin Palmer (now Archdeacon of Oxford) gave some volumes of Priestley's works with MSS. notes by Bishop Horsley.

A portrait of Mr. Coxe was painted by Mr. G. F. Watts, R.A., at the desire of a committee of subscribers, and was hung in the Library in the following year among the series of portraits of Librarians. It is a very excellent likeness, a half-length, and represents Mr. Coxe in his M.A. gown and hood. The Picture Gallery also in this year received another subscription-portrait by the same artist; that of Will. Schomberg Rob. Kerr, the eighth Marquess of Lothian, who died 4 July, 1870, in memory of whom and of his foundation in 1870 of the annual Historical Prize Essay which goes by his name, this portrait was painted.

A.D. 1877.

The Library purchased from me for £15 a very interesting Chatterton volume. It is a copy of Alexander Catcott's book on the Deluge, in two parts, 1756–68, which he had no doubt himself given to the young poet, for several fly-leaves at each end of the volume are filled with poems (of which all but a few lines are included in the printed editions) in Chatterton's handwriting. The book is now exhibited in the glass-case containing autographs at the entrance of the Reading-room. The story of my acquisition of the book, without then being aware of its interest, together with several other tattered volumes, in a little village public-house at Clifton

[1] In 1888 Sir Charles made further additions to his gift, of a similar kind.

Hampden, Oxfordshire, where they were all on the highway to destruction as pipe-lights, was related by me in *Notes and Queries* for 4 Sept., 1858, p. 182.

A collection of sixteen breviaries, exhibiting the uses of as many dioceses in France, Spain, &c., was given by Hon. and Rev. Stephen Lawley. And a copy of the Complutensian Polyglott, with a painting therein which represents Cardinal Ximenes in conference with two others upon the work, by Mrs. Marianna Phillipps.

The Chinese collection was increased by a considerable gift from Gen. L. Shadwell.

The old *Linc.* and *Jur.* galleries were removed from the central portion of the great room, because it was thought that the walls were becoming unequal to bear the weight. But it was then found that the walls had not yielded in the least since the time of their being repaired and strengthened under the direction of Sir Christopher Wren, in 1701–3 (*see* p. 169), when accurate measurements were taken. The removal of the well-lined shelves has made the walls look very bare to those who were familiar with their former aspect; while unfortunately a very large portion of the books which have consequently been transferred to a distant region are books of frequent use and reference. At the same time a new floor was laid in part of the room, raised away from the roof of the Divinity School on which the previous floor had rested, and which it was feared was cracking and giving way. The roof was repaired, and a new west window inserted, in this and the following year.

A.D. 1878.

The oldest portion of the records of the Archdeacon's Court at Oxford was transferred by the Registrar, Mr. Gorden Dayman, with the sanction of Archdeacon Palmer, to the Library, on the occasion of the removal of the Registry to a new office. A very valuable mass of material for local history and of information for genealogical enquirers within the counties of Oxford and Berks, was thus made accessible which was previously for all practical purposes lost. The papers include Proceedings in the Archidiaconal Court from the time of Q. Elizabeth, Marriage Bonds, copies of Registers of Parishes which were Peculiars, and Visitation Returns. They have since the transfer been arranged and bound. It was through the instrumentality of Mr. W. H. Turner, who had frequently been engaged at the Registry in assisting to arrange the records there preserved, that the removal was effected.

In this year a *Calendar of Charters and Rolls preserved in the Bodleian Library*, was published in an octavo volume containing (with the index) 849 pages. It was compiled by the above-mentioned Mr. Will. Henry Turner, and comprises a very large number of deeds from the collections of Ant. à Wood (formerly in the Ashmolean), Dodsworth, Tanner, Rawlinson, Gough, and others. The places to which they relate are arranged, in general, in alphabetical order under their several counties. The compiler entered the Library in the year 1870, after having gained some acquaintance with ancient documents by previous work among the records of the City of Oxford [1], among parochial and diocesan documents, and in ecclesiastical registries. He had previously been in business as a chemist and druggist, but gave up this avocation for one more in accordance with his liking, for which he prepared himself entirely as a self-taught man, with little knowledge of Latin beyond such as is found in mediæval records. His index to a portion of the Dodsworth MSS. is noticed under the year 1673. He was often engaged in researches in London and elsewhere as a record agent, and in the year 1871 edited *The Visitations of the County of Oxford* for the Harleian Society. Of this some copies were destroyed by a fire, and the volume is therefore the scarcest among the publications of that Society. His useful and persevering labours, in which he did good service, came to an early close. He died, after a lingering and painful illness, in June, 1880, aged 47.

[1] From these he published a volume of Selections, extending from 1509 to 1583, under the authority of the Corporation, in 1880.

A MS. of the fifth book of Hooker's *Ecclesiastical Polity*, containing the autograph of Archbishop Whitgift, was bought in December for £15, from a widow lady, Mrs. M. Morison, in Oxford, in the possession of whose family it had been for some time. It was collated for the seventh edition of Hooker's great work which was published in 1888, under the editorship of Dr. Church, Dean of St. Paul's, and Professor Francis Paget, who have given a facsimile of the first page.

Catalogue of the Rawlinson MSS., vol. ii. See p. 241.

A.D. 1879.

A portrait of Dr. Arthur Penrhyn Stanley, Dean of Westminster, was given by him, which had been painted by Mr. G. F. Watts. It is now in the Picture Gallery.

On July 5, the appointment of Ingram Bywater, M.A., Fellow of Exeter College, as Sub-librarian *vice* J. W. Nutt, was approved by Convocation. Mr. Nutt vacated his office at Michaelmas on accepting from his college the rectory of Harrietsham, Kent.

A.D. 1880.

Dr. Jacobson, Bishop of Chester (who died 12 July, 1884), gave a volume containing four interesting papers relative to the Book of Common Prayer and to proposals for comprehension. The first consists of suggestions for alterations in the Prayer Book, by Bishop Matthew Wren[1]. This was printed by Bishop Jacobson in 1874 in *Fragmentary Illustrations of the Book of C. Prayer.* The next is an anonymous French tract, and a translation (both in English handwriting), *Avis demandé à un théologien par delà la mer sur les articles de la comprehension*, namely, the comprehension attempted between the Church of England and the Nonconformists in the reign of William III. On this follows a copy of a tract on the same subject by Fred. Spanheim, *Comprehensionis Anglicanæ momentum, obices, ad eam motiva.* And lastly,

[1] Not Bp. *Ken*, as unfortunately misprinted in the annual List of Donations.

there is *An essay on the Liturgy for the rendering of it more plain and acceptable to many people*, to which an old annotator has affixed this note, 'by Dr. Tillotson, as I believe.' The volume was given to Bishop Jacobson on Dec. 11, 1859, by Dr. W. K. Hamilton, Bishop of Salisbury, to whose father it had been given by Dr. Rich. Terrick, who was Bishop of London in 1764-77.

Mr. Bywater resigned his office of Sub-librarian before he had held it for one year, and Falconer Madan, M.A., Fellow of Brasenose College, was approved by Convocation as his successor on 15 June.

A.D. 1881.

I end my record of four centuries of the existence of the University Library, (when I myself have in this year, 1889, lived and laboured with a glad labour therein for one-eighth of that period, in which time I have seen the Library more than doubled,) with the simple note that on July 8, 1881, Mr. Coxe, who had for a long time previously been gradually giving way to a painful disease, departed this life at the age of 69. Of his work in the Library I gave, by request, a sketch to the Library Association (of which he had been the first president, when its first meeting was held in Oxford in 1878) in a paper which was printed in 1884 in the Report of that Society's Fourth Annual Meeting held in 1881, pp. 15-17. And in the second volume of the late Dean Burgon's recently published *Lives of Twelve Good Men* Mr. Coxe's life is fully told by one who was an intimate friend, in a narrative which is an enlargement of an article contributed to the *Guardian* newspaper on 3 Aug. 1881.

From the year 1882 to 1887 the history of the Library is related by Mr. Coxe's successor, with minute details, in a *Report* to the Curators which was issued in Dec. 1888, and which fills sixty-six pages in quarto. Here, therefore, these *Annals* end. But from this *Report* (which will be annually continued) I quote the number of volumes which were found to be in the Library in Jan. 1885, when by desire of the Curators a calculation was made. The total number then 'was 432,477, of which 26,318 were MS., and 406,159 printed.' And the growth in the last forty years may approximately be represented as follows :—

	1848.	1868.	1888.
Printed *Volumes.*	220,000.	350,000.	440,000.

The annual rate of increase of *bound* printed volumes may now, it seems, be roughly estimated at 10,000, excluding all periodicals, &c.; of this number half may be reckoned as coming from Stationers' Hall. In 1867 the number was supposed to be about 3000.

APPENDIX

APPENDIX.

I.

John Leland's List of MSS.,

Noted by him as being in Duke Humphrey's Library at Oxford, c. 1534–40.

[*Collectanea*, vol. iii. pp. 58–59.]

Cf. list mentioned at p. 7, *supra.*

'*Oxoniæ in bibliotheca publica.*

Chilwardbe [Kilwardby] super 8 partes orationis. *Quoniam studium Gram.*

Epistolæ Hereberti [de Bosham], secretarii Thomæ martyris.

Bacon de cælo et mundo; cujus primi quaterniones excisi.

Summa philosophiæ Roberti Lincolniensis. *Philosophantes famosi.* Leyland: In quo libro tractat de formis, de luce, de coloribus, de iride, de cometis, de utilitate liberalium artium.

Compendium Scientiarum, eodem autore. Sed liber excisus.

Panegyrica oratio Porphyrii ad Constantinum; furto sublata.

Eulogium historiarum Angliæ.

Hampole super Psalterium.

Granarium, ingens volumen, Joannis de loco frumenti, Whethamsted, abbatis S. Albani, ad Humfredum, ducem Glocestriæ, de viris illustribus [1].'

[Leland here adds a few short extracts which he made 'ex Granario ejusdem.']

'Radulphus [de Dunstaple] est (si recte memini) ibidem, qui vitam scripsit S. Albani carmine plane docto et eleganti.

[1] Of this book Leland says, in his Lives of English Writers, 'archetypus bibliothecam propter Isidis Vadum Hunfridinam nunc incolit.' Tanner, *Bibl. Brit.* sub nom. *Joannes Frumentarius.*

Humfredus multoties scripsit in frontispiciis librorum suorum, *Moun bien moundain.*

Humfredus, dux Glocestriæ, multos codices, pulcherrime pictos, ab abbatibus dono accepit.

Apuleius de asino aureo; sublatus.

Flavius de re militari; excisus.

Claudianus, poeta.

Tragœdiæ Senecæ.

Commentarii Joannis de Serauala, episcopi Firmani, ordinis Minorum, Latine scripti, super opera Dantis Aligerii, ad Nicolaum Bubwice, Bathon. et Wellensem episcopum, et D. Robertum Halam, episcopum Sarisbur. Commentarii editi sunt tempore Constantiensis concilii.

Metamorphosis Ovidii, Gallice.

Cato Censorius; sublatus.

Opera Ciceronis.

Epistolæ Nicolai de Clamenge, cantoris Baiocensis, ad Carolum 6 Franc. regem.

Duodecim libri epistolarum Petri Candidi; sublati.

Aphorismi Damasceni.

Concordantiæ librorum Senecæ.

[Rob.] Cary super libros Posteriorum.

Epistola Lincoln. de formis, ad magistrum Adamum.

Idem de luce, de coloribus, de utilitate artium liberalium, de iride, de cometis.

Compendium Scientiarum ejusdem.

Joannes canonicus ordinis Minorum super libr. Physicorum.

Tabula [Ric.] Byllingham, justum volumen.

Algazel de Logicalibus.

Gundesalvius de anima.

Commentarii Reyneri de S. Trudo in libr. Boetii de consolatione philosophiæ.

Autosichus [*l.* Autolychus] de sphæra mota.

Esculeus de ascensionibus.

Jordanus de triangulis.'

One of the MSS. given, or intended to be given, by Tiptoft, Earl of Worcester (*see* p. 11) has very recently been found by the present Librarian among Selden's MSS. Arch. Seld. B. 50 is a fifteenth-century MS. in small folio, beautifully written by an Italian hand, of a Commentary on Juvenal. And in small red letters on a fly-leaf is written by a late hand in the same century, 'Liber hic pertinet ad Universitatem Oxon. ut cathinetur in bibliotheca.' On the lower margin of the first page is Tiptoft's coat of arms; quarterly, 1 and 3 argent, a saltire engrailed, sable, 2 and 4, or, a lion rampant, gules; and by a hand of the seventeenth century this note is attached:—'Ex his insignibus gentilitiis constat hunc librum ad Joannem Tiptoft, Wigorniæ comitem, spectasse, qui Italiæ bibliothecas diligenter lustravit, et plures libros describi curavit, et hunc bibliothecæ Oxon. donavit, ut videre est prima hujus libri pagina.' Tiptoft was beheaded 18 Oct. 1470.

II.

a. THE LAST WILL AND TESTAMENT OF SIR THO. BODLEY, KNIGHT.

[*Contemporaneous copy, Bodl. MS. Addit.* A. 186[1].]

In the name of God Amen. I Tho: Bodley of London knight being now of the age of threescore and seauen complete & more, in good disposition of memorie, though weakely affected in my health, calling to minde, y^t as death is very cirtayne, to all lyving creatures, soe the houer thereof is so vncertay̅e that I ought to be p'pared to imbrace it euery moment, in regard of my desire to geue good contentation to my kindred & freinds of the Epilogue & end of all my Actions in my life, doe therevpon make & declare my last will and Testament in manner & forme ensueinge. First I Cōmend my soule to the hande of God ye Father my Creator & maker and to his sonne Jesus Christ, my onely Sauiour & redeemer, by whose death & passion & by no other meanes, I doe stidfastly beleeve that haueing finished this course of mortalitie on Earth I shall after lyue wth him in eternall felicitie. Secondlye for my Bodye, wheresoe^r it shall please God to call me, It is my will & desire to haue it p'sently transported to Merton Coll. in Oxō, ye place of my first education in learning, there to be inteired in to ye Coll: Church as I may ꝑhapps in some poynts expresse hereafter in what manner. And touching that portion wch I must leaue behinde of those worldly blessings wth the wch God of his goodnes either hath alreadie, or shall hereafter endow me, as also of all this my last Will & Testament, I doe appoynt and constitute my Executors, my most deare and worthi freinde Sr John Bennet knight Judge of the Prerogatiue Court, & my singular good cousin M^r. Williã: Hackwell of Lincolnes Inne Counsailo^r, of whome I doe hartely request y^t they will accept of that little token of my louing affection wch I shall geue vnto them, & see those Legacies deliuered wch I shall giue to others, obseruing all ye limitations considerations & conditions, y^t I shall either specifie by this my last will in writing or hereafter by way of Appendix or Codicill

[1] Another copy is to be found in the Register of Convocation, K. ff. 108–115. That volume contains also the original Statutes, the Ordinance of the Stationers' Company in 1612, and the Accounts for 1614.

adde herevnto, w^ch^ [my] finall entent & purpose is, shall stande in as ample force & strengthe, as yf the sãe were fully comp'hended and expressly here sett-downe in this my last Will & Testament. And here first of all I doe geue & bequeath to my well beloued brother Laurence Bodley (whome onely in regard of his vnwillingnes to [be] combred wth worldly cares, I doe not make as I intended my Executo^r^) my little gould ring, wch hath in it the armes of o^r^ Familie engrauen in a blewe Saphire, wth two hundred pounds in mōy, also my basin & ewre dowble guylt, my little watch wch Michael Nowen made me sūme sixteene yeares past, & my little blacke ebeney houre glasse, besids ten pounds worthe of any of my household stuffe whereof he shall himselfe make choyce. I doe likewise conferre vpon him my yearely rents & estates of those two leases wch I haue lately graunted, one to John Carre Inholder at the signe of ye Angel wth out temple barre yeeldinge sixtie pounds yeerly, and another to one Henry Smith of Westmester yeelding by the yeare thirtie pounds cleare, of wch two leases, if it stand wth his good liking, my desire is & I would Intreate him y^t^ after his decease, ye residue of ye termes of yeeres of ye said leases may remayne to my Nevewes John and Laure: Bodley, sonnes to my late deceased brother Miles Bod:, wherein I leaue it to his discretion, to whether of the two he will geue the one or the other lease, or otherwise to reserue the one or both for his owne proper vses, bestowing vpon them as much or as little, as by there honest behavio^r^ & vertuous course of lyfe he shall finde thē worthy to enioye. And to each of my other two Nepheues Tho: and Miles Bodley I doe bequeath fortie pounds apiece in money to be deliuered vnto them at such time or times as my said broth^r^ Laurence shall thinke meete, into whose hand I would pray my foresaid Executo^rs^ to leaue ye custodie of the sãe in there behalfes.

Moreouer, I doe geue & bequeath to my said Nephew Laurence Bodley those two books of mine y^t^ I shall leaue & thirtie pounds in money for his p'sent better maintenance in studie after my departure, nothing doubting but that my said brother Lau: will take such further care y^t^ he shall not wante whatsoe^r^ shall be requisite to beare ye charges after of his continuall ꝓceeding in learning in ye vniv^r^sitie. I doe further geue to my brother Sr Josias Bodley ye sūme of one hundred pounds in money together wth the state & terme of yeares wch I holde of cirtaine tenements in the blacke ffryers of London, for wch one Jeames Trauis & Edmond his brother doe yeeld an annuall rēt of fiftie pounds, And wth all I doe remit & forgeue him whatsoe^r^ sum̄e or sum̄es of money he doth owe me at this ꝑsent.

To my sister Prothasy Sparry I doe giue a standing cuppe of Syluer dowble guylt to the valeu of xx markes in money & to euery one of her children a guylt siluer bole of x pounds price, bequeathing further to her sonne Williã Bogan ye best of my rapiers & daggers y^{t} he or his assignes shall choose. To Wiƚƚ: Helãn and Tho: his Brother sonnes to my late deceased sister Alce Carter (yf there conue^{r}sation & course of life be pleasing to my Nephew & thire brother in lawe M^{r} Wiƚƚ: Tue) I doe bequeath xx^{li} apeice & as much to there sister Marie, to be deliuered vnto thẽ when they come to ye age of [one] & twentie yeares. To eache of the children of my late brother in law Anthony Culuerwell wch he had by sister Sybyll xx^{li}, to be deliuered to eache of thẽ when they shall be of the age of one & xx yeares, or at ye dayes of there mariages, in case they shall marrie wth ye allowance of my foresaid Brother Laurence yf he shall be then liuing, or of the foresaid Willã Tue, into whose hands I am also very willing y^{t} the said childrens legaces shal remaȳe, yf so be he shall giue securitie suffitient for there particular payments at their appoynted times, reseruing the meane while to his owne conscience, to conferre vpon them, what he shall thinke meete in his discretion out of the gaine, yf any be raised by his imploȳent of their portions. To Toby Willis the eldest sonne of my brother in law Miles Willis, & to his heires, I doe geue graunt & bequeath all my right title & interest to any part of his ffathers lands in or about London, or in ye Countie of Deuõ, also ten pounds in money. To my nece Elizabeth Willis Daughter to ye said Miles I doe giue & bequeath towards her aduancement in mariage Two hundred pounds in money & twentie pounds towards her furnituer wth mariage apparell & other like necessaries. To my niece Susan Tue I doe geue a Siluer bole dowble guylt to the worth of ten pounds & my greene veluet deske. To the lady Elizabeth Winwood daughter to my late deceased wife, I geue a standing cuppe of Syluer dowble guylt to ye value of xx^{li} wth my armes engrauẽ in it & to her Eldest sonne James my godson sixe pounds thirteene shillings fore pence to buy him a Taffata dublet & hose. To M^{rs}: Anne Potman wife of Mathew Potman of London Esqr. I bequeath fore hundred pounds in money togeth^{r} wth the value of ten pounds in household stuffe such as shee or he shall choose, & to each of her Children by the said Mathew ten pounds, besids other fiue pounds wch I bequeath to his sonne Tho: Potman my Godson to buy him a Taffata suite. To my foresaid wifes graundchildren, daughters to Edmond Hampdẽ of Hartwell late deceased, I doe desire to be made & geuen fower hoope rings of gold enameled of Twentie shillings price, wth my nãe engrauen in ye inside

To my seruant George Comely & Mary his wife in regard of there long & faithfull seruice, & to the end they shall alwayes assist & helpe my Executo^{rs} when neede shall require, I doe giue Twentie pounds apeice to be quarterly payed and by euen portions wthin one yeare.

To my seruants George Bodley, Isembart Christopher and Marie Hull ten pounds apeice, & to Christo: Euans, Christo: Felps, yf they shall be in my seruice at the time of my decease (wch is not otherwise ment, as touching any portion y^{t} I doe conferre upon any of my other seruants,) sixe pounds apiece. To Dorathie Cocke three pounds, to Richard my Gardener fortie shillings & to Jo: Barrowe my Cooke fortie shillings. Besids to euery one of my Seruants so much of their wages as shall be due vnto them at the time of my departure. Besids vnto Isembart Christopher I giue whether he will choose of my two blacke Dublets, & hose of flanders Serge, & my marble riding Cloake lined wth bayes: the other blacke dublet of Serge & hose, to Geo: Bodley wth a pare of blacke cloth hose paned: my two blacke Jerkins, one of frizadoe, ye other of blacke kersey wth an open lace, I leaue to be shared betweene Christo: Euans, & Christo: ffelps.

To M^{r}. Richard Litler for a smale remēbrance of my loue I geue my newest yron Chest, and my greate stone pot trimed wth Siluer dubble guylt, together wth ye case belonging to it, & to his vertuous wife my little Danske Cabbinett in my vpper studie at ffulham, yf it be not displaced, intreating him earnestly to afforde my Executo^{rs} his counsaile & aide wherein soe^{r} they shall neede it for ye gathering of my debts or otherwise. To the poore of the ꝑrish of little S^{t}. Barthelmewes ten pounds, and as much to ye poore of the ꝑrish of ffulham to be distributed in both places as my Executo^{rs} shall thinke meete. To M^{r}. John Waterhouse who hath beene a faithfull sollicito^{r} of many causes of mine, to ye end he may continew to doe the like offices for my Executo^{rs} I bequeath ten pounds, to be payed wth in one year by fiftie shillings a quarter frō the time of my decease, And for all his ymployments by my Executo^{rs}, to be further rewarded as his travell shall deserue.

Vnto eache of my foresaid Executors I doe bequeath as a signe or peece of a signe of my affectionate loue & likeing fiftie pounds wch I knowe they will esteeme according to my loue & not value my loue according to my legacie. Moreouer I doe here acquit my ancient & speciall good frinde M^{r}. Will: Gent of Glocester hall in Oxō, of whatsoe^{r} debts or sum̃es of money he doth owe me by bond bill or otherwise. And doe bequeath vnto him my best gowne & my best Cloake, & the next gowne & Cloake to my best I doe bequeath to M^{r}. Tho: Allen of the same Hall; praying them both very kindly to interp'te my meaning to be, y^{t} although they be but tryfles & needles things to them, yet fayne I would y^{t} by wearing such memorialls, they would now & then record & refresh vnto themselves ye familiaritie & nearenes y^{t} hath beene in o^{r} ffrendship. To Merton Colledg in Oxō I doe geue for the founding & making of a new Chest to y^{e}

selfe same vse as Reads Chest was aunciently instituted in y^{t} Coll: ye sum̄e of two hundred markes in money, out of wch my meaning is, y^{t} thirtie pounds sixe shillings eight pence or about y^{t} sum̄e shall be bestowed by the Warden for ye time being & the ffellows vpon sum̄e Chest or presse for ye same purpose, wth three lockes of seuerall wardes & three different keyes to the same; The residue of the two hundred Markes shall allwayes continue as a stocke in that Chest or Presse to be imployed as ye aforesaid of Read to ye like vses of ye Students in ye Colledge. Alwayes ꝓuided y^{t} vppon the receipt of the foresaid sum̄e of two hundred Markes: ye Warden & ffellowes shall enter into bond to my Executo^{rs}: to frame a newe Booke of Statuts such as [to] them in there experience shall seeme expedient for ye safe & orderly Custodie & gouerment of the said Chest & stocke & ye same to be ꝑformed wth in one halfe yeare after the payment of the foresaid sum̄e of Two hundred Markes.

And now forasmuch as the ꝑpetuall p'seruation support & maintenance of the Publique Librarie in ye Vniv^{r}sitie of Oxō dothe greatly surpasse all my other worldly cares, And because I doe foresee y^{t} in proces of time there must of necessitie be very great want of conueyance & stowage for Bookes, by reason of the endles multitude of those y^{t} are p'sent there & like hereafter to be continuall[y] bought & brought in, I doe appoynt and my will is, y^{t} yf the intended p'sent plott for buylding ye newe schooles shall ꝓseede in such sort as ye same is all readie devised by publique consent, then ouer the tops of those two stories wch are resolued to be ye hight of ye Scholles, there shall be contriued another third rome, in case it may be ꝑformed wth good conueniencye & wth ye Vniv^{r}sities approbation, to goe in compasse round about the Scholes & so meete at each end in two Lobies or passages framed wth some speciall comlines of workmanshippe to make a faire enterance into ye northe & Southe corners of my late new enlargment Estward, for there will be gayned by this means a very large supplement for stowage of Bookes when the two Libraries shall be fully replenished, wherevpon my desire is herewth to haue it vnderstood y^{t} whatsoe^{r} charge this Additament of mine shall further occasion then was requisett in respect of ye purposed ffabrique of the Scholes (alway^{s} reconing ye rofe to be a part of the said fabrique,) shall come vnder the accompt of my expence. And in y^{t} regard I doe declare & devise that my Exec^{tors}. shall sell all my freehold lands & tenements & all my Annuities leases goods chattles & estate whatsoe^{r} to ye best aduantage they can and therewth pay my debts legases & funerals. And that ye totall value of that which shall remayne of all my lands tenements, goods leases annuities rents credits chattles & moueable[s] whatsoe^{r}, my debts legaces & funerals being first discharged, shall come to & be inioyed by the said Vniv^rsitie to be wholly imployed as they se cause about ye ordering & augmenting of these Libraries, but cheifely as I haue signified about ye erecting of the aforesaid third story & then afterwards, for soe I do determine, about the raising of a faire storie case to make ye ascent more easye & gracefull to ye first great Librarie, and thirdly about the ꝑformance of some bewtifull enlargment at the west end of the said Librarie towards Exeter Coll:, to remaine still afoote as the foresaid third story till in ꝓces of time ye occasion to put them in practise shall be offered, for as I am ꝑsuaded vppon my priuate estimate of the remaynder of my lands goods & chattles & of the totall charges whereunto these buyldings will amount, there will be a sum̃e suffitient left both for the ꝑfect ꝑformance of ye said three designes & for a competent surplusage besids to be kept still in store in their publique hutche or treasurie for such future purposes as may turne hereafter, be it sooner or later, to sum̃e further bettering of ye structure state or furnituer of ye said Libraries; my meaning is moreouer that ye fore mentioned third story & the west enlargement of ye ancient Librarie, shall be onely furnished now at ye first wth all necessarie lights & boarded floores & a reseruation made of there shelues deskes seates & othe^r needefull trim̃ings to be added hereafter when time shall enforce there vse and frequenttation. Att wch time I doe not doubt but by good endeavours and Gods blessed assistance there will be meanes enoughe found to defray that expence. And my will & meaning is that all such bonds & things as I haue in the name of Geo: Comley or any others in trust shall be put into the Inventarie of my goods as ꝑcell of my Estate. Ouerseers of this my last Will and Testament I do nominate & constitute my euer assured & specill frinde Sr Henry Sauell knight together wth the Ho^bl: Sr Raphe Winwood knight now his Ma^ts: Ambassador in y^e ꝓuinces vnited, ordayning to be geuen to Sr Henry Sauell a standing salt of Syluer dowble guylt wth my armes engrauen in it to ye value of Twentie pounds, & to Sr Raphe Winwood all my armor in my Armorie in London or wheresoe^r els it may happen to be placed hereafter, not so much in regard of ye travell & paynes y^t they may take, wch I may soone vndervalue, but for a token & rem̃ebrance of o^r mutuall loue & frindship, most instantly requesting y^t they will helpe my Executo^rs in their incident occasions & so much tender y^e ꝑfor̃ance of this my last Will as for ye trust I repose in there kinde dispositions I am confident they will.

As touching my ffunerals, I haue an earnest desire y^t my body should be conuaied frō that place whersoe^r it pleaseth God to call me to Merton Coll: in Oxō, to be buried their in the Coll. Church & whatsoe^r corner my worthy freind Sr Henry Sauell now Warden, or ye Wardē and fellowes for the time being shall thinke meete, and that wthout any chargeable monument but of sum̄e kinde of playne marble such as my Executors shall best approue, and wth sum̄e Epitaph & Inscription as I may happilye my selfe leaue in writing hereafter, or shall be devised by the Warden & my Executors in case I leaue it vndone. Vpon the day of my buriall I doe allowe for a dinner to ye Warden & sociatie wth ye rest of the said Colledge one hundred pounds, ye same to be taken in ye Coll: Hall and distributed into messes as the Coll: Bowsers wth their Wardens consent shall hold expedient, wherewth all my meaning is yt ye Vicechauncellor and Procters all the Heads of Colledges & Halls wth ye Beedles, & as many as shall weare blackes being p'sent at my funeralls shall be invited. I would haue blackes bestowed vpon my Executors & ouerseers, vppon my Brother Laurence Bodley, vppon my brother Sr Josias Bodley, vpon my Sister Sparry, my Nephew Laurence Bodley, my neece Willis, all ye seruants of my ffamilie, ye Preacher at my buriall, ye Warden of Merton Coll: for the time being, & all the ffellowes of the same, together wth ye Chaplines, keeꝑ of the vnivrsitie Libr' wth his vnderkeeꝑ & the Portor, allowing every graduate amongest theis suffitient Cloth for a schollers goune & hood. To the seruants also of the Coll: & such other there officers as reside & attende continually there, I doe allow either gowens or Cloakes as ye Warden of the Coll: shall aduise, as I doe in like manner to such as happily my Executors shall thinke fitt to haue allowance, though I haue not nāed them: for myne owne seruants my meaning is yt ye charges of as many of thē as shall be p'sent & doe seruice at my funeralls, shall be wholy defrayed by my Execurs in regard of there going & com̄inge frō the place of my decease to Oxō. To as many poore Schollers as I shall be yeares old at the day of my decease I doe giue and appoynt yt day to be worne gounes of good blacke frize made to there hands, or of sum̄ thicke blacke broad Clothe yf my Executors like it better. Howbeit I would not haue ye whole expence of my dinner and funerals to exceede ye sum̄e of sixe hundred sixtie sixe pounds thirtie shillings & fore pence, yf so be wth good conueniency it may be so excused, wch is also to much in regard of selfe, but yt I accompt such a dinner and so many gownes vppon so many good frinds deseruedly bestowed.

I doe further here ordayne that the sum̄e of ten pounds shall be at the same time distributed amongest ye poorer sort of the vulgar people yt are of the Cittie of Oxō.

Lastly my will is that my blacke Iron Chest shal be put in oyel coulers (yf it be not first done by my [selfe]), and then conveied & deliuered to the Vicechauncellor of the said vnivrsitie for ye time being, wth all the writings & deeds yt concerne the Conveyance of the lands yt I gaue & assured of late vnto thē for the lasting support and maintenance of their Librarie, wch are altogether in a boxe in one of my studdies in London wth two speciall good Padlocks, wch I caused to be made of set purpose for the vse of the foresaid Chest, accordinge to yt wch I haue formerly sett downe in a drawght of Statuts sent vnto thē wherein I haue also signified in what manner their yearely revenue geuen to ye maintenance of the said Libra[rie] shall be frō time to time disposed. And whereas by the former ꝑte of this my last will I haue devised and declared that the remaynder of the totall valew of all my lands tenements annuities goods & chattles, my debts legaces & funeralls first discharged, shall be imployed as aforesaid for ye better accomplishing of my fore mentioned designes, my will and purpose wthall is, that all my lands messuages tenements & heriditaments wch I bowght of one John Wright wthout Aldgate shall be comp'hended in the aforesaid sale and turned to those vses formerly specified. And likewise my meaning is that there shall be order taken wth ye buyers of the said lands and tent̃s wth[out] Aldgate, for the yeerly and ꝑpetuall paȳent out of the rents reuenues, yssues and ꝑfitts of the same, or out of other lands sufficiently there vnto secured, ye sum̃e of fortie pounds in money to the poore People of the Cittie of Oxō, and of the Towne of Totnes in the Countie of Deuō, and yt all such ꝑsons to whome the said lands shall hereafter come, shall yeerely for euer paye the same sum̃e of fortie pounds retayning the remayne of the said rents yssues and ꝑfitts to there one vse. And that the said sum̃e of fortie pounds a yeāre shall be yeerely payd to the said poore in manner and forme following, yt is to say to the poore people of the Cittie of Oxō, fortie markes of lawfull mōey of England uppon the feast day of St Andrew the Apostle, and the feast day of Phillip and Jacob ye Apostles yearely by euen and equall portions. And to the poore people of the Towne of Totnes aforesaid Twentie markes yearely of lawfull money of England, at the same feasts by like euen portions. And vntill such sale be made by my Executors my meaning is, that they shall pay the said Annuitie of fortie pounds out of the yssues & ꝑfitts of the said lands. And this I do in ꝑformance of the last will and Testāent of Henry Ball late of Oxō, genttleman deceased, ye charge of ꝑformance of whose will I did vndertake as Administrator, for that his Executors nāed in the same refused to take vpon thē ye charge thereof. And in consideration of this annuall payment of fortie pounds a yeare, I retayned & doe retayne to my owne vse ye sum̃e of sixe hundred pounds or thereabouts being the remayne and residue of the ꝑsonall estate of ye said Henry Ball, his debts legases and funerals being fully payd and ꝑformed as by my accompt in yt behalfe appereth, wch remayne by his will devised should be imployed in purchasing one Añuall portion to be geuen to the said poore as in and by yᵉ said my will is sufficiently specified, And for that this my will I hope shall remayne registered of record, and because the statute of Charitable Uses will euer be of force to see & cause this my order to be ꝑfor̄ed, I haue rather thus satisfied yᵉ said trust by my will then by deede to any other ꝑsons in trust, wᶜʰ might be more subiect to casualtie & losse. Now because I haue sensible reasons by meanes of the qualitie and nature of my infermities, to stand in sum̄e doubt, that my dayes will not be ꝑlonged vntill such time as I may well be able to sett downe a sound & ꝑfect ꝑiect in to whoes hands the fore said two sum̄es of fortie & twentie markes shall be frō time to time deliuered & after distributed amongest yᵉ fore said poore people, I would pray my Executors to supplie my defect in that regard auctorrie [and auctorize?] sum̄e one or more ꝑsones of worthe and reputation to vndergoe yᵗ care and charge, whereunto for the p'sent I knowe not any more fitt ꝑsons then yᵉ Proctor and one or two more of the cheefest in office of Exeter Coll: in Oxō, yf they would be so pleased to take the care and charge vppon thē, allwayes provided (for such was the will & desire of the said Henry Ball) yᵗ the townes men neither of Oxō nor Totnes shall [by] there assigneēnt or otherwise haue the dispocition [or] distribution of those his payēnts to the poore. This is my last Will & Testament, wᶜʰ because I haue sett downe wᵗʰout the advice of any lawyer or the direction of any skilfull ꝑson in their legall ꝑseedings, I do therefore make request, yᵗ all my words and manner of writings herein, may according to my meaning be construed directly and in vulgar sense as I haue indeauoured to vtter it wᵗʰ all kinde of playnes & as I take it so fully to my entended purpose, as I do there vpon reuoke and disauowe all other my former Testaments and whatsoeuer can be prodused by any ꝑson or ꝑsons for the informing hereof or any clause poynt Appendixe or Codicill that I shall annexe to this hereafter. In witnesse whereof I haue subscribed and Sealed these p'sents wᵗʰ my owne sickley hand this 2. of Januarij 1612, and in the x yeare of his Maᵗˢ. Raigne of England ffrance and Ireland and of Scotland the sixe and forteth.

THO: BODLEY.

Signed sealed deliuered and published by the said Sʳ Tho: Bodley as his last Will and Testament in the presence of

Willia: Gosnall
John Waterhouse, Scr.
Issembart Christopher
George Comley
George Bodley.

A Codicill to amēde the last Will and Testament of me Thomas Bodley knight viz.

ffor as much as [by?] ye Honott: and extraordinarie respects countenance and Comfort wch I haue euer more receaued in great aboundance frō the most Reuerend ffather in god my Lo: Archebp̄ of Canterbury his grace in all my incident and needfull occations, wth the like frō time to time from the Right Honott: ye Lo: Ellesmere Lo: Chauncellor of England, and likewise divrse yeares past frō the Hott: Sr Edward Cooke Lo: Chiefe Justice of the Comon plees, cheifely in regard of his learned aduice imparted vnto me about the securing of such lande to the Vnivrsitie of Oxō as I had purposely purchased and conferred uppon them, to continuate the maintenance of ther publique Librarie, I am greatly encouraged to be come a most instant and earnest Sutor to all there Lop̄p̄s to grace me so much more as to vouchsafe to be ioyned wth sum̄e other of my freinds as ouerseers of my will and Testament, and wth all to assist and support my Executors as the equitie of there motions in any causes of mine, for I doe vtterly renounce all other requests, shall from time to tīe require, This is I confesse a p'sumptious request to p̱sonages of there calling, in respect of the trouble, but yet, in consideration of there noble dispositions to extend the limitts of goodness to the benefit of all men that shall either craue it or neede it, I doe intreate it as a speciall fauour at their Lop̄p̄s hands, and beseech them to accept a simple remēbrāce of my gratitude in that behalfe, bequeathing to there Lop̄s three little drinking boles, made of such mettall for puritie and worthe as best might represent the [in]tegritie and puritie of there counsailes and dealings in the course of all there Actions. Moreouer in how high a degree I haue euer beene bound to the right Reuerend ffather in God the Lo: Bushoppe of London there be so many witnesses of it as I shall but labour in vayne to endeauour to expresse it, and for ye requitall it must rest in his owne brest and in his owne conceipt of my thankfull disposition, wch shall neuer faile his Lop̄s seruice that I can p̱forme vnto him or any of his, how longe soeuer the Almightie God shall be pleased to prolonge the number of my dayes. This I would declare by leauinge behinde sum̄e answerable token to my zealous affections and his Lop̄s meritts, but that I knowe right well it is farre frō his expectation, and I cannot satisfie my owne desire in the measuere of my p̱forīnge my dutie in that kinde. Neuertheles to manyfest my readinesse and to geue sum̄e little portion of contentment to my minde, I bequeath unto his Lōp my two little spoone boles double guylt, together wth my siluer fruicte basket, that com̄ing now and then to his Lop̄s table, he may thereby call to minde how much I doe honor his loue vnto mee and his incomparable good meaninge in his publique purposes and proseedings. And whereas I haue lately purchased to me and my heires for euer an annuitie of fiftie three pounds eight shillings fore pence p ann̄: of one Nicolas ffortescue Esq[r] as by the deed of conveyance thereof enroled in the Chauncerie may approue [appear ?], I doe hereby limitt, devise and appoynt that the sāe annuitie shall be likewise sold and imployed by my Executors to the vses intents and purposes in the said my last Will and Testament mentioned and expressed according as I haue limited and appoynted other my lands and psonall estate. In witnesse whereof I haue to this p'sent Codicill set my hand and seale. The 23th yeare of the raigne of o[r] soueraine Lord King Jeames of England, ffrance, and Ireland, and of Scotland the sixe and forteth.

THO: BODLEY.

Signed sealed & published in the pesence of
Isembart Christopher
George Comley
George Bodley
Jo: Waterhouse.

b. ENDOWMENT OF THE LIBRARY[1].

This Indenture made the twentith day of Aprill in the yeres of the Raigne of our Soueraigne Lorde James by the grace of God of England Scotland ffraunce and Ireland Kinge, Defendor of the faithe, &c., that is to saie, of England ffraunce and Ireland the seaventh, and of Scotland the twoe and fortith, Betwene S[r] Thomas Bodley of London Knight of the first partie, The Chauncellor, Masters and Schollers of the Vniversity of Oxford of the second partie, and John Kinge Doctor of Divinity Deane of Christchurch in the said Vniversity of Oxford, and Anthony Blincowe Doctor of the Lawe Provost of Oriell Colledge within the same Vniversity of the third partie, Witnesseth, that whereas the said S[r] Thomas Bodley beinge sometymes a member of the said Vniversity of Oxford, and a Fellowe of the Colledge of Walter Merton, out of his zealous affection to the advancement of learninge, hath lately erected vpon the ruines of the olde decaied Library of the same Vniversity a most

[1] This is printed from the original parchment roll in the University Archives. Two of the three counterparts of the indenture are preserved there in a long narrow box. They have fine impressions of Bodley's Seal attached, in ivory boxes. An imperfect copy, very badly transcribed, exists in the manuscript from which the preceding copy of the will is taken.

ample comōdious and necessarie buildinge aswell for receipte and conveyance of books, as for the vse and ease of Students, and hath alreadie furnished the same with excellent writers in all sorts of Sciences, Arts and Tongues, not only selected out of his owne studie and store but alsoe of others that were freely conferred vpon that place by many other mens guifts of sundrie states and callinges, whereby the said Library is nowe by cōmon estimation, either alreadie become or verie shortly like to prove (yf God of his goodnes shall prosper the proiect) the most absolute and sufficient for the furtheringe of students in all kyndes of knowledge of good literature, that was ever yett in beinge, in any publique place of studie: And where[as] moreover the said S[r] Thomas Bodley hath by good observation found it apparant, that the principall occasion of the vtter subversion and ruine of some of the famousest Libraryes in Christendome hath ben the wante of due prouision of some certainety in revenewe, for their continewall preservation, and beinge therevpon desirous to meete with that inconvenience (as farre as by reason and humane discourse he hath ben able) he hath prouided the landes and inheritance hereafter mentioned, to goe and be emploied, not onlie for ever to vpholde and maynteyne his foresaid Library but from tyme to tyme, and daily more and more, to augment and increase it with further supplies of books, to the honor of God, to the benefitt of the State, and ꝑpetuall renowne of his deerely affected mother the said Vniversity, And hath besides in that behalfe procured licence, both from our Soueraigne Lorde the Kinges Maiesty, and from all other lordes, mediat and immediat, of whome the messuages, landes, ten'ts and hereditaments hereafter conveyde, are holden, to geve and settle the same in mortmayne. Nowe aswell for the foresaid considerations, as for sundrie other causes inducements and motives hym therevnto perswadinge, he the said S[r]: Thomas Bodley Hath geven, graunted, aliened, enfeoffed and confirmed, and by theis p'nts doth geve graunte, alien, enfeoffe and confirme, vnto the said John Kinge and Anthony Blincowe all that Mannor Lordshipp and ffarme, called or knowen by the name of Hyndons, scituate and beinge within the ꝑishe of Cookeham, in the countie of Berkes, with the rights members and appurtenaunces thereof, And all those ffoure messuages or ten'ts with the appurtenaunces scituate or lyinge in Maydenheath in the said ꝑish of Cookeham, and every of them, now or late in the seuerall tenures or occupations of John Spratley, William Bonde, Thomas Gardener, and John Randoll, their or some of their assignes, And all those water milnes, with thappurtenaunces, called or knowen by the names of Ray Milnes, scituate and beinge in the ꝑishe of Cookeham aforesaid, And all that mese, messuage or barne there, with one close therevnto adioyninge conteyninge by estimation eight acres, called the olde Bury, And all edifices, buildings, yards, gardens, landes, meadowes, feadings, pastures, woodes, vnderwoodes, com̃ons, multures, comōdityes, profitts, ten'ts and hereditaments, whatsoever, scituate, lyinge, and beinge in the seuerall ꝑishes of Cookeham, Bray and Bisham, in the said Countie of Berks, with all and singuler their appurtenaunces vnto the said Mannor, Lordshipp, ffarme messuages, Milnes, and Close, and every or any of them, nowe belonginge and appertayninge, or nowe demysed or enioyed as part, parcell, or member of the same, And alsoe all those eight Messuages or ten'ts, with thappurtenaunces scituate lyinge and beinge in the ꝑishe of Sainct Augustine neare Paules Churche in the Cittie of London, late in the tenure or occupation of Henry Edwards or of his assignes, and nowe in the tenure, possession or occupation of Raphe Ghest, Cittizen and Plasterer of London, and John Blakey, Cittizen and Merchaunttailor of London, their assignes or vndertenaunts or of some of them, Togeather with the revertion and revertions, remaynder and remaynders, of all and singuler the aforegraunted and mentioned p'misses, and every parte thereof, And all the state, righte, tytle, clayme and demaund of the said Sr Thomas Bodley in and to the same, and every parte thereof, And alsoe all the deedes, charters, evidences, writinges, escripts and mynuments whatsoever, touchinge or concerninge the p'misses, or any part or parcell thereof: To haue and to holde the said Mannor, Lordshipp, ffarme, Messuages, Milnes, and Close, landes, ten'ts, hereditaments, and all and singuler other the premisses, with all and singuler their appurtenaunces, to the said John Kinge and Anthony Blincowe, their heires and assignes forever, To the onlie vse and behoufe of the said Sr Thomas Bodley for and during the terme of his naturall life, without ympeachment of or for any manner of waste, and with power and liberty for him the said Sr Thomas Bodley and his assignes, to cutt and carry awaye any tymber trees, or woodes, growinge or to be growinge in or vpon the p'misses or any parte thereof, And after the decease of hym the said Sr Thomas Bodley, then to the vse and behoufe of the said Chauncellor, Masters and Schollers of the said Vniversity of Oxford, and their successors forever: Vpon this truste and confidence, and to this vse yntent and purpose, That the said Chauncellor, Masters, and Schollers, of the same Vniversity, shall from and after the death of the said Sr Thomas Bodley forever employe, expende and disburse the rents yssues and ꝑfitts of all and singuler the p'misses, for and towardes the preseruation, continewance and increase of the same Librarie, And shall paye after the death of the said Sr Thomas Bodley, out of the rents and profitts of the premisses to the Keeper of the same Library for the tyme beinge, the sūme of thirty three pownds sixe shillinges and eight pence yerelie, at the feasts of Sainct Michaell the Archangell, and the Annuntiation of our Ladie the blessed Virgen Mary, or within three and thirtie daies next after every of the said feasts by even portions, And to the Assistant of the same Keeper ten pownds yerelie by even porcions, att the same feasts or within three and thirty daies after the said feaste daies: And to the servant of the same Keeper which shall sweepe, wipe and cleanse the said Library, deskes and bookes, foure powndes yerelie at the feasts aforesaide, or within three and thirty daies next after every of the said feasts: And the residue of the rents and profitts of the premisses shall dispose and expende to such vses and purposes, and in such manner and forme as is or shalbe expressed and directed in certaine constitutions and ordinances made, or to be made, for the gouernement and continewall mayntenance and increase of the said Library, by the said Chauncellor or his Vicechauncellor, with the Doctors and Masters of the same Vniversity in their Convocation house, and with the mutuall consent of the said S[r] Thomas Bodley, and enrolled or to be enrolled in the highe Courte of Chauncery. And for the more assured and stronger assurance and conveyance of the said Mannor, Lordshipp, ffarme, messuages, ten'ts, milnes, and all and singuler other the premisses, to the vses and purposes aforesaid according to the true yntent and meaninge of theis p'nts, The said S[r] Thomas Bodley doth covenaunte promise and agree to and with the said Chauncellor, Masters and Schollers of the said Vniversity of Oxford and their successors, by theis p'nts, that he the said S[r] Thomas Bodley before the feast of Pentecost nowe next cōming, shall and will acknowledge and levy one ffyne *Sur cognusauns de droit*, in due forme of lawe, with proclamations therevpon to be made according to the lawes and statuts in that behalfe made and provided, accordinge to the cōmon course of ffynes in such cases vsed, before the Justices of his Maiesties Courte of Cōmon plees att Westm. or some other person or persons therevnto sufficiently aucthorized, vnto the said John Kinge and Anthony Blincowe, or the survivor of them, of in and vpon the said Mannor, Lordshipp, ffarme, Messuages, ten'ts, Milnes, and all other the premisses, with the appurtenaunces herein before mentioned to be graunted or conveyde, in such sorte as by Counsell learned shalbe advised, with warranty only against the said S[r] Thomas Bodley and his heires: Which ffyne and all other fynes and assurances whatsoever, to be made or levied of the p'misses, or any part of them, betwene the said parties or any of them, shalbe adiudged construed and taken to be, to and for the only vse and behoufe of the said S[r] Thomas Bodley, for terme of his life, without ympeachment of waste, and with liberty and power for the said Sr Thomas Bodley and his assignes, to cutt and carrye awaye tymber, and trees, as aforesaide, and after his decease, to the vse and behoufe of the said Chauncellor, Masters and Schollers of the said Vniversity of Oxford and of their successors forever, to the vses, yntents, and purposes, and vpon the trust and confidence before expressed. And the said Sr Thomas Bodley for hymselfe and his heires doth covenaunte and graunte to and with the said Chauncellor, Masters, and Schollers of the said Vniversity of Oxford and their successors, That they the said Chauncellor, Masters, and Schollers, from and after the death of hym the said Sr Thomas Bodley shall and maie have holde, and enioye the said Mannor, Lordshipp, ffarme, Messuages, ten'ts, Milnes, and all other the p'misses aboue mentioned, ment and intended to be conveyde, with all and singuler their appurtenaunces, to the vses yntents and purposes aforesaid, freed and discharged of and from all and all manner of graunts, estats, leases, charges, and incombrances whatsoever, had, made, done, or suffered, by the said Sr Thomas Bodley, or any other by his meanes, consente or procurement (one lease heretofore made by hym the said Sr Thomas Bodley to one Christopher Smith of the said Mannor, ffarme, Lordshipp, Messuages, Milnes, and of other the landes, ten'ts and hereditaments with thappurtenaunces, in Cookeham, Maydenheath, Bray, and Bisham aforesaide, for the terme of threescore and one yeres, to be accompted from the feast of St Michaell the Archangell nowe last past before the date of theis p'nts, wherevpon the yerelie rent of Nynety one powndes ten shillings is reserved, and shall remayne and continewe from and after the decease of the said Sr Thomas Bodley yerelie due and paiable to the said Chauncellor, Masters, and Schollers, of the said Vniversity of Oxford and their successors, to and for the vses and purposes before mentioned, for and during all the residue of the said terme of threescore and one yeres then to come and vnexpired: And one lease lately made by the said Sr Thomas Bodley to the said Raphe Ghest of twoe ten'ts with thappurtenaunces, parcell of the said eight ten'ts, for the terme of threescore and one yeres, comencing from the feast of St Michaell the Archangell nowe last past before the date hereof, wherevpon the yerelie rent of twenty and twoe powndes is reserved, and shall from and after the decease of the said Sr Thomas Bodley be due and paiable vnto the said Chauncellor, Masters, and Schollers of the said Vniversity of Oxford, and their successors, to and for the vses aforesaid, for and during all the residue of the said terme of threescore and one yeres, then to come and not determined : And also one other lease lately made by the said Sr Thomas Bodley to the said John Blakey of the residue of the said eight ten'ts with thappurtenaunces for the like terme of threescore and one yeres, begynninge at the feast of S[t] Michaell the Archangell nowe last past before the date of theis p'nts, wherevpon the yerelie rent of Twenty three powndes thirtene shillings and foure pence is reserved, and shall from and after the decease of the said S[r] Thomas Bodley be due and paiable to the aforesaid Chauncellor, Masters, and Schollers of the Vniversity of Oxford, and to their successors, to and for the vses and purposes afore recited, for and duringe all the residue of the said last recited terme of threescore and one yeres, then to come and vnexpired, onely excepted and foreprized). And the said S[r] Thomas Bodley hath ordayned constituted and appoynted, and by theis p'nts doth aucthorise and appoyncte, Isembart Christofer of London, gent., and George Comley of London, gent., his lawfull attorneys for hym, and in his name, to enter into and vpon the said Mannor, Lordshipp, ffarme, messuages, landes, ten'ts, and all and singuler other the said p'misses, or into any part or parcell of the same, in the name of the said whole p'misses, and possession and seisin thereof, or of some parte thereof in the name of the whole, for hym and in his name to take; And after suche entry made, and possession and seisin soe had and taken, then, for hym and in his name, to deliver peaceable and quiett possession and seisin of all and singuler the same recited p'misses, or of any parte or parcell thereof in the name of the whole, to the said John Kinge and Anthony Blincowe, or one of them, or to their attorney or attorneys sufficiently aucthorised to receyve the same, according to the tenor effect and true meaninge of theis p'nts: And the said S[r] Thomas Bodley doth by theis p'nts rattifye, confirme, and allowe, all and whatsoever the said Isembart Christofer and George Comley shall doe or cause to be done, for hym, or in his name, touchinge, in or aboute the p'misses, as fully and effectually as yf the said S[r] Thomas Bodley were ꝑsonally p'nte, and should doe the same. And the said John Kinge and Anthony Blincowe for them and either of them doe by theis p'nts geve full power and aucthority, and doe ordeyne, make, constitute and appoyncte George Wrothe of the Countie of Bucks, gent. and Toucher Castle of London gent., joynctly and severally, their lawfull attorneys for them and in their name stead and place, to take and receyve of the said Isembart Christofer and George Comley, or either of them, the peaceable and quiett possession and seisin of all and singuler the said p'misses, or of any parte or parcell thereof in the name of the whole, accordinge to the effect and true meaninge of theis p'nts, And doe also rattifye confirme and allowe all and eu'ie thinge and things which the said George Wroth and Toucher Castle or either of them shall doe, or cause to be done, in or about the premisses, as fully and effectually as yf the said John Kinge and Anthony Blincowe were ꝑsonally p'nt att the doinge thereof. And the said Chauncellor, Masters, and Schollers of the said Vniversity of Oxford doe covenaunte and graunte for them and their successors to and with the said S[r] Thomas Bodley his heires and assignes, and to and with everie of them by theis p'nts, That they the said Chauncellor, Masters, and Schollers and their successors from and after the decease of the said S[r] Thomas Bodley shall and will from tyme to tyme yerelie forever, paie vnto our Soveraigne Lorde the Kings Maiesty his heires and successors the yerelie rente or fee ferme of ffyve powndes thirtene shillings and foure pence, yssuing and paiable out of thaforesaid eight ten'ts in the ꝑishe of St. Augustine in London and thereof shall sufficiently acquite discharge or save harmles, aswell the heires executors and assignes of the said S[r] Thomas Bodley, and their and ev'rie of their goodes chattells landes and ten'ts, as alsoe the sev'all tenaunts and lessees of the same sev'all p'misses for the tyme being, their executors and assignes, against our said soveraigne Lorde the Kings Maiesty, his heires successors officers and assignes, and ev'ie of them. In Witnes whereof to one ꝑte of theis p'nte Indentures, remayning with the said John Kinge and Anthony Blincowe, the said S[r] Thomas Bodley hath sett his hande and seale, to one other ꝑte thereof, remayning with the said Chauncellor, Masters and Schollers of the Vniversity of Oxford, the said S[r] Thomas Bodley, John Kinge, and Anthony Blincowe have sett their handes and seales, and to the other ꝑte thereof, remayning with the said S[r] Thomas Bodley, the said Chauncellor, Masters and Schollers have caused their seale of the Vniversity to be putt, and alsoe the said John Kinge and Anthony Blincowe have sett their handes and seales. Geoven the daie and yere first above written, 1609.

THO: BODLEY.

Recognit. coram me Mattheo Carew Milite, in Cancellaria Magistro, vicesimo die Maii anno suprascr. 1609.

III.

List of all the recorded Donors, from 1600 to 1700,

Who are not specially commemorated in the text of the 'Annals.'

A.D. 1600.

Thomas Cornewallis—The Aldine Eustathius.
Merton College—Thirty-eight volumes.
Philip Scudamore—Books.
Sir Thomas Lake—£10.
Thomas Case, M.D.—£10.
William Friere—£10.
William Wilson, Canon of Windsor—£10.
John Periam—£5.
Henry Stanford—Books.

A.D. 1601.

Edward James—Books.
Dean Alex. Nowell—£15 and books.
[Sir] John Crooke, Recorder of London—Books.
George Shirley—£40.
Rob. Chambrelaine and Alice his widow—£40.
Rich. Eedes, Dean of Worcester—£13 6*s*. 4*d*.
Mary Fermor, *or* Farmer—Books.
Nich. Bond, President of Magdalen College—£10 and books.
Sir Julius Cæsar—£10.
Dr. Daniel Dun—£10.
John Savile—Hebrew Lexicon.
[Sir] Arthur Atie—£10.
Sir Alex. Hampden—£10.
John Langworth, D.D., Archdeacon of Wells—£10.
Thomas Thornton, D.D.—£10.
Philip Bisse, D.D., Archdeacon of Taunton—£10.
Anth. Blincowe, Provost of Oriel College—Printed books.
John Hawley, Principal of Gloucester Hall—Printed books.

William Allen, £10; and in 1604, Printed books.
Robert Lister, Principal of Magdalen Hall—£3 6*s*. 8*d*.
Edward Fleetwood—Printed books.
Anth. Morgan—Printed books.
Walter Heath, Prebendary of Rochester—£5.
Sir John Davis—Printed books.
Benj. Heyden, Dean of Wells—Printed books.
Richard Haydocke, M.A.—Printed books.
George Upton—£4.
John Dalaber, M.D.—Printed books.
Thomas Paget—Printed books.
John Chamberlaine, London—Printed books.
Thomas Draper, M.A.—Four MSS., including that of Becket's *Epistolæ*.
Cuthbert Ridley, M.A.—Three MSS.
John Wise—Printed books.
Peter Bogan, of Totness—Printed books.
Peter Duncan—Printed books.
John Norton—Printed books.

A.D. 1602.

Toby Mathew, Bishop of Durham—£50.
Sir Will. Knollis [afterwards Earl of Banbury]—£50.
Sir Henry Davers, *or* Danvers, Knt.—Printed books.
Sir Francis Vere, Knt.—Money and books.
James Cottington, Archdeacon of Surrey—£10.
[Sir] John Bennet, Chancellor of York—£10.
Erasmus Webbe, Archdeacon of Bucks—£5.
Rob. Osberne, of Kelmarsh, Esq.—£4.
John Barcham, M.A., C.C.C.—Printed books.
Thos. Grant, Esq., of Warwickshire[1]—MSS. and printed books.
Will. Bailey, Esq.—MSS. and printed books.
Steph. Rodvey, Esq.—Printed books.
Nich. Higges, B.D.—£3.
John L[h]uid, D.D.—Hebrew MSS.
Nich. Lymbye, B.D.—MSS. and printed books.
Rowl. Searchfield, B.D.—MSS. and printed books.
Thos. Randal—MSS.
Rich. Carpenter, M.A.—Printed books.
Barth. Isaac—Printed book.

[1] His name occurs plainly as *Graunte* and *Grant*, in the books given by him in 1601 and 1602, but in the printed Register he is entered under 1602 as Thomas *Grantham*.

Will. Hakewill, Esq.—Printed books, and an Italian MS.
H. Haies, *or* Hayes—Printed musical books.
— Springham—MSS.
Will. Wroton—Printed books.
John Whetcombe, M.A.—Printed books.
John Wrothe—Koran, MS.

A.D. 1603.

Martin Heton, Bishop of Ely—£40.
Sir Edmund Udall, Knt.—£50.
Sir T. Edmundes, Knt.—£20.
Sir Rich. Farmor, *or* Fermor, of Somerton, Oxon.—Printed books and MSS.
Sir Rich. Spencer—Printed books.
Rob. Chaloner, D.D.—£20.
Thomas Docwra, of Puttridge, Esq.—Printed books and MSS.
Richard Grossevenor—Printed books and MSS.
Sir Edward Sandys—£30 and MSS.
— Helmeston, Lyme Regis—£10.
Geoffrey Perceval, B.D.—Printed books.
Sir Owen Oglethorpe, Knt.—Printed books.
Rich. Tailor, M.A., Merton College—MS. and printed books.
Rob. Dannette—£5.
Will. Canninges, London—£5.
Edw. Parvis—Printed books.
Sir John Scudamore, Knt.—£40.

A.D. 1604.

Sir Valentine Knightley, Knt.—£10.
William Allen, M.A.—Printed books.
Sir Will. Roper, Knt.—Works of Sir Th. More.
Lord Abergavenny—Printed books.
Earl of Nottingham—MSS. and printed books.
Sir Geo. More, Knt.—Thirty MSS., and £40, with which eighty-nine printed books and two MSS. were purchased.
Sir Geo. Sayntpoll, Knt.—£20.
Will. Ballow, M.A., Proctor of the University—Fifteen MSS., and four more in the following year. The list of these is printed from the *Reg. Benef.* in Dr. F. G. Lee's *Hist. of the Church of Thame*, fol. Lond. 1883, cols. 553-4.

A.D. 1605.

Sir Francis Vere, Knt.—£10, and again in 1606, 1607, and 1608, and books in 1609.
Josiah White, M.A.—Seven MSS.
Sir Thomas Lake, Knt.—£10.
Sir Will. Rider, Knt.—£10.
John Smith, of North Nibley—£5.
Sir Hen. Rolle, Knt.—£3 6*s.* 8*d.*
Will. Dun, M.D.—Five MSS.
Will. Madocks, Esq.—£5.
Will. Harrison, merchant, London—£10.
Sir Will. Billesby, Knt.—Four MSS., with printed books.
Will. Hutchinson, D.D., Archdeacon of Cornwall—Books.
Will. Cotton, Bishop of Exeter—Twenty-three MSS.
Rob. Cecil, Visc. Cranborne (afterwards Earl of Salisbury)—£66 13*s.* 4*d.*
Henry Martin, D.C.L.—£10.
Thomas Underhill, M.A.—Two MSS.
Geo. Darell, M.A., Proctor—MS. of the Statutes of the University.
John Barneston, B.D.—Two MSS.
Evan Jones, M.A.—Two MSS.
Will. Lord Paget of Beaudesert—£100.
Hen. Wriothesley, Earl of Southampton—£100.

A.D. 1606.

Dame Alice Owen, widow, London—£100.
Matthew Chubbe—40*s.*
Thomas Cutler, London—MS. of the Koran.
Ralph Barlow, B.D.—Seven MSS.

A.D. 1607.

Martin Lumley, London—£10.
Roger Braunche—£5 (with which Binius' *Concilia* were bought).
Rich. Worseley, Esq.—Ten MSS.
Sir Charles Danvers—£100[1].
John Reynolds, D.D., Pres. of C.C.C., bequeathed forty books.

[1] Eleven Chinese books are marked with his name as donor, probably as being bought with his money. Two in the same way bear Chubbe's name, seven Sir Fr. Vere's, four dean Wood's (see p. 42), four Lord Lumley's, &c. And two are assigned to Sir Francis Cleere, who was knighted in 1603, but whose gift does not appear to be recorded except in the books themselves.

A.D. 1608.

Will. Comley—40*s*.[1]
Dame Mary Hobby, widow, of Hales, Gloucestershire—£20.

A.D. 1609.

Will. Herbert, Earl of Pembroke—£100.

A.D. 1611.

Thomas Edwards, LL.D.—£10.
Laurence Bodley—£20.
Richard Townley, Esq.—£15.
Francis James, LL.D.—£20.
Sir Robert Oxenbridge—£5.

A.D. 1612.

Geo. Smith, Rector of Chelsfield, Kent—£5.

A.D. 1613.

William James, Bishop of Durham—£50.

A.D. 1614.

William Webb, Magdalen College—A Greek Martyrology.
John Glanvile, B.D., Balliol College—Printed books, including many in Italian.

A.D. 1615.

Humphrey Davenport, Esq.—£2.
Francis Harewell, Esq., of Birlingham—Printed books.
John Bust, Rector of Penshurst, Kent—£5.

A.D. 1617.

John Livesey, a London scrivener—£3.
Gabriel Barber and Lot Pierre (*qu.* Pierre Lot ?), London—£5.

A.D. 1618.

Fred. Dorville, B.D., Exeter College, of the German Palatinate—A German Bible, and the Laws of the Palatinate.
Sir George Ellis—22*s*.
Francis Matkins, Fellow of Winchester College—33*s*., being the gift of Mr. Tho. Sims, sometime Scholar of Winchester.

[1] A servant of Bodley, mentioned in his letters and will.

Sir John Walter, Brasenose College—£20.

Greg. Martyn, M.A., Exeter College, bequeathed £5.

A.D. 1619.

Hen. Reeves, *or* Rives, a London scrivener—44*s*.

Christopher Goldsmith, minister of Kingston, Sussex—22*s*.

Lady Ann Poole, widow of Sir James Harrington, Bart., of Merton, Oxon.—£5.

A.D. 1620.

Anth. Anketill, citizen of London—22*s*.

Sam. Serle, Rector of Thoydon Garnon, Essex—40*s*.

John Williams, D.D. (afterwards Archbishop of York)—£5 10*s*. Also £10 in 1621, and £5 in 1625.

Edw. Payne, merchant of Bristol, in two gifts—£4.

Sir Peter Manwood—Three MSS.

George Raleigh, Exeter College—40*s*.

Sir Will. Sedley, Bart., founder of the Sedleian Professorship of Natural Philosophy, bequeathed £100. Paid by Sir John Sedley.

Sir Nicholas Trott—Printed books.

Thomas Bancroft, Esq., of the Court of Exchequer—£3.

Thomas Bret, Esq., formerly fellow of All Souls' College—Printed books.

Thomas Gataker, B.D., of Rotherhithe—Coins, and three Hebrew and Arabic MSS.

Edmund Leigh, B.D., Fellow of Brasenose College—Coins, and printed books.

A.D. 1621.

Andrew Rivet, D.D., Professor at Leyden, incorp. at Oxford 30 Aug. 1621—Two books by himself.

Ralph Radcliff, Town-Clerk of Oxford—Medal of Frederic, Count Palatine, and a MS. 'continens apologiam pro regimine mulierum ab H[en.] H[oward] comite Northamptoniensi olim conscriptam nec unquam excusam.'

Christopher Rutinger, M.D., a Hungarian, bequeathed a gold seal attached to a charter of the Grand Duke of Muscovy, and £10.

A.D. 1622.

Sir George Coppin bequeathed £10.

Sir Richard Cox—£10.

Roger Hacket, D.D., formerly Fellow of New College, bequeathed £5.

Josiah Guy, the University carrier, bequeathed 40*s*.

Andrew Barker, merchant, of Bristol, bequeathed £3.

— Whiddon, M.A.—20*s*.

A.D. 1625.

Dame Elizabeth Craven, widow of Sir G. Craven, bequeathed £20.
William Ceely, Commoner of Exeter College—£2.
William Compton, Earl of Northampton—£30.

A.D. 1627.

Herbert Jenkes, Lincoln College—£2, and Greek Testament with short-hand summaries, &c. in MS.

A.D. 1629.

John Maltbee, Rector of Buckland, Gloucestershire—£5.
Thomas Brown, LL.B.—Printed books.

A.D. 1630.

John Trefusis, of Exeter College, a Cornish man (9 Aug.)—A specimen of what has been found to be the language of the Lampongs in Sumatra, on one long palm-leaf. In the 1697 Catalogue of MSS. it is described as being 'in lingua Malabarica.' Now numbered 'MS. Lampong, e. 1.'

A.D. 1631.

Thomas Hutchins, a London merchant—£5.
James Trussell, a London draper in Paternoster Row—£5.
John Farwell, Commoner of New Inn Hall—£2.
John Buckland, Commoner of Magdalen Hall—£2.
Daniel Norton, Commoner of Brasenose College—£2.
William Thomas, Commoner of St. John's College—£2.
[These four sums were paid as Undergraduates' fees for admission to the Library.]
Thomas Gardiner, Inner Temple, from the goods of John Brown, a London merchant, deceased—£20.

A.D. 1632.

Henry Stratford, Esq., of Halling, Gloucestershire—£2 10*s*.
George Vivian, a London merchant—Arabic astronomical MS.
John Sprot, B.D., Canon of Exeter, bequeathed £5.

A.D. 1633.

Devereux Knightley, Commoner of Lincoln College [adm. fee]—£2.
Henry Fred. Thynne [adm. fee]—£2.
Dr. Bostock—£10.

A.D. 1634.

Abr. Archdale, Esq., of Wheatley, Oxon., bequeathed £10.

A.D. 1635.

Anonymous gift through Dr. Morgan—£1.

A.D. 1637.

Conyers Darcy, jun., of Hornby Castle, Yorkshire [adm. fee]—£2.

A.D. 1639.

Edw. Peyto, Commoner of Magdalen College [adm. fee]—£2.
Edw. Harley, son of Sir Rob. Harley [adm. fee]—£2.
John Reresby, Esq., of Thribergh, Yorkshire—£2.

A.D. 1640.

John Pye, son of Sir Rob. Pye, of Faringdon, Berks [adm. fee]—£2.
Thomas Perle, a London Turkey merchant—MS. Arabic Dict.
Philip Williams, also a London Turkey merchant—Another MS. Arabic Dict.

A.D. 1649.

Cornelius Bee, the London bookseller—Two printed books.
[Probably about 1645, although under this year in the Register.] Again in 1653.
Rich. Whitaker, London bookseller—Two copies of Gerard's *Herbal*, 1636.
Roger Daniel, the Cambridge printer—His Gr.-Lat. Test., 1642.
Rob. Pinke, D.D., Warden of New College, bequeathed £10.
Maurice Abbot, Wadham College [adm. fee]—£2.

A.D. 1650.

Henry Yelverton, Wadham College [adm. fee]—£2.

A.D. 1651.

Martin Aylworth, LL.D., All Souls' College—Printed books.

A.D. 1652.

Edward Knipe, an East India merchant—Four Persian MSS.
Rich. Doydge, Esq., of Milton-Abbot, Devon—£10.
Joseph Maynard, B.D., Exeter College—£10 (and £5 in 1658).

A.D. 1653.

Christopher Elderfield, M.A., St. Mary Hall, bequeathed two MSS. and two printed books.

Rob. Nicolas [*or* Nicholls], a Judge of the Upper Bench—£10[1].

Will. Hammond, Wadham College [adm. fee]—£2.

[Sir] John Birkenhead, All Souls' College—Printed book ('De constitt. gymn. Patavini,' 1588).

— Sandbrooke—Trostius' Syriac Lexicon.

A.D. 1654.

Benj. Madock, Wadham College—Printed books.

A.D. 1655.

John Maynard, B.A., Exeter College, Serj. at Law (Sept. 30)—Printed book (Pisanus' *Astrologia*).

William Jumper, Esq.—Ogilby's Virgil.

A.D. 1656.

Thomas Ellis, M.A., Jesus College (July 13)—Printed books.

Ralph Freeman, Esq., of Aspden, Herts.—Coins.

John Newton, B.D., Brasenose College—Printed books (one in 1652), and one MS.; and on June 14, 1658, seven MSS. and three printed books.

A.D. 1657.

Thos. Pope, Earl of Down (Jan. 1)—Gruter's Map of Italy.

Sam. Woodford, Commoner of Wadham College (March 14)—Map of Rome.

Col. Edward Leigh—Printed books, including his own works.

Thomas Chaloner, formerly M.P. (June 18)—Blaeu's Globes, and Maps.

Will. Sheppard, Serj. at Law (Aug. 16)—His own books (fourteen).

A.D. 1658.

Hon. Robert Boyle (Feb. 26)—Goltzii Opera.

Judith Highlord, London—Two coins.

Robert Southwell, B.A., Queen's College—A box made of marine shells, a salamander, coins, and other curiosities not specified.

[1] With this gift twelve MSS. (chiefly Patristic) and two printed books were bought.

A.D. 1659.

Edmund Scroop, M.B., All Souls' College, Secretary to the Privy Seal in Scotland (Nov. 29)—A collection of very fine engravings from paintings by great masters, to which additions were made about the same time by John Evelyn, Sir Peter Pett, Philip Hodgson, and Capt. Silas Taylor, and four engravings subsequently by Sir Andrew Fountaine. They have recently been mounted, and re-bound in a large folio volume as 'The Scroope Album.' They number between 230 and 240 specimens, and include several drawings. A few have been added in late years.

A.D. 1660.

Griffin Higges, D.D., Dean of Lichfield, bequeathed £100.

A.D. 1661.

Maurice, Prince of Nassau, visited the Library, and left behind him on departing *Barlæi Hist. Brasil.*

A.D. 1662.

Will. Cavendish, Marquis of Newcastle—His own book on Horsemanship. Book II in 1667.

Dr. Triplett, Prebendary of Westminster—£4.

A.D. 1663.

Jeremiah Carter, an East India and China merchant—Various small Chinese curiosities, a Japanese fan, a pipe, &c.

A.D. 1666.

George Purefoy, Esq., of Wadley, Berks.—Coins.

James Hyde, M.D., Principal of Magdalen Hall—Coins.

Henry Thurscross, a London East India merchant—East Indian darts and coins, and the Malay Gospels printed in 1651.

A.D. 1667.

The Duchess of Newcastle, 'veræ virtutis imago et exemplar unicum, sui sexus ornamentum summum, politioris literaturæ decus maximum, et præsertim Philosophiæ nobilioris cultrix et ornatrix optima'!—Her own works.

A.D. 1668.

John Wildy, East India merchant—East Indian coins.

A. D. 1670.

— Fox, Gloucester—A MS. Latin Bible. [Auct. D. v. 7.]

A.D. 1674.

Will. Hunt, B.D., New College—About fifty coins.
John Roswell, B.D., Head Master of Eton—£11.

A.D. 1675.

George Ent, Esq., Middle Temple—Printed books (twice).
Sam. Jackson, M.D., Ch. Ch., bequeathed £10.

A.D. 1679.

Edw. Reynolds, D.D., Archdeacon of Norwich—£5 5*s*.

A.D. 1680.

Roger Stanley, LL.D., New College, bequeathed £20.
Moses Pitt, the well-known London bookseller, gave a volume containing Caxton's *Cato*, *Boece*, the *Knight of the Tower*, and *Æsop*, etc.

A. D. 1683.

Richard Ayliffe, Esq., Whitchurch—A MS. Latin Bible. [Auct. . v. 8.]

A.D. 1683-1688.

James Butler, Earl of Ossory (who became Earl in 1683, and succeeded as second Duke of Ormonde in 1688), gave what is described as 'totus Alcoranus' written on small round paper tablets, and enclosed in an ivory box, possibly intended to be carried about as an amulet. [Arab. Rot. G. 3.]

A.D. 1692.

John Jennings, Manciple of Hart Hall (Nov. 18)—Three small dirty and imperfect black-letter books. [8vo. V. 89 Art.]

A.D. 1697.

Sir Edw. Sherbourne—Ten editions of Manilius. He had previously (as Edw. Sherborne, Esq.) given a MS. Latin Bible. [Auct. D. v. 41.]

It is very evident that at least from the year 1668, if not earlier, to the end of the century, very few gifts were recorded, and even of the preceding entries several are gathered from the books themselves and not from any Register. No doubt there are many which still remain unnoted. But from the year 1700 the gifts become so numerous (many being trifling), that the detailed list need not be further continued. All the more important presents are noticed in the course of the *Annals*; and some are specified in Gutch's additions to the account of the Library given in his edition of Wood's *History of the University*.

Bodl. MS. 297 has an inscription recording its gift by George Broome, esq. of Holton, Oxon, but no date is given. It belongs, however, to the earliest days of benefactions.

IV.

Account of Sir Richard Lee's Muscovite Cloak,

Extracted from vol. vi. *of B. Twyne's Collections, among the University Archives, f.* 97. [See p. 51.]

'*Mr. Smyth's Relation of the Tartar Lambskinne garment in Bodleiana, Oxon.*

'Sir Rich. Lee, knight, about the later ende of the raigne of the late Qu. Elizabeth, being by her Maiestie sent ambassador into Russia, amongest other novelties of the cuntry found by the information of the inhabitants, that in Tartaria, a cuntrie neere adioyning to Muscovia and Russia, and vnder the gouernement of the Emperour of Russia, there did some yeres growe out of the ground certaine livinge creatures in the shape of lambes, bearinge wooll vppon them, very like to the lambes of England, in this manner; viz., a stalke like the stalke of an hartichocke did growe vp out of the ground, and vppon the toppe thereof a budd, which by degrees did growe into the shape of a lambe, and became a liuinge creature, resting vppon the stalke by the navell; and as soone as it did come to life, it would eate of the grasse growinge round about it, and when it had eaten vp the grasse within its reach it would die. And then the people of the cuntry as they finde these lambes doe flea of their skins, which they preserue and keepe, esteeminge them to bee of excellent vse and vertue, especially against the plague and other noysome diseases of those cuntries.

'Vppon this information, Sir Rich. Lee was very desirous to haue some of the skyns of these Tartar lambes for his money, which at that time was not to be gotten for money; for that whensoeuer any of those lambes were at any time found, it was very rarely; and then also when they were found, they were presented to the Emperour, or to some other great man of the cuntrie, as a present of great worthe.

'At this time the Emperour had a gowne or longe cloake, made after the fashion of that cuntrie with the skins of those Tartar lambes; which garment the then Duke, and since Kinge, of Swethland was very desirous to haue and offered great summes of money for, but could by no means obtayne his desire.

'At this time also Sir Rich. Lee had an agatt of so great biggenesse that he made thereof a pestle and a morter, whiche the Emperour hauinge notice of, was desirous to haue for his money. Sir Rich. Lee, vnderstandinge thereof, sent it to the Emperour as a present from him, which the Emperour would not accept as a gift, neither would he haue it but for his money. Sir Richard, beinge willinge the Emperour should haue the pestle and the morter, yet lothe to playe the marchant at that time, did therefore deliuer this pestle and morter, into the hands and custodie of the Emperour's physitian to beate his physicke in it for the Emperour; which manner of giuinge this pestle and morter did so please the Emperour, as that he caused secret enquirie to be made whether there were any thinge in those cuntries which Sir Richard was desirous to haue, and by that means had notice that Sir Richard had endeuoured to haue gotten some of their lambeskyns. Wherevppon the Emperour, after Sir Richard had taken his leaue of him, and had receaued a great gift of him as an Ambassador, and was departed one dayes iourney toward England, the Emperour sent after him the before mentioned garment so made with their Tartar lambeskyns as aforesaide, and with it some fewe skynnes loose, and gaue them all vnto him freelie.

'Sir Richard Lee, travaylinge homewards, came to the Kinge of Swethlandes court, who demaunded of him of diverse thinges of the cuntrie of Muscovia; and, amongest other thinges, asked him whether he had seene the aforesaid garment, and he answered, that he had not only seene it, but had it in his possession; whereat the Kinge of Swethland admired, sayinge he had longe laboured to get it for loue or money, but could neuer obtayne it.

'Sir Rich. Lee in this iourney had not onely gotten this garment and Tartar lambeskyns, but diverse other rich furres and other rarities of great price; the greatest part whereof the Queene tooke of him, and promised him recompence for them, which she neuer performed; which was partly the cause that he concealed this garment from her duringe her life. And when Sir Rich. Lee died himselfe, he by his will gaue it to the Library in Oxford, to be kept as a monument there, beinge, as he conceiued, the fittest place for a jewell of so great worth and æstimation as that is or ought to be.

'Sir Rich. Lee was the neere kinseman of my wife; by reason whereof, I was very familiarly acquaynted with him; and vppon conference had with him about his trauayles at sundry times, I had the true relation of all the premisses from his owne mouthe. And I comminge to Oxford to the Act, and findinge this garment in Sir Tho. Bodley's studdie or closet, without any expression made of the raritie or worth of this garment, did discouer so much as I haue herein written to Mr. Russe, the Keeper of the Library; at whose request I haue sett it downe, in writinge. And in testimonie of the truthe thereof, I haue herevnto subscribed my name, the 13th of July, 1624.

'EDWARD SMYTHE.

'Transcribed out of the originall with Mr. Russe.
'This Mr. Smyth was a Counsellor of the Temple.'

It would appear from this account that the cloak was already beginning to be neglected. Suspicion had probably been early excited as to the truth of the traveller's story which accompanied the gift, and which could scarcely have obtained entire credence later than the days of Marco Polo or Sir John Mandeville. In the Ashmolean Museum a painting is preserved (possibly the one painted for the Library in 1643, as mentioned in the note on p. 51), which represents the *Agnus Scythicus* in its fabled state; a full-grown lamb poised on the top of a vegetable stalk, with its legs dependent in the air [1]. But the key to the mystery is attached in the label on the frame: '*Polypodium Barometz.* Linn.' It is, in truth, only a large fern found in Tartary, of which the rhizoma is covered with the woolly fungus-like growth found in greater or less degree on many species of ferns. If the plant be dug up and inverted, the roots being uppermost and the fronds pendent, a strong imagination might find some resemblance in the former to a wool-clad body, and in the latter to limbs, while some of the young fronds with their spiral convolutions might be compared to the horns of a ram, such as are duly represented in the painting mentioned above. A specimen of the plant may be seen in the greenhouses of the Botanic Garden, Oxford, where it is still known by the name which the fable imposed, *Agnus Scythicus.* So great is the woolly growth found upon one species of tree-fern in New Zealand, that (as I was informed by Mr. Baxter, formerly Keeper of the Botanic Garden) tons of it are yearly imported into this country for the purpose of stuffing cushions. A finer and silkier substance is found on a fern indigenous in Mexico. It is also found in Barbadoes, and is described under the name of *Agnus*

[1] For acquaintance with this picture I was indebted to Mr. Rowell, for many years the well-qualified Under-keeper of the Ashmolean Museum. In Tradescant's Catalogue of the first contents of this Museum as formed by himself, published in 1656, occurs 'a coat lyned with *Agnus Scythicus*,' but it does not now exist in the collection.

Scythicus in Griffith Hughes' History of that island, 1750, p. 235, where its legendary story is noticed, and where it is said that Kaempfer spent a great part of his life in search for the Tartar Lamb! Three representations of it (one from the *Philos. Trans.*, another from Hunter's edition of Evelyn's *Sylva et Terra,* and the third from a drawing by Dr. De La Croix) are given in De La Croix's *Connubia florum*, with notes by Sir R. Clayton, 8vo., Bath, 1791. A description of the plant (called 'boranetz or the lambe') is found at the end of Ashmole MS. 1494.

[Since the above was in print Mr. Madan has shown me an illustrated monograph on the subject by Mr. Henry Lee, published in 1887, and entitled *The Vegetable Lamb of Tartary, a curious fable of the Cotton Plant.*]

V.

List of Books printed on Vellum,

Which have been added to the Library since the year 1830[1].

Before 1459. *Canon Missæ,* by Fust and Schoiffer. Douce.

1460. *Clementis VIII Constitutiones, cum glossa Jo. Andreæ. Ed. Pr.*, fol. Mogunt., Petr. Schoiffer de gernssheim. Bought in 1838 for 45*l.*

1468. *Justiniani Institutiones. Ed. Pr.*, fol. Mogunt. per Petr. Schoyffer de Gernssheym. Bought in 1834 for 52*l.* 10*s.*

1476. *Historia Naturale de Plinio, trad. per Chr. Landino.* fol. Ven. Nic. Janson. The borders at the commencement of each book, with the principal initial letters, are exquisitely painted, and illustrated with the portrait and arms of Ferdinand II of Sicily, to whom the work was dedicated, as well as those of — Strozzi, for whom this copy was probably executed. Bequeathed by Douce. (Douce, 310).

1480. *Breviarium Eduense,* 4to. by order of Card. John Rolin, Bishop of Autun, 'Symon de Vetericastro eius Secretarius, parisius hoc breviarium cum pluribus similibus imprimi fecit.' Bought in 1838 for 2*l.* 4*s.*

1481. *Missale Parisiense. Ed. Pr.*, fol. Par., Jo. de Prato et Desid. huym. Bought in 1842 for 10*l.* 10*s.*

1482. *Ordo Psalterii cum hymnis et canticis suis.* Small 4to. Ven. per Nicolaum Girardenguz. From the Canonici collection.

1484. *Officium diurnum secundum morem monachorum congregationis Sancte Justine, ord. S. Benedicti.* 8vo. Ven. per Bern. de Benaliis (&c.). Bought in 1843 for 1*l.* 14*s.*

1493. *Pars hyemalis breviarii fratrum Observantialium, ord. S. Benedicti, per Germaniam.* 8vo. impensis Georii Stōchs ex Sulczbach, civis Nurembergensis. Bought in 1841 for 14*s.*

N. D. Brunonis Comment. in Psalterium. Fol. [Herbip. typis Keyseri.]. Laud *MS. Lat.* 33.

[1] Supplemental to the list appended to Archdeacon Cotton's *Typographical Gazetteer* publ. in 1831. That numbered 180 separate books; the present additions amount to sixty-five, of which thirty-six are in the Douce collection.

1500, Aug. 14. *Heures a lusage de* [*Tours;* the name left blank]. 8vo. Paris, pour Anthoine Verard. With illuminations. Bought in 1844 for 6*l.*

1502. *Breviarium secundum regulam beati Hysidori.* Fol. Toleti, jussu Card. Fr. Ximenes, per Petr. Hagembach. Bought in 1853 for 200*l.* See p. 358.

1505. *Breviarium secundum usum Herford.* 8vo. Rothom., per Inghilbertum Haghe. Bequeathed by Gough.

N. D. Maps of Bay of Biscay, France, England, &c. with a Calendar; printed from blocks, in colours, probably in 16th cent., on eleven duodecimo leaves. Ashmole MS. 1352.

N. D. A small duodecimo book of prayers, in German, without any title; with woodcuts. Printed with the types of Hans Schönsperger, of Augsburg. Bequeathed by Douce. [Douce, MM. 858.]

1514. *Le Chevalier de la tour et le guidon des guerres; par Geoffroy de la Tour-Landry.* Fol. Par., pour Guill. Eustace. Bequeathed by Douce. [Douce, SS. 455.]

1514. *Missale Sarisb.* Par. Ashmole 1764. See p. 443.

1522. *Libri quattuor magnorum Prophetarum; his adduntur Threni,* &c. 12mo. Par., Petrus Vidoveus. Given by Rawlinson. [Rawl. B. N. 1.]

1529. *S. Joannes Chrysostomus in omnes Epistolas S. Pauli;* Gr. 3 vols. fol. Ven. Bought in 1843 for 45*l.*

1557. Meir ben Ephraim: Historia belli Antiochei contra Jerusalem [sive Hist. Machabæorum] *Hebraice.* 8vo. Mantuæ. Bought at — Riva's sale in 1857 for 3*l.* 15*s.* 6*d.*

1629. *Rituale monasticum secundum consuetudinem congregationis Vallisumbrosæ.* Fol. Florent. Bought in 1843 for 7*l.* 17*s.* 6*d.*

1642. *Bibliotheca Eliotæ. Eliotis Librarie.* Londini, anno Verbi incarnati M.D.XLII. A fragment, consisting of title, Proheme to Henry VIII in English, address to the reader in Latin, and table of errata; in all, five leaves.

1650. *Christlicher Agendbüchlein der Evangelischen Kirchen zu Regenspurg:* 4to. Regensp. A small directory for Lutheran worship. [Mason H. 118.]

[*c.* 1730-40.] *Some queries recommended to the consideration of the more rigid and clamorous rubricians;* pointing out the cases in which the Rubric and Canons were violated by all parties alike. 4 pp. fol.

—— Records of some of the consecrations of Non-juring bishops. fol.

1812. *Hommage au salon de la ville de Gand.* 8vo. Gand. An account of the pictures and sculptures there exhibited. Bought in 1872.

1817. List of ships employed in the service of the East India Company. Broad-side.

1859. *Rotulus Clonensis, ex orig. in Registro Eccl. Cath. Clonensis, editus cura Ric. Caulfield.* The first book printed at Cork on vellum, and the only copy so printed. Given by the late Dr. Caulfield, the editor, in 1865[1].

1861. *The Souldier's Pocket Bible;* an exact reprint of the original edition of 1643, with a prefatory note by George Livermore. 12mo. Cambridge [U.S.], printed for private distribution. This copy was given by Mr. Livermore to Archd. Cotton, and by him to the Library. It was reprinted from a copy in the possession of the editor; only one other is known to exist.

1866. ספר תגין *Sepher Taghin:* Liber Coronularum, ex unico bibl. Paris. cod. MS. a B. Goldberg descriptum, nunc primum edidit, adjectis ad calcem libri aliquot exceptis ex alio codice ejusdem bibl. inedito, J. J. L. Barges, S. Theol. facult. Paris. doctor. 8vo. Lut. Par.

1867. מעשה נסים Edited by Dr. B. Goldberg, from Pococke MS. 238. 8vo. Paris. The only vellum copy printed. Bought for 3*l.*

N. D. *Geological Map of the Environs of Oxford;* by C. P. Stacpoole. Bought in 1850 for 1*l.* 3*s.*

N. D. Dimensions of S. Peter's at Rome and S. Paul's, London. Rawl. MS. B. 367.

The following vellum-printed *Horæ* were all bequeathed by Mr. Douce:—

1498. *Les heures a lusaige de Rome.* 4to. Par., pour Simon Vostre. See list of Bindings, *infra.*

—— —— 4to. Par., per Gillet Hardouyn.

1498. *Hore secundum usum Sarum.* 8vo. Par., per Phil. Pigouchet.

1499. *Officium B. M. V. in usum Romane ecclesie.* 8vo. Lugd., Bon. de boninis.

1501. *Hore Virg. Mar. secundum usum Romanum.* 8vo. Par., Thielman Kerver.

[1501.] *Les heures a lusaige de Rome.* 8vo. Par., Simon Vostre.

1502. —— By the same printer.

1504. —— 8vo. Par., Anth. Chappiel.

1505. *Officium B. M. V. in usum Rom. eccl.* 8vo. Ven., Lucantonius de Giunta.

[1] This enthusiastic and untiring Irish antiquary (with whom I had been well acquainted for some thirty-three years) died 3 Feb., 1887, aged 63.

1508. *Hore secundum usum Romanum.* 8vo. Par., Thielman Kerver.

—— —— 8vo. Par., Guill. Anabat.

1511. —— 8vo. Par., Theilman Kerver.

[1512.] *Les heures a lusaige de Rome.* 8vo. Par., per Joh. de Brie.

[1512.] *Heures a lusaige de Sens.* 4to. Par., Jehan de brye.

1514. *Orationes et hore in usum Romanum.* 4to. (Aug. Vind.) per Jo. Schonsperger.

—— Another edition by the same printer in the same year, but without name or date.

1517. *Horæ ad usum Romanum.* 8vo. Par., Thielman Kerver.

1522. *Horæ secundum usum Romanum.* 4to. Par., Thielman Kerver.

[1522.] *Les heures a lusaige de Rome.* 8vo. Par., par Germ. Hardouyn.

1526. *Horæ secundum usum Romanum.* 8vo. Par., Thielman Kerver.

1527. *Hore in laudem B. V. Marie, secundum consuetudinem ecclesie Parisiensis.* 8vo. Par., per Sim. du bois.

[1528.] *Horæ, secundum usum Romanum, cum multis suffragiis et orationibus de novo additis.* 8vo. Par., Germ. Hardouyn.

1529. *Horæ in laudem B. Mar., secundum usum Romanum.* 8vo. Par., apud Gotofr. Torinum.

N. D. *Hore B. Marie.* 8vo. M. E. Jehannot.

—— *Hore secundum usum Romanum.* 8vo. Par., G. Hardouyn.

—— Another edition by the same printer.

—— *Les heures a lusaige de Rome.* 4to. Par., per Guill. Godar.

—— *Hore secundum usum Sarum.* 4to. Rich. Pynson.

—— *Les heures a lusaige Dangiers.* 8vo. [Par.] Simon Vostre.

—— *Heures a l'usaige de Soissons.* 8vo. [Par.] Simon Vostre.

—— *Heures de nostre dame en Francoys et en Latin.* 4to. Par., Anth. Verard.

—— *Heures.* 8vo. Par., Anth. Verard.

VI.

List of MSS. formerly in the possession of Cathedrals, Monasteries, Colleges, and Churches, in England, Scotland, and Ireland,

With some personal owners connected therewith.

Aberdeen Cathedral. Ashmole, 147 (Barth. Glanville).

Abingdon. Digby, 39, 146, 227 (fine Missal, with Calendar). Bodl. 874 (?).

—— John Crystall, a monk of. Rawlinson, C. 940.

—— Rowland, a monk of. Rawl. D. 235.

Alban's, St. Auct. F. II. 13 (Terence, 12th cent., with very humourous drawings of the *dramatis personæ*); Bodl. 569; Laud Lat. 67; Laud Misc. 264, 279 (Missal of the Altar of St. Katherine early in the 14th cent., and in the 15th transferred to the infirmary chapel), 358, 363[1], 370, 409; Rawlinson, C. 31; D. 358 (given by Abbot John Whethamstede); Rawlinson, B. N. 99 (obtained through Brother Hugh Legat, and given by Abbot John Stoke).

—— Hugh Eyton, Sub-prior. Bodl. 467.

—— Sub-sacrist. Ashmole, 1796.

Alvingham, Linc. Laud Misc. 642.

Ashridge, Bucks. Bodl. 415.

Athdare, Kildare. Rawlinson, C. 320.

Babwell. *See* Edmund's Bury.

Barking. Laud Lat. 19; Bodl. 155 (*see* p. 473); Bodl. 923 ('Iste liber constat Sibille de Felton, Abbatisse de Berkyng.')

Beauchief, Derbyshire (?). (Liber) 'Sancti Thomæ Mart.' Auct. E. *infra* 47.

Beauvale, *or* de Bellavalle, Notts. Douce, 114.

Bedford. The Minorites. Laud, 176 (given by John Grene, D.D., in 1471).

Belvoir, Linc. E Mus. 249 (*Epp. Gilb. Foliot*, given by Prior William).

Bilsington, Kent. Bodl. 127 (given by John, Vicar of Newchurch).

[1] This has a twelfth century rubric, 'Hic est liber Sancti Albani,' and also a late fourteenth century record that Bp. Rich. de Bury gave it 'domui S. Albani.' It would appear therefore to be one of the books which he bought and subsequently restored. See p. 5 *n*.

Bordesley, Warwickshire. Bodl. 168; Laud, 606 ('Bord').

Boxgrave, Sussex. Rawlinson, A. 411.

Bradsole, near Dover, Priory of St. Radegund. Rawlinson, B. 336.

Bridlington. Auct. D. *infra*, II. 7; Bodl. 357; Digby, 53.

Bristol. John Colman, 'magister domus *le Gauntes* juxta Bristolliam,' gave Bodl. 618 to John Bradley.

[—— *Printed book.* W. de Worde's *Vitas Patrum*, 1495, belonged to the Hosp. of St. John Bapt. 'in Redcliffe pitte in suburbio oppidi Bristoll;' afterwards to Bishop Tanner.

Buildwas, Shropshire. Bodl. 371.

Byland, *or* Bellaland, Yorkshire. Bodl. 842 (bought from a carpe ter by John Gillyng, a monk, in 1477), Laud Misc. 149.

Canterbury, Ch. Ch. Auct. G. *infra* 6; Bodl. 214, 379; Laud Misc. 165; Tanner, 18, 223; Rawlinson, C. 168 (Missal, given by Archbp. Warham).

—— W. Bonyngton, a monk of, 1483. Rawlinson, B. 188.

—— W. Boolde, a monk of. Bodl. 648.

—— St. Augustine's. Auct. F. VI. 3; Bodl. 299, 381, 391, 426, 464, 596 (*second half*), 600, 746 (Libri Sententiarum, 'ex adquisitione fratris Johannis Godcheap,' 'Distinctione VI^{a}, gradu II°.' It is by these shelf-marks that I have recognised the ownership, the name of the Abbey having been erased); E Mus. 223; Laud Lat. 65; Laud Misc. 225, 296; Wood Donat. 13; Ashmole, 1431; Barlow, 32; Hatton, 94; Maresch. 19[1]; Rawlinson, C. 7, 117, 159; Digby, B. N. 9 ('Liber Joh. de Lond., de librario S. August. Cant.')

Carlisle Cathedral. Bodl. 728.

—— (a House at). Laud Misc. 582.

Carmarthen, Minorites at. Bodl. 36.

Chichester Cathedral. Bodl. 142 ('de dono Seffri. primi Episc.')

Chicksand, Bedfordshire. Auct. E. *infra* 4.

Cirencester, St. Mary's Abbey. Barlow, 48; Bodl. 284.

Cokersand, Lanc. Rawlinson, C. 317.

Coventry Cathedral. Auct. F. III. 9; Digby, 33 (given by Rich. Luff, monk); Bodl. 901.

[1] This MS., a tenth-century copy of Jerome's translation of Philo, would seem from the following contemporary distich which is inscribed, to have originally belonged to Malmesbury:

'Hunc quicunque librum *Adelmo*
depresseris (*l.* deprenseris) almo,
Dampnatus semper maneas cum
sorte malorum.'

The St. Augustine's inscription of ownership belongs to the 13th cent. But there was an earlier possessor than either of these. A faint inscription, coæval with the MS., records that it was given by 'Teutbertus Levita,' *i. e.* a deacon, 'dominis suis sancto Medardo et Sebastiano,' *i. e.* to the abbey of SS. Medard and Sebastian at Soissons.

Cropthorn Worc. Rector in 1279. Rawlinson, B. N. 169.

Croyland. Rawlinson, C. 531.

Dartford Nunnery, Kent. Douce, 322. ['These booke, in whom is contente dyuers deuowte tretis and specyally þe tretis þat is callid ars moriendi, ys of þe ȝifte of Wyllãm Baron, Esquyer, to remain for euyr to þe place and nonrye of Detforde, and specially to the vse of dame Pernelle Wrattisley sister of þe same place by licence of her abbas, þe whiche Pernelle is nece to þe forseyde gentylman Willãm Baron.']

Dore, Hereford. Laud, 138; E Mus. 82.

Dover Priory. Bodl. 920 (Catalogue of the Library).

—— Hosp. of St. Bartholomew. Rawlinson, B. 335.

Dublin, Cathedral of Ch. Ch. *or* Holy Trinity. Rawlinson, B. N. 85 (a magnificent Psalter, written by direction of Prior Stephen de Derby; *see* p. 244).

—— Abbey of St. Thomas. Rawlinson, B. 500.

—— Hosp. of St. John Bapt. Rawlinson, B. 498.

—— St. Mary's Abbey, near. Rawlinson, B. 495, C. 60, D. 1236.

—— Church of St. John Evang. Misc. Liturg. 337.

Dulci Corde, De, *or* Sweet-Heart, Galloway. Fairfax, 5, (belonged to 'Dervorgoyl de Bayll'[iol], the foundress of this house, and of Balliol College. Bought by Fairfax at Edinburgh in 1652).

Dumfermline (?). Fairfax, 8.

Dunbrothy, Wexford. Rawlinson, B. 494.

Durham Cathedral (St. Cuthbert). Laud Lat. 12; Laud Misc. 359, 368, 489; Fairfax, 6; Rawlinson, C. 4.

—— Thomas Dune, a monk of. Douce, 129.

Edingdon, Wilts. Bodl. 565 (Will. Wey's Itinerary to the Holy Land, given by himself); Auct. D. V. 14 (Bible)[1].

Edmund's Bury, St. Bodl. 216, 240, 297, 582 (?), 715, 737, 860; E Mus. 6, 7, 8, 9, 26, 27, 31, 32, 33, 36, 112; Laud Misc. 233, 742; Laud Orient. 174[2]; Rawlinson, C. 697 (all between the 11th

[1] This was twice deposited, in 1463 and 1465, by *dom.* William Newton as a pledge for loans of 20*s.* from the Langton Chest at Oxford. The House at Edingdon was of the order of Bonhommes; this fact identifies the borrower with the person of that name of the order of *Boni Viri* who supplicated for the degree of B.D. 15 Feb. 14$\frac{6}{6}\frac{6}{7}$. Boase's *Reg. of Univ. of Oxf.*, 1885, vol. i. pp. 33–4.

[2] A Hebrew Psalter on vellum, with this inscription: 'Hoc Psalterium Ebraycum est de bibliotheca venerabilis monasterii Sancti Eadmundi acomodatum fratri Ricardo Bryngkelei, ordinis Minorum, sacreque theologie humilimo professori, 1502.' Few Hebrew MSS. are known as having been formerly in English conventual libraries; probably not so much from their original rarity (for

and 13th centuries); Rawl. Liturg. e. 42 (*Martyrologium;* given by Rich. Fuller, Chaplain, and Rich. Aleyne, Kerver, in 1472); Bodl. Add. C. 181.

Edmund's Bury, St. Grey Friars at Babwell. Vol. of sermons by Nich. Phillipp, preached at Newcastle-on-Tyne, Lichfield, Lynn, and Oxford, in 1430–6 (very much injured); Lat. Th. D. 1. 'Liber iste post decessum patris ac fratris Thome Goddard, bachalarii, spectat ad conventum fratrum minorum Badwellæ, exaratum Norwici Anno Dom. 1538.' Bought in 1887.

Ely. Laud Misc. 112; Bodl. Add. A. 1.

Evesham. Auct. D. I. 15; Barlow, 7 (*Officia Ecclcs.*); Rawlinson, B. N. 16; Rawl. A. 287.

Exeter Cathedral. Auct. D. II. 16, F. III. 6; Bodl. 579, 708, (all these given by Leofric[1]); Auct. D. I. 7 and 12 (given by Hugh, Archd. of Taunton), 9 (given by Adam de St. Bridget, Chanter), 13, 18; D. II. 8; D. *infra*, II. 9 (?); D. III. 10, 11 (?); Auct. F. I. 15; Bodl. 92, 137, 147, 148, 149, 150, 162 (given by Richard Brounst, Vicar Choral), 190, 206, 267, 269–70, 272, 273, 279, 286, 287, 289, 290, 293, 311 (*Pœnitentiale Gregorii*, 10th cent.), 314, 315 (given by John Stevenys, Canon), 319, 333, 335, 377, 380, 393, 463 (given by the Executors of Bp. Lacy), 482, 494 (given by Hugh, Archd. of Taunton, for the use of poor scholars), 681, 691, 707, 708, 717, 718, 720 (given by Bp. Lacy's Executors), 725, 732 (given by Bp. Grandison), 738, 744 (given by the Executors of Dr. John Snetesham, D.D., Canon and Chanc.), 748, 749, 786, 810, 829 (given by Bp. Lacy's Executors), 830, 865. Wood Donat. 15 (given by Snetesham's Executors, 1448).

—— Hosp. of St. John Bapt.; Laud, 156.

—— Conv. of Grey Friars; Bodl. 62.

Eynsham, Oxon. Laud Lat. 31 ('Liber monasterii de Heynysham juxta

several monastic catalogues witness to possession of them) as from having been generally consigned to destruction at the Dissolution through ignorance of the language. The shelf-marks of books belonging to the library at Bury are letters of the alphabet with a number sometimes in Roman, sometimes in Arabic, figures. The following MSS., in which the place-name has been destroyed, may probably by their similar marks be identified as having come hence: 'M. 23,' a twelfth century copy of Jerome on Eccles., Bodl. 582; 'B. xxv,' St. Aug. in Ps., vol. ii, Bodl. 249; 'C. xxix,' Bible, Auct. D. iii. 14; 'A. 7,' Bible, Rawl. B. N. 8; 'M. 44,' Bodl. 130. No doubt more of these shelf-marks may be found.

[1] Two of Leofric's gifts are now in Corp. Chr. Coll., Cambridge; 41, Bede's *Hist.*, and 190, Theodore's *Pœnitentiale*, &c. Two other Exeter MSS. are 93 and 191.

Oxonyham'); Bodl. 718 (a 10th cent. MS. of Ecgbert's Penitential) possibly belonged to Eynsham, as there are early entries, on a fly-leaf at the end, of moneys payable from Thame and Banbury, places at which this abbey possessed property.

Finchale, Durham. Laud Misc. 546.

Ford, Devon. Laud Misc. 606.

Fountains' Abbey. Ashmole, 1398, 1437; Laud Misc. 310, 619.

Gainford, Durham. Thomas Heddon, Vicar. Rawlinson, A. 363.

Garendon, Leic. Ashmole, 1516.

Gisburne, Yorkshire. Laud Lat. 5.

Glastonbury. Laud Lat. 4; Laud Misc. 128 (belonged to Thomas Wason, Abbot); Bodl. 80 ('domino Petro Weston monacho Glastoniensi dono dedit venerabilis pater Johannes Selwode, Abbas Glastoniensis[1]'). The Dunstan MSS., Auct. F. IV. 32, and Hatton 30, and probably 42, are said in Bp. Stubbs' preface to *Memorials of Dunstan* to have belonged to Glastonbury.

Hanworth (Middlesex?); Richard, Rector. Rawlinson, B. N. 165.

Harlaston, Staffordshire. [A beautiful Sarum Missal, printed at Paris by Wolfgang Hopyl, entirely on vellum, in 1514, which was given to Harlaston Chapel by the last will of Sir Henry Vernon, Knt., who died at Leicester 13 Apr. 1515, and was buried at Tonge, Salop, is now numbered Ashmole 1764.]

Hatfield Peverel, Essex. Rawlinson, B. 189 (given by John Bebseth, Prior).

Hereford Cathedral. Rawlinson, C. 67; Adam Dorensis. On the cover is written, by a hand of the 16th cent., 'This book belongs to the library of the cathedrall church of Hereford. Deliver it to the custos thereof to be restored to the sayd library.' As the writer failed to restore it himself, no one did after him. The next entry of ownership, with a curious irony in the opening phrase, is this: 'Suum cuique. Tho. Hearne, Aug. 19, 1731. Bought of Mr. Fletcher, of Oxford, bookseller.'

—— Vicars Choral. Rawlinson, C. 427.

—— The Minorites. Hatton, 102.

Hexham ('Hextildesham'). Bodl. 236.

Hickling, Norfolk. Tanner, 194, 425.

Holme Cultram, Cumb. (S. Mar. de Holmo); Hatton, 101.

[1] The book is a Latin translation by John Free (*al.* Phreas), Master of Balliol College, Oxford, of Synesius' tract *De laude Calvitii*. It is written and ornamented by an Italian hand, and contains as introductory matter a letter to the translator from 'Omnibonus Leonicensis,' dated at Vicenza 9 July, 1461, and a preface by the former to John Tiptoft, Earl of Worcester. The third leaf bears the arms of Bishop Beckington.

Houghton — (?). [A Breviary printed at London in 1555, 2 vols. belonged 'ad ecclesiam parochialem de Houghton, precium iiij^{s}.' Gough Missals, 171, 2.]

Jorevall, *or* Jervaulx, Yorkshire. Bodl. 514.

Kenilworth, *or* Kelyngworth, Warw. Auct. F. III. 13 (bequeathed by John Alward, Rector of Stoke Bruerne).

Kilmainham, Dublin. Hosp. of St. John Bapt. Rawlinson, B. 501.

Kime, Lincolnshire. Auct. D. IV. 15.

Kingswood, Wilts. E Mus. 62.

Kirkstall. Laud Lat. 69; Laud Misc. 216; E Mus. 195.

Langley, Norfolk. Bodl. 242 (*Registrum*).

Leedes, Kent. Bodl. 406.

Leicester, St. Mary of the Meadows. Laud Misc. 623, 625.

—— St. Clement. Bodl. 140 belonged in the 15th cent. to a friar of this Dominican house, J. de Per. Part of the book was written *c.* 1300, by one William of Glen Magna, in Leicestershire.

Lesnes, *or* Lyesnes, *alias* Westwood, Kent. Bodl. 656; Douce, 287.

Lichfield Cathedral. Bodl. 956 ('de dono Tho. Chestrefeld, Canonici residentiarii et prebendarii de Tervyn'); Ashmole, 1518.

London, St. Paul's Cathedral. Digby, 89 ('Liber magistri Thomæ Lysiaux, Decani Sancti Pauli').

—— The Carmelites. Laud Lat. 87; Bodl. 730 ('conventus Carmelitarum London. Ex ass[ignat]ione f. Thome Walden'[1]).

—— Whittington College. Auct. D. V. 10 (Lat. Bible. 'Istum librum emit magister Johannes Hychecoke de magistro Johanne Smyth, tunc presbytero parochiali ecclesie sancti Jacobi juxta collegium Ricardi Whytyngton, cujus dictus M. J. Hychecoke est socius perpetuus, pro VI. marcis et XL^{d}., anno Domini M.LXII° (*sic*! read M.CCCC.LXII) et 4° die mensis Junii ejusdem anni. Hiis testibus, magistro Thoma Englys et magistro Willelmo Twyltwyne, sociis perpetuis dicti collegii. Non venale').

—— 'Domus Salutationis Matris Dei, ord. Carthus.;' *i.e.* The Charter-House. Douce, 262; Art. 4 in Rawl. D. 318.

—— Hosp. of St. Mary of Elsyng, now Sion College. E Mus. 113.

Louth Park, Linc. Fairfax, 17.

(Ludlow Parish Church. *Printed Book*, D. 2. 13. Art. Seld.[2])

Malmesbury. Marshall, 19 (*see* Canterbury, St. Aug. *supra*).

[1] A twelfth century MS., which had formerly belonged to Reading abbey, written in the 'Romanis majusculis litteris,' which Leland specially notes as a characteristic of many of the books in Walden's large and valuable library (Tanner, *Bibl. Brit.*)

[2] *Picus Mirandula de Providentia Dei*, 1508. Given to the library of the Church by Rich. Sparchiford, Archdeacon of Salop, Oct. 19, 1557. It had previously belonged to Linacer.

Maxstoke, Warwickshire. Bodl. 182.
Melsa, *or* Meaux, Yorkshire. Rawl. C. 415; Digby, 77 [1].
Merton, Surrey. Digby, 147; Ashmole, 1522.
—— John Ramsey, Canon of. Seld. *supra*, 39.
Missenden, Bucks [2]. Auct. D. I. 10; Bodl. 729,
Mottenden, *or* Motynden, Kent. Bodl. 643 (bought by brother Richard de Lansyng in 1467 for 26*s.* 8*d.*); Auct. D. II. 20 (13th cent. Gospels, glossed: 'Constat Johanni Armorer, Vicario de Sutton Valince et Hedcorne, precio iiij^{s}, de Bukhorst, quondam fratre de Muttinden').
Muchelney, Somerset. Rich. Coscumbe, Prior. Ashmole, 189. ii.
Newark, Surrey. Bodl. 602 (*Bestiarium Moralizatum*, with pictures. John Rosse, canon of Newerke, near Guldeforde, and curate of Weylde, received it from his brother canon, Will. Thecher, 6 Oct. 1538; witnesses, Rich. Woode, canon Charles Balye, and Benedict Barslayd. On the last leaf of a 12th cent. MS. of Cassian's *Collationes*, which is bound up with this, is an entry in which the name has been almost entirely cut off by a 17th cent. binder: 'Liber prioratus de H[atford Regis?]').
New Place, Sherwood. Laud Lat. 34; Laud Misc. 428.
Northampton, S. Andrew. Auct. D. I. 8.
—— The Minorites. Auct. D. IV. 11.
Norwich Cathedral (Holy Trinity). Bodl. 151, 787 ('Liber fratris Symonis Bozoun, Prioris Norwyc.'); Fairfax, 20; Douce, 366 (*see infra*, p. 467).
Nutley, *or* Notley, Bucks. Douce, 383, iii.
Oseney, Oxford. Bodl. 655; Digby, 23 (bequeathed by Henry de Langley); Rawlinson, C. 939 (*Officia Eccles.*); Bodl. 477 (on two leaves at the beginning, mutilated by a 15th cent. binder, are lists, in red and black, of the charters of the abbey, written early in the 14th century. The name of the abbey is erased, but these words remain—'[de] dono Ricardi de Wrthe canonici nostri'); Auct. F. VI. 4 ('Liber Thomæ Corsæri, presbyteri, ex dono Radulphi Bloore, quondam canonici de Osney, 5 die Maii, A.D. 1543.')
Osyth, St., Essex. Laud Misc. 329.

[1] 'Wilflete wlt [vult] quod iste liber tradatur abathie de Mews in Holdernes, quia emit eum ab uno monacho ejusdem domus pro viij*s.* et dubitat utrum monachus habuit potestatem vendendi. Volo (*sic*) etiam quod habeant Thomam de virtutibus theologiæ ('the^{e}.') quem emit ab eodem pro iij*s.* iiij*d.*' Note at f. 147 b. The book is Grosteste's *Oculus Moralis*.

[2] Many MSS. which had belonged to Missenden are described in one of Thorpe's Catalogues for 1834.

Oxford[1], All Souls' College. Digby, 44 (written and given by John Saundre, fellow).

—— Balliol College. Bodl. 252.

—— Brasenose College. Bodl. 874.

—— Exeter College. Bodl. 42 ; Digby, 57[2].

—— (Hertford College. *Printed Tracts* on the Bangorian Controversies, 8vo. I. 237, BS.)

—— Lincoln College. Rawl. B. N. 14 (Bible : 'Liber collegii Lincoln in Oxon., ex dono magistri Johannis Kend . . ., baccallarii in sacra theologia'). Bodl. 198 ('ex dono doctoris Thome Gascoigne[3]').

—— Merton College. E Mus. 19 (given by William, Bishop of Chichester) ; Bodl. 50 (bequeathed by Thomas English), 689 and 757 (given by Henry Sever, Warden, in 1468), 696 ('ex dono Thomæ Balsall quondam socii'), 700 and 751 (given by Richard Fitz-James, Bishop of Chichester), 752 (given by Will. de Harington, D.D.) ; Digby, 67, art. 18 (given by Dr. John Reynham), 155 (given by John Burbache[4]), parts of 190 and 191, 216 ; Ashm. 835. (*Printed Book* S. 9. 14. Th.[5]).

—— New College. Auct. E. IV. 9 (*see* p. 24) ; Auct. F. V. 29 ('Liber datus collegio beate Marie Winton in Oxonia per exsecutores domini Henrici Jolypace, nuper camerarii ecclesie cathedralis Sancti Pauli London., anno Domini MºCCCCº.XXXIº. Oretis igitur pro eisdem.' The name of the college has been almost entirely erased.)

—— Oriel, *or* St. Mary's, College[6]. Bodl. 637 ; Digby, 191, art. 5

[1] St. Frideswide. Cotton MS. Tiberius C. V. probably belonged to the library of this house, as it bears the name 'Frideswide' on the top of the first page as an invocation.

[2] 'Hunc librum emit . . . . . . a magistro Philips, rectore collegii Exon, aº. Xi. 1468, una cum volvella solis et lunæ.'

[3] See p. 23 *n.* A mistaken statement of Warton's is there inadvertently repeated, that it was given by Gascoigne to Durham College.

[4] 'Liber domus scolarium de Merton Halle in Oxon. ex dono magistri Johannis Burbache, doctoris in theologia et quondam socii ejusdem domus, ut inchatenetur in libraria communi ad perpetuum usum studencium ibidem.'

[5] *Galani Conciliatio Eccl. Armenæ cum Romana*, 1650. It is satisfactory to be able to add, that the Bodleian obtained this book, as Bishop Booth obtained the Robertsbridge MS. (*infra*) 'modo legitimo ;' a memorandum records that it was 'bought of Fletcher the bookseller.'

[6] A copy of the *Chron. Martini Poloni*, *sæc.* XIV, 'legatus collegio B. Mariæ Oxon. per magistrum Rogerum, quondam socium ejusdem,' is in the Library at Berne. C. P. Cooper's *Appendix to Report on Fœdera*, App. A. p. 36.

('Domus B. Mariæ'); Auct. F.V.28 ('Liber scolarium domus beate Marie Oxonie [comparatus?] per magistrum Johannem Cobuldick anno Domini M.CCC. tricesimo septimo, pretio XX solidorum, et non accommodetur extra domum nisi consanguineis predicti magistri Johannis sub racionali caucione [1]').

—— St. Edmund Hall. Rawlinson, C. 900 (given by Hen. VIII); Cod. Liturg. 186.

—— Bostar Hall. Laud Misc. 6 ('Liber magistri Thome Wyche emptus per eum Oxonie de domino Ric. B . . . . de aula Bostaris, ultimo die Decembris,' A.D. 1455. A long subsequent inscription has been entirely erased.)

—— Staple Hall. Ashmole, 748.

—— The Minorites. Digby, 90 (given in 1388, by John de Teukesbury, with the assent of Thos. de Kyngusbury, 'Minister Angliæ').

—— (name cut off), Bodl. 215.

Paignton parish, Devon. Rawlinson, C. 314 (Canons of Bishop Quivil).

Pershore. Bodl. 209; Barlow, 3; Rawlinson, C. 81.

Pesholme (Will. Marschalle, Chaplain of), York. Bodl. 857.

Peterborough Cathedral. Barlow, 22; (*see infra*, p. 471); Bodl. 96 (?).

—— Humfr. Natures, monk of. Gough Missal, 47.

Pipewell, Northamptonshire. Rawlinson, A. 388.

Pleshey, Essex; Trinity College. Bodl. 316.

Pontefract, Holy Trinity Hospital. Barlow, 49.

Ramsey. Bodl. 833.

—— John Wellis, a monk of. Bodl. 851. See *Chron. Rames* 1886, pref. p. xlv.

—— Robert Lincoln, a monk of. *Printed Book*, Expos. Hymn. Sar. 1502. Gough Missal, 122.

Reading, St. Mary's Abbey. Auct. Digby, B. N. 11; Digby, 148, 200; Bodl. 125 [2], 197, 200 (given by W. de Box), 241, 257, 397

[1] The inscription has been in large part almost entirely erased. On the same fly-leaf with this entry there is a memorandum that M. William Bridby borrowed 20*s*. from the Gildford Chest [belonging to the University] in 1421, on depositing this volume as security.

[2] On the last leaf of this MS. there is a list, faintly written with a style, of some twenty MSS. (including 'triplices cantus' for the organ), written by one monk, to which the memorandum is added: 'Hec sunt opera fratris W. de Wicb. per quadriennium apud Leom. (*i. e.* Leominster, a cell to Reading) commorantis.' The list commences, 'Nota quod frater W. de Wicb. (*probably Wicumbe*), precibus domini J. de Abbend. tunc precentoris, hortatu vero et precepto domini R. de

(given by John Sarum), 550, 570 (given by Thos. Staunton, prior), 713, 730, 772, 781, 848; Laud Misc. 79, 91, 725; Auct. D. I. 19; D. II. 12; D. III. 12, 15; D. IV. 6 (apparently written for Abbot Roger in the middle of the 12th century); Auct. F. III. 8 (given by 'frater Alwredus'); F. *infra*, I. 2 ('de dono domini Thome Erle abbatis'); Rawlinson, A. 375.

Robertsbridge, Sussex. Bodl. MS. 132 (written by Will. de Wodecherche, 'laicus quondam conversus Pontis Roberti [1]').

Roche, *or* de Rupe, Yorkshire. Rawlinson, C. 329.

Rochester Cathedral. Laud Misc. 40.

Rossevalle, Kildare. Rawlinson, C. 32 (*Ordo servitii*).

Salisbury Cathedral. Digby, 173, art. 1 (given by Peter Fadir, Vicar Choral [2]); Barlow, 5 (a Missal, which apparently belonged to Salisbury); Bodl. 407, 516, 756, 765, 768, 835; Rawlinson, C. 400 (*Pontificale*, given by Bishop Martivall); E Mus. 2 (a fine book of the Sarum Use, given to the Library by Godfrey Goodman, Bishop of Gloucester, on condition of its restoration to Salisbury if reclaimed by Bishop, Dean, or Chapter!).

Selby. Fairfax, 12.

Sempringham. Douce, 136 (?).

Shene, Surrey, Carthusian Priory. Bodl. 797; Rawlinson, C. 57. [8vo. H. 36 Th. BS., a book printed in 1608, belonged apparently to some foreign branch of this house: 'Domus Shene Anglorum'].

Sherston, Wilts; the Church. Bodl. 733 (given by Rich. Wade, Vicar of Turvill Aston, in 1577; St. Ambrose's comment on St. Luke).

Shrewsbury, St. Chad. Rawlinson, D. 1225 (*Martyrologium* [3]).

Sion, *or* Syon, Middlesex. Bodl. 630 (given by Joan Buklonde, widow of Rich. Buklonde, citizen and fishmonger of London, to Roger Twiforde and the rest of the brethren of Syon, 'ad orandum pro

Wygorn. tunc supprioris, collectarium cotidianum secundum usum Rading correxit et de duobus unum fecit.' The book may have belonged to either Reading or Leominster.

[1] The usual anathema is subjoined on any one stealing the book from the house of St. Mary 'de Ponte Roberti,' or in any part mutilating it; which is followed by this self-exculpatory note on the part of a subsequent possessor: 'Ego Johannes, Exon. episcopus, nescio ubi est domus prædicta, nec hunc librum abstuli, sed modo legittimo adquisivi.' This *John* would seem to be John Booth, who was Bishop of Exeter from 1466 to 1479.

[2] The name of Peter Fader is found also in MS. Arch. Seld. B. 26.

[3] An extremely interesting volume. The text is of the eleventh century; to this is prefixed a fourteenth century calendar, with a large number of obits of various dates inserted, of which very many also are scattered through the volume. At the end are some hymns with music; and a list, at the beginning, of relics in the shrine of St. Chad, in Latin and English.

ea et pro anima dicti Ricardi'); Rawl. C. 781 (*Ordo servitii*); 941 (part of the *Mirror of our Lady*); Rawl. D. 403.

Southwark, St. Mary Overy. Ashmole, 1285. [*Printed Book*, Clichtoveus *De vita sacerdotum*, 1519, C. I. 5. Linc.]

—— John de Lecchelade, a Canon. Rawlinson, B. 177.

Stafford, St. Mary. Auct. F. V. 17 ('accommodatus fratri Philippo de Merston'; formerly Hatton, 44); Hatton, 74.

—— The Minorites. Auct. F. V. 18 (formerly Hatton, 39).

—— St. Thomas, near. Auct. F. III. 10.

Staindrop, Durham, The College. Rawlinson, A. 363 (given by Thos. Heddon, Vicar of Gainford, in 1515).

Tattershall, Lincolnshire. Bodl. 419.

Thorney, Cambr. Bodl. 680; Laud Misc. 364; Tanner, 10.

Titchfield, Hants. Digby, 154. [*Printed Book*, Auct. I. Q. VI. 1, possessed by Thomas Oke, Abbot of Titchfield.]

Towcester, Northamptonshire, Hugh Malyng, Provost. Bodl. 731.

Trentham, Staffordshire. Laud Misc. 453.

Tynemouth. Laud Misc. 657.

Valle Crucis, De, Denbighshire. E Mus. 3.

Waltham, Essex. Auct. D. IV. 22 (given by Walter de Nortone); Laud Lat. 109; Laud Misc. 515; Rawlinson, B. N. 62 (given by Peter, Archdeacon of London); Rawlinson, C. 330, D. 1228[1].

Wardon, Bedfordshire. Laud Misc. 447.

Warter, Yorkshire. Fairfax, 9.

Waverley, Surrey. Bodl. 527.

Westminster Abbey. Rawlinson, C. 425 (*Pontificale*).

Wilton, Wilts. Rawl. B. N. 23 (Psalter[2]).

Winchcombe, Glouc. Douce, 368. [*Printed Book*, 'Liber dompni Roberti Benet, monachi Wynchelcumbensis'; *Marsilii de Inghen Quæstt. in IV libros Sententiarum*, fol. s. l. et a.]

Winchester Cathedral ('Domus S. Swythini'). Bodl. 767. Art. 2 in Laud Misc. 368 (which belonged to Durham) written by a monk of St. Swithin.

Windsor. Bodl. 208, 822.

Witham, *or* Wytham, Somerset. Bodl. 801 ('Ex dono Joh. Blacman').

[1] This has the shelf-mark 'CLXX: al. Ca.,' in a fifteenth century hand, identifying the library; for other volumes which have the name have similar marks; 'XLV al. P., XLIII. al. P., LXXXXVIII. al. Ca.'

[2] The ownership of this book appears from the following petitions in a Litany at the end: 'Ut abbatissam nostram in bonis actibus corroborare digneris, Te r. Ut congregacionem sancte Marie sancteque Edithe et omnium sanctorum tuorum in tuo servicio conservare digneris.'

[Witney Church, Oxon, Altar of St. M. Magd. in. *Printed* Sarum Missal, Paris, 1514, bought at Oxford in 1526. Gough Missal, 25].

Worcester Cathedral. Auct. F. *infra*, I. 3; Bodl. 861 (removed in 1590), 868; Junius, 121; Hatton, 40, 76.

—— 'Fratres Prædicatores.' Rawlinson, C. 780.

York Minster (?). Rawlinson, C. 775.

—— Succentor (?). Douce, 225.

—— St. Mary's Abbey. Rawlinson, B. N. 11, 12; Arch. A. Rot. 21; (*see infra*, p. 472).

—— Hosp. of St. Leonard. Rawlinson, B. 455.

Many of Laud's MSS. came from the Carthusian monastery at Mentz, from the monastery of Eberbach in the Duchy of Baden, and from St. Kilian's at Würtzburg. It is worth mentioning that No. 233 amongst his Miscellaneous MSS. belonged to John Lydgate, and No. 576 to John Foxe. Several others had been previously in the possession of Archbp. Usher, and of Lindsell, Bishop of Peterborough. No. 702 was given, 13 Apr. 1419, by Henry Percy, Earl of Northumberland, to his confessor, brother Will. de Norham, D.D.

No. 76 of Digby's MSS. was bought by Dr. John Dee, at London, May 18, 1556, 'ex bibliotheca Joh. Lelandi.'

Bodl. 493, Grandisson's Life of Becket, was 'Reginaldi Pooli liber, 1539.'

In Auct. D. V. 12, where a long inscription has been totally erased, the following short one remains: 'Ista Biblia est fratris Andree de Averham, de ordine fratrum Minorum.' The village of Averham is in Nottinghamshire.

VII.

Notes of a few Bindings

Of some special interest, additional to those mentioned in the course of the Annals.

1459. A folio Chronicle, from the Creation, in German, written at Celle in 1459. Bound in leather ('cuir-bouilli'), with large brass bosses, and very remarkably ornamented with large hand-worked figures of men and women, with the costumes clearly represented. Douce MS. 367. *Exhibited.*

1484. *Ars dicendi*, fol. Colon., per Joh. Koelhoff de Lubeck. The contemporary binding is stamped with a variety of small devices, the Pelican in her piety, the Lamb and flag, &c., with the following curious mottos, 'Odium suscitat rixas. Litem inferre cave. Non fiant federa metu facta.' Auct. II. Q. III. 33. Bought at Heber's sale.

1486. *Liber Sextus Decretalium*, fol. Bas., Mich. Wenssler. Bound in pigskin, stamped with delicate ornamental borders and figures of *Caritas*, *Fides*, *Fortitudo*, and *Spes*. In the centre, on one side two female figures sitting, one holding in one hand a crucifix, in the other, the chalice and wafer, the other with hands clasped, looking to the Deity in the clouds, with the motto 'Impetrat alma fides Cristo quam dante salutem expectare soror spes animosa solet.' On the other side, a lady, with two infants, giving bread to a beggar; motto, 'Que vocor insigni caritum de nomine virtus Omnia que pietas suadet obire sequor.' The binding is probably about the middle of the 16th century. Auct. III. Q. III. 7. Bought at Kloss's sale.

1498. *Heures*, on vellum. 4to. Par., S. Vostre. Vellum binding, with gilt tooling, and the monogram of Catherine de' Medici, two *Cs* and two *Ms* interlaced; on one side, the Virgin crowned, with angels; on the other, the Crucifixion. Douce, 137.

Another book which appears to have the monogram of Cath. de' Medici is a copy of the 'Prymer after the vse of Sarum,' printed at Rouen by Flor. Valentine in 1556 (Douce BB. 15, formerly W. Herbert's). It has three *Cs* interlaced on the tooled binding. Douce has noted in it that it belonged to Hen. II of France, and that it came from the library at Fontainebleau.

N. D. *Horariumsecundum usum Trajecten. diocesis*. sm. 8vo. (The Easter table runs from 1492 to 1505.) Binding, black calf, with fine heraldic devices; shield with two-headed eagle, surmounted by the imperial crown, supporters, a lion and gryphon, within a border of stags, &c.; at the corners, fleur-de-lis, eagle, lion ramp., &c. Evidently it belonged to a German Emperor. Douce, 16.

—— *Lavacrum conscientie*, 12mo. Rouen; Joh. de Gersono *Opus tripartitum*, Rouen; *etc.* Contemporary binding; on one side, a female saint, with palm-branch and book, standing beside a tower; on the other, panels with fancy figures of animals, and inscription in border, 'Notam fac michi viam in qua ambulem quia ad te levavi animam meam.' Auct. I Q. VI. 3.

—— *Gemma vocabulorum*, sm. 4to., Suollis, per Petrum Os de Breda. Stamped pigskin; on one side, the Annunciation, 'Virgo Maria Mater;' on the other, the baptism of our Lord, 'Hic est Filius meus;' in the borders, the Crucifixion and the Serpent in the Wilderness, &c. Probably late in the 16th century. Auct. II. Q. *infra*, II. 20.

c. 1500. Two English MSS. which have the arms of Henry VII: one, The Mirror of our Lady; the other, a sermon on Zacchæus, St. Luke xix. 9. The second has on one side the Tudor rose, with the motto 'Hec rosa virtutis de celo missa sereno Eternū florens regni sceptrū tenet.' (*See* p. 32 *n.*) Rawl. MSS. C. 941, 942. Auct. E. *infra* 5 has also the arms of Hen. VII or VIII.

c. 1500. *Sermones Joh. Nider*; 8vo. Par. On one side four compartments with Saints; one of them St. Nicholas, restoring three children to life; on the other side, the B. Virgin, filled up with ornamental work. 8vo. N. 3 Th. The four compartments are found also (in bad condition) on the cover of 8vo. B. 269 Th.

1513. *Sermones Gilberti Tornacensis*, 8vo. Par. Bound by Nich. Spiernick, the Cambridge binder. On one side, the Annunciation, with inscription, 'Ecce ancilla domini fiat michi secundum verbum tuum.' On the other, St. Nicholas raising the children to life, with 'Nicolaus' above and 'Spiernick' underneath. On either side there is also the binder's mark, '[mark] N S'. 8vo. T. 34 Th.

[1519]. Latin poems 'in laudem Thomae Wolcii,' with a prose panegyric, by Rob. Whitinton; on fine vellum, with illuminated borders to some pages, and the Cardinal's arms on the first page. Each side of the binding has three compartments, with St. George and the Dragon, and portcullis with rose and lily. Bodl. MS. 523. *Exhibited.*

1519. The third decade of Livy, printed by Aldus, 8vo. A pair of compasses, with the motto Ουδεν ανευ λογου.

N. D. *Hore beate Virginis,* 8vo. Par. Nic. Hygman. (Calendar runs from 1520 to 1536.) The binding covered with gaudy gilt stamped ornaments, arrows, quivers, drums, &c., with the initials 'N. V.' at the four corners on each side. In the centre on one side, the B. Trinity, on the other, the Crucifixion. Gough Missal, 162.

Hen. VIII. Among Douce's specimens of bindings is one which formerly belonged to a copy of the first edition of Eginhard's *Vita Caroli Magni,* 1521, which bears on one side a very fine impression of the 'Redemptoris mundi arma,' and on the other the royal arms, with the lines 'Hec rosa,' &c.

Hen. VIII. '*Serpens antiquus de septem peccatis criminalibus,*' 8vo. Par. Brown calf, stamped with the arms of Hen. VIII and Kath. of Arragon, with the legend, 'Deus det nobis suam pacem et post mortem vitam eternam. Amen.' 8vo. S. 27 Th. This inscription (without *Amen*) is found also round the arms of England (with the Garter) on the binding of a MS. Latin Bible, Auct. D. V. 7.

1525. *Heures a lusaige de Paris,* 4to Par. Belonged to Mary de' Medici. In the centre of the finely tooled and coloured binding is the name 'Marie.' It was formerly in the library of Charles Chauncy, M.D. Douce, BB. 170.

1526. *Diomedis Grammatici opus,* 8vo. Hagenau. The emblems of the four Evangelists, with St. Paul in the centre. 8vo. B. 21 Med. B. S.

1528. P. Lombard, *Liber Sententiarum.* On one side, the B. Trinity; the Father holding up the Crucified Son, with the Dove; angels around; above, between cross-keys, the binder's (?) initials, G. P. On the other side, the Cross; at its foot, the Grave, with the Saviour (with hands folded) half-buried in it; around, the instruments of the Passion, and initials as before. 8vo. L. 4 Th.

N. D. *Prayer of Salisbury use,* sm. octavo, at Paris, by Fr. Regnault. (The Easter table from 1531 to 1546.) On one side, St. Gregory's mass; on the other, St. Barbara. In fine condition. Douce, BB. 89[1]. The same stamp, also in good condition, is found on the cover of *Summa Joh. Valensis,* Ven. 1496: Auct. II. Q. V. 20.

[1] Douce notes on a fly-leaf that he had seen a copy of Caxton's *Faytes of Armes* with the same stamps on the cover.

1533. *Missale ad usum Sar.*, 4to. Par. On one side, the arms of Hen. VIII, with dragon and greyhound as supporters, and inscription, 'laudate dominum de terra dracones et omnes abyssi, G. R.' On the other, four panels: 1. St. George; 2. St. Michael; 3. A female saint, with book and sword, and a tower in the background; 4. a female saint crowned, with book and sword, and the binder's initials again, 'G. R.' Round the panels, 'o mater dei memento mei quid quit (*sic*) agas prudenter agas respice finem.' Gough Missal, 129.

1537. Sim. Grynæus' *Novus Orbis*, fol. Basle. A beautiful specimen in the Grolier style, but without his motto. Douce, G. 300.

1540. *Biblia*, printed at Paris by Rob. Stephen, on vellum. Prefixed to the title is a painting of the royal arms of England, quarterly, three lions passant and three fleurs-de-lis, with lion and dragon as supporters, surrounded with the Garter. The morocco binding has fine Grolier-like tooling, and in the centre a shield of arms, or, a cross gules, with the motto 'Alta cernens non deficio.'

1541. Cornutus *De natura Deorum*, 8vo. Basle. The figure of *Spes*, gazing at the Cross, which has the motto *Meritum Christi*: her feet, which are marked *Charitas*, rest on the foundation-stone of *Fides*. At the side are the words *In te dñe speraui . nō confundar in eternum, in iustitia tua libera me &* eripe me. Psal.* 70. Below are the initials I. B., with a monogram or device between; and in the outer margin of the compartment the words *Quoniam in me speravit liberabo eum protegam eum quo &c.*, *Psal.* 90. A very fine specimen. 8vo. C. 24 Art. Seld. Another fine example is on the binding of 8vo. G. 8, Art. BS. (Gyraldi *Poematia*, Basle, 1540), but here the initials are I. P., with a different device.

1547. Vitruvius. In parchment, with the devices of Henry II of France, arrows and quivers, with the interlaced H. and D., for Diana of Poitiers. Douce, V. *subt.* 1.

1549. *Horæ*, large 8vo. Par. From the library of Hen. II of France and Diana of Poitiers. Fancy tooling, with the interlaced H. and D. surmounted by a crown, and the motto 'Donec totum impleat orbem.' Douce, BB. 184. An engraving of the binding is given in Dibdin's *Bibliogr. Decam.* (where the book is called a *Missal*). II. 488.

'1550. H[ieronymus] P[rims] R[atisponensis];' date and initials on stamped pigskin, with figures of our Lord, David, Isaiah, and St. John Bapt. Mason, Q. 149 (Homer, 1541).

1556. *Breviarium secundum usum majoris ecclesie Sancti Petri Geben[nensis]*; 8vo. Sides powdered with stars; tooled ornaments; legend, 'Mesire Gaspard Vincent, cure de Margni.'

1556. *Coustumes du bailliage des Sens*, 4to. Sens. Printed on vellum. Grolier binding, with the head in gold on both sides of Hen. II of France. Arch. Bodl. D. *subt.* 22.

1557. Stamped pigskin. On one side, the Crucifixion; 'Propter scelus popu[li].' On the other, the Resurrection: 'Mors ero mors tua,' within a border of figures representing Faith, Hope, Charity, and Justice. 'A. P. B. 1557.' 8vo. K. 45, Art. BS. (Melanchthon's *Historia de vita Lutheri*, 1562 &c.).

1557. *The Prymer after the use of Salisburye*, by Jhon Wayland, 12mo. A beautiful specimen of English tooling on morocco, in the early part of the last century: [by Roger Payne?] Gough Missal, 37. An armorial book-plate of twelve quarterings, with the motto 'Bende or brake,' is on the cover.

1563. Hub. Goltz's *Julius Cæsar*, fol. Bruges. Presentation copy to Philip of Spain. On the two sides is this inscription: 'Philippo Austrio Regi Hispaniae optimo maximoq. Principi Hubertus Goltzius Herbipolita Auctor devotus nomini maiestatiq. ejus D.D.' In the centre, within wreaths, on one side 'Nec spe nec metu,' on the other, 'Colit ardua virtus.' Douce, G. *subt.* 6.

1563. The Croat Version of the Augsburg Confession, with portraits, stamped in black on pigskin, of the three editors whose names are subjoined to the prefatory dedication to Philip Landgrave of Hesse, 'Primus Truber Carnio' (Creiner), 'Antonius Dalmata, exul,' and 'Stephanus Consul Istrianus [15]41.' 4to. G. 14 Jur. Seld. The same heads are found stamped in gold on the bindings of the Glagolitic Gospels printed in 1562, and the Croat New Test. in 1557. The latter book was purchased in 1887 for £28 10*s*. I am informed by Mr. W. Salt Brassington that the borders on these bindings were designed by Holbein.

1568. *La Sainte Bible, Lat. Fr., avec annotations par René Benoist*, 4to. Par. The title has an illuminated border with the arms of the family of Sanguin, seigneurs de Fontenay, of which an account by J. Holmes, dated July 31, 1832, is inserted. The binding exhibits fine tooling, with the name 'S. Magdalene Sanguin' in the centre. Douce, BB. 198.

1580. Presentation copy from Matth. Host of his *Hist. rei nummariæ* to one Jerome Tobing of Luneburg. On the calf binding on one side is stamped a portrait of John George, then Elector of Brandenburg, and on the other the arms of the Emperor Rudolph II, dated 1578. Wood, 561.

1584. G. du Bartas' *Seconde Semaine*, 4to. Par. Printed on vellum. Bound in morocco, with tasteful and delicate floriated tooling; with bows, quivers, arrows, horns, and fleurs-de-lis, and in the centre the arms of J. A. Comte de Thou, a chevron between three gadflies. Arch. Bodl. D. *subt.* 23. *Exhibited.*

1585. Aulus Gellius, 8vo. Paris. Stamped pigskin; coarse execution. On one side two female figures, as on the binding under the year 1486, *supra*; 'Impetrat alma fides Christo quam dante saliutem (*sic*) expectare soror spes animos' (*sic*; see above); on the other, two female figures, one with palm branch and spinning wheel, the other with sword, dagger, and scales: 'Fortuna fortes metuit, ignavos premit; Justicia per se exigua res est.' Auct. S. IV. 14.

1586. A volume of law tracts by Alb. Gentilis and Nic. Vigelius, printed in 1585-6 (Crynes, 547), has upon its white vellum cover a portrait of Charles Emanuel I of Savoy, with the following extravagant laudation. On one side: 'Carole, mortales dubitant homo sisne deusve. Sunt tua sceptra hominis sed tua fa[cta dei ?].' On the other side: 'Victus eras acie, fidei constantia tandem victorem ante homines fecit et ant[e Deum ?].'

'1603. Tenez le vray.' Coat of arms, arg. per fess, in chief 3 mullets sable (?) on Christoph. Gillius' *Commentationes theologicæ*, 1610. F. 1. 12 Th. And on Gretser's *Hortus S. Crucis*, 1610, B. 4. 20 Linc.

1604. *A confutation of astrologicall dæmonologie*: by John Chamber, preb. of Windsor and fellow of Eton. With a dedication to James I, dated Windsor Chapel, Feb. 2, 1603. Fol. Savile MS. 42. Beautiful gilt tooling; in the centre a falcon, crowned, holding a sceptre in its dexter claw; the badge of Anne Boleyn, used by her daughter Q. Elizabeth[1].

James I. An 8vo. Latin Bible, in minute writing of the thirteenth century, which was given to the Library by Edw. Sherborne, esq., has on a handsomely gilded vellum binding the arms of James I. An entry on a fly-leaf records that on 7 March, 1475, Richard Swan bought the book 'a domino Math., vicario de Mudford,' in Somerset. Auct. D. V. 41.

1611. *Horæ*, printed at Antwerp in 1609, 4to., presented to Mary de' Medici, in 1611, by C. M. Ab. de St. Ambroise. Prefixed on six vellum leaves are the arms of France and Tuscany, and a beautifully illuminated title-page and dedication, with paintings representing the sun-rise and the Annunciation, and a portrait of the

[1] I am informed by Mr. W. Salt Brassington that the British Museum has lately acquired a book printed in 1581 which has the same device of the falcon, and which is said to have been bound for Q. Elizabeth. Probably the Savile MS. was bound for presentation to her, and on her death the dedication to her successor was inserted, whose arms are also painted on a fly-leaf.

Queen-Regent. The binding (black morocco) is covered with the initial H. (for Hen. IV) crowned. Formerly in the possession of Dr. Charles Chauncy. Douce, BB. 169.

1611. Scottish Confession of Faith, Psalms, Catechism; 8vo. Edinb. Binding covered with gilt tooling and initials 'A^{c}S.'

1621. *La Saincte Bible*, 3 vols. fol. Par. Formerly in the Colbert, Hoym, and Lamoignon libraries. Bound in red morocco, by Le Gascon, with beautiful delicate tooling, and in the centre the arms of Count Hoym. Described in Dibdin's *Bibl. Decam.* II. 497. Douce, B. *subt.* 13–15. *Exhibited.*

1657. John Rowland's translation of John Jonston's *Thaumatographia naturalis.* Bound in a piece of coarse tapestry, with the figures of a woman and man. 4 Δ. 217.

1762. *Bullarium Franciscanum*, 1762. 3 vols. Beautiful inlaid binding, with the arms of Pope Clement XIII (Carlo Rezzonico).

VIII.

The following List of MSS. and Miscellaneous Objects of interest formerly exhibited in the Library and Picture Gallery is reprinted, with a few trifling omissions and additions, from the first edition.

Those books and curiosities which are still exposed to view are distinguished by an asterisk. But the contents of the glass cases are now from time to time varied, and many other MSS. are at present on view in addition to those here noted. As the old list, however, contains many items of interest, and sufficiently represents the variety of objects which visitors can generally examine, I here reproduce it in the main as it stood, but re-arranging its order, the better to agree with the present mode of exhibition[1].

In a glass case by the Library door[2].

* 1. Autograph book of distinguished visitors.

This book commences at the year 1820. Among the autographs which it contains may be mentioned the following in particular:—

Her Majesty the Queen, Nov. 8, 1832, with her mother the Duchess of Kent; Dec. 12, 1860.

The Prince Consort, June 15, 1841; June 4, 1856; Jan. 9, 1857 (in company with his three eldest children); Dec. 12, 1860.

Prince of Wales, Jan. 9, 1857; March 27, 1860; June 18, 1863.

Princess of Wales, June 18, 1863.

[1] This list was reprinted in part with additions by Mr. F. Madan in 1881, as a small guide-book for the use of visitors.

[2] This case now contains besides the books numbered 1–5, Pliny's *Epistolæ*, with Duke Humphrey's autograph (*see* p. 9), a volume of Bodley's letters to James; notes of Privy Council discussions in the time of Charles II (open at an amusing page, which is printed in the Clarendon State Papers, vol. iii. p. L.); the Chatterton volume (*see* p. 390); and 'The Solemne League and Covenant,' 4° Edinb. 1643, printed by Evan Tyler, having at the end some blank pages prepared for subscription of names, on which are 90 autograph signatures of peers, gentry, and divines, attached chiefly in the East Kirk at Edinburgh on 13 Oct. 1643, but some also added on 7 Nov., 22 Dec. and 8 Jan. following. Among the ministers are Robert Douglas, Moderator of the General Assembly, Rob. Barclay, Rob. Traill, David Calderwood, and James Sharpe, with the two deputed to Scotland from the English Parliament, Stephen Marshall and Robert Goodwin.

Duke of Wellington, Oct. 20, 1835 (in company with Q. Adelaide); Sept. 14, 1839; June 15, 1841; Aug. 20, 1844.

Gul. Gesenius, Aug. 5, 1820.

Sir John Franklin, 1829.

Sir D. Wilkie, June 14, 1834.

Geo. Aug. Selwyn, the first Metropolitan of New Zealand, and afterwards Bishop of Lichfield, June 30, 1837.

Chevalier Bunsen, Jan. 24, 1839; Aug. 20, 1844.

Princes of Ashantee, June 10, 1840.

Henry Hallam, Oct. 16, 1840.

Bishop of Malabar, Mar Athanasius Abdelmesih, June 12, 1841.

Pierre Ant. Berryer, Nov. 23, 1843.

W. H. Prescott, June 24, 1850.

Alfred Tennyson, June 21, 1855.

A Siamese Prince, June 29, 1858.

Lord Brougham, June 20, 1860.

Lord Palmerston, July 2, 1862.

Queen Emma of Honolulu, Aug. 14, 1865.

Chinese Ambassadors, June 7, 1866.

Until the year 1861 it was also the custom for all graduates of Cambridge and Dublin who were admitted *ad eundem* to enter their names in this book; it is to this custom that we owe possession of the signature of Bishop Selwyn [1].

[1] Many autographs of distinguished literary men are found in the old Registers of all the persons admitted to read in the Library, since in these the readers themselves generally entered their own names. The first 'Liber admissorum' contains the names of both graduates and non-academics, the names in the first case being autograph apparently from about 1617, after a first list of all the graduates at the several colleges at the time of the commencement of the book. It commences about the year 1610, and ends, in the case of graduates, arranged under their several colleges, about 1676, and in the case of strangers, at 1692. The second Register, which is 'peregrinorum et aliorum admissorum' alone, begins at 1682 and ends at 1833. The first existing register of *books* used by readers begins Jan. 3, 1647–8, and ends Dec. 30, 1649. The earlier registers appear to have been cut up for use in binding, and a few pages from the books used after 1630, which I found in the covers of various volumes, are now carefully preserved. The following are some of the names, of some special mark, which are found in the Admission books:—

John Dury, July 20, 1624.

Joh. Jonstonus, M.D., 1634, accompanying Bogeslaus, Voyvode of Beltz.

Joh. Fred. Gronovius, June 25, 1639.

George Bull, 'SS. Theol. Studiosus, per dispensat.' July 5, 1656.

Andrew Marvell, Sept. 30, 1665.

Sir Winston Churchill, Oct. 4, 1665.

Henry Dodwell, Oct. 20, 1666.

Thomas Rymer, June 20, 1683.

Edmund Calamy, 'Londinensis,' Aug. 18, 1691, and in 1722.

Sir George Mackenzie, (afterwards first Earl of Cromarty), Dec. 14, 1694, and several times subsequently.

Joh. Ern. Grabe, Nov. 10, 1697.

Thomas Madox, Sept. 21, 1705.

* 2. *Latin Translation by Queen Elizabeth*, while Princess, of an Italian sermon by Bern. Ochini, *De Christo*; written entirely by herself, and sent as a New-year's gift to her brother Edward VI[1].

It forms a small 8vo. volume of thirty-six pages, on vellum, and was given to the Library by Rev. J. Bowle, of Idmerston, Aug. 15, 1761. The following dedication (hitherto unprinted) is prefixed by the Princess :—

'Augustissimo et serenissimo Regi Edvardo Sexto. Si aliquid hoc tempore haberem (Serenissime Rex) quod mihi ad dandum esset accommodatum, & Maiestati tuæ congruens ad accipiendum, equidem de hac re vehementer lætarer. Tua Maiestas res magnas & excellentes meretur, et mea facultas exigua tantum suppeditare potest, sed quamvis facultate possim minima, tamen animo tibi maxima prestare cupio, & quum ab aliis opibus superer, a nemine amore & benevolentia vincor. Ita iubet natura, authoritas tua commouet, & bonitas me hortatur, ut cum princeps meus sis te officio obseruem, & cum frater meus sis vnicus & amantissimus, intimo amore afficiam. Ecce autem pro huius noui anni felici auspicio, & observantiæ meæ testimonio, offero M. T. breuem istam Bernardi Ochini orationem, ab eo Italicè primum scriptam, & a me in latinum sermonem conuersum. Argumentum quum de Christo sit, bene conuenire tibi potest, qui quotidie Christum discis, & post eum in terris proximum locum & dignitatem habes. Tractatio ita pia est & docta, ut lectio non possit non esse vtilis et fructuosa. Et si nihil aliud commendaret opus, authoritas scriptoris ornaret satis, qui propter religionem et Christum patria expulsus, cogitur in locis peregrinis & inter ignotos homines vitam traducere. Si quicquam in eo mediocre sit, mea translatio est, quæ profecto talis non est qualis esse debet, sed qualis a me effici posset. At istarum rerum omnium M. tua inter legendum iudex sit, cui ego hunc meum laborem commendo, & vna meipsam

Joshua Barnes, July 22, 1706.
William Whiston, Sept. 28, 1710.
C. Wesley, 'Ædis Xti alumnus,' April 19, 1729.
Joh. Dav. Michaelis, Oct. 9, 1741.
W. Blackstone, 'S.C.L.' Feb. 11, 1742-3.
Benj. Kennicott, 'Coll. Wadh. Schol.' July 15, 1746.
George Ballard, Dec. 9, 1747.
Edw. Rowe Mores, Commoner of Queen's College, Aug. 29, 1748.
John Uri, 'Korosini, Hungarus,' Feb. 17, 1766.
Edw. Gibbon, 'Coll. Magd. olim Soc. Com.' Oct. 17, 1766.
John Schweighäuser, June 13, 1769.
J. J. Griesbach, March 22, 1770.
Hen. Alb. Schultens, Oct. 16, 1772.
Philip Bliss, Feb. 9, 1809.

A list of 'extranei nobiles ac generosi, cum quibusdam Anglis, licentiati ad studendum in bibl. Bodl.,' which begins from the beginning, in 1602, and ends in 1690, is given by Wood in his MS. E. 5, but whence he obtained his earliest names does not appear.

[1] This MS. is noticed by Warton in his *Life of Sir T. Pope*, p. 73, where he also quotes Hearne's account of Elizabeth's New Testament, which is described at p. 65 *supra*. In Smith MS. lxi, fol. 1 there is a holograph Latin letter, not signed, from Elizabeth to her brother, which was also written at Enfield, as well as this volume. In it she says she had been hindered from writing before by pain in her head and eyes.

etiam dedico, Deumque precor vt M. tua multos nouos & felices annos videat & lucris ac pietate perpetuo crescat. Enfeldiæ, 30 Decembris.

'Maiestatis tuæ,
'humill. soror,
'& serua,
'Elizabeta.'

* 3. A Latin Exercise book, in 4to., which appears to have been filled up by Edward VI and his sister Elizabeth jointly.

Sentences written by the former are dated from Jan. 1548-9 to Aug. 1549. The boy-monarch has written his own name in several parts of the book. It came to the Bodleian 'ex dono doctissimi viri P. Junii, Bibliothecarii Regii, A.D. 1639.' Patrick Young also gave another book in Edward's handwriting in folio, containing Greek and Latin phrases, written, very neatly, in 1551-1552[1].

4. *Letters of Queen Henrietta Maria* to Charles I before their marriage; in French.

The volume forms part of the Clarendon State Papers. A volume of letters to her from the King, with other papers by him, is now in the glass-case.

5. Archbp. Laud's formal Letter of resignation of his office as Chancellor of the University, signed by himself, and dated from the Tower, June 22, 1641. In Latin; on parchment.

Endorsed by Ant. à Wood with this memorandum: 'Given to me by Rob. Whorwood, of Oxon, Gent., 29 Feb. 1679[2].'

[1] Mr. John Gough Nichols, in his collection of the *Literary Remains of Edw. VI*, printed by the Roxburghe Club in 1857 (vol. i. pp. cccxxiii-cccxxv), describes these volumes at length, and assigns the whole of both of them to the pen of the King, but some part of the first volume corresponds much more closely with the usual style of Elizabeth's early writing, and a memorandum by Hearne testifies that it was regarded in his day as having been written by her.

[2] A touching letter, in English, dated June 28, which Laud forwarded, together with this formal document, is printed in vol. ii. of Wharton's edition of his *Remains*, p. 217. In the same volume are included copies of all the letters which accompanied the Archbishop's gifts to the Library, and the following reply (p. 177) to a notification from the Vice-Chancellor, Dr. Frewen, of the visitation of his collection, and of the giving special charge to the Librarian respecting their safe custody, seeing that they stood unchained, and in a place frequented by strangers who came to see them.

'SIR,

'I thank you heartily for your care of my books. And I beseech you that the Library-keeper may be very watchful to look to them since they stand unchain'd. And I would to God the place in the Library for them were once ready, that they might be set up safe, and chained as the other books are; and yet then, if there be not care taken, you may have some of the best and choisest tractats cut out of the covers and purloin'd, as hath been done in some other libraries.

W. CANT.

'Lambeth, Nov. 15, 1639.'

* 6. Lord Clarendon's Letter, resigning the same office upon his going into exile; written in a secretary's hand, but signed by himself. Very touching and beautiful. It runs as follows:—

'For Mr. Vicechancellor of Oxford.

'Good Mr. Vicechancellor,

'Having found it necessary to transport myselfe out of England, and not knowing when it will please God that I shall returne againe; it becomes me to take care that the University may not be without the service of a person better able to be of use to them, than I am like to be; and I doe therefore hereby surrender the office of Chancellor into the hands of the said University, to the end that they make choyce of some other person better qualifyed to assist and protect them then I am, I am sure he can never be more affectionate to it. I desire you, as the last suite I am like to make to you, to believe that I doe not fly my Country for guilt, and how passionately soever I am pursued, that I have not done any thing to make the University ashamed of me, or to repent the good opinion they had once of me, and though I must have noe farther mention in your publique devotions (which I have alwayes exceedingly valued) I hope I shall be alwayes remembred in your private prayers as

'Good Mr. Vicechancellor,

'Your affectionate servant,

'Calice, this $\frac{7}{17}$ Dec. 1667.' 'CLARENDON.'

* 7. A volume of the Papers of W. Bridgeman, Under-secretary of State to James II (bequeathed to the Library by Dr. R. Rawlinson; *see* p. 237), open at a leaf containing the original declaration written and signed by the Duke of Monmouth, on the day of his execution, of the nullity of his claim to the Crown.

The following is a copy:—

'I declare y^t ye title of King was forct upon mee, & y^t it was very much contrary to my opinion when I was proclam'd. For ye satisfaction of the world I doe declare that ye late King told mee that Hee was never married to my Mother.

'Haveing declar'd this I hope y^t the King who is now will not let my Children suffer on this Account. And to this I put my hand this fifteenth day of July, 1685.

'MONMOUTH.

'Declar'd by Himselfe, & sign'd in the presence of us.

'Fran. Elien. [*Turner*].
'Tho. Bath & Wells [*Ken*].
'Tho. Tenison.
'George Hooper.'

Beside it was placed the Proclamation of James II, ordering the apprehension of all persons dispersing the Declaration issued by Monmouth upon his landing in England; dated but one short month previously, June 15, 1685.

The same volume contains two letters from Monmouth to the King, begging for his life, and one to the Queen. These have been frequently printed.

* 8. Latin verses in the autograph of Milton. See p. 56.

9. The original MS. of Addison's *Letter* (in verse) *from Italy to Lord Halifax.*

A Rawlinson MS.; Poetry 17.

10. Letter from Alexander Pope to H. Cromwell, Esq.; dated July 15, 1711.

The same volume contains various other letters from the same to the same, which were printed by Curll in 1727; one by Dryden, three by J. Norris of Bemerton, three short notes from Young, and several letters by Ladies Hester Pakington and Mary Chudleigh. It belongs to the Rawlinson collection; Letters 90.

11. Letter from Archbp. Laud to Sir W. Boswell, the English Resident at the Hague; dated from Lambeth, Nov. 26, 1638.

It refers to libels printed in Holland, and particularly to one against Laud, supposed to be then printing at Amsterdam, entitled, *The Beast is Wounded.* 'I thanke God I trouble not myselfe much with these things; but am very sorry for the Publicke, which suffers much by them.' Bought in 1863 at a sale at the Hague for £7 17*s.*, together with a letter on diplomatic business signed by Sir Thomas Bodley, and dated at the Hague, April 11, 1589, which is now bound in the same volume, MS. Add. C. 69.

* 12. *New Testament,* said to be bound in a piece of a waistcoat of King Charles I. See p. 67.

* 13. Another, bound by the Sisters of Little Gidding. See p. 67.

* 14. *Xiphilini Epitome Dionis Nicæi*; Gr. 4to. Par. printed by Rob. Stephens, 1551. Bound in a handsomely tooled and gilt calf binding, in the Grolier style, with the badge of Dudley, Earl of Leicester, viz. the Bear and Ragged Staff, in the centre[1]. Bequeathed by Selden.

* 15. *Bacon's Essays*; in a worked binding. See p. 65.

* Specimen of the early *Block-books*, or books printed from engraved blocks before the invention of moveable types; being the Apocalypse, represented in a series of rudely-engraved scenes, with short explanatory descriptions.

This is a copy of the edition called by S. Leigh Sotheby, in his *Principia*

[1] Another book that belonged to the Earl, having his arms on the cover, is a copy of the New Testament, printed in 1576, on vellum; probably a presentation copy from the printer, R. Jugge.

Typographica, the Second; it belonged to Douce (No. 249), who bought it for thirty guineas at Inglis' sale[1].

* 16. A French panegyrical poem, presented to Queen Elizabeth, in 1586, by Georges de la Motthe, a French refugee; with a prefatory address in prose.

Enriched with an exquisite portrait of the Queen, in all the grandeur of her wide circumference, and with golden hair of very *prononcée* hue; and with a great variety of beautifully-executed monograms, symbols, &c. around each page. The binding is richly tooled and covered with designs; while in the centre on either side, protected by glass, are brilliant bosses, formerly described as being composed of humming-birds' feathers, but really a fine specimen of enamel. Arch. Bodl. B. 73.

'Ex dono ornatissimi, simul ac optimæ spei, juvenis D. Johannis Cope, armigeri, equitis aurati, baronetti f. natu maximi, olim Reginensis Oxon, Almæ Matris ergô. 4 Cal. Jan. 1626.'

On a fly-leaf at the end is attached a fragment from some English theological treatise, in wonderfully minute, although clear, handwriting.

* 17. *Psalterium;* close of thirteenth century.

Bound in solid silver, on which are engraved the Annunciation and the Coronation of the Blessed Virgin, seen beneath a coloured transparency which gives an appearance of great richness to the otherwise uncoloured silver.

A beautifully decorated volume, given by Sir Rob. Cotton to William Butler, M.D. of Cambridge, in 1614; and to the Bodleian July 15, 1648, by Dame Anne Sadler, wife of Ralph Sadler, of Standon, Herts. Auct. D. iv. 2.

* 18. *Evangelia, secundum Matt. et Marc.* A fine Douce MS. (292) of the eleventh century, bound in thick boards, overlaid on one side with a brass plate, whereon are engraved the four Evangelists, with

[1] Of this xylographic *Apocalypse* the Library possesses two other editions, one being that called by Mr. Sotheby the Fourth, which was given by Archbp. Laud, and the other being that called the Fifth by Sotheby, but 'Editio princeps' by Heinecken, which was bought in 1853 for £120 5*s*. Other Block-books in the Library are, (1) two editions of the *Biblia Pauperum*, or Scenes from Bible History; one coloured, now exhibited in the large glass case, the other (which belonged to Douce) uncoloured; (2) the *Historia B. M. V. ex Cantico Canticorum*, being the edition called the Second by Sotheby; also exhibited; (3) *Propugnacula, seu Turris Sapientiæ*, a broadside, bought in 1853 for six guineas. A facsimile of this is given in vol. ii. of Sotheby's *Principia;* (4) *Speculum Humanæ Salvationis:* also exhibited. In this book, which is the second Latin edition of the work (formerly described as the *Editio princeps*), twenty pages are taken off from wood-blocks, and the rest from moveable type. The copy belonged to Douce. It came previously 'ex musæo Pauli Girardot de Prefond,' but is not mentioned in De Bure's catalogue of that library, published in 1757. It is said that a copy of this book has been sold for the large sum of 300 guineas.

angels; in the centre, an ivory carving of our Lord, with the Evangelistic symbols.

* 19. *Evangeliarium.* MS. in folio; of the tenth century.

A fine MS., which formerly belonged to the abbey of St. Faron, near Meaux; bought at the sale of M. Abel-Remusat's library in 1833, by Mr. Payne, and sold to Douce, apparently for the sum of £31 10*s*. On the cover is an ivory diptych; in the centre, a figure of our Blessed Lord treading on 'the lion and adder, the young lion and dragon;' around, twelve scenes from His life and miracles. Douce MS. 176.

20. Ivory triptych eleven inches high; North Italian work, of the 15th century. Transferred to the Ashmolean Museum; see p. 469.

In the centre the Blessed Virgin and Child between St. Leonard and another saint; on the wings, St. John the Evangelist and St. Lawrence[1].

* 21. The (probably) first book printed from moveable types; being a very fine copy of the grand Latin Bible (Auctarium, M. i. 1, 2) printed at Mentz about 1455. See p. 275.

A copy was sold at the auction of the library of the Duke of Sussex, in 1844, for the moderate sum of £190; when the same copy, however, was re-sold at the auction of the library of Dr. Daly, Bishop of Cashel, in 1858, it produced no less than £596. Other specimens of the Mentz press of Fust and Schoiffer are now shown in the Psalter of 1459 (Auct. M. i. 17), and the Canon of the Mass (Douce 280 b), both on vellum, and in the first Bible with date, that of 1462 (Auct. M. i. 7).

* 22. A copy of the first book printed in the English language, being *The Recuyell of the Histories of Troy*, printed by Caxton, most probably at Bruges, about 1472.

This copy wants seven leaves; it was probably given to the Library by Crynes. A second copy, which wants three leaves, is also in the Library, which was given in 1750, by James Bowen, a house-painter of Shrewsbury, well known as a local antiquarian[2]. A copy, wanting forty-four leaves, was sold at Utterson's sale in 1852 to the Earl of Ashburnham for £155.

* 23. The English Bible, translated by Myles Coverdale from the Vulgate, and printed abroad in 535. (S. Selden, c. 9.)

This copy of the first complete Bible printed in our language, is one of the largest and soundest known to be in existence, although, like almost all other copies, it wants the title. It was formerly in the possession of Selden. A facsimile title, engraved by Mr. Fry, of Bristol, from the Marq. of Northampton's

[1] Lent to the South Kensington Museum for an Exhibition in 1862, from the catalogue of which (under No. 202) the above description is taken.

Nos. 12–20 are in a glass case containing specimens of bindings, including others which are noticed in the course of this volume. Another case contains specimens of oriental binding.

[2] His Shropshire MSS. are in Gough's collection of MSS. for that county, of which they form the greater part.

copy, accompanies it, together with another leaf in facsimile, from the Earl of Leicester's copy. In 1854 a copy nearly perfect, having only two leaves in facsimile by Mr. Harris, was sold at Mr. Dunn Gardner's sale for the large sum of £364; and a very imperfect copy was sold for £100 in 1857; a nearly complete one at the sale of Mr. Perkins, of Hanworth, in June, 1873 for £400.

* 24. Hieronymus (*rectius*, Rufinus) *de Symbolo Apostolorum*; printed at Oxford in 1468. See p. 158.

* 25. *Plinii Historia Naturalis*; in folio. Printed 1476.

From the Douce collection, 318. See p. 327.

* 26. Four specimens of papyrus-rolls from Herculaneum, burnt to a crust.

Presented to the Library by George IV. See p. 290.

* 27. A Runic Primstaff, and a wooden Clog-Almanack: the former in the form of a walking-stick; the latter an oblong block, with a handle. See pp. 150, 222.

An engraving of the second may be found in the *Anglican Church Calendar illustrated*, published by Messrs. Parker. And a description of these primitive Calendars is given by Plot in his *Natural History of Staffordshire*, 1686, pp. 418–432, where there is an engraving of a Clog which was still in use in Staffordshire at that time. The Primstaff, which is well carved and in excellent preservation, belongs to the latter part of the seventeenth century, 1690-1700[1].

* 28. Eight small wooden tablets, apparently a pocket-edition of a Clog-Almanack, with very quaint figures. Made for the year 1636[1].

Given by Archbp. Laud; formerly numbered Laud D. 144.

* 29. Mexican Hieroglyphics; painted on a long skin of leather. Arch. Bodl. A. 75.

* 30. A Phœnician inscription, on stone. See p. 224.

* 31. English pocket-almanac, in brass, 1554–1579, with tidal tables for English ports, a compass, &c. On one side of its case is following inscription:—

'Ask me not, for ye Gett me not.—R. P.'

* 32. A specimen of the Papyrus-plant, in its natural state.

* 33. The *Psalter*, *Canticles*, &c., in Latin, with a Calendar; written in the first half of the eleventh century.

Noticed in Westwood's *Miniatures and Ornaments*, &c., p. 122. Douce MS., 296.

[1] The facts which determine the dates of these two Calendars (Nos. 27, 28), have been kindly communicated to me by Mr. H. F. Morland Simpson, of Fettes College, Edinburgh.

* 34. A *Bestiary*, or Natural History of Beasts, of the beginning of the thirteenth century, enriched with many very curious paintings upon a ground of brilliant gold.

Ashmole, 1511.

* 35. Another *Bestiary*, of slightly later date, illuminated in the same manner.

Bodl. 764.

36. A twelfth-century volume containing, besides various historical works, a *Bestiary*, illustrated with very curious drawings.

Laud MS. 247.

* 37. *Horæ*, formerly in the possession of Queen Mary I. See p. 52.

* 38. A *Psalter*, with the usual Canticles, Litany, &c.; written about the middle of the fourteenth century.

This magnificent volume was given by Robert de Ormesby, a monk of Norwich, to the choir of the Cathedral Church, 'ad jacendum coram Suppriore qui pro tempore fuerit inperpetuum.' It is illustrated with illuminations most beautifully executed, but, at the same time, containing the most grotesque and profanely inappropriate figures, resembling those sometimes found on the *Misereres* of collegiate churches. It is bound in a large covering of sheepskin, which by overlapping the volume has no doubt greatly contributed to preserve its freshness and beauty of condition. A facsimile from one page is to be found in Shaw's *Illuminated Ornaments*, 1833, with a description by Sir F. Madden. It belongs to the Douce collection, MS. 366.

* 39. *Boccaccio's Il Filocolo*, al. *Philocopo*; in folio, of the fifteenth century.

A beautiful MS., with five exquisite miniatures, and interlaced arabesque borders of the richest character. A facsimile, with a notice of the book, will be found in Shaw's *Illuminated Ornaments.* From the Canonici collection, 85.

* 40. *Horæ*, quarto; fourteenth century. A beautiful book.

From the Douce collection, 62.

41. *Breviary* and Psalter according to the use of the Carthusian Order; written about 1480.

A specimen of Italian art, from the Canonici collection; Liturg. 314.

42. *Horæ B. M. Virg.* 12mo. An exquisite Douce MS. (40), of the school of Albert Durer, executed by Bona Sforza. See p. 327.

43. *Horæ*, small quarto; end of the fifteenth century. The illuminations possess exquisite softness and delicacy.

Also from the Douce collection.

44. *The Miracles of the B. Virgin*, in French. A Douce MS. (374), in folio, executed about 1460, for Philip the Good, Duke of Burgundy, and enriched with most beautiful paintings of the tint called '*Camaieu gris.*'

* 45. *Horæ*, in quarto. A beautiful Douce book (144), the work of a French scribe in and about the year 1407.

* 46. *Horæ*, in duodecimo. Another gem from the Douce collection, executed about the year 1500, for the Emperor Maximilian and Mary of Burgundy his wife; in two vols. Douce, 219-20.

The margins are adorned with charming figures of birds, and in one instance a border is filled with representations of pottery and glass.

* 47. *Horæ*, in quarto, of the commencement of the sixteenth century; from the Douce collection, 112. An exquisite specimen of Flemish art. It belonged to Mary de Medicis.

* 48. *Horæ*, in small folio. A most sumptuous volume, executed towards the end of the fifteenth century. The illuminations are of the school of Van Eyck.

The borders of birds, butterflies, flowers, landscapes, &c., are marvels of nature in art; and many of the initials are distinguished by the utmost delicacy in design and finish in execution. Also from the Douce collection, 311.

49. *Horæ*. An illuminated MS. of the middle of the fifteenth century, in 4to., probably by a French scribe and artist.

From the Canonici collection.

50. Another MS. of the *Horæ*, in folio, of the fifteenth century, beautifully illuminated, with many miniatures, varying, in the treatment of some of the scenes which they represent, from the common type. Auct. D. ii. 11.

Traditionally said, but on what evidence does not appear, to have belonged to Henry VIII. In Rouse's speech on the reception of K. James the First's works it appears to be mentioned as a Breviary of Hen. Seventh then exhibited at the entrance of the Library (Hearne's *Tit. Forojul*, p. 201); if it be the same book, the tradition of its later ownership is of course then, no doubt, correct.

51. A magnificent folio volume (Bodl. MS. 270 *b*), containing a series of illustrations of Scripture History from Genesis to Job; written about the beginning of the fourteenth century; given by Sir Christopher Heydon in 1604.

Each page contains, in double columns, four pairs of miniatures painted, in medallion-form, upon a gorgeous ground of gold; the first of each pair represents some historical scene, which the second treats allegorically, and applies to the condition of the Church or of individual Christians. Two other volumes are to be found in the British Museum and in the Imperial Library at Paris. This is described in Pointer's *Oxoniensis Academia* (p. 142) as being 'a book of Scripture Cuts in curious Paint'!

52. A Hebrew *Bible*, beautifully written in the fourteenth century; in triple columns, with the Masoretic commentary written in very

minute characters, and frequently in fantastic figures, round each page.

Oppenheimer MS. 185.

53. A Russian painting upon a shell, representing a female saint called S. Parasceve, *ἡ ἁγία Παρασκευή*, who is found in the Greek Menology, but whose history is believed by the Bollandists to be a pious fiction. Removed to the Ashmolean Museum in 1887 [1].

54. A small oaken platter, bearing the following inscription: 'This Salver is part of that Oak in which his Majesty K. Charles the 2d, Concealed himself from the Rebells, and was given to this University by Mrs. Lætitia Lane.' Removed to the Ashmolean Museum in 1887 [1].

The donor was the daughter of Col. John Lane, the chief agent in the King's escape from Worcester; she died in 1709 [2]. The inscription on silver inserted in the platter was 'done at the charge of Sir Andrew Fountaine,' a well-known antiquary.

55. A specimen of Malabaric writing, upon a palm-leaf, three feet in length. 'Aug. 9, 1630. Ex dono Jo. Trefusis, generosi Cornubiensis, e Coll. Exon.'

56. A pair of long white leather gloves, worked with gold thread, which were worn by Queen Elizabeth when she visited the University in 1566 [3]. Engraved in Beck's *Hist. of Gloves*, 1883. Removed to the Ashmolean Museum in 1887.

* 57. The Book of *Proverbs*, written by Mrs. Esther Inglis. See p. 62.

* 58. A Persian poem, by Jami, on the history of Joseph and Potiphar's wife. Written A. D. 1569, and decorated with some very good paintings and arabesque borders [4].

One of Greaves' MSS.

* 59. A Persian treatise, in prose and verse, on ethics and education, entitled, *Beharistan, or, The Season of Spring*; by Nurruddin Abdurrahman, surnamed Jami.

The MS. was written at Lahore, for the Emperor of Hindustan, A.D. 1575,

[1] See *Report* for 1882-7, by the Librarian, p. 47.

[2] Pedigree of the family of Lane, p. 392 of the *Boscobel Tracts*, edited by J. Hughes, A.M., second edition, 1857.

[3] No. 7762 in the catalogue of the South Kensington Museum, in 1862.

[4] 'The poem of Joseph and Zuleikha, in the Public Library at Oxford, is perhaps the most beautiful MS. in the world; the margins of every page are gilt and adorned with garlands of flowers, and the handwriting is elegant to the highest degree.' (I. Disraeli's *Romances*, 1799, p. 52.)

by Muhammed Hussein, a famous scribe, who was called the *Pen of Gold;* and illustrated by sixteen painters. Its modern velvet binding is adorned with gold corners and bosses; and a bag in which it was kept is preserved. Elliot MS. 254, from the collection of Sir Gore Ouseley.

*60. A specimen of Telugu writing on palm-leaves; being an almanack for the year 1632.

Given by Archbp. Laud. MS. Laud Or. e. 1 (R.).

*61. The *Koran*, on a long and narrow roll, very elegantly written in minute characters.

Given by Archbp. Laud. MS. Laud Or. g. 2 (R.).

62. A fine MS. of the *Koran*, from the library of Tippoo Sahib at Seringapatam [1].

Given by the East India Company in 1806; see p. 283. Bodl. Or. 793.

63. A Burmese Pali MS., written in large black characters on thirty-nine gilded palm-leaves.

'Taken from a priest's chest in an idol-house of the deserted village of Myanoung, on the Irawaddy, thirty-five miles below Prome, April 17, 1825.' Given by Rev. Joseph Dornford, Oriel College, Nov. 8, 1830. MS. Pali a. 6.

64. A Sanskrit MS. in Telugu characters, on palm-leaves, brought from India by Sir Thos. Strange, formerly Chief Justice of Madras, together with a style employed for writings of this kind, and a leaf-cutter in sheath. Given by Sir T. Strange's daughter, Mrs. Edmund Ffoulkes, in 1864. MS. Sansk. a. 1.

65. The *Apocalypse*, illustrated in a series of very curious drawings, lightly coloured. Executed about 1250. Auct. D. iv. 17.

These illuminations Mr. Coxe at one time thought had been executed by the same hand as those of MS. Ee. III. 59. in the University Library, Cambridge, a volume which contains a Life of Edward the Confessor, in French verse (printed in 1858, under the editorship of H. R. Luard, M.A., in the Rolls Series of Chronicles), but when he was engaged in 1876 in editing this book for the Roxburghe Club he found reason to change his opinion. In the Cambridge MS. is found a particular description of Westminster Abbey, which is not elsewhere met with, and it is consequently inferred that the writer was a monk of that church. And in the course of the restorations carried on in 1868 in the Chapter House (which was built about 1250), a series of mural paintings, illustrating the history of St. John, were brought to light, one of which is a representation similar to that in our Bodley MS. of St. John 'ante portam Latinam,' and in both cases the cauldron bears the inscription of 'Dolium ferventis olei.'

[1] A MS. of the Koran, very much inferior to this, which also belonged to Tippoo Sahib, is in the Library of King's College, Aberdeen. The bulk of Tippoo's library is in the library of the Asiatic Society of Bengal at Calcutta.

* 66. A *Primer*, written about the middle of the fourteenth century.

The arms of Edw. III (England 1 and 4, France 2 and 3) are painted on the first leaf. One of Rawlinson's MSS.

67. A beautiful *Psalter*, which belonged to Peterborough Cathedral.

'Psalterium fratris Walteri de Rouceby;' followed by the Canticles, Athanasian Creed, Litany, &c. A Calendar is prefixed, with Peterborough obits, from which it appears that Rouceby died May 4, 1341. A series of nineteen miniatures, illustrating the life of our Blessed Lord and of the Virgin Mary, precedes the Psalter. The arms of Edward III appear at the head of Ps. i. One of Bp. Barlow's MSS., 22; in 1604 it belonged to one John Harborne.

68. '*þe Dreme of Pilgrimage of þe Soule*, translated out of French [of G. Guilevile] into Inglissh, with somwhat of addicions of þe translatour, þe zeere of our Lord, 1400.' Illustrated with curious coloured drawings.

A precursor of Bunyan's *Pilgrim's Progress*, with which it has been compared. It was printed by Caxton in 1483, and his edition was reprinted in 1859.

This MS. (Bodl. 770) was given to the Library, apparently in Bodley's time, by Sir James Lee, knt. Another MS., 'written in the year 1331,' was sold at the [first?] sale of the library of Thomas Britton, the small-coal-man, in Nov. [1714?].

69. '*The Mirroure of the Worlde*, that some calleth Vice and Vertu;' translated from the Latin of Laurence the Frenchman (Laur. Gallus), and illustrated with some drawings of remarkable grace and spirit, supposed to be by some Flemish artist.

A MS. of the early part of the fifteenth century; on paper. Bodl. 283.

70. *Treatise of Roger Bacon*, 'de retardacione accidentium senectutis;' with two drawings. Middle of the fifteenth century. Bodl. 211.

71. An English astrological Calendar, in six divisions, folded for the pocket; written in the latter half of the fourteenth century.

Extremely curious; contains prognostications of the weather, fatality of the seasons, &c., accompanied by innumerable figures of saints, illustrations of prognostics, the symbols found on the Runic Clog-Almanacks, the occupations of the several months, the signs of the Zodiac, and two quaint figures respectively labelled 'Harry ye Haywarde' with his dog 'Talbat,' and 'Peris ye Pyndare.' Formerly kept in a tin box. It contains the following note by T. Hearne: 'Oct. 17, 1719. This strange odd book (upon which I set a very great value, having never seen the like) was given me by the Rt. Reverend Father in God William [Fleetwood] Lord Bishop of Ely, to whom I am oblig'd upon many other accounts.' It is described pp. 47-51 of Hearne's Pref. to his edition of Fordun's *Scoti-Chronicon*. Hearne expresses surprise that St. Patrick is not found in the Calendar, although he is found in books of Salisbury use.

72. An *Historical Roll*, upwards of thirteen feet long, showing the descent of the English Kings, from the expedition of Jason in search of the Golden Fleece to the accession of Edward I (1272). Formerly belonging to the Abbey of St. Mary at York.

Illustrated with representations of various scenes up to the landing of Brute in the Isle of Wight, and thenceforward with portraits of the monarchs. Bodl. Rolls, 3.

73. *Map of the Holy Land*, on a paper roll, nearly seven feet long; written, apparently, in the first half of the fifteenth century.

Douce MS. 389. Engraved in facsimile in 1867, for the Roxburghe Club, to illustrate the Itineraries of William Wey, which were edited by Rev. G. Williams, B.D., for the same Club, from Bodl. MS. 565, in 1857. The Map in many points agrees very closely with the latter, but contains also some discrepancies, and is somewhat earlier in date.

74. German Bible, printed in 1541, with texts on the fly-leaves in the handwriting of Luther and Melanchthon, whose signatures, although much defaced by some possessor, are still very legible. See p. 322. Auct. Z. ii. 2.

* 75. *Quatuor Evangelia*; commencement of the seventh century. See p. 30.

* 76. *Psalter*, on purple vellum, written about the close of the ninth century. From the old library of the kings of France. Douce MS. 59. See p. 327.

A beautiful MS. of the *Horæ*, written on purple vellum, about 1480–1500, is among the Canonici MSS., 287. The initial letters in several instances represent classical designs.

* 77. King Alfred's Anglo-Saxon version of the treatise *De cura pastorali* of Pope Gregory the Great, being probably the copy sent by the King to Werfrith, Bishop of Worcester.

Given by Lord Hatton, MS. 20; see p. 142.

* 78. A beautiful Latin *Psalter* of the tenth century, written in Anglo-Saxon characters, with an interlinear translation, and decorated with grotesque initial letters.

Junius MS. 27. The volume is frequently called *Codex Vossianus*, from its having been in the possession of Isaac Voss, who gave it to Junius. Facsimiles are given by Professor Westwood, in his *Palæographia Sacra*, and in his splendid book of *Fac-similes of the Miniatures and Ornaments of Anglo-Saxon and Irish MSS*[1].

[1] This book contains descriptions, with facsimiles, of the Leofric, Dunstan, and Mac-Regol MSS. and of the Rawlinsonian Life of St. Columba, besides those noticed above.

* 79. The *Four Gospels*, in Latin, written in Anglo-Saxon characters, about the beginning of the eleventh century.

Noticed in Westwood's *Miniatures*, &c. (*ut supra*), p. 123.

It appears to have belonged to the abbey at Barking, a gift of tithes at Laleseie, by Adam, son of Leomar de Cochefeld, being entered on a leaf at the end by order of the abbess Ælfgiva. Bodl. 155.

* 80. The famous *Anglo-Saxon metrical paraphrase* of parts of Genesis, Exodus, Daniel, &c. called Cædmon's[1]; illustrated, as far as Abraham's journey into Egypt, with a very curious series of drawings.

The MS. is considered to have been written about A.D. 1000. One of the latest descriptions of the volume is in Westwood's magnificent book of *Facsimiles*. See p. 146. Junius 11.

* 81. *Commentary on the Passion of our B. Lord* ('Scripta super totam Passionem Christi a quatuor Evangelistis formatam'), by Michael de Massa, of the order of Augustinian Hermits.

Written (as a final colophon records) by Ralph de Medyltone at Ingham (Suffolk ?), A. D. 1405, for Sir Miles de Stapiltone. A drawing of the Crucifixion at the beginning. Bodl. 758.

The following objects of interest were dispersed in various parts of the Library :—

*1. A drawing by Holbein, framed and glazed, being a design for a cup.

On the back is the following note :—'This is an original drawing by Hans Holbein, was actually executed [for], and in the possession of, Queen Anna Bulleyn, A.D. 1534. D. Logan.' It bears, however, the initials H. and J., and was therefore executed, not for Anne Boleyn, but Jane Seymour. 'The cup was carried into Spain by George Villiers, Duke of Buckingham, when he accompanied Charles, Prince of Wales, on his romantic expedition to Madrid[2].'

* 2. The original drawing, as is supposed, by Raffaele, for his picture

[1] Cædmon was a monk of St. Hilda's Abbey, and died in 680. Bede (*Eccl. Hist.* iv. 24) tells the well-known story of his being miraculously enabled by a vision to compose vernacular verses, when previously he had been entirely unable to compose or sing a line, so that when present while a layman at feasts where, on the principle of 'no song, no supper,' every one was expected to raise a lay in his turn, he proved himself to be *no* lay-man, but was wont, when he saw the harp coming round, to rise from his place and go home supperless.

[2] *Catalogue of the South Kensington Exhibition*, 1862, p. 672. The drawing is engraved in the French journal *L'Art*, No. 541, for Dec. 1886.

of Attila stopped on his approach to Rome by the apparition of SS. Peter and Paul. Framed and glazed.

This and the preceding form part of the Douce collection.

* 3. Mahommedan lady's veil, embroidered with texts from the Koran.

* 4. Bust of Sir T. Bodley. See p. 31.

* 5. Bust of Charles I. See p. 84.

* 6. Small marble bust of Napoleon.

Bequeathed by Capt. Montagu in 1863. See p. 377.

* 7. Egyptian scroll. MS. Egypt. c. 2.

* 8. Map of England and Scotland, on parchment. Written in the fourteenth century. See p. 286, *note*.

9. Piece of wood from the south side of the curious timber Church at Greensted in Essex, built A. D. 1013. Transferred to the Ashmolean Museum.

Presented by Mr. James Dix, of Bristol, Feb. 10, 1865.

* 10. Specimen of ornamental writing by Mr. Hormuzd Rassam, whose name is well known in England, first, from his having accompanied Mr. Layard during his Assyrian researches, and afterwards, from his captivity in Abyssinia; consisting of various chapters from the Old and New Testaments, in Chaldee, Arabic, and Turkish, beautifully written in the form of two angels supporting a cross, within a border.

Presented by Mr. Rassam on leaving Oxford in January, 1849, after a stay of some months, as a mark of thanks for the manner in which he had been received. It occupied only forty-eight hours in execution, as he himself told me [1].

* 11. Sir Thomas Bodley's bell. See p. 42.

* 12. Map of Oxford, by Ralph Aggas, and a Map of Cambridge; the former dated 1578, the latter 1592; about three feet by four in size.

These extremely curious and valuable maps were bequeathed by Dr. Rawlinson. Having become decayed and dilapidated by exposure, they were some few years ago carefully mounted on canvas, on a wooden frame, and covered

[1] Another specimen of Mr. Rassam's caligraphic skill is to be seen in the Common Room of Magdalen College (in which College he was entertained for some time), where the College arms are represented in the same manner. And a third specimen, written originally for Prof. Lee of Cambridge, is now in the possession of Dr. Greenhill, at Hastings.

with glass; by which means they are effectually secured from further injury of the same kind. In a letter from Hearne amongst Bagford's papers in Harl. MS. 5906 B, fol. 73^{b}, dated 13 March 170$\frac{8}{9}$, Mr. Madan met with the following passage:—

'Ant. à Wood had in his Possession an old Map of *Oxon* which is not now in the *Museum Ashm.* but I believe is in M^{r}. Tanner's hands. M^{r}. *Dodwell* has several times told me he saw it, but I am uncertain whither 'twas printed or not. I wish M^{r}. *Bagford* would ask M^{r}. T. about it, or at least M^{r}. *Wanley*, who can give him satisfaction in several things of this nature.' Mr. Madan adds, 'See also Harl. MS. 5901, fol. 19^{b}.'

13. Four drawings of heads by Raffaele, or Giulio Romano. See p. 328. Removed to the University Gallery in 1885.

14. A Roman inscription on a brazen plate:—

FLORAE

TI. PLAVTIVS DROSVS

MAG. II.

V. S. L. M.

Given by Dr. Rawlinson, but it is believed to be a forgery. An engraving of this is extant, among the many which were executed for Rawlinson of various relics in his miscellaneous collection. It is described on the engraving as being 'Ex regiis Christinæ thesauris.'

* 15. A warrior on horseback, enamelled on copper, and marked 'Ezechias.'

16. A Greek painting on wood of St. George and the Dragon.

17. Another Greek painting on wood, on a gold ground, apparently representing two angels bowing before the Blessed Virgin, &c. These two paintings were transferred by loan to the University Gallery in March, 1885.

* 18. Heads of our Blessed Lord, and of King Charles I. See p. 201.

Metal-Work. Transferred to the Ashmolean Museum in 1887:—

i. Crucifix; enamelled.

ii. The Martyrdom of St. Sebastian; small, on brass.

iii. Four enamelled round tablets, bearing portraits of 'Le Conte de Flandres, le Conte de Champagne, le Conte de Tholoze, Duc de Normandie.'

iv. Two small enamelled representations of March and May.

v. Dolphin, with boy on his back (the Dauphin); motto, 'Qui pense ma . . . . vy advient.'

vi. Heads, enamelled, of the following Roman Emperors; Julius Cæsar, Augustus, Claudius and Otho.

vii. A small copper figure of our Blessed Lord, crowned and robed, with eyes open, and arms extended.

The following account is given by Hearne in a volume of his MS. collections[1]:—

'About five years since the workmen in digging the gardens that formerly belong'd to St. Frideswyd's, Oxford, found a crucifix; the figure in pontifical robes, enamelled and gilt, with stones in the arms and breast. It came afterwards into the hands of Mr. Edw. Thwaites of Queen's College, who gave it to the Bodleian Library, where in the Physick schoole 'tis now reserved, and seems to be very ancient.'

A drawing of the figure made for Thwaites by J. T. [alman] was given to the Library by the late Dr. Wellesley. The figure resembles a crucifix found at Lucca, of the seventh century.

The following Portraits hang in the Library:—

* 1. Sir T. Bodley[2].

In the first Binder's book and Librarian's note-book, beginning 1613, which contains also particulars of accounts of that year, is an entry of 6*d.* paid for bringing Sir Thomas' picture. And in the accounts for 1634–5 is an entry, '—for Sir Thomas Bodlie's picture drawne at Venice when he was Embassador for her late Majestie Qu. Eliz., £1 10*s.*' This would appear to refer to the picture hanging in the Library; but Bodley never visited Venice or Italy in the character of an ambassador, his Italian journeys having been made at an earlier period of his life in a private capacity. In 1636–7 there is another entry, '— to a French painter for drawing of Sir Thomas Bodley's picture, £2.' This probably refers to a portrait which hangs in the room assigned to the Bodley MSS., which represents the Founder at a somewhat older time of life. As a painting it is very poor, and bears no comparison with the beautiful picture hanging in the great reading-room. 5*s.* 6*d.* were paid for the frame of the second picture. It would seem possible from these several entries that the Library may have formerly possessed three portraits, although now there are only two.

* 2. All the Librarians from James to Bowles; with a small engraved sketch of Price; a portrait of Dr. Bandinel, taken when fresh in office, and a photograph of him, taken in the year of his resigna-

[1] Rawlinson, C. 876, f. 52.

[2] First, in old lists, by glaring error, assigned to Vandyke; then in Gutch's list to Corn. Jansen, under whose name it has continued. But chronology disproves this, if, that is, the picture was painted from life. The picture represents a man about fifty years of age, such as Bodley must have been about 1595. But Jansen was born in 1590, and began to paint in England about 1618.

tion of office; and a portrait of Mr. Coxe, painted by Watts by subscription, in 1876. See p. 390.

There are no portraits of Fysher or Owen.

* 3. Archbishops Usher and Laud; Bishops Crewe and Atterbury; Deans Nowell, Aldrich, and Hickes; Erasmus, Wanley, Lye, Gassendi, Sir Thos. Wyat, two of Chaucer, Gower, Junius (sketch by Vandyke), two of Selden (with his arms painted on panel), Sir K. Digby, Queen Elizabeth of Bohemia; Frederick, Elector Palatine; Mr. Sutherland; Dr. Stubbs, Bishop of Chester, and now of Oxford, painted by H. Herkomer, R.A., in 1885, by subscription.

* 4. Drawing of Thos. Alcock. By Cooper.

Bequeathed by Rawlinson. The following note is written on the back:—

'This picture was drawne for mee at the Earle of Westmoreland's house at Apethorpe, in Northamptonshire, by the greate (tho' little) Limner, the then famous Mr. Cooper of Covent Garden, when I was eighteen years of age.

'THOMAS ALCOCK, Preceptor.'

* 5. Drawing of Ant. à Wood, dated 1677.

6. Drawing of John Aubrey, 1666.

* 7. Drawing of F. Douce.

* 8. Small plaster busts of Dr. Pusey and Prof. Jowett.

Picture Gallery.

A Catalogue of the Pictures (which are now exclusively Portraits) was printed some years ago by the late Janitor, Norris (see p. 258). Since then, the following additions have been made [1]:—

Froben, the printer. By Holbein.

Bequeathed by Rawlinson.

Oliver Plunket, Roman Catholic Archbishop of Armagh, executed in 1681. On panel.

Bequeathed by Rawlinson.

James Edward, the 'old Chevalier,' and his wife Clementina Sobieski. See p. 233, *note*.

Bequeathed by Rawlinson.

[1] Besides some restorations from the Randolph Gallery of portraits formerly removed thither.

Pencil drawing of Pope.

Bequeathed by Rawlinson.

Sir R. Chambers, Chief Justice of Bengal.

Sir R. H. Inglis, Bart. By Richmond.

Dr. Routh, President of Magdalen College. By Thomson.

Dr. Daniel Wilson, Bishop of Calcutta.

The Earl of Derby. By Grant. See p. 360, *note.*

The Prince of Wales. By Gordon. See p. 383.

Dr. A. P. Stanley, Dean of Westminster. By Watts. See p. 393.

The following Curiosities and Models are, or were, exhibited in the Gallery :—

* 1. Chair made from the wood of Sir F. Drake's ship. See p. 134.

* 2. Chair of Henry VIII. See *ib.*

3. Guy Fawkes' Lantern. See p. 93. Removed to the Ashmolean Museum in 1887.

* 4. A series of casts of various ancient Temples and other buildings. See p. 312.

* 5. Model, in teak wood, of a subterranean passage and reservoir at Adalaj in Guzerat, built in 1499; beautifully carved, and exhibiting the whole of the interior construction and arrangement. (See *Notes and Queries*, 6th Series, V. 309).

Presented in 1842 by Sir J. W. Awdry, Chief Justice of Bombay.

* 6. Cases of Italian medals, medals by Dassier of English sovereigns, &c. See p. 247.

* 7. Two plaster casts of monuments from Nineveh, now in the British Museum, with cuneiform inscriptions.

* 8. Model, in papier-maché, of the Martyrs' Memorial, Oxford, beautifully executed.

Presented in 1844 by Rev. Vaughan Thomas, B.D.

* 9. Plaster model of the Waltham Cross.

Presented by the same donor.

* 10. Casts of the Elgin marbles.

* 11. An armillary sphere, in bronze, supported by three lions; and a brass quadrant.

Given by Capt. Josias Bodley. See p. 25.

* 12. Two small bronzes; one representing Narcissus contemplating his face in the stream; the other, Cupids disporting themselves on the backs of Tritons.

Given by Rawlinson.

* 13. A plaster cast of young Bacchanals leading the goat.

* 14. A wood carving, coarsely executed, representing Hercules spinning, and exposed by Omphale to the ridicule of two female visitors.

* 15. Bronze, in fine alto-relievo, of Curtius leaping into the gulf in the Forum at Rome.

Given by Rawlinson, 19 Oct. 1752[1].

* 16. Carving, in soap-stone, of the Judgment of Solomon.

Given by Rawlinson.

* 17. A geometrical, eleven-sided figure, inclosing an open and hollow iron ball with sixty sides, and surmounting a small pillar with columns representing the five orders of architecture. Around the base of the column are eight other geometrical figures, with vacant spaces for two which have been lost.

Probably this with the preceding articles, 10–15, came from Rawlinson.

* 18. Model, inlaid with mother-of-pearl, of the Church of the Holy Sepulchre at Jerusalem.

Bequeathed by Dr. Mason in 1841. See p. 342.

* 19. Alabaster model of the Cathedral at Calcutta.

Given by the late Bishop Wilson in 1846. This beautiful model was executed at Pisa; it was exhibited in the Italian department of the Great Exhibition in 1861.

* 20. A large and fine model in cork, of the Amphitheatre at Verona; by Dubourg.

21. Model of the Royal Yacht in 1697. Restored to the Ashmolean Museum to which it formerly belonged.

* 22. Two Chinese rolls, one silk, the other paper, containing coloured drawings of the banks of the river Tsing-Ming, with scenes illustrating the manners and amusements of the country. MSS. Chin b. 1, 2 (RR).

* 23. Collection of Indian weapons presented by Mr. Elliott. See p. 369.

[1] This apparently came from P. Le Neve's sale, for in a supplementary Catalogue of Curiosities and MSS. omitted at first and sold on March 19, 173$\frac{8}{9}$, we find 'a representation of Marcus Curtius, embossed on copper,' which was sold (as noted in Hearne's copy of the Catalogue) to 'Constable' for 14*s*.

24. Drawings and engravings of Buddhist idols; brought from a Joss-house in a Llama monastery in Pekin, in 1862; and given to the Library by Lieut.-Col (afterwards Major-Gen.) Gibbes Rigaud, of the 60th Rifles [1].

* 25. Series of clay figures, coloured, representing all degrees of rank, &c. among the Chinese.

Brought by Col. Gibbes Rigaud, of the 60th Rifles, the donor, from Tien-tsin, and given in 1862.

* 26. Handbell from a temple at Pekin. See p. 42.

* 27. Small Chinese figure of a deity, in brass; from Pekin.

* 28. Portrait, on a large roll, of the late Emperor of China, seated, with a bow and arrow in his hands.

Above is an autograph inscription by the Emperor, in verse, in praise of archery. Brought by Col. Rigaud from the 'Summer Palace.' MS. Chin. a. 1 (R).

* 29. A series of carved and coloured ivory tablets, representing Chinese life and manners, partly broken; with some grotesque figures, probably of deities, carved in wood.

Believed to have been bequeathed by Rawlinson.

* 30. A series of small Chinese paintings on ivory.

From the Douce collection.

31. Half-burned copy of a Russian translation of the *Pickwick Papers*.

Found in the Redan at Sebastopol, when that battery was stormed on Sept. 9, 1855. Given by Rev. F. J. Holt Beever in 1856. Now numbered, 256. d. 24.

* 32. Three sets of wooden roundels [2], or trenchers, of which two

[1] He died in Oxford, Jan. 1, 1885, 'full of good works and almsdeeds.'

[2] An engraving of a roundel (then, with others, in the possession of John Fenton of Fishguard) of which the exact counterpart is found in one of these sets, is given in the *Gent. Magaz.* for 1799, p. 465. As it is not known how long the Library has been in possession of its present collection, it is possible that Mr Fenton's series may now be included in it. A description of a set of the time of James I may be found in vol. xxxiv of the *Archæologia*, pp. 225–230; and a notice of the Bodleian trenchers in *Notes and Queries*, 1866, vol. x., p. 472, and other communications on the subject in the first volume for 1867. A set of twelve is described, with copies of their inscriptions (of which one is the same as the first of the two given above), at pp. 100–102 of Nicholson's *History of Kendal*, second edition, 1861. A paper on the subject by John Evans, D.C.L., Pres. of the Soc. of Antiquaries, is printed at pp. 207–216 of vol. x, second series, of the *Proceedings* of the Society, 1885, and descriptions of many sets in vol. xii. 1888, pp. 201–223.

are round (numbering thirty plates), the other square (numbering twelve); with mottos, in the former case in verse, in the latter consisting of precepts from the Bible. One of the round sets belonged in 1599 to Queen Elizabeth, and the box of the second set also bears her initials and arms. The verses are sometimes humorous, sometimes moral, and strongly dehortatory from marriage; not, however, out of any flattering deference to the condition or supposed inclination of the 'Virgin Queen,' but chiefly in accordance with the opposite view taken by some hard-hearted misogynist. Of the two classes of motto, let these stand as specimens:—

'If that a bachelor thou bee,
Keepe thou so still; be ruled by mee;
Leaste that repentance all to late
Reward thee with a broken pate.'

'Content thyselfe with thyn estate,
And send noo poor wight from thi gate:
For why? this councell I thee give
To learne to die and die to lyve.'

33. Wax impressions of seals, both early originals and modern reproductions. See pp. 248–9.

34. Model, in wood, of the Temple at Pæstum.

Carved by Mr. Thomas Wyatt, of Oxford, about 1830.

35. Wooden models of the Station Church, the Sanatorium, and the House of Rest, at Goorakhpur in Bengal.

Given in 1883 by the late E. A. Reade, Esq., C.B., of Ipsden House, Oxon[1].

36. Bust of W. E. Gladstone, M.P.; executed by Tho. Woolner, R.A., in 1866, and presented by subscribers.

37. Bust of Rev. F. Robertson. See p. 376.

38. Specimens of the Kimmeridge coal money.

39. A bronze shield, bearing the Gorgon's head.

40. A small plaster cast of the head of Torquato Tasso, from a wax model made by Mr. N. Marchant from a cast taken after Tasso's death, and preserved in the Convent of St. Onofrio at Rome, where his death occurred.

41. Various curious sets of playing cards which were collected by Douce.

[1] This gentleman also gave in 1884 some early deeds relating to his family and their property, with court-rolls, &c.

42. Albums of H.R.H. the late Duke of Albany, containing many valuable and interesting autographs and sketches; deposited by H.R.H. the Duchess of Albany.

43. Collection of Oriental and other seals, gems, moss-agates, &c.; presented by Mr. J. B. Elliott, of Patna.

44. In a separate glass case, a fine Bible printed at Glasgow in 1862, in two folio volumes, and illustrated with very beautiful photographs by Frith, which was called the Queen's Bible from its being dedicated by permission to Her Majesty.

IX.

Numismatic Collection.

The collection of Coins and Medals was commenced by the gift from Archbishop Laud of five cabinets of coins, in 1636[1], to which he subsequently made some additions. These were accompanied by a very full MS. catalogue, which is now preserved among Laud's MSS., Misc. 554. In 1657 a large addition was made by Mr. Ralph Freke (see p. 125), and numerous small gifts came from many donors in following years. A MS. catalogue of the Roman coins was made by Ashmole in 1658–1666, and given by him to the Library in the latter year; of this there is also a copy among Ashmole's MSS., No. 808. A catalogue upon which Francis Wise had been engaged for a long period was published by him in a folio volume in 1750, entitled, *Nummorum antiquorum scriniis Bodleianis reconditorum catalogus, cum commentario, tabulis æneis et appendice.* Wise remarks in his Preface, that no donation, however trifling, was rejected, and that, consequently, there was (as there is now still more) a very large quantity of Middle and Third brass coins of little or no value. From Rawlinson there came in 1755, besides coins, a collection of Italian medals (Popes, Medici family, &c.), and upwards of 700 matrices of seals, chiefly foreign. Sir Edward Blount, of Mawley, Shropshire, bart., gave a collection of Greek and Roman medals in 1751. Browne Willis contributed the most valuable portion of the whole collection, in his series of gold and silver coins[2].

[1] Laud's letter of gift, dated June 16, is printed at p. 94, vol. ii., of his *Remains*, edited by H. Wharton. A curious collection of Roman weights came among early benefactions; they are entered in Wise's catalogue.

[2] The special gems are a gold Allectus, and the famous *Reddite* and *Petition* crowns of Thomas Simon, the latter of which was struck in 1663. The Petition crown is probably the one which was sold in Dr. Mead's sale in February, 1755 (*Cat.* p. 186), and which is noticed by Rawlinson in his copy of the sale catalogue as having been purchased by — Hodsall for £12. A specimen has very recently been sold for £500. A gold Allectus was sold at Mead's sale to the Duke of Devonshire for £21 5*s*. The

Subsequent benefactors have been (amongst others) Fr. Wise, in 1760; C. Godwyn, in 1770[1]; Thomas Knight, in 1795; Douce, whose collection included those of Calder, Moore, Roberts, and Keate, and from whom came a series of tradesmen's tokens; Dr. Ingram, in 1850, whose bequest included some British and Anglo-Saxon specimens; the Queen, who gave, in 1841, a portion of the treasure found at Cuerdale (see p. 342); Mackie, 1847; Elliott, whose valuable series of Bactrian and Indian coins was presented in 1860 (see p. 369); Dr. R. Caulfield of Cork, who presented in 1866 a large collection of the Gun-money struck by James II in Ireland; and Archd. Cotton, who bequeathed a collection of tradesmen's tokens of the last century. The Ashmole coins (with Ingram's and Mackie's) were transferred from the Museum, together with Ashmole's library, in 1861. There is also a cabinet of Napoleon medals, and a collection bearing the name of 'Dr. Buck, 1741,' the source of which is not known.

No catalogue of any portion of the contents of this room (excepting a brief description of the Cuerdale coins) has been issued since the publication of Wise's volume, with the exception of an elaborate catalogue, by Stanley Lane-Poole, B.A., of the Mohammedan Coins, printed at the University Press in a thin 4to. volume in 1888. But from about 1867 until his death in 1885 W. S. Vaux, Esq., formerly of the British Museum, occasionally afforded his valuable services in arrangement and description; and as the work is still continued the whole of the collection will in course of time be arranged and described.

By the statutes of the Library, the Librarian, or one of the Sub-librarians, must always be present in the room when any coins are exhibited; nor may they be shown to more than two persons at a time, unless two of the Librarians, or a Librarian and one Curator, are present. No personal examination of coins by a visitor for the purpose of comparison with other specimens is permitted.

For further particulars reference should be made to the Report of the present Librarian, printed in 1888, pp. 42–47.

University acknowledged Browne Willis' gift by creating him D.C.L. by diploma, 10 Apr. 1749.

[1] Godwyn's collection included that of Heneage Finch, fourth earl of Winchilsea. In this portion is a silver coin bearing a fine representation of the head of Alexander of Macedon, which was engraved in 1808 for a supplemental sheet to the second edition, published in 1807, of dean Will. Vincent's *Voyage of Nearchus*, and which is inserted there at p. 313. Dr. Vincent was indebted for his knowledge of the coin to the Librarian Price. Godwyn's collection numbers over 3000 coins and medals, among which papal medals are a special feature.

X.

List of Past Librarians.

i. Chaplains to the University, and Librarians of Duke Humphrey's Library.

[The following earliest notices of the Library found in the University records, in addition to those printed in the text, are taken from the Rev. C. W. Boase's *Register of the Univ. of Oxf.* vol. i., printed by the Oxf. Hist. Soc. in 1885, p. 286 :—

1449. '24 Oct. deliberatum erat quod fieret reparacio librarie ex sumptibus universitatis.

'29 Nov. deputati fuerunt subscripti doctores et magistri ad audiendum compotum capellani universitatis de libris contentis in libraria comuni universitatis, videlicet in theologia doctor German, in jure canonico doctor Wylley, in medicine facultate dominus Cancellarius, in jure civili M. Foster, in facultate artium magistri Reynold, Warkeworth, Swan et Stokes de collegio Animarum.']

.... John Foster [Forster, B.A., 1455], M.A., resigned 1506.

1506. John Wayte, M.A., Merton, elected in place of Foster *or* Fostar. His office of Chaplain 'declared vacant because he had a benefice, 11 Oct. 1513, but he appealed.' (Boase's *Register of Univ.* i. 48).

1513. Adam Kirkebote.

.... [William] Smyth. Vacated office on being elected fellow of Eton (Boase, *ibid.* 96) 24 Sept. 1521. Rector of Everdon, Northamptonshire, in 1529 (Rawl. MS. B. 268, f. 5).

Before 1527. Edmund Fletcher, Flecher, *or* Flaccher, M.A., fellow of Exeter; afterwards B.D.

.... Whytt, *or* White.

1543. Humphrey Burnford, *or* Burford, M.A., elected 31 Oct. in place of Whytt, deceased.

ii. Bodley's Librarians.

1598. Thomas James, M.A.
1620. John Rous, M.A.
1652. Thomas Barlow, M.A., afterwards Bishop of Lincoln.
1660. Thomas Lockey, B.D.
1665. Thomas Hyde, D.D.
1701. John Hudson, D.D.
1719. Joseph Bowles, M.A.
1729. Robert Fysher, M.B.
1747. Humphrey Owen, D.D.[1]
1768. John Price, B.D.[2]
1813. Bulkeley Bandinel, D.D.
1860. Henry Octavius Coxe, M.A.

iii. Sub-Librarians.

About 1607. Philip Price[3], M.A. In office in 1612.
About 1618. John Verneuil, M.A.[4]

[1] Owen was presented by Jesus College to the rectory of Rotherfield Peppard, Oxon, 13 Aug. 1763 (the year in which he was elected Principal of his College): Turner's *Calendar of Charters*, p. 285. He gave to the Library in 1750 a copy of the St. Alban's *Fructus Temporum*, printed in 1483.

[2] Price was both a sportsman and a botanist. E. Morgan, writing to him in July, 1787, 'You may depend on my taking out a game licence for you this week,' (Bodl. MS. A. 64, f. 180); and the distinguished Botanical Professor Sibthorpe writes, 'Dr. S. considers Mr. Price a Botanist as well as the Librarian' (*ib.* 285).

[3] He was matriculated at Ch. Ch. 11 May, 1604 (A. Clark's *Register of the Univ.* 1887, II. ii. 271). On 14 Oct. 1607 a dispensation was granted him to be absent from the Schools and from lectures because of his duties 'in bibliotheca publica' (*ibid.* II. i. 67). He took the degree of B.A. 16 May, in that year, and of M.A., being then of Brasenose College, 5 July, 1611 (*ibid.* II. iii. 271).

[4] The date of his appointment is not known, but on 4 Sept. 1618 he gave as 'Hypobiblioth.' an Oxford-printed Latin treatise on logic by one S. S., which had been given to him by the author 14 June, 1613 (8vo. S. 111, Art.). A copy of T. Holland's *Oratio Sarisb. habita* came to the Library in 1619, 'ex dono Johannis Vernulii hypobibliothecarii.' He gave also a copy of P. du Moulin's *Accroissement des eaux de Siloe*, printed in 1614 (8° M. 120 Th.), in which he inscribed these words, 'Non est mortale quod opto. Mon desir n'est pas en rien d'icy bas.' His handwriting first appears in a register of books sent out for binding under the year 1647. A month before his death, on 26 Aug. 1647, he gave a volume of sermons by Jean le Fauchier, a Protestant minister at Charenton, which had been given to him by P. Richier in 1633.

1647. Francis Yonge, M.A.

1657. Henry Stubbe, M.A.

1659. Thomas Hyde, M.A., appointed Librarian in 1665.

*   *   *   *   *

About 1670. Rev. John Younger, M.A., afterwards Dean of Salisbury [1].

About 1677. Rev. John Crabb, M.A. }
1690–2. Rev. Joseph Crabb, M.A. } See pp. 180–4.

1712. Thomas Hearne, M.A.

1715. Rev. John Fletcher, M.A.

1719. Rev. Francis Wise, B.D. Appointed first Librarian of the Radcliffe Library in 1748, but he appears to have resigned his post in the Bodleian before [2].

1746. N. Foster, M.A., Balliol College [3].

1747. Thomas Winbolt, All Souls' College. See p. 219, *n*. 3.

174$\frac{8}{9}$. John Roberts, Brasenose College [4].

1750. Thomas Morres, M.A., Hertford College [5]; B.D. and D.D. in 1751.

*   *   *   *   *

1757 Oct.—1758 Apr. William Harrison, B.D., Corpus Christi College [6]; D.D. 1758.

1758 Oct.—1761 May. Adam Thomas, M.A., Jesus College [7]; B.D. 1761.

[1] 'For some time second Keeper'; Hearne's MS. *Diary*, vol. cxviii. p. 140, cited in Bloxam's *Register of Magd. Coll.* vol. v. p. 237.

[2] In 1727 and 1728 the following persons were employed by the Librarian Bowles in transcribing the copy for a new Catalogue at the rate of ten shillings for the printed sheet:—

William Walter [B.A., All Souls' Coll.]

Robert Wheeler [B.A., Univ. Coll.]

Arthur Kight [M.A., Oriel Coll.]

Samuel Wells [B.A., All Souls' Coll.]

These names are found in a small note-book (in a parchment cover) kept by Bowles.

[3] His name first appears in 1746 as making out the accounts and receiving money, and on the cover of the Register-Book which begins in Jan. 174$\frac{6}{7}$ his name is inserted in a list of officers in the place of that of Wise, which is marked out.

[4] In one of the drawers in an oak desk in the Sub-librarian's study at the east end is written 'John Roberts, e Coll. Æn. Nas. 174$\frac{8}{9}$.' He became B.A. in 1750, M.A., 1753, afterwards Archdeacon of Merioneth, and died in 1802. In another drawer in the above-mentioned desk is a memorandum that 'this desk was made in the month of July, 1716.'

[5] On 6 Oct. 1750 he signs as Under-librarian a receipt for fees, which is among the accounts for that year.

[6] He signs receipts in 1757 for salary in a memorandum-book of Owen's.

[7] *Ibid.*

1761 Oct.—1763 Oct.[1] John Price, Jesus College, afterwards Librarian. In 1765-7 acting for the Librarian.

1763 Oct.—1765 Oct.[2] James Matthews, Jesus College, B.A. 1761, M.A. 1764.

1766 Lady Day—1767 Lady Day. William Seys, Jesus College, B.A. 1761, M.A. 1764; died 1802[3].

1768. Rev. Benjamin Hall, Jesus College, M.A.; afterwards D.D. and Chancellor of Llandaff; died 25 Feb. 1825[4].

[1770. 'Jones and White, Price's representatives.'[5]]

* * * * *

1780-81. John Walters, Scholar of Jesus College, B.A. 1781, M.A. 1784[6]. See p. 268.

* * * * *

Before 1787. Rev. Edward Morgan, M.A., Jesus College[7]. [Deceased 1832].

1788. Rev. John Bown, M.A., Lincoln College[8].

* * * * *

1797. { Henry Hervey Baber, All Souls' College, B.A. 1799.
1798. { Henry Ellis, St. John's College. See p. 278.

About 1800? Rev. Samuel Rogers, M.A., Wadham College; *vice* Ellis? [Deceased, 1852.]

About 1807. Rev. Andrew Hughes Matthews, M.A., Jesus College; *vice* Baber? [Deceased 1854.]

1810. Rev. Bulkeley Bandinel, M.A.; appointed Librarian in 1813.

[1] *Ibid.* From Oct. 1757 to Oct. 1760 he signs receipts as Janitor.

[2] *Ibid.*

[3] There was also an undergraduate of the same name at the same time at Jesus College, who took his B.A. degree in 1768; but the Sub-librarian was more probably the one mentioned above.

[4] Grandfather of the late Lord Llanover.

[5] Letter from T. Astle to Price in Bodl. MS. Addit. A. 64, f. 7. Jones was the Janitor. The records are from this time forward very imperfectly kept during Price's time, and it seems impossible, amongst frequent changes, to make out a complete list of Sub-librarians.

[6] He was afterwards Master of Ruthin School and rector of Efenechtyd in Denbighshire. He died 28 June 1789, aged 30, and was buried at Efenechtyd; *Gent. Mag.* 1789, ii. 671; Rob. Williams' *Biogr. Dict. of Eminent Welshmen*, 1852. At p. 268 the year 1791 is given as the date of his death from Nichols' *Lit. Anecd.*, which seems to be a mistake. Mr. Joseph Foster, in the *Alumni Oxon.*, 1888, says that he was appointed P.C. of Tandridge, Surrey, and died in 1834; he appears to have been led into this error by the *Gent. Mag.* for the latter year, where the name of John *Waters*, P.C. of Tandridge is misprinted *Walters*.

[7] See Nichols' *Lit. Hist.* vol. v. p. 539.

[8] *Ibid.*, p. 541.

1814. Rev. Henry Cotton, M.A. } Two Sub-librarians appointed by a
—— Rev. Alex. Nicoll, M.A. } new Statute. See p. 294.
1822. Rev. Philip Bliss, D.C.L. [Assistant in Library from 1808 to *c.* 1813], *vice* Nicoll.
—— Rev. Rich. F. Laurence, M.A., *vice* Cotton.
1826. Rev. Charles Henry Cox, M.A., *vice* Laurence.
1828. Rev. Stephen Reay, M.A., *vice* Cox.
—— Rev. John Besly, M.A., *vice* Bliss.
1831. Rev. Ernest Hawkins, M.A., *vice* Besly.
1834. Rev. William Cureton, M.A., *vice* Hawkins.
1837. Rev. Herbert Hill, M.A., *vice* Cureton.
1838. Rev. H. O. Coxe, M.A., *vice* Hill. Appointed Librarian in 1860.
1861. Rev. Rob. Payne Smith, M.A. [Assistant Oriental Sub-librarian 1857], *vice* Reay.
1862. Rev. Alfred Hackman, M.A., *vice* Coxe.
1865. F. Max Müller, M.A., *vice* Smith.
1867. Rev. John William Nutt, M.A., *vice* Müller.
1879. Ingram Bywater, M.A., *vice* Nutt.

XI.

The Present Staff of the Library.

[Christmas, 1889.]

Librarian.

Edward Williams Byron Nicholson, M.A., Trinity College [Feb. 1882, after seven months' vacancy].

Sub-Librarians.

Adolf Neubauer, M.A., Exeter College, Ph. D. Leipsic [entered the Library 1868 ; appointed Sub-librarian Oct., 1873].

Falconer Madan, M.A., Fellow of Brasenose College [June, 1880].

Special Assistant in the MS. Department.

Rev. William Dunn Macray, M.A., F.S.A., Magdalen College [entered the Library, July, 1840].

Assistants.

George Parker [Sept., 1854].
William Henry Timberlake [June, 1857].
William Henry Allnutt [Oct., 1864][1].
George William Wheeler, B.A., Balliol College [May, 1889][2].
Henry Joseph Shuffrey [Jan., 1863].
William Richard Sims [May, 1867].
William Francis Thurland [Jan., 1868].

Classifier for the Subject-Catalogue.

George James Burch, B.A., Non-Coll. [July, 1887].

[1] Mr. Allnutt has long been engaged in preparing for publication a Bibliography of Provincial Presses to the year 1800. In 1878 he read a paper on the subject at the first Annual Meeting of the Library Association, held at Oxford.

[2] He succeeded F. C. Lewis, M.A., Queen's College, appointed Librarian of the South African Public Library, Capetown.

Transcribers.

Miss E. M. Sides [Feb., 1884].
Miss C. M. Sides [March, 1884].
Miss L. H. Timberlake [Sept., 1884].

Janitor at the Bodleian.

Charles Coppock [May, 1875].

Janitor at the Camera Radcliviana.

Henry James Miller [Jan., 1887].

Other Members of the Senior Staff.

Edwin Hickman [March, 1864].
William Ellis Knowles [Feb., 1872].
William Charles Baker [June, 1884].

Under-Assistants.

*Alfred Hodges Kebby [Jan., 1883].
*Alfred William Lucas Whitbread [Jan., 1883].
*James Hutt [Feb., 1885].
Benjamin Henry Hutton Mundy, Non-Coll. [Nov., 1887].
Frederick John Sweatman [Apr., 1888].
Norman Stacey Mundy [Sept., 1888].
William Frederick Wheeler [Feb., 1889].
Reginald Arthur Clayton Heslop [July, 1889].

* Assistants designate.

Other Members of the Junior Staff.

Henry James Bayliss [Feb., 1884].
Herbert George Draper [Jan., 1889].
John Smith [March, 1889].
William Edmund French [July, 1889].
Walter Sheppard [July, 1889].

[Of the Assistants and others whose names were entered in the list of officers in 1868, but of whom there is now no mention in the preceding pages, I desire to add here some particulars.

Mr. Henry Haines deceased 28 March, 1872, aged 48.

Mr. Henry John Sides deceased 25 Aug., 1883, aged 45.

Mr. W. H. Bliss, M.A. (who in 1872 availed himself of the provisions of the Clerical Disabilities Relief Act of 1870, in regard to his Orders in the Church of England) was my successor in the superintendence of the new catalogue of printed books from 1871 to the end of 1876. In 1877 he was appointed by the Record Office a commissioner for examination and transcription of records in the Library of the Vatican relating to English history; in which important work he is still engaged.

Mr. Percy W. Collcutt left before 1871.

Mr. W. F. Green left at the end of 1872.

Mr. Fred. Prickett left in 1876.

Mr. Will. Burden left in 1878.

Mr. Will. Plowman left at the end of 1877.

Mr. W. S. Plowman left at the end of 1868.

Robert Roby, deputy-janitor, resigned on account of infirmity, and died some time after 1870.

W. Bayzand (an old stage-coachman), janitor at the *Cam. Radcl.*, resigned on account of ill-health, and died (I believe) in 1886.

Of Assistants who quitted the Library shortly before the year 1868, I desire to commemorate Mr. Thomas F. Plowman, who left on being appointed Librarian of the Oxford City Library, and who now holds the office of Secretary to the Bath and West of England Agricultural Society; Mr. H. P. Molyneux, one of the first candidates to pass the now abandoned examination for the *status* of Associate in Arts, who is now in Her Majesty's Inland Revenue Office; Mr. G. D. Ham, now in Her Majesty's Customs; and Mr. John Rathbone, now in Messrs. Coutts' bank.]

XII.

Rules of the Library.

The Library is open on week-days from 9 a.m. to 3 p.m. in January, 4 p.m. in February and March, 5 p.m. in April—July, 4 p.m. in August, September, and October, and 3 p.m. in November and December. It is closed from Christmas Eve to the Feast of the Circumcision, both included; on Good Friday and Easter Eve; on Ascension Day; on the day of the University Commemoration; for the first week in October (Oct. 1–7), for purposes of dusting and cleaning; and on Nov. 7 and 8 (or Nov. 6–7, should the 8th fall on a Sunday) for the Visitation.

[These latter regulations (which considerably lessen the old number of days of closure) were finally approved in Convocation on 18 Feb. 1890.]

All graduate members of the University have the right to use the Library. Undergraduates and strangers are admitted upon being introduced by a Master of Arts or higher graduate, or upon producing sufficient letters of introduction; but every facility is afforded to strangers who make personal application to the Librarian for permission to make researches for any definite and special purpose.

The Library is under the control of a Board of Curators, consisting of the Vice-Chancellor, the two Proctors, the five Regius Professors of Divinity, Civil Law, Medicine, Hebrew, and Greek, and five Members of Congregation, elected by that House for ten years.

The *Camera Radcliviana*, formerly the Radcliffe Library, is open all the year round on week-days from 10 a.m. to 10 p.m., excepting that it is closed during the four days next before Easter, the three days ending on the first Saturday in July, the three days ending on the last Saturday in September, and on Christmas-Day and three adjoining week-days. In it are to be found most of the publications of about the last forty years, with recent magazines; and books from the old Library may be carried over for the use of readers with certain limitations.

The Statutes of the Library are printed in the general *Corpus Statutorum Universitatis.*

ADDENDA ET CORRIGENDA.

P. 9, *n.* 1. For *14th cent.* read *15th cent.*

P. 22, *l.* 3. *For* Tambaluc *read* Cambaluc.

P. 23, *n.* 2. *For* Durham College *read* Lincoln College.

P. 46. *For* Newname *read* Newmane.

" " *For* J. Wake *read* I. Wake.

P. 52, *n.* 2. *For* Stevens *read* Steevens.

P. 96. *For* Lord Sale *read* Lord Saye.

P. 118, *n.* 1. *For* about the year 1759 *read* in 1769.

P. 148. *For* see under 1696 *read* see under 1686.

P. 190. *For* Sir George Wheeler *read* Sir George Wheler.

P. 196. 1716. *Add*, A letter from Isaac Casaubon to James I, dated at Paris 12 cal. Maii, 1609, was given by — Jackson, a commoner of Hart Hall. It is bound in a volume lettered 'Orig. letters of Mary and Eliz.', Add. c. 92.

P. 197, *n.* 2. Bilstone was not sub-librarian but janitor. But the name in the book is 'John Bilson.'

P. 350. Under the year 1848 mention should have been made of the purchase from Mr. Parker of Oxford for £20 of a copy of Caxton's *Golden Legend*, 1483, (wanting 42 leaves), which had been sold out of the parish library of Denchworth, Berks.

P. 429. 1683. *For* Auct. v. 8 *read* Auct. D. v. 8.

P. 440. Canterbury, St. Augustine's. *Add* Seld. supra 30 [*Actus Apostt.*, 8th cent., with the library mark, 'Di. i. G. iii'].

P. 442. Exeter Cathedral. *Add* Bodl. Or. 135, a Hebrew grammar and a Hebrew version of Æsop, given by Bp. John [Grandison] 'ecclesiæ suæ Exon.'

P. 449. Westminster Abbey. *Add* Rawl. Liturg. *g.* 9; (a small book which belonged to a Benedictine house, with full commemoration-office of Edward the Confessor as patron).

P. 459, *n.* 1. A list of all the persons admitted to read in the Library by favour from 1603 to 1621, compiled from the *Liber Admissorum*, The Register of Convocation, and one of Wood's MSS., is printed at pp. 263–282, vol. II. of Mr. A. Clark's *Reg. of the Univ.*, printed by the Oxf. Hist. Soc. in 1887.

P. 467, no. 42. *For* by Bona Sforza *read* for Bona Sforza.

The names of Gough, Douce, and Mason were added to the roll of University benefactors by decree of Convocation on 27 March, 1847, and that of Mr. J. T. Hope in 1872.

In a thirteenth-century Psalter, numbered Auct. D. iv. 3, is the following sensible piece of advice to readers, written by a lady in the fifteenth century:—'Lerne to kepe your books fayre, and ockapy them well, and vse to clasp them whan you haue done. Rose Tressham.'

INDEX.

[1] Five other MSS. are in existence which are known to have belonged to Arethas: one is Harl. MS. 5694, and others are at Paris, Venice, and in the Vatican. *Cf.* a notice in the *Athenæum* of June 29, 1889, by T. W. Allen.

[1] It is worth noting that a Life of Tanner (by Rev. Edw. Wilton) is to be found in a quarter where it would hardly be looked for, viz. in the *Wiltshire Archæological Magazine* for May, 1872, vol. xiii. pp. 59–77.

THE END.